After Disney

The Other Orlando

Kelly Monaghan
with Seth Kubersky

After Disney

The Other Orlando

Published by The Intrepid Traveler
P.O. Box 531, Branford, CT 06405
www.intrepidtraveler.com

Copyright © 2012 by Kelly Monaghan
First Edition
Printed in the United States of America
Cover by George Foster
Maps designed by Map Gorilla
Library of Congress Control Number: 2001012345
ISBN: 978-1-937011-03-1

10 9 8 7 6 5 4 3 2 1

Trademarks, Etc.

This book mentions many attractions, fictional characters, product names, entities, and works that are trademarks, registered trademarks, or service marks of their various creators and owners. They are used in this book solely for editorial purposes. Neither the author nor the publisher makes any commercial claim to their use.

Photo Credits

Front cover :

Back cover:

(Top to bottom) Arabian Nights Dinner Show, Wet 'n Wild, and Busch Gardens Tampa photos courtesy of the Orlando/Orange County Convention and Visitors Bureau, Inc. ®
Simpsons Ride at Universal Studios Florida by Kelly Monaghan.
Orcas photo courtesy of SeaWorld Parks and Entertainment.

Table of Contents

List of Maps

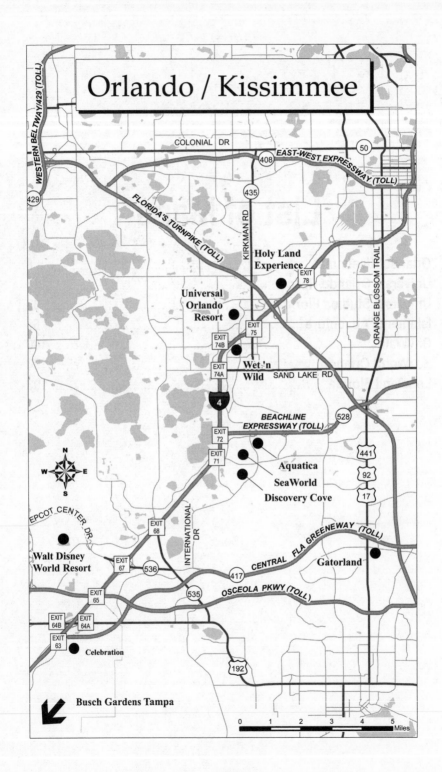

Orlando / Kissimmee

Chapter One:

Introduction & Orientation

DON'T GET ME WRONG. I LOVE DISNEY WORLD AND I VISIT MICKEY EVERY chance I get. But because Disney World is the 900-pound gorilla of Central Florida tourism, any general guidebook to Central Florida must, of necessity, devote so much space to its multitude of attractions that the area's other attractions receive short shrift, if they are covered at all. This book, then, turns away from Disney World, not out of disdain, but to lavish on Orlando's other attractions the in-depth treatment that Disney has long enjoyed. I suspect that readers of this book have already visited Disney World, perhaps many times, and are ready to explore the other possibilities of a Central Florida vacation. As you will see, they are myriad.

When's The Best Time To Come?

There are three major questions you must ask yourself when planning a trip to Orlando: How crowded will it be? What will the weather be like? When will my schedule allow me go? For those who can be flexible carefully picking the time of your visit offers a number of benefits. During slow periods, the crowds at Orlando's major theme parks are noticeably thinner than they are at the height of the summer or during the madness of Christmas week. On top of that, hotel rates are substantially lower and airfare deals abound. Likewise, Orlando in winter can seem positively balmy to those from the North. Spring and fall temperatures are close to ideal. Let's take a look at these two variables: the tourist traffic and the weather.

Orlando's Tourist Traffic

Orlando hosts nearly 50 million visitors a year and whereas most destinations have two seasons, high and low, Orlando has six. The heaviest tourist "season" is Christmas vacation, roughly from Christmas eve through January first. Next comes Easter week and Thanksgiving weekend. The entire summer, from Memorial Day in late May to Labor Day in early September, is on a par with Easter and Thanksgiving. There are two other "spikes" in attendance: President's Week in February and College Spring Break. Various colleges have different dates for their Spring Break, which may or may not coincide with Easter; the result is that the period from mid-March through mid-April shows a larger than usual volume of tourist traffic. The slowest period is the lull between Thanksgiving and Christmas. Next slowest (excluding the holidays mentioned earlier) are the months of September, October, November, January, and February. Tourism starts to build again in March, spiking sharply upward for Easter/Spring Break, then dropping off somewhat until Memorial Day.

The best advice is to avoid the absolutely busiest times of the year if possible. If you do come during the summer, as many families must, plan to deal with crowds at the major parks (Universal, SeaWorld, Busch Gardens) and console yourself with the thought that, by concentrating on the attractions covered in this book, you will avoid the worst crowds, which are inevitably at the Disney parks—with the notable exception of Harry Potter at Universal Orlando's Islands of Adventure which is frequently packed.

Orlando's Weather

Orlando's average annual temperature is a lovely 72.4 degrees. But averages are deceptive. I find Orlando's weather most predictable in the summer when "hot, humid, in the low nineties, with a chance of afternoon thunderstorms" becomes something of a mantra for the TV weather report. Winter weather tends to be more unpredictable with "killer" freezes a possibility, although it can also be quite balmy. As to those summer thunderstorms, they tend to be localized and mercifully brief (although occasionally quite intense) and needn't disrupt your touring schedule. Another thing to bear in mind is that June through September is hurricane season, with July and August the most likely months for severe weather.

Here are the generally cited "average" figures for temperature and rainfall throughout the year:

	High (°F)	Low (°F)	Rain (in.)
January	71	49	2.3
February	73	50	3.0
March	78	55	3.2
April	83	59	1.8
May	88	66	3.6
June	91	72	7.3
July	92	73	7.3
August	92	73	6.8
September	90	73	6.0
October	85	66	2.4
November	79	58	2.3
December	73	51	2.2

(Source: Visit Orlando)

Getting Oriented in Orlando

Orlando can be confusing. The Orlando metropolitan area comprises three counties and, since you will often hear location indicated by naming the county, it is worth knowing their names and relation to one another. From north to south they are Seminole, Orange, and Osceola. Orlando is in Orange County, Kissimmee is in Osceola. Most of the attractions covered in this book are in Orange and Osceola; only a few are in Seminole or more distant counties.

The area is dotted with lakes, both large and small; so streets stop, start, and take circuitous detours. In European fashion, streets change names as they cross municipal boundaries. On top of that, the area's major highway, Interstate 4, which runs east-west across the state, runs roughly from northeast to southwest through the Orlando metropolitan area and almost directly north-south in the heart of Orlando's tourist district. As a result, streets that are "east" or "south" of I-4 at one point are "west" or "north" of it at another. (See map, page 8.) All of this complicates the process of giving, receiving, and following directions.

Fortunately, most of the Orlando area's attractions are located in two fairly compact tourist districts: International Drive in Orlando and US 192 in Kissimmee, with I-4 forming a direct and easy-to-follow link between them. Attractions that are not located in these two areas are seldom more than a short drive away from an I-4 exit.

International Drive (sometimes abbreviated I Drive and pronounced "Eye Drive," just as I-4 is pronounced "Eye Four") is in Orlando. It is a meandering boulevard that roughly parallels I-4 from Exit 75 on the north to Exit 67 on the south. Many of the major attractions profiled in this book are on it or near it. At the northern end, you will find Universal Orlando (just across I-4) and Wet 'n Wild. At the southern end lies SeaWorld. In between, there are some dinner attractions and a number of smaller attractions, along with dozens of hotels, scores of eateries, several discount outlet malls, and the mammoth Orlando Convention Center. International Drive is glitzy, garish, hyperactive, and a traffic nightmare in the evening and at rush hours.

The second major tourist axis is US 192 (also called Highway 192, and Irlo Bronson Highway), which runs east to west through Kissimmee, crossing I-4 at Exit 64. West of I-4 you will find an entrance to the Disney properties; to the east of I-4 is a gaudy strip of hotels, restaurants, dinner attractions, smaller attractions, miniature golf courses, and discount shopping outlets. This strip is thoughtfully marked with numbered "Mile Markers," which I have used in the text to give directions.

Tip: Chances are you will be staying in or very close to one of the two major tourist areas. When you are traveling from Point A to Point B in the Orlando area, my advice is to travel via US 192 and I-4. This may not always be the most direct or shortest route but it will be the surest route and very often the quickest because there is less chance of getting lost en route. When I give directions in this book I try, wherever possible, to route you via these major arteries.

Keeping Posted

Every Friday, the *Orlando Sentinel*'s "Calendar" section offers an entire week's worth of information about films, plays, concerts, nightclubs, art exhibits, and the like. Music buffs will appreciate the exhaustive listings of who's playing what where and film fans will find show times for every multiplex from Orlando to the Atlantic coast. There is even a listing of area attractions and a section of personal ads just in case you start feeling lonely. You can visit the *Sentinel's* "Calendar" section on the Internet at http://www.orlandosentinel.com/entertainment.

Orlando has a free weekly newspaper, the *Orlando Weekly*, that is especially strong on the pop music scene. You will be able to find it in racks near the entrance to bookstores, coffee shops, supermarkets, and drugstores.

The Intrepid Traveler, the publisher of this book, maintains a website containing updated information about all of Orlando's attractions along with other valuable information. Log on at:

http://www.TheOtherOrlando.com/tooblog

Multi-Park Ticket Options

There's a lot to see after Disney and the major non-Disney players, Universal Orlando Resort and SeaWorld Parks and Entertainment, offer a variety of multi-day, multi-park tickets and annual passes to compete with Disney's elaborate "park hopper" system. Single day admission to the various parks is covered in the appropriate chapter.

Universal Orlando Resort

Universal Orlando Resort comprises two theme parks, Universal Studios Florida (*Chapter 2*) and Islands of Adventure (*Chapter 3*), as well as CityWalk (*Chapter 4*), a nighttime entertainment complex. There are also three on-site luxury hotels, which are not covered in this volume. This is Universal's answer to Walt Disney World's one-stop vacation concept, except that at Universal Orlando everything is within relatively easy walking distance.

Multi-Day and Multi-Park Passes

Universal Orlando offers multi-day passes in two flavors, one-park and two-park. (Online prices in parentheses.)

Base Ticket: One-Park Access
(Universal Studios Florida **or** Islands of Adventure)

	Adults	Children (3–9)
2 Days	$144.83 ($125.68)	$134.18 ($115.03)
3 Days	$166.13 ($146.98)	$153.35 ($134.20)
4 Days	$176.78 ($157.63)	$162.93 ($143.78)

Park-To-Park Ticket: Two-Park Access
(Universal Studios Florida **and** Islands of Adventure)

	Adults	Children (3–9)
2 Days	$166.13 ($146.98)	$155.48($136.33)
3 Days	$182.10 ($162.95)	$169.32 ($150.17)
4 Days	$187.43 ($168.28)	$173.58 ($154.43)

Add unlimited Wet 'n Wild visits to a 3-day or longer ticket for $32.50.

Annual Passes

Universal Orlando offers three Annual Pass options with a single price for all ages: The **Two-Park Annual Power Pass** ($170.38); the **Two-Park Preferred Annual Pass** ($244.94); and the **Two-Park Premier Annual Pass** ($372.74).

What's the difference? The Annual Power Pass (only for Florida residents) comes with about 66 blackout dates (Christmas at both parks, Spring Break, and the month of July through mid-August at IOA only), does not include parking, and offers no additional discounts. The Preferred Annual Pass is valid 365 days a year, includes free parking, and entitles the holder to a host of attractive discounts on food, merchandise, and stays at the resort hotels. Since parking is $15 a day, you need only visit five days before the additional cost pays for itself—and that doesn't take into account any shopping and dining discounts. The Premier Annual Pass adds a few nifty perks including free self-parking in the Preferred Parking area or free valet parking (gratuity excluded), Universal Express Plus access to rides and attractions after 4:00 p.m. daily, admission to all CityWalk clubs for the passholder and a guest (passholder only on weekend nights), one non-peak Halloween Horror Nights ticket, eight free bottles of water, and other benefits.

VIP Tours

Universal offers both one- and two-park **VIP Tours** for groups of twelve. They are either "non-exclusive," which means you will be with others, or "exclusive," which means the tour will be comprised of just your party. The prices are, well, pricey and do not include admission to the parks themselves. But if you can afford anywhere from $225 to $275 per person or $2,500 to $3,750 for an entire group, you can probably afford to hire someone to call (407) 363-8295 for more information.

SeaWorld Parks and Entertainment

SeaWorld Parks and Entertainment owns five properties in Central Florida, SeaWorld, (*Chapter 5*) Discovery Cove (*Chapter 6*), and Aquatica (*Chapter 12*) in Orlando and Busch Gardens (*Chapter 11*) and Adventure Island (*Chapter 12*) in Tampa.

Multi-Park Passes

These options allow for 14 days of unlimited entry to the parks included on the ticket; parking is not included. You can save on some tickets by purchasing online in advance. Here is what's currently on offer (online prices in parentheses):

SeaWorld - Aquatica
Adults:	$133.11 ($122.46)
Children (3 to 9):	$124.60 ($113.94)

SeaWorld - Busch Gardens
Adults:	$133.43 ($122.75)
Children (3 to 9):	$124.89 ($114.21)

SeaWorld - Aquatica - Busch Gardens
Adults:	$143.76
Children (3 to 9):	$135.24

Busch Gardens - Adventure Island
 Adults: $130.97 ($101.16)
 Children (3 to 9): $122.45 ($92.64)

Each park's website offers slightly different selections of ticket packages; for example, the Busch Gardens-Adventure Island option is only available on the Busch Gardens site. Tickets can also be purchased at park gates and on the phone at (800) 327-2420 or (407) 363-2559.

Annual Passes

SeaWorld Parks & Entertainment calls its annual passes Passports. They are good for one year or two years. Four parks are included in the Passport program: SeaWorld, Aquatica, Busch Gardens Tampa, and Adventure Island (also in Tampa). You can "build" your own Passport to include one, two, three, or all four parks. However, you cannot choose just the two water parks. Current pricing is as follows (including tax):

	1 Year	2 Years
One Park	$117.14	$181.04
Two Parks	$170.39	$260.91
Three Parks	$223.64	$340.79
Four Parks	$266.24	$404.69

Prices for children and seniors (65+) are $8 less than the adult price in each category. Passport holders enjoy a number of benefits. These include free parking, modest discounts on guest tickets, a 10% discount on food and merchandise, discounts on tours and other activities, 50% off preferred parking, and discounts on Discovery Cove admission. Note that Discovery Cove is *not* included in any Passport option.

Note: These perks apply only to those parks included in the Passport. If you drop in on another park for the day, your Passport won't work for parking or discounts.

The Orlando FlexTicket

Finally, Universal and SeaWorld have joined forces to create perhaps the most attractive "park hopper" of all, the Orlando FlexTicket, which neatly fits the vacation needs of most visitors to Central Florida. The participating parks are Universal Studios Florida (USF), Islands of Adventure (IOA), SeaWorld, Aquatica, Wet 'n Wild, and Busch Gardens Tampa. It's called the Orlando FlexTicket and it works like this:

Five-Park, Fourteen-Day Orlando FlexTicket:
(USF, IOA, SeaWorld, Aquatica, Wet 'n Wild)
 Adults: $293.89
 Children (3 to 9): $271.55
Six-Park, Fourteen-Day Orlando FlexTicket:
(adds Busch Gardens Tampa)
 Adults: $335.42
 Children (3 to 9): $314.12

Prices include tax. These passes offer unlimited visits to all five or six parks for two weeks and represent an excellent value. On top of that, they offer the come and go as you please convenience of annual passes, albeit for a much shorter time.

FlexTickets may be purchased at any of the participating parks' ticket booths or through your travel agent before coming. They are valid for fourteen consecutive days beginning on the day you first use them. As for parking, you pay at the first park you visit on any given day. Then show your parking ticket and Orlando FlexTicket at the other parks on the same day for complimentary parking.

All About Discounts

Getting a decent discount on the major attractions is a lot harder than it used to be. Nonetheless, it is still possible to shave a few dollars off your tourist activities here and there and those dollars can add up. Here are some suggestions (and caveats):

Dollars-Off Coupons. Coupons are distributed via attraction websites and through a variety of free visitors' guides, coupon booklets, and brochures for individual attractions. Look for them in displays at the airport, car rental agencies, hotel lobbies, and restaurants in the tourist areas. You won't have to look far.

The discounts available from dollars-off coupons are relatively modest, usually a few dollars. Some attractions make their coupons valid for up to four or six people, hence the headlines that shout "up to $16 off!" Collect as many free visitors' guides and brochures as you can. Then, in the comfort of your hotel room, select and cut out offers that appeal to you and keep them in your rental car for ready use.

If you find yourself near an attraction you'd like to visit but don't have a coupon, stop into nearby restaurants or even the entrance to a nearby attraction, and look for brochure racks. Chances are you'll find just the coupon you need.

The Orlando Magicard. Sponsored by the Orlando Convention and Visitors Bureau, the Magicard looks like a credit card. Flashing it will get you discounts at most area attractions and dinner shows, as well as at some restaurants and area hotels. You can obtain a card prior to your arrival by writing to the Orlando Visitors Center, 8723 International Drive, Orlando, FL 32819. Or call (407) 363-5872. Or order on the Web at www.orlandoinfo.com/magicard. They will send you the card free of charge. You can also pick up the card at the Center once you are in Orlando. Along with the card, you will receive a brochure with the current list of discount offers. The card is good forever; the list of attractions, restaurants, and hotels offering discounts changes periodically.

Ticket brokers. The second major source of discounts is ticket brokers. There are dozens of them scattered around the tourist areas, many of them located in hotel lobbies. Ticket brokers concentrate on the major attractions and the dinner shows. Using ticket brokers requires careful comparison shopping since discounts can vary widely from outlet to outlet. As a general rule, the discount ticket booths you find in your hotel lobby or in local restaurants seldom have the best prices. You'll do better at the free-standing ticket outlets. Virtually every reputable ticket broker will have a printed price list; collect a goodly supply of these and examine them later in your hotel room to smoke out the best deals.

Despite efforts to police the ticket broker scene, scams persist. You can be assured of a fair deal (if not the absolute lowest price) at the Orlando Visitors Center on International Drive, mentioned above.

Time Share Come-ons. Those signs you will see for "FREE TICKETS" or for ultra-cheap tickets to the big parks invariably involve sitting through a high-pressure sales pitch for a timeshare development. I have heard enough horror stories from people who have tried this ploy to advise against it.

AAA Discounts. Finally, that American Automobile Association card you probably have in your wallet is good for discounts on admission to most major (and a few minor) attractions as well as discounts on food and merchandise within the major parks. When in doubt, whip it out.

How This Book Is Organized

Chapters 2 through *8* cover the major Orlando area attractions, ones that will occupy anywhere from a half a day to several days of your time. I have attempted to cover them in some depth. *Chapters 9* through *11* cover Kennedy Space Center to the east and Legoland and Busch Gardens Tampa to the south and west. These, too, are major attractions.

Each of these chapters (with the notable exception of *Chapter 4: CityWalk*) follow the same format. Once familiar with the organization of these chapters you will be able to find the information you are looking for quickly. Before delving into descriptions of the park's rides and attractions, each chapter provides the following information:

Before You Come offers tips on how to gather the latest information along with suggestions for movies you might want to watch or books to read to enrich your experience at the park.

When's The Best Time To Come? offers some suggestions about the optimum timing for your visit, assuming you have the luxury of picking and choosing your dates.

Getting There, *Arriving At . . .*, and *Opening and Closing Times* are fairly self-explanatory. The "Arriving At" section will contain information about parking rates.

The Price of Admission covers the cost of one- and two-day visits as appropriate. This section will also contain information about annual pass options for smaller parks, if any. Information on annual passes and multi-park tickets to Universal Orlando and the SeaWorld Parks is provided earlier in this chapter.

Special Events lists seasonal events that can make a visit especially memorable.

Good Things To Know About . . . covers helpful information about such things as access for the disabled, first aid, park policies, and other practicalities.

Your Day At . . . This section provides an overview of the park and what it has to offer, followed by . . .

Best Attractions are highlighted so that you don't miss the best the park has to offer.

Touring Plans, with headings like "the One-Day Stay" or "the One-Day Stay With Kids," provide insider tips on how to make sure you see as much as possible while avoiding the crush of the crowd.

Some of these sections may be omitted or combined in the case of the smaller parks, but this list will serve as a fairly reliable guide to the order in which information is provided in these chapters.

The remaining chapters cover a number of attractions that all have a common theme. The attractions described in these chapters are scattered throughout the Orlando area. At the end of the book, there is an *Index to Rides and Attractions*, that will be most useful in locating the smaller attractions covered in *Chapters 12* through *21*. It can also be used to locate descriptions of specific attractions at the major parks.

As a general rule, I have tried to restrict the geographic scope of this book to Orlando and its immediate environs while recognizing that there are major attractions farther afield that deserve attention. That means that the farther you drive from Orlando, the more likely you will be to encounter attractions not covered in this book. For example, I have not mentioned the many things to see and do in the Tampa Bay area aside from Busch Gardens and Adventure Island, its next-door water park. Likewise, there is limited coverage of Daytona Beach and the "Space Coast."

If you would like more information about Universal Orlando Resort and the SeaWorld parks, The Intrepid Traveler, the publisher of this book, stands ready to assist you. *Universal Orlando: The Ultimate Guide To The Ultimate Theme Park Adventure* is updated every year. It features much more information than could be squeezed into this volume, including in-depth reviews of every restaurant and shop in both theme parks. There is also a chapter devoted to the three on-site hotels, Portofino Bay Hotel, Hard Rock Hotel, and the Royal Pacific Resort. *SeaWorld, Discovery Cove & Aquatica: Orlando's Salute to the Seas* offers the same in-depth coverage of the SeaWorld Parks and Entertainment family of Central Florida theme parks and water parks. It covers not only the title parks but Busch Gardens and Adventure Island in Tampa. There is also a chapter on the upscale resort hotels near SeaWorld that offer a do-it-yourself version of the on-site experience available at Universal Orlando. Both of these books were created by the same team that put together the guide you are holding now with the same attention to detail and passion for the theme park experience, all served up with a touch of humor.

Finally some highway abbreviations: I stands for Interstate; US for United States (i.e. federal) highways; SR for State Route; CR for County Road.

Accuracy and Other Impossible Dreams

While I have tried to be as accurate, comprehensive, and up-to-date as possible, these are all unattainable goals. What's most likely to change, alas, are prices. I have quoted the most recent prices. However, some attractions may decide to raise their prices later in the year. Perhaps more disconcerting will be the disappearance of entire attractions, usually smaller and/or newer ones. I sincerely hope that none of the wonderful attractions listed here close down before you get to experience them. Before driving any great distance, however, you may want to call ahead to make sure the attraction that caught your eye is still open and double check the hours and pricing.

Once again I refer you to this book's website for updated information:

http://www.TheOtherOrlando.com/tooblog

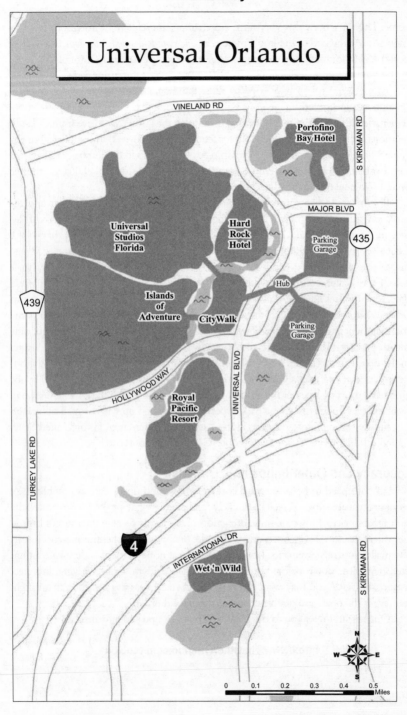

Chapter Two:

Universal Studios Florida

RIDE THE MOVIES! THE BRILLIANT OPENING–DAY AD SLOGAN COINED BY Steven Spielberg, though sadly no longer in circulation, still says it all. In creating its first Florida theme park, Universal Studios built on the lessons learned over three decades at its original Hollywood movie-themed attraction and injected a giant jolt of high-tech thrills. Over the last 20 years, much of the park's film-making "edutainment" has given way to some of the world's greatest thrill rides. But the cinematic spirit still thrives here among meticulously detailed, working movie sets that can make the simple act of sitting down to eat a hot dog seem like an adventure.

The word that visitors and locals most frequently use to differentiate Universal from Disney is "adult." Whereas Disney World is perceived by many as a kiddie park that adults will enjoy, they see Universal as a park conceived with grown-ups in mind. There are a number of reasons for this:

Adult Themes. Many Universal attractions are based on films and shows that appeal primarily to adults—*Disaster!*, *Terminator*, *Revenge of the Mummy*, and *Twister* are a far cry from *Honey, I Shrunk the Kids*.

Intensity. Whereas Disney (at least in its early days) would tend to tone down rides in the development stage lest they frighten young children, Universal Studios seems to delight in seeing just how intense they can be. *Revenge of the Mummy* is a prime example.

Beer and Wine. Beer and wine are readily available at Universal. And not just in the restaurants. Don't be surprised to see a beer vendor plying the lines on hot summer days. Some of the sit-down restaurants serve pretty decent wines by the bottle or glass and at a few places you can get a mixed drink. One of these, Finnegan's in the New York section, is a full-fledged Irish pub and a very good one at that.

Pyrotechnics. If Universal Studios Florida has a stylistic signature, something that tells you that this is a Universal attraction and not someone else's, it has to be their lavish use of fire, fireworks, and loud explosions. You can almost feel your eyebrows singe on *Disaster!*, *Twister*, and *Revenge of the Mummy*.

Before You Come

You can arrive at Universal Studios knowing nothing about any of the films or TV shows on which its attractions are based (although it's hard to imagine that being possible), and have a perfectly good time. Indeed, you don't need to understand a word of English to be entertained here, as the happy hordes of foreign tourists prove.

Nonetheless, there is one attraction that will benefit from a bit of research prior to your visit. *E. T. Adventure* will make a lot more sense to those who have seen the film. This is especially true for younger kids who might find E.T.'s odd appearance a bit off-putting if they haven't seen the film. Fortunately, this is the kind of homework that's easy and fun to do. Netflix will have all the research material you need. While you're at it, you might want to add *Shrek* and *Despicable Me* to your queue, if only to whet the kids' appetites for their visit.

When's The Best Time To Come?

With the arrival of Harry Potter at Islands of Adventure, Universal Orlando Resort is starting to look a lot more like Disney World in terms of crowds, so you are well advised to consult the Introduction to this book and try to time your visit to one of Orlando's slower periods. If you can't do that, you can console yourself with the thought that Universal Studios Florida will be less crowded than IOA no matter when you visit—at least until USF gets its own Harry Potter attraction, probably sometime in 2013. Then all bets are off.

Getting There

Universal Orlando Resort is located right next to Interstate 4 (I-4) and it has a number of entrances. If you are coming from the airport, you will approach Universal from the south; your best exit off I-4 is 75A. Coming from the north, take either 75B or 74B.

Arriving at Universal Studios Florida

Whichever route you take, Universal will cleverly funnel your car into the tollbooth-like entrance to its two massive parking garages, both within walking distance of Universal Studios Florida and Islands of Adventure. Parking is $15 for cars, $20 for RVs and trailers. Annual Pass holders can show their pass for free admission to the parking lots. Parking is $3 between 6:00 p.m. and 10:00 p.m. (except during special events), and is free after 10:00 p.m.

Tip: The leftmost open tollbooth lanes will usually have the shortest lines.

Preferred parking gets you closer to the exits from the garages and costs $20. Valet parking is $25 for a full day, less if you are coming to CityWalk for a meal.

Once parked, you've got a healthy walk ahead of you to the attractions. Universal Orlando's parking setup is divisive: some love the shelter and absence of pokey parking trams, while others hate the hike. Universal claims that the farthest parking space is just a nine-minute walk from CityWalk, assuming the frequently stalled moving walkways are operating to speed your journey. But at the end of a long day it can feel like a million miles.

Passenger Drop-Off. If you're in a generous mood, you can drop off your family near CityWalk before you park the car. Look for the signs directing you to the drop-off area, which is just across Universal Boulevard from the Valet Parking area.

Parking for Resort Guests. If you are staying at one of the on-property resort hotels, use any of the entrances and follow the signs to your hotel. All of the hotels have separate gates, with separate, paid parking facilities for guests. Non-guests can also use these lots but at rates higher than those charged to guests and considerably higher than the fee levied at the main theme park parking garages. In other words, the hotel parking does not provide an economical or more convenient alternative to regular parking.

Opening and Closing Times

Universal Studios Florida is open 365 days a year. In slow seasons, the park may open at 9:00 a.m. and close at 6:00 p.m. In high season, hours may be from 8:00 a.m. to 11:00 p.m. Universal Studios Florida sometimes opens a bit earlier than the official time, but you can't always count on this. Don't be in a rush to leave; the last guests are typically shooed out an hour after official closing.

The Price of Admission

Universal Orlando uses a tiered ticket pricing structure, "U Select," similar to Disney's "Magic Your Way." The pricing encourages purchasing longer passes by sharply reducing the premium when you add additional days and parks. All multi-day tickets must be fully utilized within 14 days after the first use, and include 14 nights of free admission to CityWalk's clubs. Whatever your choice, children under three are admitted free.

For the most recent information you should check www.universalorlando.com and click on the "Tickets" link, although as noted below, the website does not always list every type of ticket available. Another excellent source of intelligence about the latest prices and special admissions offers is www.mousesavers.com. If you'd prefer to get your information straight from the horse's mouth, you can try emailing Universal at customer.support@tickets.universalstudios.com or call (407) 224-7840.

All that being said, prices (including 6.5% sales tax and $2.15 online fees where appropriate) were as follows when this book went to press (the online prices are listed in parentheses):

Base Ticket: One-Park Access
(Universal Studios Florida **or** Islands of Adventure per day)

	Adults	Children (3-9)
1 Day	$90.53 ($92.68)	$84.14 ($86.29)
2 Days	$144.83 ($125.68)	$134.18 ($115.03)
3 Days	$166.13 ($146.98)	$153.35 ($134.20)
4 Days	$176.78 ($157.63)	$162.93 ($143.78)

For information on multi-park tickets and annual passes see *Chapter 1*.

Universal Express Plus

This program allows you to buy your way to the front of the line by purchasing a small card with a bar code that gives you one-time Express access to every ride or attraction with an Express queue. You can buy a pass for one park or both. The cards will only work on a single day starting one hour after park opening. Unlike Disney's "FastPass" system, Universal Express Plus can be utilized whenever you choose.

Pricing for Express Plus is volatile. Recently, passes have been selling in advance online for $20 for a one-park pass during slower periods, all the way up to $70 for a two-park version at peak periods like Christmas week. The online Express price calendar is also a great way to gauge how busy it will be during your visit. Prices may be higher when purchased in the parks, where they are only available for same-day use. There are very few days, it seems, on which the pass is not available; since those are usually slower days, that might not be a problem. Quantities are limited and once they're gone for the day, they're gone. At each ride, your card will be "swiped" by an attendant using a hand-held device, ensuring only one ride per attraction.

Guests staying in Universal Orlando Resort's three on-site hotels have the best deal of all. Their room card key serves as a sort of unlimited express pass allowing priority access to all but a few rides in the two parks. If you can afford the rates at these hotels, this is your best way to assure a stress-free experience in the parks. And if you add up the cost of Universal Express for your family, those hotel rates might not seem quite so pricey.

Eating in Universal Studios Florida

Universal is unlikely to draw plaudits from die-hard gourmets. Still, it seems to do a pretty good job of holding prices down while serving food most people will enjoy. And if you want a step up from the standard carnival fare, **Finnegan's** and **Lombard's Seafood Grille**, the two full-service restaurants in the park, have at least a dish or two that's better than average. Try the Catch of the Day at Lombard's or one of the Irish specialties at Finnegan's, for example, and you will feel well fed indeed. You also have the option of popping out to nearby CityWalk (*Chapter 4*) for a meal at one of the first-rate restaurants there and then returning to the park.

For most families, however, the fare will be of the standard fast-food variety—most of it edible and not too outrageously priced. Favorites in this category are **Richter's** for burgers in San Francisco and **Louie's** for Italian food in New York.

You should be aware that the prices of modest choices in the full-service restaurants are roughly equivalent to the prices at the fast food joints. So for about the same amount or just a few dollars more, you can enjoy the luxury of table service, constant refills of your iced tea, and best of all, air conditioning. It's an option worth considering. In addition to the standard eateries there are innumerable street-side kiosks, offering a wide variety of drinks and snacks, that appear and disappear as the crowds and weather dictate.

Shopping in Universal Studios Florida

It's easy to spend more on gifts and souvenirs than on admission. The standard, all-American souvenirs (T-shirts and the like) are priced slightly higher than their off-park equivalents, though some of them are very nicely designed. More upscale clothing, with the Universal logo displayed very discreetly, is sometimes available. When it is, it tends to be expensive but well made.

Rather than lug purchases with you, take advantage of Universal's package pickup service. Most shops will be happy to send your purchases to the front entrance, where you can pick them up on the way out. Or you can simply save all your shopping for the end of your visit and stop into the **Universal Studios Store** while the rest of the crowd is rushing to the gate at closing time. This shop has a good, although not complete, selection of merchandise from virtually every other shop in the park. You can also shop online at UniversalOrlando.com.

Good Things To Know About . . .

First Aid. There is a first-aid station and nursing facility on Canal Street, across from *Beetlejuice's Graveyard Revue* and just beside Louie's Italian Restaurant. You'll also find help at Family & Health Services on the Front Lot.

Getting Wet. The *Curious George* play area in Woody Woodpecker's KidZone is straight out of a water park, and kids who visit there will not be able to resist the temptation to get absolutely drenched. On cooler days when a wet child could catch a chill, bring a towel and a change of clothes.

Height Restrictions and Other Warnings. Due to a variety of considerations, such as sudden movements and the configuration of lap restraints, a few rides will be off-limits to shorter (typically younger) guests. The following rides have minimum height requirements:

Woody Woodpecker's Nuthouse Coaster	36 in. (91.4 cm.)
Despicable Me: Minion Mayhem	40 in. (101.6 cm.)
(Stationary seating is provided for shorter kids.)	
Men In Black	42 in. (106.7 cm.)
Revenge of the Mummy	48 in. (121.9 cm.)
Hollywood Rip Ride Rockit	51 in. (130 cm.)

In addition, any child under 48 inches must be accompanied by an adult on all these rides (except the *Mummy* and *Rockit*, which they can't ride at all) and must be able to sit upright without help.

PG–13 Ratings. Universal issues a "parental advisory" for kids under 13 on the following rides and attractions:

Beetlejuice's Graveyard Revue
Terminator 2: 3-D
Twister
Universal Horror Make-Up Show

In addition, *Disaster!* may be too intense for very small children. Most parents seem to ignore the warnings. In this day and age (sadly, perhaps), it's hard to imagine a child being shocked by anything.

Reservations. Both Lombard's Seafood Grille and Finnegan's accept dining reservations. They are highly recommended at any time and especially if you are visiting during the busy season, although a reservation is not an absolute guarantee of avoiding a short wait. You can make your reservations first thing in the morning when you arrive or by phone up to 24 hours in advance. The number to call is (407) 224–3613, or book online through OpenTable.com.

Single Rider Lines. To help shrink long lines, "single rider" lines can cut you to the front of the queue provided you are willing to be separated from your party. *Men*

In Black and *Revenge of the Mummy* have a single rider line open most of the time, and *Hollywood Rip Ride Rockit* offers one intermittently. Single rider entrances may shutter if there is too much demand (or not enough), so you can't always count on this option.

Special Diets. Lombard's Seafood Grille and Finnegan's can provide kosher meals with 48 hours advance notice, and offer dishes with gluten-free ingredients. Call Food Services at (407) 363-8340 to make arrangements. The 2-Park Map's list of dining spots calls out restaurants offering "healthy choices," which usually means vegetarians can be accommodated. Universal eliminated trans-fat oil from its menus in 2007. Still, if you're on a low-fat regimen, sticking with salads and fruit plates is probably the best strategy. Lombard's has a nice selection of seafood and salads.

Special Events

The year is sprinkled with special events tied to the holiday calendar. The events listed here, with the notable exceptions of Rock The Universe and Halloween Horror Nights, are usually included in regular admission, but separate admission is sometimes charged for evening events. Among the seasonal events Universal Studios puts on are:

Mardi Gras. New Orleans' pre-Lenten bacchanalia comes to Florida in the form of a nighttime parade, complete with garish and gaudy floats, plenty of baubles and beads that are flung into the outstretched hands of the crowd, and concerts by classic and current musical artists.

Christmas. Ho, ho, ho! It's a Hollywood version of a heartwarming family holiday, complete with a scaled-down version of New York's famous Macy's Holiday Parade, giant balloons included.

Rock The Universe. For one weekend in early September, Universal Studios shoos out the normal paying guests in the evening and turns the park over to Christian teens getting down with God. Top religious rockers like Switchfoot and Casting Crowns have appeared at what is billed as "Florida's Biggest Christian Music Festival." Admission to this "hard ticket" after-hours event is not included in any pass, and runs $52 for one night, $85 for the weekend.

Halloween Horror Nights. Universal's wildly popular after-hours frightfest is held on selected nights in late September through Halloween weekend. After the daytime guests depart, the park is turned into an elaborately themed bacchanalia of the bizarre, featuring famous Hollywood monsters alongside original horrors from the fiendish minds of Universal's fearmasters. The heart of the event is the half-dozen-plus haunted mazes in which visitors scream and shuffle past movie-quality tableaus of terror. Rock musicals, gory magic acts, and bawdy comedy shows (like the long-running "Bill & Ted" pop-culture satire) are staged, and most of the major rides are open. The park's thoroughfares are filled with fog and lurching "scareactors," but relax: they observe a strict "no-touching" policy.

A separate admission of roughly $82 is required, with various discounts and "frequent fear" season passes and express passes available. The event is intense in every sense: loud, claustrophobic, suggestive, scatological, and alcohol-saturated. It is not for children, nor for many adults.

The Shooting Script:
Your Day at Universal Studios Florida

Universal Studios Florida (like its sister park) is best experienced in small bites over several days. That being said, it is perfectly possible see more or less everything at Universal Studios Florida in one very full day. This is especially true if you are staying in one of the on-site hotels, which will give you preferred access to virtually all the rides and attractions. It is also true if you have heeded the advice in *Chapter 1* and arrived during one of the less hectic times of year.

If circumstances or perversity have led you to ignore this sage advice, you will have to plan carefully and perhaps purchase a Universal Express Plus pass (see above) if you are intent on seeing as much of the park as possible in a one-day time span. Even at less busy times, you might want to consider following some of the strategies set forth earlier since lines for more popular rides can grow long enough to make the wait seem tedious even in slack periods.

Universal Studios Florida uses the "back lot" as its organizing metaphor. The back lot is where a studio keeps permanent and semi-permanent outdoor sets that can be "dressed" to stand in for multiple locations. USF consists of six such sets—Hollywood, Woody Woodpecker's KidZone, World Expo, San Francisco, New York, and Production Central—in addition to the Front Lot. You will find a helpful map of the layout of the sets in the **2-Park Map** brochure, which you can pick up at the entrance gates or in many of the shops throughout the park. It will also help to have a basic idea of the different types of rides, shows, and attractions Universal Studios Florida has to offer. Each type of attraction has its own peculiarities and dictates a different viewing pattern.

Rides. As the term indicates, these attractions involve getting into a vehicle and going somewhere. Some, like *E. T. Adventure*, are the descendants of the so-called "dark rides" of old-fashioned amusement parks; you ride through a darkened tunnel environment lined with things to look at. *Men In Black* adds exciting elements of interactivity to the old formula, while *Revenge of the Mummy* blends this concept with roller-coaster thrills. Rides are the first major attractions to open in the morning and should be your first priority. Rides have a limited seating capacity, at least compared to the theater shows. They don't last long either; most at Universal are no longer than five minutes. They tend to be the most popular attractions because of the thrills they promise (and deliver). The result: Lines form early and grow longer as the day wears on and more people pack the park.

Theater Shows. Whereas the rides offer thrills, theater shows offer entertainment and, occasionally, education as well. Theater shows can be live (like the *Horror Make-Up* show), on film (like *Shrek*), or a combination of both (like *Terminator*). They occur indoors, out of the heat and sun, in comfortable theaters. They last about 25 minutes on average. Most film shows start running soon after opening time and run continuously. Live shows start about midday and have their show times listed in the 2-Park Map.

Because they seat 250 to 700 people at a time, a long line outside a theater show may be deceptive. Many times you can get in line as the next group is entering and still make the show. This is not always true during the busier times, however. Ask an attendant if getting in line now will guarantee a seat at the next show.

Amphitheater Shows. These shows differ from theater shows in that they take place in larger semi-open auditoriums that do not offer the luxury of air conditioning. They start about midday, with show times listed in the 2-Park Map brochure.

Outdoor Shows. These are small-scale shows involving a few entertainers. They occur on the streets at set times announced in the 2-Park Map.

Displays and Interactive Areas. These two different types of attractions are similar in that you can simply walk into them at will and stay as long as you wish. That's not to say you won't find a line, but, with the exception of *Fievel's Playland*, lines are rare at these attractions.

All the Rest. There's a great deal of enjoyment to be derived from simply walking around in Universal Studios Florida. The imaginative and beautifully executed sets make wonderful photo backdrops and, when things get too hectic, you can even find a grassy knoll on which to stretch out, rest, and survey the passing scene.

Academy Awards

If you have a limited time at Universal Studios Florida, you probably won't be able to see everything. However, it would be a shame if you missed the very best the park has to offer. Here, then, is a list of Academy Awards:

The Simpsons. Simulator thrills and Simpsons satire! What a combo.

Terminator 2: 3-D Battle Across Time. With this show, the award for "best 3-D show in Orlando" moved from Disney to Universal.

Shrek 4-D. Another boffo 3-D entertainment that solidifies Universal's preeminence in the genre.

Curious George Goes To Town. Just for kids and just wonderful.

Revenge of the Mummy. Eternal torment has never been such fun.

Universal Horror Make-Up Show. Fun and games with dead bodies and odd critters.

Runners-Up

These aren't on the list of the best of the best but they make many other people's lists and they are very, very good.

Hollywood Rip Ride Rockit. A one-of-a-kind coaster for thrill ride junkies and music fans alike.

Men In Black: Alien Attack. A ride-through video game pits you against the universe.

E.T. Adventure. A bicycle ride to E.T.'s home planet is like *it's a small world* on acid.

The One-Day Stay

If you are staying at an on-site hotel and thus have preferred access or you have purchased a Universal Express Plus pass (see above), then you can largely ignore the following advice and proceed as you wish.

1. Get up early. You want to arrive at the park before the official opening time. Allow at least half an hour to park your car and get to the main entrance.

2. Since you were smart enough to buy your tickets the day before, you don't have to wait in line again, at least not for tickets. Position yourself for the opening of the gates

and go over your plan one more time.

3. As soon as the gates open, move briskly to *Hollywood Rip Ride Rockit*, using the single rider line if available.

4. Make a right after exiting *Rockit* and ride *Despicable Me*.

5. Head past "Mel's Drive-In" around the lagoon to *The Simpsons Ride*.

6. Continue next door to *Men In Black*. Use the regular queue if this is your first time on *MIB*; otherwise use the single rider line.

7. Next head straight to *Disaster!*

Option: If *E.T. Adventure* is high on your list, go there first and then head for *Disaster!*; if not, save *E.T.* for late in the day when many of the kiddies and their exhausted parents will have left.

8. Ride *Revenge of the Mummy*. If the wait is over 30 minutes, use the single rider line.

9. See *Shrek 4-D*, then experience *Twister* if the wait isn't too long.

10. See *Terminator 2:3-D*.

11. Now the time has come to start checking out the theater and amphitheater shows. The *Universal Horror Make-Up Show* is a short walk from the *T2* exit, and is a must-see. Check your park map for *Beetlejuice* and *Blues Brothers* show times.

12. At this point, you will have been on the most popular rides and seen a show or maybe even two. The crowds are beginning to get noticeably larger and the sun is high in the sky. Take a break, maybe eat lunch. If the park is particularly crowded and you feel you are "running late" you may want to limit your lunch to quick snacks you can carry with you as you move from line to line. There are plenty of outdoor kiosks dispensing this kind of portable "finger food."

13. Continue your rounds of the shows you want to see and check in periodically at any rides you missed (or would like to try again).

14. As the crowd thins toward closing time, circle back to the rides you missed. A great time to find shorter lines to even the most popular rides is about an hour before the official closing time.

15. If the *Cinematic Spectacular* show is running, find a viewing location near the water about ten minutes before the performance.

16. The park doesn't lock the gates at the scheduled closing time. So this is a good time to buy your souvenirs; you'll have saved some prime touring time and won't have to lug them around for so long.

Many of the smaller eateries will be open as well, so feel free to grab a well-earned dessert. And you'll still have plenty of time to visit *Lucy* before heading to your car.

The One-Day Stay for Kids

For selfless parents who are willing to place their child's agenda ahead of their own, here is an alternative one-day plan that will serve the needs of younger children—age eleven and below, maybe seven or eight and below. Often it happens that young children are better equipped to handle the more intense rides than their elders. Presumably, you know your own child or grandchild and will be able to adapt the following outline as needed.

1. Get to the park bright and early. As soon as you are in, ride *Despicable Me* (if your kids are over 40 inches tall). Afterwards, visit *E. T. Adventure*.

2. If you have very young kids, it'll be too early for *Barney* so head to see *Shrek 4-D*.

3. Depending on your kids' tolerance, check out *Men In Black* and *Disaster!*, in that order. (Take note of height restrictions.)

4. Next, check show times for *Barney* and *Animal Actors on Location!* See them in the appropriate order. Try to steer your little ones away from *Barney's Backyard*, *Fievel's Playland*, and *Curious George*, explaining that you'll return later.

5. Break for lunch.

6. After lunch, let the kids burn off steam at *Fievel's Playland*, *Barney's Backyard*, and *Curious George* while you get some much-needed rest and plot out the remainder of the day. Remember, too, that the heat of the day is the best time for your little ones to get soaked at *Curious George*.

THE FRONT LOT

In movie studio parlance, the front lot is where all the soundstages, as well as the administrative and creative offices, are located—as opposed to the back lot, which contains the outdoor sets. Here at Universal Studios Florida, the Front Lot is a small antechamber of sorts to the theme park proper, which can be looked on as one huge back lot. On the Front Lot you can take care of minor pieces of business on your way into the park—like renting a stroller—and here you can also return when things go wrong—to register a complaint at Guest Services, or seek nursing aid for an injured child, or check Lost & Found for that priceless pearl earring that flew off in *Revenge of the Mummy*. You will find the following services on the Front Lot:

To your left as you enter the park are . . .

Lockers. There are two small bays of electronically controlled lockers. The rental fee is $8 for the day with in-and-out access, and the machines accept both bills and credit cards. If these are full, you can find more lockers (including some larger and more expensive ones that are handy if you have a lot of stuff) on the other side of the plaza.

Stroller & Wheelchair Rentals. Wheelchairs are $12 a day and strollers $15. Double strollers are $25. Slightly more elaborate strollers, called "kiddie cars," feature a kid's steering wheel and cup holders and rent for $18 and $28 respectively (when available).

A motorized "electric convenience vehicle" (ECV) is yours for $50 for the day. ECVs and wheelchairs require a $50 deposit and a signed rental agreement; ECVs can be reserved a week in advance and this is highly recommended. You must be over 18 to rent an ECV. Both ECVs and wheelchairs can be transferred from park to park.

To your right as you enter the park are . . .

Guest Services. This office performs a wide variety of functions. You can pick up information and brochures about special services and special events. If you have a complaint about anything in the park, make your feelings known here. They also field compliments. Guest Services will exchange some (but not all) foreign currency, to a maximum of $500, for a flat fee of $5. If you exchange the limit, that works out to a one percent fee, a better deal than you'll get elsewhere.

Guest Services can upgrade your one-day pass to any of Universal Orlando's multi-day pass options. The price you paid for your one-day pass will be deducted from the price of the multi-day pass. There are some simple rules: Upgrades must be purchased before you leave the park. Everyone in your party who wants one must show up with their one-day pass stub in hand. Free or complimentary passes are not eligible for upgrades. Upgrades are non-transferable and Universal enforces this feature by requiring your signature on the pass and requesting photo ID. If you really liked your visit, you can also sign up for an Annual Pass here.

ATM. Next to the Studio Audience Center is an outdoor ATM, where you can get a cash advance on your Visa, MasterCard, Amex, or Discover credit card at any time. The machine is also hooked into the Cirrus, Plus, NYCE, AFFN, and Maestro systems for those who would like to withdraw money from their bank account back home. A $2.50 fee may be charged for use, in addition to any fee levied by your institution.

Studio Audience Center. There is far less television production at Universal than there used to be, but *TNA Wrestling* is regularly produced here. If anything is being taped on the nearby soundstages during your visit to Universal Studios, this is the best place to get information and tickets. Each show will have a minimum age requirement, which can vary greatly. Tickets are free and distributed on a first-come, first-served basis. Show up early, but try not to be disappointed if you come up empty. Some tapings, including TNA, can be attended without a theme park ticket. Call (407) 224-6000 for more wrestling information.

Family & Health Services. Nursing aid is available here, under the Studio Audience Center marquee, should you need it. There is also a "family bathroom" if, for example, you need to assist a disabled spouse. A special room is set aside for nursing mothers. If you just need to change a diaper, you will find diaper-changing facilities in restrooms located throughout the park.

Lost & Found. The Studio Audience Center window does double duty as Lost & Found. Items that if lost elsewhere would probably be gone forever have a surprising way of turning up at theme parks. Universal personnel always check the rides for forgotten belongings. Items are kept for 30 days. You can call (407) 224-4244.

Lockers. Here are more of those electronic lockers, with still more lockers just around the corner in a narrow, easy to overlook passageway that leads to Hollywood Boulevard and the *T2* theater. Daily rental is $8 or $10, depending on size, and allows unlimited in-and-out access.

HOLLYWOOD

Hollywood is probably the smallest "set" at Universal Studios Florida. It is about two city blocks long, stretching from *Lucy: A Tribute* near the park entrance to The Garden of Allah motel near the lagoon. Along the way is an imaginative and loving recreation of the Hollywood of our collective subconscious.

Terminator 2: 3-D Battle Across Time ★ ★ ★ ★ 1/2

Type: A "3-D Virtual Adventure"

Time: About 20 minutes

Short Take: The most exciting 3-D theater attraction in Orlando

Most attractions based on movies are created and developed by specialists at the parks. With *T2:3-D*, James Cameron (director of box-office behemoths *Titanic* and *Avatar*) and his *Terminator* star Arnold Schwarzenegger set out to prove they could do it better themselves. And, boy, did they ever! Reports are that $60 million was spent to create this show. You'll get their money's worth.

You step off Hollywood Boulevard into the rebuilt headquarters of Cyberdyne, the not-so-nice corporate giant of the *Terminator* flicks, which is out to refurbish its image and show off its latest technology. The pre-show warm-up, which takes place in a large anteroom to the theater itself, features a delicious parody of the "Vision of the Future" corporate videos and television commercials that were all the rage in the early Aughts. The pre-show also gets the plot rolling: Sarah Connor and her son John have invaded Cyberdyne and commandeered the video screen to warn us against the new SkyNet project (which sounds remarkably like the Bush-era National Missile Defense system). According to these "terrorists" (as the Cyberdyne people describe them), SkyNet will enslave us all. The Cyberdyne flack who is our host glosses over this "unfortunate interruption" and ushers us into the large auditorium. There we settle into deceptively normal looking theater seats, don our "protective glasses," and the show begins.

And what a show it is. Without giving too much away, suffice it to say that it involves a spectacular three-screen 3-D movie starring Ah-nold himself, along with Linda Hamilton and Eddie Furlong (the kid from *Terminator 2*). In one of the more inspired touches, the on-screen actors move from screen to stage and back again, Arnold aboard a roaring motorcycle.

While the *Terminator* franchise has moved on, with two more films and a TV show released since *T2:3-D* premiered, this attraction preserves the series at its peak popularity. Though the film's celluloid projectors are showing their age, the special effects remain spectacular, and the slam-bang, smoke-filled finale still has people screaming and shrieking in their seats.

Note that the interior queue can hold over 1,100 people, while the theater holds 700 people; with shows starting every 30 to 45 minutes, the line moves fairly quickly.

The Universal Horror Make-Up Show ★ ★ ★ ★ ★

Type: Theater show

Time: 25 minutes

Short Take: Hilarious! Universal's best-kept secret

How to take something gory, gruesome, and downright disgusting and turn it into wholesome, funny family fare? Universal has solved the problem with this enjoyable (not to mention educational) foray into the ghastly art of make-up and special effects for the horror genre. The key is a horror make-up "expert" with a bizarre and goofy sense of humor who is interviewed in a studio make-up lab by an on-stage host and straight man. During a laugh-filled 25 minutes, our expert leads us through a grisly show-and-tell of basic horror movie tricks and gimmicks.

Tip: The subject matter is undeniably gross and the performers are given fairly wide latitude to ad-lib. The easily offended may find either the subject matter or the humor (or both) beyond the bounds of good taste. Universal warns "parental guidance suggested," whatever that means.

Thanks to video projected onto two screens, we get a brief history of extreme makeup from Lon Chaney to modern masters Tom Savini and Rick Baker. Also on hand are mechanical werewolf heads like those used for the still stunning transformation scene in *An American Werewolf in London*. The show ends with a preview of a new, remotely controlled monster and yet another dirty trick played on a "volunteer."

This show actually instructs while it entertains. Everyone will have a keener understanding of basic horror effects, and young children will be sternly warned about the importance of safety at all times. ("Don't do this at home ... Do it at a friend's house!")

This is the best show at Universal and it just seems to get better and better every year. The performers, all skilled improvisers, play off the audience, making every show slightly different and rewarding repeat visits.

The best seats in the house. If all you want to do is enjoy the show, the oft-repeated Universal refrain is absolutely true—every seat's a good seat. Exhibitionists hoping to be selected as a volunteer should be aware that the performers have a predilection for young women, preferably ones with limited English skills, seated in the middle, close to the stage.

Lucy: A Tribute ★ ★ 1/2

Type: Museum-style display, with video
Time: Continuous viewing
Short Take: Best for adults with a sense of history

Lucy: A Tribute is a walk-in display honoring the immortal Lucille Desiree Ball. It's hard to miss, since you bump into it almost as soon as you enter the park. There's hardly ever a crowd, so feel free to breeze on by and take it in later. Fans of the great redhead (and who isn't?) will find at least something of interest here.

The "tribute" is simply a large open room ringed with glassed-in display cases, like shop windows, crammed with Lucy memorabilia—photos, letters, scripts, costumes, and Lucy's six Emmys. One of the more interesting windows contains a model of the studio in which the ground-breaking *I Love Lucy* show was shot. It was the first show shot with the three-camera method still used today. A fascinating footnote: The sets in those days of black-and-white TV were actually painted in shades of gray (furniture, too) to provide optimum contrast on the home screen.

Selected Short Subjects

Hollywood Celebrities

Hollywood Boulevard is a great place for star spotting. **Stars of yesteryear,** like Marilyn Monroe and Lucy and Desi, as well as famous **cartoon characters** like Woody Woodpecker and Scooby Doo have been known to put in appearances. Lately, the Simpsons have been showing up in a large RV to mix and mingle with the crowds. You can have your photo taken with them or even get an autograph.

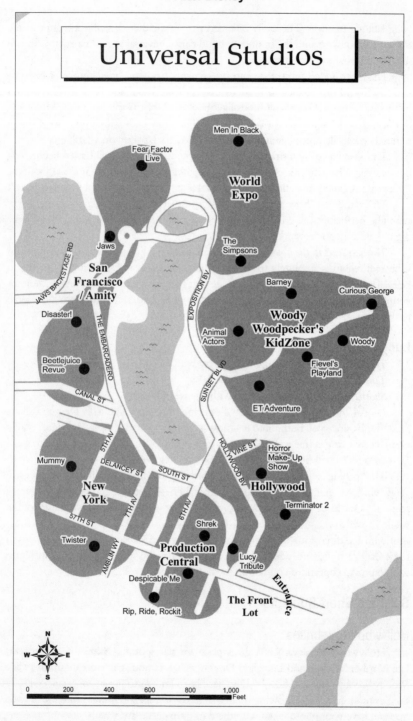

Universal Studios

Men In Black

Fear Factor Live

World Expo

Jaws

San Francisco / Amity

JAWS BACKSTAGE RD

THE EMBARCADERO

The Simpsons

EXPOSITION BV

Disaster!

Barney

Curious George

Woody Woodpecker's KidZone

Animal Actors

Woody

SUNSET BLVD

Beetlejuice Revue

Fievel's Playland

CANAL ST

ET Adventure

5TH AV

Mummy

DELANCEY ST

SOUTH ST

HOLLYWOOD BV

VINE ST

Horror Make-Up Show

Hollywood

New York

57TH ST

7TH AV

6TH AV

Terminator 2

Twister

AMBLIN WY

Shrek

Production Central

Lucy Tribute

Entrance

Despicable Me

The Front Lot

Rip, Ride, Rockit

N W E S

0   200   400   600   800   1,000
Feet

Musical Entertainment

From time to time, usually during the park's busier periods, you will find a fifties-style rock & roll group holding forth on a small stage outside Mel's Diner. The groups vary in size and composition, but the nostalgic set list is virtually guaranteed to please.

Trick Photography Photo Spot

Near the lagoon, you will find a spot where you can take your own souvenir photo using the "hanging miniature" technique pioneered in the early days of filmmaking. Position your camera on the stand and follow the fool-proof instructions. There are even footprints telling you where to place your subjects. Then you can photograph your family in front of the (real) Pantages Theater, with the (painted) Hollywood hills and the rest of the Los Angeles skyline stretching into the distance. Even if you don't have a camera, take a peek to see how it works. It's nifty.

WOODY WOODPECKER'S KIDZONE

Although its intense thrill rides have brought Universal Studios Florida a reputation as an "adult" theme park, it hasn't forgotten the kiddies. Woody Woodpecker's KidZone, located along a winding avenue off the central lagoon, is a perfect case in point. If you have children under ten, you could very easily spend an entire day here, with only an occasional foray to sample other kid-friendly attractions in the park.

Tip: At the end of the Hollywood set, past Cafe La Bamba, look for the Gardens of Allah Villas on your right. Cut through here for a shortcut to Woody's KidZone and the *E. T. Adventure.*

Animal Actors On Location! ★ ★ ★ 1/2

Type:	Amphitheater show
Time:	About 20 minutes
Short Take:	Fun for just about everybody

This awww-inspiring spectacle shows off the handiwork of Universal's animal trainers and their furry and feathery charges. It's all done with the droll good humor and audience participation that characterize all of Universal's shows. Volunteers are pulled from the audience to serve as foils for several amusing routines.

The show alternates between live action on stage and video footage on a large overhead screen showing clips of animal actors in a surprising variety of films, from comedies to horror flicks. In one especially fascinating segment, we learn how birds can be filmed in flight using a large fan and some trick camera work.

Just which animals you see will depend to some extent on which "stars" are available when you visit. But you can probably count on a display by a well-trained if slightly mercenary bird and a bit that uses a child volunteer from the audience. If you're lucky, an orangutan will provide comic relief.

In between the fun and games, the show sneaks in a few points about the serious business of producing "behaviors" that can be put to use in films. When an animal balks at performing a trick, as they do with amusing frequency, the trainer will work patiently with the animal until the behavior is performed correctly. What for us is light entertainment is serious business for the folks (both two- and four-legged) on the stage.

The best seats in the house. There really are no bad seats for this one. However, if you'd like a shot at serving as a landing strip for that mercenary bird, try sitting in the middle of the middle section.

E.T. Adventure ★ ★ ★

Type:	Gondola ride
Time:	5 minutes
Short Take:	Kids love this one (some adults do, too)

Based on the blockbuster movie that crossed sci-fi with cuddly toys, the *E.T. Adventure* takes us where the movie didn't—back to E.T.'s home planet. In a filmed introduction to the ride, Steven Spielberg, who directed the film, sets up the premise via a video message: E.T.'s home, the Green Planet, is in some unspecified trouble, although it looks like an advanced case of ozone hole, which is turning the place a none-too-healthy-looking orange. You have to return with E.T. to help save the old folks at home. How to get there? Aboard the flying bicycles from the film's final sequence, of course. The fact that Spielberg doesn't bother to explain how we'll survive the rigors of interstellar travel aboard mountain bikes tells us that this ride is aimed at the very young. After this brief setup, the doors ahead open and we line up to tell a staffer our first names and get the "passports" we will need for the journey.

Passports firmly in hand, we walk through a cave-like tunnel into the misty, nighttime redwood forests of the Northwest. This set is a minor masterpiece of scenic design and some people think it's the best part of the adventure. As we wend our way along a winding "nature trail" among the towering trees, we make out the animated figure of Botanicus, a wise elder from E.T.'s planet, urging us to hurry back. Here, too, we glimpse the jury-rigged contraption E.T. used to communicate in the film.

At the staging area, we hand in our passports and collect our "bikes" (look for E.T. to pop his head out of the basket on the front), which are actually 12-passenger, open-sided gondolas hanging from a ceiling track. They have bicycle-like seats, each with its own set of handlebars.

The best seats in the house. On the whole, the left side of the gondola provides better views than the right, especially of the city. Best of all is the far left seat in the first row.

This ride might be likened to a bike with training wheels. It has many of the aspects of more thrilling rides—sudden acceleration, swoops, and turns—but toned down so as not to be truly frightening. In the first phase of the ride, we are zipping through the redwoods, dodging the unenlightened grown-ups who want to capture E.T. for study and analysis. This section can be a little scary for small kids and a little loud for older adults. Soon, however, we are soaring high above the city in the ride's most enchanting interlude. We rise higher until we are in the stars themselves and are then shot down a hyperspace tunnel before we decelerate abruptly and find ourselves in the steamy world of E.T.'s home planet.

It's an odd cave-like environment but soon, apparently buoyed by our arrival, the place perks up and we are flying through a psychedelic world of huge multicolored flowers in wondrous shapes, past talking mushrooms and plants (or are they creatures?) with dozens of eyes. All around are little E.T.s, peeping from under plants, climbing over them, and playing them like drums It's all rather like Disney's *it's a small world* on acid.

All too soon, E.T. is sending us back to our home, but not before a final farewell when those passports pay off cleverly. Listen carefully!

E.T. is one of Universal's most popular rides for people of all ages, with the result that the lines can become dauntingly long. On busy days, there can be another wait of 15 to 20 minutes once inside before you reach the ride itself.

Tip: When the *Animal Actors* show lets out (about 25 minutes after the posted show time), the crowds stream over to get on line for *E.T.* Time your visit accordingly.

Note: There are two Universal Express entrances in this ride, one outside and a second shortly after you enter the forest inside the building.

Fievel's Playland ★ ★ ★

Type: Hands-on activity
Time: As long as you want
Short Take: For young and very active kids

Based on Steven Spielberg's charming animated film, *An American Tail*, about a shtetl mouse making his way in the New World, *Fievel's Playland* is a convoluted maze of climb-up, run-through, slide-down activities that will keep kids amused while their exhausted parents take a well-deserved break.

Don't forget to bring your camera for great **photo ops** of the kids amid the larger-than-life cowboy hats, Victrolas, water barrels, playing cards, and cattle skeletons that make up this maze of exploration.

The highlight is a Mouse Climb—a rope tunnel that spirals upwards. At the top, kids can climb into two-man (well, two-kid) rubber rafts to slide down through yet another tunnel to arrive at ground level with enormous grins and wet bottoms. Don't worry, there's also a set of stairs to the top of this water slide.

This is a place you can safely let the kids explore on their own. The ground is padded. However, kids less than 40 inches high will have to drag a grown-up (or maybe a bigger sibling) along to ride the water slide. There's seldom a wait to get in to *Fievel's Playland* but long lines do form for the water slide. If time is a factor and if you will be visiting one of the water-themed parks on another day, you can tell the kids that there are bigger, better water slides awaiting them tomorrow.

Note: Even though this attraction is aimed squarely at the kiddie set, don't be surprised if your young teens get in the spirit and momentarily forget that romping through a kid's playground is not the "cool" thing to do.

A Day in the Park with Barney ★ ★ ★

Type: Theater show with singing
Time: About 20 minutes
Short Take: For toddlers and their long-suffering parents

According to the publicity, Universal's *Barney* attraction is the only place in the United States where you can see Barney "live." For some people, that may be one place too many. But for his legions of adoring wee fans (the attraction has its own stroller parking lot) and the parents who love them, this show will prove an irresistible draw.

When the show begins, we are all ushered into a stand-up pre-show area where Mr. Peekaboo and his gaudy bird friend Bartholomew put on a singing, dancing warm-up act that wouldn't be complete unless the audience got splashed. Then, using our imaginations, we pass through a misty cave entrance sprinkled with star dust to enter the main theater. Inside is a completely circular space cheerfully decorated as a forest park at dusk. Low benches surround the raised central stage, but old fogies may want to make for the more comfortable park benches against the walls.

The show is brief and cheery and almost entirely given over to sing-alongs that are already familiar to Barney's little fans. Barney is soon joined by Baby Bop and B.J. and the merriment proceeds apace, complete with falling autumn leaves, a brief snowfall, and shooting streamers. True star that he is, Barney stays behind after the show for a well-organized meet and greet session with his young admirers. A few of the kids seem overawed to be so close to this giant vision in purple.

The theater audience empties out into **Barney's Backyard**, which is the day-care center of your dreams. Here, beautifully executed by Universal scenic artists, is a collection of imaginative and involving activities for the very young, from making music to splashing in water, to drawing on the walls. Barney's Backyard is where little kids get their revenge. Whereas many rides in the park bar younger children on the basis of height, here there are activities that are off limits to those over 48 inches or even 36 inches. Kids will love it. Grown-ups will wish there were more of it.

Tip: This wonderful space has a separate entrance and you don't have to sit through the show to get in here. Keep this in mind if the family's youngest member needs some special attention or a chance to unwind from the frustrations of being a little person in a big person's amusement park.

Woody Woodpecker's Nuthouse Coaster ★ ★ 1/2

Type: A kiddie roller coaster
Time: About 1 minute
Short Take: A thrill ride for the younger set

Woody Woodpecker's Nuthouse Coaster is described as a "gentle" children's roller coaster, knocked together by Woody from bits of this and that, running through a nut factory. The eight cars on the "Knothead Express" are modeled after nut crates; they run along 800 feet of red tubular steel track with some mild drops and tilted turns that shouldn't prove frightening to any child who meets the 36-inch minimum height requirement, although you may spot some none-too-happy grandparents.

Curious George Goes To Town ★ ★ ★ ★

Type: A water-filled play area
Time: Unlimited
Short Take: It will be hard to drag kids away

Woody's KidZone turns into a water park in this elaborate play area themed after the illustrated books about George, the playful monkey, and his friend The Man in the

Yellow Hat. Expect your kids to get sopping wet here and enjoy every minute of it.

There are some padded play areas with jets of water shooting up from the ground near the entrance, but the main attraction lies a few steps farther along, in the town square. On opposite sides stand the Fire Department and the City Waterworks, dubbed "City H2O." On the second floor balcony, five water cannons let kids squirt those below, and high above is a huge water bucket that fills with water and, with the clanging of a warning bell, tips over, sending a cascade of water into the square below as kids scramble to position themselves under it for a thorough and thoroughly delightful soaking.

When your kids are ready for a change of pace, they can repair to the **Ball Factory**, behind the town square. This cheerfully noisy two-level metal structure is filled with thousands of colored soft foam balls. The noise comes from the industrial strength vacuum machines that suck balls from the floor and send them to aim-able ball cannons mounted on tall poles or to large bins high overhead. Some vacuums send balls to stations where kids can fill up mesh bags with balls they then take to the second level balcony to feed into the ten "Auto Blasters" that let them shoot balls at the kids down below. It's a scene of merry anarchy and many adults quickly get in touch with their inner child and become active participants in the chaotic battle raging all about. Those ball bins, like the water buckets outside, tip over periodically, pummeling eager victims below and replenishing the supply of balls.

This is one attraction that can keep kids happily occupied for hours on end. It will also appeal to the older kids in your family who might find some of the other offerings in Woody Woodpecker's KidZone too "babyish."

Tip: Bring a towel and a change of clothes for the kids if the weather's cool. This is also a good activity to schedule just before you leave the park, either for the day or for a nap-time break.

Selected Short Subjects

Character Meet and Greet

Here's your chance to meet and mingle with some of Hollywood's cartoon heavyweights. That's right, Woody Woodpecker, Curious George, and animals from *Madagascar*. They show up periodically in the circular plaza at the entrance to KidZone to do a little song and dance, meet their adoring public and, yes, sign autographs. Don't expect much in the way of scintillating conversation, however; they're the strong silent type. Appearances take place on a fairly continuous basis from about midday on a schedule listed in the 2-Park Map. It's hard to predict who you'll see on a given visit, because the stars take turns making these outdoor appearances.

WORLD EXPO

The theme of World Expo is a typical World's Fair Exposition park. The result is a display of contemporary architecture and design that manages to be at once very attractive and rather characterless, although the buildings look quite zippy at night.

The Simpsons Ride ★ ★ ★ ★ 1/2

Type: Simulator thrill ride
Time: 4½ minute ride, with 10 minutes of preshows
Short Take: A wild and witty spin through Springfield

Welcome to Krustyland, the Krustiest Place on Earth™! Krusty the Clown is opening his theme park's "All-New Thrilltacular Upsy-Downsy Spins-Aroundsy Teen-Operated Thrill Ride," and you can join the Simpson family as the first suckers—um, lucky winners—to try it. Krusty's criminal nemesis, Sideshow Bob, has been spotted in the vicinity, but not to worry: as Homer says "they won't kill you in a theme park as long as you've got a dime in your pocket."

Over the last 20 years, Matt Groening's *The Simpsons* has grown from crudely animated interstitials on FOX's *Tracy Ullman Show* to the world's most popular animated family. Thankfully, the translation of *The Simpsons* to the theme-park world hasn't come at the expense of their satirical edge. From the queue video (featuring classic clips of "Itchy and Scratchy Land" and "Duff Gardens," along with sharp new skits) to the cliché-skewering signage (Ride "Captain Dinosaur's Pirate Ripoff"), this attraction pulls no punches in biting the corporate hand that feeds it.

Once inside the carnival-colorful building, you'll be separated into groups of eight and directed to a "funhouse" holding room, where you'll see a gruesomely hilarious safety warning before boarding the ride.

The Simpsons Ride retains much of the basic flight-simulator infrastructure of *Back to the Future: The Ride (BTTF)*, the attraction it replaced. The vehicles face a mammoth, curved movie screen that completely fills your line of vision and represents the true genius of this ride concept. Other simulator-based rides (like the *Despicable Me* ride here at USF) use a movie screen that serves as a window to the outside of your spaceship or other vehicle. With this concept, however, you are outside and the environment wraps around you. The illusion is startling, not to mention sometimes terrifying. (Look up as the ride starts for a vertigo-inducing effect.)

The new ride improves on its predecessor with high-resolution digital projectors, a smoother ride, and new tactile and olfactory effects. Best of all, the writing and voice acting (with nearly the entire original cast except Harry Shearer's Burns and Smithers) are worthy of an episode from the TV show's best seasons.

The best seats in the house. The best way to experience this attraction is from the front row of the middle car in the middle level of the dome. Ask the attendant at the point where the line splits for Level 2, then ask the next attendant for Room 6. You may need to wait longer, but it's worth it: you'll experience less distortion of the image and reduce any tendency toward motion sickness. Sit in the front row of the car for comfort, especially if you are tall.

Men In Black: Alien Attack * * * *

Type: Interactive ride with laser weapons
Time: 4 minutes
Short Take: This one gets addictive

Men In Black, the ride, is a bit like stepping inside a life-size video arcade game, with the element of competition thrown in just to make things interesting. The experience begins when you visit "The Universe and You," a science exhibit left over from the New York World's Fair of 1964. Soon you discover that it's just a cover to enable you to apply for admission to the elite corps of MIB. A lengthy and amusing orientation video featuring Rip Torn and Will Smith is worth watching even when there's no line. Farther along, a training film starring two amusingly retro cartoon characters, Doofus and Do-Right, provides safety instructions for the testing vehicles that await you.

Tip: If you don't mind having your party split up, look for the single rider line after your first trip through.

Eventually, you are assigned to a vehicle with five other recruits. At each seat is a laser gun and a personal scoreboard that keeps track of hits. You are cruising through a target range, testing your marksmanship, when an urgent bulletin announces that a Prison Transport full of nasty space bugs has crash landed in the middle of Manhattan. At once, you are reassigned to a dangerous but exciting mission. You and another team are dispatched, side by side, to do battle with the aliens through the dark and gritty streets of a cartoon New York.

What follows is a few minutes of chaotic fun. Aliens in every imaginable buggy shape pop up from garbage cans and taxi hoods, from around corners and in shop windows. It's a super-sized sci-fi version of those old shooting galleries down at the boardwalk. Your job is to zap them before they zap you. When the bugs score a hit, your vehicle is sent into a tailspin.

Tip: The guns auto-fire, so hold down the trigger the entire time; you'll score higher and avoid finger cramps. Hit the same target multiple times to boost your score. The maximum possible score is 999,999 and, yes, it can be done.

The vehicles are not simulators but they do allow for sudden swoops and 360-degree spins, which are both thrilling and discombobulating. And while the two vehicles depart at the same time and cruise along side by side for most of the ride, their progress can be affected by the direct hits scored by the aliens. As the battle progresses, every rider builds an individual score based on their success in targeting the enemy (you will see the tiny red dots of the laser guns dancing on the alien targets); the individual scores contribute to the overall team score. There is a sneaky way to significantly increase your score that you'll have to discover on your own.

MIB is a lot of fun and it's hard to imagine anyone having serious complaints. Video game addicts will probably want to ride again and again to improve their scores. Obviously there is at least some skill involved in wielding the laser guns because individual scores in a vehicle can vary by as much as several hundred thousand points.

Note: This ride requires that you stow all your belongings in nearby electronic lockers that are free for a short period of time but charge a hefty fee if you overstay your welcome.

HARRY POTTER AND THE GRINGOTTS AFFAIR

In January 2012, Universal closed its beloved *Jaws* ride, one of the park's original attractions on opening day in 1991, and along with it the Amity section of boardwalk games and fast food eateries leaving a gaping hole in the middle of the park. Immediately, there was feverish speculation about what would replace it. While much of the detail remains shrouded in mystery, the broad outlines of Universal's plans have slipped out from the Chamber of Secrets where they were supposed to have rested undisturbed until Universal was ready to make an official announcement.

As crystal ball gazing Muggles were quick to surmise, it seems that Harry Potter will fill the void. That makes a good deal of sense. Attendance at Islands of Adventure next door (see the next chapter) soared when The Wizarding World of Harry Potter opened and USF took an inevitable hit; a new Harry Potter attraction will certainly even the scales.

The plans, which are preliminary, strongly suggest that this new Potter "land" will center on London's Diagon Alley and, more specifically, Gringotts Wizarding Bank. The confidential plans, which were revealed by Robert Niles of ThemeParkInsider. com, seem to show a single, "secret" entrance to the area much like that described in the Rowling books. Once inside there is a large (8,900 square feet) restaurant (The Leaky Cauldron?) and a massive show building themed as the bank and housing Universal's latest spin on the "dark ride" concept.

Niles speculates that the ride will feature an elaborate queue line a la *Forbidden Journey* over at IOA, which seems a safe bet. Sketches for the ride vehicles seem to show larger versions of the little goblin-mobiles seen in the films. And since these vehicles run through torch-lit subterranean tracks to Gringotts' vaults, it seems a safe bet that the ride will take us into the mysterious bowels of this goblin-run establishment.

Best of all, the ride seems to be yet another envelope pusher for Universal—a combination of indoor roller coaster (think *Revenge of the Mummy* here in USF) with a motion simulator vehicle and 3-D projections (think *Spider-Man* over at IOA).

The preliminary plans gave no hint as to the narrative of the ride, but the likeliest scenario is that we will find ourselves caught up in some sort of break-in attempt. (I can almost hear Hagrid saying, "yeh'd be mad ter try an' rob it.") Whether it will involve the Philosopher's Stone or the Hufflepuff Cup Horcrux or something invented just for the ride is anyone's guess. But whatever the magical McGuffin, we'll wager a knut you'll be encountering dragons, wizards, and spritzes of water, and quite likely some fire (this is Universal, after all) before you're through.

As large as this ride appears to be, there seems to be room left over in the area for some other fun touches. We've heard reliable reports that there will be another Ollivander's. It's supposed to be in Diagon Alley after all and having two might ease the crush over at IOA. And Florean Fortescue's Ice Cream Parlour would be a nice touch.

A more controversial, not to mention more intriguing, aspect of the speculation about what's in store here is the notion that Universal will somehow link the IOA and USF Potter areas with a ride that starts in London and ends in Hogsmeade (and vice versa). Adding credence to that speculation, Niles reports that the preliminary plans show a second, unidentified attraction positioned exactly where you'd expect it to be if this trans-park ride comes to fruition. Unseen by visitors but visible in aerial photographs is a backstage service road that runs from the *Jaws* area almost straight to the back of the Sindbad amphitheater in IOA. Could this be the route for a new and unprecedented theme park experience?

If so, it would mean expanding the existing Wizarding World in IOA to encompass the area now occupied by the *Sindbad* show. Indeed, Universal has already announced just such an expansion of the Wizarding World and has started making some changes to office locations and parade routes in USF that suggest they are making room in those backstage areas for . . . something.

Such a trans-park ride would be a radical departure for Universal—and theme parks in general for that matter. It raises intriguing questions about how Universal would handle one-park versus two-park tickets. Or perhaps the option of paying to visit a single park would disappear altogether.

Of course all this is rank speculation, the mere ravings of mad Muggles, but isn't part of a good theme park's mission to spark your imagination?

SAN FRANCISCO

With the closing of *Jaws*, the "set" that used to be called San Francisco/Amity became simply San Francisco, but some of the odd juxtapositions that attended its former incarnation remain. *Fear Factor Live*, which has no discernible connection to the City by the Bay, is still part of it, separated from the actual San Francisco facades by a long walk past the construction barriers that mask the forthcoming Harry Potter attraction. It might have made more sense to fold *Fear Factor* into World Expo, but I'm not the one calling the shots and besides few will care.

Fear Factor Live ★ ★ 1/2

Type: Amphitheater show
Time: 30 minutes
Short Take: The TV show comes to life

For big fans of reality television shows, this live version of the recently revived NBC show may make for great entertainment. Six contestants, who have been preselected prior to each show, compete in three events. Contestants are ruthlessly eliminated and forced to take the "Walk of Shame" until the two finalists square off in a multipart test of nerves, climbing ability, and guts. The stunts are not for sissies, involving as they do considerable heights, "carnivorous" eels, and other assorted nastiness. Most impressive is the final challenge, which features two tilted convertibles raised to the rafters; contestants must climb onto the water-slicked hoods to retrieve flags attached to the grilles.

Volunteers are drawn from the audience to fill a variety of roles. Some fire water cannons and other fiendish devices designed to make the main contestants' jobs even harder. Others are given challenges like confronting creepy-crawlies and drinking yucky concoctions that might make them wish they'd thought twice about volunteering.

Note: This show is only performed "seasonally," which means at times of peak attendance. It may be gone for good by the time you visit.

Disaster! ★ ★ ★ 1/2

Type:	Show and ride
Time:	25 minutes, ride portion is 3 minutes
Short Take:	Best for the ride

Disaster! takes the "Ride the Movies" slogan to its logical extreme. Here, the ride *is* the movie and everyone who rides it is a star. Well, okay, everyone who rides it is an extra. There are chills and thrills in store, but first you have to go through some mildly amusing silliness to put you in the mood.

The experience begins with a visit to Disaster Studios, an "independent, boutique" studio, the creation of disaster flick genius, Frank Kincaid. Kincaid is quite the Renaissance man, writing, directing, and producing shoestring-budget disaster epics like *Baboom*, *Fungus*, and *300 Knots Landing*, which is about a plane crash apparently.

Once inside, you discover you have stumbled into a casting call. One of Mr. Kincaid's lackeys is looking for a few willing victims . . . er, *volunteers* to serve as actors and stunt people for Kincaid's next blockbuster. Then it's on to the next room, for the best part of the pre-ride show. Here we meet Mr. Kincaid himself, played by a subdued, but still bizarro, Christopher Walken. Through a bit of technological magic called "Musion" that will have you scratching your head and asking, "How'd they do that?" Kincaid (or at least a holographic simulation of him) strides on stage and treats us to a brief lecture on his "secret" rules of disaster films ("The annoying guy always dies") and announces his next magnum opus, *Mutha Nature*, a global warming eco-disaster flick starring Duane "The Rock" Johnson as a heroic park ranger battling evil corporate villains.

In the third room, the volunteers picked earlier are put to work filming bits and pieces that will be edited into the final film. "Time is money," Mr. Kincaid points out, so these bits are shot in an ultra-fast-paced illustration of "green screen" techniques. The big news, however, is that Mr. Kincaid has decided to cast all of us in the grand finale to his film.

This is the part most people come for, a simulated earthquake aboard San Francisco's BART (Bay Area Rapid Transit). The train (with open sides and clear plastic roof) pulls out of the Oakland station, enters the tunnel under the Bay, and soon emerges in the Embarcadero station. A voice over the train's P.A. system instructs you to scream for the camera as the earthquake reaches eight on the Richter scale and the Embarcadero station begins to artfully fall apart. Floors buckle and ceilings shatter. The car you're in jerks upward, while the car in front of you drops and tilts perilously. Then the entire roof caves in on one side, exposing the street above, and . . . well let's not give too much away.

All too soon, the terror is over and the train backs out of the station, returning us to "Oakland." As it backs out, we are treated to a trailer for *Mutha Nature*, into which have been inserted the scenes shot in the preshow and during the ride, to humorous effect.

Beetlejuice's Graveyard Revue ★ ★ ★

Type:	Amphitheater show
Time:	20 minutes
Short Take:	Best for teens and pre-teens

Beetlejuice began his career as the eponymous obnoxious "bio-exorcist" (played by Michael Keaton) of Tim Burton's breakout film. After his stint as a streetside performer on USF's New York set proved popular, he was "discovered" by Universal Studios and given his own amphitheater show. The addition of a set, pyrotechnics, and what sounds like several million dollars worth of sound equipment hasn't changed the show's basic appeal, just made it louder.

The set is a jumble of crumbling castle walls, complete with a mummy's sarcophagus and a more modern coffin. The "plot" is nonexistent. Beetlejuice, your host with the most, emerges from the mummy's tomb and immediately gets to the business at hand, summoning the Wolfman, Dracula, Frankenstein, and the ever-lovely Bride of Frankenstein from their ghostly lairs for your listening pleasure.

The choreography is straightforward, energetic, and more than a little suggestive. Anyone heretofore sheltered from modern pop concerts will find it a suitable introduction to the genre. The latest incarnation of this show is mildly raunchy, and Universal recommends "parental guidance."

NEW YORK

Compared to some others on the lot, the New York set seems downright underpopulated—with attractions, eateries, and shops, that is. Whole streets in New York are given over entirely to film backdrops. Gramercy Park, Park Avenue, the dead-end Fifty-Seventh Street that incongruously ends at the New York Public Library, and the narrow alleys behind Delancey Street contain nary a ride or shop. These sets, however, provide some wonderfully evocative backgrounds for street shows and family portraits, especially the library facade, with a collection of familiar skyscrapers looming behind it. They also include some clever inside jokes for those familiar with the movie industry. Check out the names painted on the windows of upper story offices along Fifth Avenue and see if you can spot them.

Revenge of the Mummy ★ ★ ★ ★ 1/2

Type: Indoor roller coaster and dark ride
Time: About 4 minutes
Short Take: A brilliant blend of thrills and chills

The *Revenge of the Mummy* starts innocently enough. It seems Universal is in need of more extras for this new film and you are lucky enough to be passing by as they solicit volunteers. (Don't get your hopes up. *Revenge of the Mummy* is not a real film, it's just a polite fiction for the sake of the ride.)

As you enter the queue line, it looks like one of those "The Making of..." displays that Universal used to mount. Props and set pieces are scattered about, all carefully labeled. On video monitors, director Steven Sommers, star Brendan Fraser, and others on the crew give interviews about the making of the film, dropping ominous references to ancient curses and strange happenings. A recurring character in these vignettes is Reggie, a hapless gofer who keeps losing his anti-Mummy amulet to Hollywood bigwigs.

Then the queue line takes a sharp turn through a narrow passageway and things become truly strange. There's no more video and the queue line now looks remarkably like a real Egyptian tomb in the Valley of the Kings at Thebes. Oddly, there's nothing to indicate whether this is supposed to be a movie set or the real thing, whether you're still in 21st century Orlando or back in the 1930s.

Up a rickety wooden staircase, past a massive sculpture of Anubis, the god of the Underworld, you finally reach the loading platform for the ride. Once again, there's no explanation of why you are being asked to board the 16-passenger, 4-abreast cars, or what lies ahead.

Tip: Eyeglass wearers should note that water effects in the ride (more pronounced in the front) can wet their glasses and blur their vision.

The ride itself starts deceptively. It's not too far removed from those gentle "dark rides" at a certain family park complex down the Interstate. But you're still in that nasty Imhotep's retirement home and before long things get dicey. You turn a corner and there's Reggie again, all wrapped up for Mummy take-out, warning you to turn back.

Imhotep himself appears rather dramatically and looking decidedly the worse for wear after several millennia of entombment. "With your souls, I shall rule for all eternity," he bellows, which sounds like a great slogan for a modern-day political campaign.

Around the next bend, you are given a stark choice: Get with the program and receive riches beyond imagination or resist and die a hideous death. Your cries of "I'll take the gold! I'll take the gold!" go unheeded and the ride begins in earnest.

At this point, the curse of the Mummy takes hold, and this description stops so as not to reveal too much about what follows. Universal bills this as a "psychological thrill ride" and it does, indeed, mess with your mind. Suffice it to say that the ride morphs into a supercharged roller coaster experience that takes place largely in near darkness. If you think this will be just another indoor roller coaster ride, think again. The Mummy himself puts it nicely: "Death is only the beginning."

Those who balk at mega-coasters like *The Hulk* and *Dragon Challenge* over at Islands of Adventure are still encouraged to give *Revenge of the Mummy* a try. Because the ride is so smooth, it is only slightly more intense than *Spider-Man* at IOA. If you can handle Disney coasters like *Big Thunder Mountain* and *Space Mountain*, you'll survive this one. You'll just have more fun.

Twister . . . Ride It Out ★ ★ ★ 1/2

Type:	Stand-up theater show
Time:	15 minutes
Short Take:	Amazing in-your-face special effects

Here is an attraction that will almost literally blow you away. Based on the hit film of the same name, *Twister* is a theater show without seats that leads you through three sets for a payoff that lasts all of two minutes. But what a two minutes it is!

The journey begins as you snake though a waiting line in Wakita, Oklahoma, around large props from the film. The line may seem formidable, but don't despair. This show can handle 2,400 people each hour, so the line moves fairly quickly. Once inside, the show follows a familiar three-part format. In the first chamber, themed as the prop room for the film, you watch a video that sets the scene. If you missed the movie, this segment gives you all the information you need.

The second chamber is themed as the ruined interior of Aunt Meg's house from the movie. Trees and the front end of an automobile protrude through the ceiling, where a string of video monitors continue the introduction process. There is barely any "edutainment" in this attraction, but what little there is happens here. Then it's on to the final chamber where the "real" show happens—live, in-person, and right before your eyes. You enter a set where you stand on a three-level viewing area under the deceptive protection of a tin roof. In front of you is the Wakita street that runs past the Galaxy outdoor movie theater where a "Horror Night" double feature of *The Shining* and *Psycho* is being shown. The street is deserted, but no sooner is everyone in place than all heck breaks loose and the inanimate objects before you take on a scary life of their own.

You've probably already figured out that you'll be living through the vortex of a twister. Some of the effects are versions of what you may already have seen while riding *Disaster!*, and the final funnel effect sometimes fizzles. But first-time viewers always get a big kick out of the explosive ending.

Tip: This is a wet, if not precisely soaking, experience. A poncho might be in order if you're really fussy.

Selected Short Subjects

The Blues Brothers

The Dan Ackroyd/John Belushi routine that made a better *Saturday Night Live* sketch than it ever did a movie is immortalized in this peppy street show, which currently holds forth from a makeshift stage on Delancey Street. The genial performers, who are look-alikes only to the extent that one is tall and lanky and the other short and stout, do the material justice, and Jake's hyperkinetic dance steps are a highlight of the show. If you like your rhythm and blues straight and unadulterated, you should enjoy it.

PRODUCTION CENTRAL

Production Central is modeled on a typical film studio front lot. Essentially, it is a collection of soundstages and has a resolutely industrial feel to it. But with recent additions injecting some architectural pizzazz, this area now has visual interest to match its entertainment value.

Hollywood Rip Ride Rockit ★ ★ ★ ★

Type:　　　Music-themed steel coaster
Time:　　　About 2 minutes
Short Take:　A ground-breaking (but also back-breaking) ride

Towering over the soundstages, smashing through the New York firehouse facade, and snaking its way toward CityWalk, the *Hollywood Rip Ride Rockit* has literally changed the face of Universal Studios Florida forever. Billed as "the most technologically advanced coaster in the world," this first Floridian installation from innovative European designer Maurer Söhne boasts statistics to make any speed freak salivate. It's the tallest (167 feet) and one of the fastest (65 mph) coasters in Orlando, and features a number of unique, newly engineered elements.

The experience begins in a flatscreen-festooned queue near the Blue Man Group theater, where "edgy" animated characters introduce themselves as the camera crew for your new music video. The seven 12-passenger cars are just as high-tech, with on-board video and sound systems, and color-changing LEDs that put on a carnival light show as they swoop overhead. Even the boarding process has been upgraded: a moving walkway keeps cars continuously loading, minimizing wait times.

Once in the car, you'll use a seat-mounted display to select a soundtrack from one of five musical genres, including "Classic Rock/Metal" (ZZ Top, Limp Bizkit), "Country" (Dwight Yoakam, Kenny Chesney) and "Rap/Hip-Hop" (Black Eyed Peas, Kanye West). With 30 songs to choose from, everyone should be able to find something they'll like screaming along to.

Once your music selection is made, you begin the ride by ascending a "record-breaking" vertical lift (lying flat on your back!) in only 17 seconds, then dive into a 103-foot "non-inverting" twisted loop dubbed a "Double-Take" above the plaza stage. Other maneuvers take you spiraling through the *Twister* queue facade, "crowd surfing" over waiting guests, and skirting the edge of CityWalk. The twisty track is deceptively disorienting (and surprisingly silent); you'll be back in the station before you know what hit you.

Rockit isn't as intense an experience as the *Incredible Hulk*, but delivers more kick than *Revenge of the Mummy*. It's too wild to be considered a "family coaster" (especially in the bumpy back seats) but the lack of upside-down inversions makes it a good bet for tweens ready to graduate to grown-up thrills. The best news for coaster purists (or worst for the weak-kneed) is that there are no over-the-shoulder restraints, only a large curved lap bar that holds you firmly in place while allowing bursts of out-of-your-seat airtime.

Tip: Rockit is the hottest ride at Universal Studios and it doesn't currently offer Universal Express, so do it first thing in the morning and/or use the single rider line (if available).

Despicable Me: Minion Mayhem (not open at press time)

Type: Simulator ride in 3-D
Time: About 5 minutes
Short Take: A funny, family-friendly thrill

Opening in 2012, *Despicable Me* is based on the same simulator hardware as the former Jimmy Neutron and Hanna-Barbera attractions. This newest incarnation adds cutting-edge "4K" digital 3-D projectors for ultra-sharp in-your-face visual effects. The show will be voiced by the stars of the film and at its conclusion the audience will be transformed into minions. The room containing your vehicle is actually a movie theater divided into twelve 8-seat sections. Each section is actually a simulator car, a cousin of the high-tech simulators used to train airline pilots. It hovers a few feet off the ground, like a box on stilts, and moves and tilts in sync with the on-screen action. It may only move a foot or so in any direction, but try telling that to your mind. Still, the gyrations are gentler than those of the similar *Simpsons* ride, making this a good starter thrill for those building up their courage.

Shrek 4-D ★ ★ ★ ★ 1/2

Type: Theater show
Time: 25 minutes
Short Take: Another boffo 3-D extravaganza

Welcome back to Duloc, that magical kingdom where everything is perfect—or would be if it weren't for all those pesky fairy tale characters that the late Lord Farquaad tried to do away with. As we enter Duloc we find ourselves in a dungeon antechamber where Pinocchio and the Three Little Pigs are being tortured under the direction of the ghost of Lord Farquaad. On the "Dungeon Cam" we see the Gingerbread Man tacked down to a torture table awaiting an even worse fate. Apparently, we're next.

In a very funny preshow we learn, courtesy of the Magic Mirror from the old Snow White tale, that the evil Lord still carries a considerable torch for the lovely Fiona, who is now off on her honeymoon with Shrek and Donkey. The ghost of Farquaad vows to steal Fiona and make her his spirit bride and, just to cover all the bases, decides to torture us for information as to her whereabouts.

Tip: Sidle to the right as you wait in the first chamber and take the time to read the instructions for "Duloc Express," a witty send-up of Universal's Express Plus system.

The next stop is a spacious, 300-seat 3-D theater where the story continues on film. The 15-minute film that follows would be a minor masterpiece of 3-D animation just by itself. But the clever designers of this show have added so many little extras that *Shrek 4-D* ends up in a virtual dead heat with *T2* as the top 3-D theater attraction in all of Orlando.

Both the preshow introduction and the film do a wonderful job of poking fun at the conventions of films based on fairy tales, theme park attractions, and theme parks themselves, making *Shrek 4-D* Orlando's most subversive attraction. And it must be therapeutic for theme park employees to be able to visit an attraction where guests are actually warned, "Cell phone users will be flogged. Flash photographers will be burned at the stake. Enjoy the show!"

Selected Short Subjects

Music Plaza

The Hollywood Bowl–styled stage that sits at the foot of *Hollywood Rip Ride Rock-it's* signature loop is home to Universal's seasonal concert series. The 2,400-square-foot performance space features eco-friendly lighting equipment and a bone-shaking sound system. Performers range from today's Top 40 to oldies acts; recent guests have included Nelly, Third Eye Blind, The Beach Boys, and the B-52s. Some concerts, like those during Mardi Gras and the Summer Concert Series, are included in your regular admission. Others, including the "Rock The Universe" Christian music events, require a separate ticket.

Donkey's Photo Finish

Just across the street from the *Shrek 4-D* exit, you will find a rustic stable facade where you can get your picture taken with everybody's favorite noble steed, Donkey.

Shrek shows up, too, from time to time. While Shrek is the usual theme park costumed character, Donkey is a clever animatronic who sticks his head out of his stable door and, thanks to an unseen performer doing an uncanny Eddie Murphy imitation, ad libs to hilarious effect with guests and passersby. Just eavesdropping is a great way to kill time.

EXTRA ADDED ATTRACTIONS

In the spirit of those old-time Saturday matinee specials, Universal likes to serve up a special treat just before the park closes on sultry summer evenings. It's designed to send you off into the evening toward CityWalk in a good mood and it succeeds pretty well.

Universal's Cinematic Spectacular - 100 Years of Movie Magic ★ ★ ★ ★

Type: Multimedia extravaganza
Time: To be determined
Short Take: A pleasing coda to your day

That big floating stage in the central lagoon comes to life at night, just before closing, in a seasonal show that runs only when the park is open late. This edition, not yet open at press time, replaces *Universal 360: A Cinesphere Spectacular*, a kaleidoscopic survey of Universal film history projected on four large globes. The new incarnation appears to cover much the same territory (and the rating above is based on its predecessor), but with a twist. This time around, in addition to narration by Morgan Freeman, the film clips will be projected on giant water screens as the whole lagoon comes alive with elaborate dancing water displays, representing yet another new departure for Universal's production wizards. Expect additional technical bells and whistles and a goodly dose of Universal pyrotechnics thrown in for good measure.

The French firm Aquatique seems to be heavily involved in the project and as their name suggests their medium is water. Lots of water. These are the people responsible for the water screens and other effects used in several nighttime blowouts at SeaWorld (*Chapter 5*). They've also worked for Disney, although not in any of its U.S. parks. So perhaps we can look forward to a survey of a hundred years of movie making in which every film looks a bit like *Singing In The Rain*.

Universal Superstar Parade (not playing at press time)

Type: Once-a-day parade
Time: To be determined
Short Take: Will it beat Disney?

Shades of Disney World! Another new extra at USF is a daily parade (at a time to be announced) featuring self-propelled floats that take their inspiration from *Despicable Me*, *Dora The Explorer*, *Hop*, and *SpongeBob SquarePants*. The streets of Hollywood will be alive with minuscule minions, towering stiltwalkers, skaters, dancing drummers, and of course characters like Gru and SpongeBob's buddies. When not parading, the performers will entertain around the park and the superstars of the title will appear for Meet and Greets in front of their floats.

Chapter Three:

Islands of Adventure

BILLED AS "ORLANDO'S NEXT–GENERATION THEME PARK," ISLANDS OF ADVENTURE has certainly raised the competitive bar with its assortment of cutting edge attractions, thrill rides, and illusions. And thanks to the arrival of a certain boy wizard, Orlando's "next big thing" is now even bigger. Islands of Adventure is located right next door to Universal Studios Florida, just a five- or ten-minute stroll away. Despite the proximity, Islands of Adventure is not just more of Universal Studios. It has a separate identity and, with some notable exceptions, its attractions draw their inspiration from very different sources than those in its sister park.

Guests reach Islands of Adventure through the Port of Entry, a separate themed area that serves much the same function as the Front Lot at Universal Studios Florida. Through the Port of Entry lies a spacious lake, dubbed the Great Inland Sea. Artfully arranged around it are six decidedly different "themed areas"—Seuss Landing, The Lost Continent, The Wizarding World of Harry Potter, Jurassic Park, Toon Lagoon, and Marvel Super Hero Island. The "islands" of Islands of Adventure are not true islands, of course; but the Great Inland Sea's fingerlike bays set off one area from the next and the bridges you cross to move from one to another do a remarkably good job of creating the island illusion. The flow of visitors is strictly controlled by the circular layout. If you follow the line of least resistance (and it's hard not to), you will move through the park in a circle, visiting every island in turn.

There are a number of themes, if you will, that differentiate Islands of Adventure from Universal Studios Florida (and from other Central Florida theme parks, too, for that matter):

Roller coasters. Islands of Adventure now has cut-throat competition in the world of high-end steel coasters but its heavy hitters still hold bragging rights. *Dragon Challenge* in The Wizarding World features twin coaster tracks that intertwine and come within inches of collision, while the *Incredible Hulk Coaster* on Marvel Super Hero Island zaps you to the top of the first drop with what they say is the same thrust as an F-16 jet.

Pushing the envelope. Universal's designers take obvious pride in "next generation" rides and attractions that will be like nothing you have experienced before. As just one example, the *Spider-Man* ride takes standard motion simulator technology, drops it into a simulated 3-D world right out of *T2*, puts it on a moving track, and spins it through 360 degrees along the way. *Harry Potter and the Forbidden Journey* further ups the ante by adding in-your-face animatronics and a first-of-its-kind ride vehicle.

More for the kids. While Islands of Adventure provides plenty of the kind of intense, adult-oriented thrill rides for which Universal Studios became famous, it makes a special effort to reach out to kids. Seuss Landing is almost exclusively for the entertainment and enjoyment of younger children. Toon Lagoon will appeal to slightly older kids, Marvel Super Hero Island is the perfect place for adolescents to scare themselves to death, and Harry Potter has legions of young (and not-so-young) fans.

More theming. Islands of Adventure is more heavily "themed" than its sister park and most other parks. What that means is that the park designers have made a concerted effort to stretch the theme of each island into every restaurant, every shop, indeed into as many nooks and crannies as possible. With Potter's arrival, the already excellent theming has achieved a whole new level of detail.

Music. Islands of Adventure is the first theme park to feature originally composed soundtracks—one for each island—just like a movie. Of course, music is nothing new in theme parks, but what is both new and exceptional at Islands of Adventure is the way the music is integrated into the park experience. It swells as you enter each island, changes gradually as you move from one part of the island to another, and as you cross to another island, blends seamlessly into the next island's theme. The effect is pervasive yet unobtrusive, so much so that many people may not even be aware of what a special achievement it is.

Before You Come

Reading the seven-volume Harry Potter series, and seeing the eight accompanying movies, are mandatory to get the absolute most out of the Wizarding World. You can certainly enjoy the rides and shops without any prior Potter knowledge, but at a minimum you'll enjoy the wealth of detail much more if you've at least seen the first film.

Those who have not seen the original *Jurassic Park* should really rent the DVD before visiting Islands of Adventure. This easy-to-handle research project will add to your enjoyment of what the designers have achieved in IOA's Jurassic Park. If you have not yet introduced your small children to the magical world of Dr. Seuss, this is an excellent excuse to do so. A knowledge of *The Cat in the Hat, If I Ran the Zoo*, and other Seuss books will make their visit to Seuss Landing a whole lot richer, and reading from the books is a great way to pass the time on those long car trips to Florida.

When's The Best Time To Come?

Much of the advice given in the Introduction and the previous chapter applies here as well—in brief, try to come during a slower period. Even so, the presence of Harry Potter can produce crowds that sometimes surpass those at Disney, resulting in long lines and longer wait times. If you are not staying at an on-site hotel (and thus enjoying early entry privileges) you will be well advised to arrive very early at Harry's Wizarding World or wait until late in the afternoon, when the crowds have died down a bit.

Getting There and Other Basic Information

Because Islands of Adventure is the sister park to Universal Studios Florida, all the information provided in *Chapter 2: Universal Studios Florida* about getting there, arriving at Universal Orlando Resort, parking, opening and closing times, the price of admission, and Universal Express Plus applies to Islands of Adventure as well. So rather than repeating myself, let me refer you to the previous chapter for this information. Information on multi-day passes and annual passes is provided in *Chapter 1: Introduction & Orientation*.

Eating in Islands of Adventure

Islands of Adventure's best-kept secret is the food. Those who truly care about the taste and quality of what they put in their stomachs and who despair of eating well in a theme park will find much to celebrate here.

Mythos, the full-service restaurant in The Lost Continent, is an award-winning dining experience that is exceptional by theme park standards. The food at Islands of Adventure's other full-service restaurant, **Confisco Grille**, is also very good. **Three Broomsticks** in the Wizarding World of Harry Potter draws crowds simply because of the Harry Potter theming, but the pub grub is very good and the Butterbeer is everything you imagined Butterbeer would be.

The fast food in the park is a cut above the norm, too. Best of all, given the obvious quality of the food, the prices are no more than you would expect to pay for far less adventuresome cooking at other theme parks.

Shopping in Islands of Adventure

Much of what can be said about the shopping in Universal Studios Florida can be repeated for the shopping experiences offered in Islands of Adventure. However, a number of things are worth noting.

The Middle Eastern bazaar section of The Lost Continent offers a number of shops run by some very talented artisans. Look here for the kind of gifts that won't scream "bought in a theme park!" Look, too, in Port of Entry for unusual folk sculptures and decorative items. For the child in us all, there's a satisfying selection of classic kids books for sale in Seuss Landing, and the treasure trove of comic books to be found in Marvel Super Hero Island is nothing to look down your nose at. Finally, the Wizarding World sets a new standard for theme park shopping with unique merchandise sure to have Potter fans panting.

Again, keep in mind the wisdom of saving your shopping for the end of the day. The **Islands of Adventure Trading Company** in Port of Entry has a good selection of souvenirs representing all of the park's islands, including a sampling of Potter products. There's even a **Universal Store** in CityWalk, which means you can shop for souvenirs days after your tickets to the parks have expired. You can also shop online at Universal-Orlando.com or by phone by calling (888) 762-0820.

Good Things To Know About . . .

Dining Passes. It is actually possible to eat at Mythos, IOA's top-tier restaurant, without paying admission to the park. Here's how it works: Make a reservation at Mythos (see "Reservations," below) and then stop at the "Will Call" window, to the right of the ticket booths at the front entrance to the park. Tell them you have a reservation at Mythos and want a "Dining Pass." They will provisionally charge your credit card for one-day passes for everyone in your party. You then have 2½ hours from the time of your reservation to eat and return to Guest Services. In addition, they require that you return within 30 minutes of the time you pay your check at Mythos (the time will be stamped on your credit card receipt). When you return and show your receipt, they will tear up the credit card slip; overstay your welcome and you will be charged for a one-day pass. If you find yourself running late at Mythos, alert your server to the situation and the restaurant will run interference for you with Guest Services. Although the Dining Pass program was designed specifically with Mythos in mind, you can use it to visit Confisco Grille as well, if you ask.

First Aid. There is a first-aid station with nursing facilities in Port of Entry, just past the turnstiles, in the Open Arms Hotel building. A second first-aid station will be found tucked away in the bazaar area near the Sindbad Theater in The Lost Continent (number 8 on the IOA map in this chapter).

Getting Away From It All. Each of the islands has a park-like, attraction-free section tucked away near the shores of the Great Inland Sea. They seem to have been designed as venues for private parties and corporate events. They are little visited by most guests and offer a terrific opportunity to escape the madding crowd. They also boast excellent views across the Sea to other islands. On days when the park is open past sunset, they are surprisingly private and quite romantic places to snuggle up with that special someone.

Getting Wet. Islands of Adventure has some great water-themed rides. They offer plenty of thrills but they pose some problems for the unprepared. Kids probably won't care, but adults can get positively cranky when wandering around sopping wet. The three water rides, in increasing order of wetness, are *Jurassic Park River Adventure*, *Dudley Do-Right's Ripsaw Falls*, and the absolutely soaking *Popeye & Bluto's Bilge-Rat Barges*.

So dress appropriately. Wear a bathing suit and T-shirt under a dressier outer layer. Wear shoes you don't mind getting wet; sports sandals are ideal. Bring a tote bag in which you can put things, like cameras, that shouldn't get wet. You can also pack a towel, and it might be a good idea to bring the plastic laundry bag from your hotel room. Another option: the "Haystack" full-body dryers outside *Bilge-Rat Barges* and *Ripsaw Falls*. A family of four can fit inside the big outhouse-like closets and be blasted with hot air for $5. Expect to get warm, not dry.

Height Restrictions and Other Warnings. Due to a variety of considerations, usually revolving around sudden movements and the configuration of lap restraints, a few rides will be off-limits to shorter (typically younger) guests. Here is a list of rides that have minimum height requirements:

High in Sky Seuss Ride	34 in. (86.4 cm.)
Flight of the Hippogriff	36 in. (91.4 cm.)

Pteranodon Flyers	36 in. (91.4 cm.)
Spider-Man	40 in. (101.6 cm.)
Jurassic Park River Adventure	42 in. (106.7 cm.)
Popeye & Bluto's Bilge-Rat Barges	42 in. (106.7 cm.)
Dudley Do-Right's Ripsaw Falls	44 in. (111.8 cm.)
Forbidden Journey	48 in. (121.9 cm.)
Doctor Doom's Fearfall	52 in. (131.1 cm.)
Hulk & Dragon Challenge	54 in. (137.2 cm.)

The rides in Seuss Landing require that children under 48 inches tall be accompanied by an adult.

Another problem may be encountered by taller and heavier guests. *Forbidden Journey*, the roller coasters, and *Doctor Doom's Fearfall* employ state-of-the-art harness–like contraptions to make sure that you don't go flying off into space. Unfortunately, not everyone fits into them. Anyone with a chest measurement over 50 inches may have difficulty fitting into the harness and at 54 inches (137.2 cm.) you can pretty much forget about it.

Reservations. Mythos and Confisco Grille both accept priority seating reservations. During busier periods you may spot a small kiosk in Port of Entry where you can make reservations. You can book online through OpenTable.com. If you're really planning ahead, the central reservations number is (407) 224-4012. They will take reservations up to 30 days in advance.

Single Rider Lines. To help shrink long lines, some rides open single rider lines when things get busy. You will frequently find single rider lines at *Doctor Doom's Fearfall*, *Spider-Man*, and *Forbidden Journey*. *Incredible Hulk*, *Ripsaw Falls*, *Bilge Rat Barges*, and *Jurassic Park River Adventure* offer them sporadically. Operation of single rider lines is solely at the discretion of the lead ride attendant, so don't count on this time-saving ploy.

Special Diets. The map in the 2-Park Map has a special symbol for restaurants serving vegetarian meals. Confisco's and Mythos can provide kosher meals with 48 hours advance notice. Call Food Services at (407) 363-8340 to make arrangements. These restaurants may also be able to accommodate other special dietary needs, such as gluten-free or low-carb regimens. Call the number above a few days ahead to discuss your needs.

Special Events

Islands of Adventure has fewer special events than Universal Studios Florida next door, but that may change in the future as Universal looks for ways to expand on the enormous popularity of the Wizarding World of Harry Potter.

December sees Seuss Landing transformed into a veritable winter wonderland for **Grinchmas**, complete with Seussian holiday decor and a Mannheim Steamroller-scored musical show starring the Grinch himself, who proves to be a delightful (if parentally incorrect) host.

Treasure Hunt: Your Day at Islands of Adventure

The initial excitement over Harry Potter has subsided slightly, but for now he's still drawing huge crowds, making seeing all of Islands of Adventure in one day a lot harder than it used to be. Of course, the definition of "all" will be different for everyone. For example, many people will have no interest in subjecting themselves to the intense thrills of the roller coasters, *Doctor Doom*, or *Forbidden Journey*. Teenagers, young singles, and those without children can probably skip the interactive play areas (although they're pretty nifty and worth a peek).

Those who want to see literally everything Islands of Adventure has to offer can still probably come pretty close in a single day, especially if they are willing to arrive early and step lively. If you pay for Universal Express Plus passes or enjoy the front-of-the-line privileges of staying on site, then seeing it all is much more manageable.

Islands of Adventure has many of the same kinds of attractions as Universal Studios Florida, with some notable exceptions. As at Universal Studios Florida, your first step is to consult the 2-Park Map brochure, which you can pick up as you enter the park or in many shops throughout the park. It has a great map of the six "islands," each of which will be discussed in detail in the sections that follow. Here are some general observations about what's in store for you:

Rides. The rides here come in all shapes and sizes, from relatively tame kiddie rides to slam bang simulators and coasters. They also vary widely in terms of "throughput"— the number of people they can accommodate per hour. *Pteranodon Flyers*, for example, has a minimal throughput, while *Cat in the Hat* processes a surprising number of riders each hour.

Roller Coasters. Coasters spawn long lines, although the ones at Islands of Adventure are so intense that sometimes the wait to ride is surprisingly brief. Both coasters have separate lines for the daring few who want to ride in the front row; for these folks the wait is often lengthy.

Amphitheater Shows. These operate on a fixed schedule listed in the 2-Park Map. Generally, seating is not a problem.

Theater Shows. Only *Poseidon's Fury* and *Ollivander's Wand Shop* could fall into this category and neither is an exact fit.

Displays and Interactive Areas. There are three separate interactive play areas for children; all of them can captivate your kids for hours on end. Keep that in mind when planning your touring schedule. The displays in the *Discovery Center* in Jurassic Park, while also enthralling for many children, are less likely to eat up considerable chunks of time.

All the Rest. Islands of Adventure has many more places to get away from the crowds than does its sister park. In fact, if you have a multi-day pass, you might want to bring a good book one day and just chill out along the shore of the Great Inland Sea.

Not-So-Buried Treasure

If you have limited time to spend in Islands of Adventure, or if you simply choose not to run yourself ragged attempting to see it all, here is the best the park has to offer:

Harry Potter and the Forbidden Journey. The current state-of-the-art in thrill ride technology, and quite simply the best ride in Orlando.

Spider-Man. The park's former top attraction has been dethroned by *Forbidden Journey*, but is still a can't-miss mix of high-tech wonders.

The Roller Coasters. Those who can tolerate the cutting edge coaster experience (and you know who you are) will want to ride both *The Hulk* and *Dragon Challenge*—several times. Absolutely awesome.

Popeye & Bluto's Bilge Rat Barges. A soaked-to-the-skin (but very clean) raft ride.

Runners-Up

Here are a few more suggestions that aren't at the very top of the list but are well worth considering:

Cat in the Hat. This kiddie ride manages to be both traditional and cutting edge.

Jurassic Park River Adventure. River boats, raptors, and a hair-raising splashdown.

Dudley Do-Right's Ripsaw Falls. IOA's take on the themed flume ride is a cut above most in this genre.

Seuss Landing and *Camp Jurassic.* Even if you don't go on the kiddie rides, you should at least take a slow stroll through these over-the-top wonderlands to marvel at the design.

Mythos. This is a restaurant, not a ride, but the eye-popping interior design makes even a cheeseburger a special experience.

The One-Day Stay

If you have time, you should avoid trying to cram this wonderful park into a single day; multi-day passes and the Orlando FlexTicket offer excellent value and the luxury of a more leisurely pace. Realistically, however, one day is all many visitors have. In this case, if you are staying at one of the resort hotels, the unlimited Express Plus and early admission to the Wizarding World your room key affords means that you won't have to plan your visit to the park like a military campaign. The same can be said (although to a lesser extent) for the paid Universal Express Plus passes.

However, the arrival of Harry Potter has completely rewritten all the rules for theme park attendance. On Opening Day, June 18, 2010, tens of thousands lined up beginning before 5:30 a.m., resulting in an eight-hour-long line that snaked around the entire park and out into CityWalk. Since then, Universal has experimented with various crowd-control techniques to manage the masses, including timed entry tickets to the Wizarding World, and has even closed the park to new arrivals on a few occasions.

If you are a die-hard Potter partisan who has traveled to Orlando primarily to visit his world, you'll want to join fellow fanatics at dawn. If so, it's strongly advised you stay at one of the three on-site hotels and take advantage of the hour of "early entry" each morning. With on-site privileges, you should get to the park gates 15 minutes before your early entry time; that means as early 6:45 a.m. during peak season. After entering, exit Port of Entry to the right through Seuss Landing, bearing left past Green Eggs and Ham, and cross the bridge to Lost Continent. Once inside the Wizarding World, head straight for *Ollivander's Wand Shop*, followed by *Forbidden Journey*, the roller coasters, and the remaining shops. Once you've sated your thirst for Butterbeer, explore the rest of the park counter-clockwise from Jurassic Park to Seuss Landing, using your hotel key card to enter the Express lines.

If you are staying off-site, you can try arriving at the park as early as humanly possible (at least 60 minutes before the official opening time) and heading straight to the Wizarding World, but you may find the area already filled with hotel guests. A much better idea is to follow the steps below, leaving the Wizarding World for last. Note that this plan works best when the park is open past sunset (ideally 10:00 p.m. or later).

1. Arrive at the park at least 30 minutes prior to the official opening time. As soon as the gates open, proceed straight to the end of Port of Entry and turn left.

2. Cross into Marvel Super Hero Island and enjoy the *Spider-Man* ride.

3. Hard-core thrill seekers should ride *Hulk* and *Doctor Doom*, preferably in that order. If lines are short, you may want to take the opportunity to ride *Hulk* twice. Using single rider lines (if available) can speed things up considerably.

4. Now head through Toon Lagoon to ride *Dudley Do-Right's Ripsaw Falls* followed by *Popeye & Bluto's Bilge-Rat Barges*, assuming you don't mind getting wet. It's enticing to leave these soakers until later in the day, but in hot weather you'll face a long wait by early afternoon.

5. Ride the *Jurassic Park River Adventure*.

6. Consult the park map or ask an employee if timed entry tickets to the Wizarding World are being distributed. If so, retrieve one from the kiosks in Jurassic Park (near the *Discovery Center*) or Lost Continent (near *Sindbad*).

7. Check out the *Discovery Center* and *Triceratops Discovery Trail* (open seasonally).

8. At this point, it may be close to noon and time to take stock. Take the bridge near the Jurassic Park Discovery Center to the Lost Continent. *Poseidon's Fury* is a good choice for midday since the queue is indoors and mercifully air-conditioned. Also, check the schedule for the *Sindbad* show, and consider lunch at Mythos.

9. Afternoon is also a good time to explore Seuss Landing. Don't skip *The Cat in the Hat*, and enjoy any other rides if the wait is short.

10. About three hours before closing time (or anytime after your entry ticket becomes valid), walk through Lost Continent into The Wizarding World of Harry Potter. By now the early-morning Potter fans have pooped out, and crowds should be much more manageable.

11. Stroll through the village, and then ride *Dragon Challenge*.

12. Ride *Flight of the Hippogriff* if you have kids or the line is short.

13. Ride *Forbidden Journey*. If the posted wait is over 30 minutes, ask an attendant for the "castle tour," followed by the single rider line. Use the storage lockers near *Dragon Challenge* if the line extends outside the castle.

14. Visit *Ollivander's* if the line ahead of you is under 45 minutes.

15. Save your shopping for closing time, since the stores stay open later.

Again, those who are temperamentally averse to the giant coasters and intense thrills like *Doctor Doom* will find it much easier to take in all of Islands of Adventure in a day. But as noted earlier, coaster lovers may be pleasantly surprised at how short the lines are, especially at slower times of the year, because these giants scare off a lot of people. The exception is the line for the first row, which is often lengthy.

The One-Day Stay With Kids

Many kids, especially those who are tall enough to avoid the height restrictions listed earlier, will be perfectly happy going on all the rides, in which case the strategy outlined above will work just fine. However, if you have children who are too short or too timid to tackle the thrill rides, you can adopt a much different strategy.

1. If your Potter-crazy child won't pay attention to anything else in the park once they've spotted Hogwarts' spires, bite the bullet and get there at the crack of dawn (preferably with on-site early entry). Better yet, if you have park-to-park tickets see USF in the morning and save your first IOA visit for evening.

If you decide to pass on the early-morning Potter patrol, you should make *Pteranodon Flyers* your first priority—assuming your kid is between 36 and 56 inches tall and you feel your child will enjoy it. This ride takes only two people at a time per vehicle and does not accept Universal Express Plus, so the line gets very long very quickly.

Otherwise (and if your child is over 40 inches tall), do *Spider-Man* first. Most kids will have no problem with this one, although some of their adult guardians may. After that, you can relax and take your time.

2. Take a trip to Seuss Landing for those who won't find it too "babyish." However, even kids who consider themselves too "sophisticated" for most of Seuss will get a kick out of *The Cat in the Hat* ride. Your first ride in Seuss Landing should be the *High in the Sky Seuss Trolley Train Ride*, because of its slow loading time.

3. You can pretty much pick and choose after that, using the height restrictions listed earlier and your child's preferences to guide you. Despite the cartoon violence, *Sindbad* is a fun show for kids; and don't miss the *Mystic Fountain* in front of the stadium entrance.

4. When you need a break, steer your kids to an age-appropriate play area: *If I Ran the Zoo* and *Me Ship, The Olive* for younger children, *Camp Jurassic* for older ones. The *Triceratops Discovery Trail*, when open, is also worthwhile.

5. Save the Wizarding World for late in the day when the thickest crowds have dissipated. Visit *Ollivander's* and ride *Flight of the Hippogriff* (ask for a seat near the front). Then ask for a "castle tour" to walk through the *Forbidden Journey* queue, but bypass the ride if your kid is under 48 inches tall or spooked by spiders and skeletons.

Note: Whichever plan you follow, be sure to pick up a copy of the 2-Park Map as you enter the park.

PORT OF ENTRY

The towering lighthouse with the blazing fire at the top, modeled after the ancient lighthouse of Pharos in Alexandria, Egypt, marks the gates to Islands of Adventure and the beginning of your adventure. This striking structure is only the most obvious of the metaphors used in an eclectic blend of architecture and decor that evokes the spirit of wanderlust and exploration. At the base of the lighthouse a series of sails, like those on ancient Chinese junks, shade the ticket booths for the park.

Through these gates lies Port of Entry, a sort of storytelling experience that combines evocative architectural motifs and haunting music to build your anticipation as you enter more fully into the spirit of discovery. Universal's scenic designers have outdone themselves on this one. To centuries-old Venice, they've added images of Istanbul, a soupçon of Samarkand, a touch of Timbuktu, and a dash of Denpassar to create a ravishingly beautiful example of fantasy architecture. Hurry through in the morning if you must, but if you are among the last to leave the park, you should really linger in Port of Entry and drink in the atmosphere.

As you marvel at the architectural details and the exquisite care with which the designers have "dressed" this sensuous streetscape, pay attention to the sounds that swirl around you. In addition to the chatter of your fellow adventurers, you will experience one of IOA's "next level" touches. Like all the other islands in the park, Port of Entry has its own specially composed soundtrack that unfolds as you walk along, drawing ever closer to the Great Inland Sea. But there are other inspired aural touches as well, like the muffled conversations from dimly lit upper-story windows hinting at intrigue and adventures unknown. It's a very special place.

Port of Entry serves some more mundane purposes as well. Before you pass through the gates you will find, on your left, a pale green building that houses Group Sales. If you are the leader of a group of 20 or more, this is the place to pick up your tickets. To the right of the ticket booths, you will find a Guest Services walk-up window marked "Will Call." Stop here if you have arranged to have tickets waiting for you. Nearby is the only ATM in Port of Entry, so if you are in need of ready cash, make sure to stop here before you enter the park. Other ATMs are found in The Lost Continent, The Wizarding World of Harry Potter, and Marvel Super Hero Island.

Once past the ticket booths and the entrance turnstiles, you will find a spacious semicircular plaza. Directly ahead of you is a large stone archway. The fantastic facades of the buildings to either side hide a variety of Guest Services functions.

To the left of the archway are . . .

Restrooms. Because there are some things you don't need to carry on your adventures. Nearby are phones and a phone card vending machine.

Lockers. There are four bays of electronically controlled lockers here. Rental fees are $8 for the day for smaller lockers and $10 for family size, both with in-and-out access. The machines accept bills and credit cards.

Stroller & Wheelchair Rentals. "Reliable Rentals" has a large sign outside informing you that all the jinrickshaws, gliders, submersibles, and tuk tuks are either out of service, decommissioned, hired, or, in the case of the time machine, "stuck in the 6th century." Fortunately they still have strollers ($15 for singles, $25 for doubles), wheel-chairs ($12), and electric convenience vehicles ($50) for rent. Slightly more elaborate strollers, called "kiddie cars," feature a kid's steering wheel and cup holders and rent for $18 and $28 respectively. All prices include tax. A $50 refundable deposit is required for wheelchair and electric convenience vehicle (ECV) rentals, or you can leave your drivers license or a credit card imprint.

To the right of the archway are . . .

Guest Services. Questions or complaints? The cheerful folks here can help you out. Annual passes can also be obtained here.

Lost & Found. Don't give up on that lost item. There's a very good chance a fellow tourist or a park staffer will find it and turn it in. Check back the next day, too, just in case.

First Aid. This is one of two first-aid stations in the park. The other is in The Lost Continent, near the Sindbad Theater.

Now that you have replenished your wallet, stowed your excess gear, and rented your strollers, you step through that crumbling stone archway incised with the thrilling words "The Adventure Begins" and start your journey toward the Great Inland Sea and the magical islands that ring it.

Port of Entry's main (and only) street is given over to a variety of shopping and eating establishments. At the far end of this market street, under another crumbling archway that's being propped up by a jury-rigged contraption of giant planks and chains, the street opens out into another broad plaza on the shore of the Great Inland Sea. Amid the souvenir kiosks that dot the plaza, look for a large electronic signboard that can help you plan your itinerary. The board is updated regularly with the current waiting times for the all the attractions. If no wait time is posted, the ride may be temporarily out of commission.

SEUSS LANDING

Probably best described as a 12-acre, walk-through sculpture, Seuss Landing adds a third dimension and giddy Technicolor to the wonderfully wacky world of Theodor Geisel, a.k.a. Dr. Seuss, whose dozens of illustrated books of inspired poetry have enchanted millions of children.

In its own cheerful, candy-colored way, the fantasy architecture here is just as successful and just as impressive as that in Port of Entry. Even if you have no interest in sampling the kiddie rides on offer here, you will have a great deal of fun just passing through.

If I Ran The Zoo ★ ★ ★ 1/2

Type: Interactive play area
Time: Unlimited
Short Take: Fabulous fun for toddlers

This interactive play area is based on the charming tale of young Gerald McGrew who had some very definite ideas of what it takes to create a really interesting zoo. There are three distinct areas, each of which allows little ones a slightly different interactive experience. The first is filled with peculiar animals that appear over the hedges when you turn a crank or laugh when you tickle their feet. Little adventurers can also slide down the tunnels of Zamba-ma-tant and crawl through the cave in Kartoom in search of the Natch before reaching a small island surrounded by a wading pool. There they'll be able to control bouncing globs of water and trap their playmates in cages made out of falling water. In the final area kids can stand over a grate where the Snaggle Foot Mulligatawny will sneeze up their shorts. Then they can squirt a creature taking a bubble bath, only to get sprinkled themselves when the critter spins dry.

All told, there are 19 different interactive elements to keep your child giggling all the way through this attraction. Kids will dart about eager to try them all, which may be one reason the "Zoo Keeper Code of Conduct" at the entrance warns, "Keep track of adults, they get lost all the time."

The Cat In The Hat ★ ★ ★ ★

Type: "Dark ride"
Time: 3½ minutes
Short Take: Classic storybook dark ride with a little zip

Dr. Seuss's most popular book tells the tale of what happens when two kids, home alone, allow the cat of the title to come in for a visit. Step through the doors beneath that giant red and white striped top hat and you will get your chance to relive the adventure.

This is a "dark" ride but perhaps one of the brightest and most colorful you'll ever encounter. You and your kids climb into cars that are designed like miniature six-passenger sofas and set off through a series of 18 show scenes that re-create the story line of the book. Just don't expect the static tableaux of the older generation dark rides. Brace yourself for a few quick swoops, sudden turns, and maybe a 360-degree spin.

Along the way, the ride does a remarkably good job of telling the story of the book. The fantastic animated sculptures of the cat and his playmates, Thing 1 and Thing 2, spin and twirl while furniture teeters and topples. The wise fish, who is the tale's voice of reason, cries out warnings and ignored advice until, miraculously, all is set to rights before Mom gets home. Kids familiar with the book will be delighted and those who aren't will doubtless want to learn more. This is a must-do for little ones, although a few very timid tykes still may find the swoops and spins of the ride vehicles (which have been toned down somewhat in recent years) a bit startling.

One Fish, Two Fish, Red Fish, Blue Fish ★ ★ ★

Type: Flying, steerable fish
Time: 2 minutes
Short Take: Good, wet fun

Here's an interesting twist on an old carnival ride. You know, the one where you sit in a little airplane (or flying Dumbo) and spin round in a circle while your plane goes up and down. On this ride, based on the Seuss book of the same name, you pilot a little fishy. While you can't escape the circular route of the ride, you can steer your fish up or down.

Supposedly, if you follow the directions encoded in the little song that plays during the ride ("red fish, red fish up, up, up; blue fish, blue fish down, down, down"), you can avoid being doused by the water coming from a series of "squirt posts" that ring the perimeter. There are three verses to the song and, it seems it actually is possible to stay dry for the first two by following directions. The third verse, however, tells you that all bets are off and that your guess is as good as the next fellow's. It is the rare rider who gets through the ride without getting spritzed. Not that most people care. In fact, it looks like some kids do just the opposite of what the song counsels in the hope of getting Mom and Dad soaked.

Note: On cold days, and sometimes in the cooler morning hours, the ride does not spray water on the riders, which will probably come as a relief to parents and a disappointment to little ones.

This ride is very nicely designed, with perfectly adorable little fish cars and an array of Seussian characters serving as the squirt posts. Presiding over the center of the circle is an 18-foot-tall sculpture of the Star Belly Fish from the book.

Caro-Seuss-El ★ ★ ★ 1/2

Type:	Old-fashioned carousel with Seuss figures
Time:	About 1½ minutes
Short Take:	For carousel lovers and little kids

This ride marks yet another design triumph. The old-fashioned carousel has been put through the Seuss looking glass and has emerged as a towering, multicolored confection. In place of old-fashioned horses are marvelously imaginative Seuss critters with serene smiles plastered across their goofy faces. Even if you have no interest in actually riding the thing, it's worth the time it takes to stop and admire this imaginative whirligig in full motion.

The *Caro-Seuss-El* is billed as the world's first interactive carousel. Here kids can ride on the back of a beautifully sculpted Seussian animal like Cowfish from *McElligott's Pool* or the Twin Camels from *One Fish, Two Fish.* There are seven different characters and a total of 54 mounts on the 47-foot diameter ride. The interactive part comes when you pull back on the reins and watch your steed's head shake, his eyes blink, his tail wag. A special loading mechanism for wheelchairs allows the disabled to experience the ride from their own rocking chariots.

High in the Sky Seuss Trolley Train Ride ★ ★ ★

Type:	Aerial train ride
Time:	3 minutes
Short Take:	A pleasant new perspective on Seuss Landing

Based loosely on Dr. Seuss's anti-discrimination parable about Sylvester McMonkey McBean and the Sneetches, this brief excursion over Seuss Landing is designed for the kiddies but offers rewards for their adult companions.

Cute and colorful 5-car, 20-passenger trolleys tootle along two separate tracks, each traveling a slightly different aerial route. In addition, each train has two different audio tracks, which adds up to four different experiences. This is definitely one your child will

Islands of Adventure

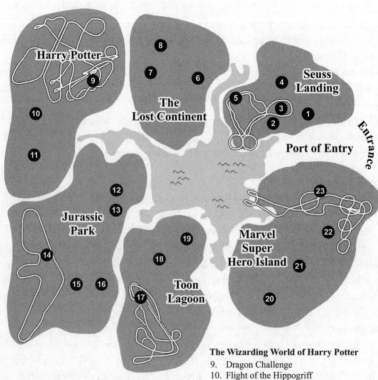

The Wizarding World of Harry Potter
9. Dragon Challenge
10. Flight of the Hippogriff
11. Forbidden Journey

Seuss Landing
1. The Cat In The Hat
2. If I Ran the Zoo
3. Caro-Seuss-El
4. One Fish, Two Fish, Red Fish, Blue Fish
5. The High in the Sky Seuss Trolley Train Ride

The Lost Continent

6. Poseidon's Fury
7. The Mystic Fountain
8. The Eighth Voyage of Sindbad Stunt Show

Jurassic Park
12. Jurassic Park Discovery Center
13. Triceratops Discovery Trail
14. Jurassic Park River Adventure
15. Camp Jurassic
16. Pteranodon Flyers

Toon Lagoon

17. Dudley Do-Right's Ripsaw Falls
18. Popeye & Bluto's Bilge-Rat Barges
19. Me Ship, The Olive

Marvel Super Hero Island
20. The Amazing Adventures of Spider-Man
21. Doctor Doom's Fearfall
22. Storm Force Accelatron
23. Incredible Hulk Coaster

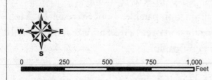

0   250   500   750   1,000
Feet

want to ride multiple times. Mom and Dad won't mind the repetition because there's plenty to see. Unfortunately, the slow-moving line may make that difficult unless you have Express Plus passes, so head here early in the day.

The train to your right as you enter the platform has the more interesting route, as it passes though the Circus McGurkus restaurant before heading out over Seuss Landing. Most of the trip is in the open air on loopy swirling tracks that take you on a bird's-eye tour of this magical land. If you weren't impressed by the design of Seuss Landing after strolling through, this ride will change your mind.

Note: This is a gentle ride, but it is "high in the sky" so those with a fear of heights might want to give it a pass.

And all the rest . . .

There are nooks and crannies of Seuss Landing that are easy to miss. These are not major attractions, to be sure, but if you take a fancy to this whimsical land, or if you have a young Dr. Seuss fan in tow, they might be worth seeking out.

Just through the woozy archway that marks the entrance to Seuss Landing from Port of Entry you will find, on your right, **McElligott's Pool**, a pretty little pond with a waterfall, some charming statuary, and some interloping ducks who have made it home. Just past this area, next to the Cats, Hats & Things shop, in a private courtyard with its own kid-sized entrance arch, lies **Horton's Egg**. Climb atop the spotted egg (a sign invites volunteers to do so) for a great **photo op**.

The Street of the Lifted Lorax is a small walk-through area next to the *Caro-Seuss-El*. It retells the story from Dr. Seuss's book, *The Lorax*, the moral of which is "Protect the environment!"

Oh! The Stories You'll Hear combines a little song and dance, a brief bit of storytelling, and a **Character Meet and Greet** with a few Seuss characters. You'll find it several times daily (see the 2-Park Map for details) either outside in the courtyard between *Cat in the Hat* and *One Fish, Two Fish*, or inside Circus McGurkus Cafe in inclement weather. From time to time, a Seuss Character Meet and Greet is also held; times and locations will be listed in the 2-Park Map.

A "How the Grinch Stole Christmas" musical show, featuring a soundtrack recorded by Mannheim Steamroller, is staged in the soundstage behind *One Fish, Two Fish* during the "Grinchmas" holiday season. The set and lighting are terrific, and the actors are all talented, but the tone is closer to the vulgar Jim Carrey film than the sweet storybook and sixties cartoon.

Tip: If you are hurrying through Seuss Landing, you can save a few seconds by turning left at Green Eggs and Ham and following the path that circles behind the shops. This takes you through a broad open area next to the Inland Sea and beneath the tracks of the *Trolley Train Ride* and lets you out a few paces from the bridge that leads to The Lost Continent, thereby avoiding the crowds that throng Seuss Landing's colorful main drag. Stop and see the beach-going Sneeches and stubborn Zax along the way.

THE LOST CONTINENT

From the color and fantasy of Seuss Landing, the intrepid adventurer plunges into the mystery of The Lost Continent. Cross a wooden bridge to the sound of mystical wind chimes, and enter a land of ancient myth.

Photo Op: The first thing you see, when you enter from Seuss Landing, is a statue of an armor-clad griffin. This grim guardian has become a favorite spot for tourists to pose for that "I was at Islands of Adventure" shot.

As you approach the Lost City, you glimpse over a craggy boulder an enormous hand holding an equally enormous trident. Only when you have walked a little farther do you realize that the boulder is an enormous head of the god Poseidon and what you are seeing are the remnants of a very large and very ancient statue that fell down eons ago. Just opposite is a brooding extinct volcano, with the faces of titans carved in its flanks. It hides Mythos, perhaps the most eye-popping restaurant in any Orlando theme park.

The grand scale and attention to detail in the architecture of The Lost Continent is exceeded only by the adjoining Wizarding World. It's rare that theme park visitors pause just to take pictures of buildings but it happens here all the time. Add to the visual splendor what many people consider to be one of the finest restaurants in any theme park in the world and The Lost Continent becomes a small but special island indeed.

Rumor holds that the neighboring Wizarding World may soon expand into this area, so portions of The Lost Continent may be lost for good behind construction walls by the time you visit.

Tip: A barely themed wooden bridge leads from near Mythos to the *Discovery Center* in Jurassic Park. This "temporary" addition, built during construction of the Wizarding World, allows you to bypass the Potter area when it's overpopulated. Look for it to be open on crowded days.

Poseidon's Fury ★ ★ ★ 1/2

Type:	Special effects extravaganza
Time:	About 25 minutes
Short Take:	Chaotic fun, but not everyone's cup of tea

Behind the ruins of Poseidon's statue lies his enormous temple, now cracked and crumbled by earthquakes, where his devotees once worshipped. Before entering, take a moment to drink in the scene. This is yet another of the park's triumphs of fantasy architecture. The scale alone is awe-inspiring. Check out the huge feet of Poseidon's now-tumbled statue and the towering trident that stands nearby. Marvel at the once-gorgeous mosaic floors now running with water diverted from its ancient course by long-ago earthquakes. Stare up at the towering facade, its massive columns seemingly ready to topple at any moment. The art direction that has created not just the iconography of an ancient and imaginary religious cult but its language as well is truly impressive.

With understandable trepidation, we step inside to something of a disappointment—a cool, dimly lit, snaking passageway. The overall design and the fragmentary murals on the crumbling walls are vaguely Minoan in appearance, but other than the flickering lights, some hard-to-read signage from "Global Discovery Group," and the ominous music, there's nothing here to hint at what lies ahead, certainly no advancing "plot line" to keep visitors informed and entertained as the line inches forward.

When we reach the front of the queue line, we are greeted by Taylor, a very young and very nervous volunteer assistant to ace archaeologist, Professor Baxter. The prof seems to have disappeared along with everyone else on the dig while Taylor was on a lunch break. Too bad, because the professor had announced the discovery of a "secret message" but disappeared before he could tell anyone what it was. Taylor, played by a young guy or gal, gamely carries on with our tour of recent temple excavations.

The first chamber, which Taylor tells us is the Chamber of Sacrifices, contains an altar and ancient wall paintings documenting an epic struggle. Legend has it that a high priest of the temple, the dumbly named Lord Darkenon, seized power from Poseidon, sparking a battle in which all perished, and that the spirits of those combatants still haunt the ruined temple. There is another terrified transmission from Professor Baxter, and then all the lights go out.

Taylor grabs an ultraviolet lamp for illumination and in so doing reveals a hidden message written on the frieze that circles the chamber. Fortunately, the ancient Greeks had the foresight to write the message in English so Taylor can read it aloud. This turns out to be a big mistake because reading the message aloud awakens the spirit of Darkenon, who is no one's idea of a gracious host.

Without spoiling it for you, suffice to say that your journey will take you into an even spookier chamber and finally into the middle of a pitched battle between Poseidon, who uses water as his weapon, and Lord Darkenon, who responds with fire. We're talking heavy artillery here, with more than 350,000 gallons of the wet stuff and 25-foot exploding fireballs. The highlight is a "water vortex" that lets you walk underneath a seemingly impossible wall of rushing water.

It should be noted that this attraction has its detractors. Some people find the story line confusing and, in the heat of the battle, some of the dialogue does get hard to hear. Others just don't seem that impressed with the effects. For many people, their enjoyment of the show will depend on how long they have waited to see it.

The best seats in the house. The entire show is experienced standing up. In the second and third chambers, the audience stands on a series of steps set in a semicircle, with a guardrail on each level. In the first two chambers, it really doesn't matter where you stand.

For the final battle scene, however, you will have a good deal more fun if you are in the very first row. It seems like most people instinctively climb the steps, not realizing that you can actually stand in front of the first guardrail, on ground level so to speak. That means that you can simply walk to the front as you enter. Despite being almost on top of the action, you won't get terribly wet, although some of those towering explosions of water find their way into the audience.

The Eighth Voyage of Sindbad ★ ★ ★

Type:	Amphitheater show
Time:	About 20 minutes
Short Take:	Slapstick stunts and dumb dialogue

In a 1,750-seat theater we get to witness the eighth voyage of the legendary Sindbad (seven just weren't enough). This is a live-action stunt show that attempts to rival the *Indiana Jones* show over at that other movie studio park (no, not Universal) but is betrayed by a clunky script.

Here Sindbad sets off on yet another search for riches untold, encountering along the way the inevitable life-threatening perils. Sindbad and his trusty but talkative sidekick Kabob (as in "Shush, Kabob!") have traveled to a mysterious cavern filled with treasure and the bones of earlier adventurers. Here the evil sorceress Miseria holds the beautiful Princess Amora in thrall and only the Sultan's Heart, an enormous ruby with magical powers, can free her. It's Sindbad to the rescue, but first he must battle Miseria for the Sultan's Heart and the ultimate power that goes with it.

Sindbad fights valiantly on the Princess's behalf. But this is no wimpy maiden in distress. Amora is a princess for the postmodern age, with hair of gold and buns of steel, who can hold her own against evil monsters, thank you very much. Together, the three heroes battle the forces of evil in its many grisly guises and (spoiler alert) eventually triumph.

It's an action-packed spectacular that features six "water explosions" and 50— count 'em, 50—of Universal's trademark pyrotechnic effects, including a 10-foot-tall circle of flames and a 22-foot-high fall by a stunt person engulfed in flames.

Note: Sadly, at press time most of the show's pyro has been eliminated, severely dampening the attraction's biggest draw. This could be an early warning sign that *Sindbad* may soon be making way for that rumored expansion of the Wizarding World.

Sindbad's set alone, with its dripping stalagmites and crumbling pirate vessels, is stupendous. The show takes advantage of every inch of it, including the wrecked prow of an ancient ship that seems to have run aground in the very middle of the audience, and the stunts are all energetically executed by the athletic cast. Unfortunately, the dialogue is packed with clumsy one-liners and pop-culture anachronisms that drag the production down. The result is a dazzling but depressingly dumb display best enjoyed by children and non-English speakers.

The best seats in the house. If you enjoy getting wet, there are two "splash zones" in this show, one toward the front to the right of the audience and the other in the middle, to the left of the wrecked prow that juts into the seating area. Otherwise, every seat gives a good view of the action, which has very thoughtfully been spread all over the enormous set. Sitting a few rows back, just to the right of the wrecked prow, offers a particularly good perspective on the action, including some bone-crunching fights that happen almost on top of you. Another good choice is the last row in front of either of the two arched entrances on the left and right. These seats give you a great panoramic view of the action, have a back rest, and offer a quick getaway at show's end. Another bonus, if you're sensitive to sound: the open archways behind you let the sound out instead of bouncing it back at you.

And all the rest . . .

The Middle Eastern bazaar section, sometimes referred to as **Sindbad's Village**, houses a number of carnival-style games, much like those found along the Amity Boardwalk in

Universal Studios Florida, just decorated differently.

Far more entertaining than another game of ring toss is the mysteriously smoking and bubbling **Mystic Fountain** that sits in front of the central entrance to the *Sindbad* show's amphitheater. Once just an interesting added touch to the fun of Lost Continent, the fountain has been elevated to the rank of a full-fledged attraction in the park map. It would appear to be dedicated to some ancient and mysterious oracle, to judge by the open-mouthed face sculpted into it. Indeed, this fountain even talks to you. Although it seems friendly enough, beware. Its hidden agenda seems to be to get you very, very wet.

THE WIZARDING WORLD OF HARRY POTTER

In 2007, Universal Orlando rocked the attraction industry by announcing a partnership with Warner Brothers and author J.K. Rowling to bring her mega-selling series about a United Kingdom conjuring academy into three-dimensional reality. Insiders speculated that securing the notoriously reticent Rowling's cooperation (in a deal that granted her unprecedented levels of artistic control over the project) could be the kind of coup that might finally allow Universal to beat Disney at its own game.

After three years of eagerly observed construction, The Wizarding World of Harry Potter premiered to the public on June 18, 2010, in a star-studded opening ceremony that was broadcast globally. Millions of Potter-maniacs, whose money helped make the books and films into a $15 billion franchise, held their breaths in anticipation. Could this new section of Islands of Adventure possibly live up to the wonders they experienced on page and screen? Well, the verdict is in, and it is a resounding "Yeeesss!"

From the moment you step under the stone archway into **Hogsmeade Village** (beneath a sign reading "Please Respect the Spell Limits"), you will be completely enveloped in this enchanted universe. The word "immersive" is ubiquitous in the themed-entertainment business, but nowhere else on earth is its application more apt. When you walk into the Wizarding World, you don't feel like you've just entered another area in an amusement park; you've seemingly been transported into the charmingly archaic Scottish hamlet where Harry and his friends relax on winter holidays, down to the worn cobblestone streets and sparkling snow-capped eaves. Everywhere you look, from the Hogwarts Express train belching steam to the exquisitely detailed storefront windows, you'll find an overabundance of exacting detail that makes this area – which was carved from the former "Merlinwood" section of Lost Continent, as well as some previously unused nearby acreage – seem far richer than its 20-acre size might suggest. Simply put, this is the most visually dense attraction in any park, Mouse-made or otherwise, with the possible exception of Tokyo DisneySea in Japan.

Universal may have somewhat oversold the scope of the expansion by initially referring to it as a "park within a park." The area is similar in size to the other "islands," and no separate admission is required. And return visitors to IOA will remember the area's re-purposed roller coasters, which may explain why they always have less of a wait than the other Potter attractions. Still, the area is enormously popular. Dedicated Potter devotees have waited hours in the hot sun just to enter their hero's home.

However, the Wizarding World's greatest asset is also its Achilles' heel: the authentically intimate scale of the streets and stores. Unlike many other oversized epic fantasies, the Potter books and films depict a more human-scaled world of congested markets and narrow alleyways. Confines here are just as cramped as Rowling imagined, which is great for preserving the illusion but poor for pedestrian management.

On busy days, in order to keep this compact area from being overwhelmed by eager visitors, Universal distributes free timed-entry tickets from electronic kiosks located in Lost Continent and Jurassic Park (consult the 2-Park Map for details). Use the kiosk touchscreen to select the number of guests in your party, then return later with the resulting tickets during your assigned entry time. There may be a line for the ticket kiosks, but it typically moves swiftly. Alternatively, except on the most crowded days, you should be able to enter without a timed ticket by early evening, when crowds are thinner and nighttime illumination makes the area even more entrancing.

If you aren't already a Potter-head, you'll want to pick up at least the first few novels or films to better appreciate the area, which is currently focused on the first four "years" in the seven-book series. Even if you're merely a Muggle with no prior Potter interest, the beauty and wit you'll find here may inspire you to start reading once you return home.

Harry Potter and the Forbidden Journey ★ ★ ★ ★ ★

Type: Next-generation dark thrill ride
Time: About 30 minutes for the tour, 4 minutes for the ride
Short Take: The best theme-park ride in the Western Hemisphere

As you emerge from Hogsmeade and round the corner, you'll catch sight of an awe-inspiring vision: the majestic spires of **Hogwarts Castle**, home to the ancient school where Harry and his schoolmates learn the ways of wizardry. Perched high atop a craggy cliff face, the edifice is actually an empty shell perched atop a massive camouflaged show building, but thanks to clever use of forced perspective it appears even larger and more imposing, if less colorful, than Cinderella's digs down the road. Pass between the school's stone gates (which mystically glow with the attraction's name at night) and enter the castle dungeon to begin your adventure.

Tip: Duck into the first left-hand cliff crevice for a glimpse behind the scenes.

Forbidden Journey is actually comprised of two attractions in one. The first is the queue, cleverly disguised as an elaborate walking tour of Hogwarts, which has opened its doors to non-magical Muggles like yourself for the first time in its ten-century history. (For serious continuity nerds, your visit occurs on a day "frozen in time" outside of the Potter canon, sometime between the events of *Goblet of Fire* and *Half-Blood Prince*.) Waiting in line is rarely considered entertainment, but here is the exception; with more details and effects than most entire attractions, this surpasses Disneyland's *Indiana Jones Adventure* as America's most impressive holding pen. If you were to walk slowly through the queue with no one ahead of you, examining the artifacts and watching all the effects, it would take almost 30 minutes. The production values are high enough that even those uninterested in the ride should still experience the castle tour.

Tip: Universal Express Plus is not valid on this attraction, but there is a non-rider experience offered which includes almost all of the normal line's magical effects, including a private portrait gallery, with little or no wait. Ask the first attendant you encounter inside the castle for the "castle only tour." At the end, ask how to transfer to the single rider line, which starts in the final chambers. You'll experience most of the castle queue plus the ride for only about one-third to one-fourth of the standard wait time!

Warning: Spoilers Ahead!

The tour begins in the dungeon, where you'll see screen-accurate reproductions of artifacts like the "One-Eyed Witch" and "Mirror of Erised," and pass by the "Potions Classroom" where Neville Longbottom can be heard being upbraided yet again for his ignorance. Emerge from the dark dungeon into the sunny greenhouse, where Professor Sprout's magical herbs, like hanging pitcher plants and mandrakes (thankfully silent), are raised.

Note: If the extended queue outside the greenhouse is in use, anticipate at least an hour wait before entering the air-conditioned interior.

Once inside the castle corridors, you will spend 20 to 30 minutes exploring some of Hogwarts' most iconic locations. Begin by passing a series of ancient-looking statues, including one of the school's architect, and the regal stone griffin that guards the Headmaster's office. Next you'll encounter a portrait gallery, featuring one of Universal's most startling effects: paintings that move and speak, appearing even up close to be oil on canvas instead of video projections. The four founders of Hogwarts (Godric Gryffindor, Rowena Ravenclaw and Helga Hufflepuff, and the never-before-seen Salazar Slytherin) greet you and bicker about the presence of Muggles inside their school. (This is where the non-rider tour begins.)

Next, you'll enter the spectacular set of Headmaster Dumbledore's office, exactingly reproduced from the films, right down to the Pensive in the corner. Dumbledore (played by actor Michael Gambon in a startlingly real upgrade of *Disaster!'s* "Musion" hologram effect) welcomes you, warning that "the time may come when you must choose between what is right, and what is easy." Oh, and look out for Hagrid's pet dragon, which has apparently gotten loose again.

Exiting the office, you encounter the Defense Against the Dark Arts classroom, festooned with skeletal beasts and other occult artifacts, where you are promised a multihour lecture on Hogwarts history. Luckily, Harry Potter himself (played by Daniel Radcliffe), along with his friends Ron (Rupert Grint) and Hermione (Emma Watson), materialize on a balcony above you from beneath Harry's Invisibility Cloak (another amazing Musion). They invite you to play hooky with them, skipping the boring lecture in favor of a game of Quidditch (the series' flying-broom-based sport). Soon you are swept past the "Fat Lady" portrait that guards the Gryffindor Common Room into the lounge's comfy confines, where a quartet of new paintings prepare you to board the "enchanted benches" that will take you on your adventure.

Tip: Look in the cabinet on the left immediately after the Fat Lady for props actually used in the Potter films.

The final step in your preparation comes courtesy of an animatronic Sorting Hat, which delivers the inevitable safety spiel in rhyming verse. Finally, you enter the floating candlestick-filled Room of Requirement, which doubles as the boarding area. Four guests at a time step onto a two-stage moving sidewalk and are fastened side-by-side into one of 40-odd golden, high-backed benches, that flow by in a constantly moving stream. The purple seats feature overhead restraints similar to a roller coaster, but with a curved handlebar to grip, and partitions that prevent you from looking at other riders.

With John Williams' theme music twinkling in your seat-mounted speakers, you glide sedately sideways until Hermione scatters some "Floo powder" over you. All at once your feet lift off the ground as you lean backwards, flying up through a network of chimneys, and floating into the castle's towering Observatory. Next, you are summoned by Harry and Ron, riding by on their broomsticks, and you plunge through the window after them, skimming precariously along Hogwarts' rocky foundations. Catching up with the boys, who assure you they haven't lost anyone on these "dodgy" devices yet ("this week, anyway"), you are confronted with Hagrid's missing dragon. Putting your Quidditch match on hold, you hide from the creature inside the creaky old Covered Bridge; you can spot his massive wing beating against the windows, and scorch-marks appear on the walls. Suddenly the floor collapses, dropping you eye-to-eye with the fire-breather, who delivers a warm blast of steam in your face. That sends you spiraling down into the Forbidden Forest, lair of Aragog the enormous Acromantula and his web-spitting kin.

Before you say I've given it all away, that's barely the first third of the adventure! Before you're done, you'll be whacked by the Whomping Willow, watch a Quidditch play close-up, and see a Dementor suck your soul right out of your body. It's a dark, discombobulating, and often startling experience that will leave you breathless (and moist). Naturally, all ends well, with cheering throngs in the Great Hall, a wizardly admonishment to "tuck your elbows in," and a final tumble down the Floo Network back to the room where you began.

End of Spoilers!

After your journey, all that remains is to tumble downstairs into Filch's Emporium (see Shopping below), check out your souvenir photo, and sprint to rejoin the line for another flight.

Tip: For re-rides, use the single rider line, which starts in the dungeon across from the lockers. You'll skip the tour, going straight to the safety spiel room, and cut your wait considerably.

The best seats in the house. All four seats on each bench are excellent, but the middle two give the least-distorted view of the curved screens. The "front" seat (far left when seated) gets the biggest "boo" scares, while the "back" seat (far right when seated) experiences the most motion.

How did Universal Creative create this masterpiece? By starting with the template they pioneered with *Spider-Man*: motion-simulator seats moving through a seamless blend of physical effects and projection screens. This time, they upgraded the sets from *Spider-Man's* comic-book stylization to fully sculpted environments that seem to extend in all directions, then stuffed them with animatronic monsters that aggressively lunge within feet of your face. As for the video, it ditches the 3-D (the glasses would go flying), but makes up for it with high-definition footage featuring the film stars, projected onto vision-encompassing domes: think smaller-sized *Simpsons* screens, mounted on a clever carousel contraption that gives every car a sweet-spot perspective.

What elevates *Forbidden Journey* above those predecessors is the KUKA Robocoaster, a world-exclusive new technology that takes an industrial robotic arm and for the first time mounts it on a moving track. The result is not a roller coaster. There are no sustained speeds, big drops, or upside-down moments. Nor is it a traditional simulator. With your legs dangling free, you have an unprecedented feeling of "floating" that will have you flat on your back and leaning dynamically from side to side. The motion is extraordinarily smooth, with little jerking or jarring, though its intensity will be disorienting to those prone to motion sickness; even thrill ride veterans may stumble off somewhat woozy.

Most amazing is the way that this next-generation underpinning is completely invisible to the rider. As long as you keep your head back in your seat as instructed, you'll never see the arm holding you aloft. Nor should you see any other ride vehicles, making it seem like a uniquely personal adventure. That is an amazing feat when you consider that a new vehicle can be dispatched every seven seconds.

Tip: After your first few times through, try sitting in an outside seat and leaning slightly forward for insight on how the magic happens.

Just because *Forbidden Journey* is the new attraction champion of Orlando (and possibly the world) doesn't mean it's perfect. The trip is dizzyingly chaotic, and the barebones plot boils down to a greatest-hits mishmash of memorable action moments from the films. The projected sequences seem somewhat blurry, likely due to your extreme proximity to the screen and the rapid movement of the action. And a few of the spooky animatronics appear unconvincing after repeated rides. But these are minor quibbles that don't detract from this being a five-star attraction in the truest spirit of that score.

Note: Although Universal has reconfigured the seats, some visitors with larger chest, tummy, or thigh dimensions may have difficulty with the ride's safety restraints. If you have any doubt, test out the sample seats outside the attraction entrance. If you pull down the harness and get a green light, you're golden, but if you get the yellow ask an attendant about special seating. You may be retested before boarding; don't take it personally, the attendants are only looking out for your safety.

An alternate stationary loading platform (complete with theming) is available for those needing to transfer from a wheelchair, or anyone physically unable to navigate the moving belt. Just ask an attendant for assistance, though it can get backed up on busy days.

Note: This ride requires that you stow all your belongings in electronic lockers located immediately inside the entrance. They are free for a period of time that varies with the queue length, but charge a hefty fee if you overstay your welcome. Be aware that long items like wizards' wands may not fit in the lockers, though you can use the "baby swap" as a "wand swap." Better yet, save your shopping until the end of the day, after your ride.

Tip: If a line extends outside the castle, it may be for the lockers, located to the right of the entrance. If you don't have any loose belongings, proceed past the line to the left. If you do, consider using the lockers outside *Dragon Challenge*. There is a small compartment in the back of each rider's seat, just big enough for your keys, wallet, and cellphone or compact camera. Don't forget your belongings when your journey ends!

Dragon Challenge ★ ★ ★ ★ 1/2

Type: Twin roller coasters
Time: 1.5 minutes
Short Take: Close–call coaster nirvana

An easily overlooked stone archway marks the entrance to this immense inverted steel roller coaster, hidden behind the stone wall through which the Hogwarts Express appears to emerge. Actually, two separate roller coasters lurk back there, travelling along separate but closely intertwined tracks that diverge and then converge to terrifying effect.

Note: This ride requires that you stow all your belongings in electronic lockers located immediately outside the entrance, in a shelter disguised as a train station. They are free for a period of time that varies with the queue length, but charge a hefty fee if you overstay your welcome.

This coaster (formerly known as *Dueling Dragons*) is themed after the first of three tasks comprising the "Triwizard Tournament," the wizarding competition seen in the fourth Potter tale, *Goblet of Fire.* Begin by walking the meandering path toward the small (compared to Hogwarts) castle ahead. Along the way, you'll pass banners supporting Harry Potter and his competitors (Fleur Delacort, Victor Krum, and Cedric Diggory) and the Weasley's flying Ford Anglia, which has crashed into a nearby tree. Pass into the stone structure and you enter the Champions' Tent, where the Goblet of Fire stands spewing an otherworldly blue flame. Further ahead, you'll find the Triwizard Cup itself on a pedestal, a trio of golden dragon eggs, and a chamber filled with flickering floating candles. Those who remember the wonderfully macabre theming of the *Dueling Dragons* queue will be disappointed by the labyrinth of featureless stone walls that follows, but eventually you will be asked to turn left toward the red "Chinese Fireball" or right to the blue "Hungarian Horntail." While waiting for your coaster, look up at the shadowy dragons battling above the ruined ceiling.

This is an inverted coaster, which means that the cars, completely dressed to look like dragons, hang from a track over your head. Your feet dangle in the air below your seat. When the cars are fully loaded the passengers look as though they are hanging from the dragons' claws. Then it's off on a 90-second ride over a lake that is actually shaped like a dragon, a fact that few people who ride this attraction are likely to notice.

The two coasters share the same lift to the top of the first drop, but then the Chinese Fireball peels off to the left as the Hungarian Horntail swoops to the right. After that, their separate trips are carefully synchronized so that, as they loop and swirl their way around, they meet in mid air at three crucial moments. A computer actually weighs each coaster and then makes the appropriate adjustments to get the timing just right. Perhaps the scariest close encounter comes when they come straight at one another on what is obviously a head-on collision course. At the last moment, they spin up and apart with the dangling feet of the riders coming within a foot or two of each other at nearly 60 miles per hour. At another point, both coasters enter a double helix, spinning dizzily around one another. All told there are three near misses in the 50 seconds or so it takes to travel from the first drop to the point where the coasters slow down to reenter the castle. If you've ever asked yourself what could be more terrifying than the current generation of high-speed steel roller coasters, ask no more.

Note: Shortly before press time, following a couple of unfortunate injuries involving flying debris during the near-misses, Universal suspended synchronized operations of the dueling tracks. Hopefully a solution will be found soon; after over a decade of safe operations, it would be a shame for future guests not to experience the dragons' most dramatic feature. In addition to tempering the thrills, staggered dispatches of alternating trains slow down the line, so ask an attendant how they are operating (or observe from just inside the entrance) before getting in line.

Some people find this ride so extreme, the motion so violent, and the experience so short that they can't decide whether they liked it or not. Indeed, you'll notice many people exiting in stunned puzzlement.

Tip: If you'd like to get a preview of this ride, look for the exit. It's to your left as you face the entrance. A short way up, you will find a viewing area behind a high metal fence; most likely a number of departing riders will have paused here for another look. This vantage point gives you a pretty good view of the twin coasters' routes. For those who have no intention of ever strapping themselves into this coaster, it's a pretty entertaining attraction in and of itself.

It's also possible to enter the queue line itself for a peek. Just a short way in is a spot where you can witness two of the ride's close encounters up close. You'll actually feel the wind rush through your hair as the coasters spiral past. If this dissuades you from venturing farther you can turn back.

The best seats in the house. The first row is the clear choice for the thrill seeker. Otherwise, the outside seats in each row give a better view (if you have your eyes open!) and are less likely to induce motion sickness. Seats farther back in the vehicle offer a different ride experience, partly because you can't see what's coming and partly because the back rows snap about with a bit more zip. Finally, the left hand track is more "aggressive" than the right one; that is, it has a few more spins to it and moves a bit faster at some points. Overall, the best seats are the first row inside on the Hungarian Horntail, and the last row outside on the Chinese Fireball.

Flight of the Hippogriff ★ ★ ★ 1/2

Type:	A junior roller coaster
Time:	About a minute
Short Take:	Best for the view of Hogsmeade

Just past Hogsmeade Village and just before you enter Hogwarts Castle, you'll find a stone monolith marking the entrance to this cute coaster. Formerly known as *The Flying Unicorn*, the ride was re-themed around one of the favorite pets of Rubeus Hagrid, Hogwarts' "care of magical creatures" instructor. Eager riders wind around Hagrid's pumpkin patch and stone hut on the fringe of the Forbidden Forest, listening as the gentle giant instructs us on the proper way to approach the proud Hippogriff.

We board one of the two 16-rider trains, which appear to be made of woven wicker, and are urged to bow respectfully to the life-size animatronic eagle/horse that sits nodding in its track-side nest. After a slow climb to the first drop, which provides a spectacular view of The Wizarding World and beyond, the coaster glides briefly through a series of dips and swoops before returning to the wooden hut that serves as the station.

Smaller kids will delight in the gentle ride from the slower front seats, but even adults have been know to squeal when sitting in the surprisingly zippy back rows. Though the "Vekoma Junior" track is similar to Woody Woodpecker's coaster next door in USF, the *Hippogriff* is 400 feet longer, 15 feet taller, and 7 mph swifter. Striking vistas and rich theming make this a worthwhile spin even for childless grown-ups.

Ollivander's Wand Shop ★ ★ ★ ★

Type: Small-scale show
Time: About 5 minutes
Short Take: A charmingly magical moment

A mysteriously levitating wand in the window marks this Hogsmeade storefront, behind which hides the sleeper attraction everyone will be talking about back home. Though it doesn't even appear on the park map, people line up for hours to enter this Rowling-approved franchise of the famous Diagon Alley purveyor, "maker of fine wands since 382 BC."

Groups of 20-odd guests are allowed at a time into the tiny shop, its towering shelves stocked with dusty boxes. The kindly proprietor greets you and selects one or two lucky customers (almost always children) to test out a wand. As Potter followers know, wands have embedded in their cores various magic substances like unicorn hair or a phoenix feather, and each wand must choose its own master. As the volunteers test the "wrong" wands, a range of disastrous special effects is triggered. Flowers wilt and shelving collapses, requiring the shopkeep to magically repair the damage. Finally, the destined wand is found, as signified by a swirl of light and wind straight out of the cinema.

Afterwards, the volunteers are sent into the adjoining Owl Post store to pay for their new wands (or another of their choosing), and the next group is ushered in. There is no charge to attend or participate in the show, but if you want to take your wand home it will run about $30.

The entire show lasts about five minutes, the queue can be daunting, and the effects are sweetly simple. But the actors involved are so engagingly "in character" (all with exhaustive knowledge of wand arcana and credible accents) that it's worth the wait, especially if your child is the one selected.

Tip: There are multiple "spells" rigged throughout the shop, so repeat visitors will experience slightly different shows.

And all the rest . . .

There are no formally scheduled theater shows within the Wizarding World. Nor are there any strolling actors portraying "Harry Potter" or any other named characters (you'll have to enter Hogwarts to see them). But there are a number of interactive entertainments involving less-famous Potter characters that are worth seeking out.

The **Hogwarts Express Conductor** watching over the train at the area's Lost Continent entrance is more than a living prop for **photo ops**. He's a veritable wealth of knowledge about the attraction and all Potter lore; just try to stump him.

Several times daily, one of two performances is presented in front of the pseudo–Celtic, rune-covered monolith across from the friendly frozen snowman. Both are good fun, but operate on an unpublished schedule. No set show times are listed on the park map, but performances usually occur a couple times each hour, so hang around and see what pops up.

The **Frog Choir,** briefly seen in *Prisoner of Azkaban*, is an a cappella choir consisting of four Hogwarts students and two bass-singing toads (psst, they're puppets). The group, led by an emphatically gesticulating conductor, performs beat-box versions of songs from the Potter scores, such as "Hedwig's Theme" and "Something Wicked This Way Comes."

At the **Triwizard Spirit Rally**, the visiting students from the Beauxbatons and Durmstrang show off their school pride. First the lovely French ladies demonstrate their ribbon-dancing talents to a classical soundtrack. Then the Russian lads show off their martial arts skills with some fighting-stick acrobatics. Afterwards, everyone poses for pictures.

When you are exhausted from your adventures, seek refuge from the sun in **The Owlery,** a pleasantly shaded area beneath the innards of a rustic clockwork bell tower. Animatronic owls roost in the rafters, depositing realistic droppings on the beams below although not, it should be noted, on you.

The restrooms, located across from Ollivander's, are an attraction in and of themselves. If you listen over the flushing, you can hear the ghostly **Moaning Myrtle** sighing and weeping. Of course, if you're a parent you're probably already used to hearing a little child cry while you try to pee.

But the greatest Potter attraction is the one most likely to be overlooked in the rush to the headliner rides. Each street-facing window, including the ones that front inaccessible facades, contains delightfully detailed dressing and animated illusions. Hidden touches abound, from dueling chess pieces to rolling eyeballs. Here are a just few to keep an eye out for:

The goblin-run bank Gringotts has an ATM branch near the back patio. Spintwitches sporting goods sells quivering quidditch equipment (spot the runaway Golden Snitch flying in their window). Tomes & Scrolls displays living pictures of Gilderoy Lockhart (Kenneth Branagh), while Scrivenshaft's & Pottage's stock quills and cauldrons that work by themselves. Inside Dogweed & Deathcap Exotic Plants you'll spot a potted Shrieking Mandrake and other freaky flora. Gladrags Wizardwear has Hermione's Yule Ball gown from the fourth film, with an animated kitty made of measuring tape pawing at its hem. In Dominic Maestro's second-story music shop, when the enchanted cello hits a bad note, sheet music flies. And outside the Three Broomsticks, dishes wash themselves!

JURASSIC PARK

If you've seen the movie *Jurassic Park*, you will recognize the arches that greet you as you enter. If you haven't, you should make sure to rent the original film from your local video store before coming. Knowing the film will help you understand a lot of the little details of Jurassic Park, including the frequent references to velociraptors.

Here, Universal's design wizards have re-created the theme park that the movie's John Hammond was trying to create before all prehistoric heck broke loose, and the lush and steamy jungle landscape they have devised fits in perfectly with Florida's humid summers.

As in the movie, we are asked to believe that we are in a park containing actual living dinosaurs, some of which are quite dangerous. Periodically, roars are heard, and more than one child has been seen starting in terror when an unseen critter growled in the underbrush. Unfortunately, the surprisingly realistic atmosphere has been somewhat disrupted by the boy wizard's arrival. It's understandably difficult to hide a huge honking castle, but it would be nice if they'd at least give its backside a coat of "go-away green" in the future.

Discovery Center ★ ★ 1/2

Type:	Interactive displays
Time:	Unlimited
Short Take:	Best for young dinosaur buffs

This is lifted almost straight from the film and houses a fast food restaurant, a shop and, on the ground floor, a children's "science center," which blends fantasy and reality in such a way that you might have to explain the difference to your more trusting kids. Kids will certainly recognize the huge T-Rex skeleton that perches menacingly on a rock outcropping and pokes its head through to the circular railing on the upper level.

A nursery carefully incubates dinosaur eggs. Nearby, kids can handle "real" dino eggs and put them in a scanner to view the developing embryo inside. Periodically an attendant appears and conducts a deadpan scientific show-and-tell as you watch an adorable baby raptor emerge from its shell.

Closer to reality is an actual segment of rock face from the North Sea area containing real fossilized dinosaur bits from the Triassic, Jurassic, and Cretaceous eras. A series of clever "neutrino data scanners" let kids move along the rock face looking for dinosaurs. When a fragment is found, the scanner analyzes it and then identifies and reconstructs the dinosaur from which it came. In somewhat the same vein is an exhibit of life-sized dinosaurs that supposedly lets you see the world as the dinosaurs saw it by looking through high-tech viewfinders mounted periscope-style into the model dinosaurs' heads and necks and moving the creatures' heads around (unfortunately, it rarely seems to work properly).

On the zany side is a DNA sequencing exhibit that explains the cloning premise on which the movie is based and then lets you combine your own DNA with that of a dinosaur to create a saurian you. And completely over the top (but a lot of fun) is a quiz show with the rather naughty name, "You Bet Jurassic." Here you and two other tourists compete in a game of dinosaur trivia. But don't get your hopes up; the grand prize is a lifetime supply of Raptor Chow, which is apparently manufactured from losing contestants!

On the back wall of the lower level you'll find a large mural depicting life in the Jurassic era. If you entered the *Discovery Center* from the upper level, you might want to take a peek through the massive double doors in the middle of this wall. They open out onto a spacious park-like terrace that descends to the shores of the Great Inland Sea. This is one of the loveliest open spaces in the park and offers a stunning view back to the Port of Entry and the lighthouse that welcomes arriving guests. With its tropical foliage, it's secluded and romantic at night. Near the dock area once used by boats that ferried guests back and forth from Port of Entry is a bridge leading to the Lost Continent area near Mythos restaurant.

Jurassic Park River Adventure ★ ★ ★ ★

Type: Water ride
Time: 5 minutes
Short Take: A wild, wet dino-tour with teeth

This is the attraction that will draw people to Jurassic Park. The pre-ride warm-up plays it straight. Video monitors in the queue line emphasize proper boarding procedures and ride safety, just as you would expect in the "real" Jurassic Park.

River Adventure itself is an idyllic boat ride that gives you an opportunity to view from close range some of Jurassic Park's gentlest creatures. Unfortunately, on the trip you take with 25 other guests, things go very, very wrong. Your first stop is the upper lagoon, where you meet a 35-foot tall mama ultrasaur and her baby. Then you cruise past the park's north forty where you glimpse stegosaurs and the playful hydrosaurs. Too playful, unfortunately.

Before you know it, you're off course in the raptor containment area and on the lunch menu. In a desperate attempt to save you, the boat is shunted into the environmental systems building, that huge 13-story structure at the back of Jurassic Park. It is in this vast, dark, and very scary setting that the ride reaches its climax. After narrowly escaping velociraptors and those nasty spitting dinosaurs, you come face to face, quite literally, with T-Rex himself. After that, the 85-foot plunge down what was billed as the "longest, fastest, steepest water descent ever built" in pitch blackness will seem like a relief.

Tip: You can speed your way through this ride by asking the attendant to point you toward the single rider line (if available).

This is a great ride to experience at night, especially once you enter the main building. The bright Florida sun tends to give away the approach of the final breathtaking drop; at night it comes as a real surprise.

The best seats in the house. Clearly the first row of the boat is where you thrill seekers want to be; just be warned that you will get wet. Of course, you'll probably get wet no matter where you sit, although seats in the center of the craft are a little more protected. The ride attendants are more likely to accommodate a request for a seat that gives you some protection from a drenching than they are to put you in the front row. However, if you come early in the day or late in the evening, when the crowds are thinner, you may be able to pick any seat you want.

Camp Jurassic ★ ★ ★ ★

Type: Interactive play area
Time: As long as it takes
Short Take: Terrific fun for pre-teens

This 60,000-square-foot interactive kids' play and discovery area is about four times the size of *Fievel's Playland* over at Universal Studios Florida and will appeal to a slightly older age group, although kids of all ages will find plenty to keep them occupied. The place is a minor masterpiece of playground design and is highly recommended for kids who are getting antsy or who just need to burn off some excess energy. Even adults will enjoy sampling its pleasures.

Camp Jurassic transports you to a jungle on the slopes of an ancient active volcano. The roots of banyan trees snake around ancient rock outcroppings and an old abandoned amber mine offers exciting networks of rope ladders and tunnels, as well as subterranean passageways, to explore. There are corkscrew slides, cascading waterfalls, secret hideaways, and a place where kids can do battle with water cannons made up to look like the deadly spitting dinosaurs from the film.

Aside from the water cannons, all the fun here comes from kids burning off energy and exercising their imaginations as they run, climb, and slide their way through this intricate and imaginative maze of a prehistoric environment. Don't be surprised if your kid gets lost in here for an hour or so, and don't be surprised if you find yourself enjoying it just as much.

Pteranodon Flyers ★ ★ 1/2

Type: A mild, hanging coaster
Time: 80 seconds
Short Take: Not worth waiting for

Taking off from the back of *Camp Jurassic* is this "family" ride that glides gently around the camp's tropical perimeter for an enjoyable but all-too-brief soaring experience. The ride vehicle consists of a pair of swing-like seats, one behind the other, that dangle from a metal pteranodon. Pteranodons, you might remember, were flying dinosaurs with long mean-looking beak-like faces and hooks on their leathery wings. These pteranodons are not at all threatening. In fact, you hardly notice them once you are seated.

Your vehicle glides rather than rides along the overhead track, taking you on a journey that lets you survey *Camp Jurassic* below and the Great Inland Sea in the distance. This ride is a little more "aggressive" than the sky rides you may have encountered at other parks and offers a few mild "thrills" as the flyers bank and curve.

The main problem with this ride is that it accommodates so few riders. Universal has tried to remedy this situation by imposing a 36-inch minimum and 56-inch maximum height requirement; if you are taller than this, you must be accompanied by a child who falls within the range. This has helped somewhat, but compared to all the other rides in the park, its hourly "throughput" is still laughably low. The result is that the line forms early and lasts a long, long time. You won't be alone if you decide that an hour and a half wait for an 80-second ride is a tad on the absurd side. And Universal Express

Plus is not accepted at this attraction. So if you think this is the kind of thing your kid will demand to ride, plan on coming first thing in the morning. The wait also tends to be more reasonable shortly before the park closes.

Note: Be aware that some children, especially those with a fear of heights, might find this ride terrifying. And if they do, they won't have Mommy or Daddy to cling to since the two seats are quite separate.

Triceratops Discovery Trail ★ ★ ★

Type: Walk-through display
Time: About 5 minutes
Short Take: An entertaining example of robotic wizardry

After sitting dormant for half a decade, Universal resurrected this opening-day attraction to help absorb Potter-generated crowds. Groups of a couple dozen guests are ushered into an animal paddock, where a paleo-veterinarian tends to a 24–foot long, 10-foot high Triceratops. A masterpiece of animatronic engineering, these massive creatures appear to move, breathe, sneeze, and even pee (seriously) with remarkable realism. The vet will explain a bit about his charge's care and feeding, then ask for any questions from the audience. Unless there's an especially curious kid in the audience, the whole affair lasts just a few minutes. If you can suspend your disbelief, you'll be enthralled; if you can't it's still an impressive piece of hardware.

Tip: There are three different trikes on display ("Cera," "Topper," and "Chris") each with slightly different personalities and behaviors, so if you enjoy the attraction you can see it multiple times.

Note: This attraction only operates during peak summer and holiday periods.

TOON LAGOON

After the intensity of *Forbidden Journey* and Jurassic Park, the zany, colorful goofiness of Toon Lagoon is a welcome change of pace. Many of the characters you have come to know and love through the Sunday funnies in your hometown newspaper can be spotted here—some appear in blow-ups of their strips, some have been immortalized in giant sculptures, and some will actually be strolling the grounds and happy to pose for photos. A visit here offers a unique opportunity to live out a child's daydream of stepping into the pages of the comic strips and exploring a gaudy fantasy world filled with fun and laughter.

Toon Lagoon's main drag is **Comic Strip Lane**, a short street of shops and restaurants, including those described below. It is an attraction in itself. Nearly 80 comic strip characters call this colorful neighborhood home, including Beetle Bailey (on furlough from Camp Swampy no doubt), Hagar the Horrible, and Krazy Kat. The concept makes for all sorts of serendipitous juxtapositions. Hagar's boat hangs over a waterfall that falls into a big pipe that bubbles up across the way at a dog fountain where all the dogs from the various comic strips hang out.

Turning off Comic Strip Lane is the zany seaside town of **Sweet Haven**, a separate section of Toon Lagoon containing a variety of Popeye-inspired rides and attractions. Water is a recurring theme in Toon Lagoon and you can get very wet here. See *Good Things To Know About...Getting Wet* in the introduction to this chapter for a strategy to follow.

Dudley Do-Right's Ripsaw Falls ★ ★ ★ ★

Type: Log flume ride
Time: 6 minutes
Short Take: Laughs and screams

In Dudley's hometown of Ripsaw Falls, as you might expect, Nell is once again in the clutches of the dastardly Snidely Whiplash. That's all the excuse you need to take off on a rip-roaring log flume ride that, like so many other attractions in this park, takes the genre to a whole new level.

The build-up takes us through a series of scenes in a "moving melodrama" in which the much-loved characters unfold a typically wacky plot that includes not just Dudley, Nell, and Snidely but Inspector Fenwick and Horse, too, as our five-passenger log-boats rise inexorably to the mountainous heights where Snidely has his hideout. Along the way we pass animated tableaux that advance the tie-her-to-the-railroad-tracks plot. The landscape is dotted with signs that echo the off-the-wall humor of the old cartoons.

At one point the boat detours into the abandoned Wontyabe Mine, at another we pass a billboard advertising Whiplash Lager ("made with real logs"). Of course, Dudley triumphs almost in spite of himself. Anticipating victory a bit too soon, he strikes a heroic pose with his foot on a dynamite plunger, precipitating a plunge through the roof of a TNT storage shack as the riders are seemingly shot beneath the water surface only to pop back to the surface 100 feet downstream. Another nice touch is that the final drop is curved rather than a straight angle; the result is that, as the angle steepens, you could swear you're hurtling straight down.

Tip: You can speed your way through this ride by asking the attendant to point you toward the single rider line (if available).

This is one ride that just may be as entertaining to watch as to take. If you'd prefer not to take the plunge and actually go on the ride, you can stand and watch others take the steep 60-foot drop into the TNT shack. Or you can use the Water Blasters (25 cents) to spray the riders as they pass below you—good, clean, evil fun.

Note: The lap bar restraints on this ride can be extremely confining. Be prepared to suck in your stomach to get them secured.

Popeye & Bluto's Bilge-Rat Barges ★ ★ ★ ★ 1/2

Type: Raft ride
Time: About 5 minutes
Short Take: Super soaking good fun

You may get spritzed a bit on the *Jurassic Park River Adventure* and on *Dudley Do-Right's Ripsaw Falls*, but for a really good soaking, you have to come to Sweet Haven, home to Popeye, Olive Oyl, and the gang. The barges of the name are actually circular, 12-passenger rubber rafts that twirl and dip along a twisting, rapids-strewn watercourse.

Just as Dudley has his Snidely, Popeye has Bluto. Their lifelong enmity and rivalry for the affection of Miss Olive form the basis for the theming on this ride, which involves Olive, Wimpy, Poopdeck Pappy, and all the rest. Water splashes into the sides of the raft in the rapids and pours in from above at crucial junctures. And at least one person in your raft is sure to get hosed by the little devils (actually someone else's kids) manning the water cannons on *Me Ship, The Olive* (see below) before the raft is swept into an octopus grotto where an eight-armed beast holds Popeye in its tentacled grip, preventing him from reaching his lifesaving spinach. Before it's all over, the hapless rafts have been spun into Bluto's fully operational boat wash, which is just like a car wash except it's for boats.

This is the spiffiest raft ride in town and the ride to take at the hottest, stickiest part of the day. Because the free-floating rafts spin and twist as they roar down the rapids, how wet you get is somewhat a matter of luck; you certainly will get damp and you may be drenched. The rafts have plastic covered bins in the center in which you can store things you'd rather not get wet. They do a pretty good job, too. Many people are smart enough to remove and stow their shoes and socks since plenty of water sloshes into the rafts along the way.

Tip: The heavier the raft, the faster the ride. So if you want a little extra oomph in your ride, get in line behind a bunch of weight lifters or opera stars.

Me Ship, The Olive ★ ★ ★

Type:	Interactive play area
Time:	Unlimited
Short Take:	Nice, but can't beat *Camp Jurassic*

Resist the temptation to come here after the raft ride and throttle the little darlings who were squirting you with the water cannons. Instead, let your littlest kids loose in this three-story interactive play area representing the ship Popeye has named after his one true love. Older kids will find this spot of limited interest.

The ship theme is clever and well executed but makes for cramped spaces. Still there are some good reasons for at least a brief visit. The top level offers some excellent views of *Dragon Challenge*, all of Seuss Landing, and an especially good angle on the *Hulk* coaster. Videographers and photographers will definitely want to take advantage of these **photo ops**. Also on the top level is a tubular slide that will deposit little kids on the middle level where they will find, on the starboard side, four water cannons they can aim at hapless riders on the *Bilge-Rat Barges* ride—and they're free! Also on this level is a "Spinach Spinnet," a cartoon piano that little kids will enjoy banging on. Yet another corkscrew tubular slide takes your tykes to the bottom level, where they can play in Swee' Pea's Playpen. For those who cannot climb the many stairs of *Me Ship, The Olive*, a small elevator is thoughtfully provided.

Toon Lagoon Amphitheater Shows ★ ★ ★ to ★ ★ ★ ★

Type:	Seasonal amphitheater show
Time:	About 20 minutes
Short Take:	Usually worth watching

This large amphitheater marks the boundary between Toon Lagoon and Marvel Super Hero Island. It hosts an irregular series of short-run live shows and special events (Rosie O'Donnell once taped here, for example). The television show *iVillage Live* broadcast from here before moving to Chicago. It's impossible to anticipate what, if anything, will be on when you visit. Most recently, "Max Hoffman's Agro Circus" stunt shows involving skateboards and BMX bikes have performed. Whatever's on tap will be listed in the 2-Park Map. It may be that these shows will be back or you may encounter something completely different. Or perhaps another television show will recognize the special opportunities this venue offers.

The best seats in the house. During the stunt shows, bikers will periodically zoom out into the audience, fly up a short ramp, and come to a deft stop right in front of the first row of the upper section of seats, making this the prime seating location.

These shows are "seasonal," meaning they run during the summer, at Christmas, and over Spring Break. If something is going on here during your visit, don't miss it.

And all the rest . . .

There are regular **Character Meet and Greet** sessions in Toon Lagoon, either along Comic Strip Lane or in front of the Pandemonium amphitheater. The characters, naturally, are your funny paper favorites like Popeye and Olive Oyl, Beetle Bailey, and Woody Woodpecker. During busier periods, these events may be called out on the 2-Park Map.

Toon Lagoon's **Comic Strip Lane** offers some terrific **photo ops.** There are cut-outs that put you in the comic strip and many of the palm trees are mounted with comic strip speech balloons. You pose underneath and get a nice shot of you saying things like, "It must be Sunday...We're in color!" or "Don't have the mushroom pizza before you ride Ripsaw Falls."

Perhaps the best is a trick photo involving Marmaduke, that playful Great Dane. You'll find it on the facade of Blondie's restaurant (see below), and a nearby sign tells you exactly how to set up the shot.

If you turn to the right at *Me Ship, The Olive* and follow the path over the raging rapids of the *Bilge-Rat Barges* ride, you'll find yourself in a delightful snarl of walkways along the Great Inland Sea, another of the park's wonderful get-away-from-it-all spots.

MARVEL SUPER HERO ISLAND

Those from another planet may not know that Marvel is the name of a comic book company that revolutionized the industry way back in the sixties with a series of titles showcasing a bizarre array of super heroes whose psychological quirks were as intriguing as their ingeniously conceived superhuman powers. As might be expected, this cast of characters offers rich inspiration for some of the most intense thrill rides ever created.

After the extensive theming of the other islands, Marvel Super Hero Island can seem a little, well, flat. Some people suspect, erroneously, that Universal was cutting corners or had run out of money when it came to designing this section of the park. Not at all. Marvel Super Hero Island is, in fact, a brilliant evocation in three dimensions of the visual style of the comic books that inspired it. Marvel used strong colors and simple geometric shapes to create a futuristic cityscape with an Art Deco flavor. Against this purposely flat backdrop, they arrayed their extravagantly muscled and lovingly sculpted heroes. Marvel Comics had a profound effect on American visual design, not to mention its effect on contemporary notions of the body beautiful.

But enough art history. What you've come here for are the thrill rides and Marvel Super Hero Island has some of the best examples of the genre you're likely to find in Central Florida. Interestingly, while Disney bought Marvel Comics in 2009, Universal retains the theme park rights in Florida indefinitely, so Spidey and pals are staying put for the time being.

The Amazing Adventures of Spider-Man ★ ★ ★ ★ ★

Type: 3-D motion simulator ride
Time: 4½ minutes
Short Take: An astounding spin into the comic pages

Until Harry Potter's arrival, Universal's publicity powerhouse trumpeted this as "the next threshold attraction," the one that takes theme park entertainment to a new level, just as *Back to The Future . . . The Ride* (since closed) and *T2* did when they opened over at Universal Studios Florida. An upgrade of *Spider-Man* with digital 3-D projectors and newly re-animated imagery is currently underway; when complete in 2012, it will make Spidey an even more detailed and immersive experience.

Visitors step into the offices of the *Daily Bugle* only to discover that the evil villain Dr. Octopus and his Sinister Syndicate have used an antigravity gun to make off with the Statue of Liberty and other famous landmarks as part of a plot to bring New York City to its knees. Since cub reporter Peter Parker and all the rest of the staff are mysteriously absent, crusty editor J. Jonah Jameson drafts his hapless guests into a civilian force with the mission of tracking down the evildoers and getting the scoop on their nefarious doings.

Guests board special 12-passenger vehicles and set off through the streets of the city, where they discover Spidey is already on the case. What ensues is a harrowing high-speed chase enhanced through a variety of heart-stopping special effects.

The vehicles are simulators, much like the ones in *The Simpsons* in Universal Studios Florida. Underneath they have six hydraulically operated stalks that can be used to simulate virtually any kind of motion. But these cars can also move through space, and they do, along tracks that allow for 360 degrees of rotation. The combination of forward motion, rotation, and simulator technology creates startling sensations never before possible.

Further heightening the experience is the environment through which the cars move. This is the world of Marvel Comics sprung vividly to life and startlingly real. Intermixed with the solid set elements (that include enormous chunks of a cut up Statue of Liberty) are almost undetectable screens on which three-dimensional films add an extra measure of depth and excitement. Both villains and heroes seem to leap directly at you. At several points, various villains and Spidey himself drop onto the hood of the vehicle with a thud and a jolt. They are insubstantial three-dimensional cartoons, of course, but the effect is amazingly real.

As your ill-fated journey proceeds, it is your bad luck to keep interrupting the evildoers at awkward moments, and they do their utmost to destroy you, with deadly bursts of electricity, walls of flame, and deluges of water. They narrowly miss each time, sending your vehicle spinning and tumbling to its next close encounter with doom.

Finally you are caught in the irresistible force of an antigravity ray that sucks the vehicle ever upward as Spider-Man struggles valiantly to save you. The ride culminates with a 400-foot drop through the cartoon canyons of New York to almost certain death on the streets below. It's quite a ride.

The best seats in the house. Logically, the first of the three rows in the vehicle should be the best, since you don't have the heads of fellow passengers in your field of vision. Still, the other rows, because they are slightly farther from the screens, provide better 3-D effects.

Tip: *Spider-Man* usually offers a single rider line to speed your wait.

Doctor Doom's Fearfall ★ ★ ★ 1/2

Type: A free-fall ride with oomph
Time: 30 seconds
Short Take: A big buildup with a slow letdown, best for the view

Near the Bugle building is Doom Alley, a part of town that has been completely taken over by the bad guys of the Sinister Syndicate: Dr. Octopus, The Hobgoblin, and The Lizard. Here the archfiend Doctor Doom has secreted his Fear Sucking Machine, in which he uses innocent, unsuspecting victims (that's you in case you hadn't guessed) to create the Fear Juice with which he hopes to finally vanquish the Fantastic Four.

The payoff is a fiendish twist on the freefall rides that have long been a staple of amusement parks and which were artfully updated in Disney's *Tower of Terror.* But whereas those rides take you up slowly and drop you, *Doctor Doom,* in the true Universal spirit, turns convention in its head.

Sixteen victims, that is, passengers, are strapped into seats in small four-person chambers. Suddenly they are shot upward 150 feet at a force of four G's. There is a heart-flipping moment of weightlessness before the vehicles drop back, gently bouncing back upward a few times before all-too-quickly returning to terra firma. Most people scream on freefall rides, but this one happens so quickly (less than 30 seconds) and becomes so anticlimactic after the brief takeoff that many riders won't remember to scream until the ride is over.

Tip: You can speed your way through this ride by asking the attendant to point you toward the single rider line, inside the nearby arcade.

The best seats in the house. Chambers 3 and 4 look out over the park, while 1 and 2 give a less glamorous view of the interstate.

The Incredible Hulk Coaster ★ ★ ★ ★ ★

Type: Steel coaster
Time: 1½ minutes
Short Take: Aaaargh! An unforgettable blast

In the scientific complex where Bruce Banner, a.k.a. the Incredible Hulk, has his laboratories, you can learn all about the nasty effects of overexposure to gamma radiation. No, it's not more edutainment, it's the warm-up for another knock-your-socks-off roller coaster.

In a high-energy video pre-ride show, you learn that you can help Bruce reverse the unfortunate effects that have so complicated his life. All you have to do is climb into this little chamber which is, in fact, a 32-seat roller coaster. This is no ordinary roller coaster, however, where you have to wait agonizing seconds while the car climbs to the top of the first drop. It seems to get off to a fairly normal start, slowly climbing a steep incline, but thanks to an energizing burst of gamma rays you are shot at one G 150 feet upward, going from a near standstill to 42 mph. From there it's all downhill so to speak as you swing into a zero-G roll and speed toward the surface of the lagoon at 58 mph. This is no water ride though, so you whip into a cobra roll before being lofted upwards once more through the highest (109 feet) inversion ever built. After that it's under a bridge—on which earthbound (i.e. "sane") people are enjoying your terror—through a total of seven inversions and two subterranean trenches before you come to a rest, hoping desperately that your exertions have, indeed, helped Bruce out of his pickle.

Here's an interesting note for the technically minded: The initial thrust of this ride consumes so much power that, if the needed electricity were drawn directly from Orlando's electric supply, lights across town would dim every time a new coaster was launched. So Universal draws power at a steady rate from the city's power grid and stores it in a huge flywheel hidden in the greenish building by the Inland Sea labeled "Power Supply." This enables them to get the power they need for that first heart-stopping effect without inconveniencing their neighbors.

Tip: This can be a very discombobulating experience. If you feel a bit weak in the knees at ride's end, look for the Baby Swap area on your right. Here you can sit down in air-conditioned comfort for a few minutes to regain your composure before striding out pridefully into the Florida sun.

Note: This ride requires that you stow all your belongings in nearby electronic lockers that are free for a period of time that varies with the queue length, but charge a hefty fee if you overstay your welcome.

Tip: You may be able speed your way through this ride by asking the attendant to point you toward the single rider line, if open.

And on your way out, don't forget to check out the photo of your adventure. The high-speed cameras capture each of the eight rows of the coaster as it zooms past, so one of the frames is likely to have a good shot of you.

Storm Force Accelatron ★ ★ ★

Type:	Spinning cup ride
Time:	1½ minutes
Short Take:	A dressed-up standard carnival ride

Tucked behind the *Hulk* coaster and Cafe 4, under a futuristic purple and blue dome, is this Marvelized version of a fairly standard amusement park ride. A large circular spinning platform contains four smaller circles that spin independently. Each of these small circles holds three cup-like cars that also spin independently. When the whole thing gets up to speed, there are three levels of spin. An added bit of oomph comes from the circular control in each car that allows the riders to control just how fast their car spins.

The cars are designed to hold four adults but with kids aboard the number can increase; apparently the record is eight passengers in a car. The spin control works quite well and with some vigorous turning you can add quite a bit of momentum to your brief spin cycle whirl. Even if you skip the ride, it's worth strolling back here to take a peek at the back end of *Hulk*.

Tip: To get the full effect of the strobe lights that represent Storm's lightning, ride this one at night.

And all the rest . . .

Kingpin's Arcade, admittedly, seems less out of place here than its equivalents elsewhere. That's because the world of video games is, after all, a comic book world and some of the machines in here represent the current state of the art in this genre. The games run on tokens, which you can obtain from a vending machine. No refunds are given so you're forced to use them all, which might not be all that much of a challenge since some of the fancier games require six tokens. If you ride *Doctor Doom's Fearfall*, you will exit through this incredibly loud emporium. Look for the hole blasted in the wall that leads to Cafe 4.

Several times a day, according to a schedule listed in the 2-Park Map, there is a **Character Meet and Greet** in the plaza opposite the entrance to the *Spider-Man* ride. Several characters from the X-Men comics—Rogue, Storm, Cyclops, and Wolverine— along with Spidey and Captain America, ride out in a parade of all-terrain three-wheelers to give autographs and pose photogenically with your kids. Unlike the costumed cartoon characters encountered elsewhere, these heroes will actually talk to you.

Chapter Four:

CityWalk

Orlando's nightlife epicenter has shifted several times over the decades. In the 1970s and 80s, downtown's historic Church Street Station was world-famous for its entertainment (and is now attempting a comeback). In the 1990s, Disney's Pleasure Island (currently defunct and under redevelopment) cornered the after-hours adult market. But today, the preferred place for post-attraction partying is at Universal Orlando. CityWalk is a hip enclave of heavily themed restaurants, nightclubs, shops, and movie theaters that rocks long after the nearby theme parks have closed up for the night.

Orientation

The layout and setting of CityWalk is ingenious. It is a 30-acre lozenge-shaped area plopped right down between Universal Studios Florida and Islands of Adventure. It is impossible to get from your car to either of the parks, or from one park to the other, without passing through CityWalk. On top of that, a river runs through it—or rather a man-made waterway that separates most of CityWalk from the theme parks and links CityWalk to the Hard Rock and Portofino Bay Hotels, and the Royal Pacific Resort.

There are three major streets: a straight avenue that leads from the parking structures, a curving boulevard that leads from Universal Studios to Islands of Adventure near the waterway, and the Promenade that runs past the major nightclubs. Smaller streets wind between CityWalk's few freestanding buildings; one of these is a zigzag stairway that descends from the upper exit of the Cineplex to the waterway. It used to be called Lombard Street and that's how it will be referred to in this chapter because "Zigzag Stairway with No Name" is awkward. Along the waterway runs an esplanade in the middle of which is an outdoor performance space for special concerts and other events. Also along this esplanade is a dock where you can pick up an elegant complimentary motor launch for the short trip to the resort hotels.

Smack dab in the middle of CityWalk is a large open space called simply the Plaza. On one side, a series of grass and stone platforms descends toward the water, forming a seating area for the performance space at water's edge. On the other, a stage sits over a sloping, waterfall-like fountain. Here you are likely to see a band entertaining the passing crowd with high-decible cover tunes. From time to time you may see other off-the-wall entertainers – jugglers, stilt-walkers, and the like – roaming the grounds spreading smiles and good cheer.

With one exception, the nightclubs in CityWalk are located along the Promenade, which rises gradually from Plaza level, curving behind the Plaza, to the upper exit from the Cineplex. This clever arrangement makes the nightclub area a separate and easily policed enclave within an enclave. The exception is Hard Rock Live (a concert hall more than a nightclub), which is connected to the Hard Rock Cafe and lies across the waterway along a short walk that connects Universal Studios Florida and Islands of Adventure.

Getting Information

There are a number of ways to get information about what's going on at CityWalk prior to your visit. On the Internet, you can get information on upcoming events by visiting www.citywalkorlando.com. CityWalk advertises prominently in the *Orlando Sentinel's* Friday Calendar section and the free *Orlando Weekly*, which also carry listings of many CityWalk entertainment events. The main CityWalk number for "additional information" is (407) 363-8000; follow the automated prompts for an extensive inventory of recorded announcements about CityWalk's various restaurants and clubs. For dining reservations, dial (407) 224-3663 or surf to OpenTable.com

Arriving at CityWalk

You arrive at CityWalk just as you would arrive for a visit to Universal Orlando's theme parks. You park in the same parking structures and pay the same parking fee. Of course, you also have the option of valet parking, if you wish (see *Chapter 2*).

If you arrive between 6:00 p.m. and 10:00 p.m., parking will be $3. Parking after 10:00 p.m. is **free**. If you are arriving just for lunch and plan to stay for less than two hours, valet parking is free with restaurant validation (see below).

You enter CityWalk itself down a long broad avenue that passes by the Cineplex on your right (see map, below). That bridge you pass under is the Promenade and it leads from the upper exit of the Cineplex past CityWalk's string of nightclubs. An escalator to the bridge is available if you can't wait.

Note: If you are arriving by motor launch from one of the resort hotels, you will disembark at a dock just below the NASCAR Sports Grille.

Also by the bridge and the escalator is a kiosk called **Dining Reservations and CityWalk Information**. Here you can peruse menus of the various CityWalk restaurants, make dining reservations and priority seating requests (a process described below), and get pretty decent advice on how to plan your evening. Pick up here a brochure called **City Guide**, which is published monthly. It contains a colorful if hard-to-read map of the enclave and an extremely helpful list of events at the various clubs. You can also pick up maps and show schedules for the two theme parks here, although they sometimes run out.

Just past the bridge, on your left, you will see the **Guest Services** window; come here with questions and problems. A short walk will bring you to the Plaza, CityWalk's broad open center. From here you proceed straight ahead to Islands of Adventure, turn right to head to Universal Studios Florida, or turn left to make your way to the Promenade and the nightclubs.

The Price of Admission

Officially, there is no admission to CityWalk, but that's only partially true. First, if you are coming to Universal Orlando just to visit CityWalk, there's the parking fee to consider – unless, of course, you arrive after 10:00 p.m., which may be the perfect time to begin a visit to what is primarily a nighttime attraction. More importantly, CityWalk's biggest draws, the nightclubs, all levy a $7 cover charge for the live evening entertainment starting at 9:00 p.m. Hard Rock Cafe never charges a cover, even when there's entertainment (which is rarely), and Hard Rock Live is not really a nightclub, so cover charges don't apply there. The Cineplex also charges admission.

If you are coming simply to enjoy the pleasures of CityWalk, you have a choice of paying each cover or admission charge individually or purchasing a one-day **CityWalk Party Pass**, which is sort of an "open sesame" to all the entertainment venues except Hard Rock Live, which always charges its own, separate admission. The Party Pass costs $12.77; annual passholders receive a 20% discount. You can add a movie at the AMC Cineplex for $3.99; upgrade to 3-D for an extra $3, IMAX for $4, or IMAX 3-D for $5.

If you have purchased a FlexTicket or any multi-day pass to the theme parks (a very likely scenario), then you already have 14 consecutive days of access to CityWalk's clubs, starting on the day you first use your ticket or pass. Be aware that the Party Pass will not be honored at clubs with special events and some clubs will occasionally levy an additional cover charge on Party Pass holders.

To purchase your Party Pass, turn left at the Plaza and look for the box office windows outside the groove discotheque. If these windows are closed, check with the Guest Services window between the Endangered Species store and the Pastamoré Market Cafe.

CityWalk also offers a **Meal and Movie Deal** ($21.95 including tax and gratuity), which combines a meal at your choice of CityWalk restaurants (except Emeril's or Hard Rock) and an upgradable ticket to the Cineplex; a **Meal and Party Deal** ($21 including tax and gratuity) combines a meal with a Party Pass. The selection of entrees offered is limited to a half-dozen options at each restaurant; a non-alcoholic beverage is included, but not appetizer or dessert. Standbys like NASCAR cheeseburgers and Pastamoré lasagna are on the menu, but so are more exciting options including Fusion sushi rolls, Bob Marley's curry chicken, Latin Quarter's arroz con pollo, and Pat O'Brien's jambalaya. Depending on how you order, the meal side of these deals is worth $16 to $20, making the movie ticket or Party Pass practically free.

What's The Best Price?

If you purchased a multi-day theme park pass, then price is not a consideration: 14 consecutive days of CityWalk club access is included. Go. Boogie. Enjoy. Otherwise, you may want to spend a few moments considering your options. If you plan on visiting most, if not all, of the clubs on a single night, the Party Pass is a fabulous deal. Of course, it's nearly impossible to visit all the clubs in one night, so you'll miss a lot. But even if you only visit two, the Party Pass pays for itself.

However, be aware that it is possible to visit two clubs and pay only one cover charge. It works like this: The cover charge clicks in at 9:00 p.m., but they don't go around from table to table to collect the cover from those already in the club. So you could arrive at, say, Marley's half an hour before the cover takes effect, grab a good seat and catch the first show. Then you could move on to, say, Rising Star, paying the $7 cover there. If you call it a night then, you've only spent $7 in cover charges and saved a little money – $5.77, to be exact.

Since the additional cost of a Party Pass is so small, why not go for it? That way you can satisfy your morbid curiosity about clubs you otherwise wouldn't try. And who knows? You might discover a place you really love.

Good Things To Know About . . .

Discounts. Your Universal Orlando Annual Pass is good for a 20% discount for up to four people on the CityWalk Party Pass. At some times of the year (which seem to vary), your Annual Pass is good for a complimentary Party Pass from Sunday to Thursday. A Preferred Annual Pass will also get you a 10% discount on food and beverages (excluding alcohol) at many restaurants and clubs, and 2-for-1 beer at the groove; Premier passholders get an additional 5% (except at Bubba Gump) plus 2-for-1 well liquor at the groove and Rising Star. Members of the American Automobile Association (AAA) are eligible for discounts at some restaurants (indicated in the City Guide brochure) and shops.

However, which card gets what discount where is subject to constant change, so the best policy for the traveling tightwad is to ask about discounts every time you have to pay for something.

Drinking. The legal drinking age in Florida is 21 and the law is strictly enforced in CityWalk. The official policy is to "card" (i.e. ask for identification) anyone who appears under 30. So if you fall into this category make sure to bring along a photo ID such as a driver's license or passport to prove your age. Once you've passed muster, your server will attach a plastic bracelet to your wrist, so you don't have to produce ID for the rest of the evening.

Alcoholic beverages are sold quite openly on the streets of CityWalk and from walk-up stands at the various clubs along the Promenade. To prevent those over 21 from purchasing drinks for underage friends, a standard policy is to sell one drink per person. Just to make sure, CityWalk maintains a very visible security presence (see below).

First Aid. And speaking of drinking, if you fall down and injure yourself, or have another health problem, there is a first-aid station located near Guest Services. Just follow the passage to the restrooms and look for the door at the end of the passage.

Happy Hour. Many restaurants and clubs in CityWalk have a generous happy hour that starts as early as 3:00 p.m. and ends as late as 10:00 p.m. Details vary, but 2-for-1 draft beers, $3 well drinks, and cut-price appetizers are typical. Even Emeril's has a happy hour now, though the bar in Cigarz sadly does not.

Money. There is an ATM on your left as you enter CityWalk, near the Guest Services window. There are others just outside the upper exit from the Cineplex, near Cigarz, and near the groove.

Private Parties. Most of CityWalk's restaurants have facilities for private parties. The central number for information is (407) 224-CITY (2489) for groups of more than 20 and (407) 224-FOOD (3663) for smaller groups.

Reservations. All of the table-service restaurants except for Hard Rock Cafe and Bubba Gump accept reservations by phone at (407) 224-3663, or online through OpenTable.com. Emeril's accepts reservations up to six months in advance by calling (407) 224-2424 or faxing (407) 224-2525.

Note: If you are a guest at a Universal Orlando resort hotel, you can flash your room key card at the restaurant for priority seating at the first available table.

Restrooms. Most restrooms are inside the restaurants and nightclubs. You'll find "public" restrooms tucked away down corridors next to Guest Services, near NAS-CAR Sports Grille, and near The Latin Quarter on the Promenade.

Security. CityWalk's security is so pervasive and so visible that some people might wonder if there's something to be worried about. In addition to the in-house security staff with their white shirts emblazoned with the word "SECURITY," you will see armed members of the Orlando police force. What you won't see are the undercover security personnel who mingle with the crowds.

The primary mission of all these security elements is to prevent any abuse of state liquor laws. For example, while you can stroll around CityWalk with your beer or cocktail, you are not allowed to carry it back to your car or into the parks.

Valet Parking and Validation. Most restaurants will validate your valet parking ticket during lunch hour (11:00 a.m. to 2:00 p.m. Monday through Friday only). A two-hour stay is free. Emeril's validates anytime including Saturdays and dinner. The Cineplex does not validate parking.

Shopping in CityWalk

The designers of CityWalk had a difficult challenge when it came to creating retail spaces that would both complement and enhance their entertainment district. How do you create an upscale shopping experience that has the strength and credibility of major "brands" without offering "the same old thing," familiar big-name shops just like the ones holiday-goers have back home? And to hold its own against the entertainment venues, the shopping has to be pretty entertaining in its own right, without overwhelming CityWalk's prime reason for being. By and large, management has met the challenge.

The shopping here is fun without being overbearing, and the range of goods for sale fits in very well with the customers who come here—people on vacation, bent on having fun rather than purchasing necessities. There's probably nothing here that you can't live without, but there's also plenty of stuff you'd love to have, either as a special treat for yourself or as a gift for friends and family who couldn't make the trip with you. Prices, on the whole, are surprisingly moderate. Oh sure, you can drop a bundle if you want, but there's plenty here to appeal to a wide range of budgets.

The **Universal Studios Store**, which dominates the Plaza, offers you the chance to continue your theme park shopping any old time you please. Other shops allow you to broaden your horizons. Breezy, summery women's clothing is on offer at the stylish **Fresh Produce**, while men are sure to find a suitable Tommy Bahama shirt at the **Island Clothing Store**. Younger, hipper styles are to be found at the **Quiet Flight Surf Shop** and **Element**, which caters to the skateboard crowd. For something a little more out of the ordinary, visit the walk-in humidor at **Cigarz** or stroll into **Hart and Huntington** for a tattoo (or a T-shirt if you chicken out).

The Talk of the Town

Just as the theme parks have their must-see attractions, there are some very special things in CityWalk. No star ratings are supplied for CityWalk, but here is a highly subjective list of personal favorites in a number of categories.

Best food. Emeril's has to be the choice here. Best wine list, too. There's really no serious competition.

Best bar. The funky bar at the back of Cigarz, a cigar shop near the upper exit of the Cineplex, is hip and hidden. The bar at Hard Rock Cafe with its spinning Caddy takes second prize.

Best food value. When you factor in what you pay for what you get, Pat O'Brien's comes out on top, with Bubba Gump a close second.

Best place to take the kids. Hard Rock Cafe is the best, but NBA City, NASCAR Sports Grille, and Margaritaville all have kid-friendly aspects.

Friendliest service. Bubba Gump.

Best burgers. The Hard Rock Cafe. Have yours with one of their rich chocolate milk shakes.

Best dessert. Emeril's elaborate creations take the cake in this category.

Best for the midnight munchies. Finding food after midnight is not always possible, but if Pat O'Brien's is serving late, that's the clear winner. Otherwise, check Margaritaville, or the food court upstairs.

Most romantic. If you're idea of "romantic" is letting your date know you're dropping a bundle on the meal, then Emeril's is the place for you. Otherwise, the Latin Quarter has mucho mood lighting and live music. For free romance, take a moonlight cruise to the resort hotels on a shuttle boat.

Most fun. Jimmy Buffett's Margaritaville, with its wild and wacky decor and exploding volcano, wins the prize here.

Best decor. The the Latin Quarter features Meso-American stonework and a stunning dance floor beneath a fiber-optic starry sky. The Hard Rock Cafe's memorabilia collection is equally memorable.

Coolest. The hip and witty Red Coconut Club is one of the best clubs in Orlando. At the opposite end of the style spectrum, the funky cigar shed bar at Cigarz offers its own brand of hipness.

AMC Universal Cineplex 20 with IMAX

This is the mall multiplex writ large and it's hard to miss because it's the first thing you see on your right as you arrive from the parking lots. Given its 4,800 seats in 20 theaters on two stories, it's unlikely you have anything quite like it at home.

The soaring lobby is decorated with giant black and white banners depicting cinema heartthrobs, and escalators whisk you past them to the nine theaters upstairs. The theaters range in size from an intimate 150 seats to nearly 600. Unfortunately, 20 theaters does not mean 20 films. Expect the usual assortment of first-run features with the very latest releases playing in multiple theaters and midnight screenings of cult favorites. If you live in or near any moderately sized city in the United States, chances are all the films playing at the Cineplex are playing back home; it's just that here they're all under one roof. Of course, all the theaters here have stadium seating with plush high-backed seats that rock gently, and the screens are about twice the size of those you are probably used to. The Cineplex shows "RealD" digital 3-D films, and you can keep the glasses. Every theater is also equipped with digital video projectors and Sony Dynamic Digital Sound (SDDS), touted as "the most advanced digital cinema sound system in the marketplace today." So all in all, catching a movie here is a viable option for a rainy Florida afternoon.

There is also an IMAX screen in the Universal Cineplex. If you're wondering how they removed the roof to install one of those massive screens you remember from the science museum, don't worry: they didn't. For this new all-digital version of IMAX, an existing theater (in this case screen 17, already the Cineplex's largest) was retrofitted with dual 2K projectors and a beefier sound system. The original screen was replaced by one marginally larger and closer to the audience, and the first couple rows of seats were removed (though not enough to make sitting in front on the sides anything but nauseating). This "patented geometry" is supposed to create the illusion of a much larger picture, but it isn't worth the premium for normal films. IMAX 3-D, on the other hand, is more immersive than its RealD competition, and may be worth the extra bucks. If you want the "real" giant-screen IMAX experience, you'll have to drive down Universal Boulevard to Pointe Orlando's Regal Cinema.

Admission (including tax) for adults is $10 for evening shows; bargain matinees (all shows that start before 3:55 p.m.) are $8. Children 2 to 12 pay $7. "A.M. Cinema" (shows that start before noon on weekends and holidays) are $5. Seniors (60+) pay $9 ($5 on Tuesdays), and students pay $7 on Thursdays. Add an additional $3 per ticket for RealD 3-D, $4 for IMAX, and $5 for IMAX 3-D. Annual Pass holders save $2 on shows after 4:00 p.m.

In addition to the regular box office windows, there are vending machines to your right that allow you to skip the line and purchase tickets, at no extra charge, using your credit card. More detailed information can be downloaded at amctheatres.com/universal or obtained from a human being by calling (407) 354–3374. Or purchase tickets in advance online at www.fandango.com. Fandango charges a "convenience fee" of "up to" $2; tickets can be printed out at home or picked up at the box office.

Don't worry about going hungry while you watch. There is the usual array of soft drinks, popcorn, and candy, all at inflated prices. More interesting are the mini-pizzas, nachos, and ice cream sundaes. There's even a coffee bar if you crave a latte and a full liquor bar serving up exotic cocktails and coolers. The 32-ounce draft beer is the best brew bargain on property.

Anyone who has suffered through a serious drama with a munchkin kicking the back of their the seat will appreciate AMC's "Distraction-Free Entertainment" policy. To quote: "In order to provide the most enjoyable experience for adults attending R-rated features in the evenings, no children younger than 6 will be admitted to these features after 6 p.m." Bravo!

Universal occasionally screens classic and foreign cinema or hosts film festivals, but it's a shame it doesn't dedicate one screen to fare outside the modern Hollywood mainstream. On the other hand, the Cineplex has regular midnight performances of cult classics like *The Rocky Horror Picture Show*, complete with a live cast of bizarro fans in costume acting out on stage, so film buffs shouldn't be too disappointed (visit www.richweirdoes.com for midnight movie information).

Tip: You may want to exit on the upper level, even if you are seeing a film on the Cineplex's bottom level. From there you can either descend the narrow zigzag street lined with shops, or stroll along the sloping Promenade, home to CityWalk's row of restaurants and nightclubs.

Hollywood Drive-In Miniature Golf

Opening in early 2012, Hollywood Drive-In is a pair of elaborately themed 18-hole mini-golf courses that Universal has somehow shoehorned into the narrow area near valet parking. Featuring detailed outdoor and indoor environments created by Universal's theme-park designers, these 36 greens go beyond any putt-putt you're likely to have at home. The theme of this attraction is inspired by the cheesy classics of the drive-in movie era, as you'll probably guess from the 40-foot tall robot and haunted house set-pieces. As guests play through "The Haunting of Ghostly Greens" or "Invaders from Planet Putt" they'll encounter movie-style sets and interactive effects straight out of a sci-fi or horror B-movie. LED lighting lets you golf through graveyards or putt through a flying saucer day or night.

Guests can get a preview of the greens by looking down over the side of the moving walkway as they approach CityWalk. The entrance to the course is to the right of the Cineplex box offices. Information on pricing, operating hours, discounts for annual passholders, and so forth were not available at press time.

Restaurants at CityWalk

Some of CityWalk's restaurants offer terrific entertainment (usually at night, usually with a cover charge) and some nightclubs serve excellent food. The main distinction seems to be that "restaurants" open early in the day and serve full meals, while "nightclubs" open in the late afternoon or early evening and serve only a limited food menu. Among the restaurants, Jimmy Buffett's Margaritaville and Latin Quarter turn into nightclubs, with cover charges, in the evenings. NASCAR Sports Grille offers the occasional entertainer in its al fresco dining area, and NBA City screens great moments in basketball history all day. All the others are strictly dining establishments. All restaurants (except Emeril's) serve the same menu at the same prices all day.

In the reviews that follows, I have attempted to estimate the cost of an average meal, without alcoholic beverages. In the case of full-service restaurants, estimates are based on a "full meal" consisting of an appetizer or salad, an entree, and dessert. Restaurant prices are rated as follows:

$	Under $15
$$	$15 - $25
$$$	$25 - $40
$$$$	Over $40

Hard Rock Cafe

What:	American casual cuisine
Where:	Across the waterway
Price Range:	$$ - $$$
Hours:	11:00 a.m. to midnight (kitchen closes at midnight)
Reservations:	None
Web:	www.hardrockcafe.com

The immense structure across the water, with the peculiar hodgepodge architecture, the Caddy sticking out of the facade, and the huge electric signs, is the world's largest and busiest Hard Rock Cafe. Those who have visited other Hard Rocks will know what to expect—just expect more of it. For the uninitiated, the Hard Rock Cafe is a celebration of rock and roll history and lifestyle that has become an international marketing and merchandising phenomenon. From its auspicious beginnings in London's Mayfair section, Hard Rock has grown to a mega-chain, with restaurants in virtually any city that has pretensions to world-class status.

The Hard Rock's primary claim to fame is its extensive and ever-growing collection of rock memorabilia that is lovingly and lavishly displayed. As befits the largest Hard Rock in the world, the Orlando outpost has some spectacular mementos. After your meal, take the time to wander about and drink it all in. The staff won't mind; they're used to it. If you're lucky, they will be running free tours of the memorabilia collection.

There is dark paneling and deep carpeting on the floors and winding wooden staircases. There are rich gold frames on the photos, album covers, gold records, and other memorabilia that fill every inch of wall space. "Rock and roll is here to stay," they like to say. "We've got it screwed to the walls!" Upstairs, take note of the two circular rooms, one at each end, dedicated to the Beatles and the King. There's even an elegant wood-paneled library.

At the heart of the restaurant, downstairs, is a circular bar open to the second level. A magnificent 1961 pink Cadillac convertible spins lazily over the bar and above that is a splendid ceiling mural straight out of some domed chapel at the Vatican. Except that here the saints being serenaded by the angels are all dead rock stars, most of whom died from drug overdoses. To one side is a trio of towering stained glass windows paying homage to Chuck Berry, Elvis Presley, and Jerry Lee Lewis. All in all, this expansive Hard Rock has the look and feel of a very posh and very exclusive men's club—which is perhaps what rock and roll is, after all.

Tip: If your party is small, the bar is an excellent place to eat. The bar offers the full menu and quicker seating when the place is crowded. A seat here gives you an excellent vantage point from which to soak up the ambiance. If the downstairs bar is full, there is another upstairs.

The Hard Rock Cafe chain is also justly famous for its American roadhouse cuisine, which gives a nod to the black and southern roots of rock. Burgers, barbecue, and steak are the keynotes, with sweet and homey touches like milk shakes, root beer floats, and outrageous sundaes. It's no wonder the place was an instant hit when it opened in the midst of London's culinary desert. The menu also reminds us that, in its heyday, rock's superstars were scarcely more than kids. This is teenybopper comfort food prepared by expert cooks for people who can afford the best.

Probably the heart of the menu is the selection of barbecue dishes ($12 to $24), with the chicken and ribs combo a popular favorite. For those who prefer their barbecue Carolina-style, there's a pulled-pork sandwich. A big step up in sophistication are steaks like the succulent New York Strip.

Of course, if you're still a teenager at heart, you'll order a burger ($10 to $15). The best is the Hickory BBQ Bacon Cheeseburger, but there's also a Veggie Burger to keep Sir Paul happy. If you want to return to your pre-cholesterol-crisis youth, you'll have a milk shake or a root beer float with your burger. The fries that go with them are very good, too.

Tip: Root beer floats aren't on the menu, but they'll whip one up if you ask nicely.

Lighter appetites can be satisfied with one of the appetizers ($10 to $19) or a salad ($10 to $12), while bigger appetites can order a small Caesar salad to go with their entree. But save room for dessert ($6 to $8) because the HRC Hot Fudge Brownie lives up to its fabled reputation.

Your meal comes complete with a soundtrack and the excellent choice of songs leans heavily to the glory days of rock in the late sixties and early seventies. Television monitors, dotted around the restaurant and gold-framed like the rest of the memorabilia, identify the album from which the current track is taken. The volume has been turned up (this is rock and roll, after all) but not so high as to make conversation impossible.

No self-respecting Hard Rock Cafe would be without a shop hawking Hard Rock merchandise, and this one has two. They are labeled simply **Hard Rock Store** in big bold letters. Believe it or not, the shops sometimes have lines just like the restaurant and they are handled the same way, with a roped-off queue filled with people who can't wait to add another Hard Rock shot glass to their growing collection.

NBA City

What:	American casual cuisine
Where:	Across the waterway
Price Range:	$$ - $$$
Hours:	Sunday through Thursday 11:00 a.m. to 10:30 p.m.; Friday and Saturday to 11:30 p.m. During busy times they will stay open later.
Reservations:	(407) 363-5919 or OpenTable.com
Web:	www.nbacity.com

choice the ever-changing Catch of the Day, prepared to order. The rest of the menu runs heavily to salads, sandwiches, and junk food (in the best possible sense of the term). There are nachos, conch fritters (super!), and fried calamari, and the servings are generous to a fault. Prices are moderate; only a couple of choices are over $20. A separate kids' menu features meals for $7.

Perhaps the spicy Louisiana- and Jamaican-inspired dishes like Jambalaya and Bayou Shrimp Pasta fare best. The Cheeseburger in Paradise ($12), alas, is merely a large but otherwise undistinguished example of the genre. Far better are sandwiches like the Pulled Pork, about $11. Better still is the King Crab and Shrimp Salad ($15), which is served as an entree in a huge shell-shaped bowl. There's good news on the desserts ($4 to $6). The Key Lime Pie is a winner and the Chocolate Banana Bread Pudding is to die for.

Beer drinkers will appreciate the wide selection of premium bottled brews (about $5). For those who like their drinks on the sweet side, the specialty drinks run about $7 and are available in non-alcoholic versions for less.

A restaurant by day, Margaritaville transforms itself after the dinner crowd thins out into a cross between a nightclub and a full-fledged performance space showcasing bands and live performers that reflect in one way or another that certain indescribable Jimmy Buffett style. The house bands here are very good, alternating between Buffett standards and a mix of calypso, easy-going rock, and country-western. Every great once in a while, Buffett himself drops by.

Jimmy Buffett has been very savvy in marketing himself, so it's no surprise that there's a very well stocked gift shop, the **Margaritaville Smuggler's Hold**, attached to the restaurant with a second entrance from the Plaza. Here Parrot Heads can fill in the gaps in their Buffett CD collection or buy one of his books (he's a pretty good writer it turns out). In addition, there are plenty of T-shirts, gaudy Hawaiian shirts, and miscellaneous accessories that the well-dressed beach bum simply can't afford to be without.

Latin Quarter

What:	Nuevo Latino cuisine
Where:	Next to Jimmy Buffett's
Price Range:	$$$
Cover:	$7 after 9:00 p.m.; entertainment Thursday to Saturday only
Hours:	Daily 4:00 p.m. to 10:00 p.m. for food; club stays open until 2:00 a.m. Thursday to Saturday
Reservations:	(407) 224-3663 or OpenTable.com

This restaurant and part-time nightclub salutes one of the largest ethnic groups to get stirred into the cultural menudo that is the United States—the natives of the 21 Spanish-speaking nations that lie south of the border. It does this most notably through its pan-South-American cuisine.

The large, two-level space with its arching blue walls creates the illusion of a sultry tropical night in the ruins of an ancient city. The first-floor stage and spacious dance floor is flanked by two massive Aztec gods and backed by what surely must be the Andes.

CityWalk

To Blue
Man Group

15

To Universal
Studios

8

1

16

9

**Entrance
and
Parking**

14

Plaza

The Promenade

2

10

13

11

12

3

4

7

5

6

To Islands of
Adventure

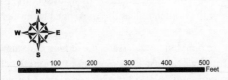

1. Universal Cineplex
2. Bubba Gump (ground floor)
   Red Coconut (Promenade level)
3. Bob Marley - A Tribute to Freedom
4. Pat O'Brien's
5. the groove
6. Latin Quarter
7. Jimmy Buffett's Margaritaville
8. NASCAR Sports Grille
9. Shops
10. Pastamoré (Plaza Level)
11. Rising Star
12. Emeril's Restaurant
13. NBA City
14. Hard Rock Cafe & Hard Rock Live
15. Blue Man Group
16. Water Taxis

N
W E
S

0   100   200   300   400   500
Feet

The food here is hearty but unexceptional. The kitchen makes a stab at so-called Nuevo Latino cuisine, with its elaborate presentations, but falls far short of the standards set by the best restaurants in this genre. Among the appetizers ($8 to $14), the cheese-stuffed, bacon-wrapped grilled shrimp is a real winner. Salads ($4 to $14) are delicious and make an excellent choice if you'd like a light meal. Try the chicken breast or the grilled Chilean salmon over greens.

The entrees ($10 to $29) were designed with the meat-lover in mind. The Churrasco Skirt Steak takes the humble skirt steak, rolls it up into a tower and serves it over a bed of garbanzos, ham, and chorizo. Among the seafood entrees the more interesting choices include the Caribbean crusted mahi mahi and the red snapper topped with chorizo sausage. They also do a daily special with Chilean sea bass that is worth considering. There is a separate menu section highlighting a variety of fajitas ($15 to $16).

The desserts ($6) include a caramelized banana custard and mango cheesecake. To ease the strain on the family pocketbook, a kids' menu featuring $6 meals is offered.

Drinkers have their choice of a lengthy menu of specialty drinks that salute various Latin American countries ($7 to $10). Mixed drink enthusiasts could do worse than set a goal to sample them all. For the less adventuresome, beer is also served and it makes an excellent accompaniment to most of the dishes. A small wine list is offered ($24 to $48).

Upstairs, on a balcony overlooking the stage, Latin Quarter now offers an all-you-can-eat churrascaria "dining experience." Start with the gourmet salad bar featuring sushi, cured meats and cheeses, and lobster bisque alongside the standard greens. Then, when you are ready to meet the meat, grab your tongs and flip the paper disk on your table from red to green. An endless parade of skewer-slinging gauchos will appear and slice a variety of grilled meats at your table-side. Some, like the house specialty picanha sirloin, mango-marinaded spareribs, and smoked sausage, are excellent; a few, like the pork shoulder and bacon-wrapped chicken, are inedibly dry. Most of the rest, including filet mignon, ribeye, and leg of lamb, fall under "acceptable." At $37 for adults (kids are half-price, under 6 is free) you'll need to be a hard-core carnivore who likes their meat medium-well to really get your money's worth, though to be fair similar restaurants elsewhere in Orlando cost more. You can order the salad bar only for $20, a better value.

In the evening, Latin Quarter features low-key, live entertainment. Typically it will be an excellent flamenco guitarist, playing on the outdoor patio when the weather co-operates or indoors when it doesn't. At 10:00 p.m. on Thursdays (Ladies Night) through Saturday, Latin Quarter turns up the heat with a Reggaeton D.J.

Emeril's Restaurant Orlando

What:	Gourmet dining
Where:	On the Plaza
Price Range:	$$$$+
Hours:	Lunch 11:30 a.m. to 3:00 p.m.; dinner 5:00 p.m. to 10:00 p.m. Sunday through Thursday; to 10:30 p.m. Friday and Saturday
Reservations:	Mandatory. Call (407) 224-2424, fax (407) 224-2525, or OpenTable.com
Web:	www.emerils.com

Emeril Lagasse, the popular TV chef and cookbook author, brings his upscale New Orleans cuisine to Orlando in this lavish eatery decorated (if that's the word) with over 10,000 bottles of wine in climate-controlled glass-walled wine cases. This is an extremely handsome restaurant that evokes and improves upon Emeril's converted warehouse premises in the Big Easy. The main dining room soars to a curved wooden roof and the lavish use of glass on the walls facing the Plaza makes this a bright and sunny spot for lunch. The exposed steel support beams contrast with the stone walls and rich wood accents, while stark curved metal chandeliers arch gracefully overhead. It's a hip, modern look that matches the food and the clientele.

The cuisine is Creole-based, but the execution is sophisticated and the presentation elaborate. Many dishes follow a standard Emeril architectural template: A layer of hash, relish, or puree is topped by the main ingredient, which in turn is topped by an antic garnish of potatoes, onions, or some other vegetable sliced in thin strips and flash fried; the plate is then decorated with a few swirls or dots of various sauces, sprinkled with spices and greenery, and delivered to the table with a flourish. Many dishes are based on home-style comfort foods like barbecue, fried fish, or gumbos, and there's an unmistakable spiciness to much of it. The result is a cuisine that is fun and festive with only the occasional tendency toward self-conscious seriousness, making Emeril's a great choice for a celebratory blowout.

Despite its noisy, bistro-like atmosphere, this is a first-class restaurant where dining is theater and a full meal can last two and a half hours, with the per-person cost, with drinks and wine, easily rising to over $100. In the European fashion, Emeril's closes after lunch to allow the kitchen a chance to catch its breath and ready itself for a different and more extensive dinner menu.

Appetizers ($8 to $15 at lunch and dinner) include Panko-crusted fried green tomatoes and fried calamari along with the occasional more exotic creation. Soups and salads ($6 to $13) enjoy their own section on the menu and typically include a sturdy gumbo, savory seafood stew, and some artfully presented and deceptively simple green salads.

Entrees are in the $14 to $24 range at lunch, $26 to $50 at dinner. They include the odd-sounding but delicious andouille-crusted Texas redfish at dinner (a pecan-crusted version is offered at lunch). A multi-course "degustation" menu with wine pairings is sometimes served, and a tasting menu at a Chef's Table is also sometimes offered. At lunch, the three-course "Big Easy Lunch Crunch" ($22) is a terrific value.

Desserts ($8 to $12) are equally elaborate, although it says something about the chef that his signature dessert is a homey banana cream pie served with chocolate shavings on a latticework of caramel sauce.

Dining here is a special experience. Emeril's is not the kind of place where you will feel comfortable in full tourist regalia, even though the management officially draws the line only at tank tops and flip-flops. Stop back at your hotel to change and freshen up.

Tip: If you are dining alone or there are just two of you, you might want to try the "Food Bar," a short counter with stools that looks into the kitchen. The primo dining location is the L-shaped dining area by the windows; VIPs are seated here, so reserve well in advance if it's your preference.

Emeril's, by the way, is strictly a restaurant; there is no entertainment. For most people, the tongue-tingling food will be entertainment enough.

If you want to sample Emeril's but still stay within your budget, visit the bar for the daily happy hour (5:00 to 8:00 p.m.), when discount appetizers and half-price beer and cocktails are available.

Special note on reservations: Emeril's accepts reservations six months in advance and often books up completely several weeks in advance, especially during the height of convention season (February and March). So if you are planning on visiting at a busy time or are planning a special-occasion meal here, you will be well advised to book as early as possible. A day or two before your visit, the restaurant will call you to remind you of your reservation. By the way, the concierges at the resort hotels have no special pull with Emeril's.

So how do you get seats at the last minute? Most often you don't, but your best shot is to call at 3:15 p.m. on the day you want to dine. If all else fails, show up early and ask for a seat at the main bar, where people are seated on a first come-first served basis and can order from the full menu. Generally, it's easier, but by no means a slam-dunk, to come by a table on short notice at lunch.

Pastamoré

What:	Home-style Italian
Where:	On the Plaza
Price Range:	$$ – $$$
Hours:	5:00 p.m. to 10:00 p.m.
Reservations:	(407) 224-3663 or OpenTable.com

This cheerful and noisy Italian eatery blends contemporary decor with the homey touch of that old neighborhood Italian restaurant you loved as a kid. The decor is trendy postmodern with terra cotta walls and blue banquettes. Decorative accents are provided by Roman stone heads and words like "cucina," "pizza," and "antipasto" spelled out in cursive red neon. The menu features the kind of comfortable Italian dishes that won't have you reaching for your Italian-English dictionary.

Appetizers and salads ($4 to $13) include fried calamari, fried cheese ravioli, and Italian wedding soup. Pasta dishes ($12 to $19) range from straightforward lasagna and spaghetti to blue crab ravioli and shrimp pasta with a spicy red pepper sauce. They also serve up some very tasty personal pizzas ($8 to $9) from a wood-fired pizza oven.

Meat and poultry dishes ($14 to $24) include such Italian staples as veal and chicken prepared parmigiana, marsala, or piccata style, along with grilled ribeye and pork chops. Among the seafood entrees ($18 to $20) the Seafood Fra Diavolo is a standout. Vegetable side dishes ($3 to $5), include a wonderful broccoli with roasted garlic and lemon.

The wine list features Sangiovese reds for $23 to $110; half bottles of California wines are considerably less. Desserts ($3 to $5) are of the standard Italian variety and for $12 you can pig out on your choice of three of them.

Because everything is a la carte, the bill can add up quickly, though the kids' buffet ($10) can soften the sting. A 15% gratuity is added to the bill for parties of six or more.

Pastamoré has an attached deli and espresso bar that opens early; see the *Fast Food* section, below.

NASCAR Sports Grille

What:	All-American cooking
Where:	Near the bridge to Universal Studios Florida
Price Range:	$$ - $$$
Hours:	11:00 a.m. to midnight
Reservations:	(407) 224-RACE or OpenTable.com
Web:	www.nascarsportsgrille.com

Just by the bridge that leads to Universal Studios, the large building that houses the NASCAR Sports Grille is an ode to speed. It swoops and leans and looks for all the world as if it's doing 120. NASCAR, in case you don't know, stands for National Association of Stock Car Automobile Racing, the organization that sets the rules for stock car racing and owns the tracks on which hard-driving, all-American folk heroes are created. Stock car racing is a distinctly American sport, with roots in the rural and blue-collar south. But if you were expecting a restaurant in which a grease-smeared good ole boy might feel at home, think again.

NASCAR Sports Grille is more upscale sports bar than down-home beanery. The decor is chic and sleek, with brown-on-brown booths, banquettes, and marble-topped bars. The design references to racing are mostly muted and discreet, although upstairs two race cars hang from the ceiling and periodically roar to life as their wheels spin furiously.

In true sports bar fashion the place is alive with television screens, small ones in the booths, plasma screens on many columns and a 37-foot "media wall" on the main level. They are just as likely to be tuned to baseball or football as racing, although on race days, the majority are given over to NASCAR.

There is seating on two levels. Downstairs, an entire wall can be opened up to the verandah on nice days creating a wonderfully spacious ambience. Upstairs, there is a narrow outdoor balcony that is a great place to dine on a balmy evening. Also upstairs is a small racing-themed arcade where you can let those antsy kids loose while mom and dad eat.

Tip: If you want to eat upstairs, let the hostess at the main entrance know. She will pass you on to the upstairs hostess.

The food follows the sports bar model, with an accent on steaks, ribs, and burgers and with seemingly no desire to dazzle. Appetizers ($7 to $17) include coconut shrimp, fried onion rings with a dipping sauce (excellent!) and nachos. There is also chili and a variety of salads.

Steaks ($17 to $25) range from a top sirloin to filet mignon. More affordable (and often better) are the chicken and ribs dishes ($12 to $23), including BBQ ribs and grilled pork chops. Seafood and pasta ($12 to $17) includes mahi mahi and "points leader" shrimp alfredo pasta. Burgers and other sandwiches ($10 to $12) are probably the most reasonable choices on the menu. The desserts, alas, are merely serviceable.

A small NASCAR shop with a separate entrance is filled with some nice logo-ed clothing and other NASCAR souvenirs.

Bubba Gump Shrimp Co.

What:	Seafood with a Southern flair
Where:	At the entrance to CityWalk
Price Range:	$$ - $$$
Hours:	11:00 a.m. to midnight
Reservations:	None
Web:	www.bubbagump.com

The infectious charm of the hit Tom Hanks film, *Forrest Gump,* suffuses the rambling, ramshackle bayou shrimp shack that greets you as you arrive at CityWalk. The wooden walls are covered with license plates, photographs from the film, little signs with pithy sayings, and flat-screen TVs that show the film over and over, without sound but with subtitles should you want to follow along. The place seems deceptively small from the outside, but it seats 500 in a series of dining rooms and two bars. Cajun music and 50s rock plays constantly and everyone seems to be in a great mood.

The servers are every bit as peppy as the soundtrack, smothering you with attention and good cheer. A signaling system at each table uses license plates to flag down passing servers should you need anything and before your meal is through it may seem like everyone in the place has stopped by to see how you're doing or challenge you to a *Forrest Gump* trivia test.

Shrimp is the order of the day here. It's everywhere on the menu and the cooks obviously know their way around this tasty little crustacean. Everything sampled here is very good indeed, but if you need guidance, the menu helpfully calls out "Bubba's All Time Best" choices with a little Bubba Gump shrimp logo. Appetizers ($5 to $14) feature breaded popcorn shrimp and the marginally more healthy Cajun shrimp, which is sauteed in butter and served with Gump's signature garlic bread for sopping up the sauce. Neither is too spicy. The Hush Pups also deserve special mention.

Salads and sandwiches ($10 to $13) include a Dixie Fishwich, a Shrimp Po'Boy, and a Tossed Chicken Cobb. The entrees ($16 to $24) showcase shrimp in a dazzling variety of guises, including fried, boiled in broth, stuffed, sauced, and in a spicy New Orleans style preparation over rice. A separate list features "Forrest's Favorites," such as Bourbon Street Mahi Mahi, a Salmon (or Mahi Mahi) Veggie Skillet, and non-shrimp dishes like fried chicken and baby back ribs. Desserts ($5 to $10) include "That Chocolate Thing" and an architecturally striking strawberry shortcake.

There is, of course, a gift shop offering Gump T-shirts and souvenir glasses, but perhaps the best choice here is a container of Bubba Gump shrimp boil and the restaurant's own cookbook that will let you take the taste of Bubba Gump's home with you.

Fast Food at CityWalk

There are a few less elaborate, less costly dining choices in CityWalk for those looking for morning coffee, a quick bite, or a budget-saving alternative to a full-course, full-price blowout meal. There are also a few al fresco spots to grab a quick drink!

Pastamoré Marketplace Cafe

This annex to the Pastamoré restaurant opens bright and early (at 8:00 a.m.) to serve strong coffee and strength-building pastries to the crowds arriving for a busy day at the theme parks. They also have "breakfast pizzas" that are worth a try. At lunch, the emphasis turns to Italian-style panini, pizza, pasta, and antipasto salads. Finally, late in the day, you can stop by again for dessert or a glass of wine. Indoor seating is limited and the few outdoor tables let you survey the passing scene.

Cinnabon

Across the street from the Pastamoré Marketplace Cafe is this branch of the nationwide chain famous for its oversized, gooey and delicious cinnamon buns at moderate prices. Ice cream and a small selection of desserts are also available. Seating is very limited and all outdoors. This place opens early to snag the breakfast crowd.

TCBY

This outpost of the popular frozen yogurt chain serves up the usual variety of cold and creamy treats.

Starbucks

The best thing about this airy coffee shop is the view over the Plaza and the crowds below. Otherwise, it's pretty much like every other Starbucks you've ever been in, which is presumably the point. If you like the jolt of Starbucks, note that this one opens at 8:30 a.m. and stays open late. No wireless Internet access, though.

Fusion Bistro Sushi & Sake Bar

This small, sleek outlet outside the Cineplex's second-story exit, serves serviceable, if not exquisite, sushi rolls and nigiri. The stainless-steel bar isn't actually that inviting to sit at, but you can watch the chef inside through the window or on the closed-circuit TVs. Appetizers ($3 to $7) include miso and edamame, and rolls ($5 to $12) range from simple California to Dancing Eel and Red Dragon (spicy tuna with jalapeño). Bento boxes ($4 extra) include soup, salad, and a cookie; they are a slightly better value than buying a la carte. For dessert, try an oddly addictive Mochi rice cake ($4 for 3 pieces). Beverages include Japanese beer ($4 to $5) and hot or chilled sake ($5 to $15).

The sushi here is a cut above your local supermarket and should give a satisfactory fix to vacationers in wasabi withdrawal. Just don't look for "expert" items like mackerel, yellowtail, or soft-shell crab on the menu; you'll have to go to the Orchid Bar at Loews Royal Pacific for that (see the next Chapter).

Whopper Bar/ Panda Express/ Moe's Southwest Grill

Three familiar franchises fill this mall-style food court, strategically located near the upper exit of the Cineplex. Burger King's outlet is the first in a spin-off chain centered on their signature sandwich. For a little more than your local drive-thru ($6 to $8 with small drink and fries) you can get a Whopper covered in gourmet toppings like guacamole, peppercorn bacon, and "angry onions." Panda Express serves passable stir-fry combo plates for $7 to $8, and Moe's tacos and burritos ($3 to $7) come with a free fresh salsa bar. A narrow balcony offers limited seating with a view of the Plaza.

Big Kahuna Pizza

Nicely framed by gaudy pizza-themed surfboards, this simple stand serves up cheese or pepperoni pizzas, whole ($14 to $16) or by the slice ($3 and $4). Chicken wings are $6. You can wash it all down with draft beer ($5 to $6) or a soft drink.

Fat Tuesday

Did you know that Louisiana allows drive-through alcohol sales? New Orleans staple Fat Tuesday has set up shop beside its hometown neighbor Pat O's to offer the next best thing: a stumble-through daiquiri bar. A chorus-line of slushy machines spin merrily and dispense frozen concoctions ($7, or $10 in a souvenir cup with $6 refills) in flavors ranging from strawberry and mango to the aptly named "Cat 5 Hurricane" and "190 Octane." $1 Jello shots and "tooters" are available for those who really want to get their party on, along with beer and soda.

Latin Express

Most of the nightclubs along the Promenade have walk-up windows dispensing specialty alcoholic drinks, but the Latin Quarter also serves up some tasty and inexpensive munchies for about $5 to $7. Choices include Cuban sandwiches, empañadas, and ropa vieja. Latin Express has irregular hours, but is generally open Wednesday through Sunday evenings.

Galaxy

No fast food, just fast booze. This walk-up full-service bar has a small seating area in the Plaza framed by the groove, the Latin Quarter, and Emeril's. A nice place to sit and people watch.

Lone Palm Airport

Just outside Margaritaville stands a palapa-shaded bar that uses Jimmy Buffett's Hemisphere Dancer plane as the perfect backdrop. Makeshift tables are scattered about, surfboards lean against palm trees, and a sandy area is filled with kids' digging toys. It all evokes the kind of beachside dives Jimmy sings about so eloquently. Sit at the bar and watch Buffett music videos while munching on snack food and sipping (what else?) margaritas. Every weekday, a 3:00 to 5:00 p.m. Happy hour offers discounted appetizers and drinks, featuring half-price margaritas.

Entertainment at CityWalk

There are two theatrical entertainment venues at CityWalk, both located conveniently on either side of Hard Rock Cafe. One hosts a resident attraction while the other welcomes touring artists.

Blue Man Group

What:	Avant garde theater performance
Where:	Across the waterway next to Hard Rock Cafe
Tickets:	Adults $84.14 to $94.79 at box office, $68.16 to $78.81 online

Hours: or by phone; children 9 and under $26.63. 20% annual pass-
holder discount

Hours: Vary widely; call (888) 340-5476 or (407) 258-3626

Web: www.blueman.com or www.universalorlando.com

Back in the 80s, three "performance artists" created Blue Man Group in New York's seedy East Village. They were weird, hip, edgy, incomprehensible. They were the most avant of the avant garde. Today they are family entertainment. Such is cultural progress.

Now an international phenomenon, the Orlando edition of the troupe holds forth in an industrial-looking thousand-seat theater at the end of a long, winding pathway next to the Hard Rock Cafe.

And just what awaits at the end of that path? Well, perhaps the greatest compliment that can be paid Blue Man Group is that it is pretty much indescribable. Three very bald, very blue, very silent guys in black pajamas (could they be space aliens?) appear on a stage that seems to be part of a strange factory and do a series of odd things, some of which take real skill, some of which are very funny, and some of which are just plain wacky. They are at once consummate masters of ceremony and befuddled innocents who seem constantly surprised by the presence of the audience.

Some of the best segments involve the trio's considerable skill as percussionists (a four-man, day-glo combo assists from overhead). And who could have guessed how much entertainment value there was in pouring colored liquids onto drum heads? There's plenty of audience interaction and the show wraps up with a chaotic finale that involves everyone and sends the crowd out in a festive mood.

So what's it all about? Some see a critique of modern society, others detect commentary on the pretensions of modern art. Perhaps the best advice is to check your brain at the door and let the fun of the evening take over; the more you try to analyze, the less you'll enjoy the experience. They do not recommend the show for children under 3; that could be stretched to 5 or 6.

There is a tendency to compare this show to *La Nouba*, the Cirque du Soleil show over at Downtown Disney. This is unfair. *La Nouba* is a multi-million-dollar extravaganza with a large cast. *Blue Man* is, essentially, a three-man show that has grown over the years but that still sticks close to its Off Broadway origins. It's really an apples and oranges comparison.

Tip: The show lasts 1 hour and 45 minutes, there is no intermission, and beer vendors work the crowd beforehand. You have been warned! (At least there's appropriate music in the restrooms.)

The best seats in the house. All things being equal, the closer and more centrally located your seat, the better. The first four rows are designated as the "poncho zone" and those seated there are issued cheap plastic coverups, just in case. But it's a far cry from a "splash zone" at SeaWorld and more marketing than anything else. Besides, the ponchos are a bit uncomfortable. Unless you're a die-hard fan, sitting a few rows farther back won't decrease your enjoyment one little bit. Zone 1, center is just about ideal. The "cheap seats" (Zones 3 and 4) are on a steeper incline and offer good sight lines of the whole stage.

Tickets can be ordered over the phone by calling (888) 340-5476 or (407) 258-3626 from 9:00 a.m. to 7:00 p.m. daily; you can also order online at the two websites above (follow the prompts). There is a box office at the theater as well. You may also see offers combining a Blue Man ticket with theme park admission and a CityWalk Party Pass (typically saving around $15). College students with a valid school ID or ISIC card can get "rush" tickets at the box office on the day of the show for $30 each (limit two per ID).

The show schedule is somewhat erratic. Typically there are two shows a day at 6:00 and 9:00 p.m. But some days there is just one show at 8:00 p.m., or three shows at 3:00, 6:00, and 9:00 p.m. Some days there are none. Call or check the websites for show times during your visit.

Hard Rock Live

What: Rock performance space

Where: Across the waterway next to Hard Rock Cafe

Tickets: $10 and up, depending on the act

Hours: Most shows start at 8:00 p.m.

Web: www.hardrocklive.com

The Orlando Hard Rock Cafe may be the world's largest, but what really makes it special is its next door neighbor, Hard Rock Live, the chain's first live performance venue. Underneath that retro take on Rome's ancient Coliseum is a cutting-edge rock performance space loaded to the gills with sound, light, and video technology, including two video walls flanking the stage. In its standard configuration the joint holds 1,800. If they pull out the seats and turn the first floor into a mosh pit they can pack in 2,500, which still makes it "intimate" by rock standards. At the other end of the spectrum, they can use flywalls and props to shrink the space to the size of an intimate club.

The large stage (60 feet wide and 40 feet deep) offers bands plenty of room in which to rock and the computerized lighting system, strobes, and fog machines create the kind of dazzling effects that rock fans used to have to roll up and bring with them. Most important for the true aficionado, the sound system answers the burning question, "What does it sound like at ground zero of a nuclear explosion?" In other words, the place totally rocks.

Given the limited capacity, it's unlikely that the real giants of rock will be able to play here (at least not too often), but Elton John has fluttered like a candle in the wind and recent shows have featured current artists like Matisyahu, 3 Doors Down, Rodney Carrington, and the Arctic Monkeys, alternating with classic acts like Weird Al Yankovic, the Pet Shop Boys, Peter Frampton, and Elvis—Costello, that is. Standups like Bob Saget, Louis C.K., and Jim Gaffigan also appear here, as do magicians Penn and Teller.

If the music isn't blowing you away, you can repair to one of six bars and, depending on the show, you may be able to get something to nosh on from the Hard Rock Cafe kitchen, like hot dogs, wood-oven pizzas, or nachos.

Ticket prices are moderate, with most acts checking in at between $25 and $35 with the occasional show rising to $75 or so. Every once in a while you can catch an evening of rocker wannabes for as little as $10. Tickets can be purchased at the box office or, for an additional fee, from TicketMaster at (407) 839-3900. Tickets for some events can also be purchased online at www.hardrocklive.com. Most shows begin at 8:00 p.m., with the box office opening at 10:00 a.m. Information about upcoming events is available by calling (407) 351-5483 or online at the address just given.

Nightclubs at CityWalk

As mentioned earlier, nightclubs at CityWalk are those entertainment venues that open only in the evening and serve either no food at all or a limited food menu. Fortunately, the food served in the clubs is very good indeed. A brief rundown on the clubs, but very little additional information, can be found online at www.citywalkorlando.com.

Note: All clubs have a **$7 cover charge** that clicks in at 9:00 p.m. See *The Price of Admission* and *What's The Best Price?* at the beginning of this chapter for advice on how to avoid or, at least, minimize these cover charges.

Red Coconut Club

What: Hip, retro dance club
Where: On the Promenade
Hours: 8:00 p.m. to 2:00 a.m. Sunday to Thursday; 6:00 p.m. to 2:00 a.m. Friday and Saturday

It's the Rat Pack meets the Jetsons in this witty evocation of 50s-era Las Vegas-style futuristic chic. Step inside and it's as if you are entering the living room of Frank Sinatra's Palm Springs getaway. Continue on and you step onto the palm-fringed outdoor patio, where the swimming pool serves as the dance floor and many-pointed stars hover in the dark blue night sky above. But this isn't a nostalgia trip. The club has a hip, ironic edge that's very twenty-first century. The tone is captured perfectly by Paul Anka, in his best Sinatra mode, crooning "*Smells Like Teen Spirit*" just like Old Blue Eyes himself might have put it across at the Copacabana. If Kurt Cobain ever heard it, he'd kill himself all over again.

The club has a surprisingly large capacity, yet it manages to seem quite intimate. The upstairs balcony offers a great perspective on the dance floor and bandstand below. It is usually open only on weekends, but it is available for private rental throughout the week. There's live music, too, of course, with a hip combo holding forth from a raised platform behind the patio bar.

The band tailors its repertoire to suit the crowd, moving easily from laid-back sophistication to more upbeat and harder edged selections. Late at night, a D.J. takes over to keep the crowd rocking until closing.

Martinis and Cosmopolitans ($10) are the featured drinks here, but you can also get mojitos and tropical specialties like Mai-Tais and Zombies ($9) as well as Red Coconut Clubs ($8), which are chilled shots mixed with Red Bull. There's wine, too, most of it Californian, but with a smattering of Australian and New Zealand imports. When it comes to champagne, the Club doesn't mess with success and offers a generous selection of French classics.

There is a brief and evolving menu of appetizer-sized nibbles ($7) including mini beef filets, coconut fried shrimp, sesame chicken skewers, and vegetable spring rolls with a citrus soy dipping sauce.

A nightly happy hour (8:00 to 10:00 p.m. Sunday to Thursday; 6:00 to 9:00 p.m. Friday and Saturday) offers discounts on select drinks and appetizers. Thursday is "Ladies Night," with complimentary admission and drink specials for females. "Hospitality Tuesdays" offer the same for local industry workers.

What sets the Red Coconut apart from all other theme-park clubs is its bottle service. Order up a full bottle of premium liquor, wine, or champagne for your party ($120 to $420) and your table instantly becomes its own private club, complete with a red velvet rope limiting access to you and your guests. The bottle is delivered on a silver tray with your choice of two mixers. Pour it yourself or have your server do the honors. What a great way to impress your friends or business associates! And when you consider what it would cost to order drinks a la carte, it can be surprisingly cost-effective.

Bob Marley—A Tribute To Freedom

What:	Reggae club
Where:	On the Promenade
Hours:	4:00 p.m. to 2:00 a.m.; kitchen closes at 10:00 p.m. Sunday to Thursday, 11:00 p.m. Friday and Saturday
Reservations:	(407) 224-3663 or OpenTable.com
Web:	www.bobmarley.com

Reggae fans will appreciate this salute to Bob Marley, the Jamaican-born king of reggae, where the infectious backbeat of Marley's lilting music mingles with the spicy accents of island cooking. Created under the watchful eye of Marley's widow, Rita, who has contributed Marley memorabilia for the project, this venue is as much a celebration of Marley's vision of universal brotherhood as it is a restaurant or performance venue.

When Marley first hit the U.S. scene, he was regarded as something of a dope-smoking revolutionary barbarian. Like many black artists, he suffered the indignity of having his songs "covered" by white artists (like Barbara Streisand!). But music hath charms to soothe the conservative as well as the savage breast and Marley's infectiously charming music gradually became domesticated, despite his occasionally radical-sounding lyrics. Today, his lilting "One Heart" is the unofficial national anthem of Jamaica, made universally familiar through the magic of television commercials.

Marley was a member of the Rastafarians, a religious sect with roots in 1920s Harlem, that believes in the divinity of the late Emperor Haile Selassie and the coming of a new era in which the African diaspora will return in glory to the Ethiopian motherland. "Rastas" shun alcohol, adhere to a vegetarian diet, and smoke copious quantities of ganja, or marijuana, which is seen as a gift from God and something of a sacrament. The nightclub that bears his name violates all those principles; there's plenty of booze, meat on the menu, and no ganja.

One thing close to Marley's heart that does get full expression here is the theme of universal brotherhood. It is preached by the M.C. and practiced by the patrons, making Bob Marley's perhaps the most multicultural entertainment venue in Orlando, a place that turns up the volume and lives out the words of Marley's most famous song: "One love. One heart. Let's get together and feel all right."

The exterior is an exact replica of 56 Hope Road, Marley's Kingston, Jamaica home. Inside you will find two L-shaped levels, each with its own bar, opening onto a spacious palm-fringed courtyard with a gazebo-like bandstand in the corner. Because both levels are open to the courtyard, Marley's is not air-conditioned but fans do a good job of keeping a breeze going.

The predominant color scheme is yellow, red and green, the national colors of Ethiopia; the lion statues evoke Haile Selassie's title of Lion of Judah, a motif that is repeated in the mural on the bandstand. The walls are covered in Marley memorabilia and the sound system pumps out a steady stream of Marley hits.

The nighttime entertainment, which kicks off at about 8:00 p.m., typically consists of a house band of skilled reggae musicians performing a mix of Marley hits, other reggae classics, and the occasional pop standard adapted to the reggae beat. The music of the house bands is good, but not so good that it makes you forget how much better Bob Marley and the Wailers were. Still, their main job is to get people out onto the dance floor, and they accomplish that task easily. After a few drinks and once you are gyrating with the crowds, you'll find no reason to quibble.

The "Rastafarian Tings" ($3 to $6) are non-alcoholic. However, the "Island Favorites," "Frozen Tings," and "Extreme Measures" ($8 to $9), fueled with island rum and other potent potables, are designed to help get you past your inhibitions and onto the dance floor. Of course, Red Stripe, Jamaica's favorite beer, is also available.

The food is designed more as ballast for the drinks than anything else, but it is quite good and a nice introduction to Jamaican fare for the uninitiated. The portions are about appetizer size, so you could well sample several in the course of a long evening.

Appetizers ($6-$12) include Stir It Up ($9), a cheese fondue laced with Red Stripe and served with vegetables for dipping, and Jammin' Caribbean chips and salsa. The "Catch a Fire" chicken sandwich ($11) is marinated in "jerk" seasoning (a sort of all-purpose Jamaican marinade), grilled, and served with a creamy cucumber dipping sauce.

There are also both meat and vegetarian versions of Jamaican patties ($9 or $10), filled flaky pastries. More substantial fish entrees ($12 to $17) include grilled mahi mahi and fried tilapia. Several dishes are served with yucca fries, which look deceptively like French-fried potatoes but have a taste and texture all their own. Desserts ($5 to $7) are worth sampling, with the Is This Love mango cheesecake especially good. Fresh fruit on a skewer is also available.

A small shop counter in a downstairs corner hawks Marley T-shirts and polos as well as Marley CDs. This is probably as close as you'll get to finding the complete Marley discography in one place, a perfect chance to fill in the gaps in your collection. There is a small selection of books on reggae and Marley for those who would like to learn more.

"Legendary" Thursdays feature half-price appetizers and drink specials from 9:00 p.m. to close, and Sundays are "Ladies' Night."

Bob Marley's is a popular joint and on weekends can spawn long lines of people waiting for one of the 400 spaces inside to open up. Even early in the week, space can be hard to come by for those who don't arrive early. If you want to be in the thick of it, you'll definitely want to be downstairs. If you're not the dancing type, a row of stools along the railing of the upstairs balcony offers excellent sightlines to the stage. For a change of scenery, you can take your drink onto a second floor balcony that looks out over the Promenade.

Anyone looking for a fun evening of dancing and drinking and infectious music to go along with it will find little to complain about here. True Marley devotees will find everything they are looking for.

Everything but the ganja.

Pat O'Brien's

What:	The original dueling pianos, plus New Orleans cuisine
Where:	On the Promenade
Hours:	4:00 p.m. to 2:00 a.m.
Reservations:	(407) 224-3663 or OpenTable.com
Web:	www.patobriens.com

Step into Pat O'Brien's and you'll believe that you've been magically transported to the Big Easy. At least you will if you've ever visited the original Pat O'Brien's in New Orleans' French Quarter, because CityWalk's version is virtually a photographic reproduction. This was the first attempt to transplant the O'Brien's experience and word is that when O'Brien's owner visited CityWalk he marveled that Universal's design wizards had captured the place "right down to the cracks in the walls."

There are three main rooms at Pat O'Brien's. The Piano Bar houses the famed copper-clad twin baby grand pianos that are an O'Brien's trademark. This is strictly a bar, its brick walls and wooden beams hung with dozens of gaudy German beer steins that let you know this is a place for serious drinkers. Here a steady stream of superbly talented pianists keeps the ivories tickled almost constantly as patrons sing along, pound on the tables, and shout requests. In fact, Pat O'Brien's is credited with inventing the "dueling pianos" format that has been copied so often. The word seems to have gotten around that this is a great place to bring a bunch of old friends (or new acquaintances from the latest convention to blow through town) to drink and blow off some steam.

O'Brien's draws a somewhat older crowd than Marley's or Buffett's. If you're old enough to remember when popular music meant songs with lyrics you could actually understand, you'll probably have a good time here, especially if you can carry a tune and aren't shy about singing along.

Across from the Piano Bar is a smaller version, called the Locals Bar, minus the pianos but with a jukebox and large-screen projection TV that always seems to be tuned to some sporting event. Out back is a delightful open-air patio dining area. Here, at night, the ambiance is highlighted by yet another O'Brien's trademark—flaming fountains.

Upstairs is given over to private party rooms, but you can mount the stairs and find your way to a narrow balcony overlooking the Promenade. It's a great place to sip a drink and survey the passing scene.

And speaking of drinks, Pat O'Brien's (for those who don't know) is the home of the Hurricane ($10), a lethal and lovely concoction of rum and lord knows what all else that has made the place famous worldwide. In fact, the original New Orleans location pulls in more money than any other bar its size in the world.

Pat O'Brien's hasn't skimped on the food side of the equation. Devotees of New Orleans' spicy Creole- and French-influenced cuisine won't be disappointed even though the presentation and service are decidedly casual. Your meal arrives in little fake skillets lined with shamrock-dotted wax paper. Plates and utensils are black plastic. But the offhand presentation belies the sophistication of the cuisine. Prices are moderate, too, with nothing on the menu over $17 and many choices under $10.

The Jambalaya is a spicy medley of shrimp, chicken, andouille sausage, and rice flecked with vegetables. The blackened Louisiana redfish is a signature New Orleans dish and done well here. Perhaps best of all is the Cancun Shrimp, with its coconut-tinged frying batter and sweet, fresh fruit salsa. It's served over Pat O'Brien's signature French fries, dusted with paprika and ever-so-lightly spiced with cayenne before being fried to the perfect texture, and at $10 it's a real bargain. The Shrimp Gumbo appetizer comes in a small portion just right for the lighter appetite.

The Po' Boy sandwich is another Big Easy signature dish. It's a Creole take on the heroes and hoagies from up north. Pat O'Brien's version is a heaping portion of popcorn shrimp, fried oysters, or fried crawfish served on an open-faced baguette with a rich Cajun mayonnaise on the side. Eating it as a sandwich is a bit of a challenge, but worth it as the bread, veggies, seafood, and rich Cajun sauce play off each other very nicely indeed. It's served with those magnificent spicy French fries.

The Crawfish Nachos sounds better than it tastes. The delicate flavor of crawfish etouffé (very nice on its own) doesn't stand up well against the tortilla chips, melted cheese, and sour cream. For dessert ($4 to $6) choose from the Strawberry Hurricane Cheesecake or Pat O's Bread Pudding, redolent of nutmeg and cinnamon and served with a whisky sauce that packs a 100-proof wallop. There is also a kids' menu, featuring simple meals for about $5.

"2 For Tuesdays" specials include 2-for-1 domestic drafts and specialty drinks, including Hurricanes (souvenir glass not included).

Out front, facing the Promenade, you'll find a small gift shop offering Pat O'Brien's souvenir glassware and other gewgaws.

the groove

What:	High-tech, high-gloss disco
Where:	On the Promenade
Hours:	9:00 p.m. to 2:00 a.m

the groove (the lower case is intentional) is CityWalk's dance club and it sets out to compete head to head with the legendary nightspots that have caught the public imagination in urban centers like New York, Chicago, and Los Angeles. It is also the only venue that does not come with a recognizable brand name. No Jimmy Buffetts or Bob Marleys to give this place instant name recognition. This joint stands or falls on its own merits.

It succeeds remarkably well by providing a place where a mostly young crowd (you must be at least 21 to enter) can come and boogie the night away in a cacophonous atmosphere that duplicates big city sophistication. The main difference is that here you will be let in even if you don't meet some snotty doorman's idea of what is currently cool and hip. Intimate it's not, with a maximum capacity of 1,277 on multiple levels, but with crowds comes excitement.

The design conceit is that you are in a century-old theater that is in various stages of renovation, but the dim lighting and pulsing light effects negate much of the intended effect. The various areas of the club provide ample space for those who want to thrash and writhe under pulsating lights to ear-splitting music while offering some refuge to those who just want to watch.

The main dance floor is dominated by a soaring wall of video monitors that operate separately and then coalesce to form a single image. Patterns of light swirl across the floor to disorienting effect. There is a small seldom-used stage for visiting groups. Most nights the nonstop sound assault is provided by a D.J. The music is eclectic; typically the evening starts off with the more widely popular forms of dance music, with the mix changing gradually as the night wears on. Late at night, the music is predominantly "progressive house." If you don't know what that means you probably won't like it. But those who know it love it.

On Thursdays, the groove is successfully pursuing the time-warped clubgoers left homeless by the closure of Disney's "8-Trax" with its own "80's Nights." Admission is **free** before 10:00 p.m., and drink specials are available to get you in the new wave mood.

Wednesdays are often "**Teen Nights**" ($10 to $15), alcohol-free dance parties for 15- to 19-year-olds, lasting from 8:00 p.m. to midnight. The first soft drink is **free**. On these nights, the groove reverts to adult form at the witching hour. Teen Nights are more frequent during the summer months and are listed in the City Guide brochure.

Fortunately, there are some relatively quiet corners (50- to 80-seat bars actually) where you can get better acquainted with that special someone you just met on the dance floor. These are the Red, Blue, and Green Rooms, respectively, and each is decorated differently. The Red and Green Rooms are dim and deliciously decadent but the Blue Room is lit with a ghastly pallor that will flatter only Goths and vampires and seems designed to convince you you've had too much to drink. When it all becomes too much, you can repair to a balcony over the Promenade and look down on the latecomers standing in line.

Rising Star

What:	Karaoke club
Where:	On the Promenade
Hours:	Sunday through Thursday 8:00 p.m. to 1:00 a.m.; Friday and Saturday 7:00 p.m. to 2:00 a.m.

Located in an octagonal building almost at the geographical center of CityWalk, Rising Star is your neighborhood karaoke bar given an extreme makeover. The canned "tiny orchestra" on a portable CD player is gone, replaced by a live band and backing singers with concert-quality lighting and sound systems. The only thing they can't upgrade are the vocal talents of the eager volunteers who line up for their shot at small-scale stardom.

The club's two-story design combines the intimate ambiance of a jazz club (its former incarnation) with the great sightlines of a conventional theater. A scattering of memorabilia from *Downbeat* magazine's Jazz Hall of Fame remains on the walls, with the rest covered by velvet curtains. The color scheme of soothing browns and rich reds, along with the plush banquettes, creates an aura of ultra-cool sophistication. The overall effect is at once festive and laid-back.

The format should be familiar: choose a song from their slender list of about 100 selections (classic rock standards and a smattering of Top 40), write it on a slip of paper, and wait your turn. You (and one friend) can join the band on stage, belting away with teleprompter lyrical assistance, while overhead video screens broadcast your performance to the back row. The musicians do a professional job of staying in time no matter how inebriated the intonations, though it's a wonder they don't go mad repeatedly recycling their short set list.

The food and beverage service is also fairly standard. You can have the bartender pour the usual well drinks for about $5, but there are also martinis ($8.50), wines by the glass ($4 to $8) and a variety of specialty drinks ($7 to $10). Food ($5 to $12) is something of an afterthought and includes potato skins, buffalo wings, and chicken fingers.

Rising Star opens at 8:00 p.m., and the band begins performing at 9:00. If you want to sing, get your request in early, as the club can fill up quickly, especially on weekends. On Sundays and Mondays the live band takes a break, so you and your and backup choir will be singing to prerecorded instruments.

Chapter Five:

SeaWorld Orlando

"I'VE BEEN TO DISNEY," PEOPLE WILL TELL YOU, "BUT Y'KNOW WHAT I THINK is the best thing they've got down there in Orlando? SeaWorld!" I heard it over and over again. In a way this reaction was somewhat surprising. After all, compared to the Magic Kingdom or Universal, SeaWorld is downright modest, with only a smattering of thrill rides.

Of course, this "I-liked-SeaWorld-best" attitude may be one-upmanship—that quirk of human nature that makes us want to look superior. After all, SeaWorld is educational and how much more flattering it is to depict yourself as someone who prefers educational nature shows to mindless carnival rides that merely provide "fun." I'm just enough of a cynic about human nature to give some credence to this theory.

However, I think the real reason lies elsewhere. No matter how well imagined and perfectly realized the attractions at Universal or Disney might be, the wonders on display at SeaWorld were produced by a creative intelligence of an altogether higher order. The animated robotics guys can tinker all they want and the bean-counters in Holly-wood can give them ever higher budgets and they still will never produce anything that can match the awe generated by a killer whale soaring 30 feet in the air. No matter how much we are entertained by Universal and Disney, at SeaWorld we cannot help but be reminded, however subliminally, that there are wonders in our world that humankind simply cannot duplicate, let alone surpass.

It's a feeling of which many visitors probably aren't consciously aware. Even if they are, they'd probably feel a little awkward trying to express it. But I am convinced it is there for everyone—believer, agnostic, or atheist. It's the core experience that makes SeaWorld so popular; it's the reason people will tell you they liked SeaWorld best of all. To paraphrase Joyce Kilmer's magnificent cliché about human inadequacy,

> I think that Walt will never do
> A wonder greater than Shamu.

Before You Come

You can get up-to-date information on hours and prices by calling (407) 351-3600 and pressing "2." Between 8:00 a.m. and 8:00 p.m., you can speak to a SeaWorld representative at this number.

For the latest on SeaWorld's animals, you can check out SeaWorld Parks & Entertainment's animal information site on the Internet. The address is www.seaworld.org. For late-breaking SeaWorld Parks updates, visit their official blog at www.seaworld-parksblog.com, or follow them on twitter @SeaWorld. There's also a free app featuring interactive park maps available for iPhone and Android; search your app store for "seaworld parks."

When's the Best Time To Come?

This is a tough call. Many people like to come to Orlando when the tourist traffic is thinner (see *Chapter 1*), but SeaWorld stays open later and adds extra evening shows during the summer months and over Christmas. Some of them are terrific and it would be a shame to miss them. Even at the height of summer the crowds at SeaWorld are quite manageable compared to those you'll encounter at, say, Disney. Crowds in January are negligible and the weather cool to moderate, perfect viewing conditions for the outdoor shows, although it can get quite chilly.

Even if you come when the parks are open late, I would recommend arriving early and planning to stay until the park closes. There are two reasons for this. Early arrivals breeze right in; as the morning wears on, the lines at the attractions lengthen. As for staying until the bitter end, all of the added summer shows are performed in the hour or two just before closing. Compensate for the long day with a leisurely lunch.

Getting There

SeaWorld is located just off I-4 on Central Florida Parkway. If you're coming from the south (i.e. traveling east on I-4) you will use Exit 71 and find yourself pointed directly toward the SeaWorld entrance, about half a mile along on your left. Because there is no exit directly to Central Florida Parkway from Westbound I-4, those coming from the north (i.e. traveling west on I-4) must get off at Exit 72, onto the Beachline Expressway (Route 528). Don't worry about the sign that says it's a toll road; you won't have to pay one. Take the first exit and loop around to International Drive. Turn left and proceed to Central Florida Parkway and turn right. It's all very clearly marked. This route, by the way, offers a nice backstage peek at *Kraken*, SeaWorld's first roller coaster. As you get close to SeaWorld, tune your AM radio to 1540 for a steady stream of information about the park. This will help while away the time spent waiting in line at the parking lot.

Arriving at SeaWorld

Parking fees are $14 for cars and $15 for RVs and trailers and are collected at toll booths at the entrance. If you'd like to park close to the front entrance, you can opt for Shamu's Preferred Parking, available for cars only, for $20. Annual passholders pay nothing for regular parking and pay $10 for preferred parking; Platinum passholders park anywhere they please for free.

Handicapped Parking. Several rows of extra large spaces near the main entrance are provided for the convenience of handicapped visitors. Alert the attendant to your need for handicapped parking and you will be directed accordingly.

The SeaWorld parking lot is divided into sections, and you will be ushered to your space in a very efficiently controlled manner. While the lot is not huge, it's still a very good idea to make a note of which lettered section and numbered row you're parked in. If you are parked any distance from the entrance, you may be directed to a tram that will whisk you to the main entrance, although trams don't run as often as they used to. If you arrive after noon, however, you may find yourself on your own. Fortunately, the farthest row is never too far from the park perimeter. You can orient yourself by looking for the centrally located *Skytower*. It's the blue spire with the large American flag at the summit.

Once you reach the beautifully designed main entrance, you will find a group of thoughtfully shaded ticket booths where you will purchase your admission. To the left of the ticket windows are the Guest Relations window and the annual pass center. Once inside the park, walk straight ahead to the Information Desk. There you can pick up a large map of the park. On the back you will find a schedule of the day's shows as well as information on any special events happening that day.

Opening and Closing Times

SeaWorld operates seven days a week, 365 days a year. The park opens at 9:00 a.m. and remains open until 6:00, 7:00, 8:00, 9:00, 10:00, or 11:00 p.m.—or even until 1:00 a.m.—depending on the time of year. Unlike Universal and Disney, SeaWorld does not practice soft openings (admitting guests early). During very busy periods, they will start admitting people at 8:30, but these early arrivals are held in the Entrance Plaza (or "mall") just inside the gates, until the park proper opens at 9:00. By the time the last scheduled shows are starting (about 45 minutes to an hour prior to the posted closing time), most of the park's other attractions have either shut down or are in the process of doing so.

The Price of Admission

SeaWorld has several ticket options, including some that offer admission to its sister park, Busch Gardens, in nearby Tampa. At press time, one-day admission prices (including sales tax) were as follows:

One-Day Admission:

Adults:	$87.32
Children (3 to 9):	$78.80

Children under age 3 are admitted **free**.

An ever-changing array of incentives is offered for ordering your tickets online in advance. At press time, you can buy a one-day ticket online with a bonus "second day free" for $10 less than the one-day gate price. Alternatively, you can buy children's tickets at half-price with a full-price adult admission. Special deals for Florida residents are also announced on the website.

Information on "Length of Stay" tickets, which combine two or more parks; the

Orlando FlexTicket, which includes five or six parks; and "Passports" (annual passes), which also offer access to multiple parks, will be found in *Chapter 1*.

The Discovery Cove Option

If you are also planning to visit Discovery Cove (described in *Chapter 3*), be aware that your admission fee there includes a 14-day pass to SeaWorld (or Busch Gardens Tampa, if you prefer). The pass is valid for 14 consecutive days, starting the day of your first visit, and can be activated either before or after your Discovery Cove visit. To get the pass, stop into Guest Relations and show your Discovery Cove confirmation letter. You will be issued a nontransferable credit-card-sized pass. You may be required to produce a photo ID each time you enter the park using this pass.

Quick Queue

Love thrill rides but hate the wait? SeaWorld has a solution, but it will cost you. In exchange for $24.95 per person, the Quick Queue pass will permit you one front-of-the-line ride each on *Manta, Kraken, Journey to Atlantis,* and *Wild Arctic.* If once is never enough, you can get Unlimited Quick Queue access for $34.95. Both options also include one ride on the paddlewheel boats. Quick Queue isn't as useful as Universal's paid Express Plus program, nor is it free like Disney's FastPass. But if you visit during peak season and fail to follow my touring plan, the price may seem a pleasant alternative to an hour-plus wait for a roller coaster.

VIP Tours

For those short on time and long on cash, SeaWorld offers a guided seven-hour VIP touring option that guarantees you will hit the highlights and be treated like a celebrity along the way. You'll get to feed stingrays, dolphins, and sea lions and pet a Magellanic penguin. You will also be given reserved seats at the Shamu show, *One Ocean,* which means very good seats indeed. Similar preferred seating is offered at either the sea lion or dolphin show, depending on scheduling on the day of your visit. Guests on VIP tours who meet the minimum height requirements (see ride reviews, below) also get one-time front-of-the-line privileges at the big thrill rides, *Manta, Kraken, Journey to Atlantis,* and *Wild Arctic.*

None of this comes cheap. The cost is $100 for adults and $75 for children 3 to 9 (younger children tour free)—and that's in addition to the regular price of admission! At least tax and lunch with a choice of sandwich, salad, dessert, and soft drink are included in these prices.

A few bucks cheaper ($75 adults, $55 children) and three hours shorter, the **Family Fun Tour** is a kid-centric spin on the VIP tour that swaps coasters for Happy Harbor kiddie rides and adds a meet & greet with "Shamu" (the huggable fuzzy costume kind, not the giant sea mammal). During the Christmas season, holiday-centric variations on the VIP tour ($100 adults, $75 children) and Family Fun Tour ($65 adults, $50 children) are available. And when the park is open late, a special **Summer Nights VIP Tour** ($125 adults, $100 children) is offered, focusing on the seasonal nighttime shows.

Whichever tour you choose, there are only 12 spaces in each group, so you may want to reserve a spot online. Tours leave at varying times in the late morning; there may just be one tour a day during slower periods and as many as four or five during the busier tourist seasons.

If that's not exclusive enough, you can opt for a private version of the VIP Tour, dubbed the **Elite VIP Tour**. This private tour offers the same privileges, but is limited exclusively to your party and includes a full-service meal at Sharks Underwater Grill. The tab is $275 per person (with a two-guest minimum) plus the regular one-day admission. Book online at least two weeks ahead for the Elite Tour.

Special Events

SeaWorld doesn't hold extra-cost after-hours events as often as Disney and Universal do, but that doesn't mean they don't go all-out for the holidays. It just means that SeaWorld's seasonal perks all come included in the price of your regular ticket.

The biggest annual event is SeaWorld's **Christmas Celebration**, which runs from Thanksgiving thru New Year's Eve. It features special seasonal variations on many of their popular animal shows, and a *Polar Express* overlay at the *Wild Arctic* attraction (see the following reviews for details). There is also a compact but competent ice skating show presented at the Atlantis Bayside Stadium (a rarely used venue across the lake from the *Waterfront* area, formerly used for a now-defunct waterski show). SeaWorld's holiday decor is tastefully restrained compared to the Magic Kingdom, and periodically features "snow" flurries, a treat for Floridian children who may never see the real thing. The season concludes with a midnight musical fireworks display to ring in the New Year.

At the opposite end of the calendar, SeaWorld's **Summer Nights** offers extended operating hours from mid-June through mid-August, along with special after-dark animal shows and the *Reflections* fireworks finale (see later in this chapter for details). In between, weekend **music festivals** each February/March and April/May celebrate country and Latin artists with live concerts, plus food and drink menus to match. Finally, SeaWorld's **Halloween Spooktacular** (weekends in October) is a fright-free festival for little kids in costumes to trick-or-treat and see seasonal stage shows.

Eating in SeaWorld

Dining at SeaWorld is almost entirely of the fast-food and cafeteria variety, a lot of it quite good. There is only one full-service restaurant, **Sharks Underwater Grill**, but it is a winner and highly recommended if only for the stunning view into the shark tank that it offers. However, there is much more to recommend it. The food is of exceptionally high quality for a theme park, nicely prepared and beautifully presented. The wine list is limited but serviceable.

Tip: Sharks Underwater Grill is popular and long waits for a table are common. You can avoid the crush by telling the greeter that you are heading for the bar. There you can enjoy the full menu, either at the bar itself or at one of the nearby hightop tables. The bar offers an excellent view of the shark tank.

SeaWorld also offers a number of what might be called "dinner shows," including a Polynesian luau, the **Makahiki Luau**, which is reviewed in *Chapter 13: Dinner Attractions*. It does not require purchasing admission to the park and thus is best enjoyed on a day when you are not touring the park. The others, which revolve around Shamu, do require purchasing a ticket to the park. One, the **Shamu Rocks Dinner Buffet** is seasonal, which means that it is offered only during busier times. Between Thanksgiving and Christmas, it has a (you guessed it) Christmas theme, with visits from Mr. and Mrs. Claus. One benefit of paying the additional price (about $30, $20 for kids) is that you get great seats for the *Shamu Rocks* show.

Another dinner show, **Dine With Shamu**, has been on hiatus for a while since the unfortunate death of a SeaWorld trainer after one of the shows. There is no word on when the show will resume, if ever. If it does, you can look forward to a buffet dinner served poolside while trainers conduct an informative and entertaining session with some of their orca charges.

There is beer to be had at most eateries, but there is precious little else on offer. If you have a hankering for a glass of wine or a mixed drink, you'll have to head for the Sharks Underwater Grill.

You can also get great desserts here. They're made right on the premises and most of the casual eateries offer them. I especially recommend the chocolate cherry and carrot cakes, but those whose taste runs to fruit for dessert won't be disappointed. Fresh strawberries are readily available.

Virtually every cafeteria style restaurant offers a moderately priced (under $10) "Kid's Meal." The main component varies from place to place, but the selection leans heavily to hot dogs and chicken fingers. Kids Meals are served in a reusable Shamu souvenir lunchbox.

SeaWorld lets you eat while waiting for or watching the big outdoor stadium shows; there are even snack bars (offering ice cream bars and nachos) conveniently located near the entrances to the stands, but I've seen people bringing in trays from restaurants some distance away. Not all eating establishments are open throughout the park's operating hours. A "Dining Guide," listing the various restaurants and their operating hours, is available at the Information Desk in the Entrance Plaza.

Shopping in SeaWorld

Of course, SeaWorld is dotted with strategically located gift and souvenir shops ready to help you lessen the heavy load in your wallet. The merchandise in the various shops, not to mention the shops themselves, change with such regularity that SeaWorld has given up on listing them on the park map. So rather than attempt a shop-by-shop or section-by-section description, I will touch on the overall shopping scene here and call out a few shops that I feel are deserving of special note.

Most of the wares on display are of the standard tourist variety but some items deserve special mention. Many of SeaWorld's shops offer some very attractive figurines and small sculptures. They range from quite small objects suitable for a bric-a-brac shelf to fairly large pieces (with fairly large price tags) that are surely displayed with pride by those who buy them. Prices range from under $20 to well over $2,000. If you're in the market for a special gift or are a collector yourself, you will want to give these items more than a cursory look. Among the shops to seek out for these art objects are **Shamu's Emporium** in the main entrance plaza and **Under the Sun** in the Waterfront area.

Another, more affordable souvenir is a Shamu-themed beach towel (which can come in handy after sitting in the splash zone at Shamu Stadium!) or one of the many plush dolls for kids, many of which are irresistible. The animals you will encounter depend on which attraction you've just exited, each of which seems to have its own gift shop. My personal favorites are the polar bears and baby seals in the **Arctic Shop** at the exit to *Wild Arctic*.

The shops in the Waterfront section, that flow one into another, offer some very nice clothing items. Most of it is for women, but men might score a good quality Hawaiian-style shirt. Also in these shops is a constantly changing variety of decorative items for the home that might make good gifts for you or someone you love.

A shop that will draw the curious as well as shoppers is **The Oyster's Secret**. Here you can watch through underwater windows as divers plunge downwards in search of pearl-bearing oysters. And if you decide to buy one and want it placed in a custom setting, you will be accommodated. There is also a good selection of pearl jewelry. Some of it is quite expensive, but the small, irregular shaped fresh water pearls worked into intricate necklaces are both attractive and affordable.

Most of the shops offer a free package pick-up service that lets you collect your purchases near the front entrance on your way out, so you needn't worry about lugging things about for half the day. Inveterate shoppers can soothe their conscience with the thought that a percentage of the money they drop at SeaWorld goes toward helping rescue and care for stranded sea mammals.

Good Things To Know About . . .

Access for the Disabled. All parts of SeaWorld are accessible to disabled guests and all the stadium shows have sections set aside for those in wheelchairs. These are some of the best seats in the house. Wheelchairs are available for rent at $12 per day. Electric carts are $45 per day.

Babies. Little ones under 3 are admitted free and strollers are available for rent if you don't have your own. Single strollers are $13.15 for the day, double strollers are $17.84. There are also diaper changing stations in all the major restrooms (men's and women's). In addition, there are "non-gender changing areas" at *Wild Arctic*, the Friends of the Wild shop, and behind Voyagers restaurant, where you will find diaper vending machines. There are nursing areas near the Friends of the Wild shop and at the Baby Care station near *Shamu's Happy Harbor*, where you can also buy a limited menu of baby food and baby care products.

Education Staff. It's hard to say too much in praise of the education staff at Sea-World. There are some 100 employees whose job it is to hang around and answer your questions. They are invariably friendly, enthusiastic, and more than happy to share their considerable knowledge with you. Don't be shy. Taking advantage of this wonderful human resource will immeasurably increase the enjoyment and value of your visit to SeaWorld. Just look for the word "Education" on the employee's name tag. In fact, even employees who are not with the Education Department will likely have the answer to your question.

Emergencies. As a general rule, the moment something goes amiss speak with the nearest SeaWorld employee. They will contact security or medical assistance and get the ball rolling toward a solution. There is a first-aid station in a tent behind *Stingray Lagoon* in the North End of the park and another near *Shamu's Happy Harbor* in the South End.

Feeding Times. Feeding time is an especially interesting time to visit any of the aquatic habitats. Unfortunately, there is no rigid schedule. By varying feeding times, the trainers more closely approximate the animals' experience in the wild and avoid, to some extent, the repetitive behaviors that characterize many animals in captivity. However, you can simply ask one of the education staff at the exhibit when the animals will next be fed. If your schedule permits, I would recommend returning for this enjoyable spectacle. Of course, at some exhibits—the dolphins, stingrays, and sea lions—you can feed the animals yourself—for a hefty fee!

Kids' ID System. SeaWorld may be less crowded than Disney World, but it's still remarkably easy to lose track of your little ones here. Stop by Guest Services to pick up wristbands for your young children—Guest Services will label them with your name and cell phone number so staff members can easily get hold of you if they encounter your child on the loose. Wristbands are available free of charge and are uniquely numbered, so that even if the writing on the wristband smears, they can still use this number to look up your information back at Guest Services should the need arise.

Lockers. Lockers are available in the Entrance Plaza behind Shamu's Emporium. The all-day fee is $7 for small lockers, $10 for large. One-time-use lockers are also available near *Shamu's Happy Harbor* and the thrill rides *Manta, Kraken,* and *Journey to Atlantis.* They cost 50 cents for small lockers, $1 for large (quarters only).

Special Diets. Vegetarians can stop at the Information Desk and request the Food Services staff's list of meatless dishes and the restaurants that serve them. Similar lists of seafood and low-fat selections as well as other dietary notes are available from the same source.

Splash Zones. All of the stadium shows give the adventuresome the opportunity to get wet—in some cases very wet. One advantage of the splash zones is that they are some of the best seats at SeaWorld. But the threat is very, very real.

I am a believer in splash zones for those who come prepared. Those inexpensive rain ponchos that are sold at every major park will hold the damage to a minimum (although there is probably no real way to guard against a direct hit from Shamu!). Kids, especially young boys, will enjoy the exquisite machismo of getting thoroughly soaked.

One word of warning: In the cooler periods of the year, a full soaking will be extremely uncomfortable, and may be courting a cold, or worse. Bring a big towel and a change of clothes, or be prepared to shell out for new duds at the SeaWorld shops.

Sailing the Sea: Your Day at SeaWorld

SeaWorld can be seen quite comfortably in a single day, without rushing madly around or otherwise driving yourself crazy. This is especially true if you've arrived during one of Orlando's slack periods or if you will be forgoing the thrill rides. But even during the most crowded times, SeaWorld is still more manageable than other parks in the area.

SeaWorld is not a large park, but its comfortable layout and the large Bayside Lagoon at its center make it seem larger than it is. Much of the North End of the park is lushly landscaped with large shady trees and bird-filled pools along the walkways. The South End, on the other side of the Lagoon, is open and airy with a gently rolling landscape. In look and feel, it is quite a contrast to the more tightly crammed spaces of the Magic Kingdom and Universal Orlando. Many parts of SeaWorld have the feel of a particularly gracious public park or botanical garden.

One of SeaWorld's key differentiators is the fact that the vast majority of its attractions are either shows that take place in large, sometimes huge, outdoor auditoriums or "continuous viewing" exhibits through which people pass pretty much at their own pace. My observation is that most people pass through pretty quickly, so even if there's a line, the wait won't be unbearable. Once inside you can take your own sweet time. Here, briefly, are the different kinds of attractions at SeaWorld:

Rides. There are just four "rides" at SeaWorld but they are doozies.

Outdoor Auditorium Shows. These are SeaWorld's primo attractions—Shamu, the sea lions, the dolphins, and some others. There are plenty of shaded seats for these shows (anywhere from 2,400 to 5,500), but even in slower periods they fill up, which should tell you something about how good the shows are. It is possible to enter these auditoriums after the show has begun if they are not full.

Indoor Theater Shows. Some shows take place indoors, in darkened air-conditioned theaters. None of them involves sea mammals and none of them falls into the must-see category. When these shows begin, the doors close and latecomers must wait for the next performance. Be aware that it is difficult to leave these shows in the middle.

Seasonal Shows. Some shows are only put on when the park is open late, which means summer and Christmas. They are designed for twilight or after dark viewing and thus run only in the hours just before the park closes. I have called these shows out in the reviews in this chapter.

Aquatic Habitats. This is SeaWorld's term for its continuous viewing exhibits of live marine animals. The habitats range from huge tanks like those you may have seen at aquariums to elaborate stage sets the likes of which I can almost guarantee you've never seen before.

Guided Tours. These are small group experiences that operate on a limited schedule and charge a moderate additional fee. They offer unique access to SeaWorld's "backstage" areas and a chance to learn a bit more about some of the park's most interesting inhabitants.

Catch of the Day

If you had very little time to spend at SeaWorld, I would venture to suggest that you could see just a handful of attractions and still feel you got your money's worth—if you picked the right ones. Here, then, is my list of the very best that SeaWorld has to offer:

The three major open-air animal shows—**One Ocean**, **Clyde & Seamore**, and **Blue Horizons**—are the heart and soul of SeaWorld. Anyone missing these should have his or her head examined.

Close behind are the major "aquatic habitats"—**Wild Arctic** (and the ride that introduces the experience), **Shark Encounter**, **Key West at SeaWorld**, and **Turtle-Trek**. I have omitted **Pacific Point Preserve** only because you are likely to see its close equivalent elsewhere.

If you have the time, the **Pets Ahoy** show is very entertaining and holds up to repeat viewing. Finally, for thrill seekers, there are the stupendous roller coasters, **Kraken** and **Manta**.

The One-Day Stay

1. Get up early, but not as early as you would if you were heading for Disney or Universal. Remember, when SeaWorld says the park proper opens at 9:00, it means it. Get there a little earlier perhaps (you can get a bite to eat or browse the shops in the Entrance Plaza starting at 8:30 a.m.), but there's no need to kill yourself. The exception is for guests at SeaWorld's six "Official" hotels, who receive early entry on select days during peak season (see the concierge desk for details).

2. After purchasing your tickets and entering the park, thrill seekers and ride freaks should head immediately to *Manta*, followed by *Kraken* and *Journey to Atlantis*. (Bear left after the entrance mall and follow the signs and the running kids.) Then plan on doing *Wild Arctic* and its exciting ride later in the day, preferably during a Shamu show when the lines for *Wild Arctic* tend to thin out.

If, for one reason or another you are taking a pass on the thrill rides, proceed immediately to *Wild Arctic*. (Just keep bearing right until you see the Lagoon and circle it in a counterclockwise direction.) If you're not interested in taking the ride, the line for the stationary version is always a good deal shorter, so coming later may be okay. Also, if you'd like to skip the ride portion altogether, it is possible to slip quietly in through the exit in the gift shop and just see the animals.

3. Now's the time to review the schedule printed on the back of the map you got when you entered. First, check the times of the "big three" shows—*One Ocean, Clyde & Seamore*, and *Blue Horizons*. Whatever you do, don't miss these. Don't try to see two shows that start less than an hour apart. Yes, it can be done but you will be making sacrifices.

Instead, schedule your day so you can arrive at the stadium about 20 minutes before show time, perhaps longer during busier seasons. That way you can get a good seat, like dead center for *One Ocean* or in a splash zone for the kids. There is almost always some sort of pre-show entertainment starting 10 or 15 minutes before the show. It's always fun and, in the case of the warm-up to the sea lion show, often hilarious.

4. Use your time between shows to visit the aquatic habitats. Use the descriptions in the next section and geographical proximity to guide your choices. For example, you can leave the dolphin show and go right into the turtle exhibit. Or you can see *Clyde & Seamore* and visit *Shark Encounter* immediately after.

5. If you have kids with you, you will miss *Shamu's Happy Harbor* at your peril. Adults, of course, can give it a miss.

6. Fill in the rest of the day with the lesser attractions or return visits to habitats you particularly enjoyed. In my opinion, several of the non-animal shows and attractions can be missed altogether with little sacrifice. If your time is really limited (e.g. you got to the park late), I strongly urge you to take my advice. You can always come back another day and prove me wrong.

7. If you stay until the end, as I recommend, you will not want to miss *Sea Lions Tonight* and *Shamu Rocks* (if they're playing during your visit).

This plan should allow you to see everything you truly want to see in one day and maybe even some attractions you wished you hadn't bothered with.

The Two-Day Stay

If you have the luxury of spending two or more days at SeaWorld (Discovery Cove visitors and Passport holders take note), I recommend relaxing your pace, perhaps leaving the park early on one day to freshen up and catch a dinner show elsewhere. With two days, even a very relaxed pace should allow you to see everything in the park, several of them more than once.

Another strategy to adopt is to use the first day to concentrate on the shows and the second day to concentrate on the rides, the animal habitats and, perhaps, take a guided tour or two.

THE NORTH END

SeaWorld is not neatly divided into "lands" like some other theme parks I might mention (although Key West and the Waterfront are a step in that direction). However, a convenient division of the park is provided by Bayside Lagoon. If you look at the map you collected on arriving at the park, you will notice that the vertical line formed by the *Skytower* effectively divides the park in two: the northern side ("The North End") is to the left of the tower; the southern side including most of the Lagoon ("The South End") is to the right. In this chapter I have adopted this North End/South End division. Please remember that this is my terminology and not SeaWorld's. If you stop a SeaWorld employee and ask, "How do I get to the North?" you may be told to get on a plane and fly to Philadelphia.

The layout and open landscaping of the southern half, combined with the sheer size of the stadiums located there, make getting your bearings relatively easy. In the northern half, however, the layout and lusher landscaping, while pleasing to the eye, can be confusing. When traveling from Point A to Point B in the northern half of the park, use the map to get you started in the right general direction. Then rely on the directional signs, which are posted at nearly every turning, to guide you to your destination.

I begin with the northern half of the park for the simple reason that this is where you enter the park past the Shamu lighthouse in the artificial harbor that graces the airy entrance area. I describe the attractions in geographical, rather than thematic order, starting with *The Waterfront*. From there I proceed in a roughly clockwise direction, returning full-circle to *The Waterfront* and the fabulous *Pets Ahoy* show located there.

The Waterfront ★ ★ ★

Type: Themed shopping and dining venue
Time: Continuous viewing
Short Take: Lovely to look at

Although it is home to two major attractions—*Skytower* and *Pets Ahoy*, *The Water-*

front is primarily a place to dine, stroll, and shop. Themed beautifully as a fantasy Mediterranean seaside village esplanade, this area is the gateway to the sole walkway across Bayside Lagoon to the southern end of the park.

The Waterfront is home to three large restaurants, **Voyagers Smokehouse**, **Seafire Inn** and **The Spice Mill**. All are cafeteria style, all are moderately priced, and all are above average.

Between these lies a series of shops offering some of the nicest merchandise in Sea-World. Each has its own entrance but they are all linked inside, making for seamless, not to mention cool, shopping. Outside is the esplanade, dotted with coffee stands and snack kiosks, and the setting for periodic street shows. On the lower level is a children's water play area and a sea wall where waves crash every few minutes, soaking the delighted kids who gather there precisely for that reason.

Just off shore, on a tiny island at the base of the *Skytower*, is the **Sand Bar**, an outdoor bar and one of the nicest places in Orlando to sip a beer al fresco.

Skytower ★ ★ ★

Type:	Bird's-eye view of Orlando
Time:	6½ minutes
Short Take:	For those who've seen everything else they want to see at SeaWorld

The *Skytower* is a circular viewing platform that rotates slowly while rising from lagoon level to a height of 400 feet. From there you can see the dome of *Spaceship Earth* at Epcot and *Space Mountain* at the Magic Kingdom, as well as some of the Orlando area's high-rise buildings. Closer by, you will get a superb view of the layout of *Kraken* and, across the street, Aquatica. If your timing is right you will get to see a load of terrified riders make a complete circuit on the awesome coaster.

There are two levels, each offering a single row of glassed-in seating that circles the capsule. You pick the level of your choice as you enter. The upper level would seem the better choice, and most people head that way, but it only gives you a 10-foot height advantage that doesn't really affect your enjoyment of the experience.

Riding the *Skytower* is an enjoyable enough way to kill some time if you aren't eager to see anything else and don't mind paying the extra charge. Seeing SeaWorld from the air can be fascinating. You will also gain an appreciation for the cunning way the park is laid out and see why you've been having difficulty navigating from place to place in the North End.

The *Skytower* ride is at the mercy of the elements. Any hint of lightning in the area closes it down, as do high winds, which might buffet the top of the tower even when it's perfectly calm on the ground.

Pets Ahoy (at Seaport Theatre) ★ ★ ★ ★

Type:	Indoor theater show
Time:	25 minutes
Short Take:	A must for pet lovers

If you saw *Animal Actors* at Universal Studios Florida, you might be tempted to skip this one. However, if you are a pet lover, you'll want to put this charming show on your list. It also offers a pleasant break from the hot Florida sun.

The SeaWorld twist here is that almost all the animals in the show were found in Central Florida animal shelters and rescued from an uncertain fate. As a result, the cast list runs heavily to cats and dogs, although there is an amusing pig, a skunk, and even a mouse.

Ace trainer Joel Slaven (of *Ace Ventura: Pet Detective* fame) has done an amazing job here, especially with the cats. Not only do Slaven's pussycats do every doggie trick and do them better but there is a cat who does a tightwire act and one who bounds over the heads of the audience, jumping from one tiny platform to another.

Abby and Elmo's Treasure Hunt (Seasonal) ★ ★ ★

Type: Indoor theater show
Time: 25 minutes
Short Take: Strictly for tots

During the summer months and holiday seasons, the characters from Sesame Place, a sister park in Pennsylvania, come south to entertain the hordes of kids in Orlando at the Seaport Theatre. There are typically three shows a day, in the morning and very early afternoon.

This one promotes reading with a silly story about finding clues to a riddle that will allow Elmo, Abby, Rosita, Grover and Cookie Monster to open a talking trunk filled with kids' books. There's plenty of loud music and the characters run into the audience, much to the delight of their tiny fans.

On weekends in October, during SeaWorld's Halloween Spooktakular, a similar kid's show called "Countdown to Halloween" (featuring *Sesame Street's* The Count, of course) is performed in this theater.

Entertainment at The Waterfront ★ ★ ★

Type: Indoor and outdoor acts
Time: Irregular and unpredictable
Short Take: Pleasant enough

There is a regular and ever-changing menu of entertainment on tap in and around the Waterfront. Some of the entertainment takes the form of street acts that could be animal show and tell, strolling musicians, or cut-up physical comedy. Fairly typical is **Groove Chefs**, an act that has shown some staying power. Three young guys, who are ostensibly chefs at the nearby Seafire Inn, take a break with garbage cans, pots, pans, and drumsticks and rustle up a rhythmic ragout that is sure to get your toes tapping. The rhythms are intricate, the footwork fancy, and the variety of sounds that emerge from their oddball collection of implements quite amusing.

There's indoor entertainment, too, on the stage in the back room of the Seafire Inn. The acts that appear here are unpredictable and tend to be in the variety show tradition. Most recently, there was a show called **Wild Things** that showcased "nature's most misunderstood creepy creatures" in an easygoing show-and-tell format. The best part is that you can either enjoy these shows while eating or stroll in just for the show. Sometimes

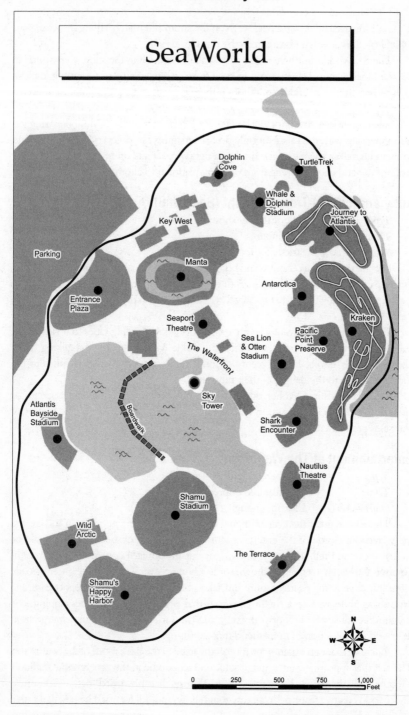

SeaWorld

Dolphin Cove

TurtleTrek

Whale & Dolphin Stadium

Key West

Journey to Atlantis

Parking

Manta

Antarctica

Entrance Plaza

Seaport Theatre

Kraken

Pacific Point Preserve

Sea Lion & Otter Stadium

The Waterfront

Sky Tower

Boardwalk

Atlantis Bayside Stadium

Shark Encounter

Nautilus Theatre

Shamu Stadium

Wild Arctic

The Terrace

Shamu's Happy Harbor

N
W   E
S

0   250   500   750   1,000
Feet

these shows are listed in the show schedule on the SeaWorld map you picked up on entering the park.

Dolphin Nursery ★ ★ ★

Type: Small shaded outdoor pool
Time: Continuous viewing
Short Take: Not much to see but hard to resist

This is where dolphin moms get to enjoy a little maternity leave with their newborns during the bonding process. A barrier fence prevents you from getting right to the pool's edge, so at best you will just be able to glimpse the little ones as they swim by in close formation with mom.

Still, even a glimpse of a baby dolphin is a hard lure to resist and you will probably want to pause here for a look. Education staffers are on hand to answer your questions. Feedings usually take place in the morning and late afternoon, making those the best times to visit.

Manta ★ ★ ★ ★ ★

Type: Flying roller coaster
Time: 2½ minutes
Short Take: First of its kind in Orlando

In summer 2009, SeaWorld unveiled its latest entry in the ongoing Orlando roller coaster sweepstakes. This is not a "me-too" coaster but another new departure that has drawn coaster enthusiasts in the thousands.

Manta celebrates the ray, one of the sea's most majestic and graceful creatures. The queue line for the coaster begins with a total immersion in an aquarium filled with 300 rays of all descriptions—shark rays, spotted eagle rays, leopard rays, cownose rays, and oscillate river rays—along with an amazing giant Pacific octopus. (Thoughtfully, non-riders get their own exclusive entrance to observe the aquarium.)

Then you get a chance to actually be a ray, a supercharged one, in fact. The business part of *Manta* is a so-called "flying" roller coaster, the ride vehicles themed to resemble the creatures they celebrate. The coaster starts off looking like a standard "inverted" model with seats hanging chairlift-style below the track. But just before the coaster takes off, the seats tilt to face downward, leaving you lying prone on your well-padded chest harness. This unique posture gives the distinct sensation of zooming, superhero-like through the air. The ride features lighting and sound effects, as well as rushing waterfalls, to take riders high overhead, then speed them to within inches of the simulated sea below.

A remarkable aspect of this coaster is the way it changes depending on which row you ride in. From the front, the ride feels unexpectedly gentle, with swooping turns providing a largely visual thrill. But in the back row, the 98-foot tall pretzel loop can make even hardened coaster addicts "grey out" from the extreme G-forces. Whichever level of intensity you prefer, make sure to make this your first destination in the morning if you plan to ride, as *Manta* attracts the park's longest lines.

Key West at SeaWorld

Key West at SeaWorld is not so much an attraction as a collection of related attractions wrapped in a single theme. The attractions here are aquatic habitats featuring the denizens of warmer waters and the theme, of course, is the casual sophistication and good times atmosphere for which Key West has become famous. On both scores, SeaWorld acquits itself admirably.

Turtle Point ★ ★ ★

Type: Aquatic habitat
Time: Continuous viewing
Short Take: Best when a staffer is present

Turtle Point is small by SeaWorld standards, a shallow seawater pool fringed by white sand beaches. It is home to four species—loggerhead, Kemp's ridley, hawksbill, and green sea turtles, all of them rescued animals.

Turtles, it must be said, are not the most lively creatures SeaWorld has on display. No leaps and twirls here. So, for most folks, this habitat will warrant no more than a quick look. Fortunately, SeaWorld staffers are often hanging out by the pool ready to answer questions. When a group of people gathers and starts exercising its curiosity, a visit to *Turtle Point* can be quite interesting.

Stingray Lagoon ★ ★ ★ ★

Type: Aquatic habitat
Time: Continuous viewing
Short Take: Your best shot at touching a SeaWorld critter

Under a shading roof lies a long, shallow pool with a smaller "nursery pool" in one corner. Its edge is at waist height for easy viewing and interaction. Scores of stingrays lazily circle the main pool, while their "pups" navigate the nursery pool. The mature rays may look scary, but they are remarkably gentle creatures that will tolerate being petted (they feel a bit like slimy felt) and will almost always appreciate a free handout. A small tray of tiny fish called silversides can be purchased for a staggering fee of $15 or $20 depending on the crowds (annual passholders get a 10% discount). Despite the high cost, there are plenty of takers. Once again, SeaWorld education staffers make regular appearances here, providing a steady stream of information about these fascinating creatures and answering any questions you might have.

Thanks to the accessibility of the stingrays, this is a very popular attraction. If the pool edge is packed, be patient. Eventually you will be able to make your way forward where your patience is sure to be rewarded.

Dolphin Cove ★ ★ ★ ★ 1/2

Type: Aquatic habitat
Time: Continuous viewing
Short Take: A spectacular SeaWorld habitat

Dolphin Cove lets you get up close to these delightful creatures—at a price. This extensive Key West habitat allows petting and feeding on one side and viewing on the other, from both a raised platform and an underwater observation post. Most people start at poolside.

Here you can lean over a low wall and reach out to touch a passing dolphin. Since dolphins are naturally curious and gregarious animals, they often pause to check out the curious tourists who are checking them out. For many people, passing their fingers along the sleek flanks of a passing dolphin is the highlight of their day at SeaWorld.

Unfortunately, if you want to grab the best viewing spot and maximize your chances of touching one of the inhabitants here, you will have to pay for the privilege—and queue up to do so! You see, dolphin feeding here is carried out by paying customers and a prime section of the water's edge is roped off for those who are performing this job. A line, often a long one, forms for the purpose of purchasing a small paper tray of three smelt-like fish for (gasp!) $20. Only those who have purchased fish are allowed into the prime viewing area alongside the dolphin pool.

Note: The amount of fish sold is limited, because the staff wants to make sure the dolphins don't over-indulge—unlike the human guests who are, in fact, encouraged to eat to excess! So, while you can purchase more than one tray, there may be a limit on your total purchase depending on the size of the crowd.

If you don't wish to buy dolphin snacks, you are relegated to a much smaller viewing area at the far end of the pool, where your chances of interacting with a dolphin, while not precisely nil, are certainly much diminished.

Having fish to offer will definitely increase your chances of touching a dolphin, although they will occasionally swim close enough to the edge to allow a foodless hand to sweep along their flanks. But you can't just show up any old time and buy food. It's sold only at specified feeding times and only up to the quantity that SeaWorld's marine dietitians have determined is appropriate to keep the dolphin fit and not fat. If touching a dolphin is a priority for you or your child, I would advise checking out feeding times and arriving a bit early to get on line to purchase food. Otherwise, there is a good chance you will be disappointed.

A number of SeaWorld photographers roam the far shore and snap just about everyone who makes it to poolside. The photos can be previewed on video screens in the photo hut just a few yards away. A single 6-by-8-inch photo will set you back $20, but you can get every picture they took of you and your family on a CD for $60. There are frames, too, including one held by a plush doll dolphin for $20.

While touching dolphins seems to be the first order of business for most visitors, don't overlook the **underwater viewing area** (as many people obviously do). It offers a perspective on these graceful beasts that you just don't get from above and, not incidentally, is a wonderful place to wait out those afternoon summer thunderstorms for which Orlando is famous. It will also give you a deeper appreciation of the skill and craft that went into designing the reef-like pool in which the dolphins live. To get there from the petting and feeding area, walk around the pool to your left.

As at all the habitats, SeaWorld staffers make occasional educational presentations. There is usually a staffer sitting on a life guard's raised chair on the beach across from the petting area. Feel free to hail him or her from the sidelines if you have any questions.

Blue Horizons (at Key West Dolphin Stadium) ★ ★ ★ ★ 1/2

Type: Live water show with dolphins, pseudorcas and acrobats

Time: 25 minutes

Short Take: Cirque du Soleil meets Flipper

This show, which rounds out the Key West experience, is Shamu in miniature, with a large dose of Cirque du Soleil-style pizazz thrown in for good measure. Instead of giant killer whales we have the far slimmer bottle-nosed dolphins and pseudorcas, or "false killer whales." The setting is a swirling, multi-level, multi-platform blue extravaganza of flying manta rays and sea foam over the large dolphin pool.

The show is conceived as the fantasy of Marina, a girl who dreams of "a place where our dreams come true." She dives out her window (don't try this at home) and finds herself in a watery world of wonder where she meets Delphis, a dolphin spirit who transforms into a hunky guy in an anatomically correct wet suit, and Aurora, a bird spirit in gaudy red plumage who soars overhead in an aerial ballet.

Dolphins, pseudorcas, acrobats, high divers, parrots and lorikeets, and even an immense buzzard get in on the act in what is one of SeaWorld's most elaborate spectacles. I counted 18 performers, 9 dolphins, and 2 pseudorcas, as well as a passel of parrots.

The debt to Cirque du Soleil is obvious and they carry it off well. An elaborate aerial harness apparatus enables the performers to soar over the pool in graceful circles and gives the razzle-dazzle divers a quick route back to their high platforms for another spectacular leap.

The marine mammals are no slouches either. At one point, all nine dolphins are in the pool in a three-ring circus of amazing behaviors. At one point, two dolphins propel their trainer in a corkscrew pattern through the water. At another, Delphis and Marina take turns riding a pair of dolphins chariot style around the pool, a foot on the back of each animal.

The show ends with all the performers soaring and diving while the air is alive with multi-colored birds. It's a sure-fire crowd pleaser that marks yet another triumph for the SeaWorld creative team.

TurtleTrek ★ ★ ★ ★ ★

Type: Aquatic habitat

Time: Not available at press time

Short Take: For everyone in the family

You don't expect a natural history exhibit to pack an emotional wallop, but this one sure does—and does it very deftly. It is unlikely that anyone in your family will emerge from this experience unaffected. As we go to press, SeaWorld is in the final stages of an extensive renovation of the attraction formerly known as *Manatee Rescue*. Beginning in spring 2012, the habitat's original inhabitants will be joined by a group of sea turtles, adding a whole new dimension, not to mention a new name, to the attraction.

The manatee is a large, slow-moving marine mammal that favors the shallow brackish waterways along the Florida coast, the very same areas that have become a recreational paradise for boaters and fishermen. As man's presence in their habitat has increased, the manatees' numbers have dwindled. The good news is that, thanks in part to the rescue efforts of SeaWorld, the manatee population is on the rebound.

But manatees are not out of danger yet, a fact brought home when we realize that all of the small manatees in the exhibit are orphans and that some of the larger animals have been grievously wounded by their encounters with civilization. One has lost most of its tail, another a front flipper. One of the themes of this exhibit is SeaWorld's ongoing rescue efforts of manatees and other marine mammals. The news that at least one released manatee has reproduced in the wild seems like a major victory.

After viewing the manatees from above—in a pool that re-creates a coastal wetland, with egrets and ibises looking on—we pass into the underwater viewing area where the majesty and fragility of this odd beast become even more apparent. Their slow, graceful movements and their rather goofy faces make the manatee instantly appealing. The aquatic setting is lovely too.

The new underwater habitat, this one filled with salt water instead of fresh, is home to a dozen sea turtles and over 150,000 fish. Interactive touch-screen video monitors provide a self-guided wealth of additional information about the sealife on display and the problems they face from habitat destruction and pollution. Staffers from SeaWorld's education department stroll the viewing area on a somewhat irregular schedule. If any are there when you visit, they will be more than happy to answer your questions.

For the attraction's finale, we enter a circular underwater theater that SeaWorld has transformed into what they describe as "a first-of-its-kind 3-D/360-degree dome theater experience that is completely immersive." What that seems to mean is that the audience stands against circular railings in the center of the room, while high-definition 3-D footage is projected onto the curved ceiling and wall surrounding them. The result is a "hyper-realistic" first-person perspective of the sea turtle's harrowing and heartwarming natural migration, providing a first-ever "turtle's-eye view" of the alien (to us) universe beneath the ocean's surface.

I found this attraction (at least in its previous incarnation) a profoundly moving experience and one to which I return eagerly on each visit. Signs along the exit ramp challenge you to make a personal commitment to help the manatee and other endangered animals. What will you do?

Photo Op: As you leave the exhibit, look for the sculpture of the manatee cow and her calf floating artfully above the pavement. If it's still there, it makes an excellent backdrop for a family photograph.

Journey to Atlantis ★ ★ ★ 1/2

Type: Combination flume ride and roller coaster
Time: About 6 minutes
Short Take: Wet and wild

It just goes to show you: always heed the warnings of crusty old Greek fishermen, no matter how crazy they seem. Of course, the tourist hordes ignore Stavros' sage advice and set sail on a tour of the ancient city of Atlantis, which has mysteriously risen from the Aegean.

Rising some ten stories, Atlantis looks gaudily out of place at SeaWorld, yet it sure looks pretty in the golden glow of the setting sun. But it's not the architecture that draws us here. It's the dizzyingly steep water flume emerging from the city walls and the happy screams of those plunging to a watery splashdown. Wend your way through the Greek-village-themed waiting line and be entertained by the news coverage of the eerie reappearance of Atlantis as you wait for your boat.

The voyage gets off to a peaceful start, but after a benign and quite lovely interlude, the boat is seized by the evil Allura, who I gather is a vengeful ancient spirit of some sort. You are winched higher and higher before being sent on a hair-raising journey that combines the scariest elements of a flume ride and a roller coaster. It's a nifty engineering feat but most people probably won't care as they plunge down the 60-foot flume into a tidal wave of water. Another slow ascent gives you a chance to catch your breath before you zip through a fiendishly hidden mini-roller coaster to another splashdown, as Allura cackles gleefully. It's all over quickly—too quickly for my taste—but you can always head immediately for the end of the line for another go.

It must be said that the story line for this ride is a bit confusing and hard to follow, which bothers some purists. Most people don't seem to care.

Tip: This is a very wet ride, especially if you are in the front row of the eight-passenger boat that serves as the ride vehicle. An inexpensive poncho (which you can get at any of the theme parks) provides pretty good protection. Expensive cameras and other items that might not survive a soaking can be checked as you enter the boat, but they are placed in unlocked lockers and no guarantees are provided. Pay lockers are available near the entrance to the waiting line; they cost 50 cents and if you don't have the change you will have to walk over to the nearby lockers for *Kraken*, where a change machine is available.

As you exit the ride, don't miss the lovely **Jewels of the Sea Aquarium**, just off the inevitable gift shop. Hammerhead sharks and stingrays swim above you in a domed aquarium, while angelfish inhabit the aquarium beneath your feet. Around the walls, don't miss the moon jellyfish that glow enchantingly when you press the light button. Just outside the aquarium and gift shop, playful hidden fountains await to soak the unwary.

Photo Op: Just outside the Jewels of the Sea Aquarium is a plaza with a splendid view of the 60-foot flume plunge. If you don't want to take your own pictures, shots of every boatload of happily terrified cruisers are on sale at the ride exit.

Kraken ★ ★ ★ ★ ★

Type:	Roller coaster
Time:	2 minutes
Short Take:	Aieeee!

When *Kraken* opened, SeaWorld clearly set out to compete head to head with Universal and Disney for coaster bragging rights and, by Neptune, they've succeeded.

Kraken may not be the tallest or fastest coaster in Orlando, but it more than holds its own in the thrills department. One of the neatest (or scariest) things about *Kraken* is that the seats are raised slightly so your feet dangle free. So even though the track is beneath your feet at all times, you don't have the same feeling of connectedness you get on other coasters. Nor do you have the comfort of the overhanging superstructure you get in an inverted coaster. The effect is subtle, yet undeniably terrifying.

For a coaster this fast (they claim speeds "in excess of" 65 mph), *Kraken* is also remarkably smooth. Your head may be pressed against the headrest by the G-forces but it won't be buffeted about. Another thing you may notice (if you aren't screaming too loudly) is that *Kraken* is an unusually quiet coaster. Even if you are standing right next to the fence where *Kraken* dips underground at the end of its run, you can barely hear it. Farther away, it is only the shrieks of the riders you hear in the distance. Another item of note is that the ride designers have made a special effort to accommodate those with large upper torso measurements; specially modified seats in rows four and five of each car can handle those with chest measurements of up to 52 inches. There is also a minimum height requirement of 54 inches.

This is an extremely "aggressive" ride, to use the phrase preferred by the designers. They even have a sign urging those with prosthetic limbs to make sure they are securely fastened! So you will be well-advised to stow everything that's not firmly attached to your body in the pay lockers at the entrance to the ride. Smaller lockers are available at modest cost. A change machine is provided.

Now you're ready for the experience itself. As you make the excruciatingly slow climb to the 15-story apex of the first hill, show off just how cool you are by taking in the panoramic view of the park you get from the top. It may be the last time on this ride you have your eyes open.

As you enter the first drop, you begin to fully appreciate the exquisite horror afforded by *Kraken's* unique design. The effect is less like riding in a roller coaster than like being shot through the air on a jet-propelled chair, all the while turning and twisting head over heels. There are seven loops—at least I think there are seven loops, because I keep forgetting to count—as the coaster soars over water and dips below ground along over 4,000 feet of torturous turquoise and yellow track.

The 119-foot vertical loop, the 101-foot diving loop, the zero-gravity roll, and the cobra roll may all have their equivalents on other coasters, but experiencing them in *Kraken's* raised, exposed seats adds a heightened level of sheer terror that beggars description.

As astonishing as the engineering is, one of the best moments of the ride occurs thanks to the scenic design. It occurs when the coaster dives underground into what is described as the "monster's lair," a tunnel that appears to be on the brink of being totally inundated by a thundering waterfall. But before you have a chance to drown, you are whipped back above the surface and into a flat spin before returning to the starting point. Truly amazing!

On the downside, the experience is short, about two minutes altogether and a full minute of that time is consumed getting you to the top of the first hill and returning you to the starting point after the coaster brakes at the end.

If you'd like to get a preview of *Kraken*, perhaps to decide if you want to subject yourself to its special brand of terror, there are two good vantage points. The first is just to the left of the main entrance, where a viewing area has been thoughtfully provided for the faint of heart. This spot gives you a good view of the first drop and the end of the ride. Over at *Pacific Point Preserve*, you can get a good view of the main section of the ride.

Photo Op: If you have high speed film and a fast shutter speed, you might try for a shot in the viewing area near the large Kraken head where the cars dip underground, just at the ride's end.

And speaking of photos, you can pick up one of you and your terrified fellow riders at the exit to the ride in a variety of mountings, including key chains and snow globes. There is, of course, a fee which can run well over $20.

For those who care about such things, *Kraken* takes its name from a mythical sea creature that, in SeaWorld's version at least, looks a lot like a giant dragon eel, a multicolored cousin of the moray. In a cave near the viewing area by the main entrance, you can see actual dragon eels pretending to be embryos in giant Kraken eggs.

Antarctica—Empire of the Penguin (not yet rated)

Type: Aquatic habitat, plus
Short Take: Wait and see

In late 2011, SeaWorld shuttered their popular but aging walk-through penguin habitat for demolition and redevelopment. When the project, which is projected to take at least 18 months, is complete in spring 2013, the former penguin home will be replaced with an Antarctica-themed experience that SeaWorld describes as their "biggest-ever attraction expansion." Details are scarce at press time, but your journey to the "bottom of the world" is expected to incorporate animal observation areas with a state-of-the-art indoor dark ride to the South Pole, featuring technology that makes each family-friendly trip unique. If the enormous prototype artificial ice walls spotted behind the scenes are any indication, this ride will even grander in scale and more elaborately detailed than the excellent North Pole-themed *Wild Arctic* across the park.

Fear not for the penguins amidst all the construction. They will have a prominent home in the new attraction, which is being billed as "the coldest theme park attraction in the world." In the meantime, SeaWorld is housing their frigid feathered friends in a newly expanded backstage facility.

Pacific Point Preserve ★ ★ ★ ★

Type: Outdoor aquatic habitat
Time: Continuous viewing
Short Take: Don't miss feeding the sea lions

Over 50 sea lions roar and bark with delight in this two-and-a-half-acre, open-air, sunken habitat. SeaWorld's design team traveled to the Pacific Northwest to take molds of the rock outcroppings along the coast to build this remarkable re-creation. Adding to the verisimilitude is a wave machine, similar to those used in the water theme parks, that creates waves of anywhere from a few inches to two feet in height. The viewing area extends entirely around the exhibit, and while the sea lions (and a smaller number of harbor seals) are safely out of reach, it's almost as if you can touch them.

But if you can't pet them, you can feed them. Small trays of fish are available at certain times for the princely sum of $15 or $20, depending on the crowds, (Passport holders get 10% off) and their contents will very quickly disappear down a sea lion's gullet. It's all great fun and, if you aren't careful, you can spend more for their dinner than you will for your own. The sea lions, for their part, have learned how to part you from your smelt and will bark furiously and even leap decoratively up onto the edge of the pool until their hunger is satisfied, which it never is. Fortunately, watching other people feed the sea lions is almost as entertaining as doing it yourself. The feeding stations are open regularly and it is rare that they sell out before closing time.

While their feeding behavior might lead you to believe these animals are tame, they are not. The sea lions you see perform in the *Clyde & Seamore* show just around the corner live separately from their cousins in *Pacific Point*. They have been trained for years and habituated to interacting with humans. The animals in *Pacific Point Preserve* are wild and like all wild animals unpredictable. In other words, don't dangle little Susie over the edge to get her within smelt-tossing range.

Tip: You might want to ask someone on the education staff when the main feeding will take place that day. While the public certainly helps with the feeding, the staff has to make sure that their charges are adequately fed. They do this by serving up fish by the bucketful at least once a day. This is a highly entertaining ritual so it's worthwhile to check the schedule. Also, the handlers have to hand-feed some of the older sea lions and seals who don't compete well for food with their younger rivals. You and your kids will undoubtedly find this part of the feeding particularly touching.

Clyde & Seamore Take Pirate Island (at Sea Lion & Otter Stadium) ★ ★ ★ ★

Type:	Live water show with sea lions, otters, walruses
Time:	25 minutes
Short Take:	The funniest show at SeaWorld

Forget about education. This one's all about high spirits and low humor and it's a sure-fire crowd pleaser. Clyde and Seamore are sea lion versions of Laurel and Hardy, or Ralph Kramden and Ed Norton, or maybe two of the Three Stooges. In any event, they're bumblers.

There's a plot about a search for gold (and fresh fish), a treacherous otter, and (of course) pirates, but it's almost beside the point. The real point of this show is watching Clyde and Seamore cavort up, down, and around the multilevel set and into and out of the pool that rings the lip of the stage. The humor is broad and the little kids love it. One thing that makes the show such a hoot is the slapdash way in which the human performers carry it off, bloopers and all. Some of the gaffes are due to the unpredictability of the animals but other boo-boos seem to be written into the script, although few will suspect as much unless they see the show several times.

If you are lucky, you might get to see a walrus or two make a cameo appearance. Walruses, I am told, are nowhere near as tractable as sea lions and, given their considerable bulk and potential for wreaking havoc, they only appear when they're in the mood. Even then, they may balk at performing, just like a Hollywood star, and the trainers know better than to argue with several tons of balky blubber. As usual, a small child is summoned from the audience to help out (and shake Clyde's flipper). And, of course, there are the usual dire warnings about splash zones, although the wetness quotient is far lower here than at the Shamu show.

Tip: If you arrive more than about 10 minutes early, you will be entertained by **The SeaWorld Mime**. If you arrive fewer than 10 minutes before show time, you may become one of his victims. This is not mime in the cutesy Marcel Marceau tradition—there's no getting trapped inside an invisible box or walking against an imaginary wind. This is mime with an attitude, that mimics, mocks, and plays pranks on the steady stream of people arriving for the show. Those familiar with the work of David Shiner, the clown prince of this genre, will know what to expect. For others, I don't want to give too much away. This is, far and away, the best of SeaWorld's pre-show entertainments. It is an attraction in its own right and not to be missed.

Sea Lions Tonight (Seasonal) ★ ★ ★ ★ ★

Type: Live show
Time: 25 minutes
Short Take: Hilarious sendup

As the title suggests, this show is performed only at night, only once a day, and only when the park is open late. If you are here when this show is being offered, don't miss it!

The goofy guys who brought you Clyde and Seamore let their hair down even farther to bring you this truly funny (and occasionally biting) satire on the *other* shows at SeaWorld. But instead of dolphins and whales, they use sea lions, walruses, and otters. The SeaWorld Mime is dragooned into the show and doesn't seem to be too happy about the dumb things he's called on to do, including standing in for the birds of *Blue Horizons* and donning a whale fluke headpiece for their version of *One Ocean*.

The show pokes good-natured fun at the pretentiousness that lurks just below the surface of shows like *Blue Horizons* and *One Ocean*. Maybe there's a wee bit of jealousy involved, too. In one of the show's funniest bits, the cast members strut and preen as orca trainers, their wet suits bulging with artificially enhanced muscles, while an enormous lumbering walrus stands in for Shamu. There are jabs taken at *Pets Ahoy* and *Kraken* as well. All in all, it adds up to one of the best shows at SeaWorld.

Shark Encounter ★ ★ ★ 1/2

Type: Aquatic habitat
Time: 15 to 20 minutes
Short Take: Up close and personal with some scary fish

In *Shark Encounter*, SeaWorld has very cleverly packaged an aquarium-style display of some of the sea's scariest, ugliest, and most dangerous creatures. The tone and lighting of this exhibit is dark and foreboding, with appropriately ominous soundtrack music, but you needn't worry about any unpleasant surprises. When you get right down to it, it's fish in tanks and far too fascinating to be truly scary to any except perhaps the most suggestible kids.

The attraction wraps around **Sharks Underwater Grill** and, in fact, the restaurant has commandeered what used to be the big attraction—a massive tank brimming with a variety of shark species, with huge picture window viewing areas. You still get a nifty view of the sharks, as we shall see, but something was lost from the attraction when the restaurant was added.

You enter this habitat to the left of the restaurant. A short corridor leads to a clear acrylic tunnel through an artificial tropical reef. This is home to the moray eels—nasty-looking snake-like fish. The moray's coating of yellow slime over its blue flesh gives it a sickly green tint. At first, all you see are the many varieties of reef fish swimming about, but closer inspection reveals the morays poking their heads out of their holes. The more you look, the more you see. There are dozens and dozens of the creatures hidden in the crevices of the reef. From time to time one swims free, undulating its long body right overhead. Looking up you see the surface of the water. The tank has been designed to mimic the natural habitat as closely as possible; the lighting comes from a single over-head source, standing in for the sun.

The tunnel curves around and into a viewing area in which several tanks hold specimens probably best kept separate. First is the delicate and intricately camouflaged lion fish. Looks are deceiving here, because the lion fish's feathery appendages are actually poisoned spines that are highly toxic to swimmers unfortunate enough to come in contact with them.

Tried any fugu at your local sushi bar? You may want to reconsider after viewing the puffer fish on display here. Fugu, as the fish is known in Japan, is one of the world's most poisonous fish. The Japanese consider its edible portions a delicacy, and licensed fugu chefs carefully pare away the poisonous organs. Despite their precautions, several people die each year from fugu poisoning. Swimming unconcernedly with the puffer fish are surgeon fish, a pretty species that carries the marine equivalent of switchblades concealed near the tail. When attacked (or grabbed by unwary fishermen), they lash out with their hidden weapon, inflicting a nasty gash. Across the way are barracuda, looking every bit as terrifying as when I first encountered them while snorkeling in the Caribbean. Had I been to SeaWorld first, I would have known that an attack was unlikely and probably would have made less of a fool of myself.

As you walk down the long tunnel toward the shark encounter that gives the attraction its name, wall displays fill you in on little known shark facts. For example, did you know that a shark's liver takes up nearly 90% of its body cavity and accounts for nearly a quarter of its weight? Scientists theorize that, since the liver contains a great deal of oil and since oil is lighter than water, the shark's huge liver may contribute to its buoyancy.

Look for a series of rectangular windows on your right. Here you can get a glimpse of what the lucky diners in the restaurant are seeing. It's a spectacular sight, even from this somewhat restricted vantage point and it may be enough to make you decide to have lunch there.

At the bottom of the zig-zag tunnel, you reach the attraction's culmination—a slow, stately ride on a conveyer belt through a 124-foot tunnel that takes you right down the middle of the shark tank. About a foot thick, the clear acrylic walls of the tunnel are supporting 450 tons of man-made salt water over your head. Don't worry, you're perfectly safe; the acrylic can withstand a tromping by 372 elephants (as you are informed on exiting).

All around and above you swim small sawtooth sharks, brown sharks, nurse sharks, bull sharks, lemon sharks, and sandpiper sharks. There are no giants here but what the specimens lack in size they more than make up for in number. If you ever encounter sharks in the wild, hopefully there will be nowhere near this many of them.

The next stop is the exit and the blinding Florida sunshine. If you overlooked the pool at the entrance to Sharks Underwater Grill when you entered, take a moment to check it out as you leave. Look for the bridge over a shallow pool in which some of the smaller and less threatening shark specimens are displayed. Here are small hammerheads and nurse sharks along with a variety of rays, including the jet-black bat ray.

Tip: You can satisfy your curiosity and get a great view of the restaurant's shark viewing windows by heading for the bar and having a cool drink. It's seldom crowded at the bar and often you can walk right in, past families waiting for a table. If you're hungry, the full menu is served at the bar and at a number of nearby raised tables.

A'Lure, The Call of the Ocean (at Nautilus Theatre) ★ ★ ★

Type: Indoor stage show
Time: 25 minutes
Short Take: An undersea dance and acrobatic fantasy

If you can't afford the astronomical ticket prices of Cirque de Soleil over at Disney, this wordless blend of acrobatics, mime, and dance makes a passable substitute.

The pantomimed plot, such as it is, is fairly standard: boy meets mermaid, boy loses mermaid to wicked sea-witch, boy engineers a coup and installs his fishy friend on the undersea throne. The pseudo-Atlantean story is as insubstantial as the soap bubbles that drop from the ceiling; it's an excuse to shove as many Cirque-style acrobatic acts on stage as possible. There are pole climbers bouncing off trampolines, girls tossing yo-yo-like spinning "diablos" skyward and catching them on lengths of string, and acrobats soaring overhead on long strands of fabric. One act follows another in an overwhelming flood. These talented athletes all perform interesting stunts; I especially liked the guy who spins inside a sort of steel hula hoop. Sadly, they are saddled with clichéd dance choreography and costumes that look salvaged from Siegfried and Roy. But the show is colorful and kinetic enough to keep the kiddies occupied if you're looking for a 20-minute break in the A/C.

Note: From time to time, acts change. Contortionists become acrobats and vice versa. However, the overall shape of the show has remained remarkably stable since it first opened.

Paddle Boats ★ ★ 1/2

Type: Just what it says
Time: As long as you want, one half hour at a time
Short Take: Can be skipped

In Bayside Lagoon you can rent large, pink, flamingo-shaped paddle boats for a leisurely outing on the lagoon. The boats seat two adults comfortably and cost $5 per person for a half hour. If you have the time and enjoy this sort of activity, you may want to give them a go.

Life jackets come with your rental and are required wearing. You must be at least 56 inches tall to take a boat out alone, smaller children (except handheld infants) may ride with an adult. Check the park's daily calendar for opening hours, which vary.

THE SOUTH END

The southern half of SeaWorld lies to the right of the *Skytower* on the official park map, most of it across the Boardwalk, the wooden walkway that takes you over Bayside Lagoon to Shamu Stadium. The whole feel of this side of the park is quite a bit different, with its large open spaces between huge modern stadiums and buildings.

Once again, I describe the attractions in geographical rather than thematic order, starting from The Terrace restaurant (reviewed later) and continuing in a clockwise direction around Bayside Lagoon.

Arcade and Midway Games ★ 1/2

Type:	Video and "skill" games arcades
Time:	As long as you want
Short Take:	For video game addicts

My feelings about these money-siphoning operations, located near the Shamu Stadium, can be summed up pretty easily—why bother? The main reason you paid good money to come to SeaWorld is just paces away and everything you can do here, you can do elsewhere for less money. That being said, these venues are clean and attractive and the prizes at Midway Games are better than most.

One Ocean (at Shamu Stadium) ★ ★ ★ ★ ★

Type:	Live stadium show
Time:	25 minutes
Short Take:	The acme of the SeaWorld experience

Could there be a more graceful animal on Earth than a 5,000-pound orca? You won't think so after seeing this visually dazzling demonstration of "tricks" put on by the Shamu family.

Actually, they aren't "tricks" at all in the common sense of the term. They are simply extensions of natural behaviors that have been reinforced by the whales' trainers with patient attention and liberal handfuls of smelt. Nor is *One Ocean* to be confused with mere entertainment. In keeping with SeaWorld's commitment to conserving the marine environment and saving endangered marine species, this show teaches implicit lessons about the inter-connectedness of nature and the importance of the marine mammal husbandry practiced at SeaWorld Orlando and its sister parks around the country.

The stars of the show are members of the family *orsinus orca*, commonly known as killer whales and affectionately known by nearly everyone who visits SeaWorld as Shamu. The first killer whale ever captured was named Namu after a town in British Columbia. Shamu means "mate of Namu" in the language of British Columbia's native people. Of course, different whales appear in different shows, so the mammoth performers in this show are, in a sense, playing the role of Shamu.

The "stage" is a huge 7-million-gallon pool filled with man-made salt water kept at a chilly 55 degrees (although the whales are used to much chillier water in their natural habitats) and completely filtered every 30 minutes. At the back is a small island platform for the trainers, above which looms a large structure in the shape of a killer whale's tail fluke and four video screens that move, merge, and spin as the moment requires. The front of the stage is formed by a 6-foot high Lucite wall that gives those in the first several rows an underwater view. Downstage center is a shallow lip that allows Shamu to "beach" herself for our enjoyment.

SeaWorld's latest signature show dispenses with the sappy video testimonials from trainers that slowed down its predecessor, *Believe,* in favor of largely wordless marine wildlife footage. There are also high-powered fountains installed around the stadium that shoot plumes of water into the pool, adding to the razzle-dazzle. But the real focus of the show is the awe-inspiring and absolutely delightful interaction of the whales and their trainers. The whales leap, glide, dive, and roll with a grace that belies their huge size. Many times, two trainers working with two whales will perform in perfect synchronization. They make it look easy and natural, but my guess is that it is fiendishly difficult to pull these tandem tricks off.

The warnings of a "big wave" that precede the show's grand finale are in deadly earnest. If you're sitting in the first 14 rows, you'll likely get very, very, very wet. Actually, it's possible to sit in this section and escape a drenching—I've done it. But if you happen to be in the direct line of one of the salvos of chilly salt water hurled into the audience by the cupped rear fluke of a five-ton whale, you will be soaked to the skin. It's pretty much a matter of luck. Some of the biggest laughs come when people who have fled the "splash zone" for the higher ground of the first promenade get nailed anyway by a particularly forceful fluke-full of water.

It must be noted that the tragic 2010 drowning death of trainer Dawn Brancheau has significantly altered how SeaWorld presents its shows. Until new safety technology (like a quick-lifting pool floor) is developed, you won't see SeaWorld trainers riding whaleback or being shot 30 feet into the air off the nose of an orca as in performances past.

The best seats in the house. Many kids (especially 9- to 13-year-old boys) will insist on sitting in the splash zone and will feel cheated if they don't get soaked. But adults should consider sitting here as well. If you wear a rain poncho (which you may already have from a visit to another park) you can protect yourself relatively well, and these seats do offer an excellent view, especially underwater. But the seats higher up, where you are assured of staying dry, offer excellent sight lines and the video coverage of the show assures that you won't miss anything.

Tip: Between shows, follow the pathways that ring Shamu Stadium to locate the ramp to the **Underwater Viewing Area** around back. This is a not-to-be-missed perspective on these magnificent creatures. Especially enchanting is the opportunity to watch Shamu and her much smaller calf, Baby Shamu, swimming gracefully in tandem. The whales are rotated through this viewing pool, so there's no guarantee that a specific whale will be there when you drop by. There are benches in front of the picture windows and if the crowds are thin enough you can rest while you watch.

Shamu Rocks (Seasonal) ★ ★ ★ ★

Type: Rock show with killer whales
Time: 20 minutes
Short Take: Shamu and trainers at play

When the park is open late, this is the last show of the day in Shamu Stadium. It is somewhat shorter and different in tone but no less exciting and enjoyable. This time around, there's little or no attempt to "educate" you. Instead, the focus is on ear-splitting rock (with a live guitarist making a splashy cameo appearance) and a dazzling computer-generated video show that really puts those spinning video screens through their paces. The trainers appear in glitzier wet suits, some with red sashes around their waists, and do some disco dance routines designed to coax the audience into joining in.

The whales seem almost an afterthought, which is too bad. Still, they do some amazing things like leaping in tandem or soaring completely out of the water and doing a back flip. I would have liked less rock and more Shamu, but you can't have everything.

Some things don't change, however. The show still ends with a barrage of water to the lower seating area. Why tamper with success?

During the holiday season, this show is tweaked to become *Shamu Christmas Miracles*. Imagine the standard Shamu shtick set to religious and secular seasonal music, and you get the general idea.

Shamu's Happy Harbor ★ ★ ★ ★ 1/2

Type: Play area
Time: 30 minutes to an hour
Short Take: Great for young kids, toddlers, and their long-suffering parents

If *Wild Arctic* (below) represents an attempt to reach out to the thrill-seeking segment of the tourist population, *Shamu's Happy Harbor* seeks to appeal to the youngster too antsy or uninterested to sit still for a fish—no matter how big it is. Here is a way for even very young children to be entertained in that most effective of ways—by doing things for themselves.

Shamu's Happy Harbor is dominated by a four-story, L-shaped, steel framework painted in shades of sea green and pink. At first glance it looks like a construction site gone very wrong. Closer inspection reveals it to be an intricate maze of cargo netting, plastic tubes, and slides that kids can climb up and through to their heart's content. Some chambers in this maze contain tire swings, just like the ones in backyards across America, except that these are two stories above ground level. The cargo netting is completely enclosed in smaller-mesh black netting. While there's no danger of falling, the upper reaches of the structure are quite high and some smaller children may become frightened.

It's not just for kids, either. Adults can join in, too, although some of the parents I watched obviously wished they weren't allowed. While the corridors of netting are big enough to accommodate anyone, the tubes are designed with smaller people in mind. Thus, the average sedentary grown-up will get quite a workout going through them. You're allowed to climb up the netting but stairs are provided for the trip down. Too many middle-aged sprained ankles is my guess.

The larger structure of *Shamu's Happy Harbor* is complemented by any number of lesser activities, called "elements," all of them action-oriented. These will keep kids busy for hours unless you can drag them away to the next show at the Sea Lion and Otter Stadium. There are four-sided, canvas "mountains" that kids can climb with the help of knotted ropes and then slide down, and large inflated rooms in which kids 54 inches and shorter can bounce and tumble.

Standing in front of it all is a kid-sized schooner, the **Wahoo Two**, just waiting to be explored. Nearby, the **Water Works** offers a jumble of tubes and netting that is constantly splashed with jets of water. The perimeter of the Harbor is ringed with a series of smaller kiddie rides, the most elaborate of which is the **Sea Carousel**, a cute kiddie-friendly ride with a capacity of 64 aboard colorful sea creatures in four concentric rows. The choices of critter range from the cute to the rather scary, so guide your child accordingly. On the other side, you will find **Flying Fiddler** (42 in. minimum height) **Jazzy Jellies** (42 in. minimum), **Ocean Commotion** (42 in. minimum), **Swishy Fishies** (36 in. minimum), and, most interestingly, the **Shamu Express** (38 in. minimum), a kiddie roller coaster with cars cleverly themed with Shamu-like tail flukes. At the other end of the Harbor, you'll find **Shamu's Splash Attack**, where you can pay to sling water bombs at a friend. Buckets of seven water-filled balloons are two for $5, and **Op's Beat**, where kids can bang on hanging steel drums to their heart's content.

Shamu's Happy Harbor is an ideal place for parents to take the squirmy baby of the family when he or she gets restless with the more grown-up attractions at SeaWorld.

Photo Op: Just opposite *Shamu's Happy Harbor* is a made-to-order photo backdrop. It's a life-sized model of Shamu and Baby Shamu perfectly posed under a sun awning (to protect your shot from that annoying glare). Place your kid on Shamu's back and click away.

Wild Arctic ★ ★ ★ for the ride ★ ★ ★ ★ ★ for the habitat

Type: Simulator ride plus a spectacular habitat

Time: 5 minutes for the ride; as long as you want for the habitat

Short Take: A SeaWorld must-see

That large, techno-modern, warehouse-like building near Shamu Stadium houses one of SeaWorld's most popular attractions—a devilishly clever combination of thrill ride with serene aquatic habitat. All in all, this is one of the most imaginative attractions in Orlando. Mercifully, the waiting line snakes through an area that is shielded from the blazing sun, because the lines can get long.

Tip: To avoid long waits, you will be well advised to see *Wild Arctic* early in the morning. Another option is to visit during performances at nearby Shamu Stadium. But time your visit carefully; the waiting line fills up very quickly when the Shamu show empties out.

During our wait, we are entertained by a fascinating video presentation on the lifestyle of the Inuit peoples who inhabit the frozen realm of the Arctic. And during our slow journey through the line, we are asked to make an important decision: Do we want to take the helicopter ride to the base station or do we want to go by land? It's a choice between "motion" and "non-motion" and it can be important.

The Wild Arctic Ride

If you choose to take the helicopter, be prepared for a whale of a simulator ride (you should pardon the expression). We begin our journey by crossing a metal bridge into the vehicle itself. Once all 59 voyagers are strapped in, the staff exits, the doors close, and the "helicopter" takes off.

The ride, which lasts all of about five minutes, simulates a flight aboard an amphibious (not to mention submersible) helicopter to a research station deep within the Arctic Circle. Despite the gale warnings crackling over the radio, our friendly pilot can't help doing a little sightseeing—including putting the rotors into "whisper mode" so we can drop in on a polar bear family and dipping below the waves for a glimpse of a narwhal. But his unscheduled detours exact their price and soon we are caught in that gale. At first the pilot prudently puts down on a glacier to await a better reading on the weather but the glacier gives way and we plummet headlong toward the icy waters below.

At the last second, the pilot gets the rotors whirling and we zoom away from certain death. Next, he decides we'll be safer flying through a crevasse, away from the howling winds, but we fly straight into and through an avalanche. Finally, we break through into the clear and the Arctic base station lies dead ahead.

It's a real stomach-churner; as I write these words I realize that I'm becoming a little queasy just remembering it all. The action is fast, abrupt, and violent. You'll find yourself being tossed from side to side as you grip the armrests and scream—in excitement or terror, depending on your mood. Alas, the quality of the visual effects and motion simulation in this attraction has not kept pace with the times, and its virtual reality suffers greatly in comparison with Disney's revamped *Star Tours* and Universal's *Simpsons* simulators.

Those who choose the "non-motion" alternative for their voyage to the *Wild Arctic*, are escorted past the three simulators to a stationary room where they watch the same video, before entering the Arctic base station.

Tip: The non-motion line moves much, much faster than the line for the simulator ride. If you are pressed for time, you might want to consider making the ultimate sacrifice (or use this as an excuse for missing what can be a very scary ride).

Note: You may want to take an over-the-counter medication before you head for the park if you are prone to motion sickness but would like to experience the ride.

The Wild Arctic Aquatic Habitat

Once you wobble off the simulator ride, you enter SeaWorld's most elaborately conceived aquatic habitat, one that would have been a five-star attraction even without the exhilarating thrill ride that precedes it.

The conceit here is that scientists have discovered the wrecked ships from the expedition of John Franklin, a real-life British explorer who disappeared in 1845 while searching for the nonexistent Northwest Passage. The wreck, it seems, has drawn a wide variety of wildlife seeking shelter and prey, so the scientists "stabilized" the wreck and constructed their observation station around it.

The first "room" of the habitat simulates an open-air space, with the domed ceiling standing in for the Arctic sky. A sign informs us that we are 2,967 miles from SeaWorld in Florida. Gray beluga whales (the name is derived from the Russian word for "white") are being fed in a pool directly in front of us. Thankfully, SeaWorld has not attempted to mimic Arctic temperatures.

Next, we enter the winding tunnels of the research station proper. The walls alternate between the ancient wood of the wrecked vessels and the corrugated steel of the modern structure. We view the animals through thick glass walls; on the other side, temperatures are maintained at comfortably frigid levels for their Arctic inhabitants.

Art imitates reality here in the form of the SeaWorld research assistants, clad in their distinctive red parkas. They are here to answer guests' questions but they are also carrying out valuable scientific research by painstakingly recording the behavior patterns of the polar bears and other animals in the exhibits in an attempt to find ways to short-circuit the repetitive motion patterns that befall many animals in captivity. One strategy has been to hide food in nooks and crannies of the habitat, encouraging the animals to use true-to-nature hunting behaviors to find their food. By the way, the fish swimming with the polar bears usually avoid winding up on the dinner table, although the bears sometimes just can't resist taking a swipe at them.

For most people, the highlight of this habitat will be the polar bears, including the famous twins Klondike and Snow, born in the Denver Zoo, abandoned by their mother, nursed through infancy by their zookeepers, and then placed with SeaWorld as the facility best equipped to nurture them to adulthood. They're adults now and usually aren't in the habitat at the same time. Indeed, adult polar bears are solitary creatures in the wild so this arrangement mimics reality to a great extent.

There are also enormous walruses swimming lazily in a separate pool. Harbor seals appear in a video presentation showing the animals in their natural habitat. The narration is cleverly disguised as the radio transmissions of the scientists gathering the footage for research purposes.

After viewing the animals on the surface, we walk down a series of ramps to an underwater viewing area for a completely different and utterly fascinating perspective. Video monitors show what's happening on the surface and simple controls allow visitors to move the cameras remotely to follow the animals when they climb out of the pool. The set decoration below the surface is every bit as imaginative as it is above, simulating the Arctic Sea beneath the ice shelf.

There's much to explore here, including displays that let kids crawl through a simulated polar bear den or poke their heads through the ice, just like a seal. Dotted throughout the exhibit are touch-sensitive video monitors that let us learn more about the animals we are viewing and the environment in which they live. Just before the exit ramp, a small room offers a variety of interactive entertainments.

One lets you plan a six-week expedition to the North Pole, selecting the mode of transportation, date of departure, food supply, and wardrobe. Then you get to find out how wisely you planned. Another computer offers up a printout that tells, among other interesting facts, how many people have been born since the date of your birth.

Note: During the past several holiday seasons, SeaWorld has transformed this attraction into the *Polar Express Experience*, based on the popular picture book and creepy CGI Tom Hanks film. Incoherently edited clips from the movie are poorly synchronized to the shaking simulators of the ride portion (redressed as train cars) making the ride even more discombobulating than usual. However, the giant Christmas tree and Santa photo-op added to the walk-through are quite charming and well worth a look.

Tip: The exit is through the Arctic Shop and a prominent sign says "No Re-Entry." However, late in the day, it appears to be easy to sneak back in through the back door if you'd like another peek at this fabulous habitat.

Reflections (Seasonal) ★ ★ ★ ★ 1/2

Type:	Light show and fireworks
Time:	20 minutes
Short Take:	A fitting finale

During peak season (particularly summertime), guests are invited into the rarely used Atlantis Bayside Stadium after sunset for some eye-candy to end the day. SeaWorld has tried some of the elements in *Reflections* before, but now they have been all wrapped up in what's billed as the largest and most spectacular finale in the park's history.

Positioned as springing from "one drop of water," *Reflections* is a phantasmagoria of water- and sea-themed special effects that unfold in the lagoon just offshore from *The Waterfront*. Hundred-foot-tall walls of water spray serve as screens on which laser images of the sea are projected, as flames erupt and fireworks shoot skyward. There are even underwater light effects. It's a joyful (if cloying) mishmash that's sure to dazzle and send folks off to the parking lots in a jolly mood, though it's unlikely to make anyone forget *IllumiNations* down the road at Epcot.

Tip: Even if the stadium is full, you can still see most of the show's effects by standing along the water's edge anywhere outside the venue.

OTHER ADVENTURES

Yes, you can interact with the animals at SeaWorld—if you have the money and can meet these programs' age and height requirements. SeaWorld offers a number of "Behind the Scenes" guided tours, as well as animal interactions and educational activities. The guided tours carry a not-so-nominal additional charge (ranging in price from $40 to $399 including tax), over and above your admission price, but offer some opportunities to interact with or learn about the animals here that you'd be hard-pressed to find elsewhere.

Despite the high prices, the programs are very much in demand and arrangements have to be made well in advance of your visit. Reservations for all these programs can be made by calling (800) 406-2244 or (407) 363-2380. Or you can book online through seaworldparks.com.

Reservations can also be made at the Tour desk near the front entrance to the park. You'll find it almost directly ahead as you pass through the entrance turnstiles. Most program fees are non-refundable, although you may be able to reschedule. When you purchase your tours, you will be given a chit with the name and time of your tour. This serves as your "ticket" and lets the guide know who belongs to the tour and who doesn't. Tours begin at different points in the park. The meeting points are marked with signs. You will be given directions to them when you sign up.

Behind the Scenes Tour

SeaWorld is far more than "just" a theme park. This engrossing and entertaining 90-minute "backstage" tour highlights SeaWorld's role as a major rescuer and rehabilitator of aquatic—and other—animals. What you see on this tour will depend on which animals are currently in the park's care. You will likely get to see manatees and sea turtles that have been injured, typically by the carelessness of Man. You may see some dolphins, but they are usually here for reasons other than injury. Thanks to its reputation, SeaWorld is sometimes given injured animals that are not part of its usual stock in trade—like snakes, rabbits, and exotic birds. These, too, are on display. You'll also get to touch a shark, explore a hidden polar bear den, and interact with a penguin. 10% of your $40 admission ($10 ages 3 to 9) will be donated to the SeaWorld & Busch Gardens Conservation Fund to support conservation projects around the world.

Dolphins Up-Close Tour

If you're not including a visit to Discovery Cove (see *Chapter 6*) in your vacation, you can still interact with a dolphin, maybe two or three, by taking this informative 45-minute tour. It has the additional advantage of being one of the least expensive ways to play with dolphins (at $50 per adult, $30 ages 3 to 9) and having no age restrictions.

The experience begins at the animal rehab section where dolphins, manatees, and sea turtles are cared for when they're sick or just need a little R&R. The education staffers who run these tours are extremely knowledgeable, so feel free to pepper them with questions; it's a great chance to get a free education on dolphin lore.

The culmination and undeniable highlight of the tour is a private visit to the dolphin feeding area at *Dolphin Cove*. The tour group is broken up into family units and each family gets plenty of face time with a dolphin or two. You will have an opportunity to touch, rub and scratch these delightful creatures, shake their flippers and have them respond to some simple commands. Feeding is handled by staffers. In its own way, this experience is just as much fun as actually swimming with the dolphins at Discovery Cove. And photographers record it all for posterity.

If you want an "Up-Close" animal experience but dolphins aren't your priority, or you want to save a few bucks, similar one-hour tours are also offered focusing on either penguins or the sea lion stars of *Clyde and Seamore*. Both tours include opportunities to touch, feed, and take photos with your preferred creature, for $40 per person ($10 ages 3 to 9).

Marine Mammal Keeper Experience

Think you'd like to rescue injured manatees or care for beluga whales, seals, and other marine mammals? If you've got $399 (discounted 10% for passholders), are at least 13 years old, 52 inches tall, and can climb a flight of stairs and lift 15 pounds, and can get yourself to the park by 6:30 a.m., here's your chance to find out. Up to four guests per day get to work with SeaWorld's caregivers, helping to prepare the mammals' food (each species has a special diet) and feed and care for them. The experience lasts eight hours (6:30 a.m. to 2:30 p.m.) and the price includes park admission, lunch, and a souvenir T-shirt.

Beluga Interaction Program

SeaWorld's latest animal encounter revolves around the snowy white beluga whales that inhabit the *Wild Arctic* exhibit. This innovative two-hour experience allows you to step into the artfully designed Arctic environment and actually dangle your feet in the chilly 55-degree water of SeaWorld's simulated Arctic Ocean.

The adventure begins when you and up to three other intrepid souls don a much needed wet suit and take a tour of the behind-the-scenes area of the exhibit. Then you become part of the show for the tourists as you step into the exhibit itself and sit on the simulated icy shore of the whale's tank. Under the watchful eyes of two trainers, you will have a chance to pet and feed Spooky, a 1,700-pound bundle of beluga. You'll even get a cold peck on the cheek. Sadly, or perhaps fortunately, you never get a chance to slip into the bone-chilling water.

The fee is $149 per person ($199 with a souvenir photo package). Participants must be at least 13 years old.

Family Adventures

SeaWorld offers a smorgasbord of special activities, including Shamu-themed birthday parties ($850 plus tax for up to 20 kids and adults), day camps ($210 to $289), and sleepover programs for kids from kindergarten through the eighth grade (roughly ages 5 through 13). Year-round sleepover programs offer bonding experiences for kids and their parents, including such treats as a Halloween outing to *Shark Encounter*. These overnight events cost $78 per person (including tax).

For more information on these programs call (866) 479-2267 or (407) 363-2380; passport holders can call (800) 406-2244 for information on discounts. The email address is education@seaworld.org. A brochure spells out the registration process in some detail. A complete health history and medical release form must accompany all registrations.

Chapter Six:

Discovery Cove

NOT TOO LONG AGO, THE NEWSPAPERS CARRIED A SHORT PIECE ABOUT A 14-year-old Italian boy saved from drowning in the Gulf of Manfredonia by a dolphin. The lad, a non-swimmer, fell off a sailboat and was sinking under the waves when he felt something pushing him upward. "When I realized it was Filippo, I hung on to him," the boy was quoted as saying. One can only assume that Filippo is Italian for Flipper!

This is only the latest example of a tale that has been told since antiquity. The frescoes of the ancient Minoan civilization of Crete are alive with playful dolphins, and Greek literature is peppered with accounts of dolphins saving wrecked sailors. So humankind's fascination with this playful and occasionally lifesaving creature has a long and honorable pedigree. And as the story about the boy from Manfredonia illustrates, *Flipper*, the hit TV show about a preternaturally precocious dolphin and his towheaded sidekick, clearly has a hold on the world's imagination many years after its original prime time run.

The marketing geniuses at SeaWorld were not blind to this intense fascination with the stars of their animal shows and some years ago instituted a program (now discontinued) that allowed a small number of guests to duck backstage at SeaWorld and actually meet and swim with the stars of the show. Out of this somewhat makeshift idea, SeaWorld has created Discovery Cove, a whole new class of theme park, the first one to be designed specifically for one-to-one human-animal interactions. At Discovery Cove you can not only swim with dolphins but cruise with stingrays, have tropical fish nibble at your fingers, and let exotic birds perch on your head and shoulders while you feed them by hand.

Because of its unique mission, Discovery Cove has been carefully designed to accommodate a limited number of visitors. Only 1,000 people can come to Discovery Cove each day and only 750 of them will be able to swim with the dolphins. Consequently, reservations are mandatory, whether you will be swimming with the dolphins or not. Discovery Cove will admit walk-ups for its "non-swim" program (i.e. you don't get to interact with the dolphins) *if* there is room. That is a very iffy proposition during the warmer months, but your odds of getting in on short notice improve dramatically in the winter.

This limited-capacity policy is, first and foremost, for the protection of the animals, but it has undeniable benefits for the human visitor. The park clearly has room for more than a thousand, so there is plenty of space to spread out on the expansive beaches. No scrambling for lounge chairs, no shoulder-to-shoulder sunbathing and only the very occasional traffic jam at prime snorkeling spots.

Before You Come

Because of its limited capacity and obvious popularity, a visit to Discovery Cove demands advance planning. Reservations are mandatory and making reservations six months or more in advance is not such a silly idea. In fact, reservations can be made up to a year in advance. Somewhat to the surprise of Discovery Cove's marketing people, more visitors (over 50%) want to swim with the dolphins than had been anticipated. So if a dolphin interaction is your goal, the sooner you book, the better your chances.

While it is extremely unlikely that you will be able to book a dolphin swim on short notice, it can happen, especially if you can be flexible on dates. Cancellations do occur. If you want to visit Discovery Cove and not swim with the dolphins, your chances of getting in at the last minute are only slightly better.

The best plan is to phone regularly before your visit and drop by in person once you have reached Orlando. Obviously, the more people in your party who want to swim with the dolphins, the less likely it is you will be successful. It is also possible that there will be openings for just two people when you have a party of four.

There are two ways to make reservations, by phone or on the Internet. The toll-free reservation line is (877) 434-7268. Overseas visitors can call (407) 370-1280. You can make a reservation for the day you visit but you cannot reserve a specific time to swim with the dolphins until you arrive at the park, which is a good incentive to arrive early on the day of your visit. More on this later. The Internet address is

www.discoverycove.com

When's the Best Time To Come?

Although I don't generally recommend coming to Orlando at the height of the summer if you can possibly avoid it, the tropical island beach resort ambiance of Discovery Cove makes it a delightful place to spend a blistering hot summer's day. The salt water pools are kept nice and cool for the animals and make for a bracing dip. Of course, summer brings with it the increased likelihood of stormy weather. Dolphin interactions will be held in the rain, but will be cancelled if there is lightning in the area.

In late spring and early fall, the weather should be closer to ideal. Winter in Orlando can range from the pleasant to the chilly. At this time of the year, the weather may not be ideal for lounging on the beach but the water temperature may be warmer than the air temperature. On the other hand, crowds are generally smaller during the cooler months and the non-swim package is discounted in January and February (see below). Wet suits are available to ease any discomfort of in-the-water activities.

Getting There

Discovery Cove is located just off I-4, near SeaWorld, on Central Florida Parkway so the driving directions are similar. From the south (i.e. traveling east on I-4) use Exit 71 and you will find yourself pointed directly toward Discovery Cove; it's a little more than half a mile along on your right, a short distance past the SeaWorld entrance on the left.

From the north (i.e. traveling west on I-4), get off at Exit 72, onto the Beach-line Line Expressway (Route 528). Take the first exit and loop around to International Drive. Turn left and proceed to Central Florida Parkway and turn right. The Discovery Cove entrance will be on your left, almost immediately after turning.

Self-parking is **free** and just a short walk from the entrance. Unfortunately, there is no valet parking. You can drop members of your party at the front door, but you will then have to handle the parking chores yourself.

Opening and Closing Times

The official opening hours are 9:00 a.m. to 5:30 p.m. but since the first dolphin swim begins before 9:00 (as early as 7:30 or 8:00 during peak periods), the doors are open earlier. It is also possible to linger until 6:00 before you are politely pointed to the exit. My personal recommendation is to arrive early, about 8:00 or 8:15, if you are participating in the dolphin swim. I provide some more advice on timing your dolphin swim later. On the other hand, if you are coming in winter, when the first dolphin swim isn't until 10:00 a.m., you can afford to sleep in a bit. If you choose the "Twilight Discovery" package, you don't have to arrive until three in the afternoon.

The Price of Admission

Prepare yourself for a shock. Discovery Cove is probably the most expensive theme park you will ever visit. But before you flip immediately to the next chapter, read on. On closer examination, Discovery Cove offers extremely good value for your investment. In my opinion, this very special park is worth every penny, especially when you consider that your Discovery Cove admission brings with it 14 days of "free" admission to either SeaWorld or Busch Gardens Tampa, your choice.

There are a multitude of "seasons" at Discovery Cove, each with its own pricing. The lowest (read: cheapest) season is in January; peak season runs from mid-June through early August. In between, prices can vary from day to day. The best way to check prices during your visit is through discoverycove.com. At press time, prices (including tax) for everyone over 6 years of age were as follows:

All-Inclusive Day Package (includes the dolphin swim):
　　　Lowest season:　　　$211.94
　　　Highest season:　　　$318.44

Non-Swim Day Package:
　　　Lowest season:　　　$137.39
　　　Highest season:　　　$179.99

Children under 3 are **free**, but all others are charged the same rate as adults. Children must be at least 6 years old to swim with the dolphins, so kids between 3 and 6 will pay the non-swim rate.

If those prices didn't take your breath away, perhaps you'd like to upgrade to the **Trainer for a Day** program. For a mere $530.37 (including tax) in peak season, or $423.87 during low season, you will be treated to a "enhanced dolphin interaction and training encounter" as well as a number of other behind-the-scenes activities. Participants must be at least 6 and those under 13 must be accompanied by a paying adult.

Eating in Discovery Cove

Discovery Cove has moved to an all-inclusive model, which means that a hot breakfast buffet and an all-you-can eat lunch are included in the price of admission. Both are served cafeteria-style at the **Laguna Grill**, an imposing Polynesian-style structure about halfway into the park. Although the service style may bring back memories of your high school lunch room, the food is surprisingly good if somewhat limited in choice. All seating is outdoors, most of it well shaded.

There are two **beach bars** located elsewhere in the park, one near the *Dolphin Lagoon* and the other near the stingray pool and *Aviary*. Here you can get soft drinks, iced tea, fruit punch, and lemonade as well as beer and wine coolers. Chips, cookies, and fresh fruit are also available, as are more elaborate frozen alcoholic concoctions (for an additional cost).

Shopping in Discovery Cove

The relentless merchandising that characterizes virtually all theme parks is mercifully muted at Discovery Cove. The major shopping venue, **Tropical Gifts**, another Polynesian-style building, is strategically located near the main entrance, so you can pick up the bathing suit you desperately need as you enter and the high-priced souvenir you almost certainly do not need as you leave. There is a large variety of dolphin figurines and sculptures in all price ranges; the more elaborate sculptures can range up to $20,000.

Farther into the park is an open air shop artfully located *across* the path, so you pretty much have to walk through it. It specializes in more practical items, like sunglasses and such.

Good Things To Know About . . .

Access for the Disabled. Discovery Cove has provided ramps with handrails into many of the water areas. Those who can maneuver themselves into the shallows of the Dolphin Lagoon, will be able to experience the dolphin swim. Special wheelchairs that can negotiate Discovery Cove's sandy beaches are available and work is under way to provide a "platform" that will enable guests to get around in their own wheelchairs. Eventually, Discovery Cove plans to introduce special "flotation chairs." Phone ahead to see what will be available when you visit.

Cancellation Policy. Because the number of daily visitors is carefully controlled, a visit to Discovery Cove is more like a tour package or a cruise than a visit to a "regular" theme park. The advance reservation and cancellation policies reflect this fact.

All reservations must be prepaid 45 days prior to your visit, or immediately if your planned visit is less than 30 days away. If you have to cancel your reservation you may incur a penalty. Cancellations made more than 30 days before the reserved date get a full refund; between 15 and 29 days, a 50% refund; between 8 and 4 days, 25%. If you cancel fewer than eight days out, you forfeit the entire amount.

Discounts. The best way to get a discount is to book early. Bookings made 100 days or more out qualify for a ten percent discount. Florida residents can also qualify for a discount as long as one member of their party does the dolphin swim. Discovery Cove has offered occasional discounts, during slower periods, to Passport holders, conventioneers, and via radio station promotions. Promotional discounts may not include the 14 days of admission to the theme parks. Conventioneers can call (866) 781-1333 for information about special offers just for them; these are typically offered on selected dates during the low season.

Dolphins. Dolphins have such a wonderful public image as cute and cuddly critters that it's easy to forget that they are, in fact, large, powerful, and unpredictable wild animals. The dolphin PR machine likes to play down the fact that, in their natural state, they vie for dominance by biting, scratching, and fighting. Those scrapes and scars and nicks you'll see on your dolphin friend bear mute testimony to this fact of ocean life.

I mention this not to frighten or dissuade you—it's not like you'll be diving into a pool of man-eating sharks—but to encourage you to approach these magnificent creatures with the respect they deserve. Follow your trainer-host's directions and you'll do just fine. Do something stupid and you run the slight but very real risk of injury.

Emergencies. The park is dotted with fully certified lifeguards, but any nearby attendant should be your first stop in an emergency. A first-aid station is located near the Tropical Gifts shop not too far from the front entrance.

Getting Oriented. Discovery Cove does not hand you a paper map as other parks do. Since the park is quite compact, there's really no need. The main axis of the park is a paved walkway, with lockers, changing rooms, and restaurant to your right (as you walk from the main entrance) and the beach, lagoons, and river to your left. It's hard to get lost but, just in case, mosaic tile maps called "Points of Discovery" are dotted about on low-slung rocks to help you get your bearings.

Lockers and Changing Rooms. Lockers are free and plentiful. There are two locker locations. There is one near the Dolphin Lagoon and another between the dolphin and stingray pools. You will be directed to a locker location depending on the time of your arrival, but if you have a preference it will most likely be honored. Both locker areas are next to spacious and well-appointed changing rooms complete with showers, extra towels, hair blowers, and toiletries.

Money. The best way to handle money at Discovery Cove is not to. The laminated ID card you receive on arrival bears a bar code that can be linked to your credit card. If you prefer the old-fashioned way, all the shops and refreshment stands accept cash and credit cards.

Sunscreen. Don't bother lathering yourself with sunscreen prior to your visit. You'll just be asked to shower it off. Discovery Cove provides its guests, free of charge, a special "dolphin-friendly" sunscreen. Take care when applying it, because a little goes a long way. It doesn't seem to disappear as readily as most commercial sunscreens, so if you use too much you'll look a bit like you've dipped your face in flour. If you like it, you can pick up more in the gift shops.

Getting Into the Swim: Your Day at Discovery Cove

At first blush, it may seem there are only a few things to "do" at Discovery Cove, but they somehow manage to add up to a very full, relaxing, and rewarding day. Think of your day at Discovery Cove not as a visit to a mere theme park but as a day spent at a very exclusive tropical resort with some highly unusual amenities and you will not only approach the experience with the right attitude but increase your odds of getting the most from your investment.

Even if you are not planning to swim with the dolphins, I recommend arriving early. And if you *are* swimming with the dolphins I strongly advise being among the first to arrive. Your dolphin swim time slot will be assigned on a first come, first served basis upon arrival at the park. So the earlier you arrive, the more choice you will have.

My personal feeling is that you are better off being in one of the first dolphin swims of the day. The theory is that in the morning the dolphins are more active and curious, because they've had a night to rest and haven't yet spent a day with overexcited tourists. I'm not actually sure how accurate this theory is. After all, the dolphins have been specifically trained for this duty and each dolphin is limited to just six sessions a day. What's more, if a dolphin shows signs of losing interest, the trainers will simply call for a replacement. Still, I find the theory has a certain appeal. Besides, by doing the dolphin swim first thing, you get your day off to a smashing start and you can relax for the rest of the day, without keeping one eye on your watch for fear of missing your appointment with dolphin destiny. And in the summer, a morning swim slot means you will avoid the afternoon thunderstorms that are an Orlando trademark. So, assuming you are arriving early, here's how your day at Discovery Cove might play out.

My first bit of advice is to arrive dressed for the water. This is Orlando, remember, and no one at your hotel will think it odd that you are strolling through the lobby dressed in a swim suit, T-shirt, and sandals. If you like, you can bring along "regular" clothes to change into at the end of the day.

Arriving at the main entrance is a bit like arriving at a nice hotel. The large airy lobby, with its exposed wooden beams and a peaked, thatched roof, is what you might expect at a Polynesian resort. Suspended above you, sculpted blue dolphins frolic amid schools of tiny fish. Arriving guests have their bags inspected and are then directed to one of ten check-in counters, so your wait will be minimal.

Your host will find your reservation and check you in. Your photo will be taken with a digital camera and put on a laminated plastic ID card that you can wear around your neck. The card has a bar code that can be linked to your credit card. That way, you can "pay" for anything in the park with your ID card and settle a single bill on leaving the park. It's a terrific convenience and highly recommended.

If you are booked for a dolphin swim, you will also pick a swim time and be assigned to one of three cabanas. The cabanas are not changing rooms, as the term might suggest, but staging areas where you will be briefed prior to your dolphin encounter. It is your responsibility to arrive at your assigned cabana at the appointed time.

Once checked in, you will join a group of eight or so other guests to be escorted into the park itself. Your guide will tell you a bit about what to expect during your stay and direct you to the lockers and cabanas. During this brief introduction, each family group will pose for a picture, which is included in the cost of admission; you can pick it up later in the day or as you leave the park.

You will be issued a mask, snorkel, towel and dolphin-friendly sunscreen. The snorkel is yours to keep, the mask must be returned. You will also be issued a black and neon-yellow neoprene vest that is a cross between a wet suit and a flotation device. The vest is required wearing in the water. It is actually a clever way to keep you buoyant and visible (and therefore safe) without making you feel dorky. And, like a wet suit, it provides some comfort in the chilly waters of the *Dolphin Lagoon* and *Grand Reef*. If you'd like more wet suit warmth, you can request an actual wet suit, very much like those worn by the trainers. This one comes to mid-thigh and offers more coverage than the vest alone. For non-swimmers and little ones, stiff yellow life vests are also available. If you mislay your towel during the day, replacements are readily issued.

Your next stop will most likely be the lockers. They are simple wooden affairs located in shaded palapas. The doors of unclaimed lockers will be open and inside you will find the key, which is on a lanyard so you can wear it around your neck. (The ID card and key, by the way, tuck neatly inside your vest, so they don't get in your way during the day.) Near each locker area is a changing room, should you need it.

If your dolphin swim is later in the day, it is now time to take advantage of the hot breakfast buffet, scope out the beach area, and choose a lounge chair or two to accommodate your party. Take your time and pick a spot that offers the ideal combination of sun and shade to suit your tastes.

If you have followed my advice and arranged an early dolphin swim, it will now be time to head to your assigned cabana to begin your experience; you can have breakfast after your dolphin encounter. Or you might want to head straight for the rays in the *Grand Reef*. This is because the rays will be hungriest in the morning. Trying to feed a full stingray in the afternoon can be a daunting challenge.

Otherwise, you can pretty much take things easy for the rest of the day, basking in the sun, swimming in the river or saltwater pools, visiting the *Aviary*, or eavesdropping on the later dolphin swims as the spirit moves you.

The Twilight Discovery Option

If you choose the Twilight Discovery option, which is available only on select nights during the summer months, your day begins at three o'clock in the afternoon and ends at about nine. Pricing and schedules are not yet available for 2012, but costs are comparable to a peak-season daytime admission. Your experience, though shorter, will be much the same as if you had opted for a full day, but with a few important differences. For one thing, there will be fewer of you. This program is limited to just 150 guests.

Most important to my way of thinking, is that the dolphin interaction is a "wade" rather than a "swim." In the evening, all interactions with the dolphins take place in shallow water. That means you will miss out on the thrill of being towed by the dolphin, which is one of the great highlights of the daytime experience. Of course, that dolphin ride takes time, so without it you get a little more one-on-one time with your flippered friend. Although the evening interaction is the same 30 minutes as during the day, many people who have done both report that it seems longer.

Obviously lunch is not included in the evening option, but dinner is and it is a decided step up from the midday fare. Chefs personally prepare delicacies like blackened sea scallops or grilled steak and shrimp. They'll even help you create your own pasta dish. Desserts are more lavish as well and include flaming bananas Foster.

Live music is part of the experience, too, and you can expect lively limbo dancing on the Laguna Grill patio. Because the crowds are smaller in the evening, it's possible to slip off somewhere relatively quiet with that special someone and savor the sunset in this very special place.

Attractions at Discovery Cove

Discovery Cove has a limited number of "attractions" but they are some of the best to be found in the Orlando area. They are enjoyable enough that you may be surprised to find a very full day seems all too short.

Swim with the Dolphins ★ ★ ★ ★ ★

Type: Animal interaction
Time: About 30 minutes
Short Take: An unforgettable experience

Your dolphin encounter begins when you arrive at your appointed cabana at the appointed hour for a briefing. This is primarily an exercise in heightening your anticipation with a brief video, but a trainer does put in an appearance to offer some pertinent safety tips, such as keeping your hands away from the dolphin's blow hole. ("It'd be sorta like me sticking my finger in your nose," she points out helpfully.)

Following the briefing you and your "pod" of anywhere from six to nine people will be led to the lagoon. I have heard conflicting reports on the maximum group size for the dolphin encounter. Nine people is said to be the maximum and seven or eight the preferred number. I have been in groups of six and eight. At water's edge you meet the two trainers who will guide your encounter. Your first challenge is getting used to the chilly water, which is kept between 72 and 76 degrees Fahrenheit for the comfort of the dolphins.

The dolphins make a splashy entrance, zipping from their holding pen and leaping into the air in greeting before splitting off to head to their respective human pods. Eagerly, you wade to the edge of a sharp drop-off to meet your new dolphin friend. The dolphin you meet may have been specially trained for duty at Discovery Cove or may be an old pro. I once swam with Capricorn, an aging movie star of sorts who was 36 and had appeared in *Jaws III*.

Here at the edge of deep water, you and the other members of the group will get to rub down your dolphin, a tactile interaction the dolphin obviously enjoys. Then you take the plunge into deep water for the main part of the experience. How many people go out at one time is a function of the size and makeup of your group. Our trainers said they usually try to take people out as couples, but sometimes they go out in threes.

Exactly what you do with your dolphin will depend to some extent on what behaviors the dolphin has been trained to perform, but you will almost certainly be able to give some hand signals to which the dolphin will respond by chattering excitedly or spinning in a circle. The interaction is carefully planned so that every member of your group gets equal access to the dolphin and no one feels cheated of one-on-one time with their frisky friend. You will also have a chance to feed your new friend several times in the course of the interaction. This tends to keep the dolphin interested, but don't be surprised if your dolphin decides to take an unscheduled break to check out something of greater interest elsewhere in the pool. This is normal apparently and if your dolphin shows sufficient lack of interest in the proceedings the trainers will simply call in an understudy.

For most people, the highlight of the interaction comes at the end when they place an arm over the dolphin's back and cup their other hand over a flipper and get towed back to the shallows. There they pose in a sort of hug with their new-found friend for the still and video photographers who have been carefully documenting the entire dolphin interaction for posterity and profit.

Before you leave, you can stop by the photo pick-up area (to your left, across from Guests Services) and see the photos and videos taken of your dolphin interaction. They're available for purchase, of course, in a variety of formats. The pricing system is complicated and you can quickly run up an enormous tab. Everything is available "a la carte," but if you order one of two packages, the a la carte pricing for other options goes down. To give you an idea, here are some sample prices, which do not include tax.

The Ultimate Package ($219) includes seven 6x8 prints, one 4x6, two key ring photo viewers, a DVD video of your interaction, and a CD-ROM with all the photos from your experience, along with a photo album and poster. The Adventure Package ($139) consists of five 6x8 inch prints, a 4x6 with two key rings, and a photo CD. The basic Island Package ($69) is three 6x8 prints, one 4x6, and two key rings. To these you can add a DVD of your dolphin interaction for $50 ($75 a la carte) or photo CD for $75 ($125 a la carte). The least expensive a la carte offering is a single 6x8 inch print or one 4x6 inch print and two key rings for $20. Of all the elements at Discovery Cove, the pricing of the photos and video was the only thing I heard the slightest complaint about.

Tip: Pick your photos up early and stash them in your locker. A line starts forming at around 3:00 p.m. and it gets longer as the day wears on.

Unfortunately, you are not allowed to take those nifty disposable underwater cameras along with you—the dolphins might pinch them and do themselves an injury, I was told. But if a non-swimming member of your party is an accomplished photographer with a telephoto lens, he or she may be able to get some great shots from the shore. The trainers will be more than happy to direct them to the best vantage points.

Wind-Away River ★ ★ 1/2

Type:	Circular river
Time:	Unlimited
Short Take:	Best for the *Aviary*

If you've visited a water park, you've probably experienced a variation of this attraction. It's a circular fresh water "river," varying in depth from 3 to 12 feet, with an artificial current that will bear you lazily along. The river rings the *Freshwater Oasis* and takes about 20 minutes to circumnavigate at an easy pace. This is strictly a one-way river;

swimming against the current is discouraged by the lifeguards stationed along the route and it is virtually impossible to be out of sight of a lifeguard. The river is kept several degrees warmer than the saltwater pools. After visiting a saltwater pool like the *Grand Reef*, the river will feel like a warm bath.

Most people bring along their snorkels, although there are no fish in the river and very little to see. An attempt has been made to add visual interest by studding the bottom with chunks of Mayanesque ruins and visitors seem to have created their own decorative touches by arranging stones on the bottom in the form of peace symbols, smiley faces, and hearts.

The high, rocky banks are landscaped with lush, tropical foliage so there are only four places to enter or exit. The main entrance, near the *Dolphin Lagoon*, broadens out into a large lagoon-like pool called **Serenity Bay** backed by a very pretty waterfall behind which is a cool cave-like area.

The best section of the *Wind-Away River* is the one that passes through the *Aviary*. Heavy waterfalls at either end prevent the birds from escaping. Inside is a tropical paradise and you may be surprised at how closely you can approach birds perched at the water's edge. You can step out of the river here and visit the birds at even closer range.

Aviary ★ ★ ★ ★ 1/2

Type: Animal interaction
Time: Continuous viewing
Short Take: Discovery Cove's best-kept secret

Imagine a jungle paradise where the birds are so tame they'll eat out of your hand and foot-high deer peek about the blossoms as you pet them. This is what you'll find if you step out of the *Wind-Away River* into the very special world of Discovery Cove's jungle aviary.

The *Aviary* is populated with some 200 exotic birds representing 100 species from the four corners of the world, many of them so intriguingly colored that they look more like products of the vivid imaginations of folk artists than creatures from the natural world. Since many of the birds found here have been hand-raised by Discovery Cove trainers, they are completely tame and will happily eat out of your hand. Food is readily available from some of those same trainers, who can also answer your questions about which bird is which. Typically there are one or two examples of each species, but in some cases, like the gaudily colored conures, you will see a small flock flying through the trees or perching on the branches. There are actually three aviaries here. There is one on each side of the river and the far aviary has a smaller aviary within it housing tiny birds like hummingbirds.

The type of food you choose—grain pellets, fruit, or meal worms—will determine which birds you attract, and unlike the dolphin encounter, your time here is unlimited. You can also feed the tiny muntjac deer, which have their own special diet. If you'd like to develop your bird-watching skills, ask one of the attendants for a laminated chart that identifies the species.

Tip: Most people discover the *Aviary* while cruising down the *Wind-Away River,* but there are some unmarked land entrances not far from *Freshwater Oasis.* They make visiting the *Aviary* several times during the course of the day a very tempting option. Remember, there are three separate areas in the *Aviary*. Don't miss any of them.

Freshwater Oasis (not open at press time)

Type: Wade-through animal habitat
Time: Continuous viewing
Short Take: Sounds promising

After opening the *Grand Reef* attraction (below), Discovery Cove's designers immediately set about re-imagining the park's original saltwater snorkeling experience as a tropical rainforest habitat that will be available for guests to explore in spring 2012.

Visitors can enter the habitat from a number of entrances and wade through warm, fresh water and wander along island trails. Playful Asian small-clawed otters from Indonesia swim alongside waders while pint-sized marmoset monkeys, native to the rainforests of South America, leap from branch to branch in the lush rainforest canopy overhead. The otters are cleverly separated from waders, but the marmosets fly free above.

Most of the water is waist-deep or shallower making this attraction especially attractive to families with younger children, who will be able to roam freely. If you get tired of wading and animal-watching, you can sink into one of the in-water "relaxation stations" that dot the area and enjoy a cool drink while soaking up the sunshine.

Grand Reef (with SeaVenture) ★ ★ ★ ★

Type: A swim-through aquatic habitat
Time: Continuous viewing
Short Take: A great snorkeling experience guaranteed

Having been disappointed on several snorkeling outings in the real tropics, I was impressed by the variety of multicolored tropical fish on display in this clever re-creation of a coral reef. It's not real coral, of course, but a thin film of algae encourages fish to nibble at the simulated coral outcroppings very much as they do on the real thing.

Grand Reef, which opened in 2011, is the first major expansion to Discovery Cove. It replaced the park's original saltwater reef attraction, which has been transformed into *Freshwater Oasis*, the new otter and marmoset habitat. Here in the reef you can snorkel to your heart's content without worrying about visibility being lessened by churning surf. Nor do you have to worry about those nasty little things—jellyfish, fire coral, and moray eels—that frequent real reefs. And the sharks and barracudas are thoughtfully kept behind thick (but virtually invisible) sloping glass walls. You get the illusion of swimming above them without the bone-chilling fear that typically arrives with the realization that you are swimming a few feet from something that might eat you.

The fish are fed periodically, and when the water around you is swirling with bits of food, it will also be alive with a kaleidoscope of fish. Put out your hand and the bolder among them will nibble hopefully at your fingertips as large eagle rays cruise the depths below.

If you don't want to wear a snorkel mask, there are an array of paths and bridges along the water's edge that lead to a complex of hidden grottoes and observation points, affording views of the underwater world from every angle.

On the other hand, if you really want to delve beneath the surface, consider signing up for **SeaVenture**. For an additional $59 per person, groups of six can descend a ladder and take a stroll on the reef floor. You won't need to grow gills, because you'll be wearing a 75-pound space-age diving helmet that provides an unencumbered view of your aquatic environment (and even keeps your hair dry). SCUBA certification or prior diving experience is unnecessary; a pre-swim briefing will tell you everything you need to know. During your 20-minute undersea experience, a guide will identify species swimming by, including sharks (thankfully separated from guests by invisible barriers). For the finale, your guide will feed the inhabitants, ensuring that you're enveloped in a colorful swarm. If you're not claustrophobic and have the extra cash, this is an undeniably unique experience.

Horticulture Tour ★ ★ ★ 1/2

Type: Show and tell from the gardening staff
Time: About 30 minutes
Short Take: How Discovery Cove was created

I have rated this attraction with gardeners and landscaping aficionados in mind. Others might find it less compelling, but I would encourage you not to dismiss this short tour out of hand. It is well worth taking, especially if you are a fan of Discovery Cove and this is your second visit. It will give you a much deeper appreciation of what the landscapers and grounds crew have accomplished.

The tour is simplicity itself. A member of the groundskeeping staff meets you near Guest Services and takes you on a short stroll up the walkway toward the main entrance, pausing as he goes to explain how what looks to most visitors like a jungle—with all the randomness that the term implies—is actually a cleverly designed bit of theatrical stage setting. I was particularly impressed with the way a wall of bamboo trees was ingeniously placed so as to mask the hum of traffic from a street that lies just a few yards away. You'd never know.

Conservation Cabana ★ ★

Type: Fun facts and critters, too
Time: Continuous viewing
Short Take: Worth a peek

When you reach the beach area of Discovery Cove, look to your left for two square, open-sided, tent-like structures. This is the *Conservation Cabana*, where members of the education staff wait to satisfy your idle curiosity about what you are seeing and provide a deeper understanding of Nature and the importance of protecting it.

The cabana is stocked with a small collection artifacts from the natural world—eggshells, bones, coral, and the like—to pique your interest and encourage discussion. Several times during the day, the conservation staffers bring out animals for show and tell and a brief walk around the park to show them off. You might see a macaw or, my favorite, a two-toed sloth.

Chapter Seven:

Gatorland

THOSE BORN DURING WORLD WAR II OR EARLIER, MAY REMEMBER THE ROADSIDE attractions that dotted the tourist landscape. Half carnival side-show, half shanty town, these entrepreneurial "attractions" served as living proof of Mencken's maxim that "no one ever went broke underestimating the taste of the American public." Trading on actual freaks of nature ("See the two-headed calf!") or objects of less certain provenance ("Mummified Indian chief!"), the typical roadside attraction tended to spread incrementally along the highway as the owner figured out new ways to lure the passing parade of cars with stranger wonders or larger souvenir shops featuring the latest in joy buzzers and whoopee cushions. Each year, it seemed, the advertising budget would finance a few more garish billboards, a few more miles away, until tourists knew hundreds of miles in advance that something extraordinary lay ahead. The old roadside attractions were a blight on the landscape. They were tacky, lowbrow, often smelly, and altogether marvelous. They represent one of the most cherished memories of my youth and I wish they were still around.

At Gatorland, they still are—in a way. Gatorland is a modern and evolving nature-themed attraction. It is well-run, clean, and in spite of the 5,000 alligators crammed into its 110 acres, remarkably smell free. But its roots are firmly in the roadside attraction tradition. In fact, that's how it started out back in 1949.

Owen Godwin was a local cattle rancher—Florida was once America's second-biggest cattle producer, after Texas—who decided to turn a liability into an asset. Alligators were the Florida cattleman's nemesis. They would hunker down in water holes and kill unsuspecting calves. This intolerable loss of income prompted a vendetta against the gator, and cattlemen became adept at capturing and killing the scaly predators. Godwin realized not only that there was a market for the hides and meat of the gators he killed but that few of the tourists who whizzed past on Highway 441 had ever seen an alligator and might pay for the privilege. So Godwin rounded up some gators and a passel of the snakes that thronged his property and the "Snake & Reptile Village" was born, beckoning to the southbound tourist traffic. Even today, in spite of Orlando's phenomenal post-Mickey growth, Gatorland's location seems a bit out of the way. In 1949, it really must have seemed in the middle of nowhere.

Gatorland has come a long way since its early days, not so much in its look and feel as in its focus and attitude. For a while Godwin followed the pattern of many roadside attractions. As he prospered, he traveled farther afield, adding "exotic" animals to his collection. Those days are long past and only a few holdovers from that era remain.

For many years, Gatorland was a working alligator "farm," sending over 1,000 gators to market each year. So successful was the Gatorland model that it sparked a renaissance in alligator farming across the American south. So Gatorland phased out its farming operation to concentrate on the zoological side of the operation and the conservation of Florida species. Gatorland is also a partner with the University of Florida in alligator research and is the only place on earth where alligators are bred through artificial insemination.

Compared to the big attractions in town—Disney, Universal, and SeaWorld—Gatorland is downright modest. Many of the exhibits are made of simple cinder block construction painted white and green, and I'm sure the appearance of much of the park hasn't changed a whole lot since the sixties. Rather than a being a drawback, I find this homey quality to be a large part of Gatorland's charm. If you don't come with exaggerated expectations fueled by Hollywood scenic artists and are willing to accept the park on its own low-key terms, you won't be disappointed.

Before You Come

There is no pressing need to do in-depth research prior to a visit, but if you'd like to check prices or hours you can call Gatorland at (800) 393-5297 or (407) 855-5496. The website is www.gatorland.com. On the website, you will find a "virtual tour" with Frequently Asked Questions about the park and an "Ask Ally Gator" educational page where you can ask questions about crocodilians in general.

When's the Best Time to Come?

Even at the height of the tourist seasons, Gatorland will be far less mobbed than the larger attractions. The best time to visit, then, is dictated more by the patterns of the animals than those of the people who come to see them.

Alligators are cold blooded and derive their warmth from the sun and surrounding atmosphere. Thus, in the winter they tend to be slow moving and sluggish, not that they're particularly lively in the best of circumstances. April and May is breeding time and if you visit then you will be entertained by the bellowing of amorous males attracting their mates. It sounds a bit like a lovesick Harley if you can imagine such a thing. Alligators lay hard-shelled eggs in nests on the ground. So by June you may be able to see nests in the *Alligator Breeding Marsh*. The hatchlings emerge in late August and early September, when visitors will be treated with dozens of joyous events in the **Gator Grunts Nursery**. Birds have their own migratory and mating patterns. Nesting in the *Breeding Marsh* begins in January or February, hits its peak in April and May, and continues through the summer, as various species arrive to hatch and raise their young. Regardless of when you come, don't arrive too late in the day. If you arrive mid-afternoon, you may miss some of the shows.

Getting There

Gatorland is located at 14501 South Orange Blossom Trail, also known as US Routes 441, 17, and 92, in the southern fringes of Orlando. It is seven miles south of the Florida Mall and 3.5 miles north of US 192 in Kissimmee. To reach Gatorland from I-4, take either the Bee Line Expressway (SR 538) or Central Florida Parkway east to Orange Blossom Trail and turn right.

Gatorland will be on your left as you drive south, made prominent by its trademark alligator jaws entrance. There is parking for about 500 cars, which gives you an indication of the size of the crowds they expect. Parking is **free** and all spaces are a short walk from the entrance.

Opening and Closing Times

Gatorland is open daily from 10:00 a.m. until 5:00 p.m. Call ahead or check the website before your visit for exact hours and show times. The park, which is largely out of doors, operates rain or shine, 365 days a year.

The Price of Admission

At press time, admission prices (not including tax) were as follows:

Adults:	$24.99
Children (3 to 12):	$16.99

Annual passes are $45.99 and $31.99 (tax not included), for adults and kids, respectively. You can upgrade to the annual pass before leaving the park on the day of your visit. If you think you will return within a year, this is a good deal. I suspect it will appeal most to bird watchers and nature photography buffs, who will find plenty to keep them occupied at various times of the year. Gatorland's annual pass is good only for admission to the park. It does not give you a discount on food or at the gift shop, nor does it allow you to bring in guests at a discount.

Gatorland offers a couple of upgraded admission options for the deeply gator-obsessed. The "Grunt" Package ($32 adults, $25 kids) combines park admission with railroad rides, one "Rookie Wrestlin'" experience (photos extra), and a package of gator chow. "Gator Night Shine" ($20) is an after-hours guided tour of the breeding marsh; gator food, flashlights, and bug spray are provided. "Trainer for a Day" ($125, age 12 and up only, 5 people max) is the ultimate two-hour backstage tour, featuring hands-on encounters with several "creepy crawlers." All special tours must be booked in advance via website or telephone.

Serious nature photographers will be especially interested in the $100 Annual Photo Pass. From February to July, this pass allows holders to enter the park at 7:30 a.m. and stay until dusk on Fridays, Saturdays, and Sundays. This enables access to the *Alligator Breeding Marsh and Bird Sanctuary* and the *Swamp Walk* (both described below) when conditions for photography are at their best and there's no risk of tripods being knocked over by hordes of tourists.

Discounts. Members of AAA, CAA (Canadian Automobile Association), AARP, and the military receive a 20% discount on admission. Also check the Gatorland website, where tickets can be purchased online, for additional discount offers. Discounts cannot be combined. Gatorland also offers a series of special discount offers to Florida residents, so locals should inquire about current offerings.

Good Things to Know About . . .

Access for the Disabled. The entire park is accessible to the disabled (with the exception of the third level of the Observation Tower in the *Alligator Breeding Marsh*) and wheelchairs are available on a rental basis for $10 (plus tax) per day. There is also an electric scooter available for $20 per day. Both rentals require that you leave your driver's license or other photo ID as a deposit.

Babies. Strollers are available from the same location as wheelchairs, also require an ID as deposit, and rent for $7 a day for singles, $10 for doubles (plus tax). Diaper changing facilities will be found in all restrooms.

Leaving the Park. When you pay your admission, your hand will be stamped with a gator symbol. It allows you to leave (for lunch perhaps?) and return on the same day.

Money. An ATM hooked up to the Cirrus, Plus, PULSE, and STAR systems is located in the gift shop.

Safety. Alligators may look like they never move a muscle but they can move with surprising speed when a meal is in the offing. And to an alligator your toddler looks an awful lot like lunch. The railings over the alligator lake have been fitted with green mesh guards to discourage leaning over the sides. Nonetheless, I have seen people lift their children onto the railings and lean them over for a closer look or to help them feed the gators. DON'T DO THIS! You will not only give people like me heart failure but if your child wriggles loose and falls he or she could very well be killed.

Special Diets. Gatorland's eateries are not equipped to handle special diets, though their website lists a limited menu of gluten-free items. However, Gatorland welcomes picnickers, so feel free to bring your own meals. In fact, feel free to bring an entire cooler. There are several nice areas to eat your own meals; just ask a park employee. No alcoholic beverages are permitted and Gatorland requests that you do not bring any glass containers into the park.

Eating in Gatorland

Your choice of restaurants at Gatorland is easy; there's really only one. **Pearl's Patio Smokehouse** is a wood-sided, tin-roofed, Florida-style fast-food stand, with paper plates and outdoor seating. A few steps away is a covered seating area, closer to the *Alligator Breeding Marsh*. Here you can sit at a small counter facing a pen holding a pair of emus, who will cruise by looking for a handout.

The featured attraction at Pearl's is alligator served as breaded, deep-fried "nuggets" for about $8 a serving. It would really be a shame to come to Gatorland and not try this local delicacy. My observation, however, is that many people are not yet ready to take the plunge. If you are one of them, you needn't worry about going hungry. Good old reliable hot dogs, hamburgers, fried shrimp, grilled chicken breast sandwiches, and

French fries are all available at modest prices. Beer is $4.

Tip: Pearl's is right next door to the *Gator Wrestlin'* arena. Consider taking your lunch over there and eating while you grab a good seat and wait for the show to begin.

Other than Pearl's your only choice is the **Snack Bar**, near the *Gator Jumparoo* attraction. The menu is a pared-down version of Pearl's, plus pizza but minus the gator.

Shopping in Gatorland

What better way to commemorate your visit to Gatorland than with a photo of yourself with a real, live alligator. No, you don't get a chance to pose with any of the 12-foot whoppers you saw in the pool, but you can have your picture taken while holding a small gator whose jaws have thoughtfully been taped shut. If gators aren't your cup of tea, you can also have a boa constrictor draped decoratively over your shoulders. Photo prices start at $10.95 for prints, and $14.95 for T-shirts. The stand can be found right next to the *Gator Jumparoo* area.

But the real shopper's paradise is the gift shop through which you stroll on your way out of the park. For such a modest park, Gatorland has a surprisingly upscale gift shop, with an extensive range of alligator skin products. The price tags are truly heart-stopping but if you've done any comparison shopping you will realize there are some real bargains to be had here, from gorgeous boots for men to purses for women to wallets and belts for everyone.

In addition to the pricier items, the gift shop carries a full assortment of standard tourist souvenirs, from mugs and refrigerator magnets to alligator claw backscratchers and games for kids. There's lots to see here and you can always return to shop another day without paying admission to the park.

Swamp Thing: Your (Half) Day at Gatorland

Gatorland has trademarked the phrase "Orlando's best half-day attraction." That seems about right to me. Many people stay for a shorter period and it's doubtful you will stay longer unless you are an ardent bird watcher or a wildlife photographer willing to wait for that perfect shot. In any event, you can take your time here. There is never any need to rush madly from place to place to avoid long lines or crushing crowds.

As I mentioned before, Gatorland is modest in both scale and execution. Unlike the bigger parks, it's not filled with attendants and hosts; you are pretty much on your own, although you can certainly feel free to collar one of the "gator wranglers" with your questions. These guys take turns hand-feeding and wrestling gators and handling deadly snakes. They are knowledgeable, charming, and maybe just a little nuts. They are one of Gatorland's major assets. You will recognize them by their distinctive swamp explorers' outfits that grow wetter and sweatier and dirtier as the day wears on.

The park is an elongated rectangle divided lengthwise into three main parts. The first is a huge alligator-clogged lake that stretches the entire length of the park. When you enter the park from the Gift Shop after paying your admission you step onto a large wooden platform over this lake. The platform is honeycombed with open areas filled with sunbathing and swimming gators. One of these openings is the site of the *Gator Jumparoo* show, Gatorland's signature attraction. Also on this platform is a space set aside for children's birthday parties.

Across the wooden platform, you will find *Alligator Alley*, the second major area of the park. It is a long, narrow, shaded concrete walkway that runs north and south through the middle of the park. It is instantly recognizable by the wavy, blue-green, snake-like line down its middle. Along this walkway you will find a variety of displays, animal pens, and scientific work areas, as well as (at the southern end) the *Gator Wrestlin'* arena and Pearl's Smokehouse.

On the other side of *Alligator Alley* is the third major area, a 10-acre *Alligator Breeding Marsh*, with its wooden walkway and Observation Tower, and behind that the crocodile exhibits. The *Swamp Walk*, reached through a gate at the south end of the park, comprises a separate fourth area.

The Half-Day Stay

When you pay your admission, you will be given a folded Gatorland map with a list of permanent attractions, and a schedule of the day's shows printed on a paper slip and tucked inside. Check to see the starting time of the next show. If you have more than half an hour before show time, spend it gawking at the huge gators in the main pool. This should whet your appetite for what's to come.

Your first order of business should be the live shows. It doesn't much matter in which order you see them. You may want to consider seeing the wrestling show twice. In between shows, you can check out the smaller exhibits dotted along the spine of the park.

Give yourself at least 20 uninterrupted minutes or more to take in the *Alligator Breeding Marsh and Bird Sanctuary*, more if it's nesting season. You'll probably want to spend some time at the highest level of the **Observation Tower** for a great bird's-eye view and then take a leisurely stroll along the water level walkway for a closer look. The *Swamp Walk* is restful but not a must-see unless you're a bird-watcher. Remember to bring along your binoculars for a closer look at the wildlife.

Attractions at Gatorland

There are three live shows at Gatorland, each presented several times a day, and they form the heart of the Gatorland experience. The shows let us get close—but not too close—to critters that alternately fascinate and repel us. Since alligators, crocodiles, and other reptiles are a natural source of curiosity for most of us, it's easy for these shows to jump right in and start answering our unasked questions about these scaly creatures. The result is that staple of the modern-day theme park: effortless "edutainment."

A group of about five young men and women, all Florida natives, takes turns starring in these exhibitions. They have mastered an easy, laid back, aw-shucks, country boy style that is most ingratiating. The humor—and there's lots of it—is self-deprecating while at the same time letting us city slickers know who's got the really cool job. These guys are the living embodiment of Gatorland and I think you'll find it hard not to like them.

Gator Jumparoo ★ ★ ★ ★

Type: Outdoor show
Time: 15 minutes
Short Take: As close as it gets to performing alligators

The scene is a large open square in the wooden platform over the alligator lagoon. The cause for gathering: there's been a mishap in the previous gator wrestlin' show, and now there's an opening for a new gator wrestler. Two enthusiastic backwoods kids, suited up in denim overalls and tagged with goofy country names like Bubba and Lulu Belle, will compete for the slot by feeding the resident gators with increasing daring and dramatic flair. The two are supervised by a slightly more civilized announcer, who warms up the crowd and separates the two wannabes when emotions run high and squabbles break out (such as when Bubba "flips" his chicken at his opponent—get it? He "flipped" her the bird...).

After the opening skit, each half of the audience is assigned a key word to encourage the gators to leap for the chicken parts temptingly dangled over the water, the host rings the bell, and the fun begins. Alerted by the commotion, mammoth gators swim lazily into view. Slowly, they zero in on the morsels over their heads. They begin to lunge upwards at the bait, urged on by cheers from the crowd. Alligators jump by curling their tails on the shallow bottom and thrusting upwards. A successful leap is something to see and will make a great snapshot if your timing's right.

Once the gators are suitably excited and the contestants riled up and raring to win the points that will ensure their position as Gatorland's newest wrestler, the host ups the ante. After a brief interlude that involves the use of whole chickens as boxing gloves and an explanation of the difference between crocodiles and alligators ("the spellin'," asserts Bubba, while the other eagerly corrects him: "no, my mama taught me this... crocodile goes best with a merlot, but alligator is nicest with a pinot grigio..."), the competitors retreat to raised platforms on either side of the beach, armed with several whole chicken carcasses, and commence hand-feeding the now lively gators. The thick leather belts around their waists, attached to thick chains, ensure that while a gator might make off with an arm, the rest of the contestant will be spared.

And despite the clowning and hijinks, they are clearly skilled handlers, expert in the ways of gators and genuinely respectful of the animals. There's no denying that the stars of the show are the imposing carnivores, and the banter is low-key enough to keep the gators at the forefront.

This show appeals to some of our most primordial fascinations with animals and it's an appeal that's hard to deny. Most people find this show very entertaining. Precisely how exciting the show is will depend to some extent on when you visit. During the cooler months, alligators tend to be sluggish. Under optimum conditions, the gators leap lustily, flashing their pale undersides and gaping maws as they snare lunch.

The best seats in the house. First of all, there are no seats, just a railing. If you're not in the first row, your view will be somewhat impaired. The best view is to be found along the side directly facing the small beach and platforms. Arrive about ten minutes early to secure a spot by the rail.

Gator Wrestlin' ★ ★ ★ ★ ★

Type:	Outdoor show
Time:	15 minutes
Short Take:	Best show at Gatorland

Gatorland's best show takes place in an open-air arena next to Pearl's Smokehouse. Covered bleachers face a sunken sandy platform surrounded by a small moat and a raised border that (we hope) keeps the gators from getting out. Twelve gators, about seven or eight feet long, lie on the sand sunning themselves.

This is a two-man show. Ostensibly one is the host and the other the gator wrangler, but I suspect the second man is there in case the wrangler gets in trouble. This show is obviously for real and there's no disguising the fact that it's hard work. ("I never finished school," the wrangler says. "So you kids out there study real hard or you might wind up doin' this.")

Alligator wrestling began, we are told, as a matter of necessity. Alligators would hide in water holes and take the occasional calf. The cattle boss would order the hands to get that gator out. Their courage bolstered by a little moonshine, the ranch hands would oblige. Eventually, the practice became a competitive sport that gave young men a chance to show off their courage and prowess. Which is exactly what happens in this show. The show begins with the wrangler kicking the gators off their sunny perch into the moat. They hiss their annoyance. Then a kid picked from the audience carefully picks out the biggest one for the wrangler to wrestle. Resigned to his fate, the wrangler drags the wriggling, hissing, and none too cooperative beast onto the sandy platform.

Along with an informative patter about alligators, often made breathless by the exertion of keeping a 150-pound gator motionless, the gator wrangler shows off a few of the tricks of the trade—like pulling back the gator's head and placing his chin across its closed jaws. Despite his assurance that it doesn't take much pressure to hold a gator's jaws closed, you respect and admire his gumption. At one point, the wrangler pries the gator's jaws apart to show us his teeth. "If this works, it's gonna make you a pretty nice little snapshot," he says and then adds with perfect backwoods sang froid, "If this don't work, it's gonna make you a pretty nice little snapshot."

Maybe there's less to wrestling gators than meets the eye, but I wouldn't bet on it. The casual machismo and sly good humor with which these fellows put their charges through their paces makes for a thoroughly entertaining 15 minutes. After the show, the stage area is mobbed with audience members eager to ask questions ("Didja ever get bit?") and shake the hand of someone with the guts to wrestle a gator.

Photo Op: For $10, you (or your child) can be a "Rookie Wrestler" and briefly pose sitting on the back of a gator. There is an additional charge for prints of the photo that the park photographer will take of you. The gator's jaws are securely taped shut, and a gator wrangler is close at hand, so there's no real danger. A limited number of opportunities are provided on a first-come-first-served basis before and after selected *Gator Wrestlin'* performances.

Up Close Encounters ★ ★ ★ 1/2

Type: Outdoor show
Time: 15 minutes
Short Take: Poisonous snakes and other creepy-crawlies

This show comes by its name honestly, so if getting personal with an assortment of creepy-crawlies isn't your cup of tea, you may want to skip this one in favor of something a bit less heavy on audience participation. Surprise also plays a major role in the unveiling of the various critters, so don't count on your ability to pick and choose which animals you'll want to be friendly with.

That said, this is a fun, irreverent, and highly informative presentation. The hosts explain to us that Gatorland frequently has to deal with surprise drop-offs, as locals unload their unwanted exotic pets here by leaving them in unmarked boxes outside the entrance. Given the indigenous wildlife's propensity to use venom, stingers, and other nasty surprises on unsuspecting box-openers, the staff at Gatorland have tired of risking their lives at this pursuit and so opted to turn the tables and have us, the audience, take over the dirty work—literally. They scamper through the seats, distributing small wooden crates and taking the names of the folks sitting next to them. One by one, they call these audience members onto the stage and introduce them—and the rest of us—to the contents of their crates, which range from scary-looking but mild-mannered tarantulas to venomous snakes. "Don't step over the Line of Death," the hosts cheerfully warn. Most audience members seemed quite happy to comply.

Gatorland Express Railroad ★ ★

Type: Swamp train ride
Time: 15 minutes
Short Take: Easy intro to gator lore

The *Gatorland Express Railroad* leaves about every 20 minutes from a small station behind Lily's Pad. It's a scaled-down steam engine that takes you on a lazy loop circling the *Alligator Breeding Marsh* and crocodile exhibits (see below). While not the most exciting of experiences, it provides a painless introduction to Gatorland and alligator lore. There is, however, an additional $2 charge for this attraction, which is probably not worth it unless your kids insist. On the other hand, the charge lets you ride as often as you wish. In the humid summer months, a chance to sit down in the shade, feel the breeze as the train chugs along, and let someone else show you around shouldn't be underrated.

The engineer/narrator is a gator wrangler taking a break from his more strenuous chores at the live shows. He points out sights of interest along the route and fills you in on Gatorland's purpose and the range of its attractions. The train makes a stop by Pearl's Smokehouse, near the entrance to the *Jungle Crocs*; you can get off here but can't get on.

Alligator Breeding Marsh and Bird Sanctuary ★ ★ ★ ★ 1/2

Type: Observation platforms and walkways through a
             wildlife sanctuary
Time: As long as you wish

Short Take: Bring your binoculars

This is one of Gatorland's more recent attractions and one of its most successful, in its own low-key way. The concept was ingenious: Build a natural setting in which some 100 female and 30 male alligators would feel free to do what comes naturally and provide a steady stream of new alligators to enthrall visitors and serve the growing market for gator meat and hides. But because birds like to nest over alligator holes for the protection they provide against predators like raccoons, opossum, snakes, and bobcats, Gatorland hoped for a bonus population of wild birds. They built it . . . and they came. So happy with their surroundings are the gators, that some females have taken to setting up their nests underneath the wooden boardwalk, prompting Gatorland staff to build additional barriers at these points to keep protective Mama 'Gator and Foolhardy Tourist safely apart.

Today there are over 1,000 bird nests in active use at Gatorland. Here you will find the magnificent, bright white great egret with its majestic plumage alongside the more dowdy green and blue herons. There are also snowy egrets, cattle egrets, and tricolor egrets. With a bit of luck you might also spot an osprey perched high in a pine tree, surveying the alligator pool below and weighing his chances for a fish dinner.

The *Alligator Breeding Marsh* has three entrances. To the north near *Lilly's Pad* and to the south near *Pearl's Smokehouse* you can gain access to the wooden walkway that runs the length of the alligator lake. In the middle of the park is a bridge that takes you directly to the Observation Tower. Starting in June you will be able to see alligator nests, some remarkably close to the walkway. Shortly after the eggs have been laid, Gatorland staffers remove them to an incubator to insure hatching. Signs left behind document the date of laying and the number of eggs.

Large, shaded gazebos with wooden benches offer a chance to rest, relax, and contemplate the serenity of the preserve. It's hard to believe some of Florida's scariest critters are basking just feet from where you sit. You'll see plenty of gators from the walkway. They wallow in the mud, float almost submerged in the water, and sun themselves on logs and the opposite shore. But for a really great look, you'll want to climb the Observation Tower.

The **Observation Tower** is a three-story affair located in the center of the walkway. It is accessible from the walkway, of course, but you can also reach the second level via a bridge directly from the park's central spine. An elaborate zigzag ramp next to the bridge makes the tower's middle level accessible to wheelchairs.

If you brought binoculars to Florida, don't forget to bring them to Gatorland. Climb to the top level, where signs point out the direction and distance to major Florida landmarks. Look straight down at the alligator lake and you will see dozens of 10-footers clustered around the base of the platform.

Look across at the opposite shore and you will see more gators amid the foliage; the longer you look, the more you'll see. Look at the trees in spring and you will see dozens of egrets tending their nests. Look closer and you will see the drabber species well camouflaged amid the leaves. A quarter will get you a brief look through a telescope mounted on the railing, but when a hawk appears in the high branches, the line gets long.

Screamin' Gator Zip Line ★ ★ ★ ★

Type:	Extra-cost aerial adventure
Time:	About 2 hours, including safety briefing
Short Take:	Uniquely exhilarating but expensive

Always dreamed of dangling above the jaws of a cold-blooded killer with only a steel string between you and consumption? Gatorland's newest attraction takes you up a seven-story tower overlooking its crocodile habitats and alligator marsh. Then they make you step off a small platform and slide a total of 1,200 feet along a series of zip-line segments, each between 230 and 500 feet long. You'll be hitting speeds of up to 30 mph, so hold tight to the provided protective harness. The price: a princely $70; at least park admission is included.

Note: Advance reservations are required. No open-toed shoes allowed. Participants must be over 37 inches tall, under 275 pounds (they weigh you!), and sign a liability waiver (parents or guardians must sign for minors). Are we scared yet?

Jungle Crocs ★ ★ ★ ★

Type:	Walk-by animal exhibit
Time:	Continuous viewing
Short Take:	Keep an eye out for Blondie, the "leucistic" croc

It's not quite equal time, but this exhibit gives the alligator's crocodilian cousins a chance to bask in the sun. Down a wooden walkway at the southern end of the *Alligator Breeding Marsh*, Gatorland has assembled one of the largest collections of crocodiles, which can be distinguished from alligators by their pointy snouts and snaggly, protruding teeth. There are saltwater crocs ("salties") from Australia and Southeast Asia, Nile Crocs from (where else?) the Nile, as well as a representative cross section of American and Cuban crocodiles.

Swamp Walk ★ ★ ★

Type:	Wooden walkway through a cypress swamp
Time:	5 minutes or as long as you like
Short Take:	Best for bird-watchers

Through an iron gate, across a heavy swinging wooden bridge over an algae-tinged moat with yet more alligators, lies what Gatorland bills as the headwaters of the Everglades. From here, so the sign says, water flows through the Kissimmee lake system to Lake Okeechobee and, thence, to the Everglades.

What we see on this leisurely walk is a wilderness setting with a quiet calm and a very special type of beauty, made all the more enjoyable because, thanks to the raised wooden walkway, we don't have to wade through the muck and the cottonmouth moccasins and the poison ivy to appreciate it. Most folks walk through at a brisk pace, but if you linger you are likely to be rewarded with glimpses of birds and other wildlife that more hurried tourists miss out on.

Much of the Orlando area looked just like this before people started draining the wetlands to farm and, later, build shopping malls. Only the soft whoosh of traffic on nearby highway 441 reminds us that we are in modern, not primordial, Florida.

Giant Gator Lake ★ ★ ★ ★

Type: Huge alligators in huge observation area
Time: As long as you wish
Short Take: Rewards patient viewing

This is the huge lake that lies right next to the Gift Shop and park entrance. The place is home to Gatorland's largest specimens, giant 12-footers who are truly awesome, whether in catatonic repose in the sun or cruising ominously through the murky waters.

Other than feeding them (below), there's not much to do here except watch. At first it will seem that there's nothing much going on. It may even seem that some of these critters are statues. But your patience will be rewarded. As you continue looking you will be able to sort the alligators from the crocodiles and start to notice those nicely camouflaged gators lurking in the shadows or lying submerged and motionless.

Photo Op: If you've got a video camera try for a shot of a white heron hitching a ride on the back of a floating gator. Also, look for a large plaster model of an alligator on the boardwalk; it makes a good prop for a photo of your fearless kids.

Feed the Gators ★ ★ ¹⁄₂

Type: Audience participation
Time: A few minutes
Short Take: Fun for the kids

Near the *Gator Jumparoo* platform is a stand selling five turkey hot dogs for $2.50 (with discounts available for those who prefer to buy in bulk) to those who'd like to feed a gator. Don't expect to be able to dangle your hand down like the gator wrangler in the *Jumparoo* show. The trick to feeding gators is to loft your hot dog gently so it lands to either side of the gator's head. They can't see directly in front. Many of the dogs wind up in the beaks of the ugly wood storks that patrol this area. Resist the temptation to hand feed these scavengers; their beaks can draw blood.

Tip: Take your hot dogs over to the *Alligator Breeding Marsh* and feed the gators from the Observation Tower. The gators over here are not as well-fed as those in the *Giant Gator Lake* and will show more interest in your free handouts.

Alligator Alley Animal Exhibits ★ ★

Type: Zoo–like walk-by exhibits
Time: 15 to 30 minutes
Short Take: Worth a stroll by; kids will enjoy feeding the parakeets, goats, and deer

Alligator Alley is lined with a hodge-podge of cages, pens, and glass-walled displays that hearken back to the days when Gatorland was building its collection of "exotic" animals. Today, most of the animals on display are Florida natives like "Judy" the black bear and a small collection of emus, along with a variety of turtles, gators, and crocs.

The newest addition to the Alley is the **White Gator Swamp**, home to four of the world's largest leucistic (not albino) ivory-colored gators inside Cajun-themed glass cubicles. The **Snakes of Florida** display is one of the more elaborate, housing a representative sample of Florida's 69 snake species behind glass windows and accompanied by helpful bits of written information. The walk-through **Very Merry Aviary** houses a scruffy band of parakeets that you can feed ($1 per serving); it is open for hour periods on a regular schedule posted on the door.

Many of the animals, like the macaws and emus (not Florida natives), and the farm animals in **Allie's Barnyard** can be fed. Convenient dispensers at a number of enclosures contain appropriate treats (at 25 cents a modest handful) for the kids to feed to their favorites. Like the aviary, Allie's Barnyard opens up for half-hour to hour-long up close sessions about four times a day, and ice cream cones of critter food sell for $2, or three for $5. Across the way from Allie's Barnyard, look for **Flamingo Lagoon**, home to a small flock of American flamingos. The graceful pink birds, immortalized by millions of tacky lawn ornaments, are actually a light grey at birth. They get their reddish color from their diet of brine shrimp.

Shell Shack ★ ★ ★ 1/2

Type:	Walk-by exhibit with occasional opportunities for interaction
Time:	Continuous viewing, or scheduled times as posted
Short Take:	Low-key fun for families with small fry

Most of the traffic seems to flow through the right half of *Alligator Alley*, but to the left lie a few treasures worth seeking out. Some of the more impressive inhabitants dwell in an unassuming little enclosure, with a small shed helpfully labeled "Shell Shack." This spot is the home of three Aldabara tortoises, mammoth creatures that range from 500 to 550 pounds apiece. The species comes from an island off the coast of Africa, though these particular tortoises retired here from Busch Gardens. The individuals on display are each over 90 years old, and have a life expectancy of over 150 years. While they're striking enough just to look at from outside the enclosure, an occasional "Meet the Keeper" event, with times helpfully announced on a whiteboard near the shack, affords an opportunity to get closer to these gentle giants.

For a $5 fee, the keeper supplies children with a few quartered carrots skewered on long wands, to permit kiddies to feed the tortoises without getting their fingers too close to their powerful beaks. This seems an excellent interaction for young children in particular; it is quiet, low-key, and the tortoises, while impressive (and often more than thigh-high to a parent) are slow-moving and so less likely to spook the little ones. Toddlers here look both more at ease and more excited at the chance to feed and walk around a giant tortoise than the mostly stunned-looking tots getting their photos taken in the gator-wrestling ring. As an added bonus, one parent per child is permitted to enter the enclosure for free, for a better photo opportunity.

Gator Gully Splash Park ★ ★ ★

Type:	Wet play area
Time:	As long as you wish
Short Take:	For kids unimpressed by alligators

Located just a hop, skip, and a jump away from the *Gator Jumparoo* arena and next to the Aldabara tortoises, *Gator Gully Splash Park* is a quarter-acre of splashing, spritzing contraptions guaranteed to cool off your overheated brood. They'll find sculpted gators with back-mounted water guns, giant egrets with spouting beaks, and "Grandma's Wet Shack" full of squirting fountains.

An adjoining playground offers refuge for squirmy toddlers. This small play area is geared to the wee set with small-scale frog-themed slides and other fun things to do. It's all dry so you don't have to worry about junior getting sopping wet and there is a small shaded area that gives parents some relief from the sun. A clothes changing station is conveniently close at hand.

Chapter Eight:

The Holy Land Experience

WHEN THE HOLY LAND EXPERIENCE, ORLANDO'S NEWEST THEME PARK, OPENED IN February 2001, it garnered worldwide publicity, much of it tinged with controversy. It received hoots and sniggers from secularists for whom religion is, at best, a quaint anachronism. It also took flak from some religious leaders who took exception to the very idea of the new park. Aside from referring one and all to the First Amendment of the U.S. Constitution, I do not wish to get involved in whatever controversy there may be about The Holy Land Experience. I would, however, like to report that, taken on its own terms, it is a remarkably successful endeavor.

Using popular media for religious messages has a long and honorable tradition, from the mystery plays of medieval Europe, that sought to teach Bible stories to the illiterate, to the Mitzvah-Mobiles of modern day New York that reach out to lapsed Jews. So why not a theme park that seeks to bring to life the Jerusalem of the time of Jesus Christ and teach, nay preach, a religious message to those who come to gawk? It may not be for everyone but the medium just might get the message across to people unlikely to pull out and dust off that Gideons Bible in their motel room.

Reflecting the Jewish heritage of its founder, Marvin Rosenthal, The Holy Land Experience originally placed considerable emphasis on the Jewishness of Jesus and his milieu. While the current owner, Trinity Broadcasting Network (TBN), has directed the park's current focus squarely towards the evangelical Christian audience the network serves, the park staff still greets you with a hearty "Shalom!" Ancient Hebrew hymns highlight some of the live performances, several of the exhibits pay homage to the Judaic traditions of the Old Testament, and Jewish prayer shawls and menorahs are sold in the gift shops. Much of the merchandise is imported from Israel.

The Holy Land Experience is not a large park, just 15 acres, about the size of a small "land" at one of the major Orlando parks. It is also worth noting that, scenically, The Holy Land Experience is extremely well executed. The lead design firm was ITEC Entertainment Corp., the same outfit responsible for much of the theming of Islands of Adventure over at Universal Orlando. They've also done work for Disney and their experience shows, although they were obviously working with a more limited budget here. Still, the results are impressive and The Holy Land Experience compares favorably with other "minor" parks in the Orlando area.

Those drawn to the evangelical Christian message will find a visit to The Holy Land Experience to be enlightening and moving. Secular sceptics are unlikely to be swayed, and kids of any faith may wonder why Mickey has better toys than Jesus. But religious belief or religious yearning are not prerequisites for admission, and non-believers should not dismiss The Holy Land Experience out of hand. Lovers of history, theology, or archeology will find much of interest, and the park is as scenic and well-maintained as any in town.

Before You Come

If you would like current information about operating hours and schedules, you can call, toll-free, (800) 447-7235. The local number is (407) 872-2272. The website for the park, www.holylandexperience.com, contains basic information and is a good place to check for late-breaking developments.

If you haven't already read the Bible, it's unlikely you'll do so just to prepare for a theme park visit, but here's a fairly painless assignment anyway. Pull out the Bible in your hotel room and glance through the closing chapters of Exodus, starting at Chapter 36, to learn a bit about the construction of the wilderness tabernacle. If you like, continue on into the first several chapters of Leviticus to learn about the practice of blood sacrifice. One of the more interesting presentations at The Holy Land Experience is based on these sections of the Good Book.

When's The Best Time To Come?

I generally advise against visiting theme parks during the busiest times of the year if you can possibly avoid it, but because of Holy Land's seasonal pageants (described below) I will make an exception here. At Christmas and Easter The Holy Land Experience mounts some rather elaborate shows that are worth watching and that can be profoundly moving for believers.

Getting There

The Holy Land Experience is located at 4655 Vineland Road at the corner of Conroy Road. It is just off Exit 72 on I-4 and can be clearly seen from the highway. Coming from the south (that is, traveling east on I-4), turn left at the top of the exit ramp, cross the bridge, and take the first right. Coming from the north (west on I-4), keep turning right from the top of the exit ramp. This will take you into the parking lot of The Holy Land Experience. Parking is **free** for all vehicles.

Opening and Closing Times

The Holy Land Experience is open year-round every day except Sundays. Normal operating hours are Monday to Saturday, 10:00 a.m. to 6:00 p.m. During holiday periods, hours may be changed or extended. Call for more information.

The Price of Admission

The Holy Land Experience has several ticket options. Because it is a not-for-profit ministry, no taxes are levied on the admission charges.

One-Day Pass

Adult: $35
Youth (6–12): $20
Child (3–5): $7

Children under 3 are **free**. Everyone 6 and older gets admission for 50% on their birthday (proof of age required). One-day passes can be upgraded to a second admission, which must be used within 30 days, for $15. There is no annual pass option.

Good Things To Know About . . .

Access for the Disabled. All of The Holy Land Experience is wheelchair accessible. A limited number of non-motorized wheelchairs are available for **free** from Guest Services on a first-come/first-served basis. No motorized scooters are available; if you need one you must make your own arrangements. American sign language interpretation is available free with two weeks advance reservation; call (800) 447-7235.

Babies. A limited number of strollers are available for free in the Old Scroll Shop. Diaper changing areas are available in all the restrooms in the park.

Dress Code. The Holy Land Experience expects its guests to dress appropriately. While recognizing that most people are here on vacation, the management draws the line at halter tops, short-shorts, and other forms of dress deemed (in their opinion) to be immodest. They also refuse entry to those who arrive "in costume."

Bible Study and Church Services. The Holy Land Experience offers **free** Thursday night Bible study sessions at 7:30 p.m. and Sunday church services at 10:30 a.m. when the park itself is closed. Parking is also **free** for these events.

First Aid. First-aid facilities are available in the Guest Services office near the front.

Group Rates. If you have a group of 10 or more adults, you can qualify for reduced rates. You must reserve ahead, and the total cost must be paid in full four weeks prior to your visit. Your tickets will be held at Guest Services pending your arrival. Call the park for current group rates.

Leaving the Park. If you wish to leave the park during the day, make sure to retain your ticket. You can use it to regain admittance later in the day. Leaving for lunch is an option, and there are numerous restaurants a short drive away at the Millennia Mall complex.

Lost and Found. If you lose something during your visit, chances are it will turn up at Lost and Found in Guest Services. This is a religious theme park after all.

Money. ATMs are located in Guest Services and the Shofar Shop.

Pets. The Holy Land Experience has no pet boarding facilities, and no animals (other than seeing-eye dogs) are allowed in the park. Plan accordingly.

Prayer and Religious Activity. The management of The Holy Land Experience expects some exhibits to move visitors to prayer. However, they reserve the right to eject those whose religious activity (in their opinion) is creating a disturbance.

Sun. Much of The Holy Land Experience takes place outdoors under the broiling

Florida sun. The *Plaza of the Nations*, an uncovered marble square, can get brutal on the warmest days. Although some events are moved indoors during the height of summer, head coverings and sunscreen are highly recommended.

Rain. In the event of rain, outdoor presentations may be moved inside to the Shofar Auditorium. However, the actors are game for performing outdoors in a drizzle, since "the rain falls on the just and unjust alike."

Smoking and Alcohol. The Holy Land Experience is a non-smoking, alcohol-free facility.

Weddings. Using the Temple and the Plaza of Nations can make for a spectacular wedding. Call (866) 872-4659 for more information.

Eating in The Holy Land Experience

You have five dining choices, two indoor quick-service cafes and three outdoor stands. The **Oasis Palms Cafe** is a small cafeteria seating just 120 people, half of them outside at tables overlooking the Oasis Lagoon and its towering jet-like fountain. The menu is American with a smidgen of Middle Eastern. In true theme park style they even serve "Goliath Burgers," which are hearty American fare, as are the herb-roasted potatoes you can get to accompany them. Other entrees include grilled chicken sandwiches, chicken tenders, and turkey drumsticks. The gyros (with pita chips and hummus on the side) are particularly tasty. Expect to pay about $11 for a sandwich, side, and soda. **Centurion Treats** is a take-away window attached to the back of the cafe, serving pretzels and ice cream. **Simeon's Corner** is an outdoor snack stand serving hot dogs, pretzels, and cold drinks. The **Royal Portico Eatery** serves hot turkey legs, ice cream, and smoothies. All the above locations also offer bagged Chick-fil-A chicken sandwiches for significantly above drive-thru prices. A final option is **Holy Grounds**, a wittily named coffee shop with cold snacks and cakes.

Shopping in The Holy Land Experience

There are no money changers in the Temple, but there is shopping nearby, much of it near the front entrance. A lot of the merchandise is from Israel, including some lovely Havdalah candles, cups and plates, and Nativity scenes carved from olive wood. There is original religious art at prices (up to $5,000) that might make you say a quick prayer. You can also find Bibles and a variety of devotional books, audiotapes, and videos, many featuring prominent television evangelists associated with TBN. A section of The Old Scroll shop near the entrance has a children's area featuring a big-screen TV and biblical videos.

The Pilgrim's Way:
Your Day at The Holy Land Experience

The Holy Land Experience is recommended as a full-day experience, although to fully absorb all the park has to offer will require coming back for at least a second visit. When you arrive, you will be given a map that contains information about the park's amenities and services. You will also get a separate schedule of live shows and other events that you can use to plan your day.

I found the most workable strategy was to arrive early and see a few of the live performances first. Most of the shows have just one performance each day, but the schedule is such that you have a comfortable amount of time to move from one show to the next and get a good seat. During the hottest part of the day (for you summer visitors), you can see the indoor presentations.

This touring strategy will take you into the late afternoon. The entire park population turns out for the afternoon *Passion Play*, so pick your seats early. If you leave early, you might want to return at closing (remember to save your ticket) for the **Living Waters** show. During the holidays, the parking lot stays open late so you can admire the illuminated displays outside the park gate.

Attractions at The Holy Land Experience

The Holy Land Experience's attractions include both indoor presentations that operate more or less continuously, and live productions (both indoor and outdoor) that perform on a limited schedule. It is unlikely that you will be able to see all of the live shows. For one thing, not all shows are presented every day, and if you try to catch every live show offered, you will not only have to skip lunch but probably won't have time for the indoor presentations, most of which are very much worth seeing. My best advice is to scan the schedule, pick out the live shows that appeal the most and plan your day accordingly.

In addition to the below attractions, the 2,000-seat Vatican-meets-Vegas **Church of All Nations** is where TBN's *Praise the Lord* is produced each Friday evening; studio audience admission is free. And at park open and closing, the **Living Waters** 15-minute synchronized fountain show, set to inspirational music, makes a fitting punctuation for the day, especially after sunset. Holy Land's map also lists several "points of interest" that are simplistic static tableaus, like the "authentically reproduced" Bethlehem Bus Loop and the Garden of Eden's out-of-scale menagerie. You'll stumble over most sites naturally; don't sweat any you miss.

Qumran Cave Presentations ★ ★ ★

Type: Walk-through exhibit and communion
Time: About 15 minutes
Short Take: Worth a quiet moment

The real Qumran caves are where a trove of ancient biblical texts belonging to the Essenes (an ascetic sect of Jews who were Jesus's contemporaries) was discovered in 1947. Here, they are an imposing facade that conceals two unrelated experiences, each with its own entrance. "The Tiny Town of Bethlehem" is a detailed model of the manger site, sculpted in Italy from soapstone; it's followed by a replica of the Church of the Nativity birthplace shrine. "Holy Communion with Jesus" is a Last Supper nosh of *matzoh* crackers and grape juice (served in a complementary wooden thimble) held a dozen times daily in a richly decorated chamber.

Smile of a Child Adventure Land ★ 1/2

Type:	Outdoor play area
Time:	As long as the kids want
Short Take:	Interactive biblical fun

This is as a play area where kids can burn off some excess energy when they aren't feeling particularly devotional. Simple displays depict Moses, Noah's Ark, and Jonah in the belly of the whale. There's a small-scale climbing wall for kids age 8 and up and a couple offbeat **photo ops** like Jesus on a motorcycle.

Seasonal Pageants ★ ★ ★

Type:	Multi-location musical dramas
Time:	40 minutes
Short Take:	Large-scale expressions of faith

During the Christmas and Easter seasons additional live performances with an appropriate holiday theme will almost certainly be added, oftentimes displacing one or more of the shows already mentioned. Some, but by no means all, special holiday shows may require an additional charge.

During the Christmas season, you might see *Bethlehem's Miracle Night*, while at Easter you might see *Follow Me: The Road To Resurrection*. These shows are more elaborate versions of the year-round shows described above and below. The Christmas show I saw, for example, featured a dramatic entrance by the three wise men, and quasi-operatic music in the Andrew Lloyd Webber mode; many of the vocal performances are quite accomplished. If you are planning on visiting during a holiday period, it's a good idea to call ahead or visit the Holy Land website to find out what will be playing when you arrive.

The Wilderness Tabernacle ★ ★ ★ ★

Type:	Stage show with special effects
Time:	25 minutes
Short Take:	Interesting evocation

Of all the attractions at The Holy Land Experience, this is the most theme-park-like. In a darkened theater, we see a dramatized re-creation of the tabernacle God commanded Moses to build in the wilderness after the exodus from Egypt. As a voice-over narrator tells the history of the tabernacle, an actor representing Aaron, the very first High Priest, mimes the rituals and sacrifices being described. Because the Bible (Exodus, Chapter 36ff) gives fairly complete instructions for building the tabernacle, the re-creation is remarkably evocative.

The presentation progresses from the sacrificial altar and bronze laver (or purification bath) outside into the tabernacle itself, where the Arc of the Covenant resided and into which the High Priest entered just once a year. The presentation ends with a "Shekinah Glory" special effect that is straight out of *Raiders of the Lost Ark*. All in all, I found this show a fascinating use of theme park show biz to teach a religious and archaeological lesson.

Passion Play (at Calvary's Garden Tomb) ★ ★ ★ 1/2

Type: Drama set on a re-creation of Christ's tomb
Time: 35 minutes
Short Take: Moving and dramatic

In a sunken garden setting, the approach lined with white lilies at Easter time, lies an imaginative reconstruction of Christ's tomb. The huge circular stone door is rolled aside as it was on the third day when the women who came to anoint Christ's body discovered He was risen. If you step inside you see a typical tomb of the period, the winding cloths in disarray, and a small sign that says. "He is not here for He is risen."

Above the tomb rise the three crosses of the crucifixion. Shaded seats and benches in front of the tomb allow a place for quiet contemplation most of the day, and provide audience seating during one of the daily *Passion Plays* depicting Jesus's final earthly moments.

"The Passion of Jesus Christ" is a fast-paced dramatization of the life and death of the Nazarene. A winged angel announces Mary's immaculate impregnation; then we fast-forward to the Garden of Gethsemane for Judas' kiss. Pilate, perched atop a nearby tower, washes his hands. Then Roman soldiers beat Jesus bloody, scourge him with whips, and lead him through the crowd to the cross on Calvary Hill above the Garden Tomb. The entire event is presented in graphic, even gory detail, and parents with young children may want to beware.

Tip: A family seating section is designated to shield young eyes from the most graphic moments. Use it.

The show concludes with the rolling back of the empty tomb, and a call to group prayer set to a dramatic Contemporary Christian pop soundtrack. Holy Land's "CENTURY" acting ensemble performs with obvious emotion and commitment befitting the subject.

In the rear of the seating area is the small **Judean Village Stage** where you may see small-scale devotional skits, such as "The Woman at the Well," about a shady Samaritan who meets Jesus.

Note: Many of the plants in the park have signage explaining their biblical connections. Here at the tomb, for example, a sign in front of an aloe plant tells us that the plant was often used for embalming and offers a Bible verse (John 19:39) in which the plant is mentioned.

Temple of the Great King and Plaza of the Nations ★ ★ ★

Type: Historical re-creation
Time: Continuous viewing
Short Take: A fitting setting for the shows

The *Temple of the Great King* is a one-third scale re-creation of Herod's Temple, which stood on Jerusalem's Mount Moriah in the first century A.D. What we see is actually just the Temple's facade and a courtyard in front of it surrounded by 30 Corinthian columns with golden capitals. Supposedly, this is all archaeologically accurate. Be that as it may, the *Plaza of Nations*, as this space is called, is a dazzling centerpiece for The Holy Land Experience. Add a high priest in white robes and bulbous turban, blowing a shofar to summon the faithful, and a uniformed Roman solider striding purposefully about and you have a nice, if pared down, evocation of ancient Jerusalem.

Some of the live performances take place here, using the semicircular steps to the Temple as a stage. Seating is provided by folding chairs arranged in a semicircle facing the Temple. The signature show performed here is "We Shall Behold Him," a glitzy gospel pageant visualizing Jesus's triumphant return, accompanied by sequin-wearing angels, that immediately follows the Passion presentation. It is also used for the day-ending "Miracle Moment" prayer session.

Theater of Life ★ ★ ¹ᐟ²

Type:	Religious films
Time:	30 to 90 minutes
Short Take:	Well done

A 150-seat theater hidden away behind the facade of the *Temple of the Great King* is used for the screening of films that speak directly to believers. Twice each day, *The Seed of Promise* is shown. This handsomely produced film, shot on location in Israel in high-definition video, encapsulates the religious message of The Holy Land Experience. Beginning with a depiction of the Roman sack of Jerusalem in 70 A.D., the film travels back in time to the Creation, where we see Adam and Eve in the Garden of Eden, and forward again to the almost sacrifice of Abraham atop Mount Moriah. The 30-minute film ends with Jesus, arisen from the dead, visiting the lands around Jerusalem and making Himself known to His followers.

The rest of the day, a selection of feature-length films produced by TBN—currently *Lion of Judah*, *The Emissary*, and *One Night with the King*—are screened in their entirety. Between films, the theater hosts "Make a Joyful Noise to the Lord" karaoke, where guests can get up and sing spiritual standards; think of it as *Aramaic Idol*.

Jerusalem Model A.D. 66 ★ ★ ★ ★

Type:	Large city model
Time:	Continuous viewing
Short Take:	Come for the informative talks

A large room in a building past the *Plaza of the Nations* houses a fascinating scale model of Jerusalem as it existed in 66 A.D. Why 66 A.D.? Because, with the completion of the northern wall, this was the largest the ancient city ever grew. Four years later, it was obliterated by the Romans in retaliation for Jewish uppityness.

The model, which measures 45 feet by 25 feet, is historically accurate with one exception. The houses have been enlarged to show detail. The housing was actually six times as dense and the streets 15 times as narrow as depicted. In fact, the houses were packed so closely together that in Jesus's time you could leap from roof to roof and traverse the entire length of the city without ever touching the ground.

That last tidbit was gleaned from the fascinating half-hour talks that are given here. I strongly urge you not to miss these entertaining mini-lectures. Without them, the display is merely interesting, but the talks make this the best attraction at The Holy Land Experience.

Several times a day, a knowledgeable biblical scholar (most if not all of them are preachers) steps onto a small open space next to the Temple Mount and, with the aid of a laser pointer, conducts a guided tour of the Jerusalem that Jesus knew. In a fascinating blend of Bible stories with historical records and archaeological excavation, he brings oft-told stories of the work and especially the Passion of Jesus to life. I was fascinated to learn, for example, that Jesus's description of Gehenna (Hell) was a direct reference to the trash heap that burned ceaselessly outside Jerusalem's walls. His contemporary listeners would have known immediately what He was talking about. A DVD version of this talk is available for purchase and may make an excellent souvenir of your visit.

Shofar Auditorium Shows ★ ★ ★ to ★ ★ ★ 1/2

Type: Theatrical presentations
Time: 15 to 40 minutes
Short Take: Religious theater for every taste

Behind the model of Jerusalem lies the 510-seat Shofar Auditorium. Here, a half-dozen stage shows are presented beginning about an hour after park open. "Lengua" is a broad comedy about the influence of angels on everyday lives, with a tongue-in-cheek retelling of "Daniel and the Lion's Den" that will tickle kids. "Why I Love Him" dramatizes the agony of Jesus's female followers after his arrest. "Forgiven" follows three wayward Israelites (King David, Hosea's wife Gomer, and Saul) on their return to righteousness. All three are extremely professional, performing passionately even if their glitzy costumes aren't exactly authentic. Striking lighting and slick soundtracks add to the drama. Other offerings include a patriotic musical revue and a worship concert, both rousing examples of their kind. Shows change frequently so read the descriptions in the printed schedule; if the topic appeals to you, the production values are likely to satisfy.

The Scriptorium ★ ★ ★ 1/2

Type: Guided, themed museum
Time: 55 minutes
Short Take: Well done, but for the serious-minded

Themed after a fourth century Byzantine monastery, the Scriptorium houses the Robert and Judith Van Kampen collection of biblical manuscripts, codices, incunabula, and other rare books that document the history of how the Bible has been preserved, published, and disseminated through the ages.

This is not your typical museum, however, with its treasures arrayed in well-lit rooms and accompanied by explanatory text. The Scriptorium's designers, seemingly inspired by nearby theme parks, have created a richly themed walking tour that uses set elements, decoration, smoke effects, dramatic lighting, and speaking mechanical figures to tell, not the Bible story but the story of the Bible, which is touted in media-savvy terms as "the best-selling book of all time."

This is a guided tour in the sense that a voice-over narration (some tours are in Spanish) offers tidbits of information about the articles on exhibit as changes in lighting signal guests to move on to the next chamber. Along the way, the narrator offers a distinctly evangelical interpretation of the propagation of the Christian faith, the Protestant Reformation, and the subsequent spread of various Christian sects to the New World. Highlights include 4,000-year-old cuneiform tablets, a "Tyndale Bible" reputedly stained with the blood of a martyr who died for possessing it, a re-creation of Gutenberg's printing press, and a narrow escape through Wycliffe's fireplace to elude persecutors. The tour culminates with a soul-stirring recitation of the Ten Commandments, complete with Charlton Heston-worthy lighting effects.

Serious Bible students and lovers of rare books will find much of interest here. Committed Christians will doubtless be moved by some moments in the tour. Others might be less impressed, I'm afraid. The tour's length and stately pace could well prove a problem for younger visitors and the easily bored. There is no exit once the tour commences.

Near the exit, in a small room, the Ex Libris Book Shoppe features a video presentation called **A Day In The Life Of A Monk**, which chronicles the daily routine of the pre-Reformation monastics who played such a pivotal role in preserving ancient scriptures (and along with them a great deal of the wisdom of ancient Rome and Greece, although this isn't mentioned). It's in black and white and runs on a continuous loop. The more historically minded should find it interesting.

Chapter Nine:

Legoland Florida

LEGOLAND IS THE YOUNGEST OF FLORIDA'S MANY THEME PARKS, BUT ITS ORIGIN IS intertwined with the oldest. In the opinion of many, the Central Florida theme park phenomenon actually began when Dick Pope carved a man-made paradise out of a patch of swampy cypress forest along the east shore of Lake Eloise to create Cypress Gardens in 1936. Most people thought he was nuts. One newspaper called him "the Swami of the Swamp." But Cypress Gardens soon became world-renowned for its spectacular botanical gardens and its innovative water ski spectaculars. As theme parks boomed in the 1970s, Cypress Gardens retained much of the easygoing, leisurely air that characterized its early days, relegating it to perennial also-ran status and gaining a reputation, partially deserved, as a park for senior citizens.

Cypress Gardens limped into the new millennium before closing in 2003, a victim to changing tastes, declining attendance, and mounting financial losses. An amusement park owner from Georgia attempted to rescue Cypress Gardens by tacking on an assortment of off-the-shelf carnival rides, but it folded for good in 2009. It looked like the park's prized lakeside real estate would be turned into luxury home sites.

Instead, enter Merlin Entertainment, operator of Euro-centric tourist attractions like Madame Toussauds, Alton Towers, and the London Eye. In January 2010, Merlin announced their purchase of the former Cypress Gardens site, and presented their plans to convert it into America's first East Coast Legoland, the fifth park in a family-focused chain that stretches from Billund, Denmark, to Carlsbad, California.

The resulting park premiered in October 2011 (a remarkably short time to develop a 150-acre attraction) and represents a departure from the high-tech, thrill-seeking theme parks found in Tampa and Orlando. Legoland is entirely successful when viewed from the perspective of its intended audience: 2- to 12-year-olds who have been raised on LEGO's ubiquitous building block toys. Legoland also retains just enough of Cypress Gardens' original treasures to appeal to people who remember the park in its horticultural heyday. Childless people between those demographics will be hard-pressed to find enough to occupy themselves for a full day, or justify the substantial admission fee. But for many toddlers to tweens, Legoland's less-overwhelming scale and hands-on interactivity might make it even more appealing than Mickey's Magic Kingdom, at a slightly smaller price.

Before You Come

If you'd like to get advance information on what will be going on at Legoland during the time of your visit, give them a call at (877) 350-LEGO (5346). They'll be happy to fill you in on the events calendar or send information. Legoland also maintains a colorful website at http://florida.legoland.com.

When's the Best Time to Come?

Legoland is too new to provide accurate crowd predictions, but you can expect attendance to follow along with Orlando's larger parks, peaking during summer, Christmas, and other school holidays. I recommend spring and fall, since the weather is close to ideal; the summer can be stifling and winter is unpredictable, with temperatures ranging from pleasant to quite chilly. Be sure to check Legoland's online calendar before planning your trip, since from September through May the park is closed on most Tuesdays and Wednesdays.

Getting There

Legoland is a leisurely one-hour drive from Orlando (less, if you drive like the locals who take the 65 mph speed limit as a suggested minimum). The easiest way to get there is to follow I-4 West to Route 27 South. Turn right at State Route 540. Legoland is a bit less than four miles along on your left.

If you prefer not to drive, Legoland operates a shuttle bus service from Orlando for $10 per person round trip, which was available at press time for a "preview price" of $5. Pickup is at 9:00 a.m. daily from the Orlando Premium Outlet shops on Vineland Road. Riders are asked to arrive 30 minutes prior to departure. Return service is provided back to the same location at the park's closing time. You can book reservations on the Legoland website at the same time you buy your park admission.

Parking at Legoland

Legoland's parking is $12 for cars, $15 for RVs and trailers, and $6 for motorcycles. Handicapped parking is available close to the entrance for those with a valid placard, and "preferred" parking spots go for $20. If you leave the park, hold onto your parking receipt for free same-day re-entry.

Opening and Closing Times

Unlike many area theme parks, Legoland does not open early and rarely boogies late. The park opens every operating day at 10:00 a.m. Closing time varies from 5:00 p.m. during slower periods to 6:00, 7:00, 8:00, or 9:00 p.m. The schedule is somewhat erratic; a color-coded calendar on the website will be invaluable in planning your visit. Note that the park is closed on Tuesdays and Wednesdays during off-peak months.

The Price of Admission

Legoland sells admission by the day and by the year. At press time, prices (not including tax) were as follows:

One-Day Pass:
Regular $75 ~ Child (3 to 12) $65 ~ Seniors (60+) $65

Two-Day Pass:
Regular $90 ~ Child (3 to 12) $80 ~ Seniors (60+) $80

Water Park Admission (open seasonally, theme park admission required):
Ages 3+ $12 ~ Under 3 $3

Standard Annual Pass (one year of main park admission only):
Regular $129 ~ Ages 3 to 12 and 60+ $99

Plus Annual Pass (includes parking plus food and merchandise discounts):
Regular $159 ~ Ages 3 to 12 and 60+ $129

Premium Annual Pass (Plus Pass benefits and seasonal water park admission):
Regular $179 ~ Ages 3 to 12 and 60+ $149

Garden Pass (one year of main park admission with parking, valid Monday to Friday only)
Seniors (60+) only $85

Ambassador Annual Pass (Lifetime admission to Legoland Florida):
All Ages $2500

The standard annual pass, is only valid for one year of admission, and does not include parking or any discounts. Since the Plus Pass costs only $30 more, and includes free parking and a variety of discounts. If you plan to visit more than twice in one year, it is clearly the way to go.

The Premium Pass adds admission to the water park, which will be open seasonally starting in summer 2012. Without a Premium Pass, a visit to the water park requires a $12 additional fee ($3 for kids under 3). The annual passes make the most sense for Florida residents or others who find themselves in the Winter Haven area on a regular basis. If you decide you want one, stop by the Annual Pass Center near the entrance; they will create your photo ID Pass while you wait.

Eating in Legoland

Your dining choices at Legoland are mostly of the fast-food variety and very little of it justifies the prices being charged, although they say they use fresh ingredients. The best value is the unspectacular **Pizza & Pasta Buffet**, which at least offers a delightful view from the open-air terrace. One exception is the signature Granny's Apple Fries, an addictive combination of sliced apples, cinnamon, and sweet whipped cream.

Otherwise, the cafeteria-style **Market Restaurant** promises "freshly prepared healthy family meals" with salad, stir-fry, roast chicken, and salmon featured on the menu along with the usual burgers and chicken strips for those who just don't want to be all that healthy.

Shopping in Legoland

Like the dining, the shopping is not a reason in itself to visit the park, unless of course you are a LEGO nut, in which case you can complete your collection (and empty your bank account) while here. So if you need to stock up on LEGO toys, games, or branded merchandise of any kind, seek out the **LEGO Studio Store** and **Big Shop** and knock yourself out. There are also some nice things to be found at the **Garden Shop** that offer a welcome relief from the non-stop LEGO merchandising.

Good Things to Know About . . .

Access for the Disabled. Almost all of the park is wheelchair accessible, although some of the inclines are best negotiated with the help of a companion. Ask at Guest Services about accessibility for individual attractions, but be warned that many of the child-scaled rides are challenging for even able-bodied adults to get in and out of. The park seems to be built for European-sized backsides, not American. Both wheelchairs and electric scooters can be rented just inside the entrance on a first-come-first-served basis. Wheelchairs are $10 per day. Electric scooters (ECVs) are $35.

Babies. Strollers can be rented near the entrance, immediately to your left as you enter. Single strollers are $9 per day, doubles are $14. A baby care center near the Fun Town Theater features bottle warmers, nursing rockers, a microwave, and other amenities. Diaper changing stations can be found in all restrooms, men's and women's.

Emergencies. There is a first-aid station next to the Fun Town Factory Tour. Automated External Defibrillators are available throughout the park. If you or someone in your party has a problem, contact one of the park employees, otherwise known as "Model Citizens."

Leaving the Park. You may leave the park and return during the day. Just make sure to have your hand stamped as you leave.

Lockers. Cash and credit card-operated lockers are conveniently located to the left of the main entrance. All-day rental with in-and-out access costs $7 for a "large" locker (holds two backpacks) or $12 for a three-bag "jumbo" locker.

Money. There are ATMs located to the right of the main entrance, and near the baby care center; locations are marked on the park map. A fee of about $2 is charged for their use.

Pets. Other than trained service animals, pets are not permitted on park property. There is a small kennel for cats and dogs to the west of the main entrance, but space is limited. Ask at Guest Services about availability and pricing.

Safety. Like Cypress Gardens before it, Legoland is open to all the birds and animals who take it into their minds to pay a visit. The park warns people not to feed the birds or other little critters because they are wild and unpredictable and may become aggressive. That's good advice, but the squirrels are hard to resist. It's unlikely that you'll see an alligator during your visit but, if you do, remember that feeding wild alligators is not only stupid but illegal.

All attractions have height requirements listed on the map. Most have a minimum of 36 inches or less, and kids under 48 inches can ride on many with an accompanying adult. Even so, be sure to supervise small ones at all times, as the hands-on nature of many of the attractions can make their motion unpredictable.

Special Diets. If you have special dietary needs, ask at Guest Services for a special

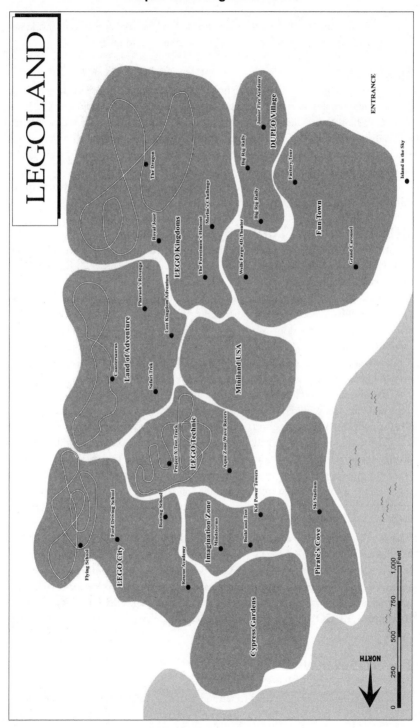

brochure. Guest are not allowed to bring outside food or beverages into the park, but exceptions are made for those with special medical needs and infants.

Special Events

For Christmas, Legoland celebrates the holiday with a 30-foot-tall tree made entirely of bricks. A different family is chosen nightly to aid in a tree lighting ceremony. On New Year's Eve, the park presents a fireworks display at midnight "kids standard time," which is 7:00 p.m. for the rest of us. There are also spectaculars for the Fourth of July (Red, Brick, and Boom) and Halloween (Brick or Treat). All of these are included with regular park admission.

Legoland has also retained Cypress Gardens' open-air amphitheater (where musical acts used to hold forth) for potential future concerts or special events.

Brick by Brick: Your Day at Legoland

Legoland can easily be seen and appreciated in a day. You may not see everything, but as you read through the descriptions that follow, you will probably find there are some things you won't mind missing.

Rides. While no competition for Disney or Universal's mega-bucks attractions, Legoland features a nice variety of kid-friendly rides, including a quartet of junior roller coasters, an interactive indoor dark ride, and an array of creatively decorated carnival-style attractions.

Entertainment. Legoland presents a limited schedule of family-style entertainment, from 3-D films to slapstick comedy and a water-ski stunt show.

Exhibits. Cypress Gardens' original botanical displays are preserved here, albeit in reduced form, alongside elaborately detailed dioramas made entirely of plastic bricks. The combination makes Legoland one of the best parks anywhere for quiet observation.

This is good-sized park, and when you take into account the meandering (and inconsistently signed) paths through the many themed areas, you can walk a fair distance during your visit. The park comprises 150 acres and runs north to south along the shore of Lake Eloise; the sole entrance is at the south end and it is a long walk to the far northern reaches of the park. The park is divided into 11 named areas. **The Beginning** is your colorful introduction to the park, and primarily a dining and shopping venue. It leads to **Fun Town**, modeled on a quaint village square, from which you branch out to other areas of the park. Moving north along the shore of Lake Eloise, you'll pass the lands of **Miniland, Pirates' Cove, LEGO Technic**, and **Imagination Zone**, ending at the historical **Cypress Gardens** botanical display along the park's northern border. Continuing clockwise inland from the shore, you'll encounter **LEGO City, Land of Adventure, LEGO Kingdoms**, and **Duplo Village** before returning back to Fun Town.

The One-Day Stay

As you enter the park, pick up a copy of the park map. Scan this for the show times of the entertainments you most want to see and plan accordingly. If times are not printed inside, they will be displayed on a marquee in Fun Town.

If you arrive at opening time, proceed through Fun Town and bear right into LEGO Kingdoms towards *The Dragon* indoor roller coaster, which will soon develop the park's longest line. Exit to your right to Land of Adventure for the *Lost Kingdom Adventure*, followed by *Beetle Bounce*, *Coastersaurus* and *Safari Trek*. Then cross through LEGO City to *Rescue Academy*, then the *Driving*, *Flying*, and *Boating Schools*. Follow those with the *Test Track* and *Aquazone* in the LEGO Technic area.

At this point you have hit all of the park's major rides. Check the show schedule again for the performances you had your eye on, and experience any of the other minor rides you come across if wait times seem reasonable.

Now you have the afternoon to tour the Miniland displays and botanical gardens, visit the water park (for an additional fee, in season), or enjoy a leisurely lunch. Crowds should be an issue in the park only on the busiest days, but lines can build by midday due to the rides' low carrying capacities. *Island in the Sky* is a fun diversion that can be squeezed in just about anytime you like; it only takes five minutes.

Another option is to save your visit to the botanical gardens for late in the day, toward sunset if operating hours allow. Photographers, especially, may find the afternoon sun and the lengthening shadows a plus.

The Beginning

At the park's front gate stands a large overhead marquee announcing the attraction's name in bold primary colors, fronted by the word "Welcome" formed from thousands of LEGO bricks. It's only the first of many block-based statuary displays that you will encounter during your day. Pass under the archway to approach the entrance turnstiles, with windows of ticket vendors located to your right. Once through the gates, you'll see that, apart from some large-scale LEGO sculptures, the entrance plaza looks strictly utilitarian. The park's largest eating and shopping outlets are located here, along with Guest Services, stroller and wheelchair rentals, and the processing center for annual passes. There is only one attraction in this area, but it is a classic well worth experiencing.

Island in the Sky ★ ★ ★ ★

Type: Aerial platform ride
Time: About 3½ minutes
Short Take: A too-short bird's-eye view

Tucked away behind the shops of The Beginning is a 370-ton counterbalance that is used to loft a circular platform 153 feet in the air (roughly 16 stories high), where it rotates to give its passengers a panoramic view of Legoland and Lake Eloise. Off in the distance, you can see the silhouette of stately Bok Tower, 11 miles away. Seating is single-file around the edge of the platform and once the platform is airborne, you can stand and move to the rail for a better look. Recorded narration points out the spectacular sights, making a credible case for Legoland as "one of the most beautiful theme parks in the whole world."

One of the newly restored classic attractions from the Cypress Gardens era, this is a fun way to get another perspective on the park, and the lofty vantage point offers photographers many wonderful **photo ops**. At under four minutes from start to finish, this ride is a bit too short for my taste, but you can ride as many times as you wish (or until your camera battery dies). The location of this attraction and the mobile platform itself have been cleverly hidden behind trees and buildings. You can see the raised platform from elsewhere in the park, but you could spend all day in Legoland and never suspect it was there.

Note: Children under 48 inches must be accompanied by an adult.

Tip: If the park is open late, ride this one at sunset, several times.

Fun Town

Just past the comparatively bland Beginning section lies Fun Town, the navigational hub of the park disguised as a quaint old-fashioned town square. A classic carousel ride is found here, along with a movie theater and walk-through exhibits. This section also boasts the biggest concentration of shopping and eating outlets. Paths branch off from here to the east, toward LEGO Kingdoms and DUPLO Village, and to the north into Miniland.

The Grand Carousel ★ ★ ★

Type: Double-decker merry-go-round
Time: 2 minutes
Short Take: A beautiful boardwalk classic

Every good amusement park needs a classic carousel, and the centerpiece attraction in Fun Town certainly qualifies. This charming traditional merry-go-round features both stationary benches and moving stallions, all decked out in fanciful frills. But what makes it unique is its two-story design. Riders can climb stairs to the second level for a birds-eye ride.

Note: Children under 48 inches must be accompanied by an adult.

Wells Fargo Fun Town 4D Theater ★ ★ ★

Type: 3-D films with effects
Time: About 12 minutes
Short Take: Best for the air conditioning

It's practically Florida law that every theme park must have a "4-D" theater mixing 3-D film with spritzes of water, wind, and similar tactile effects. Legoland has a trio of flicks that play in repertory, rotating every 45 minutes or so throughout the day on the same screen. All three feature LEGO toys, brought to life via computer graphics, whizzing around on G-rated adventures. You can pick between *LEGO Racers*, *Spellbreaker* wizards and skeletons, or *LEGO City*, starring jetpack-wearing adventurer Clutch Powers. All place a premium on ADHD-inducing kinetic action, as opposed to plot or character.

Nothing here will make you forget Disney or Universal's more polished 4-D attractions, but they're fit for young fans of the LEGO brands. The theater provides a passable distraction in a cool room for a quarter hour, but the seats are unfortunately too uncomfortable for a quick nap. Just don't arrive too early unless you want to sit through repetitive advertisements for the park's sponsors.

Tip: If show times aren't printed on your map, check the sign in front of the theater.

Factory Tour ★ 1/2

Type:	Walk-through exhibit
Time:	Less than 10 minutes
Short Take:	A major disappointment

If you were hoping for an impressive demonstration on how LEGOs are made, on the order of the famous Hershey Chocolate World tour, then just keep walking. This simplistic exhibit is barely worth the time it takes to walk through the building. After viewing a brief video about the LEGO legacy, guests enter a single small room with barely animated displays mimicking the stages of LEGO brick production. This faux factory wouldn't fool even the most gullible child, and the pace of the automated exhibits is too slow to hold youngsters' attention. You don't even get a free brick at the end, though there is a store with every size and shape, conveniently sorted by color and priced at a pricey $9 per quarter pound.

And All The Rest...

A small **conservatory**, not yet open at press time, serves as a glassed-in horticultural exhibit.

Miniland

The geographical and thematic heart of the park, Miniland only has one attraction, but it is the area most people, regardless of age, will remember from their visit. Paths on opposite ends of this area lead to Land of Adventure, Pirates' Cove, and back to Fun Town. Signage can be confusing, so check your bearings before heading uphill from this sloping section.

Miniland Displays ★ ★ ★ ★ ★

Type:	Detailed dioramas of national landmarks
Time:	20 minutes to 10 hours
Short Take:	An amazing achievement in model making

More than 25 million factory-standard LEGO building bricks were used to build Legoland, and the majority of them went into this, the park's centerpiece. Eight elaborate displays —I hesitate to call them miniatures, since some tower over ten feet tall—recreate scenes from famous American cities with exacting detail and witty humor. The Las Vegas strip (including Elvis and the Rat Pack), Washington D.C.'s mall of monuments, New York City's Times Square and Central Park, and California from the Golden Gate to Hollywood Bowl are all incarnated in plastic bricks. Unique to this Legoland is a Florida tribute, starring Kennedy Space Center (with a model of the recently retired space shuttle) and Daytona Speedway, along with a Pirate Shores lagoon filled with floating buccaneers.

Each of the displays, which you are free to walk around and photograph at your leisure as long as you don't cross protective railings, features a number of push buttons that activate effects, from racing cars to spraying water. Plaques provide information on the models' real-life inspirations. You could literally spend all day here without seeing all of the careful details lovingly worked into these displays, and for many adults Miniland alone may make the whole trip worthwhile.

Pirates' Cove

This slim area along the lake shoreline is named for its only attraction. It also is home to a hamburger stand, but is chiefly notable as a passage to the Imagination Zone, LEGO Technic, and Cypress Gardens sections. A second lakeside stadium here is usually dormant, except during special concerts and events.

Battle For Brickbeard's Bounty ★ ★ ★

Type: Water-ski stunt show
Time: 15 minutes
Short Take: Moist and tepid

Water skiing has been a Cypress Gardens trademark since the early 1940s. Those who remember Cypress Gardens from the "old days" will find this show a pale shadow of the park's past glories. But for the target audience, who have likely never seen such a stunt show before, this is a gentle introduction to the genre.

A slender plot encourages the audience to root for Miranda, a plucky privateer, as she leads the "imperial guard" in battling pirates over evil Brickbeard's ill-gotten booty. There are a few daring water stunts, and some soaking audience interaction, but the pacing is slow and the skiers (hampered by oversized suits fashioned to look like LEGO figures) move even slower.

Note: The audience "splash zone" is not well marked. Stay away from the front half of the theatre near the big ship if you want to stay dry.

LEGO Technic

This area is inspired by LEGO's "expert builder" mechanical toys. It's among the park's least decorated sections, but is home to a couple of its best thrill rides. This area opens to LEGO City on one end, and Pirates' Cove at the other.

Project X Test Track ★ ★ ★ 1/2

Type: Wild Mouse roller coaster
Time: About 2 minutes
Short Take: A "pink knuckle" thrill for all ages

Though it shares nomenclature with the high-tech E-ticket at Disney's Epcot, Legoland's take is a far-simpler "wild mouse" style roller coaster, similar to what you might find in a local amusement park. This one is larger and taller than most, however, delivering some surprisingly swift dips and tight turns to thrill adults and adventurous kids alike. Watch that first drop, it's a doozy!

Note: Riders must be at least 42 inches. Children under 48 inches must be accompanied by an adult. Wheelchair users must be able to transfer to the vehicle.

Note: This ride's seats are especially unfriendly to riders with larger bottoms.

AQUAZONE Wave Racers ★ ★ ★ 1/2

Type: Spinning ride on water
Time: About 3 minutes
Short Take: Unexpectedly exhilarating

At first glance, this twin set of turning vehicles might look like a simple carnival attraction dressed up with a jet ski theme. But watch out; these waves can pack a punch. Each rider boards a small open-air boat, which is bound to a central turntable by a metal arm. As the two spinning circles of riders sharing the shallow pool pick up speed, blasts of air under the water shower them with a welcome spray. Non-riders can join in the fun by spraying participants with nozzles from the water's edge. The best part is that guests have control over their vehicle's rudder, allowing the craft's rear to swing out with the pull of a lever.

Tip: For maximum centrifugal excitement, use the rudder control to pull your jet ski all the way in towards the center, then quickly swing to the outside.

Note: Riders must be at least 40 inches. Children under 52 inches must be accompanied by an adult. Wheelchair users must be able to transfer to the vehicle.

And All The Rest...

The final carnival-style attraction here, the **Technicycle**, is a "zany" spinning machine that uses pedal-power to send airborne riders turning in circles. You'll also find stands selling snacks, along with the obligatory outlet to purchase a photo package of yourself screaming on the coaster.

Imagination Zone

Imagination Zone parallels LEGO Technic, squeezed between Cypress Gardens and LEGO City. This locale is home to several hands-on interactive attractions, which require kid-power and creativity to activate. In addition to the attractions below, there is a counter serving fried chicken (which may morph into a panini shop if rumors prove true). Don't miss the giant Albert Einstein bust at one end of the area and the cartoon bunny with a chainsaw (seriously!) at the other.

Kid Power Towers ★ ★ ★

Type: Self-powered drop tower
Time: Under 1 minute
Short Take: Best for the view

Here's a scaled-down version of the freefall rides found in many thrill parks, with an interactive twist: pairs of riders must pulley-pull their seat to the top before their smooth descent to the ground. While no *Tower of Terror*, it will give you a brief upper-body workout, and a swell view of the lake.

Interactive Building Areas ★ ★

Type: Hands-on toy activities
Time: Varies
Short Take: A building-block playland

Inside the industrial-looking building that makes up the bulk of the Imagination Zone you'll find a trio of interactive play areas. **LEGO Mindstorms**, **Build & Test**, and **Hero Factory** are each geared to different age groups and brand franchises, but all are self-guided playrooms filled with a vast array of LEGO products. It's either nirvana for creative children or a giant toy commercial, depending on your perspective.

Cypress Gardens

What was once Florida's first theme park has been pared back to a small section of Legoland, but it's still the area's botanical crown jewel. You can access today's Cypress Gardens, which comprises the central portion of the original attraction, from a foot-bridge across from the Pirates' Cove stadium.

Note: There are no restrooms inside the botanical gardens.

Botanical Gardens ★ ★ ★ ★ ★

Type:	Beautifully landscaped gardens
Time:	20 to 30 minutes or as long as you wish
Short Take:	Among the best of its kind in the world and a photographer's paradise

By definition, botanical gardens are a sort of museum. Most botanical gardens seem to strive for order. Succulents here, pines there, palms over there. Tropical plants in this area, temperate plants in that area. That way people can study them better. Completeness is also a goal, trying to have more epiphytes than the next botanical garden, for example. The aesthetics of display, while important, often seem to be a secondary concern, except in the more formal gardens.

The designers of Cypress Gardens, however, seem to have started by asking a simple yet powerful question—"How can we produce the most stunning visual spectacle possible?"—and letting everything else follow from there. The result is a remarkable blend of over-the-top landscaping and serene beauty.

These gardens contain over 8,000 different kinds of plants, trees, and flowers collected from 90 different countries. There are over 60 varieties of azaleas alone. I have no idea whether that means the collection is unusually complete (I mention azaleas only because it's a flower I recognize). Nor do I know if the designers have carefully segregated tropical plants from the temperate varieties (I suspect they have not). But I can't imagine anyone will care. Here the purely aesthetic experience is paramount. A leisurely stroll, with open eyes and a receptive soul, will yield abundant treasures. And if you're a typical vacation photographer, bring along a few more rolls of film (or memory cards) than usual. You'll find ample use for them. As large as it is, the garden is not a maze and there's little likelihood of getting lost.

Tip: The garden is dotted with wooden benches. Bring a handkerchief or paper towel, as many of them are wet in the morning hours, before the sun has had a chance to dry them off.

As you enter the gardens, you cross a bridge onto a chain of man-made islands. To your left is Lake Eloise, its shore guarded by stately cypress trees emerging from the shallow water. To the right is a man-made canal. Must-see sights along this archipelago are the **Big Lagoon** and the massive **banyan tree**. This behemoth began its tenure at Cypress Gardens as a 50-pound sapling in a bucket. Today it's larger than your average castle, with its aerial root system creating a charming maze of paths through its very heart.

Perhaps the most beautiful spot in the entire gardens is the **Gazebo**. This is no rustic wooden affair but a resplendent white-domed structure, inspired by Greek architecture, supported by eight fluted columns, and flanked by gently bubbling fountains. Also known as the "Love Chapel," it was the site of the over 300 weddings that took place at Cypress Gardens each year. The Gazebo stands at the top of a rise that looks down across the Big Lagoon and out to Lake Eloise; the view from here is as fine as the reverse view from below.

The current gardens aren't as large or lush as they once were, but they look better now than at any time since the destructive 2004 hurricanes, and the new owners have committed to continued restoration. The posing Southern Belles have not returned (except in LEGO brick statue form), nor have the botanical boat rides (yet), but there is still enough beauty here to put this treasure at the top of your Legoland must-do list.

LEGO City

This area is the furthest from the front entrance, but it is worth the walk. Some of Legoland's most innovative interactive attractions can be found here, along with its best live show. You can access the area from a hub between LEGO Technic and Imagination Zone, or from the Land of Adventure near the *Big Test* stage.

Rescue Academy ★ ★ ★ ★ 1/2

> *Type:*　　　　Competitive fire-fighting simulation
> *Time:*　　　　About 3 minutes
> *Short Take:*　A pulse-raising blast for the entire family

Better than any other attraction, *Rescue Academy* represents Legoland's admirable design strategy that gets whole families to interact in an imaginative, hands-on environment. It also happens to be wet, exhausting, and a whole lot of fun.

Several teams of participants board life-sized toy fire trucks and pump a handcar-style handle to propel it a dozen yards toward a two-story building engulfed in painted "flames." After hopping out of the truck, some of the players pump another fireplug-mounted handle, while the rest race to aim the water hose at overhead targets. Once the targets are down, each team climbs back into the truck and sprints (at a snail's pace) back to the starting point in pursuit of victory and *Rescue Academy* bragging rights.

There are no fancy flame and smoke special effects here to spice things up, but they aren't necessary to engage all members of the family. You're likely to end your fire fighting career smiling broadly and (if you do most of the heavy pumping) short of breath.

Note: Participants must be at least 34 inches tall. Children under 48 inches must be accompanied by an adult. Wheelchair users must be able to transfer to the vehicle.

FORD Driving School ★ ★ ★ ★ 1/2

> *Type:*　　　Driving course for tweens
> *Time:*　　　About 3 minutes

Short Take: Unfair that only kids get to drive!

Outsaide, the full-sized Explorer assembled from bricks ballyhoos this attraction's corporate sponsor, but let the commercialism pass. LEGO City's second signature attraction looks so much fun, I wish I was still between the mandatory age range of 6 to 13 so that I could try it.

Plenty of parks have miniature driving courses, starting with Disneyland's *Autopia*, but Legoland's is unique in that the cars aren't on rails. The child drivers have complete control of their car's direction, but this is no bumper-car arena. The puttering pathways form a reality-based urban streetscape, complete with working traffic lights, stop signs, and even a roundabout. Employees are on hand to play traffic cop and strictly enforce the rules of the road, which the kids seem to enjoy even more than causing vehicular chaos. Consider this the park's must-do attraction for any budding automotive enthusiasts under the age limit.

For tykes between 3 and 5 who are too small for the full experience, LEGO City also has a scaled-down "Junior" version of the *Driving School*.

Boating School ★ ★ ★ 1/2

Type: Kid-sized motorboat ride
Time: About 5 minutes
Short Take: It's fun to float, but frequently frustrating

Take the *Driving School* attraction, put it on the water, and you've got the basic idea behind *Boating School*. Up to two kids can board a miniature motorboat and pilot it along a twisting canal dotted with nautical LEGO statues. Though outwardly as attractive as the cars, these boats can be challenging for children to pilot in a straight line, and the waterway doesn't allow much freedom of movement. Luckily, employees patrol the shore to give errant vessels a friendly push, but the queue can still become frustratingly slow.

Note: Riders must be at least 34 inches tall. Children under 48 inches must be accompanied by an adult. Wheelchair users must be able to transfer to the vehicle.

Flying School ★ ★ 1/2

Type: Junior suspended roller coaster
Time: About 90 seconds
Short Take: An uncomfortable intro to inverted coasters

An obscure footpath behind the *Driving School* leads to the final institution in Legoland's educational system. This coaster is a holdover from Cypress Gardens' final days, when it was known as *Swamp Thing*. Despite the aeronautical overlay (including a kid-operated propeller plane in the queue) this is still the same rough ride. The seats on this 1,122-foot-long, 48-foot-tall coaster hang below the steel track, leaving riders' legs swinging freely. With no upside-down flips and a top speed of only 26 mph, this should theoretically be ideal for all ages of thrill seekers. Unfortunately, these skies fly unfriendly thanks to excessive side-to-side shaking, leaving guests with jostled jaws. Pliable tweens are liable to jump back in line after riding, but adult aviators will feel one flight is more than enough.

Note: Riders must be at least 44 inches tall. Children under 52 inches must be accompanied by an adult. Riders over 6-foot-5 are also prohibited from riding.

The Big Test Live Show ★ ★ ★ 1/2

Type: Slapstick live show
Time: About 20 minutes
Short Take: Goofy and genial

This physical comedy skit loosely themed around fire safety isn't as hyped as the ski show, but for my money it's more fun. A motley quintet of high-school stereotypes (the jock, the nerd, the cute girl, etc.) compete to become full members of the volunteer fire department and pratfalls ensue. The song and dance sections are nothing to shout about, but the stunts get impressively elaborate by the end. The high-flying finale, featuring a flailing fire-truck ladder, might make even silent stunt legend Buster Keaton crack a smile.

Tip: Audience members in the first few rows may get sprayed or even soaked.

Land of Adventure

With a blend of primeval and Egyptian environments, Land of Adventure is among the most exotic environments in the park. Though short on dining and shopping, it is home to Legoland's most sophisticated ride, along with its only wooden roller coaster. The land connects to LEGO City on the north end and LEGO Kingdoms to the south, with a couple paths branching off to Miniland found between.

Coastersaurus ★ ★ ★

Type: Wooden roller coaster
Time: Under 1 minute
Short Take: Rickety in just the right way

Coastersaurus used to be known as the *Triple Hurricane* and is the second roller coaster salvaged from Cypress Gardens. Unlike its steel siblings, this one uses vintage wood construction to zip you past clever brick statues of life-size (but non-threatening) dinosaurs.

This coaster used to be known for the surprisingly strong G-forces in its final "widow maker" curve, but Legoland's engineers have slowed down the ride, making for a more child-friendly experience. Even with diminished intensity, *Coastersaurus* grants a great view from the top, and a few fun pops of floating "airtime" on the way down.

Note: Riders must be at least 36 inches tall. Children under 48 inches must be accompanied by an adult. Wheelchair users must be able to transfer to the vehicle. The train seats are a tight squeeze for larger guests.

Lost Kingdom Adventure ★ ★ ★ 1/2

Type: Interactive indoor dark ride
Time: About 3 minutes
Short Take: Small-fry shooting gallery on steroids

Climb aboard a jeep-like vehicle and grab a light-blasting pistol for an Indiana

Jones-esque adventure into an Egyptian tomb. Don't worry; the mummies inside are more silly than scary, the four-passenger cars move at a crawl, and you're guaranteed to beat the baddies by the end.

Legoland's most high-tech attraction isn't quite as advanced as Orlando's similar *Men In Black* and *Buzz Lightyear* shooting rides, with simplistic sets and stiffly animated characters. But younger kids raised on video games will likely love this life-size version, tagging the dozens of lighted targets, then trying again for a higher score.

Tip: Hit a lit target, then shoot it again when it changes color for extra points.

Note: Riders must be at least 34 inches tall. Children under 42 inches must be accompanied by an adult. Wheelchair users must be able to transfer to the vehicle.

Beetle Bounce ★ ★ ★ 1/2

Type:	Bouncing tower ride
Time:	Under 1 minute
Short Take:	Whee!!!

At only 15 feet, this pair of tween-scaled drop towers don't look tall enough to be in the same class as their multi-hundred-foot cousins. But think again; these scarab-topped obelisks, each bearing a seven-passenger bench with secure lap restraints, prove big air can come in small packages. Riders are lifted to the top, dropped to the bottom in a buoyant series of short bounces, then sent back to the top for a few more cycles. Though brief, this ride makes thrill veterans and timid tykes alike squeal with giddy delight, without being extreme enough to bring up anyone's lunch.

Note: Riders must be at least 36 inches tall. Wheelchair users must be able to transfer to the vehicle.

Safari Trek ★ ★ ★

Type:	Kiddie car ride past LEGO animals
Time:	Under 2 minutes
Short Take:	Well done, but not worth a long wait

Legoland's land-based spin on Disney's *Jungle Cruise* serves up tiny track-bound safari trucks, which travel a short outdoor path past life-sized LEGO sculptures of African wildlife. The elephants, zebras, lions, and such are remarkably detailed and accurate (as far as brightly colored plastic bricks can be) and the models sport some limited movement and sound effects. Unfortunately, the ride attracts a slow-moving crowd, and once on board kids quickly discover they can't steer like in the *Driving School*.

Tip: You can get a view of many of the attraction's animals by walking past it.

Note: Riders must be at least 34 inches tall. Children under 48 inches must be accompanied by an adult. Wheelchair users must be able to transfer to the vehicle.

And All The Rest...

Pharaoh's Revenge is a small Egyptian-styled sheltered playground featuring foam balls. **Adventure Games** is a grouping of extra-cost midway come-ons. You can likely find similar versions of both (minus the LEGO dressing) back home.

LEGO Kingdoms

You can't build a Florida theme park without a castle, and the medieval fortress that dominates here fills the bill. This modest edifice lacks the lofty architecture of Hogwarts or Cinderella's digs; instead, think of one of LEGO's old-school plastic playsets enlarged to several stories high. You'll find one of Legoland's signature rides here, alongside several small diversions. Exits from here lead west through DUPLO Village to Fun Town, or back north to Land of Adventure.

The Dragon ★ ★ ★

Type: Indoor dark ride meets kiddie coaster
Time: Just over 3 minutes
Short Take: *Revenge of the Mummy* for munchkins

Arguably the headliner attraction at Legoland, *The Dragon* re-purposed Cypress Gardens' second small steel roller coaster, a virtual clone of Universal's *Hippogriff* kiddie ride. They cleverly connected it to indoor "dark ride" scenes depicting a Dark Ages royal court, complete with a jester, a wizard, and the titular overgrown iguana.

The brief vignettes, all constructed from LEGO bricks, display remarkable craftsmanship, but their movement is limited like a department store window display. Special effects are confined to a few flashing lights, and the transition into the outdoor coaster portion is awkwardly unthemed. But it's convincing enough to elicit "oohs" at the opening dioramas from precocious dragonslayers who then squeal as they swoop through the coaster's mild spirals.

Tip: Despite the impressive-looking facade, the slow-moving queue is in the un-air-conditioned outdoors, so ride early in the day. The back seats provide the biggest (though still mild) thrills.

Note: Riders must be at least 40 inches tall. Children under 48 inches must be accompanied by an adult. Wheelchair users must be able to transfer to the vehicle. The train seats are a tight squeeze for larger adults.

Royal Joust ★ ★ 1/2

Type: Horse-inspired kiddie ride
Time: Under 2 minutes
Short Take: A jousting simulation for little Lancelots

Like an ancient English echo of the *Safari Trek*, *Royal Joust* lets little squires age 12 and under try their hand at knightly combat, safely reinterpreted as a ride along a snaking track atop plastic stallions. The twists are that the single-seat conveyances gently buck in imitation of galloping steeds, and the scenery depicts comical medieval characters with a mini-Monty Python wink.

Note: Minimum height is 36 inches; maximum age is 12; maximum weight is 170 lbs.

And All The Rest...

Merlin's Challenge is a barely disguised version of the spinning Himalaya ride you'll find at every traveling fair. (Riders must be at least 36 inches tall. Children under 48 inches must be accompanied by an adult, who should sit toward the outside.) **Jester's**

Games are more unexciting carnival money-suckers. The **Forestmen's Hideout** is a multilevel play structure, like what you'd imagine Robin Hood clambering around as a kid. There is also a small stage in front of the castle where **seasonal shows** may intermittently pop up.

DUPLO Village

The last and smallest of Legoland's lands is based on the spin-off toys designed for the youngest children. Here you'll find a **Playtown** and **DUPLO Farm**-themed playgrounds, along with a handful of preschool amusement rides starring circling jalopies and big rigs. The most elaborate is the **Junior Fire Academy**, a water-squirting carousel styled after its bigger brother across the park. Where this area intersects with LEGO Kingdoms and Fun Town, behind the 4-D theater, you'll find the park's well-equipped baby care center.

Legoland Water Park

Immediately after debuting Legoland Florida, the developers disclosed plans to resurrect and restyle Cypress Gardens' shuttered *Splash Island* attraction into a Legoland water park, scheduled to open by summer 2012. Only accessible to paid guests of the main park, admission to the water rides costs an extra $12 per day ($3 for kids 3 and under) and is included for Premium Annual and Ambassador passholders. With just two "rides" Legoland's version hardly qualifies as a full-fledged water park, but it is a thoughtful addition to the park for those looking for a break from the summer heat.

Circling the area is **Build–A–Raft River,** where you can customize an inner tube with big buoyant LEGO-style attachments and take a lazy float along a 1,000-foot long stream. Another great way to relax is to sun yourself on the shores of the **LEGO Wave Pool,** a medium-sized generator of gentle surf. For active kids, there is **Joker Soaker**, a colorful, multi-level, water-soaked play area that is the best thing here. At its apex, a 300-gallon bucket held by a giant LEGO figure fills with water and periodically tips over, much to the delight of the kids below.

Splash Out consists of three speed slides. Two are fairly straightforward, but the third is a completely enclosed tube with a zippy corkscrew near the top. Next door is **Twin Chaser**, where you grab your own inner tube and climb to the top to descend through one of two twisting flumes, with both open and enclosed sections, to a splashdown in a small pool. Finally, **DUPLO Splash Safari** is a series of small slides and splash fountains designed specifically for toddlers.

Chapter Ten:

Kennedy
Space Center

ABOUT AN HOUR FROM ORLANDO (AND DISNEY'S TOMORROWLAND) IS A PLACE
where the fantasy drops away, replaced by awe-inspiring reality. It is here, at the John F.
Kennedy Space Center, smack in the middle of a wildlife refuge, that real people, riding real live spaceships, were blasted into outer space on a variety of scientific missions.
Nearby Cape Canaveral handles military and commercial launches. On the fringes of
this very serious enterprise, the Kennedy Space Center Visitor Complex (a separate
entity) lets us earthbound types get a peek at this very special world and imagine—just
for a moment—what it must be like to be on the cutting edge of tomorrow. Though
the space shuttle program ended in 2011, if you time your visit just right you can still
see an actual rocket roaring into the heavens.

The Kennedy Space Center (or "KSC" for short) is immense, one-fifth the size of
the state of Rhode Island. Only 6,000 of its 140,000 acres are used for operations; the
rest is a wildlife refuge. Most people are amazed to learn that this monument to high-
tech is home to more endangered species (15) than any other place in the United States
except the Everglades. There are also 310 types of birds flitting between the launch pads.
Yet over the years, the complex has logged some 3,000 launches. As you might expect,
you will only get to see a small sliver of Kennedy Space Center's vastness but the access
you are granted is remarkable.

For those who care about such things, I should note that no taxpayer money is
used to support the visitor facilities, tours, or other tourist activities at Kennedy Space
Center. All of these are run by a private company, Delaware North Parks Services, and
are entirely self-supporting.

Before You Come

Doing homework for your visit to Kennedy Space Center is not absolutely necessary,
but it helps if you have at least some background knowledge of the space program. A
painless way to get that background is to head down to the video store and rent *The*

Right Stuff and *Apollo 13*. Both films are a lot of fun to watch and offer great insight into the human as well as the technical dimensions of the space program. And search YouTube for the 1994 Discovery Channel special, *The Space Shuttle*.

For information about the Kennedy Space Center Visitor Complex itself, call (866) 737-5235 or log on at www.kennedyspacecenter.com. Another way to get an advance look at the Center is to call the above number or visit www.thespaceshop.com and order the *Kennedy Space Center Visitor Complex* tour book. It is $7.99, plus tax and takes about a week to arrive. It doesn't provide tour and film times but it will certainly whet your appetite and help you decide how to focus your time during your visit.

When's the Best Time to Come?

KSC is open every day except Christmas. To a great extent, attendance reflects the seasonal ebb and flow of tourists described in *Chapter 1*. However, attendance is also greatly affected by the launch schedule at the Kennedy Space Center.

The days before and after a launch tend to be busier than usual as excitement builds in anticipation of the big event. The day of a launch, the Visitor Complex may close for the hours preceding the blast-off. If the rocket launches before 9:00 a.m., the center is open all day. Given the fact that launches are frequently delayed, however, the pre-launch closing can mean that the Visitor Complex will be open for just a few hours or not at all on a launch day.

So even though seeing a launch is one of the neatest things to do while you're in Florida, a visit to Kennedy Space Center at that time may not be an ideal choice—unless you don't mind missing some things or will be able to spend more than a day on the Space Coast.

For a recorded message giving dates and other information about upcoming rocket launches dial (866) 737-5235 and chose option 2. If you are interested in seeing a launch, see the discussion at the end of this chapter.

Getting There

The easiest way to reach KSC from Orlando is to get on the Beachline Expressway (SR 528) headed east. The tolls will set you back $3.25 each way but it's the fastest route (about an hour or so). Turn off onto SR 407 North, and then onto SR 405 East, which will lead you directly to the Visitor Complex. You can also take SR 50 (Orlando's East Colonial Drive) to route 405. It takes a bit longer but it's free.

Once you get on SR 405, don't be misled by the *Astronaut Hall of Fame*, which you will pass on the right. The main entrance to Kennedy Space Center is farther along, also on the right, and also graced with a life-size replica of the space shuttle. The *Astronaut Hall of Fame* is owned by KSC, but is a semi-separate attraction and is described in *Chapter 14: Another Roadside Attraction*.

Once you get to the KSC Visitor Complex, parking is provided **free** in lots with sections named after shuttle craft.

Opening and Closing Times

Hours for the Visitor Complex vary throughout the year. Opening time is invariably

9:00 a.m. and the standard closing time is usually 6:00 p.m. However, you should call for or check the website for exact times.

Tours and IMAX films begin at 10:00 a.m. Tours stop departing about three hours prior to the closing time of the Visitor Complex. The last showing of the IMAX films is usually about one or two hours prior to closing. Some attractions at the Visitor Complex also close early.

The Price of Admission

You enter the Kennedy Space Center Visitor Complex through a Ticket Plaza that is themed to evoke the International Space Station. The ticket booths take the form of space station modules, while the overhead shading is provided by large solar panels. A few space-walking astronauts float above, adding to the effect. There are about 20 ticket windows, with the Will Call windows located to your far left as you approach the Ticket Plaza.

Kennedy Space Center offers a number of admission options. Prices, before tax, are as follows:

Standard Admission:

Adults:	$43
Children (3 to 11):	$33

This is a one-day admission ticket that includes access to all the exhibits at the Visitor Complex, the main Kennedy Space Center bus tour, and admission to the IMAX films. It also includes one admission to the *U.S. Astronaut Hall of Fame* and its simulator rides which must be used within seven days of your Visitor Complex visit.

Specialty Tour Tickets (Cape Canaveral: Then & Now/ KSC Up-Close):

Adults:	$21/$25
Children (3 to 11):	$15/$19

These prices are per tour, and in addition to the cost of regular admission. In other words, you can't show up just to take one of these tours.

Annual Pass:

Adults:	$56
Children (3 to 11):	$46

The annual pass allows unlimited access to the Visitor Complex, the KSC bus tour, and the IMAX films, plus priority purchase of tickets to view launches. Annual passholders also get a discount of $4.50 on tickets for each of up to six guests as well as 10% off select Space Shop merchandise. Passholders must show the pass and a photo ID each time they enter.

Which Price Is Right?

This is a tough call and the answer will depend on your level of interest in the space program and how much time you can devote to visiting KSC. If you have just one day, many people will be perfectly satisfied with the standard one-day admission. The special interest tours are well worth taking; just be sure to check the departure schedules, as departures are limited. The annual pass will appeal primarily to space junkies who live nearby or who visit the area several times a year.

Eating in Kennedy Space Center

While you won't have to subsist on the powdered drinks and squeeze-tube dinners that were once standard fare for astronauts, neither can you expect a gourmet dining experience at KSC Visitor Complex. The eateries here are geared to processing hundreds of generally young diners in a quick and efficient manner, and the food quality seldom rises above fast-food or cafeteria level. One of the management's best inspirations has been to dispatch dozens of freestanding food carts to various points in the Visitor Complex. They offer everything from ice cream snacks to fruit to more substantial fare like hot dogs. Given the difficulty of squeezing everything into a one-day visit to the Center, it makes a lot of sense to eat on the run from these carts and save the big sit-down meal for later in the evening.

The Orbit Café, the park's main eatery, is a large, noisy fast-food emporium with various service stations dispensing beverages, salads, sandwiches, and desserts. You can get pizzas and pasta dishes, burgers and hot dogs, and BBQ pulled pork. Domestic beer is served. There is fast food at the Apollo/Saturn V Center's **Moon Rock Cafe**. If you are trying to pack as much as possible into a one-day visit, grabbing a hot dog here during the *KSC Tour* (see below) and eating it while waiting for the bus is a good strategy.

For a fee ($25 adults, $16 kids), you can sit down to lunch with an authentic astronaut through the aptly named "Lunch with an Astronaut." Seating for the one-hour event begins at 12:15 daily. Salad, chicken marsala, canneloni, penne, and pie are on the menu, along with a face-to-face personal moment with someone who has slipped the surly bonds of earth and survived to tell the tale.

Shopping in Kennedy Space Center

The largest selection of KSC souvenirs and outer-space themed merchandise to be found anywhere is yours to browse through in the mammoth, two-level **Space Shop** that lies between Information Central and the bus depot. Here you will find everything from T-shirts priced well under $20 to leather bomber jackets with the NASA logo for over $200. There are smaller shops with much the same merchandise, including one at the Saturn V facility that is visited on all of the bus tours.

Tip: For a nifty (and cheap!) souvenir or gift, buy a postcard and stamp and mail it here. It will arrive with a special Kennedy Space Center cancellation. Philatelists take note.

Good Things to Know About . . .

Access for the Disabled. All of KSC Visitor Complex is wheelchair accessible. **Free** wheelchairs may be obtained at the Information counter in Information Central, the first building you enter after paying your admission. The IMAX films are equipped with devices for the hearing impaired.

Audio Tours. Audio tours of the Visitor Complex are available at the Information counter in Information Central. They are complimentary for guests with vision or hearing impairments. In addition to English, audio tours are available in Spanish, French, German, Italian, Portuguese, and Japanese. In fact, these tours seem to be most popular with non-English speakers.

Babies. Stroller rentals are **free** at KSC (at the Information counter in Information Central). Diaper changing tables are located in some restrooms, including the men's room at the Orbit Café.

First Aid. There is a well-equipped first-aid station with a nurse on duty from 9:00 a.m. to 5:00 p.m. It is located near the bus boarding area.

Leaving the Park. Since the Kennedy Space Center is far from any population center, it is unlikely you will want to leave during your visit but if you decide to do so, just get your hand stamped at the exit and you will be able to reenter.

Money. You will find ATMs to the right of the Ticket Plaza, on the wall of the Space Shop across from the *Astronaut Encounter,* and at the Apollo/Saturn V Center. They are connected to all the major bank systems and credit cards.

Pets. Pets will be boarded **free** of charge during your visit. The pet kennel is to your right as you approach Information Central.

Security. Security is exceptionally tight. All visitors must pass through metal detectors and a battery of additional security personnel stands ready to conduct more detailed searches. Coolers and backpacks are banned and no lockers are available, so plan on leaving your excess stuff in the car and traveling light.

Blast Off: Your Day at Kennedy Space Center

I have found that it is impossible to see everything at Kennedy Space Center in one day. It is, however, possible to see most of it if you get there early and step lively for the next 8 to 10 hours. Even a delay of a few hours will decrease your chances of seeing as much as possible. It will help to understand that there are three main components to the KSC experience: the Visitor Complex houses most of the exhibits and the wonderful IMAX films; the bus tours leave from the Visitor Complex and let you explore the working end of the Space Center; the *Astronaut Hall of Fame* is a separate attraction about a mile from the Visitor Center that houses a museum and a number of space-program-themed simulators.

When you arrive at the Visitor Complex, your first stop is the Ticket Plaza where you collect your access badge. Once you have your badge, you proceed through a building called Information Central. This is really just a spacious antechamber containing the Information counter, which doubles as Lost and Found. Pass through this building and you are in the Visitor Complex itself. Kennedy Space Center and the adjacent Cape Canaveral Air Force Station cover a great deal of territory. The Visitor Complex, by contrast, is quite small; you can walk from one end to the other in about five minutes. Your visit to Kennedy Space Center will be centered here—except when you leave on the bus tours.

The One-Day Stay

Getting the most out of a one-day visit to Kennedy Space Center requires early arrival and careful planning.

When you purchase tickets, you will be handed a map of the Complex and a schedule of tours, IMAX film showings, and other events. Pause a moment in the coolness of Information Central to orient yourself with the map and plan your day with the schedule. Note that the bus tour of Kennedy Space Center, called simply *KSC Tour*, has continuous departures (ending between about 2:15 p.m. and 2:45 p.m., depending on closing time), while the *Cape Canaveral Then & Now Tour* has just one departure and the *KSC Up-Close Tour* has only a few. So if you have paid the premium to take either of the latter tours (you can realistically take only one), plan your day around it. (Since both special interest tours drop you off at the Saturn V Center, you have the option of skipping the main *KSC Tour*; if you do, your time constraints are lessened considerably.) Seeing both IMAX films in one day may prove tricky. Whatever you do, don't miss the *Space Shuttle Experience*.

If you plan on doing all or most of the major, scheduled attractions, you will discover that once you have mapped out your schedule, you will have a half hour or an hour here and there during the day to see what's left and eat. I suggest grabbing your food on the run if you want to maximize your touring time. There are plenty of freestanding kiosks scattered about, making this a viable strategy.

You can use the descriptions below and your own taste to determine which of the "what's left" will most appeal to you. I strongly recommend the *Launch Status Center* and the *Astronaut Encounter*.

Attractions at the Visitor Complex

Most of the attractions at the Visitor Complex are available for continuous viewing, except the IMAX films and the *Astronaut Encounter* which have scheduled showings throughout the day. The exhibits range from the compelling to the easy to miss. They are described here starting from Information Central and proceeding in a roughly clockwise path to the back of the Complex. Since distances are short, see the ones that appeal most first, then visit the others as time permits.

Robot Scouts ★ ★ ★

Type:	Walk-through presentation with animated displays
Time:	20 minutes
Short Take:	A well-done introduction to unmanned space exploration

Our host for this clever overview of current unmanned space exploration missions is Starquester 2000, a robot himself who has been temporarily grounded by a faulty navigational system. As we walk along a twisting, darkened corridor, we pause at six windows where we get a quick and painless overview of the Voyager, Viking, Cassini, and other missions, as well as the Hubble Space Telescope. These robot scouts attempt to determine if life exists elsewhere in the solar system, whether humans can survive on the various planets and moons they have visited, and in general just how the universe works.

It's a reminder of how many stunning discoveries have been made in the last few decades by these "trailblazers for human exploration," as Starquester never tires of calling them. Even though this attraction looks forward to a human presence on Mars, it is also a reminder that unmanned space exploration will be standard operating procedure for the foreseeable future.

Astronaut Encounter ★ ★ ★ ★

Type: Meet a real live astronaut
Time: About 20 minutes
Short Take: Best for the astronaut Q&A

This is one of the Visitor Complex's more inspired attractions, despite some unnecessary padding. A perky host warms up the audience with some space program trivia and then clowns around with two young volunteers from the audience. That's the unnecessary part. But about ten minutes into the show, a real live veteran of the space program shows up and things get considerably more interesting.

All the astronauts who appear in this show are the real McCoy, with at least one space flight to their credit, and some of the big names of the space program have appeared on this stage. The astronaut chats for a bit and then segues effortlessly into a question and answer period that can be great fun. The host circulates through the audience with the mike so everyone can be heard. For some reason, the show always seems to end with a kid asking how the astronauts go to the bathroom in space. Just like a space mission, this show is planned to the last detail. After the Q&A, the astronaut hangs around for **photo ops**.

This theater is also used for live presentations blending pop culture with various aspects of space and the space program. These shows change regularly, with the most recent themed around the "Star Trek" franchise. Scripts are typically aimed at a younger audience, and the acting is less than compelling. A time-waster at best, but don't discount the appeal of air conditioning.

Nature & Technology ★ ★

Type: Diorama
Time: Continuous viewing
Short Take: Can be skipped

Tucked around the corner from the *Astronaut Encounter* theater is this small display about the Merritt Island National Wildlife Refuge (see *Chapter 17: Gardens & Edens*). It consists of an "immersive" diorama depicting the wildlife and natural scenery that surround the Space Center.

Children's Play Dome ★ ★ ★

Type: Playground and jungle gym
Time: Unlimited
Short Take: A great place for the little ones to let off steam

Beneath this geodesic dome, kids and their parents will find a small jungle gym, riddled with climbing tunnels and thoughtfully equipped with cubby holes for sneakers and other valuables, as well as a kid-sized space shuttle, where you can enthusiastically reenact the historic moments you've just witnessed. Parents will appreciate the picnic tables tucked under the dome, perfect for resting one's feet while the small fry tear around, and a nice spot for a snack break away from the Florida sun.

Early Space Exploration ★ ★ ★ 1/2

Type: Space program museum
Time: Continuous viewing
Short Take: An eye-popping encounter with history

A portion of the original control room from the Mission Control building used during the Mercury and early Gemini missions has been transported here from its original home on Cape Canaveral. I found this small room, which looks a bit like a set from a low-budget 1950s television series, absolutely entrancing. It bears mute testimony to the speed at which our technology is exploding. The view you get is the same President Kennedy once enjoyed when he came to the Cape to witness a launch.

Otherwise, this is a once-over-lightly history of the early space program. Sometimes, the Beatles seem to get equal billing with the Mercury astronauts, but if you take the time to read the signage, you'll learn quite a bit. And the few artifacts on display, actual Mercury and Gemini capsules prominent among them, are fascinating.

Rocket Garden ★ ★ ★

Type: Outdoor display of rockets
Time: Continuous viewing
Short Take: Great photo backdrops

This may remind you of a sculpture garden at a museum of modern art. Indeed, some of the rocket engines on display look just as arty and a lot prettier than some modern art. The stars of the show, however, are the big rockets. A plaque gives the vital statistics for each object for the technically inclined, but most people will be content to gawk and have their pictures taken in front of these amazing machines.

The *Rocket Garden* can be appreciated from a distance, but the Apollo-Saturn service arm, once part of the gantry that served the giant Saturn rockets, is worth a visit. Armstrong, Aldrin, and Collins strode down this metal walkway en route to the moon. Also worth a closer look is the mammoth Saturn 1B rocket lying on its side on the far side of the garden; this behemoth generated a thrust of 1.3 million pounds as it lofted Skylab astronauts into orbit back in the seventies.

Guided tours of the area are available twice daily, with the schedule posted on a sign. This is a great chance to hear some stories that illuminate the human dimension of the space program.

Exploration Space: Explorers Wanted ★ ★ 1/2

Type: Displays on space exploration
Time: Continuous viewing
Short Take: On and off fun, if you have the time

This walk-through grab bag of displays and short films explores the future of space exploration, and asks younger guests if they might have a role in it. A mix of giant video screens and arcade-like interactive kiosks let you try your hand at docking a spaceship and other futuristic menial labors. Twice an hour, a live show recruits audience volunteers to become "space pioneers of tomorrow." Wander through at your leisure if you have a gap in your schedule, but don't go out of your way.

IMAX Theater Exhibits ★ ★ 1/2

Type:	Various displays
Time:	Continuous viewing
Short Take:	If you have the time

A number of exhibits and displays are scattered about the large building that houses the IMAX film theaters (see below). If you have a few moments to spare before or after the show—or have ducked inside to escape a rain shower—you might want to take a quick look around.

At one end of the building is an art gallery featuring works commissioned by NASA to commemorate the space program. They range from hyperrealism to the surreal to the completely abstract and are worth at least a quick look. At the other end is a space used for temporary or traveling displays; these can range from the excellent to the merely interesting. In a passage between the two theaters you will find a small display explaining the process whereby shuttles were prepared, launched, retrieved, and prepped yet again for flight.

Astronaut Memorial (Space Mirror) ★ ★ ★

Type:	Memorial to fallen astronauts
Time:	Continuous viewing
Short Take:	Intricate, intriguing, and moving

At first this monument to those who have lost their lives in the space program struck me as a bit of overkill. But as I examined the intricate mechanism that uses the sun's beams to illuminate the 16 names on this massive memorial, I came to realize how fitting it is to blend the high-tech and the heavenly to honor these special people. The entire memorial tilts and swivels to follow the sun across the sky as mirrors collect and focus the sun's rays onto clear glass names in a huge black marble slab. From the opposite side the effect is startling. The memorial is handsomely sited at the end of a large pool at the back of the IMAX Theater; a small kiosk on the side of that building houses computers that offer background information on the astronauts honored on the memorial.

Shuttle Plaza/Atlantis Orbiter

Type:	Real space shuttle
Time:	Continuous viewing with the possibility of long waits
Short Take:	Not yet open at press time

The full-scale model of the space shuttle that stood for years on this spot was removed shortly before press time to make room for the real thing. The actual Space Shuttle Atlantis orbiter, decommissioned into a museum piece after the end of the shuttle program, will live here starting sometime in 2013. Plans call for a $100 million, 65,000 square foot indoor display facility, including interactive features on accomplishments of the shuttle program like the International Space Station and Hubble Telescope.

Assuming the presentation of the orbiter itself remains similar, the opportunity to be close enough to touch a real space shuttle is impressive. But don't be surprised if you find a visit a bit of a letdown, especially if you've had to wait 40 minutes or an hour for a glimpse. What stuck me most about the old exhibit was how cramped the space allotted to the crew is. Not even a New York landlord would have the gall to call this a studio apartment. Guided tours of the Shuttle Plaza area, which also contains two booster rockets, are offered from time to time.

Shuttle Launch Experience ★ ★ ★ ★

Type: Space launch simulator
Time: 5-minute ride with 15 minutes of preshows
Short Take: Not to be missed.

This attraction is KSC's first and only E-ticket ride in the Orlando theme park tradition. While it can't compete with Disney's dizzying *Mission: Space* in sheer G-forces, it is a thrilling taste of what shuttle astronauts once experienced. Before you board this $60 million space ship simulator, famed former shuttle commander Charlie Bowden will brief you (via video) on the awesome power behind a launch, including an earth-shakingly loud simulacra of main engine ignition.

After what seems like an interminable wait , you finally board the simulator cabin, dressed as the inside of a shuttle cargo bay. Firmly strapped into one of 44 seats, you watch an unconvincing CGI view of your flight on video screens in the cabin's nose, while Bowden coaches you through your training flight. In true theme park tradition, something goes wrong before you safely dock, revealing the spinning Earth through the bay doors above (another iffy video effect). The five-minute ride itself only tilts slowly back and forwards to mimic microgravity (no spinning) so you shouldn't have to worry about losing your lunch. Just don't look too long on the simulated space view below as you stumble down the spiral exit ramp, which serves double duty as a time-line of space exploration milestones.

Tip: Lines can build here, so hit this attraction early in the day.

Launch Status Center ★ ★ ★ ★

Type: Live briefings and educational displays
Time: Briefings last about 20 minutes
Short Take: The best thing at the Visitor Complex

The modest looking, almost anonymous, white geodesic dome near the Explorer mock-up in Shuttle Plaza houses what is, in my opinion, the best thing at the Visitor Complex. There are models and displays here of the retrievable solid rocket boosters and their motors, a manned maneuvering unit, even an outer-space soft drink dispenser. Perhaps the most fascinating artifact is an actual solid rocket booster nose cone from the 66th shuttle mission; usually these sink to the bottom of the ocean and are replaced, but this one remained afloat long enough to be retrieved.

The main attractions here, however, are the live briefings that occur every hour on the hour from 11:00 a.m. to 5:00 p.m. Held in front of a set of simulated mission control panels like those used in astronaut training, they feature a live "communicator" and live shots from remote video cameras strategically stationed around the working heart of the Space Center, including the Vehicle Assembly Building and the launch pad itself.

No matter when you visit, there will always be something going on at the Space

Center and this is your opportunity to get the inside scoop. Obviously, the most interesting time to come here is in the days and hours before a launch. However, a visit is worthwhile no matter where they are in the launch cycle. The communicators are veritable encyclopedias of information about the space program, and I would urge you not to be shy about asking questions once the formal briefing is over.

Center for Space Education ★ ★ ★

Type: Hands-on science displays open to public
Time: Continuous viewing
Short Take: For teachers and budding astronauts

On the opposite side of the Visitor Complex grounds from Shuttle Plaza, set well away from the other attractions, this large building houses the educational outreach component of the Kennedy Space Center. Inside, teachers will find a library and resource center just for them. Special programs for visiting school groups are also held in this building. The **Exploration Station** is open to the general public. It is a largish room filled with hands-on, interactive exhibits that demonstrate basic principles of science. This will probably most appeal to younger kids.

The Bus Tours

The only way to see the working end of the Space Center is by taking a guided bus tour. Three tours are offered, representing the past, present, and future of the space program. All tours leave from an efficient bus terminal at one end of the Visitor Complex. The buses are much like regular city buses except they have much larger windows. No food is allowed aboard the buses and the only beverage allowed is bottled water, which is available for purchase at the Visitors Complex and each stop of the *KSC Tour*. It's not a bad idea to bring some, especially in the warmer months.

The *KSC Tour*, included in the price of admission, visits the Kennedy Space Center on Merritt Island. This tour is quite clearly the star of the show, with continuous departures starting at 10:00 a.m. and continuing until about three hours prior to closing. There are two stops on this tour and you can stay as long at each of them as you wish because the buses run continuously. This system has obvious advantages but the downside is that crowds can build up, making the bus loading process slow and chaotic. So it's best to take this tour early in the day.

There are also two "special interest tours" that cost an additional fee. The *Cape Canaveral Then & Now Tour* ($21 adults, $15 children) has one departure daily and the *KSC Up-Close Tour* ($25 adults, $19 children) has about five or six; each of these tours is limited to a single busload, about 50 people. On a one-day visit you will be able to take only one special interest tour in addition to the *KSC Tour*, not both.

The ticketing procedure is also somewhat cumbersome. You must first purchase your tickets at the Ticket Plaza, then proceed to the Information counter in Information Central to make your reservations for a specific departure time. There are additional security procedures that require signing in and showing photo ID such as a drivers license. Foreign visitors should bring their passport. Failure to follow these procedures can result in confusion at tour time; you may even be denied boarding.

There is one thing that all tours have in common: they all finish up with visits to the Apollo/Saturn V Center and the International Space Station Center (ISSC). For that reason alone, I have given all tours the same five-star rating.

Special Note: Because of the steady stream of commercial launch activity at Cape Canaveral, the Cape tour is sometimes curtailed or unavailable. And during times of heightened security, both of the special interest tours may be cancelled.

Another unpredictable element, in terms of what you will see, is the wildlife at the Center. Alligators, sometimes jokingly referred to as part of the security system, are sighted frequently and there are bald eagle nests along the tour routes.

The standard narration on the tours will be supplemented—or interrupted—whenever the driver feels it's time to add his or her own commentary or release a late-breaking news bulletin ("Wild hogs on the left!"). Narration, in French, German, Spanish, and Portuguese, is available on tape on a first-come, first-served basis.

Kennedy Space Center Tour ★ ★ ★ ★ ★

Time: 2 to 3 hours

Short Take: The next best thing to becoming an astronaut

The bus tour of Kennedy Space Center, with the Apollo/Saturn V Center, is yet another "must-see" stop on the Central Florida tourist circuit. And no wonder. This tour takes you to the sites where the space shuttle was prepared and launched. It also gives you an opportunity to gape and gawk at an actual Saturn V rocket. It's as close as you'll come to being launched into space without joining the astronaut corps.

There are two stops on this tour—the LC-39 Observation Gantry and the Apollo/Saturn V Center. You will also get to drive by the Vehicle Assembly Building, where the space shuttle was mated with its immense fuel tanks prior to each launch.

The **LC-39 Observation Gantry** ("LC" stands for "launch complex") is a four-story tower that offers a bird's-eye view of launch pads 39A and B, from which all shuttle flights departed. You'll also get close to the VAB itself. One of the largest buildings in the world, its roof covers five acres. It encloses so much space that it has its own atmosphere and it has actually rained inside. It was here that the gigantic Saturn V rockets used in the Apollo program were assembled. The shuttles seem tiny by comparison.

The undisputed highlight of this tour is a visit to the **Apollo/Saturn V Center**. The building is massive—and it has to be to house a refurbished, 363-foot-tall Saturn V moon rocket, one of only three in existence. Before you get to see the star of this show, you enter the **Firing Room** where the actual mission control consoles used during the Apollo missions form a backdrop for a video and audio re-creation of the launch of Apollo VIII, the first manned lunar mission.

Then you step into the massive building that houses the Saturn V, suspended horizontally in one long open space. No description can prepare you for just how immense this thing actually is. The word "awesome" moves from hyperbole to understatement. Arrayed around, alongside, and under the rocket are interpretive displays filled with astounding facts about this magnificent achievement.

Before you leave, be sure to visit the **Lunar Theater**, where you will see a re-creation of the first landing on the moon and be reminded of just how touch-and-go this mission was up to the very last second. After the show, you step into the **New Frontiers Gallery** for a preview of space missions yet to come.

If you don't linger at the various stops, you can complete this tour in about two hours, but rushing through is a mistake. Take your time, invest three or four hours and enjoy yourself. There are places to eat at each stop and the Apollo/Saturn V Center even boasts the **Moon Rock Cafe,** the "only place on earth where you can dine next to a piece of the moon." Between stops a taped commentary plays on ceiling-mounted video monitors; it provides some interesting background information on the Center and its operations. This tour is an exciting experience for anyone. For Americans, it should be a source of deep patriotic pride.

Tip: Try for a seat on the right side of the bus as you shuttle from stop to stop.

KSC Up-Close Tour ★ ★ ★ ★ ★
Time: 90 minutes
Short Take: In the footsteps of the astronauts

In a sense *KSC Up-Close* begins where the *KSC Tour* leaves off, offering you extra special access to places you glimpsed from afar on the main tour. With the expert guidance of a space program expert who is a gold mine of little known facts, you get to stop near **Launch Pads 39A and B** at a special seaside viewing platform that offers one of the best **photo ops** to be had at KSC. With the towering pads to one side and the Atlantic Ocean to the other, you'll get a terrific view of the rotating service structure that swings away for the actual launch, the flame trench that harnesses and channels the inferno created by the rockets, and the massive lightning rods that protect the craft from Florida's stormy weather.

For the first time since 1978, you can now get inside the **Vehicle Assembly Building** exclusively on this tour. It looks immense from the vantage point offered on the *KSC Tour,* but inside it is positively awe-inspiring. This opportunity may be discontinued at any time, but at the moment you may see a decommissioned shuttle orbiter as it is prepared for permanent display.

Every mission begins with an inch-by-inch journey on the **Crawler Transporter**, which you'll revisit on this tour. The tour ends at the Apollo/Saturn V Center, described above. From there, you can take a bus straight back to the Visitor Complex, or proceed to the International Space Station Center.

Note: If you take this tour, you may want to skip the main *KSC Tour.* Yes, you will miss the LC-39 Observation Gantry, but you will get a closer look at pads 39A and B on this tour.

Cape Canaveral Then & Now Tour ★ ★ ★ ★ ★
Time: Approximately 3 hours
Short Take: Stirring history for true space buffs

This tour is sometimes changed or modified to accommodate launch activity, making it difficult to predict what you will actually see on the day of your visit. It also requires a much greater exercise of the imagination than does the *KSC Tour* (although that's probably a good thing). Still, I suspect there will be those who will slightly prefer this tour to the other. The main reason is that on this one you actually get to enter the places where space history was made, even if those places are now mere empty concrete spaces where towering launch gantries once stood.

It was from Cape Canaveral that the first Americans were launched into space. You can walk through a blockhouse that housed mission control for the early Mercury missions and stroll out to the pad from which puny looking Redstone rockets launched the first Americans into space using a gantry jury-rigged from an old oil drilling rig. The room-sized computer used for these launches could be replaced by a modern laptop, with plenty of room left over on the hard drive for games. Next door is a small museum with a collection of artifacts relating to the early days of the space program. Much of the launch pad area has been turned into a sort of outdoor sculpture garden displaying two dozen or so rockets and missiles, including my personal favorite, the sleekly magnificent and rather sexy Snark.

Another powerful moment comes on a visit to the actual launch pad on which Apollo astronauts Gus Grissom, Ed White, and Roger Chaffee lost their lives in a tragic fire during a dress rehearsal of the first Apollo flight. The site is now a monument to their memory. Another monument of sorts that is glimpsed on this tour is the Minuteman missile silo in which the remains of the Space Shuttle Challenger were placed after the investigation of that accident.

Cape Canaveral entered the space age in 1950 with tests of captured German V-2 rockets. But it is far from being a dusty museum or a monument to the past. It is a bustling modern spaceport from which a wide variety of unmanned military, scientific, and commercial satellites are launched into orbit, including many of the satellites that provide our telephone communications and weather forecasting. As you drive around, you may catch glimpses of preparations for upcoming launches.

The narration for this tour is handled by both the driver and a guide, who banter back and forth much in the style of co-hosts on a morning news program. Their knowledge is considerable and their devotion to their jobs and the history entrusted to them apparent. Either side of the bus is okay since you get to walk up to and into the most interesting sights. As with *KSC Up-Close*, you will be dropped off at the Apollo/Saturn Center at the end of your tour, where you may take a bus straight back to the Visitor Complex, or proceed to the International Space Station Center.

The IMAX Films

If you've never seen an IMAX film, this is an excellent place to remedy that situation. IMAX is an ultra-large film format, ten times larger than standard 35mm film and three times the size of the 70mm films you see at your local movie theater. It is projected on a screen some five and a half stories high and 70 feet wide. The sound system is equally impressive, producing bass tones you will feel in your bones.

The IMAX Theater at the Visitor Complex contains two back-to-back IMAX theaters, the first such IMAX "multiplex" in the world. The auditoriums are small relative to the size of the screen, so I would recommend showing up early so you can grab a seat toward the back of the house. There are doors on five levels and I find the seats in the middle of the third level to be just about ideal.

Space Station 3D ★ ★ ★ ★ 1/2

Time: 45 minutes

The 3-D is far more than a mere gimmick in this enthralling film narrated by Tom Cruise about the International Space Station. The sequences featuring the launches of the Russian Soyuz and the U.S. Shuttle, with debris and smoke rushing toward you at dizzying speed as the powerful sound system makes your seat vibrate, are incredible, but they are just a warm-up for the shots in space. There are some jaw-dropping, vertigo-inducing shots of astronauts working outside the space station while earth drifts serenely by 250 miles below. And there are plenty of shots of the astronauts taking care of business and just horsing around in the zero-G interior of their orbiting home. Watch out for those free-floating oranges!

Hubble 3D ★ ★ ★ ★ 1/2

Time: 40 minutes

The newer of KSC's two IMAX 3-D films tells the inspiring story of the Hubble Space Telescope, as narrated by Leonardo DeCaprio. The crews of Shuttle Atlantis's mission STS-125 brought an IMAX 3-D camera on board to document their painstaking spacewalk repairs of the most complex optical device ever built. Due to the weight of the film, only 8½ minutes of footage could be shot in space; it is fleshed out with earthbound footage, and stunning computer-generated flythroughs of helix and butterfly nebulas as detected by Hubble's historic lens. Both films are first rate, so select the smarmy celebrity narrator you prefer.

Seeing a Rocket Launch

You've probably seen film clips of rocket launches on TV dozens of times. But, to quote Al Jolson, you ain't seen nothin' yet! Seeing a launch live and in person is one of the truly great experiences a Florida vacation has to offer. Catching at least a glimpse of a launch is surprisingly easy. On a clear day, the rising rocket is visible from the Orlando area. Getting a closer look, however, requires a bit of planning.

While they don't have the same cachet as the shuttle launches (which ceased in 2011), the launches of commercial and military satellites on Delta and Atlas rockets that still take place on Canaveral are pretty fun to watch. When they are in the offing, visitors are given advance notice and will be advised as to the best places along the *KSC Tour* from which to get a view of the big event. The latest launch status information can be found at http://www.nasa.gov/centers/kennedy/launchingrockets/index.html.

First, you must understand that you don't have to be close to the launching pad to get ringside seats. In fact, no one can be close to the launching pad. The greatest danger a launch poses to bystanders is, surprisingly, the noise generated by the awesome engines. Unless you're a credentialed reporter, a federal official, or have some inside pull at NASA, you will be a good bit away. But you can still have an excellent view and an experience you will remember for the rest of your life.

At the Center, tour buses may run on a limited schedule on launch day, depending on the time of launch, or they may not run at all. But the entire Visitor Complex plays a live broadcast over the PA system of the events unfolding, including updates from mission control, and a jumbo TV screen in the *Rocket Garden* plays a live TV feed.

Viewing a launch from the best vantage point requires a modest investment and some advance planning. The Kennedy Space Center Visitor Complex sells a limited number of tickets for its buses to the viewing area. The cost is $20 for all ages, in addition to regular admission (required). Tickets may be purchased a couple weeks pre-launch by calling (866) 737-5235 or (321) 449-4444, or on the Internet at www.kennedyspace-center.com. (See below for a free alternative.)

Launch viewing details were in flux at press time, and may not be offered for certain flights. Demand for these tickets is unpredictable, and has been considerably less intense since the end of the shuttle program. Given the uncertainty of the actual launch date, you will have to check back regularly to plan your visit. KSC's website and a re-corded message at (321) 867-4636 provide the latest information.

On Launch Day

Plan on pulling on to SR 405 (from the west) or SR 3 (from the south) several hours before the scheduled launch time. Park your car in the Visitors Complex parking lots, purchase your tickets to enter the facility, and head for the buses that will shuttle you to the viewing area. Once there, remember you are on government property and in a wildlife refuge to boot, so there are a few simple rules. Cooking and fires are prohibited, as are alcoholic beverages. You are not allowed to fish, wade, swim, or feed the wildlife. If you have a pet, you'll have to leave it behind at KSC's free air-conditioned kennel.

I was lucky. The launch I observed went up on the dot. But you should be aware that, more often than not, the rocket doesn't go up on schedule. If there are delays for weather or technical glitches, you will be kept posted. If the launch is scrubbed (that is, canceled) you can still enjoy the Visitor Complex.

Seeing a Launch for Free

If you'd rather not pay the KSC admission fee and the $20 extra charge to be bussed out to the viewing location, you can still get an excellent view of the launch from numerous locations in nearby Titusville and Cocoa Beach. NASA maintains a website of suggested viewing locations at http://www.nasa.gov/centers/kennedy/launchingrockets/view-ing.html. One of the best is Space View Park on Broad Street in Titusville. Take Exit 80 from I-95 (SR 406, Garden Street). The park is two blocks south of SR 406.

Chapter Eleven:

Busch Gardens Tampa

BUSCH GARDENS TAMPA IS A SOMEWHAT SCHIZOPHRENIC MIXTURE OF zoological park and amusement park, with a dash of variety show thrown in. Given the seemingly disparate demands of these elements, the designers have done an admirable job of creating an attractive whole. Aesthetically, a stroll through Busch Gardens is one of the most pleasing in Central Florida.

Like any good theme park, Busch Gardens has one. In this case it's Africa, the mysterious continent so linked in the popular imagination with wild animals and adventure. Borrowing a page from the Disney manual, the park is divided into "lands," or as they are called here, "themed areas." With few exceptions, they take their names from countries or regions in Africa. The metaphor works wonderfully for the zoo side of things, although it results in the occasional oddity (kangaroos in Africa?). However, it is largely extraneous to the park's other elements. A roller coaster is a roller coaster, whether it's named after an Egyptian god (*Montu*) or a term in a Congolese dialect (*Kumba*).

So why schlep to Tampa for another theme park? There are two main answers: the animals and the roller coasters. Disney's Animal Kingdom has created some competition to Busch's great apes and white Bengal tigers, but it has just one major roller coaster. SeaWorld has animals and thrill rides, too, but it is short on land-based mammals.

There are other reasons, as well. For early risers at least, Busch Gardens is a very doable day trip from Orlando. And Busch even provides shuttle service from SeaWorld, to spare you the hassle of driving. The inclusion of Busch Gardens in SeaWorld's reasonably priced Passports and its participation in the Orlando FlexTicket program (see *Chapter 1: Introduction & Orientation*) adds another incentive to make the trip.

Finally, Busch Gardens Tampa has an allure all its own. The innovative animal habitats temper the frenzy of the rides, and the rides give you something to do when just sitting and watching begins to pale. The park is beautifully designed with some absolutely enchanting nooks and crannies. While it's a great place to do things, Busch Gardens is also a delightful place simply to be.

My only caution would be that the amusement park side of the equation can tend to overshadow the zoo. Many of the animal exhibits reward quiet, patient observation, but the excitement generated by the smorgasbord of giant roller coasters and splashy water rides will make it hard to cultivate a contemplative state of mind, especially for the younger members of your party. Perhaps the best strategy is to use exhibits like the *Myombe Reserve* (great apes), *Edge of Africa* (lions and hippos), and the walk-through aviary to chill out and cool down between bouts of manic activity. Another strategy is to devote one visit to the amusement park rides, another to the zoo exhibits.

Before You Come

You can hear some recorded information and, if you're lucky, reach a real live person by calling (888) 800-5447. In Tampa, you can call the Guest Relations number, (813) 987-5888, during park hours.

For the latest on Busch Gardens' zoo animals, you can check out the park's animal information site at www.buschgardens.org.

Another website provides information for the amusement park side of Busch Gardens Tampa. The address is www.buschgardens.com. An unofficial fan website, www.bgtnation.com, is a good source of late-breaking news.

When's the Best Time To Come?

Plotting the best time of year at which to visit is less of a consideration than with the other major theme parks of Central Florida. Busch Gardens gets the fewest visitors of the major theme parks in central Florida. On the other hand, attendance continues to grow and on several recent visits large groups of foreign tourists and American high school kids were much in evidence.

Getting There

Busch Gardens is roughly 75 miles from Universal Orlando, about 65 miles from the intersection of I-4 and US 192 in Kissimmee. You can drive there in about one and a quarter to one and a half hours depending on where you start and how closely you observe the posted speed limit. Drive west on I-4 to Exit 7 (US 92 West, Hillsborough Avenue). Go about 1.5 miles and turn right on 56th Street (SR 583); go another two miles and turn right on Busch Boulevard. Busch Gardens is about two miles ahead on your right.

Shuttle Bus Service

If you'd rather not drive from Orlando, you can take advantage of the shuttle bus service that Busch (in association with Mears Transportation) operates from a lengthy list of hotels in the Orlando area. The roundtrip fare is $10 per person, but if you have a five-park FlexTicket the service is free. Buses depart between roughly 8:30 a.m. and 10:00 a.m. with return journeys at 6:00 or 7:00 p.m., depending on the current closing hours at Busch Gardens Tampa, which vary seasonally (see below). Be aware that there may be as many as three stops en route and that arrival time at Busch Gardens can be as late as 11:30 a.m., so if you'd like to arrive bright and early, driving is your best option.

Reservations are required. To make one, or to check the latest schedule and pick-up points, call (800) 221-1339.

Arriving at Busch Gardens Tampa

You know you're almost at Busch Gardens when you see the giant roller coaster *Montu* looming overhead. You'll probably also hear the screams as you pull into the parking lot. Actually, there are a series of parking lots with room for 5,000 vehicles. Lots A and B are near the park entrance and are reserved for handicapped and preferred parking, respectively. There is much more parking across the street, which is where you will most likely be stowing your car. Trams snake their way back and forth to the entrance, but if you're in A or B it's just as easy to walk.

Motorcycles and cars park for $14, campers and trailers for $16, tax included. If you have any Busch Gardens annual pass, parking is free. Preferred Parking, in Lot B, costs $21 ($11 for most Passport members, free for Platinum Passport holders). Valet parking is $27 ($23 for Passport members).

Opening and Closing Times

The park is usually open from 10:00 a.m. to 6:00 p.m. every day of the year. However, during the summer months and at holiday times the hours are extended, with opening at 9:00 a.m. and closing pushed back until 7:00, 8:00, 9:00, or 10:00 p.m. The Morocco section stays open a half-hour or so later than the rest of the park to accommodate last-minute shoppers. Call Guest Relations at (813) 987-5888 for the exact current operating hours.

The Price of Admission

Busch Gardens sells only one-day admissions, but you can get a discount if you purchase your tickets in advance on the Internet. The following prices include tax. The discounted price is given in parentheses.

One Day Admission:

Adults:	$85.59 ($74.89)
Children (3 to 9):	$77.03 ($66.33)

Children under age 3 are admitted **free**.

Two-Park Ticket (SeaWorld):
(One day each at Busch Gardens and SeaWorld)

Adults:	$133.43 ($122.75)
Children:	$124.89 ($114.21)

Two-Park Ticket (Adventure Island):
(One day each at Busch Gardens and Adventure Island)

Adults:	$130.97 ($101.16)
Children:	$122.45 ($92.64)

Information on "Length of Stay" tickets, which combine two or more parks; the Orlando FlexTicket, which includes five or six parks; and "Passports" (annual passes), which also offer access to multiple parks, will be found in *Chapter 1*.

Quick Queue

Just like SeaWorld, Busch Gardens offers an express entry option for roller coaster fans unwilling to wait in line. For $19 to $32 (prices vary seasonally) you can cut the line once at each of the park's coasters and water rides, plus Rhino Rally. An extra $13 to $17 upgrades you to "Quick Queue Unlimited," which allows (you guessed it) unlimited trips on the rides of your choice. Busch Gardens has many more thrill rides than SeaWorld, making its version of Quick Queue more useful (and more expensive). On a peak attendance day, you may find the cost worthwhile to bypass the epic *Cheetah Hunt* line alone.

Special Events

Busch Gardens Tampa hosts a growing number of razzle-dazzle themed events timed to the calendar. The oldest of these is an alcohol-free New Year's Eve celebration for young people and families. Halloween shenanigans are in evidence during October. These are typically after-hours affairs that require a hefty separate admission (a recent **Howl-O-Scream** event was $78 plus tax). However, if you purchase your tickets in advance or have an annual pass, discounts are substantial.

From early June to mid-August (the exact dates differ each year), when the park is open to 9:00 or 10:00 p.m., Busch Gardens presents **Summer Nights**, a varied menu of outdoor entertainment at venues throughout the park. You might see a comic ventriloquist, an aerial act, juggling acts, or a DJ. Music festivals catering to country, oldies, and Latin demographics occur through the winter and spring.

During the **Christmas** season there are nightly tree lighting ceremonies and from fall through spring the park hosts a series of music festivals celebrating the country, oldies, and Latin genres. To learn more about what events may be planned during your visit and to get the latest on ticket prices, call toll-free (888) 800-5447.

Eating in Busch Gardens Tampa

On the whole, the dining experience at Busch Gardens is a step down from that at its sister park, SeaWorld, in Orlando. While **Crown Colony House**, the sole full-service restaurant in the park (in the Egypt section) can't hold a candle to Sharks Underwater grill at SeaWorld, it has a few tasty dishes. The main draw here is the great view of the *Serengeti Plain*.

For more casual dining, I recommend the **Desert Grill** in Timbuktu, where you can be entertained in air-conditioned comfort while you dine, the **Zambia Smokehouse** for better than average barbecue amid the roars and screams of *SheiKra* in Stanleyville, and the outdoor **Zagora Cafe** in Morocco. And speaking of Morocco, I find it disappointing that Busch Gardens has not chosen to extend its African theme to its restaurant menus. I found myself wishing for something akin to the first-rate Moroccan restaurant at Epcot in Walt Disney World Resort. All the restaurants mentioned here are reviewed later in this chapter.

(An interesting note: No straws are provided at any of the park's restaurants or fast-food outlets in deference to the safety of the animals.)

Shopping in Busch Gardens Tampa

The souvenir hunter will not leave disappointed. There are plenty of logo-bearing gadgets, gizmos, and wearables from which to choose. The T-shirts with tigers and gorillas are especially attractive. Tiger fanciers will also be drawn to the beach towels with the large white Bengal tiger portrait.

Best of all are the genuine African crafts to be found here and there around the park. Look for them in Morocco and Cheetah Hunt, but they sometimes show up elsewhere. The prices can be steep for some of the nicer pieces, but there are some very attractive (and attractively priced) smaller items to be found. Clothing is another good buy at Busch, with most of the better shops located in Morocco.

Most of the shops offer a free package pick-up service that lets you collect your purchases near the front entrance on your way out, so you needn't worry about lugging things about for half the day. You can avail yourself of Busch Gardens' mail order services by dialing (800) 410-9453 or (813) 987-5060, or visiting www.buschgardensshop.com.

Good Things To Know About ...

Access for the Disabled. Handicapped parking spaces are provided directly in front of the park's main entrance for those with a valid permit. Otherwise, physically challenged guests may be dropped off at the main entrance. The entire park is wheelchair accessible and companion bathrooms are dotted about the park. Some physically challenged guests may not be able to experience certain rides due to safety considerations. An "Access Guide" is available at Guest Relations near the main entrance.

Wheelchair and ECV rentals are handled out of a concession next to the Jeepers and Creepers shop in Morocco. Wheelchairs are $15 a day. Motorized carts are $45. ECVs are popular, so get there early to be sure you get one.

Animal Observation. Busch Gardens does an excellent job of displaying its animals in natural settings. One consequence of that is that they can sometimes be hard to see. So if spying out elands or catching a glimpse of a rare rhino baby is important to you, consider bringing along a pair of binoculars. They will come in handy on the *Skyride*, the *Trans-Veldt Railroad*, and even at lunch in the Crown Colony House restaurant.

Babies. Diaper changing tables are located in restrooms throughout the park. A nursing area is located in Sesame Street Safari of Fun.

If you don't have your own, you can rent strollers at the concession next to Jeepers and Creepers in Morocco. Single strollers are $14.02 for the full day with tax, double strollers are $18.69.

First Aid. First-aid stations are located in Timbuktu behind the Desert Grill restaurant and in the *Skyride* building in Cheetah Hunt. If emergency aid is needed, contact the nearest employee.

Getting Wet. The signs say, "This is a water attraction. Riders will get wet and possibly soaked." This is not marketing hyperbole but a simple statement of fact. The water rides at Busch Gardens are one of its best kept secrets (the mammoth roller coasters get most of the publicity), but they pose some problems for the unprepared. Kids probably won't care, but adults can get positively cranky when wandering around sopping wet.

The three major water rides, in increasing order of wetness, are *Stanley Falls Log Flume*, *Congo River Rapids*, and the absolutely soaking *Tanganyika Tidal Wave*. (The *Swamp Stomp* section of Sesame Street Safari of Fun can also get tykes very wet.) Fortunately, these three rides are within a short distance of each other, in the Congo and Stanleyville, allowing you to implement the following strategy:

First, dress appropriately. Wear a bathing suit and T-shirt under a dressier outer layer. Wear shoes you don't mind getting wet; sports sandals are ideal. Bring a tote bag in which you can put things, like cameras, that shouldn't get wet. You can also pack a towel and it's probably a good idea to bring along the plastic laundry bag from your motel room.

Plan to do the water rides in sequence. When you're ready to start, strip off your outer layer, put it in the tote bag along with your other belongings, and stash everything in a convenient locker. There are lockers dotted throughout the Congo and Stanleyville. A helpful locker symbol on the map of the park will help you locate the nearest one. Now you're ready to enjoy the rides without worry.

Once you've completed the circuit, and especially if you rode the *Tidal Wave*, you will be soaked to the skin. You now have a choice. If it's a hot summer day, you may want to let your clothes dry as you see the rest of the park. Don't worry about feeling foolish; you'll see of plenty of other folks in the same boat, and your damp clothes will feel just great in the Florida heat. In cooler weather, however, it's a good idea to return to the locker, grab your stuff, head to a nearby restroom, and change into dry clothes. Use the plastic laundry bag for the wet stuff.

The alternative is to buy a Busch Gardens poncho (they make nice souvenirs and are readily available at shops near the water rides) and hope for the best. This is far less fun and you'll probably get pretty wet anyway.

Kids' ID System. Stop by Guest Services to pick up wristbands for your young children. Guest Services will label them with your name and cell phone number so staff members can easily get hold of you if they encounter your child on the loose. Wristbands are available free of charge and are uniquely numbered, so that even if the writing on the wristband smears, they can still use this number to look up your information back at Guest Services, should the need arise. If you become separated from your child, contact the nearest employee. Found children are returned to the Security Office next door to the Marrakesh Theater in Morocco.

On Safari: Your Day at Busch Gardens

The bad news is that it's difficult—probably impossible—to see all of Busch Gardens in a day. The good news is that most people will be happy to forego some of the attractions. The more sedate will happily pass up the roller coasters to spend time observing the great apes, while the speed demons will be far happier being flung about on *Montu* or challenging their fear limit on *SheiKra* than sitting still for a show in The Desert Grill.

In many respects, Busch Gardens is a "typical" theme park. Each area of the park is decorated and landscaped to reflect its particular "theme," which is also reflected in the decor of the shops and restaurants (although not necessarily in the merchandise and food being offered). The attendants wear appropriate uniforms and a variety of rides, exhibits, attractions, and "streetmosphere" compete for your attention. If you've been to any of the other big theme parks in Central Florida, it's unlikely you'll find anything radically different about Busch Gardens. Here, then, are some of the elements in the Busch Gardens mix:

The Zoo. Home to over 2,000 animals, representing hundreds of species (the numbers will probably have risen by the time you visit), Busch Gardens is one of the major zoological parks in the nation. It is also a highly enlightened zoo, embodying the latest thinking about how animals should be housed and displayed to the public. You will receive an understated but persistent message about the importance of conserving and protecting the planet's animal heritage. Like SeaWorld, Busch Gardens boasts a zoological staff that is friendly, visible, approachable, and more than happy to answer questions.

Meet The Keepers. One way in which the staff helps spread the conservation message is through regular Meet The Keepers shows built around feeding and caring for the animals. The presence of food means that the animals are usually at their most active during these shows; the attendants also attempt to coax their charges into appropriate poses for those with cameras. You can pick up a schedule of Meet The Keepers sessions when you enter the park.

Roller Coasters. Busch Gardens boasts one of the largest concentrations of roller coasters in the nation. They range from the relatively modest *Scorpion* to the truly awesome *SheiKra*. Even the smallest of these rides features elements, like loops, that are not to be found on just any roller coaster. You will be well advised to take advantage of the coin-operated lockers located near every roller coaster to store your loose gear. Anyone who is serious about their roller coasters will definitely want to put Busch Gardens on their must-see list for their Central Florida vacation.

Water Rides. Busch Gardens is also home to a group of water rides that are designed to get you very, very, very wet. They are great fun, but require some planning and strategizing. Unless, of course, you're a young boy, in which case you simply won't mind walking through the park sopping wet from the top of your head to the toes of your $100 sneakers. See *Good Things to Know About … Getting Wet*, above.

Live Shows. There is a regular schedule of entertainment throughout the day in open-air amphitheaters and indoor, air-conditioned theaters. A few are animal-oriented, but most are pure variety entertainment shows that change periodically. Most shows don't gear up until 11:00 a.m. or noon. Thereafter, they run pretty regularly until closing time. A show schedule is available near the main entrance.

Your very first step on any visit to Busch Gardens Tampa is to pause near the main entrance and pick up a copy of the park map, with a listing the times of the various shows and the schedule of Meet The Keepers sessions printed on the back. As you will see by perusing the map, Busch Gardens is divided into ten "themed areas" most of them named after a country or region of Africa although a growing number are named after the attractions they house. As the park has evolved, Busch has rejiggered the geography a bit, which can result in some odd juxtapositions (great apes in Morocco?). Each area is relatively compact but the entire park is quite large (335 acres), making covering the entire place a bit of a challenge.

In describing the ten areas, I will start with Morocco, the first area you encounter as you enter the park, and proceed clockwise around the park, ending with Egypt. I am not suggesting that you tour Busch Gardens in this order (although it would be the most direct route if you were to walk the entire park). Use the descriptions that follow, along with the suggestions given above, to pick and choose the attractions that best suit your tastes and that you can comfortably fit into the time available. Remember that you can use the *Skyride* between Stanleyville and Cheetah Hunt to cut down on the walking.

In addition to the attractions listed below, Busch Gardens features a number of strolling groups of entertainers designed to put a bit of bounce back in your step as you stroll the grounds. The **Jungala Characters** are a coterie of fanciful jungle creatures in psychedelic colors who cavort on stilts or leap about on "PowerSkips," ingenious footgear that really puts pep in the step. Some of the creatures are actually elaborate puppets that ingeniously incorporate the puppeteer who operates them. The **Men of Note** offer up the kind of close harmony, a capella doo-wop music more associated with the streets of Philadelphia than the souks of Morocco. Still, they can often be found entertaining departing guests there or holding forth at the Marrakesh Theater.

Big Game

For those with limited time or who want to skim the cream of this multifaceted park, here are my selections for the trophy-winning attractions at Busch Gardens:

For coaster fans, **SheiKra**, **Cheetah Hunt**, **Montu** and **Kumba** are musts and you'll want to ride **Gwazi** just to be complete. Of the water rides, **Congo River Rapids** is my favorite and the **Tanganyika Tidal Wave** is highly recommended for those who want to get totally drenched.

Animal lovers will not want to miss the chimps and gorillas in **Myombe Reserve** or the tigers in **Jungala**. **Edge of Africa** is another must-see animal habitat, but the **Serengeti Safari Tour** (for an extra charge) is the best way to get close to the animals. **Rhino Rally** is a fun way to get an all-too-brief glimpse of some other veldt dwellers. And finally, if you have preschoolers in tow, you will not want to miss the spectacular **Sesame Street Safari of Fun**.

The One-Day Stay for Ride Fans

1. Plan to arrive at the opening bell. As soon as the park opens, grab a map just inside the turnstiles and proceed directly to *Cheetah Hunt*.

2. Backtrack toward the entrance, then continue clockwise to *SheiKra* in Stanleyville (bear left), bypassing *Gwazi* for now. If crowds are sparse, and if you dare, ride *SheiKra* more than once. (If *Rhino Rally* is on your list, try to get there first thing in the morning, before you ride anything else; lines form quickly and the ride handles many fewer riders per hour than the coasters.)

3. After *SheiKra*, continue to the Congo and ride *Kumba*. If the *Skyride* is operating, you can use it to head to *Montu* in Egypt; otherwise just walk. Then, walk back through Egypt, Cheetah Hunt and Morocco to *Gwazi*.

4. Once you've done the coasters, head back to Stanleyville and ride *Stanley Falls* and the *Tanganyika Tidal Wave*, finishing up with a ride on *Congo River Rapids*. Now

head south, pausing to admire the tigers in Jungala as you check the map and Entertainment Guide. If the timing's right, catch the *Skyride* again and head back to the Moroccan Palace Theater to catch the ice show.

5. After lunch, you have several choices. You can hit your favorite rides again, try the lesser rides, or (my personal suggestion) visit the various zoo attractions, perhaps catching another show at some point in the afternoon. Don't forget to check the schedule of Meet The Keeper shows.

The One-Day Stay for the More Sedate

1. If you are not a ride fanatic you don't have to kill yourself to get there at the minute the park opens, although a full day at Busch Gardens, taken at a moderate pace, is a full day well spent. For now, I'll assume you are arriving early. Grab a park map and the Entertainment Guide and bear to the right as you stroll towards Cheetah Hunt. En route, peruse the times for the variety shows and the Meet The Keeper sessions.

2. If you plan to take the *Serengeti Safari Tour*, sign up now. Take a leisurely tour of *Edge of Africa*, and if you're interested and the lines aren't too long, you might want to walk to Egypt and pop into *King Tut's Tomb*. Otherwise, stroll to Nairobi for a visit to *Myombe Reserve* and *Jambo Junction*. Don't dismiss *Rhino Rally* out of hand; the ride is very mild and the wildlife worth a look.

3. Now board the *Trans-Veldt Railroad* at the Nairobi Station for the journey around the Serengeti.

4. Now you're ready to see some shows. You can walk to Timbuktu for the musical variety show at the Desert Grill (and have lunch if you haven't grabbed a bite yet) or you can stroll the other way to catch *Iceploration* at the Moroccan Palace.

5. Round out your day with a visit to Bird Gardens and the *Critter Castaways* show. If you have little ones in tow, don't forget to let them have their own special time in Sesame Street Safari of Fun.

Morocco

Morocco is your first stop in the park, so some of the available space is given over to housekeeping. Here you'll find Guest Relations and the Adventure Tour Center, where you can make arrangements for the special tours described at the end of this chapter. Just around the corner to your right is the stroller and wheelchair rental concession. Since Morocco is also the exit to the park, a fair amount of space is given to souvenir and other shops, the better to lure those on the way out.

Note: On especially busy days, they open the Nairobi Gate, which is directly to the right of where the parking lot tram drops off new arrivals. This entrance lets visitors into the park at a point about equidistant from Nairobi, Cheetah Hunt, and Morocco.

Otherwise, the main business of Morocco is stage shows of one sort or another. There are two theaters (reviewed below) and an **alligator pond**, where several times a day a Meet The Keepers show takes place. It's a zoologically correct version of the more popularized shows you get at Gatorland and other gator-themed attractions. A raised platform called the **Sultan's Tent** hosts **photo ops** with animals during busier times.

Rock A Doo Wop (Marrakesh Theater) ★ ★ ★ 1/2

Type: Live stage show
Time: 25 minutes
Short Take: Rock down memory lane

On a thrust stage with Moorish arches and purple curtains, this peppy revue pays homage to the early days of rock and roll, when simple melodies and a snappy beat swept across the nation and transformed a generation, not to mention the generations that followed. A four-man combo, some of whom look old enough to remember the era first-hand, provide solid backing for a troupe of eight youngsters, four men, four women, who run through a repertoire that seems oh so familiar to the mostly grey-haired crowd this show attracts. Despite the title, just one number is in true a capella doo-wop style, but it is "In The Still of the Night" and it is a smashing success. After the show, some of the performers mingle with the audience for **photo ops**.

Note: This show changes from time to time, but the theme remains the same—pop rock standards with an accent on oldies.

Iceploration (Moroccan Palace Theater) ★ ★ ★ ★

Type: Indoor theater show
Time: 30 minutes
Short Take: Around the world on ice

The 1,200-seat Moroccan Palace Theater is an extremely well-appointed performance space capable of Broadway-quality spectacle, as illustrated by the now departed (and spectacular) *Ka Tonga*. But the theater has a proud tradition of hosting ice shows and *Iceploration* is the most elaborate yet.

The new show revolves around young Austin, who thinks that electronic technology connects him to the entire world. His grandfather proves otherwise by taking him on a whirlwind tour of the planet's wonders. In a visit to the Serengeti, ingenious, large-scale puppets re-create an African watering hole, while acrobatic skaters tell a story of a cheetah on the hunt for antelope. At Australia's Great Barrier Reef, black light and helium-filled balloons depict a world filled with exotic fish, sea turtles, and a moray eel.

Back on land, they're off to the Arctic, where in a dazzling display of theatrical artifice they witness the stunning aurora borealis while live sled dogs and a Siberian lynx grace the stage. Their final stop is the lush tropical rainforests of the Amazon where monkeys and birds fill the air and you won't even think to ask why the ice isn't melting.

A company of some 20 talented, not to mention acrobatic, skaters carry the story with ease. And thanks to a creative team that includes the Tony-winning costume designer Gregg Bates (*The Drowsy Chaperone*), Busch proves yet again that it can beat Broadway at its own game.

Myombe Reserve: The Great Ape Domain ★ ★ ★ ★ ★

Type: Ape habitat
Time: Continuous viewing
Short Take: The zoo's crown jewel

Of all the animal habitats at Busch Gardens, this is the hands-down winner. The beautifully imagined setting here would be almost worth the visit without the chimps and gorillas. But it is these fascinating primates that we come to see, and the scenic designers and landscape architects have given them a home that provides plenty of variety for the animals while making it easy for us to spy on them. The achievement is remarkable and ranks right up there with the spectacular habitats at SeaWorld.

The habitat is divided in two, with the first area given over to a band of nine chimpanzees in a rocky, multi-leveled environment complete with spectacular waterfalls, calm pools, and a grassy forest clearing with plenty of climbing space. Best of all is a glassed-in viewing area that allows us to spy on the chimps' private behavior.

Passing through a tunnel, we reach the lowland gorilla habitat. There's a wonderful theatricality to this entrance as we pass through a simulated jungle fog to "discover" the gorillas grazing on our left. Talk about gorillas in the mist! In addition to a glassed viewing area, this habitat features a small amphitheater for extended observation and video cameras that allow us to observe individuals in the far reaches of the habitat.

Plenty of explanatory information is provided via blackboards (the conceit here is that we are visiting a jungle outpost of a scientific expedition), photos and "field notes" containing tidbits of animal lore posted on signs, and voice-over narration in the hidden viewing area. If you only have time for one zoo exhibit between roller coaster rides, make it this one. The entrance to *Myombe Reserve* is opposite the Moroccan Palace Theater; the exit leads you into the Nairobi section.

Bird Gardens

As the name suggests, Bird Gardens houses most of the birds in the Busch Gardens zoo collection. In addition to the few larger bird displays mentioned below, the area is dotted with flamingos and other exotic water fowl, their wings obviously clipped, in beautifully landscaped open settings with ponds and streams. They are joined by a rotating group of visiting Florida species. Some of the walkways are lined with gaudy parrots in free-hanging cages. Over all, the effect is enchanting, rather like the private gardens of a rich and tasteful eccentric.

Bird Gardens is also home to *Gwazi*, a mammoth twin-track wooden roller coaster that greets you as you enter. Behind the coaster entrance is Gwazi Park, a stage reserved for special events. Near *Gwazi*, you will find **Xtreme Zone**, where you can climb a simulated cliff or bounce on a trampoline. There is an additional charge for these activities. A short stroll away and often overlooked is **Eagle Canyon**, a quiet corner devoted to these magnificent raptors.

Gwazi ★ ★ ★ ★ 1/2

Type:	Dueling wooden coasters
Time:	About 2½ minutes
Short Take:	Up-to-date nostalgia

For those who remember the days when all roller coasters were made of wood, *Gwazi* will be like a stroll down memory lane—until the first drop reminds you that this isn't your father's coaster.

The "gimmick" here, of course, is that there are two separate coasters, each holding

24 passengers, one representing a tiger, the other a lion. As you snake your way to the departure platforms, you get to choose which one you'll take on and each route has its own theming—the lion territory evokes an African desert environment, while the tiger territory is reminiscent of the jungles and streams of Asia. The dueling trains depart simultaneously and "race" to the finish with six "fly-bys" along the way. The close encounters may not be quite as scary as on some of the dueling steel coasters—the realities of wooden coasters mandate a decent amount of space between the rail and the edge of the superstructure—but they are pretty scary nonetheless. Likewise, the ride itself may seem tamer. After all, it's hard to do an inversion on a wooden coaster. But the rumble and rattle of wood makes *Gwazi* seem faster than its 50 miles per hour and on some of the turns the cars seem to be at right angles to the ground. Wooden coasters also have a liveliness that steel coasters don't. Coaster enthusiasts would say, "it's alive!" which is another way of saying that the give in the wood makes each ride seem different from the last.

Tip: Any serious coaster buff will want to ride at least twice, once on each track. After many rides, coaster mavens seem to agree: the lion coaster has the steeper first drop, but the tiger coaster is, over all, the more intense experience.

Gwazi was upgraded in 2011 with new "Millennium Flyer" trains and rehabilitated tracks, resulting in a less spine-wrenching (though still plenty wild) ride. There are some other good things to be said about *Gwazi*. It lasts longer than some of its zippier competitors and because the height restriction here is only 48 inches, more members of the family will get a chance to ride. *Gwazi* is also quite beautiful, in a way in which the more modern steel coasters aren't. The wood is weathered rather than the more traditional white and blends in nicely with the African conical thatched roof motif of the entrance. And from the top you get a fascinating (but brief) glimpse of one of the park's "backstage" areas, as well as the surrounding terrain.

Critter Castaways (in Bird Theater) ★ ★ ★ 1/2

Type:	Live amphitheater show
Time:	About 20 minutes
Short Take:	A potpourri of pettable performers

The creators of this show seem to have borrowed heavily from *Pets Ahoy* over at SeaWorld and the kiddie show next door in Sesame Street Safari of Fun. The result is a harmless bit of fluff that should appeal to most, especially the littler ones in your party.

The backdrop is a fairly elaborate set depicting the wreck of the Amazon Queen, an old tug boat by the looks of her. Our singing hostess, Jane, lives here in harmony with a few shipwrecked friends and a passel of animals from around the world. Jane is one of those annoying, sugar-sweet types you see on early morning TV shows aimed at tots. She sings a saccharine song about "living in harmony" until you want to go up on stage and throttle her.

But to give Jane and her fellow cast members their due, this is not about musical theater. This is about the animals. They range from humble cats and dogs (all alumni of local rescue centers, apparently) to emus and kangaroos, and a variety of multicolored birds of all shapes and sizes. For good measure, there are cameos by a mouse, a skunk, and two pigs.

There is less "edutainment" in this show than there was in previous incarnations, although we do learn that the maribou stork can fly almost as high as an airplane and we get to see how a lesser anteater uses its long tongue to slurp jelly out of a tube. The joy and the fun of the show derives quite simply from our age-old fascination with animals of all types. Just watching them walk across the stage—which is all most of them do—qualifies as entertainment. Some of the dogs and cats do considerably more, performing some nifty tricks. And a beautifully plumed parrot flies around the auditorium, neatly zipping through a series of hoops. It's enough to make you forget that annoying song.

Note: This show seems to change more than most, but given the elaborate set I suspect the current edition will be around for a while. Although I have liked some versions better than others, it has always been worth seeing.

Walkabout Way ★ ★ ★ ★

Type: Walk-through animal exhibit
Time: Continuous viewing
Short Take: An overload of adorable

This latest addition to Bird Gardens injects a slice of the Australian continent into the park's otherwise African atmosphere, but never mind the thematic dissonance. The free-roaming wallabies and hand-fed kangaroos who inhabit the **Kangaloom** section of this outdoor habitat are so achingly cute and affectionate, you may loose many minutes making friends with these curious marsupials.

Check at the exhibit entrance for the feeding schedule; at a few appointed times each day, you can buy a cup of roo-chow for about $5, which will be eagerly slurped from your palm. Supplies are limited, but the animals are plenty attentive even if you don't have treats to dispense.

At 11:15 each day, ten guests get to feed a joey (a baby roo) a bottle of apple juice. There are only ten $10 bottles available each day on a first-come first-served basis, so plan of getting there early if you want to enjoy this very special experience.

In addition to the kangaroos and wallabies, the exhibit incorporates a free-flight aviary, the **Kookabura's Nest**, filled with native Australian birds, and the **Tuckerbox**, a place for kids to have up-close encounters with tawny frogmouths and other Down Under fauna on an erratic schedule.

Aviary ★ ★ ★ 1/2

Type: Walk-through animal exhibit
Time: Continuous viewing
Short Take: A lovely place to pause

This is a smallish habitat compared to others in the park, but its size belies its enchantment. Essentially a large tent made of a dark mesh fabric, the aviary lets you visit a wide variety of tropical birds in a remarkably realistic setting, instead of peering at them through the bars of a cage. Benches allow for long and leisurely viewing. Some, like the roseate spoonbill, may look familiar but others, like the odd Abdim's Stork and a beautiful blue Victoria Crowned Pigeon that thinks it's a peacock, will probably be new to you. The longer you sit and relax here, the more the mesh tent fades from your consciousness. What remains is a charming encounter with some very lovely birds.

Sesame Street Safari of Fun

This play area was enlarged and improved in 2010 to welcome the lovable Muppet characters from PBS's *Sesame Street* into the park. Other theme parks in Central Florida have similar kiddie areas but nowhere will you find the concept pulled off with as much wit and verve as the Safari of Fun. Here, the clever design of *Fievel's Playland* at Universal and the size of *Shamu's Happy Harbor* at SeaWorld come together to create the only five-star kiddie attraction in this book.

There are animals to be seen here, too, of course. At one end are iguanas, monitor lizards, and komodo dragons. At the other, in a separate circular area, is *Lory Landing*, described below. But the emphasis is on fun and little ones will not be disappointed.

Interactive Play Areas ★ ★ ★ ★ ★

Type: Hands-on activity
Time: As long as you want
Short Take: The best of its kind in Central Florida

Most of the Safari of Fun is given over to a series of loosely connected climb-up, crawl-through, slide-down play areas that can keep little ones occupied for hours. I have given them the rather cumbersome name of "interactive play areas," but each has its own identity and special attractions, as we shall see.

Dominating the north end of the area is **Cookie Monster's Canopy Crawl**, an elaborate two-story structure colorfully painted and shaded by a large tarp covering and towering live oak trees. On the lower level, it features a net climb, an "air bounce" (a large inflated floor on which kids can jump to their hearts' content), and a "ball crawl" (a pit filled with colored plastic balls into which kids can literally dive). The upper level is reached either via the net climb or, for less agile adults, a stairway. There you will find a two-level, kid-sized, climb-through, maze-like environment forming a delight-ful obstacle course. No one higher than 56 inches is allowed in this one, so Mom and Dad are excused.

From this upper level extend two rope bridges. Both go to **Elmo's Tree House**, one directly and the other via an intermediate tower, from which kids can zip down a corkscrew slide to ground level. The Tree House itself is a kid's fantasy of a humongous old tree girdled by a spiral wooden staircase leading to a "secret" room at the top. Along the way, climbers can detour into jungle gym-like environments that snake off through the Safari of Fun. Kids will love it; nervous parents may find it hard to keep track of their little ones. At the foot of the Tree House lies **Oscar's Swamp Stomp**, a watery play area where kids can really get soaked. The swamp leads through and around the old tree and comes complete with a friendly sea serpent whose snake-like body appears and disappears beneath the water. Set apart and surrounded by a fence is **Slimey's Sahara Sand**, a large and ingeniously designed sandbox with adorable playhouses, and an area for adults to relax.

The overall effect of these interlocking entertainments is pure delight. Not only is virtually every activity conceived by the preschool mind represented here, but the design and attention to detail are wonderfully imaginative.

Tip: If your kids are old enough to be turned loose in the Safari of Fun, you can draw some comfort in the knowledge that there is only one way out, at the southern end. There is no exit at the north end, near *Lory Landing*.

Kiddie Rides ★ ★ ★

Type: Mechanical rides for toddlers
Time: A few minutes each
Short Take: Variations on a single theme

Sprinkled around Safari of Fun are small kiddie rides. You know the kind of thing: tiny vehicles that go round and round in a tiny circle with tiny little people sitting in them. The ones here are better designed and executed than most, with cutesy names like *Snuffy's Elephant Romp, Elmo's Safari-Go-Round,* and *Big Bird's Whirlie Birdie*.

Of special note for slightly older kids (minimum 38 inches, under 42 inches must be accompanied by an adult) is *Air Grover,* a junior roller-coaster with gentle dips and dives that makes a fine first step for budding thrill-riders.

A for Africa (Sunny Day Theater) ★ ★ ★ 1/2

Type: Live outdoor show
Time: About 15 minutes
Short Take: Entertainment for tots

This is a delightful little sing-a-long and audience participation show for the kids. Adults should check their sophistication at the door. Elmo, the eternally hyperactive red Muppet, goes on an imaginary musical adventure to Africa with his friends Abby Cadabby, Zoe, Grover, and Cookie Monster, and the audience comes along for the ride. The choreography is energetic, especially considering the heavy costumes the performers wear, and the music is insistently upbeat. It's all good fun and the little tots at whom this show is aimed seem to love every minute of it.

Lory Landing ★ ★ ★ 1/2

Type: Walk-through animal exhibit
Time: As long as you like
Short Take: Close encounters with inquisitive charmers

Lorys and lorikeets are the main attraction in this aviary within an aviary. About halfway between parakeets and parrots in size, lorys are as curious as they are colorful. As you walk through their jungle-themed aviary, they are likely to land on your head, shoulder, or arm to check out your shiny jewelry or angle for a handout. Busch Gardens encourages this by selling "lory nectar" ($5) just in case you forgot to bring your own.

This is great fun for kids (grown-ups, too!) and well worth a visit. In the antechamber to the lorys' digs are large cages displaying their larger cousins—cockatoos, macaws, and the like.

Stanleyville

Stanleyville is a compact, cleverly designed area that quite literally has something for everyone. At the southern end is what is arguably the best roller coaster in all of central Florida, the first stop we encounter on the park-circling *Trans-Veldt Railroad,* as well as a quite nice barbecue restaurant. At the other end are two delightful water rides and in the middle is a spacious theater that serves up some first-rate live entertainment on a somewhat erratic schedule. The *Skyride* (described in the Cheetah Hunt section, below) offers a shortcut to Cheetah Hunt and Egypt. The only downside is that there are very few animals to be seen here, but I seriously doubt you'll care.

SheiKra ★ ★ ★ ★ ★

Type: Floorless vertical dive coaster
Time: 3 minutes
Short Take: Gulp!

SheiKra (pronounced SHEEK-rah) was America's first "vertical dive roller coaster" and its presence cements Busch Gardens' reputation as *the* Central Florida destination for coaster freaks. And just to add to the fun, they removed the floor, adding an extra layer of terror to the experience. If pushing yourself to the limit is your idea of having a good time, then you will not want to miss this fall-filled fear-fest.

Although *SheiKra* officially lasts a full three minutes, the first 70 seconds or so are taken up by the slow crawl to a height of 200 feet where, after a tight U-turn, you reach the first drop. There you pause just over the lip for several hours (okay, three or four seconds) as you contemplate your fate. Then you drop straight down at a 90 degree angle before swooping upwards to do it all again. The second drop takes you straight through the mist-filled center of a ruined tower, underground, up again for another tight turn, and down for a watery splashdown that slows you for a quick return to safety.

The best seats in the house. The ride vehicles are broad and compact, with three eight-seat rows. On top of that, they feature "stadium-style seating," meaning that each row is a little higher than the one in front of it. The result is that virtually every seat gives you a great view of the terrors that face you. Still, the true believers will want to ride until they get into the first row for the unobstructed view of the first drop during that eternal pause.

One of the best touches in this ride is a simple engineering trick used in that final splashdown. Twin tubes mounted on the outside rear edges of the ride vehicle dip into the water on either side of the track, sending up two towering plumes that crash down on the kids who have eagerly gathered at pool's edge. And thanks to the clever siting of the ride, you will have plenty of time to figure out exactly how it's done.

In fact, *SheiKra* offers the best views for non-riders of any Busch Gardens coaster, so you can walk under and around it and get an excellent idea of exactly what you are missing. That is almost as much fun as riding. Almost.

Trans-Veldt Railroad ★ ★ ★

Type: Steam railroad journey
Time: 30 to 35 minutes for a complete circuit

Short Take: Shuttle with a view

Right under *SheiKra*, you can board a reconstruction of the type of steam railroad that served as mass transit in Africa circa 1900, rest your weary feet, and get some great views of the animals of the *Serengeti Plain*. This is one of two vehicular viewing venues for the Serengeti (the *Skyride*, described below, is the other).

It makes a leisurely counterclockwise circuit of the park with stops in Nairobi (the closest stop to the main entrance) and the Congo (near Timbuktu). Since you can board or exit at any of the three stops, the *Trans-Veldt* is a great way to cut down on your walking time, and it provides glimpses of animals you probably wouldn't see otherwise.

As you travel from Stanleyville to Nairobi you will get a tantalizing preview glimpse of *Rhino Rally* and *Cheetah Hunt* (described below), which might help you decide if you want to brave their long lines. Continuing through Egypt on your way to the Congo, you will pass right through the superstructure of *Montu* and enter the Serengeti where you will see giraffes and a variety of veldt antelopes. Too bad you can't stop for a longer look. A narrator on the train helps make sure you don't miss any of the animals and offers interesting facts about the ones you do see.

After the Congo stop, the train loops past Jungala and back to Stanleyville. This portion is the least scenic, although it does provide some fun "backstage" glimpses of the park, including a close-up look at some portions of *Kumba*. In fact, the route of the *Trans-Veldt* takes you past every roller coaster in the park.

Tip: The left-hand side of the train offers the best views of the Serengeti.

Stanleyville Theater ★ ★ ★ to ★ ★ ★ ★ ★

Type: Live entertainment
Time: Varies
Short Take: Keep your fingers crossed

It's hard to predict what, if anything, you'll be able to see here when you visit. The schedule is erratic and anything but predictable. But if you're lucky, you may be able to catch your favorite stars of yesteryear in live performance, making this the hottest show in town. Past acts that have played here include Gary Lewis and the Playboys, Herman's Hermits, and Juice Newton. There have been Big Bands, too, like the Tommy Dorsey, Glenn Miller, and Les Brown Orchestras. Performances tend to be from Thursday through Sunday only, so plan accordingly if this sort of thing interests you. Usually, there are three shows a day and tickets, which are free, are required. You can get them near the theater.

Stanley Falls Log Flume ★ ★ ★ 1/2

Type: Water ride
Time: About 2 minutes
Short Take: The last drop is a doozy

This is a fairly ordinary log flume ride, especially when compared to more recent variations on the theme. On the other hand, it is one of the longest in the nation, they say. The car in which you ride is a log-shaped contraption with two seating areas scooped out of it. Each car holds four people, adults or children. However, when the lines aren't too long you can ride two to a car.

Your log rumbles along at a moderate pace in a water-filled flume, takes a few turns, and then climbs slowly to a modest height. The first small drop is merely preparation for the finale, a slow ride up yet another steep grade and an exhilarating drop to the bottom in full view of the passing crowds. Like all water rides, this one has a warning about getting wet, but the cars seem designed to direct the wave generated by the final splashdown away from you. It's unlikely that you'll get seriously soaked on this one.

Tanganyika Tidal Wave ★ ★ ★ ★

Type:	Water ride
Time:	About 2 minutes
Short Take:	A first-class soaking

If the nearby *Stanley Falls Log Flume* lulled you into a false sense of security about staying dry, this one will dispel any such notions. Like the log flume ride, this is all about the final drop. In fact, until then, this ride is far tamer. It snakes lazily through a narrow waterway past stilt houses, whose porches are piled high with Central African trade goods, before taking a slow climb to the top.

Then, all bets are off as the 25-passenger car on which you're riding plunges wildly down a sharp incline into a shallow pool of water, sending a drenching wave over not just the passengers but the spectators who have eagerly gathered on a bridge overhead. No two ways about it. This one really soaks you. Even with a poncho you'll still be pretty darned damp. Since you're probably soaked to the skin anyway, why not top the ride off by standing on the bridge and waiting for the next car to come by? For those who don't want to take the ride or get soaked on the bridge, there is a glassed in viewing section that offers the thrill of a wall of water rushing at you, without the soaking effects.

See *Good Things to Know About ... Getting Wet*, earlier in this chapter, for some tips on negotiating Busch Gardens' water rides.

Jungala

With Jungala Busch Gardens Tampa ditches the geographic metaphors used in most of the park. Jungala is a made-up word designed, I suspect, to suggest this section's blend of spectacular animal habitats and fun activities for kids. Besides, it is home to animals that are not native to Africa but to India and Southeast Asia. And what animals they are! Tigers and orangutans are some of the most fascinating animals on display at the park. Of course, they are also some of the least active, so what you actually get to see is somewhat "luck of the draw." If you have the luxury of time, repeat visits will be rewarded.

If Safari of Fun is for preschoolers, Jungala is for tweens, that "awkward" age, roughly 8 to 13, between child and teenager. Some of the non-animal attractions here have been specifically designed for that age group, with others thoughtfully excluded.

Orangutan Habitat ★ ★ ★ ★

Type:	Animal habitat
Time:	Unlimited
Short Take:	Another winner

This is the first habitat you encounter, to your left, as you cross the bridge to Jungala from Stanleyville. A shaded portion of the bridge allows a good view of the entire enclosure, which is a sort of raised island surrounded by steep cliffs and water. Don't overlook the ingenious video binoculars here that allow for a closer look.

Orangutans are powerful and agile climbers and the habitat has been designed to let them show off their skills. There are three large metal towers topped with platforms (no attempt at jungle verisimilitude here); the towers are linked by vine-like ropes that allow the orangs to shuttle between them.

At the end of the bridge, to your left, you will find **Orangutan Outpost,** an indoor (but not air-conditioned) viewing area with glass walls looking into the enclosure. A sort of shelf made of logs rims the viewing area and the orangs, seemingly as curious about us as we are about them, often come up for a closer look at the odd creatures in the theme park habitat. A great touch here is a plexiglass section of the floor that looks down on a square rope hammock where the orangs like to come and chill out. There are Meet The Keepers sessions a few times a day here. At other times, signs around the room and interactive video screens provide information about this fascinating species.

Tiger Enclosure ★ ★ ★ ★ ★

Type: Animal habitat
Time: Unlimited
Short Take: Ingenious and enchanting

This sprawling habitat has been cleverly designed to provide the tigers plenty of variety while allowing the visitor many options for viewing. The space is divided in two separate enclosures, with a rocky tunnel, punctuated with windows, running between them.

Tiger Lodge is an indoor, air-conditioned viewing area with floor to ceiling windows that allows for comfortable long-term viewing of one of the enclosures. Outside, **Tiger Trail** runs through the tunnel separating the enclosures allowing you to peer into both. Overhead is a glass paneled walkway that lets the keepers move tigers from one enclosure to the other. Usually it is closed off, but sometimes you will see tigers lolling in this passageway, apparently drawn by the warmth of the small enclosure (hey, they're cats). The trail then curves around the outside of the second enclosure offering a number of views, including an underwater view of one of the tigers' pools. (Alone among the big cats, tigers tolerate, even enjoy, water.) There's also a great view from a wooden bridge into a sort of canyon, with waterfalls and large dead trees that let the tigers climb from one level to another.

Best of all is the **Tiger Pop-Up Viewing** hole. Reached via a cramped tunnel, it allows you to stick your head up inside the tiger enclosure offering a chance for a truly up-close and personal view. When a tiger is lying near this observation post, lines form quickly.

There are more Meet The Keepers sessions here than at the orangutan habitat and Tiger Lodge provides much the same sort of signage found at Orangutan Outpost. Of course, tigers are cats, so most of the time they are napping. As with the orangs, repeat visits will eventually be rewarded.

Treetop Trails ★ ★ ★ 1/2

Type: Interactive play area
Time: Unlimited
Short Take: Adults follow kids at their peril

This is Jungala's version of *Safari of Fun* and like that larger space it is a sprawling interactive play area that encompasses a number of other attractions. At ground level, there are two water play areas, one set aside for toddlers. Above rises the **Canopy Walk**, a maze of climb-through mesh tunnels, rope bridges, and walkways that wind past several small animal habitats showing off gibbons, gharials, and flying foxes. The gharial habitat (they are needle-nosed crocodilians) has a kid-sized tunnel with glass sides that give an underwater view of the denizens within.

Adults are allowed here, but no concessions have been made for aging bones. Many parts of this maze are designed for tween-sized explorers, so proceed at your own risk.

Wild Surge ★ ★ ★ 1/2

Type: Mini thrill ride
Time: About 2 minutes
Short Take: Strictly for kids

This is a scaled-down version of a standard amusement park ride. Two rows of seven seats are positioned back-to-back around a central tower. The seats are raised to a height of 35 feet, offering a view of the *Treetop Trails* area, and then dropped for a sequence of three bounces, then raised and dropped again. A final drop falls all the way to the bottom of the shaft and a return to terra firma. The ride sits in a sort of cave and raised viewing areas let non-riders share the fun vicariously.

Jungle Flyers ★ ★ ★ ★

Type: Zip-line ride for youngsters
Time: 20 seconds (that's not a typo!)
Short Take: I wanna ride, too!

This is far and away the most popular ride at Jungala and waits of 90 minutes are not uncommon. To reach it, you must climb a set of stairs from the *Canopy Walk*, but not so fast! The ride is for those 48 inches tall and 6 to 13 years of age. Anyone older cannot weigh more than 220 pounds and must be accompanied by a kid who meets the height and age requirements. How do they know your weight? They weigh you!

From the launch platform, three twin zip lines head off in different directions. Riders are seated in a sling chair, hoisted to a height of 63 feet above ground level, and let free to slide over the *Treetop Trails* area to a distant post and back again. It all takes just 20 seconds!

Because of the long wait times, unless your kid absolutely needs mommy or daddy nearby to summon the courage to ride, I would suggest adults sit this one out and give the kids a chance.

The Congo

The Congo is even more compact than it used to be, having ceded much of its land to Jungala. It remains a cleverly designed area with twisting tree-shaded walks and a number of spectator bridges over rides offering vicarious fun for non-riders. All of the space—there is no dining and very little shopping here—is given over to some of Busch Gardens' best thrill rides, so expect lots of excited kids and teenagers jostling for space. The predominant architectural motif is round buildings with conical wooden stick roofs.

In addition to the two major attractions profiled below, the Congo contains a bumper car ride (**Ubanga-Banga Bumper Cars**) and remote control trucks and boats. There is also a stop for the *Trans-Veldt Railroad* (described above).

Kumba ★ ★ ★ ★ ★

Type: Steel roller coaster
Time: Just under 3 minutes
Short Take: Yet another superb roller coaster

Once, *Kumba* was Busch Gardens' blockbuster ride. It's since been overshadowed by *Montu* and *SheiKra*, but it's still pretty amazing and is the largest of its kind in the southeastern United States. *Kumba* means "roar" in a Congolese dialect, the PR people say, and it's well named. Riders are braced with shoulder restraints into 32-seat vehicles (eight rows, four abreast) that roar along almost 4,000 feet of blue steel track that winds up, around, over, and through the surrounding scenery. There are loops, camelbacks, and corkscrews to terrify or thrill you, as the case may be. One of the more disorienting maneuvers takes you on a "cobra roll" around a spectator bridge, which is a great place for the faint of heart to get an idea of what they're missing. Remember to wave to Aunt Martha as you whiz by.

Congo River Rapids ★ ★ ★ ★ ★

Type: Water ride
Time: About 3 minutes
Short Take: The best of the water rides

It doesn't have the steep drops of the flume rides in Stanleyville, but for me *Congo River Rapids* provides the most enjoyable overall water ride experience in Busch Gardens. Here you climb aboard 12-seater circular rafts that are then set adrift to float freely along a rapids-filled stretch of river. The raft twists, turns, and spins as it bumps off the sides and various cunningly placed obstacles in the stream. In addition to the raging waters, which periodically slosh into the raft, there are waterfalls and waterspouts, all of which have the potential to drench you to the skin. The most insidious threat of all comes from your fellow park visitors, who are encouraged to spray you with water cannons (at 25 cents a shot) from the pedestrian walkway that skirts the ride.

Despite all the white water, the raft proceeds at a relatively stately pace and the "river" drops only several feet over its quarter-mile course. The real excitement is generated by the ever-present threat of a soaking. How wet you get is only somewhat a matter of chance. It seems that the wetness quotient has been increased since the ride first opened. Time was that some people emerged virtually unscathed, while others got soaked. Now it seems that almost everyone gets thoroughly doused. On a hot Florida afternoon, that seems to be just the ticket, which makes this my favorite water ride and explains the five-star rating.

Timbuktu

Timbuktu is, of course, the legendary sub-Saharan trade crossroads that figures prominently in the popular imagination of adventure and exploration. Here at Busch Gardens, Timbuktu is an open, sun-drenched plaza dotted with palm trees and featuring architecture that mimics the mud towers of its namesake. There is precious little shade here unless you venture indoors. The attractions in Timbuktu are a mismatched assortment, having little to do with either Timbuktu or even Africa. But then, Timbuktu is emblematic of far-flung trade, so perhaps it's not so farfetched that it contains an eclectic grab bag of themed attractions from around the world.

There are no zoo animals here. In their place are a variety of typical **amusement park rides**, including Busch Gardens' only **carousel** and several other **kiddie rides**. Also at hand are a collection of **midway games**, cleverly disguised as a sub-Saharan marketplace, and a **video arcade**.

The Scorpion ★ ★ ★ 1/2

Type: A beginner's roller coaster
Time: About a minute
Short Take: Roller coasters 101

This is the place to come to decide if you have what it takes to tackle the bigger coasters in the park. *The Scorpion* is far and away the tamest of the lot, although it does have one up-and-over loop. So if you've never been "inverted," this is as good a place to start as any. Otherwise, it's no more terrifying than, say, Disney's *Big Thunder Mountain*.

SandSerpent ★ ★ ★

Type: A "baby" roller coaster
Time: About a minute and a half
Short Take: Take the kiddies

If the *Scorpion* is too much for you, head here. It's what's known in the amusement park trade as a "wild mouse" ride. Little four-seater cars zip along a sinuous elevated track with sharp turns and a few mild drops. Kids love it but adults sit high in the little cars and may feel exposed, which can be fun (or not) depending on your taste. The ride does give you a nicely elevated view of the surrounding Timbuktu area.

One downside to the ride is that only a few widely spaced cars are on the track at any given time. This is for safety reasons, but it does lead to slow loading times, which can translate into long waits in line.

Pirates 4-D and Sesame Street 4-D (Timbuktu Theater) ★ ★ ★

Type: 3-D films
Time: About 25 minutes each

Short Take: 3-D shows that make a splash

With this pair of shows, which rotate performances within the park's "4-D" theater during the day, Busch Gardens takes on Disney and Universal in the 3-D movie sweepstakes and comes in a solid third.

First up is *Sesame Street Presents: Lights, Camera, Imagination!,* a lighthearted diversion aimed at the same preschool set entertained by the *Safari of Fun.* Big Bird, Grover, Oscar the Grouch, and their fellow furry friends join together for the first "Sesame Street Film Festival," featuring gentle spoofs of classic flicks like *Superman* and *King Kong.* The humor is warm and charming, though not nearly as laugh-out-loud funny for adults as the similar *Muppet Vision 4-D* attraction at Disney's Hollywood Studios. Be warned: this show employs some of the most ubiquitous and uncomfortably soaking water effects of any 3-D film I've experienced.

In the afternoons, the *Sesame Street* gang steps aside to make room for pirates. Starring the late Leslie Nielsen as Captain Lucky and Eric Idle as his sidekick Pierre, *Pirates 4-D* tells the tale of an evil pirate—that would be Captain Lucky—who returns to Dead Man's Cave to reclaim his buried treasure. What the crew doesn't know is that Captain Lucky buried his former crew along with the treasure and plans to do likewise with his current collection of scalawags.

What Captain Lucky doesn't know is that one member of his old crew—the cabin boy—survived and has rigged the entire island with devilishly clever booby traps. Much of the fun of the film comes from setting off those traps, which involve crabs and spiders and bats and bees, along with an array of seat-side special effects that place the creepy crawlies in our midst. It's all great fun and not really very scary, although very young tots don't seem to know that.

An additional attraction is the air-conditioned Timbuktu Theater, making this a great show to catch during the hottest part of the afternoon.

Best seats in the house. The seats in the front half of the house get the best (or worst, depending on your perspective) of the water effects.

The Phoenix ★ ★ ★

Type: Amusement park ride
Time: 5 minutes
Short Take: Only if you haven't done it before

This is a very familiar amusement park ride. A curved boat-like car seating 50 people swings back and forth, gaining height. At the apex of its swing, it pauses and the passengers hang briefly upside down, screaming merrily. Then on the next swing it goes completely up and over. Chances are, there's a ride like this at an amusement park somewhere near your home, which leads to the question: Ride this one or spend the time doing things you can't do near home? I'd recommend the latter.

Musical Variety Show at the Desert Grill Restaurant ★ ★ ★ ★

Type: Musical variety show
Time: About 20 minutes
Short Take: Best with a meal

What you see here during your visit to Busch Gardens is hard to predict. That's because the stage at the spacious and blessedly cool Desert Grill plays host to a constantly changing roster of musical and dance variety troupes. What's easy to predict is the quality of the shows, which in my experience have been uniformly excellent.

Typically, you will be entertained by a young, energetic, and talented cast. Some shows I've seen have involved intricate percussion and acrobatics. Others have featured championship ballroom dancers, strutting their stuff in a variety of dancing styles. Many times the show will spill out into the audience and they always seem to be looking for a way to get the kids involved. It's all bright and cheerful and makes for a pleasant way to end a meal.

The Desert Grill Restaurant is a cafeteria-style eatery. The food line is to the side of the main auditorium, but all seating is in the theater itself, at long trestle tables set perpendicular to the stage. It's best to arrive a half an hour or so before the posted show time. That should give you time to get your meal and eat most of it before the show starts, so you can enjoy the musical entertainment over dessert.

Nairobi

This is Busch Gardens' most zoo-like themed area. To the east, the plains of the Serengeti stretch as far as the eye can see. On the other side are a string of animal exhibits ranging from the merely interesting to the truly wondrous. In addition to those described below, there are displays of **rhinos** and **Asian elephants**, with occasional Meet The Keepers and Animal Encounter sessions. The *Trans-Veldt Railroad* (described in the Stanleyville section, above) stops right in the middle. The showpiece of Nairobi, however, is the *Rhino Rally* attraction, which is an African animal encounter disguised as an adventure ride.

Rhino Rally ★ ★ ★

Type: Drive-through animal tour
Time: 5 minutes
Short Take: Nifty idea that's more clever than thrilling

Rhino Rally artfully blends safari-style animal encounters with a tame jeep ride through a 16-acre patch of the *Serengeti Plain* offering glimpses of water buffalo, zebras, antelope, elephants, and rhinos. This attraction was shortened in 2010, removing an often-malfunctioning "white water" river finale to make room for the new *Cheetah Hunt* coaster. The resulting ride isn't as thrilling, but at least it operates more reliably with a somewhat shorter wait.

The adventure begins as you board a 17-passenger converted Land Rover with your guide and driver to take part in the 34th annual running of Rhino Rally, an off-road race along the Zambezi River across the rugged and dangerous terrain of the African veldt. One adult in the group is chosen to ride next to the driver (a great seat, by the way) and serve as the navigator who, in off-road rally tradition, will be blamed if anything goes wrong. Along the way, your sturdy vehicle splashes through crocodile-infested waters and comes almost face to face with elephants, rhinos, and other wild critters. The course has been cleverly designed to allow the Land Rovers to nosedive into streams and water holes and cross narrow bridges over deep ravines.

The trip provides close-up, although brief, encounters with elephants, Grant's zebras, cape buffalo, and scimitar-horned oryx. The ancient Egyptians, we learn, domesticated these beasts and forced their long curving horns to grow together into a single horn, creating the myth of the unicorn. After driving past two rare white rhinos (they are actually gray), the vehicle fords a stream filled with real crocodiles cruising just a few feet away. Fortunately, your intrepid guide is able to navigate the stream and drive up the riverbank, bringing everyone safely to the finish line.

A great deal of the fun of this ride is supplied by the driver/guide. The best ones really get into the spirit of things, teaching you a few handy Swahili phrases and getting everyone involved in the action. So you may want to ride more than once. The problem with that is the line can grow to daunting lengths on busy days. Figure on up to an hour's wait during peak season unless you arrive at opening time.

Tip: If you are alone or if there are just two of you, you may be able to get in a vehicle a bit sooner by following the sign for the single riders line. If you are waiting in the main line, you can accomplish much the same thing by holding one or two fingers aloft during the boarding process. Ride attendants sometimes look for singles or couples to fill in empty spots on the Land Rover that's about to depart.

The best seats in the house. The seats on the left-hand side of the vehicle offer the best views of the wildlife.

Animal Care Center ★ ★ ★ ★

Type: Walk through exhibit of exotic animal husbandry
Time: About 20 minutes
Short Take: A clever idea well executed

A lot of fascinating stuff happens behind the scenes at a major zoo. Busch has had the clever idea of turning that into an attraction to delight and inform its visitors. Here, in a spotlessly clean 16,000-square-foot facility guests make their way through a series of state-of-the-art facilities where they can watch through glass walls what goes in to the care and feeding of Busch Gardens' 200 different species.

In the Nutrition Center, which looks like something you might expect in the studios of the Food Network, animal nutritionists conduct regular demonstrations on how they prepare meals for their animal charges; from time to time guests can join in. The Treatment Rooms allow surgery on animals from small to large while overhead critter cams allow onlookers a closer look. In the diagnostic area, visitors can watch the routine procedures like sonograms and teeth cleaning that are performed on a variety of exotic creatures every day.

Obviously there's no way of telling exactly which animals will be having what procedures on the day of your visit, but a variety of interactive exhibits is available to keep guests occupied on slow days.

Jambo Junction ★ ★ ★

Type: Animal exhibit
Time: Continuous viewing

Short Take: Lifestyles of the cutest and cuddliest

Busch Gardens Tampa maintains a cadre of "Animal Ambassadors," a team of smaller critters who make public appearances around the park, at nearby schools, and even on television. The senior ambassador, Harry, a two-toed sloth has appeared on the major late-night talk shows. The ambassadors' job is to foster greater awareness of the animal kingdom and mankind's responsibility for protecting it. This is where they live between gigs. A visit here is most entertaining when a member of the education staff is on hand to answer questions and maybe even help you pet a flamingo.

Curiosity Caverns ★ ★ 1/2

Type: Walk-through exhibit
Time: Continuous viewing
Short Take: A real "Bat Cave"

Decorated to evoke a prehistoric cave, complete with wall paintings, this darkened walk-through tunnel displays, behind plate glass windows, a variety of critters that most people think of as "creepy," although the nocturnal marmoset is positively cuddly. Aside from the snakes and reptiles, the main attractions here are the bats. Fruit bats cavort in a large enclosure decorated with bare trees artfully draped with bananas, apples, and other yummy treats. Nearby, in a smaller display, are the vampire bats (yes, they really exist!), the animal blood on which they thrive served up on dainty trays hanging in their cages.

Cheetah Hunt

Cheetah Hunt is the newest of Busch Gardens' "lands." It was created by shaving off a sliver of the former Crown Colony, now part of Egypt. Cheetah Hunt also has the distinction of being the first of Busch Gardens' themed areas to be named after a roller coaster, which is reviewed below. Also here is the *Skyride*, which links this corner of the park with Stanleyville.

Cheetah Hunt ★ ★ ★ ★ ★

Type: Launched roller coaster animal habitat
Time: About 3½ minutes
Short Take: A sensational sensation of speed

Technically, Busch Gardens' newest roller coaster is not part of Egypt but its own tiny "land." But since the attraction forms the gateway to the Egypt section for guests coming from Nairobi or the front of the park, and the crumbling sandstone decor sports a distinctly Middle Eastern look, I'm incorporating it here.

Did you ever watch *Return of the Jedi* and wish you could zoom through the trees on a speeder-bike? So did the designer of this family-friendly coaster, who was inspired by that film to engineer a ride emphasizing smooth, ground-level maneuvers and multiple high-velocity launches over big drops or loops.

Your adventure begins in the *Skyride* station, which now shares real-estate with the *Cheetah Hunt* loading station. As you wait in the slow-moving queue (at only 1,370 riders per hour, this popular ride attracts long lines), there are video monitors and signs featuring cheetah trivia to entertain you.

Once aboard the 16-rider trains, you'll be shot out of the station at 30 mph by electromagnetic motors, skipping the standard slow climb up an initial lift hill. A brief swoop around the neighboring cheetah habitat brings you to the second launch segment, accelerating you at 60 mph to the top of a 102-foot "windcatcher" tower that looks like a precariously balanced pile of pick-up sticks.

Diving 130 feet off the tower into a trench, your train leaps over the passing *Skyride* gondolas, then navigates a gracefully engineered "heartline" roll (the only upside-down element in the ride). That's followed by a series of ground-hugging banked turns along the river rapids once part of the *Rhino Rally* ride. A final 40-mph launch leads to a series of airtime-inducing hills and speed-sapping curves, ending up back in the station.

With a modest 48-inch height requirement and a minimum of scary loops, *Cheetah Hunt* makes a perfect stepping stone for tweens braving their first big-boy ride. Perfect for coaster-cravers and more moderate thrill-seekers alike, the ride is refreshingly smooth and comfortable, especially compared to its more intimidating siblings like *Kumba* and *Montu*.

Cheetah Run ★ ★ ★ 1/2

Type: Animal habitat
Time: Unlimited
Short Take: A fun display when the cats are at play

For those still unwilling to ride the coaster, the adjacent *Cheetah Run* exhibit makes an ideal place to wait for the more adventuresome in your party. Much like the aquarium incorporated into SeaWorld's *Manta* coaster, the designers have ingeniously integrated an animal habitat around the ride, with careful soundproofing to prevent the animals from being disturbed; much like your house cats, these cheetahs seem to largely ignore the tourists whizzing past, along with almost everything else besides food. A dozen of the African cats, including from time to time cubs, are on view through giant glass panels. Keepers appear several times a day to feed the animals and exercise them with sprints along their 220-foot long running path. For the curious, touch-screen computers provide additional information on these amazing animals.

The Skyride ★ ★ ★

Type: Suspended gondola ride
Time: 5 minutes
Short Take: Shortcut with a view

If you've been on the sky ride at any amusement park, you know what this one's all about. This isn't intended as a tour of the *Serengeti Plain*, although it does pass over *Edge of Africa* and *Rhino Rally* and offers a glimpse of the plains animals in the distance. Rather, this is a one-way shortcut from Crown Colony to Stanleyville, or vice versa. Your vehicle is a small four-seat gondola suspended from an overhead cable. You can board at either end, but you cannot stay aboard for a round trip. The ride dips down for a dog-leg left turn at a checkpoint on the northern end of the *Serengeti Plain*. This is not a disembarkation point but is used primarily to adjust the spacing between gondolas to assure a smooth arrival.

You can get good views of the *Serengeti Plain* on this ride, although most people will take the opportunity to check out the action on *Montu, Kumba,* and *Cheetah Hunt,* whose track briefly passes over the *Skyride* cable, or perhaps to spot the towers of Adventure Island, Busch Gardens' water park, down the road.

Egypt

Egypt was once one of Busch Gardens' smallest lands. Its primary purpose was to give the mega-coaster *Montu* a home. The *King Tut* attraction seemed a bit of an afterthought, and the only eatery here was a kiosk dispensing snacks. Then Busch decided, somewhat incongruously, to make *Edge of Africa* part of Egypt even though the animals on display there flourish a good ways to the south. More recently the adjacent Crown Colony House was assigned to Egypt, which means that the area now has a major eatery, a very nice full-service sit-down restaurant with a spectacular view of the *Serengeti Plain.*

The design of Egypt proper evokes upper Egypt, that is the part well south of present day Cairo, as it might have looked about the time Howard Carter was unearthing King Tut's treasure. The scale is appropriately grandiose but the statuary and wall carvings fall well short of the originals. Still, it's pleasant enough. There's a clever "archaeological dig," called **Sifting Sands**, that is, in fact, a shaded sandbox in which little ones can uncover the past. A small selection of **midway games** is also offered.

For most people, however, Egypt will be glimpsed briefly en route to the massive temple gates at the end, beyond which lurks the terrifying *Montu.*

Edge of Africa ★ ★ ★ ★ ★

Type: Brilliant animal habitat
Time: Continuous viewing
Short Take: Up close and personal with lions and hippos

Edge of Africa is an animal habitat to rival *Myombe.* Here, on a looping trail that evokes a number of African themes, are displayed a compact colony of adorable meerkats, a pride of lions, a pack of hyenas, a few hippos, and a troop of ring-tailed lemurs. The genius of the design is in the glass walls that allow you, literally, to come nose to nose with some of these animals.

The best display is built around the metaphor of a scientific encampment on the Serengeti that has been invaded by lions or hyenas (the zoo operation alternates these species in the exhibit). Two Land Rovers are built into the glass wall that separates you from the beasts, allowing you to climb into the vehicles and re-create an actual safari experience. At feeding time, the handlers drop meat morsels into the enclosure from above the Land Rovers, encouraging the animals to climb into the backs and onto the hoods of the vehicles. The effect is breathtaking as you sit a hand's breadth away from these snarling carnivores.

The hippo exhibit evokes an African river village with the huts raised over the water on stilts. The viewing area is nicely shaded by the huts and the extensive glass wall allows a terrific underwater perspective on these beasts. While they may seem lumbering on land, under water they are surprisingly graceful as they lope past swarms of freshwater tropical fish. One visitor compared them to flying pigs.

The key to really enjoying *Edge of Africa* is to come at feeding time when the animals will be at their most active and most visible. At other times they will most likely be off relaxing in the shade somewhere. The attendants doing the feeding are all experienced animal handlers who are more than happy to share their extensive knowledge with you, so don't be shy about asking questions. Unfortunately, there is no regular feeding schedule. Feeding times are varied to mimic, to some small extent, life in the wild, where animals can never predict when—or even if—their next meal is coming.

The solution is to ask the attendants at the attraction when feeding time will be. You may have to be persistent and you must also be willing to drop whatever you're doing elsewhere in the park to return at the appointed time. Take it from me, it's worth it.

Serengeti Safari Tour ★ ★ ★ ★ ★

Type: Guided tour
Time: 30 minutes
Short Take: A safari for those who can't get to Africa

First the bad news: There is a hefty extra charge for this attraction of $34 for everyone 5 and older (Passport holders get a $2 discount). That will probably be a budget-buster for many families; but if the cost doesn't scare you off, this one will provide experiences you'll remember for a good long time. If it's any consolation, it's a heck of a lot cheaper than going to Africa.

The tour begins when about 20 people are loaded on to the standing-room-only back of a flatbed truck. A small awning provides some shade at the front, but since it is lowered for the animal feedings much of the time you will be in the searing sun; a hat, not to mention water, is not a bad idea. Your friendly tour guide, a Busch Gardens' education staffer, lays down a few simple safety instructions and then it's off to the interior of the *Plain* for the real highlight of the tour—a chance to hand feed the giraffes and elands. Along the way, you will see ostriches and maribou storks, but the giraffes are the stars of the show.

The adult giraffes tower over you, while the youngsters just get their heads over the edge of the truck. They are remarkably tame and will let you pet their stiff, tawny necks and soft muzzles. You may also get a demonstration of how they use their long black tongues to pluck the dainty leaves off thorny acacia bushes. For most people, this is the highlight of the tour. To have two or three of these gentle giants leaning into the back of the truck as you feed them and stroke their powerful necks is a very special experience indeed.

The best seats in the house. The back of the truck where you stand has a padded rail around the rim. I suggest positioning yourself at one of the back corners since the giraffes will often trail after the slow-moving vehicle looking for another handout.

Tip: The trucks have a maximum capacity of 20 people and on a typical day there are just five tours. While the high price keeps the crowds down, tours do fill up quickly. You can reserve ahead for the first tour of each day only, which departs at 11:15 a.m. and is the only morning tour. The morning tour also offers the advantage of beating the heat of midday. Call (813) 984-4043 to make your reservation. When you arrive at the park, look for the Adventure Tour Center in Morocco (on your left), where you can pay for your tour with cash or credit card. If you don't reserve ahead, you must sign up in advance for one of the afternoon tours when you get to the park; it is wise to do so early.

Serengeti Plain ★ ★ ★

Type:	Extensive animal habitat
Time:	Continuous viewing but access is limited
Short Take:	Takes persistence to see it all

This is one of Busch Gardens' major zoological achievements, a 50-acre preserve that evokes the vast grasslands of Eastern Africa. (Serengeti is a Masai word meaning "plain without end.") Here, Busch displays a representative cross section of African plains dwellers, from charming curiosities like giraffes and the endangered black rhinoceros, to the herd animals—lithe gazelles and lumbering wildebeest (or gnus). There are some African birds here, too, like the maribou stork, but most of the birds you will see are what Busch Gardens calls "fly-ins," Florida species that recognize a good deal when they see one. The rule of thumb is that if it's a bird and white, it's a Tampa Bay local.

It's a brilliant idea and, by and large, well executed, although it still looks far more like Florida scrub land than the real Serengeti. The concept and the design involve a number of tradeoffs. By mimicking nature, the designers have made the animals hard to see—just like in the wild. Although you can see into the *Serengeti* from Nairobi or the terrace of the Crown Colony House, the only way to get a good look is to go inside. Unless you are willing to pay the stiff extra fee for the *Serengeti Safari Tour*, that can be accomplished only by the *Skyride* (see above) and by the *Trans-Veldt Railroad* (see the Stanleyville section, above) that circles the perimeter.

So your routes through the *Serengeti* are predetermined as are the lengths of your visits. This creates a number of minor problems. There's no guarantee that the animals will be in prime viewing position (or even visible) when you pass by, although it's unlikely that you will miss much. And, if an animal catches your fancy or is doing something particularly interesting, your vehicle simply keeps on going; you don't have the luxury of stopping. You also have no control over how close you can get to the animals (with the notable exception of the *Serengeti Safari Tour*). The nature of the park experience, however, suggests that most people will glimpse the animals briefly on the short rides. And that's too bad.

That being said, the *Serengeti Plain* remains a major feather in Busch Gardens' zoological cap. The animals enjoy a much more spacious and natural environment than they would have in a more "traditional" zoo, and we probably shouldn't complain too much about the compromises we must make for their comfort.

Montu ★ ★ ★ ★ ★

Type:	Inverted roller coaster
Time:	About 3 minutes
Short Take:	The next best (i.e. scariest) thing to *SheiKra*

This one is truly terrifying. It is also, for those who care about such things, the tallest and longest inverted steel roller coaster in the southeastern United States.

Montu (named for a hawk-headed Egyptian god of war) takes the formula of

Kumba and quite literally turns it on its head. Instead of sitting in a car with the track under your feet, you sit (or should I say "hang") in a car with the track overhead. Once you leave the station, your feet hang free as you climb to a dizzying 150 feet above the ground before being dropped 13 stories, shot through a 360-degree "camelback loop" that produces an eternity of weightlessness (actually a mere three seconds), and zipped, zoomed, and zapped along nearly 4,000 feet of track that twists over, above, and even into the ground. Fortunately, when you dip below ground level you do so in archaeo-logical "excavation trenches," in keeping with the Egyptian theme. There's not much to see in these trenches, but then you don't spend much time in them and you'll probably have your eyes jammed shut anyway.

Each car holds 32 passengers. At maximum capacity, 1,700 guests can be pumped through this attraction each hour. Nonetheless, lines can be formidable. If this is your kind of ride, plan on arriving early during busy seasons.

The best seats in the house. The best (and scariest) seats are in the front row. Oth-erwise, the outside seats are the ones to hope for. Given the overhead design of this ride, the interior seats offer a very obstructed view, which may not be a problem if you tend to ride with your eyes shut most of the time. Getting the front seats is pretty much the luck of the draw, although every once in a while you may be able to step in when the faint of heart opt out of the front row.

Even if you can't or don't ride roller coasters, *Montu* is worth a visit for a close-up view of the crazy people who are riding. Position yourself at the black iron fence that you see as you pass through the massive temple gates that lead to the ride. Here you'll get an exhilarating close-up look of 32 pairs of feet as they come zipping out of the first trench. If you do ride, don't forget to look for your terrified or giddy face on the instant photos they sell.

King Tut's Tomb ★ ★ 1/2

Type:	Walk-through attraction
Time:	About 10 minutes
Short Take:	A "spirited" guide to an ancient tomb

Here's your chance to walk in the footsteps of Howard Carter, the legendary ar-chaeologist who discovered King Tut's tomb in the 1920s. As you wait in the darkened entrance to the tomb, old newspaper headlines and period newsreels re-create the ex-citement and wonder of the discovery. Then, the projector jams, the film melts and, as you enter the tomb proper, the spirit of Tut himself takes over as tour guide.

What you see is a re-creation of the tomb as it looked at the time of discovery, the many treasures and priceless artifacts piled in jumbled disarray. As lights illuminate specific artifacts, Tut tells us about his gilded throne, his golden chariot, and his teenage bride. Moving to the burial chamber, we see his solid gold sarcophagus and the golden goddesses who guarded the cabinet containing alabaster urns filled with his internal organs.

For newcomers to Egyptology, this attraction will serve as an intriguing introduc-tion. The marvelously air-conditioned tomb also makes for a pleasant break from the burning Florida sun. Those who are familiar with Tut may want to skip this one.

Guided Tours

Busch Gardens Tampa offers a number of special tours in addition to the *Serengeti Safari Tour* (see Egypt, above). These offer special perks, behind-the-scenes access, and up-close encounters with some of its animal charges. There is a hefty extra charge for these special experiences, but if you have the budget I think you'll find it money well spent. The fees given below (which do not include tax) are in addition to regular park admission and only some tours offer very modest discounts to Passport holders. Prices were accurate at press time but are subject to change, so it's best to call prior to your visit to double check prices and availability. You can book online at buschgardens.com, or call toll-free at (888) 800-5447 and ask to be connected to the tour department. The direct line is (813) 984-4043. Tour tickets can also be purchased in the park at the Adventure Tour Center, to your left as you enter the park; at the Heart of Jungala, a small counter in the Tiger Lodge viewing pavilion in Jungala; and at the Park Information counter in the entrance to Desert Grill in Timbuktu.

Children under 5 are not permitted on any animal interactions, although they can participate in other elements of some tours. Bilingual guides can be arranged with prior notice.

Endangered Species Safari

This $40 45-minute tour adds a visit to the endangered white rhinos to the giraffe feeding of the *Serengeti Safari Tour*, described above. Participants also learn a bit about conservation efforts and the good work of the World Wildlife Fund, which gets a donation of $2 from the cost of the tour.

Sunset Safari

This is an adults-only version of the *Serengeti Safari Tour*. It features opportunities to feed the giraffes and visit the rhinos while knocking back a few premium lager brews. Presumably, they make sure no one is FUI (feeding under the influence). This 45-minute experience is $40 per over-21 head.

Serengeti Night Safari

If you liked the *Sunset Safari,* you'll love this two-and-a-half hour after-dark version. You'll begin with appetizers and alcohol in the exclusive Safari Club, followed by a moonlight stroll through the *Edge of Africa* to "explore the nighttime mysteries" of hippos, lions, and hyenas. Next, take a guided tour of the *Serengeti Plain* for unique views of the animals through night vision goggles, then settle in by a bonfire to hear your guide share African folklore. Finally, you head back to the Safari Club for desserts, coffee, and a nightcap of African liqueur. Admission costs $60 and is available to adults only.

Jungala Insider

Here's a chance to get up close and almost personal with the tigers and orangutans of Jungala. This is a 45-minute tour, and the fee is $20, a portion of which goes to the SeaWorld-Busch Gardens Conservation Fund.

The tour begins with a walk backstage to the subterranean quarters of the tigers who are not on display in the outdoor habitat. You will get to watch them being fed (blood popsicles, anyone?) in their cages while an extremely knowledgeable keeper explains the intricacies of caring for these magnificent beasts. Don't expect any "interaction." These are wild animals, after all, and no one at Busch Gardens touches them except when they've been anesthetized for veterinary exams.

Next, it's off to the orangutan compound for a similar show-and-tell. Here the orang is behind glass and the keeper demonstrates the way the critter has been trained to respond to simple hand signals. A few of these are "tricks," but most have to do with making veterinary procedures easier on the keepers. Finally, you will get to meet two "Animal Ambassadors" from the bird kingdom, such as a golden conyer and a gaudily colored macaw.

Keeper for a Day

This is Busch Gardens Tampa's ultimate animal encounter experience, not to mention the most costly. But the $250 you pay for this six-and-a-half hour tour will probably seem worth it to animal and zoo fanatics. Because there is hard work involved, this one has some additional restrictions. Participants must be at least 13 years old and 52 inches tall and able to lift 15 pounds and climb a flight of stairs. You have to follow instructions, too, something not every tourist seems capable of doing. Your time is divided between caring for and feeding giraffes and antelopes in the morning and birds in the afternoon, all in the *Serengeti Plain* area of the park. Reservations are required, and must be made at least a week in advance.

If the Keeper for a Day program is too much, there are shorter "Keeper Experiences" available focusing on either elephants or tigers and orangutans. The 90-minute tours, which have the same restrictions as the Keeper for a Day program, cost $200 for a group of up to six participants, bringing the cost down to $33 each if you can gather five other friends; 24-hour advance reservations are required.

Guided Adventure Tour

This five-hour guided tour combines the animal encounters of the *Serengeti Safari Tour* with visits to *Edge of Africa* and the park's major rides and shows. Guests on this tour get front of the line access to several of the major coasters and the best seats in the house for the shows, as well as lunch at a "family favorite" restaurant (which means one of the more casual, cafeteria-style eateries). You also receive a 20% discount on all park merchandise and free stroller and wheelchair rental.

The tour costs $95 for adults and $85 for kids 5 to 9 and is limited to 15 people. Make a reservation before arriving or look for the "Guided Tour Adventure Center" in the entrance plaza to the park. Tours depart once a day at 10:20 a.m.

Roller Coaster Insider

This 45-minute tour is for those fascinated with the mechanics behind the "big iron" rides. For $20 (ages 10 and up only), you get to visit *Montu's* maintenance facility to witness the "nuts and bolts" behind keeping the coaster running. Next, take a walk up to the braking platform for a bird's-eye view of the ride's seven inversions. Finally, skip the queue to take a front-row ride.

Elite Adventure Tour

This $200 per person all-day extravaganza is Busch Gardens' VIP tour and it can last as long as you wish, although at this price you'll probably want to arrive early and stay until the park closes. The *Elite Adventure Tour* offers the front of the line access, priority seating, and discounts of the *Guided Adventure Tour*, plus a free continental breakfast, lunch, and free parking and bottled water. This one must be booked at least 24 hours in advance, but large groups should book at least a week in advance.

Adventure Camps

If you really want to be nice to your kids, you won't just take them to Busch Gardens Tampa, you'll leave them there. Busch Gardens operates a number of sleepover camps for kids from grade six through high school. There's even a program that takes college kids. With nifty names like Zooventures and Young Explorers, these camps last from three to nine days and cost from $900 to over $2,000. Housing is dorm style on Busch Gardens property.

And if you think it's unfair that kids have all the fun, ask about the Family Sleepovers that let adults tag along. For more information and to request a catalog of camp programs at all of the Busch parks (the SeaWorlds in Orlando, San Antonio, and San Diego also offer programs), call (877) 248-2267 or (813) 987-5252.

Chapter Twelve:

Water Parks

ORLANDO IS THE HOME OF THE WATER PARK AS WE KNOW IT TODAY. GEORGE D. Millay, a former SeaWorld official, started it all in 1977 with the opening of Wet 'n Wild. Since then, the concept has been copied, most noticeably by Disney, whose near-by complex has two water-themed parks—Typhoon Lagoon and Blizzard Beach—both beautifully designed in the Disney tradition. Despite its deep pockets and design talent, Disney hasn't buried the competition. Wet 'n Wild is still going strong, SeaWorld has created a beautiful new water park down the road in Aquatica, and, to the west, there is Adventure Island, right next to Busch Gardens Tampa. All of these water parks offer plenty of thrills at a competitive price.

An often overlooked selling point of these non-Disney water parks is that they all have numerous hotels and motels just a short drive away. Wet 'n Wild has many hotels within walking distance. This makes them especially easy to visit. If you are staying near one of these parks, there is little need, in my opinion, to trek all the way to Disney for a water park experience.

Like any self-respecting theme park, a water park has rides. But the rides here don't rely on mechanical wonders or ingenious special effects. Indeed they are the essence of simplicity: You walk up and then, with a little help from gravity and a stream of water, you come down. The fun comes from the many variations the designers work on this simple theme.

Slides. These are the most basic rides. After climbing a high tower, you slide down a flume on a cushion of running water, either on your back, on a rubber mat, in a one- or two-person inner tube, or in a raft that can carry anywhere from two to five people. Virtually every slide will have a series of swooping turns and sudden drops. Some are open to the sky, others are completely enclosed tubes. All slides dump you in a pool at the bottom of the run.

Speed Slides. Speed slides appeal to the daredevil. They are simple, narrow, flat-bottomed slides; some are pitched at an angle that approaches the vertical, others descend in a series of stair steps. Most culminate in a long, flat stretch that allows you to decelerate; a few end in splash pools. They offer a short, intense experience.

Wave Pools. These large, fan-shaped swimming pools have a beach-like entrance at the wide end and slope to a depth of about eight feet at the other. A clever hydraulic system sets waves running from the wall to the beach, mimicking the action of the ocean. Most wave pools have several modes, producing a steady flow of varying wave heights or a sort of random choppiness. Sometimes rented inner tubes are available for use in the wave pool.

Good Things to Know About . . .

Dress Codes. Simply put: wear a swimsuit. Most parks prohibit shorts, cut-off jeans, or anything with zippers, buckles, or metal rivets, as these things can scratch and damage the slides. Those with fair skin can wear T-shirts if they wish. Some rides may require that you remove your shirt, which you can usually clutch to your chest as you zoom down. Most people go barefoot, as the parks are designed with your feet's comfort in mind. If you prefer to wear waterproof sandals or other footwear designed for water sports, they are permitted.

Leaving the Park. All the parks reviewed here let you leave the park and return the same day. Just make sure to have your hand stamped before leaving.

Lockers. All water parks provide rental lockers and changing areas. Most people wear their swimsuits under their street clothes and disrobe by their locker. At day's end, they take their street clothes to a changing area, towel down, and get dressed, popping their wet suits into a plastic bag. The plastic laundry bag from your hotel room is ideal for this purpose.

Safety. Water park rides are safe, just as long as you follow the commonsense rules posted at the rides and obey the instructions of the ride attendants. You are more likely to run into problems with the sun (see below) or with physical exertion if you are out of shape. You will climb more stairs at a visit to a water park than most people climb in a month. If you're not in peak condition, take it slow; pause from time to time and take in the sights.

The Sun. The Central Florida sun can be brutal. If you don't have a good base tan, a day at a water park can result in a painful sunburn, even on a cloudy day. Don't let it happen to you. Use sun block and use it liberally. Most overlooked place to protect: your feet. The sun also saps your body of moisture. Be sure to drink plenty of liquids throughout the day.

Towels. At Wet 'n Wild you can rent towels for a modest fee. Adventure Island, at my last visit, was not renting towels but said they were considering doing so, "because we get so many requests." It's easy (not to mention cheaper) to bring your own, even if it's one borrowed from your hotel.

Eating in the Water Parks

Water parks are like a day at the beach. Consequently, dining (if that's the right word) is a pretty basic experience. Most park eateries offer walk-up window service, paper plates, plastic utensils, and outdoor seating, some of it shaded. The bill of fare seldom ventures out of the hot dog, hamburger, pizza, barbecue, and ice cream categories. The prices are modest. You really have to work hard to spend more than $15 per person for a meal, except at Aquatica, which features some more upscale eating choices. In short, food at the water parks has been designed with kids and teenagers in mind, so I have not covered the restaurants in the reviews that follow. Suffice it to say you won't go hungry.

However, in my opinion, the best way to eat at the water parks is to bypass the fast-food eateries altogether and bring your own. If you are the picnicking type, I don't have to tell you what to do. Others should be aware that Florida supermarkets are cornucopias of picnic supplies. The folks at the deli counter will be more than happy to fix you up with a sumptuous repast. You can even pick up an inexpensive cooler while you're there along with ice to keep things cool. All the parks prohibit alcoholic beverages and glass containers.

Most people simply find a suitable picnic bench when they arrive and stake it out with a beach towel and their cooler, returning at lunch time. If you feel uncomfortable doing this, you can leave your cooler in the car and retrieve it at lunch time. (Don't forget to get your hand stamped!) Another option would be to use one of the rental lockers. Note that Aquatica's picnic area is just outside the park.

Shopping in the Water Parks

The casual attitude of these parks toward eating is echoed in the shopping. Don't worry, you'll be able to get that nifty T-shirt or the key chain with the park's logo if you must. But the shops are fairly basic even at their most spacious. The best thing about them is the canny selection of merchandise. If you get to the park and find yourself saying, "Oh no, I forgot my . . ." chances are you'll be able to find it in the shop.

In addition to the usual gamut of souvenirs and T-shirts are swimsuits (some of them quite snazzy), sandals, sun block and tanning lotions, film, combs, brushes and other toiletries, towels, sunglasses, trashy novels—in short, everything you need for a day at the beach. Forgetful picnickers will also be pleased to know that they can find soft drinks, snack foods, and candy bars at most of the shops.

Wet 'n Wild

6200 International Drive, Orlando, FL 32819 ~ (800) 992-WILD; (407) 351-1800
www.wetnwildorlando.com

The original Orlando water park is still the best. Add to that its location in the heart of Orlando's tourist country and its partnership in the Orlando FlexTicket program (see *Chapter 1: Introduction & Orientation*) and you have a real winner.

The park layout is compact and efficient with little wasted space. The style is sleekly modern and the maintenance is first rate—even though Wet 'n Wild is the oldest water park in the area, it looks as if it opened just last week.

Getting There

Wet 'n Wild is located in the heart of Orlando's prime tourist area on International Drive at the corner of Universal Boulevard, right off I-4 Exit 75A. Parking is $12 for cars, $16 for RVs and vans.

Opening and Closing Times

Thanks to heated water on its slides and in its pools, Wet 'n Wild is open year-round, although it can get plenty chilly in the winter months. The hours of operation vary from 10:00 a.m. to 5:00 p.m. from late October to around the end of March to 9:30 a.m. to 9:00 p.m. at the height of the summer. Call the information lines above for specific park hours during your visit.

The Price of Admission

The following prices do not include tax:

> ***One-Day Admission:***
>
> | | |
> |---|---|
> | Adults: | $48.99 |
> | Children (3 to 9): | $42.99 |
> | Children under 3 are **free**. | |
> | Seniors (55+): | $42.99 |
> | Annual Pass (all ages): | $79.88 |
> | Weekday Annual Pass (all ages): | $52.00 |

For the best prices on annual passes, check Wet 'n Wild's Internet site. Prices may be higher at the gate.

Wet 'n Wild participates in the **Orlando FlexTicket** program described in *Chapter 1: Introduction & Orientation*. In addition, the park offers discounts for entry in the afternoon year round. See their website for details.

Rentals

The following are available for rent or loan at the round kiosk located to your right as you enter the park:

Lockers are $5 for small, $8 for standard size, or $10 for the family (large) lockers, plus a $3 refundable deposit.

Towels are $4, plus a $3 deposit.

Life vests are **free**, as are inner tubes at the rides that require them.

Cabanas can be rented, and include lounge chairs, towels, a lockbox, and a fridge full of Coke products. During peak attendance times, Express passes to cut the lines may be sold. Prices vary seasonally; see the website for reservations.

Rides and Attractions at Wet 'n Wild

Wet 'n Wild is a compact and tightly packed park that somehow avoids feeling cramped. For the purposes of describing its attractions I have divided the park into three slices. I will start on the left-hand side of the park (as you enter the front gate), then proceed to the center section, and finally describe the slides and such on the right-hand side.

Kid's Park

This delightful, multi-level water play area is a sort of Wet 'n Wild in miniature for the kiddie set, those 48 inches and shorter. At the top, there are some twisting water slides that can be negotiated with or without tiny inner tubes. On the other side is a mini-version of the *Surf Lagoon* wave pool surrounded by a Lilliputian *Lazy River*. In between are shallow pools with fountains, showers, water cannons, and a variety of other interactive play areas, all watched over by vigilant lifeguards. Looming overhead is a gigantic bucket that slowly fills with water and periodically tips over, sending a cascade of water onto the squealing kids below. Surrounding the *Kid's Park* is a seating area filled with shaded tables and chairs where Mom and Dad can take their ease while junior wears himself out nearby.

Mach 5

The massive tower that houses *Mach 5* and two other rides looks like a giant pasta factory after a nasty explosion; flumes twist every which way. At the entrance, you grab a blue toboggan-like mat; the front end curves up and over two hand holds. Then there is a very long climb to the top where you will find three flumes labeled A, B, and C. They all seem to offer pretty much the same experience, but you'll probably want to try all three anyway. I sure did.

You ride belly down on your mat and take a few gently corkscrewing turns. But then there is a quick drop followed by a sharp turn followed by another drop and so on until you zip into and across the splashdown pool. Keeping your feet raised will decrease the coefficient of drag and give you a slightly zippier ride.

The Blast

This two-passenger tube ride, which shares the *Mach 5* tower, is one of Wet 'n Wild's "themed" rides. It whisks you through a multicolored and fanciful landscape that is part psychedelic daydream and part factory floor. As you whish past funny looking machines, pipes and chutes blast you with water at unexpected moments, usually when you've just been disoriented by another twist or turn in the chute. The real fun, however, is saved for last, with an exhilarating waterfall plunge into the pool that marks the ride's end.

The Flyer

This newer ride also shares the *Mach 5* tower and, while it starts at about the same height as *Raging Rapids*, it's a much faster, scarier ride. This time there's nothing to drag to the top with you; your vehicle awaits at the launching area. It's a bright green two-, three-, or four-person raft (no single riders), with built-in hand grips. Hang on tight because the turns are sharp and the raft gets thrown high up the curved side walls as you zoom quickly to the bottom. This is a justifiably popular ride with a lot of repeat riders.

The Surge

The Surge shares a tower with *Disco H2O*. The lines for both attractions are parallel, and can get quite lengthy, so be sure to get in the correct line at the beginning, lest you end up at the wrong attraction when you get to the top! For *The Surge,* riders board rafts, large four-person circular affairs. You sit in the bottom of the raft, facing toward the center, and grab hand holds on the floor. Then the attendant gives the raft a good spin as he sends you on your way down the first fall. The flumes are larger versions of those at *Mach 5* and the descent seems somewhat slower. The turns, however, are deceptive. Depending on where you're sitting as the raft enters a turn, you can find yourself sliding high on the curved walls, and when you hit one of the frequents drops backwards you'll feel your tummy do a little flip.

Disco H2O

Missed the disco era? Well, hustle on over to this ride and climb aboard one of the four-person rafts for a plunge down a time warp that takes you back to the groovy seventies. There, in a darkened circular chamber, you'll spin round and round a watery disco dance hall filled with funky music and fun light effects as you are drawn ever closer to a hole that sucks you back to the well-lit present. It's almost enough to make me like disco. Almost.

The Black Hole: The Next Generation

The last slide ride on this side of the park, *The Black Hole* works an interesting variation on the theme. Here you ride a two-person inner tube down completely en-closed black tubes. It's not totally dark, however; projectors create cosmic "explosions of color" on the curving walls around you. Although the lighting and sound effects add a special thrill, *The Black Hole* is not especially scary or fast, especially compared to, say, *Mach 5*. If you choose the tube to your right as you enter the launch area, you'll get a few extra bumps. A single person can ride alone, occupying the front hole in the inner tube.

Knee Ski/Wakeboarding

Rounding things off on the left side of the park is something completely dif-ferent—a modified water-skiing experience. You kneel on a small surfboard specially designed for this sort of thing; molded rubber impressions make it easy to stay on and a mandatory life-jacket protects you if you fall off. And instead of a speedboat, your tow line hangs from a sort of cable-car arrangement that tows you in a long circle around a lake. The entire course is surrounded by a wooden dock and, should you fall, you are never more than a few strokes from the edge. Ladders like those in swimming pools are provided at regular intervals, making this a very safe ride.

Dunkings are rare, however. Given the special design of the board, the low center of gravity, and the moderate speed of the tow line, most people complete the circuit easily. So don't let a lack of experience with water skiing keep you from enjoying this ride.

Note: This attraction is only open May through September.

Surf Lagoon

Moving to the center section of the park we find, appropriately enough, the centerpiece of Wet 'n Wild. This is an artificial ocean. Well, actually, it's a fan shaped swimming pool with a hydraulic system that sends out pulsing waves in which you can jump and frolic. You can also bounce around on top of them in an inner tube. At the "ocean" end of the pool, a waterfall splashes off the back wall and onto swimmers bobbing in the waves below. At the "beach" end of the pool, you'll find plenty of lounge chairs for soaking up the sun.

Volleyball Courts

Squeezed between the back of the wave pool and the lakeside terrace are two side-by-side volleyball courts. The surface is soft beach sand. Balls can be obtained free of charge at the Courtesy Counter at the front of the park. If there are people waiting, you are asked to limit games to 15 minutes or 11 points, whichever comes first. The courts are occasionally reserved for the use of private groups visiting the park.

Wild One

Head past the volleyball courts on to the dock and hang a right. Down at the end is *Wild One*, the only ride at Wet 'n Wild that requires an additional charge over and above the admission to the park ($7 including tax for one rider, $10 for two). The ride is worth the extra expense. You are towed in a large inner tube behind a jet ski as it races around the Wet 'n Wild lake. The fun here is in the turns, as the two inner tubes being towed accelerate sharply in wide arcs to keep up with the jet ski's tight turns. The ride lasts about two minutes.

Note: This attraction is only open May through September.

Bubble Up

As you move to the right side of the park, you encounter *Bubble Up*. This attraction is just for kids. Too bad, because it looks fun. In the center of a pool stands a large blue and white rubber mountain; at the top is a circular fountain producing a steady downpour. The object is to grab the knotted rope hanging down from the summit and pull yourself to the top up the slippery sides. Once there you can slide back down into the pool.

Bubba Tub

This is a deceptively simple ride that packs a wallop. Five-person circular rafts zip down a broad, straight slide that features three sharp drops on the speedy trip to the bottom. The ever-helpful attendant gives the raft a spin at takeoff so it's hard to predict whether you'll go down backwards or not. It's a short ride, almost guaranteed to raise a scream or two, and a lot of fun.

Lazy River

Circling *Bubble Up* and the *Bubba Tub* is a swift-moving stream, about 10 feet wide and 3 feet deep, cleverly themed to evoke old Florida, complete with boat docks and rustic billboards. There are a number of entrances and you can enter or exit at any of them. Grab one of the floating tubes and float along with the current; it takes about five minutes to make one complete circuit. It is also possible to swim or float down *Lazy River* unaided, and many people choose this option.

The Storm

Riders of *The Storm* zip down a towering chute into an open air bowl, where they spin wildly around at speeds of up to 45 mph as spectators cheer them on. Then they drop through a hole in the middle of the bowl into a waiting splash pool.

Der Stuka

Behind the *Bubba Tub*, you will find a high tower housing three slides—*Der Stuka*, *Bomb Bay*, and *Brain Wash*—billed as among the tallest and fastest in the world. Like all speed slides, *Der Stuka* is simplicity itself. You lie down on your back, cross your ankles, fold your arms over your chest, and an attendant nudges you over the edge of a precipitously angled free fall. You'll reach speeds approaching 50 mph before a long trough of shallow water brings you to a halt.

Bomb Bay

Bomb Bay is right next to *Der Stuka*. Its slide is precisely the same height, length, and angle of its neighbor. So what's the difference? Here you step into a bomb-shaped capsule that is then precisely positioned over the slide. The floor drops away and you are off to a literally flying start down the slide. Thanks to the gravity-assisted head start, this slide is even faster than *Der Stuka*, or at least it seems that way.

Brain Wash

After *Der Stuka* and *Bomb Bay*, *Brain Wash*, which shares the same tower with the two speed slides, seems tame by comparison. But looks are deceiving. *Brain Wash*, which takes off from a point slightly below the top of the tower, consists of an enclosed tube that takes a twisting 53-foot drop into a giant 65-foot sideways funnel; think of it as a family-friendly variation on *The Storm's* toilet bowl design.

You ride in a two- or four-passenger inner tube, which swirls and sloshes back and forth up the banked funnel walls before spitting you out the bottom. The "mind altering" psychedelic lighting and soundtrack surrounding you promise to leave you with a "clean and happy brain." At the very least, you may get a nose-full of water as you splash down at the end of this exhilarating twist-a-rama.

Aquatica by SeaWorld

5800 Water Play Way, Orlando, FL 32821 ~ (888) 800-5447 or (407) 351-3600
www.aquaticabyseaworld.com

SeaWorld's newest venture, Aquatica, is a spacious and beautifully designed park, with a signature SeaWorld touch—dolphins! The addition of sea creatures to the water park formula gives Orlando's new entry an edge that's not likely to be matched any time soon and for the first time gives Disney some serious competition in this niche.

I still give Wet 'n Wild the edge because its rides are a lot more fun, but Aquatica offers more in the way of lounging areas and food choices. It's more of a "family" park than Wet 'n Wild, which appeals to a younger crowd, and that may be just fine for a lot of folks.

Getting There

Aquatica is located just across International Drive from the SeaWorld property, conveniently close to Exit 1 of the Beachline Line Expressway (Route 528). Whether you are traveling east or west on the Beachline, you will turn left at the bottom of the exit ramp onto I-Drive. Look for the entrance to Aquatica on your left almost immediately. Turn onto Water Play Way, which is the cutesy name given to the driveway to the parking lot.

If you are approaching from the north or south along International Drive, just watch for the signs; it's all very well marked. There is also a free shuttle service from just outside the entrance to SeaWorld.

Arriving at Aquatica

The entrance from International Drive leads you to the far side of the park where the parking lots and main entrance are located. Parking is $12 for cars, $16 for RVs and vans. Preferred parking, which is somewhat closer to the entrance, is $15 ($7 for Passport holders). If you have visited SeaWorld or Discovery Cove the same day, parking is free; just show your parking receipt.

Once you have parked, make your way up the beautifully landscaped walkway, past rocky waterfalls, to the ticket booths. If you have booked online, you will find electronic kiosks off to the side where you can print out your tickets.

Opening and Closing Times

For most of the year, Aquatica opens at 10:00 a.m. During busier times, opening is moved to 9:00 a.m. The 9:00 a.m. opening is sometimes reserved for those who have purchased Saturday or Sunday tickets online; this perk allows for first dibs on prized beach locations. The parking lot opens one hour prior to the official opening time and many people will get there early to queue up at the entrance.

Closing time varies with the season; 5:00 or 6:00 p.m. are the most common closing times, but during some holidays periods, the park stays open as late as 10:00 p.m. You can find current hours on the website or by calling (888) 800-5447 or (407) 351-3600.

The Price of Admission

If you are only visiting Aquatica, here are your options. The following prices do not include tax:

One-Day Admission:

Adults:	$49.99
Children (3 to 9):	$44.99

Children under 3 are **free**.

If you order your tickets online at www.aquaticabyseaworld.com you can get $5 off each ticket. You may also be able to get in an hour early at certain times of the year, although this perk is not always offered.

Information on the **Orlando FlexTicket**, which includes five or six parks and "Passports" (annual passes), which also offer access to multiple parks, will be found in *Chapter 1: Introduction & Orientation.*

Rentals

Lockers are $15 for small and $30 for large, plus a $5 refundable deposit. They offer all-day in and out access.

Towels are $4, $2 of which is refundable when you return them.

Cabanas, which feature amenities like refrigerators, soft drinks, sunscreen, and even tables, rent for $60 to $600 depending on the time of year and the level of luxury.

Rides and Attractions at Aquatica

Aquatica is laid out in a large, lazy circle, with the zippy *Roa's Rapids* as its centerpiece. I will describe the attractions in approximately the order you will encounter them on a counterclockwise circumnavigation of the park, starting from the park entrance.

Dolphin Plunge

This ride is far and away the most popular in the park, so expect long lines and be patient. It is a long, but scenic, climb to the top, across a wooden suspension bridge to a staircase that circles a tall, narrow tower. At the top are two flumes, one on either side of the summit platform.

Riders sail down on their backs as they snake through some 250 feet of enclosed tubes, which turn transparent as they enter and pass through the *Commerson's Dolphin Habitat* (below) before splashdown in a small exit pool. It takes some practice to slow yourself down to survey the habitat and its denizens at leisure. Most people ride several times before they glimpse the dolphins that give the attraction its name.

Tip: The translucent tubes are subject to fogging, which can make it difficult to see the dolphins. Regular riders suggest riding in the afternoon, when the sun has had a chance to "burn off" the fog.

Commerson's Dolphin Habitat

As you continue into the park, you have no choice but to pass by the large pool that is home to Aquatica's signature attraction—the pod of Commerson's dolphins that give the *Dolphin Plunge* its name and raison d'être. These adorable critters, native to the waters of Australia, bear black and white markings that give them an unmistakable resemblance to Shamu. Of course, the resemblance is purely coincidental, but it makes for great subliminal marketing.

Chances are a staffer will be posted by the pool, so don't forget to ask him or her when feeding times will be the day of your visit. If you return at the appointed time, you will be treated to a display of enchanting "behaviors" as the frisky dolphins earn their daily bread... er, fish.

At other times, you have a variety of options for checking out these fascinating cousins of Flipper. The surface of the pool is one spot, although the best chance of seeing them break water is during the aforementioned feeding times. The next option is to continue into the park proper, down the stairs, and take a left turn into an underwater viewing area called **Dolphin Lookout** where you can watch them zip about the pool, over, under, and around the clear tubes of *Dolphin Plunge*.

The best option, however, is the underwater window that is part of *Loggerhead Lane,* reviewed below.

Whanau Way

There are four slides at the top of this five-story tower, two on each side. Riders use two-seater tubes to swoosh down 340 feet of curving flumes, through open and closed segments marked by cascading waterfalls, to splashdown. Each flume has a 360-degree corkscrew, either near the top or near the bottom.

The ride is situated in such a way that members of your party who are not riding can get a good view of the entire superstructure and the tubes it supports. It is also just a short stroll away from the left-hand end of the artificial beach and *Cutback Cove* (see below).

Omaka Rocka

This pair of slides, named after a South Seas phrase meaning "rocking river," was added to the front of the *Whanau Way* tower in 2010 as part of the park's first expansion. Riders in single-seater tubes descend through a first-of-its-kind mix of semi-transparent pipes and massive funnels (three per slide) that send you spinning up their sides like a skateboarder in a halfpipe. You must be 48 inches tall to ride (with or without a life vest) since its speed and near-weightless moments make it more disorienting than most of Aquatica's other slides.

Cutback Cove & Big Surf Shores

These twin wave pools are arranged side by side (the only such arrangement in the world, apparently) facing an enormous 80,000-square-foot artificial white sand beach filled with beach chairs. Most people will head here soon after arrival to stake their claim to the beach chairs that will form their party's base of operations for the day, and I recommend that you do the same. A towel, a T-shirt, a beach bag, or other item is sufficient to mark a lounge chair as "taken." Most of the chairs are in the open sun, although a few offer some shade, yet another reason for getting here early.

Despite the name, *Big Surf Shores* is the calmer of the two wave pools, with gently rolling surf. It is also shallower than *Cutback Cove*, where the depth reaches six-and-a-half feet. The waves in *Cutback Cove* reach five feet and are a lot of fun.

The wave action in both pools operates on a 20-minute schedule, 12 minutes off and 8 minutes on, although they don't always seem to adhere to that schedule. Electronic signs at the edge of the water variously announce the time, the air temperature, or the remaining minutes left on the current wave cycle.

Back on the beach, you can relax in your lounge chair and look past the twin wave pools to SeaWorld, just across International Drive. You will easily spot the *Skytower,* the golden cupola of *Journey to Atlantis,* and the steel spaghetti sprawl of *Kraken.* Be aware that the lounge chairs here are placed quite close together, so there is little opportunity for real privacy. Be prepared to get to know your neighbors.

Roa's Rapids

Just opposite the twin wave pools is one of the main entrances to *Roa's Rapids,* which occupies the center of the park. There is another entrance opposite *Walkabout Waters* (see below).

This is Aquatica's jazzed-up version of the "lazy river," which is a water park staple. Most lazy rivers gently float folks along on a roughly circular path. But, as the name suggests, *Roa's Rapids* kicks things up a notch.

Here the water zips along at a brisk 4 feet per second (or 2.72 mph!) along a twisting, 1,500-foot course, which makes for a very different experience from the usual lazy river.

No inner tubes are available on this one. Brightly colored neoprene life jackets are required for little ones, but they are highly recommended for all. With a life jacket on, you can simply surrender yourself to the current and float along with little or no effort. Try rolling on to your back with your feet pointed downstream!

Water splashes onto the water course from streamside spouts or waterfalls as you pass under bridges. Periodically, the stream is bisected by small islands, which forces the water into narrower streams with simulated rapids. As noted earlier, there are two spots where you can exit, which can be a bit of a challenge given the strength of the current. But I have noticed that most people are having too much fun to think about exiting after just one circuit.

Roa, by the way, is a Maori word meaning "long time."

Kata's Kookaburra Cove

This delightful area is a self-contained water park designed just for Aquatica's littlest visitors, a fact brought home by a sign announcing a *maximum* height of 48 inches. It is, in effect, a miniature version of the larger park. Its centerpiece is a shallow pool, with depths ranging from six inches to a foot and half, all of it nicely heated, with temperatures ranging up to 104 degrees. There is a raised platform in the middle where the more mischievous will find water cannons they can train on unsuspecting waders.

There are a number of places where little ones can stand under cascading water, including an ingenious station where conical buckets fill with water until their own weight causes them to tip over and splash anyone below.

Around the perimeter are arrayed a number of kiddie-sized slides that mimic the park's grown-up attractions; all of them dump riders into the central pool. **Racer Chaser** is a very mild slide with four flumes. **Slider Rider** is slightly more advanced, with more active water providing a faster ride. **Slippity Dippity** is another zippier slide with a curving "S."

Zippity Zappity is a double inner-tube ride that forces parents to get involved, with the grown-up sitting in the rear of the tube. There are two side-by-side slides here, with two mild curves on the way down.

All slides in this area are staffed with lifeguards and the rules require that all little ones under age 6 need a "supervising adult" to ride with them. Should anything go amiss, Aquatica's first-aid station is nearby.

Taumata Racer

Taumata is the abbreviated form of the longest place name in the world, Taumatawhakatangihangakoauauotamateaturipukakapikimaungahoronukupokaiwhenuakitanatah, a hilltop in New Zealand. Maybe that's Aquatica's way of signaling that it's a long way to splashdown on this combination of corkscrew and speed slide.

There are eight enclosed flumes in a single row at the top of this seven-story tower. Riders travel head first, prone on rubber mats with curved fronts that hide two hand holds. Sped along on an energetic stream of water, they zap through a 360-degree spiral before opening out onto steep speed slides that end in long slow-down lanes. Interestingly, the outside tubes at the top emerge in the middle of the speed slide section, while those at the center open onto the outer lanes of the speed slide.

Walkabout Waters

How to describe this water-soaked extravaganza? Imagine *Shamu's Happy Harbor* at SeaWorld or *Safari of Fun* at Busch Gardens Tampa. Then add water. Lots and lots of water.

This multi-level, multi-component play area seems to have been designed with tweens in mind. That certainly is the major demographic represented. It is decorated in dazzling shades of pink and blue, with Maori designs interspersed throughout and spinnaker-like sails at the top. Water sprays, spritzes, pours, and cascades everywhere. When you get in the middle of the maze-like structure, the noise from falling water is positively deafening.

Topping off this intricate structure are two immense buckets that fill with water and then tip over every several minutes, sending a wall of water to splash off a roof below and onto the excited kids at ground level. You will find rope walks and water cannons on the upper levels. There are a few slides, too. Nothing too extreme, but fun enough for the target audience.

Even though this attraction is obviously aimed at kids from 8 into their teens, a lot of adults seem to take guilty pleasure in sampling its attractions.

Walhalla Wave

This is one of two slides that share the same superstructure. *Walhalla Wave* is a "family raft ride," which means that up to four people share a round rubber raft, thoughtfully fitted with hand holds. They zip down a 600-foot series of twists and turns, partly open and partly enclosed and dotted with waterfalls to douse you as you enter or emerge from the tunnels. It's an exhilarating and somewhat disorienting ride to the bottom.

The rafts that this ride uses are brought to the top by a conveyor belt, so you don't have to lug your own. A thoughtful touch.

HooRoo Run

Right next to *Walhalla Wave*, *HooRoo Run* is a broad, straight, open speed slide that zips riders to the bottom in three steps. This requires a minimum of two people per raft (a max of four). Both *HooRoo* and *Walhalla* have a 600-pound maximum load limit, so if you are a "big" family, be aware that you may be split up!

Loggerhead Lane

Here is a "lazy river" ride that lives up to the name. The three-foot-deep water course describes a short, meandering circle punctuated with the requisite water spouts and waterfalls. Most people ride in the one- or two-seater inner tubes provided. Most of them are already in the water, so the river is sometimes clogged with unused tubes.

Given its short length, this would be a disappointing lazy river if it were not for a very special feature. At one end, the river passes through a tunnel with a large picture window looking into the *Commerson's Dolphin Habitat*. The effect is spectacular. Not only will you get a great view of the peppy little dolphins as they cavort around the tubes of *Dolphin Plunge*, but you'll see that slide's riders swishing by on their way to splashdown. The current is gentle enough that it's an easy matter to maneuver your tube to water's edge, where you can grab the shore and pause for a longer look. Many people do just that.

A short distance away is a shortcut that links the two sides of the river. Here, under shelter, you will find **Fish Grotto**, a large aquarium filled to bursting with colorful tropical fish.

Note: There are plenty of lawn chairs all along the broad walkway that circles around (but does not completely surround) *Loggerhead Lane*. If you'd prefer not to deal with the sand of the beach in front of the wave pools, this makes an ideal alternative as your base of operations for the day.

Tassie's Twisters

You have to wade across the river of *Loggerhead Lane* to reach this ride. Grab an inner tube as you do. Once you've climbed the tower, you sit in your tube—friends can share a two-holer—and zip down one of two curving water chutes into large bowls where you whirl in a circle until gravity inevitably draws you to the hole in the bottom to splashdown zones right next to the lazy river. From here you can exit the ride or hang on to your tube for a spin along *Loggerhead Lane*. And if you haven't seen the dolphins yet, you'd be foolish not to do just that.

Conservation Cabana

This simple cabana-style tent, just across the way from the Kiwi Traders shop, is home to members of SeaWorld's conservation staff, who have stocked it with various marine artifacts and an aquarium. From time to time, some cute little critter will join them.

There is no formal schedule of shows or presentations, but feel free to stop in whenever you're passing by to get an impromptu briefing on the importance of marine conservation, to explore their collection, or to ask any questions that have sprung to mind during your visit.

Adventure Island

10001 McKinley Drive, Tampa, FL 33674 ~ (888) 800-5447; (813) 987-5660
www.adventureisland.com

Busch's entry into the Central Florida water park market is a winner, and if your only shot at a water park is during a visit to Tampa, it's the obvious choice. While I give a slight edge to Wet 'n Wild for its rides and to Aquatica for its ambiance, Adventure Island, with its artful design and pleasing layout, has nothing to be ashamed about.

Getting There

Adventure Island is right across the street from Busch Gardens Tampa, two miles west of I-75 and two miles east of I-275. Drive past the Busch Gardens parking lots (heading north) and keep a sharp lookout for the entrance on your right. The main gate is easy to miss if you're not careful.

Parking is $12 per car or camper, motorcycles park **free**. If you hold a Busch Gardens passport that includes Adventure Island, parking is **free**.

Opening and Closing Times

Park hours vary with the calendar. At the beginning (March) and end (September and October) the park will be open from 10:00 a.m. to 5:00 p.m. and usually only on weekends. As crowds grow and days lengthen during the warmer months, the weekend hours may extend from 9:00 a.m. to 9:00 p.m. The best way to know when the park will be open during your visit is to check the website at the address given above.

The Price of Admission

At press time, Adventure Island was offering a single one-day admission option, with $5 off each ticket purchased online. The following prices do not include tax:

One Day Admission:

Adults:	$44.99
Children (3 to 9):	$40.99

Children under 3 are **free**.

Rentals

Lockers are $12. You receive a $3 gift card, redeemable only at Adventure Island, when you return the key.

Cabanas are $100 to $160 depending on the season. Less expensive "Chiki Huts" are $50 to $100.

Strollers and wheelchairs are $15.

Volleyballs are **free** with a photo ID or annual pass.

The admission price includes **free** use of inner tubes in designated areas of the park and life vests for all guests.

There are no towels for rent.

Rides and Attractions at Adventure Island

Adventure Island is laid out in a sort of figure eight. I have described its attractions in the approximate order you would encounter them on a counterclockwise circumnavigation of the park.

Beach Areas

As you move from the entrance plaza and walk down the steps into the park proper, you see a delightful sandy expanse in front of you. It's ideal for sunning and relaxing (although not for picnicking) with its many lounge chairs. Many people prefer to spread a beach towel on the pristine white sands. The entire area is ringed by an ankle-deep stream, so as you exit you can rinse the sand off your feet. Similar areas are dotted around the park.

Runaway Rapids

This series of five water slides is so ingeniously snaked through a simulated rocky canyon that you are hard-pressed to spot the flumes as you wend your way to the top. To the left are two child-sized slides on which parents and tots can descend together. To the right and higher up are the three adult flumes. Here, as at other slides in the park, red and green traffic lights regulate the flow of visitors down the slides.

You ride these slides on your back or sitting up; there are no mats or tubes used. As a result, they can get off to a slow start but they pick up speed as you hit the dips and turns about a third of the way down. Of the three adult slides, the one on the left seems the zippiest, while the one in the middle is the tamest. None of them are super scary, however, and most people should thoroughly enjoy the brief ride to the shallow pool below.

Wahoo Run

Adventure Island's newest ride is a twisty, turny mega slide designed for large rafts holding up to five riders. As you zip down 600 feet of corkscrewing blue tunnels at up to 15 feet per second, you pass under four waterfall curtains that guarantee a thorough drenching before you are deposited in a splash pool at the bottom. This is a great family ride.

Paradise Lagoon

This is a swimming pool with pizzazz. At one end, two short tubes (one slightly curved) let you slide down about 15 feet before dropping you from a height of about 3 feet into 10-foot-deep water. A short distance away, you can leap from an 8-foot-high rocky cliff, just like at the old swimmin' hole. Although the pool seems deep enough (10 feet), head-first dives are not allowed. At the pool's narrowest point, you can test your balance and coordination by trying to cross a series of inflated stepping stones while holding on to an overhead rope net.

Endless Surf

Adventure Island's 17,000-square-foot wave pool generates 5-foot-high waves for body surfing as well as random choppiness for what is billed as a "storm-splashing environment." This is the smallest of the adult wave pools at the three parks reviewed here, with a correspondingly small lounging area at the beach end. Waves are set off in 10-minute cycles, with a digital clock at the deep end counting down the minutes until the next wave of waves.

Fabian's Funport

Adventure Island's kiddie pool follows the formula to a "T." The ankle- to calf-deep pool is abuzz with spritzing and spraying water fountains, some of which let kids determine when they get doused. A raised play area features mini water slides and water cannons with just enough range to spray unwary adults at the pool's edge. A unique touch here is an adjacent mini version of the wave pool, scaled down to toddler size. A raised seating area lets grown-ups relax while keeping an eagle eye on their busy charges.

Rambling Bayou

Adventure Island's version of the continuous looping river is delightful, with a few unique touches—a dousing waterfall that is marvelously refreshing on a steamy day, followed by a gentle misting rain provided by overhead sprinklers.

Spike Zone

This is by far the nicest volleyball venue at the water parks reviewed in this book. In fact, these 11 "groomed" courts have hosted professional tournaments. Most of the play, however, is by amateurs. Even if you're not into competing, the layout makes it easy to watch.

Water Moccasin

Three translucent green tubes descend from this moderately high tower. The center one drops sharply to the splashdown pool, while the two other tubes curve right and left respectively for a corkscrew descent. This is a body slide (you ride lying down on your back) that offers the thrill of a speed slide in the middle tube and a rapidly accelerating descent through the others.

Key West Rapids

The tallest ride at Adventure Island attracts long lines due in part to slow loading times. Fortunately the wait is made easier to take by the spectacular view of next-door Busch Gardens. In the distance, past the loops and sworls of *Montu*, you can see the downtown Tampa skyline.

Here you pick up a single or two-rider tube at the bottom and climb up for a looping and swooping descent on a broad open-air flume. The ride is punctuated twice by rapids-like terraces where attendants (I call them the Rapids Rangers), regulate the flow of riders. Thanks to the two pauses, this ride never attains the speed of similar rides at the other parks, but it offers an enjoyable descent nonetheless.

Splash Attack

This is a more elaborate version of *Fabian's Funport* and draws an older crowd—kids from 8 to about 15. The multi-level play area (much like that found in *Safari of Fun* at nearby Busch Gardens) is alive with spritzes, sprays, spouts, and hidden geysers that erupt to catch the unwary. A variety of ingenious hand-operated devices lets kids determine to some extent who gets doused and when. A huge bucket at the summit tips over every now and then, soaking everyone below.

Caribbean Corkscrew

This ride is almost identical to *Blue Niagara* at Wet 'n Wild, although to my untutored eye the angle of descent seems slightly narrower. You probably won't care as you spiral down and around one of these two tubes, which are twisted around each other like braided hair, picking up speed until you are deposited in the long deceleration pool. Holding your nose is highly recommended for this one.

Riptide

Riptide adds the thrill of competition to the speed slide concept. A pair of twin enclosed speed slides, one red, one blue, take off from a single high platform. One pair of tubes swerves left, the other right, before rejoining for parallel splashdowns. No one knows who's winning until the final moments of the ride.

Gulf Scream

Right next to *Riptide*, these two slides offer a toned down speed slide experience and, by comparison, the ride down is leisurely. If you're uncertain about tackling *Riptide*, test your mettle here.

Aruba Tuba

Aruba Tuba shares a tower with the *Calypso Coaster*. As with *Key West Rapids*, you pick up your single or double tube at the entrance and climb to the top. This ride, as the name implies, descends through a tube which is mostly enclosed with a few brief openings to the sky. Periodically, you are plunged into total darkness, adding to the excitement generated by the speed, sudden turns, and sharp dips of the ride. All in all, one of Adventure Island's zippiest experiences. You emerge into a pool with a convenient exit into *Ramblin' Bayou*, just in case you feel a need for a marked change of pace.

Calypso Coaster

Unlike its sister ride, *Aruba Tuba*, *Calypso Coaster* is an open flume. It is also wider, allowing for more side-to-side motion at the expense of speed. But there's no drop-off in excitement as you are swooped high on the sides of the flume in the sharp turns you encounter on the way down. Of the two, I give *Aruba Tuba* slightly higher marks in the thrills department, but it's a very close call.

Everglides

This ride is unique among the parks reviewed in this book. It is a slide—a speed slide in fact—but instead of descending on your back or in a tube, you sit upright on a heavy yellow, molded plastic gizmo that's a cross between a boogie board and a sled. As you sit in the ready position, held back from the steep precipice by a metal gate, you might start to have second thoughts. But then the gate drops, the platform tilts, and you are sent zipping down the slide. The best part of the ride is when you hit the water. Instead of slowing down quickly, you go skimming across the surface for about 20 yards before slowing to a stop. If you're doing it right, you'll hardly get wet. The major error to be made on this ride is placing your center of gravity too far back. If you do, you're liable to be flipped over backwards for a very unceremonious dunking.

Chapter Thirteen:

Dinner Attractions

THE CONCEPT OF THE "DINNER ATTRACTION" IS NOT UNIQUE TO ORLANDO, BUT even though the area has lost several long-running dinner show establishments in recent years, there can be few other places on earth where there are so many and such elaborate examples. At a typical dinner attraction (there are exceptions) the dinner is not a separate component; instead, the meal and the theme of the show are closely intertwined and usually something will be going on as you eat. Beer and wine (along with soft drinks) are frequently poured freely from pitchers throughout the evening. The shows have been created specifically for the attraction; everything from the decorations on the wall to the plates you eat off reflect the theme.

Dinner attractions are unabashedly "touristy." You'll have plenty of opportunity to buy souvenir mugs, a photo souvenir (often in the form of a key ring), and other tourist paraphernalia. There is plenty of audience participation; in fact, sometimes it's the best part of the show. Many (but by no means all) dinner attractions have an element of competition built in, with various sections of the audience being assigned to cheer on various contestants. And finally there is the matter of scale. Many of Orlando's dinner attractions are huge productions put on in large arenas and halls, some of which seat over 1,000 people. There are exceptions to these rules, but they describe the Orlando dinner attraction experience.

In this chapter, I have reviewed all the non-Disney dinner attractions in the Orlando area. For pageantry and large-scale spectacle there are *Arabian Nights*, *Medieval Times*, and *Pirate's Dinner Adventure*. For musical variety entertainment there are the *Makahiki* and *Wantilan Luaus*, *Capone's*, and *Treasure Tavern*. For magic fans there is the *Wonder-Works* magic show on International Drive. Finally, for comedy/mystery fans there are *Capone's* (again) and *Sleuths Mystery Show*. I have tried to give you a good idea of the nature of each experience, bearing in mind that not everyone shares the same taste.

In my opinion a trip to Orlando is not complete without a visit to one of these attractions. If you have the time (and the stamina), catch two or more shows representing different genres. I don't think you'll regret it.

Tip: Discounts to most dinner attractions are readily available. Look for online specials on their websites, dollars-off deals in coupon booklets, and reduced-price tickets at ticket brokers (see *Chapter 1: Introduction & Orientation*).

Arabian Nights

3081 Arabian Nights Boulevard, Kissimmee 34747 ~ (800) 553-6116; (407) 239-9223 from Canada: (800) 533-3615

www.arabian-nights.com

Prices:	Adults $66.99, children (3 to 11) $41, tax and fees included. 25% discounts for online booking. Prices do not include tip.
Times:	Daily. Usually 6:00 p.m. Sunday to Tuesday and Thursday; 8:30 p.m. Wednesday, Friday, and Saturday. Show times vary and there are occasionally two shows a night, so check. Matinees sometimes available.
Directions:	I-4 to Exit 64, then east on Route 192 for less than a quarter of a mile. The entrance road is on your left, with the theater itself set well back from the highway.

Orlando residents have frequently voted *Arabian Nights* their favorite dinner attraction, and it's easy to see why. Beautiful horses, impeccably trained and put through their intricate paces by a young and vivacious team of riders, are hard to beat. The show may appeal most to horse lovers and riders, but the old clichés "something for everyone" and "fun for the whole family" are not out of place here.

Arabian Nights is huge; it has to be to accommodate the 20,000-square-foot arena the horses need to strut their stuff. Each side of the arena is flanked by seven steeply banked rows of seats; all told, the house can hold 1,200 spectators and every seat provides a good view of the action.

The "seats" are actually a series of benches, each seating 12 people at a small counter on which you will be served your dinner. The fare is simple but satisfying—a choice of pot roast, sirloin steak, pork loin marsala, grilled chicken, or chicken tenders, with garlic mashed potatoes and a medley of vegetables, plus dessert. Vegetarian lasagna is also available. Unlimited soft drinks are included in the price. Add $5 if you want Bud Light or blush wine, $15 for premium drinks including margaritas and sangria.

The doors open about an hour and a half prior to show time if you'd like to come for pre-show drinks and live entertainment that sets the mood for the entire evening: exotic, but family-friendly. There's a belly dancer who pulls kids from the audience on stage for impromptu dancing lessons (and some great **photo ops** for proud parents), and henna "tattoos" offered for an additional fee. A **free** appetizer buffet (chips & salsa, veggies & dip) and a cash bar are also available.

An hour before show time, the arena doors open for younger kids to participate in stick horse races (sticks provided), while guests who have upgraded to the "Sneak Peak

Stable Tour" ($10 extra per person) get to interact with the equine stars; those under 18 can sit on one for a photo. At thirty minutes before show time, a new preshow performance demonstrates how the show staff prepare their animal charges to perform, as a trained Mustang illustrates "a day in the life of an *Arabian Nights* horse."

For the show itself, we are introduced to "all-American girl Sherry Smith," a champion horse rider who discovers on her 21st birthday that she is secretly Princess Scheherazade. The real emcee is Abracadabra, a wise and experienced genie who defends the Princess against the machinations of evil Prince Vaneer. Together they travel the world in search of Scheherazade's true love Prince Khalid, witnessing spectacles of horsemanship along the journey. It's just enough of a "plot" on which to string a series of scenes that show off the beauty and skills of *Arabian Nights'* multimillion-dollar stable of 52 horses.

While there are plenty of stunts involved in this show, the main emphasis is on the horses themselves, with their trainers and riders playing important supporting roles. Much of the evening involves intricate dressage and group riding in which the training of the horses and the precision of the riders are essential. Horses dance, prance, and strut to the music. A *toreador* demonstrates his proficiency with the *garrocha* pole; Gypsy acrobats leap from one galloping horse to another. In one sequence, horses and riders do a square dance. One of the evening's most stunning moments comes when a magnificent, riderless black stallion performs an intricate series of movements in response to the subtle signals of his trainer.

Note: Each December, the show transforms into "Scheherazade's Wish," which takes the same characters and stunts, and cross-culturally combines them with Jack Frost, Santa Claus, and acrobatic elves.

All of this is performed by a remarkably small cadre of talented performers who change costumes and wigs with amazing rapidity to reappear over and over in new guises. Still, it is the horses that command our admiration. At show's end, many of the equine performers romp about spiritedly in the arena; many people linger just to watch them play. Before, during, and after the show, flash photography is permitted and performers offer lots of **photo ops** to those quick with the shutter, but video recording during the show is prohibited.

Note: Priority seating in the first three rows is an additional $5 per guest. A VIP ticket ($15 additional for adults, $12 for kids) combines priority seating, the "Sneak Peak" preshow tour described above, and a 50% discount on drinks. A 25-minute postshow "Backstage Tour," including a beverage in a souvenir cup, is $20 per person. The "most exclusive" Horse Lovers Package blends both the VIP and Backstage options, plus a poster and program, for $40 per person.

Capone's Dinner & Show
4740 West Highway 192, Kissimmee 34746 ~ (800) 220-8428; (407) 397-2378
www.alcapones.com

Prices:	Adults $53.99, children (4 to 12) $33.99. Plus tax and tip. 50% discounts frequently available.
Times:	Generally 7:30 p.m. nightly, or 5:00 p.m. and 8:30

p.m. 1:00 p.m., matinees on select days.

Directions: On the south side of 192, a short distance east of
                  the junction with SR 535, between Mile Markers
                  12 and 13.

Somewhere along the tawdry, commercial strip of Route 192 in Kissimmee you'll find an innocent ice cream parlor. But as with so much in the Orlando area, there's more here than meets the eye. For you see, the ice cream parlor is just a front for a speakeasy, Prohibition style. Yes, we've gone back in time again to 1930s Chicago, where the action owes a lot to Damon Runyon via *Guys and Dolls* and the Chicago accents sound straight outta Brooklyn.

Capone's Dinner & Show is a cheerful mishmash of Broadway show, nightclub cabaret, sketch comedy revue, and all-you-can-eat Eye-talian buffet—that's buffet, as in Warren or Jimmy. Dinner includes the usual soft drinks, plus beer, wine, and cocktails (rum runners, vodka cranberry, rum and cola). In addition, there's a cash bar for serious drinkers; arrive at least 30 minutes early and buy a drink at "Al's Secret Hideaway Bar" upstairs to get early seating and first crack at the buffet.

The fun begins when you arrive and pick up your tickets at the box office. You're instructed to knock three times at the secret door and give a password. Then you get in line outside, where black-vested waiters warm up the crowd with the wisecracking rudeness that is to become the evening's hallmark. So be forewarned: Don't wear garish tourist garb unless you can take some good-natured ribbing. Feather boas and fedoras are sold for those wishing to better blend in.

Once the show's ready to begin, each party is led to the secret door, knocks three times, and gives the password—and they don't let you in until you get it right. Once inside, you're in a spacious nightclub with a large stage. The waiters—with names like Babyface—take drink orders and keep up a cheerful patter laced with film noir gangster patois. Much of the seating is in long rows of tables, so you'll have a chance to chat with the folks on either side of you; it's a fun way to get an idea of the wide cross section of types and nationalities drawn to Orlando.

The show, which revolves around two pairs of star-crossed lovers, freely borrows plot elements from *Guys and Dolls*, *Some Like It Hot*, and any number of old gangster movies. Best of all is the kewpie doll leading lady, dumb and delicious, with a voice that would shatter fine crystal. The cast relies heavily on intentionally bad jokes and audience interaction to generate laughs. More often than not they succeed. Throw in some leggy chorines, a bit of torch singing, and a better than average buffet dinner and you have a winning combo that has stood Orlando's test of time. It's hard not to like this bunch, even if they don't always shoot straight.

Makahiki Luau

In the SeaWorld park ~ (800) 327-2424; (407) 351-3600
seaworldparks.com/en/seaworld-orlando/Dine-and-Shop/Dining/Makahiki-Luau

Prices: Adults $46, children (3 to 9) $29, plus tax and tip.
              Park admission not required.
Times: Daily at 6:00 p.m.

Directions: In SeaWorld, in the Seafire Inn restaurant

At dusk, a ceremonial procession makes its way through *The Waterfront* in the Sea-World park, heralding the approach of a Polynesian tribal chieftain. A warrior blows a conch shell to announce the arrival of the Grand Kahuna. A welcoming ceremony complete with dancing briefly enlivens the wharfside while the park's visitors look on. Then, those who have ponied up for the luau are ushered into a spacious theater in the back of the nearby Seafire Inn restaurant where they are transported to the lush South Seas. Giant tikis flank the raised semicircular stage and family-style tables radiate outwards to give everyone a good view.

The show, which begins as the crowd settles in, is hosted by the Grand Kahuna himself, a sumo-sized mountain of a man, with the assistance of a guitar and ukulele trio singing songs of the island from the authentic to the hokey commercial variety.

Most of the show is given over to the dancers, four bare-chested men and four lissome young women who constantly reappear in new and ever more colorful costumes to evoke a variety of styles and moods. The sets change along with the costumes and the wide variety of colorful backdrops makes this one of the most scenically lavish luaus I've seen. The dancing is never less than enchanting and in the war chant numbers rather exciting. What's more, the dancing never veers towards the offensive, making this a perfectly G-rated show.

The Grand Kahuna and his female counterpart are charming hosts as they take us on a guided tour of the folk dances of the islands of Polynesia, from Hawaii to New Zealand, with stops at Tonga and Fiji along the way. The story reaches its climax with a Fire Dance finale that is literally incendiary, as a dancer wearing nothing but a loincloth twirls a flaming baton and rests the burning ends on his tongue and the soles of his feet.

All of this, our host explains, to illustrate "the light of life that shines in the sky and in every one of us." The sentiment is typical of the gentle spirit of this show, which is apparently a family affair. At one point, the Grand Kahuna introduces his son, who seems to be having just as much fun as the audience.

The food may not be quite as good as the show, but there is plenty of it, all served family style. First comes a salad, followed by three entrees, fish in piña colada sauce, sweet and sour chicken, and BBQ pork, along with rice and mixed steamed vegetables, followed by "island sweets" for dessert. The admission price includes the meal, one complimentary cocktail, and complimentary soft drinks, coffee, or unlimited iced tea. For the drinkers in the crowd, a cash bar is available.

Note: From November through New Year's, SeaWorld presents the *Makahiki Christmas Luau,* which adds a big dollop of "O Holy Night" to the Polynesian polyglot performance. Prices and menu are the same as the regular show; see the website for exact times and dates.

Medieval Times

4510 Highway 192, Kissimmee 34746 ~ (888) 935-6878; (407) 396-1518
www.medievaltimes.com

Prices: Adults $59.95, children (3 to 12) $35.95. Plus tax and tip. Discount codes available online. See below

	for upgrade options.
Times:	Nightly. Show times vary from month to month.
	See website for current schedule.
Directions:	On the south side of 192, between Mile Markers
	14 & 15.

Back in time to the year 1093 we go as we cross a drawbridge over a murky moat and enter a "climate-controlled castle," guided by wenches and squires with a decidedly contemporary look about them. *Medieval Times*, in Kissimmee, is a cheerfully gaudy evocation of a time most of us know so little about that we'll never know if they've got it right—although I strongly suspect that Ethelred the Unready wouldn't recognize the joint.

Actually, *Medieval Times* tells us more about American tourism than it does about eleventh century Europe. The emphasis here is more on showing visitors an old-fashioned good time than on chivalry and historical accuracy. The medieval theme is merely a convenient excuse on which to hang a display of horse-riding skills.

Medieval Times is a bit like a large ride at one of the nearby theme parks. Just outside the castle moat, a small eight-cottage village depicting Dark Age arts and crafts (including a display of ghastly torture devices) serves as a waiting area; arrive early to explore it. As you enter the castle, you are issued a color-coded cardboard crown and have your picture taken for the inevitable (and optional) souvenir photo of yourself in chivalric garb. The large, banner-bedecked anteroom in which you wait for the show to begin does a brisk trade in tourist items and souvenirs, including some lovely goblets and very authentic-looking swords.

A burly bearded lord is your host. His booming voice, with its idiosyncratic mock-formal cadences, will become familiar over the course of the evening as he explains the seating process, exhorts you to be of good cheer, introduces you to the players, narrates the ongoing pomp and pageantry, and chides one and all for not having enough fun.

The dinner show itself takes place in a long, cavernous room in which guests are arrayed on 6 tiers of seats flanking a 70-yard-long, sand-covered arena. Each row consists of a long bench-and-counter arrangement so that everyone can eat and have a good view of the show. Each side of the arena has three color-coded sections that correspond to the color of the crown you have been given. Where you sit determines which of the color-coded knights you cheer for during the festivities.

The meal and the show unfold simultaneously. The meal is simple—soup, half a roasted chicken, a pork rib, a roasted potato—but the herbed chicken is roasted to perfection and the ribs melt off the bone. In addition, you get to eat with your fingers! It's 1093, remember. I can't explain the psychology, but it helps put you in a suitably barbaric mood to cheer on your knight. (Vegetarians will be accommodated on request.)

The show begins slowly and builds to a climax of clashing battle-axes and broadswords that throw off showers of sparks into the night. Demonstrations of equestrian skills and the royal sport of falconry give way to our six mounted knights, young men who race back and forth on their charging steeds, plucking rings from the air and throwing spears at targets. Before long the crowd is pounding the tables and cheering lustily for their armor-clad champions. Successful knights are awarded flowers that, in the spirit of chivalry, they share with young women in the crowd who have caught their eye. These guys are good at what they do and you may find yourself wondering if there's a career in this and, if not, what their day job is.

The show plays out to a specially composed score with stirring classical overtones (it was recorded in Kiev in the Ukraine) that sets just the right martial tone. The main event is the joust in which the knights compete against each other, charging full tilt down the lists, shattering their lances on their opponents' shields, and taking theatrical falls to the soft earth beneath. The battle continues on foot with mace and sword and at least as much verisimilitude as you get in professional wrestling.

There is actually a simple "good vs. evil" plot woven into the show, which is scheduled for a revamp in early 2012. Whatever the new storyline, you can expect it will include treachery and intrigue, the love of a feisty princess, and a surprise ending that brings the crowd to its feet. This ain't art but it's a lot of fun. And the folks putting on the show not only know their business but keep getting better at it. I've seen three versions of this show and the upcoming one promises to be the best yet. Even if you've been to *Medieval Times* before, a return visit is worth considering.

Note: *Medieval Times* offers a dizzying array of upgrade options to increase the cost of your ticket. The "Royalty Package" grants second or third row seating, a cheering banner, and a souvenir program and DVD, for $10 more per person. The "Celebration Package," aimed at parties and groups, adds a slice of cake and a framed photo to the Royalty benefits for $16. For $20, the "King's Royalty Package" includes the photo and souvenirs, plus front-row "VIP" seating. The improved views and tchotchkes are nice, but not strictly necessary; your mileage may vary.

Pirate's Dinner Adventure

6400 Carrier Drive, Orlando 32819 ~ (800) 866-2469; (407) 248-0590
www.piratesdinneradventure.com

Prices:	Adults $61.95, children (3 to 11) $37.45. Prices do not include tax or gratuity.
Times:	Show nightly, times vary. Usually 7:30 p.m., or 6:00 and 8:30 p.m. Call to check. Doors open an hour prior.
Directions:	From I-4 Exit 74, go east (Sand Lake Road), left on International Drive, then right on Carrier.

If there were Academy Awards for Orlando dinner shows, *Pirate's Dinner Adventure* would have to get the best set award. This cheerful mélange of old-time Technicolor pirate movie, Broadway musical, and big top circus unfolds in a fog-shrouded domed arena dominated by a towering and ghostly pirate vessel a-sail on the watery deep. They're pretty generous with the special effects, as well, and pyrotechnic wizardry is very much in evidence. Parents with very young children, who may be alarmed by all the crashing and booming, may want to consider a more low-key dinner show. Older kids, however, should have a blast with this rollicking performance.

The fun starts in a large antechamber where the Treasure Bay Archaeological Society is welcoming arriving guests to their First Annual Gala with Gypsy fortune tellers, face painting for kids, and a mini-maritime museum. There are hors d'oeuvres, and a cash bar, and even a tiny arcade for die-hard video game freaks. The show proper gets under way as renowned archaeologist Katherine Eriksson explains her discovery of Treasure Bay, a perfectly preserved pirate seaport. Katherine and her explorer friend Freddy, naturally trigger a mystical curse, and have to battle buccaneers over Poseidon's cursed treasure through stunts, slapstick, and original Broadway-style songs.

We know these pirates can't be all bad when they announce that they will serve us a sumptuous meal, just to prepare us for the torture, maiming, and certain death that will follow shortly. They even take the time to bond with their captives, as each pirate works his color-coded section into a frenzy, to ensure that they'll cheer him on and boo his opponents in any contests of wit, skill, or luck that might come up.

The meal served is a hearty one: yellow rice with roasted pork and chicken. Considerate pirates that they are, vegetarian lasagna is also available upon request, although guests are advised to alert the staff ahead of time to be sure they'll have some ready to go. There are also menu upgrades, including filet mignon and lobster tail, available when you arrive at the box office. Then we settle back for a celebration of swashbuckling derring do on the high seas.

Pirate's plot was radically revamped in 2011 to celebrate the theater's 15th anniversary, but the show still involves old standards like aerial stunts, choreographed swordplay, trampoline acrobatics, and crew rivalries that will require the audience's participation to be settled. New to the production is a romantic subplot, modern pop-culture references, and—would you believe?—Britney Spears music.

Punctuated by song, the fast and furious action moves left and right, up and down, comes from behind us, and soars high over our heads. The pirates compete in wacky games of skill, and kids from the audience are taken aboard to be sworn in as swashbuckling buccaneers. All too soon the story seems resolved, though sit tight—there's a twist ending after dessert.

All this cheerfully chaotic mayhem is carried forward by a game and talented young cast. The male pirate chorus is especially fine. Don't be surprised if you find yourself singing along to the refrain of "Drink, Drink, Drink." And speaking of drinking, beer, wine, and soda flow freely during the meal and afterwards. After the show, there is a "Pirate's Buccaneer Bash" where cast members are available for photos, the cash bar re-opens, and guests are invited to stick around for dancing, sing-alongs, and socializing.

Pointe Performing Arts Center

9101 International Drive, Orlando, FL 32819 ~ (407) 374-3587
www.pointearts.org

Prices:	$40 for dinner and the show, $20 for just the show
Times:	Show times are Friday and Saturday at 8:00 p.m. and Sunday at 7:00 p.m.; dinner before or after
Directions:	From I-4 Exit 74, go east (Sand Lake Road), right on International Drive, then straight ahead to the Pointe★Orlando Shopping Center on your left.

Like a hermit crab borrowing a shell, FantasyLand Productions, a low-budget, non-Equity theater company, slipped into one of several vacant retail spaces at Pointe★Orlando (a once-tony shopping strip on I-Drive now notable mostly for its IMAX cinema and mid-range restaurants) to create the Pointe Performing Arts Center and reintroduce the dinner theater concept to Orlando. It's not "true" dinner theater since you enjoy your meal not in the theater but at a nearby restaurant (the Southern fried BBKing's Blues Club or the Greek Taverna Opa). Still, it's as close as you'll get in Orlando and not a bad concept at all. The Dinner and a Show option, as they call it, includes your meal. When you buy your ticket, you receive a voucher for the meal, which can be used either before or after the show. If you want to dine before the show, they advise picking up your voucher an hour and a half prior to show time. The voucher covers one drink, a selected entree, and parking validation; appetizers, dessert, drinks, and tip are additional. You can also opt to see just the show.

The company carved their modest, 108-seat theater, out of a cavernous room formerly occupied by a dance club, so anticipate awkward acoustics and limited sightlines. They have presented an interesting mix of shows, ranging from serious plays like *History Boys, Proof,* and *The Guys* (about 9/11) to comedies such as *Nunsense* and *Greater Tuna* to musicals like *Xanadu* and *Rent*. Thus far, these ambitious titles have consistently outstripped the fledgling troupe's talents and production capabilities, and none of the actors are paid, so don't come expecting Broadway.

Note: A separate series of ultra-low budget shows for young audiences is presented on Saturday afternoons at 1:30 p.m. ($5).

Sleuths Mystery Show & Dinner

8267 International Drive, Orlando 32819 ~ (800) 393-1985; (407) 363-1985
www.sleuths.com

Prices:	Adults $55.95, children (3 to 11) $23.95. Prices do not include tax or gratuity
Times:	Varies. Call or see website for current schedule
Directions:	From I-4 Exit 74 go east on Sand Lake, then left on I-Drive; the theaters are on the left just south of *Ripley's Believe It Or Not*.

Nestled incongruously in a suburban-style strip mall in the middle of the gaudy International Drive tourist strip is one of Orlando's most enjoyable attractions. *Sleuths* presents a rotating menu of 13 hilarious whodunits served up with relish before, during, and after dinner.

You may find yourself invited to Lord Mansfield's Fox Hunt Banquet or discover yourself one of the alumni attending a reunion at genteel Luray Academy. Whatever the premise, the hilarity is virtually guaranteed, thanks to an ensemble of accomplished (and wonderfully hammy) local actors with a gift for improvisation and the quick comeback. Most of the fun and the biggest laughs come from the unscripted interactions with the "guests" who are made to feel very much part of the action. There are over a dozen different shows served up by *Sleuths*, so if you find this sort of thing to your liking you'll be able to return many times before you start to get bored or run out of new material.

As you arrive for dinner, you will meet some of the cast members ushering guests to their tables and passing hors d'oeuvres. After the salad course, the murder mystery proper unfolds on a minuscule set at the front of the house. Don't be surprised if you're called from your seat to participate in some bit of lunacy. At one show I saw, four people found themselves galloping through the house on make-believe horses while the rest of the audience bayed like hounds. But, if you're shy, don't fret; cast members seem to have an uncanny knack for not disturbing those who'd rather not be chosen for "stardom."

The humor is broad, with a healthy dose of double entendre. The cast members throw themselves into their parts but occasionally drop out of character in gales of suppressed laughter. And the audience never hesitates to pitch in, gleefully pointing out telltale clues that those on stage have missed. Before long, someone turns up dead and everyone in the cast seems to have a motive.

Now it's your turn to play detective. Each table of diners is asked to name a spokesperson. During dinner, each table mulls over the clues and tries to come up with one telling question that will uncover some yet-unknown fact that will point to the murderer. Each audience member is asked to write down their solution to the crime—who dunnit, with what, and why.

Another bit of good news is that the food, while simple, is quite tasty. The choices are limited—Cornish hen, prime rib (for a $3 extra charge), and vegetarian or meatball lasagna. I'd recommend the Cornish hen. Beer, wine, and soft drinks are poured freely, and a full cash bar is available before and during dinner.

After dinner, the cast reappears and submits itself to the interrogation of the audience. This is no dry exercise in forensic logic. Thanks to the expert ad-libbing of the cast, the laughter continues virtually nonstop. Ultimately, the wrongdoer is identified and audience members who guessed right win a prize.

Sleuths has become so popular that it now supports three separate theaters in its strip mall home. Three nights a week the bar and one of the theaters stay open late for *Sleuths'* "It's No Mystery" after-dinner series. Thursday it's "A Little Night Magic." Friday features "Mama's Comedy" improv games; and Saturday sees a "Stand-Up Comedy Spotlight." Shows start around 10:00 p.m. and cost $10 each; all are well worth their modest price.

One indicator of the success of the *Sleuths* experience is that, by show's end, the audience feels part of the family. The cast members graciously thank you for your attendance and point out the valuable service you perform in helping a local business survive and thrive without being owned by Disney or NBC. Hear! Hear!

Treasure Tavern

6400 Carrier Drive, Orlando 32819 ~ (877) 318-2469; (407) 206-5102
www.treasuretavern.com

Prices:	Adults $60.65, price includes tax but not gratuity.
Times:	Tuesday through Saturday at 8:00 p.m. Call ahead to check. Doors open 30 minutes prior.
Directions:	From I-4 Exit 74, go east (Sand Lake Road), left on International Drive, then right on Carrier.

Make a left on Canada Avenue for parking.

Right next door to *Pirate's*, that attraction's owners have built a separate, more intimate dinner experience with a decidedly adult focus. Unlike other attractions in this chapter, those under 18 are actively discouraged. That's reflected in both *Treasure Tavern's* more upscale menu and its atmosphere of envelope-pushing double entendres.

The cozy dining hall's opulent yet oddball decor should make fans of Disney's defunct Adventurers Club feel right at home, as will the trio of Stooges-inspired sidekicks performing slapstick stand-up at your tableside. Our hostess Madame Gretta (a Mae West-ian broad in a banana brassiere) introduces the club's sing-along credo, and a pair of puppets protrude from a picture frame to snark at the proceedings. The attractive cast clowns their way through about two hours of audience participation, crude comedy, and comely choreography, never letting up even while you're noshing.

I'd have to rank the meal among the best I've had at any Orlando eating attraction. Chef Wania de Mattos' salad, prime rib ($3 extra), and chocolate-almond "opera" cake are all a cut above. Other entree options include beef tenderloin with shrimp, roast chicken, salmon, or vegetarian lasagna. Hot appetizers are available a la carte (about $10). There is a cash liquor bar available if you'd like drinks with dinner. Presentation is absurdly elaborate, with Gretta's "Jewels"—attentive serving wenches who double as exuberant dancers—dishing dinner while singing smirk-inducing songs like "Toss My Salad" and "You Can't Beat the Meat."

The show's highlight is a rotating roster of amazing variety acts from around the world. I've seen a marvelous mime, amazing Mongolian contortionists, and Russian quick-change magicians who must be seen to be believed. Along with the risque (but not overly raunchy) comedy, they combine to create a cheerfully dumb vaudeville that recalls Ed Sullivan meets Benny Hill. If that blend sounds like fun to you, this may be the best time you find in town.

Wantilan Luau

6300 Hollywood Way, Orlando 32819 ~ (407) 503-3463

Prices:	Adults, $60 plus tax; children under 13, $33
Times:	Saturday at 6:00 p.m. year round; Tuesday and Saturday at 6:00 p.m. seasonally
Directions:	At Universal's Royal Pacific Resort off I-4 Exit 74B (westbound) or 75A (eastbound)

Wantilan is Indonesian for "gathering place" and at the outdoor Wantilan Terrace, at the Royal Pacific Resort folks gather together on Saturday nights for that tried-and-true staple of warm weather tourism, a Hawaiian luau complete with roast suckling pig on your plate and Hawaiian hams on stage, but thankfully no poi.

The generous buffet meal starts with fruits and salads, continues with Lomi Lomi Chicken Salad, the "Catch of the Day," Teriyaki Chicken, Flank Steak, and the aforementioned Pit-Roasted Suckling Pig, before wrapping up with a dessert station featuring goodies like White Chocolate Macadamia Nut Pie and Chocolate Banana Cake. Wine, beer, Mai Tais, and soft drinks are included in the price and a cash bar is available. The entertainment is as rich and filling as the meal, featuring a medley of Polynesian song stylings and hula dancing.

There is a cancellation fee of $20 per person unless you cancel prior to noon on the day of the performance.

WonderWorks Magic Show

9067 International Drive, Orlando 32819 ~ (407) 351-8800
www.wonderworksonline.com/magic.html

Prices:	Adults $43.99, children (4 to 12) and seniors (55+) $33.99, includes admission to WonderWorks; for show and food only, adults $24.99, children and seniors $16.99; prices do not include tax
Times:	6:00 p.m. nightly, and 8:00 p.m. Friday to Saturday
Directions:	From I-4 Exit 74, drive east on Sand Lake Road, turn right on International Drive; the show takes place in WonderWorks, next door to the Pointe★Orlando shopping center.

As I watched this enthralling show, I was reminded of what a terrific disappearing act top-notch magic has done over the last few decades. Thanks to the demise of the great television variety shows of the fifties and sixties, there's a good possibility that your kids (or maybe even you!) have never seen a really good magician perform up close. You can remedy that sorry circumstance by heading for WonderWorks, the interactive attraction in the upside down house (see *Chapter 14: Another Roadside Attraction*).

Every night, in a small 130-seat nightclub-like room at the back of Mazzarella's Pizzeria, you can catch a one-hour show featuring some truly first-rate prestidigitation. The show changes from time to time (I have seen shows called *Shazam* and *Night of Wonder*) but *Tony Brent's The Outta Control Magic Comedy Dinner Show* is featured most nights (except Sundays). The basic formula remains pretty much the same, whether the accent is on Vegas-style razzle dazzle or broad comedy. Most shows progress from standard playing-card and ball tricks to some truly amazing stunts. Often you will see some personal object borrowed from an audience member get smashed or burned beyond recognition only to reappear in perfect condition elsewhere. Some tricks involve elaborate contraptions in which the stars are locked and sometimes chopped, sliced, and diced (or so it would seem).

There is great emphasis placed on audience involvement, with pride of place given to the youngsters, whose sense of awe and wonder is evident in their fresh faces. Adults get their chance to shine as well in routines that are as light-hearted and humorous as they are mystifying. The result is a thoroughly entertaining interlude.

What makes this a dinner attraction is the all-you-can eat pizza and all-you-can drink beer, wine, and soda. The pizzas, which are quite good and don't skimp on the cheese, are half plain and half pepperoni, and as one disappears another arrives to take its place. The doors open and food service begins about 30 minutes prior to show time and service continues throughout the show.

The "Magic Combo" package includes admission to both the show and the WonderWorks attraction and touring the attraction after seeing the show makes for an enjoyable and entertainment-packed evening. You can also opt just to eat and see the show, in which case the show becomes one of Orlando's best entertainment bargains. Reservations are recommended, especially during busier periods, because seating is limited. The only nearby parking is in the lot of the next door Pointe★Orlando shopping mall. Unfortunately, WonderWorks does not validate parking tickets, so expect to pay about $4 or $5 for it, depending on how long you linger at the attraction.

Chapter Fourteen:

Another Roadside Attraction

EARLIER, I MENTIONED THE GREAT AMERICAN TRADITION OF THE ROADSIDE attraction—those weird, often wacky, always wonderful come-ons that beckoned from the highway's edge, all designed to amuse or entertain or mystify, all designed to part the tourist from his money and keep him happy while they did it.

Fortunately for us, the tradition is alive and well and flourishing in the fertile tourist environment of Central Florida. Of course, a lot has changed; the attractions listed here are clean and modern, there's nothing suspect or fraudulent going on, and no one is trying to con you out of anything. But a lot remains the same. This chapter then is a cornucopia of museums, monuments, mysteries, and amusements that, in my opinion, partake of this noble legacy of American showmanship. Enjoy!

American Police Hall of Fame and Museum

6350 Horizon Drive, Titusville 32780 ~ (321) 264-0911
www.aphf.org

Admission:	Adults $13, children (4 to 12) $8, seniors (60+) and military $10
Hours:	Daily 10:00 a.m. to 6:00 p.m., except Thanksgiving, Christmas Eve/Day, New Year's Eve/Day
Location:	On SR 450, just east of US 1

This attraction honors the more than 7,000 peace officers who have died in the line of duty since 1960, each of their names carved in marble. More names are added each year. Surrounding the memorial hall are exhibits of police memorabilia. There are badges from across the country and police hats from around the world. One section highlights forensic methods, another depicts the training and handling of K-9 dogs, while others display classic firearms and a memorial to terrorism victims. On a more whimsical note, there are Segway two-wheeled scooters and a police car used in *Blade Runner*. Helicopter rides ($25 to $153) and biplanes ($80) take off just outside the front entrance and an attached gun range allows visitors to test their skills.

Nearby: Enchanted Forest, Kennedy Space Center, Warbird Air Museum.

Astronaut Hall of Fame

6225 Vectorspace Boulevard, Titusville 32780 ~ (866) 737-5235

www.kennedyspacecenter.com/astronaut-hall-of-fame.aspx

Admission:	Adults $20, children (3 to 11) $16, plus tax
Hours:	Daily noon to 7:00 p.m.
Location:	On SR 405, just off US 1

Just before you reach Kennedy Space Center you pass a beautifully designed museum/simulator attraction called the *Astronaut Hall of Fame.* Admission here is included in all of the ticket options offered by the Space Center Visitors Complex, but it can be visited separately. For more information on admission packages, see *Chapter 10: Kennedy Space Center.*

The museum portion of the experience pays homage to the 7 Mercury and 13 Gemini astronauts who worked in the days when space travel was new enough that we could all keep track of who was who. More recently, 22 Apollo and Skylab astronauts were added to the *Hall of Fame.* Also on display are actual Mercury, Gemini, and Apollo capsules. There is even a Mercury model into which you can squeeze yourself—or try to. If you ever wondered why the early astronauts referred to the Mercury program as "man in a can," this experience will explain it all.

Probably of more interest to most visitors, especially the younger ones, will be the variety of simulated experiences this attraction has to offer. **G Force Trainer** puts you in a centrifuge that simulates 4-Gs of acceleration. A video screen in front of you shows what a jet pilot might see while zooming through the wild blue yonder. Amazingly, there is no sensation of spinning, just eight minutes of the rather uncomfortable pull of rapid acceleration. A newer educational exhibit is **Science on a Sphere**, a giant video-screen globe that gives a space-eye view of Earth's ecosystems. The adjoining education center is the site of **Camp Kennedy Space Center**, a $295 week-long summer camp for kids 8 to 14, and the **Astronaut Training Experience**, a one-day program designed for adults who are jealous of all that fun the kids are having.

Allow about two to three hours to fully experience this attraction. If you just want to hit the highlights, it will take far less time. Since many Kennedy Space Center visitors stop here late in the day, it can get very crowded after 4:00 p.m.

Nearby: Enchanted Forest, Kennedy Space Center, Police Hall of Fame, Warbird Air Museum.

Citrus Tower

141 North US 27, Clermont 34711 ~ (352) 394-4061

http://citrustower.com/clermont

Admission:	(Elevator to top of tower) Adults $4, children (3 to 15) $2, plus tax
Hours:	Monday to Saturday 9:00 a.m. to 5:00 p.m.
Location:	Half a mile north of SR 50

Clermont's *Citrus Tower* is a monument to a vanished industry. While I was visiting, another tourist told of coming here as a child in the fifties. "All you could see was miles and miles of orange trees," he remembered. "There's not much to see now." A series of devastating freezes over the past two decades has forced Florida's citrus industry farther south. Today, the fields around the *Tower* are more likely to hold a new subdivision than orange groves.

From the observation platform at the tower's top you can see 35 miles in all directions. You can even make out downtown Orlando and the taller buildings at Disney World in the hazy distance. Later, you'll be able to argue that you were as high as it is possible to get in the state of Florida. (*Bok Tower Gardens* in Lake Wales, see *Chapter 17*, also claims this distinction.)

Nearby: Lakeridge Winery, Presidents Hall of Fame.

Fantasy of Flight

1400 Broadway, Polk City 33868 ~ (863) 984-3500
www.fantasyofflight.com

Admission:	Adults $28.95, children (6 to 12) $14.95. Annual pass $69.95
Hours:	Daily 10:00 a.m. to 5:00 p.m. Closed Christmas and Thanksgiving. Restaurant open 11:00 a.m. to 3:00 p.m.
Location:	Exit 44 off I-4, about 50 miles west of Orlando

Vintage aircraft collector Kermit Weeks has turned his avocation into an irresistible roadside attraction that is definitely worth a visit if you are traveling between Orlando and Tampa. Just off I-4, *Fantasy of Flight*, with its Compass Rose restaurant, makes a great place to take a breakfast or lunch break. You can tour the exhibits and have a meal in less than two hours. Come for a leisurely lunch and then spend the afternoon if you want to take the **free** tours.

There are three major sections to *Fantasy of Flight*. The first is a **walk-through history of manned flight**, with an accent on its wartime uses. Using dioramas, sound, film, and life-sized figures, it's the equivalent of a Disney World "dark ride" without the vehicles. You start your journey in the hold of an old war transport. Suddenly, the jump master is ushering you out the open door of the plane. The engines roar, the cold wind whistles through your hair, you step out into the pitch blackness of the nighttime sky; all you can see is stars. Soon you find yourself at the dawn of flight, as a nineteenth century hot-air balloon is preparing to take off. Then you are in the trenches of World War I, a tri-plane about to crash into your position. Next you are at a remote World War II airstrip. As a new replacement in the 95th Bomber Group, you receive a briefing and then step aboard a restored B-17 Flying Fortress. As you walk through the aircraft you hear the voices of the crew during a mission over Europe, anti-aircraft fire bursting all around you. Stepping across the bomb bay catwalk, you see the doors open beneath you as 500-pound bombs rain down on the fields and cities below. All of this is beautifully realized. The sets are terrific, the lighting dramatic, the soundtrack ingenious, the planes authentic in every detail. I found the B-17 mission to be truly moving.

The second section is a large, spotless, sun-filled **hangar** displaying Weeks' collection. There are reproductions of the Wright brothers' 1903 flyer and Lindbergh's "Spirit of St. Louis." There are a few oddities, like the 1959 Roadair, an attempt to build a flying automobile. But most of the planes are the real thing. The oil leaks, captured in sand-filled pans, tell you that many of these planes still fly. You'll see the actual 1929 Ford Tri-Motor used in the film *Indiana Jones and the Temple of Doom*. There are World War II immortals as well, the B-24J Liberator, a heavy bomber, and the Grumman FM2 Wildcat, the U.S. Navy fighter that shone in the early days of the war. There's even a Nazi short-take off and landing plane, the Storch, that once saved Mussolini's neck by plucking him from a remote mountain resort.

There are several **guided tours** given in the afternoon; arrive by 11:30 if you want to take them all. The **Tram Tour** provides a good overall look at the hangar and some otherwise restricted areas. Other tours focus on various aspects of vintage aircraft restoration and will be especially interesting to aficionados. The **aerial demonstration of the day**, however, which takes place in the late afternoon (weather permitting), will appeal to just about everyone.

By this time, you may wish you were able to get behind the controls of one of these great machines. Fortunately the price of admission includes unlimited flight time aboard the eight simulators in **Fighter Town**, *Fantasy of Flight's* third main section. Aboard the Yorktown aircraft carrier, you can strap yourself into a virtual Corsair and go gunning for Zeroes over tropical islands in "Battle over the Pacific." Each sortie lasts seven minutes. The experience is surprisingly realistic. A flight instructor monitors your progress and provides helpful hints—like don't fly upside down. You can fly against the computer or against another pilot in a different simulator. It's also possible for teams to fly against each other. After your own flight, you'll probably want to go to the control tower to see how things look from the flight instructor's point of view.

When you leave the hangar area, you find yourself back where you began. If you'd like to walk through the dioramas again (and you might), help yourself. Otherwise you can visit the gift shop (leather bomber jackets just $300!) or stop into the **Compass Rose restaurant**, a beautifully designed re-creation of the kind of Art Deco restaurant you might have found at a fancy airport in the 1930s. The Compass Rose opens at 11:00 a.m. and makes a good choice for lunch. If a visit puts you in the mood to take to the air, check into the hot air balloon and plane rides available here (see *Chapter 19: Moving Experiences*).

The latest addition to *Fantasy of Flight's* arsenal is **Wing Walk Air,** a "confidence course" comprised of a 40-foot-high ropes obstacle course, and a 600-foot zip-line suspended over water. The ropes course alone costs $12, the zip-line $15, and $22 for both; get up to $10 off by combining it with regular attraction admission.

If you are a buff of vintage cars as well as aircraft, be sure to check online for *Fantasy of Flight's* seasonal lineup of "land and sea" special events, including "Roar N Soar" in November and "Mustangs & Mustangs" in March. Budding ghost busters will get into periodic "NightFlight" paranormal investigations.

Nearby: Frank Lloyd Wright Buildings, Polk Museum of Art, Water Ski Experience.

Florida Air Museum

4175 Medulla Road, Lakeland Linder Airport, Lakeland 33807 ~ (863) 644-2431
www.sun-n-fun.org

Admission:	Adults $10, seniors (55+) and active military $8, children (8 to 12) $6, children under 8 **free**
Hours:	Monday to Friday 9:00 a.m. to 5:00 p.m.; Saturday 10:00 a.m. to 4:00 p.m.; Sunday noon to 4:00 p.m.
Location:	In the middle of nowhere. From I-4 Exit 25, drive south on County Line Road, turn left on Medulla Road.

Small, even tiny, personal aircraft, hand-built from scratch, from plans, or from kit, are the focus of this small spic and span museum. In addition to more familiar types of craft are gliders, ultralights, and gyrocopters. My favorite was a replica of the 1913 wood, wire, and cloth Laird Baby Biplane, built by aviation pioneer Matty Laird when he was just 16. One wall is given over to a chronological history of Florida aviation from 1900 to 1941 and other displays remember National Airlines, Howard Hughes' 1938 flight around the world, and his fabled "Spruce Goose" megaplane. A hangar a short drive away houses larger World War II military planes; their latest addition is a DC-3 circa 1943.

Reaching the Florida Air Museum takes some stick-to-itiveness. It's truly off the beaten path, but if you're really into this type of aircraft the trip will be worthwhile. Every April there is a fly-in for personal plane enthusiasts.

Fun Spot Orlando

5551 Del Verde Way, Orlando 32819 ~ (407) 363-3867
www.fun-spot.com

Cost:	$3 to $35 as explained below; kids ride **free** with paying adult. $150 for annual pass., $75 for week-day-only annual pass (valid at both locations)
Hours:	Noon to 11:00 p.m. Monday to Thursday; to midnight Friday; Saturday 10:00 a.m. to midnight; Sunday 10:00 a.m. to 11:00 p.m.; extended during holidays to 10:00 a.m. to midnight.
Location:	Just off International Drive near the intersection of Kirkman Road and International

Fun Spot easily wins the Orlando go-kart sweepstakes with its intriguing, twisting, up and down, multilevel tracks. There are four of them here, with the 1,375-foot, three-level *QuadHelix* the most popular. There are also bumper cars, bumper boats, and a 101-foot high Ferris wheel that offers a panoramic view of the upper end of International Drive and Universal Orlando across the Interstate. A 10,000-square-foot video arcade (tokens at 25 cents each or $25 for 120) and a snack bar round out the offerings at this compact amusement park. An expansion, planned to open in 2013, will add two roller coasters and a water park.

Rides cost $3 each and go-kart runs are $6, although most people will opt for a package deal. You can buy an armband that gives you unlimited access to all rides and the go-kart tracks for $35. For $25 you get access just to the "kiddie" and "family" rides and for $15 your child can get unlimited access to six kiddie rides.

Nearby: iFly, Ripley's Believe It Or Not, Titanic, Universal Orlando, Wet 'n Wild, WonderWorks.

Fun Spot Kissimmee

2850 Florida Plaza Boulevard, Kissimmee 34746 ~ (407) 397-2509
www.fun-spotusa.com

Cost: *SkyCoaster:* $40 for one person, $70 for two, $90 for three

Go-Karts & Rides: $3 to $9 each; $15 to $35 for unlimited armbands (see above); see above for annual pass information

Hours: Daily noon to midnight on weekends, varies during the week

Location: On US 192 near Old Town, between Mile Markers 9 and 10

Those odd-looking white towers, floodlit at night, that stick up over the Kissimmee tourist strip will lead you to the "world's tallest" **SkyCoaster**, the centerpiece of Fun Spot's Kissimmee branch. The experience begins when you are strapped into a full body harness, on your stomach, in a prone position. Up to two friends can ride with you, with discounts for the additional riders.

Next you are hoisted 300 feet in the air to the rear tower and . . . well, dropped. But this is not bungee jumping. There is no gut-wrenching jolt at the bottom. Instead you glide suspended on stainless steel airline wire along a path mathematicians call an "arcuate curve" between the other two towers. The result is a remarkably smooth and— once you recover from the initial shock—relaxing ride. After about three swings of ever decreasing arc, you are lowered to a platform and released. For $16 you can have your adventure immortalized on video.

Aside from the *SkyCoaster*, Fun Spot Kissimmee features a selection of four go-kart tracks and carnival rides similar to its I-Drive sibling; the most notable is *Power Trip*, a clone of the spinning coaster at Disney's Animal Kingdom. Pricing is identical to the Orlando attraction detailed above, with a discounted two-park pass sometimes offered.

Note: The adjacent Old Town complex (described below) is not associated with *Fun Spot*; ride tickets from one aren't valid at the other.

Nearby: Arabian Nights, Old Town.

iFLY

6805 Visitors Circle, Orlando 32819 ~ (407) 903-1150
www.iflyorlando.com

Cost: All ages 3 and older, $49.95 and up, plus tax

Hours: Daily 9:30 a.m. to 10:30 p.m.; reservations suggested

Location: Off I-Drive, opposite Wet 'n Wild

iFLY (formerly called *SkyVenture*) is a freefall skydiving adventure housed in an odd-looking tower that packs quite a punch. Inside is a powerful fan that creates a 120-mph rush of air in a vertical wind tunnel.

Following a course of instruction in the fine art of skydiving, you are suited up and walked high into the tower where, along with your instructor, you step out into mid air and learn to fly. The upwards rush of air keeps you aloft as your instructor takes your hand and shows you how to negotiate the updraft. Around you, a 360-degree virtual reality display heightens the sensation of free falling thousands of feet above the ground below. The entire experience takes about an hour, although the freefall portion lasts only about two minutes, which they say is about as much as first-timers can take. A DVD of your adventure costs about $25.

Nearby: Fun Spot Orlando, Magical Midway, Ripley's Believe It Or Not, Titanic, Universal Orlando, Wet 'n Wild, WonderWorks.

The Jesus Film Project Studio Tour

100 Lake Hart Drive, Orlando 32832 ~ (800) 225-3787, (407) 826-2300
www.jesusfilm.org

Admission:	**Free**
Hours:	Tours Monday to Friday, 10:30 a.m., 1:30 p.m., and 3:00 p.m.
Location:	In southeastern Orlando; call for directions or get map on website

Campus Crusade for Christ (CCC) has set a goal to dub *Jesus*, a two-hour 1979 film based on the Gospel of Luke, into 1,800 languages. At 1,120 and counting, they're nearly two thirds of the way there. This modest but cleverly designed 30-minute guided tour illustrates the challenges and payoffs of this ambitious project.

At one point, a tour member gets to test his or her skill at dubbing the words of Peter; at another, in a simulated outdoor "theater," guests witness the reaction to a screening of the film at a remote village in India. Along the way, picture windows provide a glimpse into the actual translating, recording, and editing process. At tour's end, you can purchase the film in many different languages.

Nearby: WordSpring Discovery Center.

Lakeridge Winery Tour

19239 U.S. 27 North, Clermont 34711 ~ (800) 768-WINE; (352) 394-8627
www.lakeridgewinery.com

Admission:	**Free**
Hours:	Monday to Saturday 10:00 a.m. to 5:00 p.m.; Sunday 11:00 a.m. to 5:00 p.m.
Location:	About 5 miles north of SR 50 and 3 miles south of Florida Turnpike exit 285

Believe it or not, American wine making began in Florida, thanks to some French Huguenot settlers who started fermenting the local wild Muscadine grapes near present-day Jacksonville in about 1562. Viticulture was a thriving Florida industry until the 1930s, when a plant disease wiped out most of the vines. Now, thanks to Lakeridge, the only winery in Central Florida, wine making is starting to make a comeback in the Sunshine State. Lakeridge currently produces some 200,000 gallons. Perhaps one day it will fill up all the acres abandoned by the citrus industry. (See *Citrus Tower*, above.)

The attractive Spanish-style building set atop a small hill on a bend in the highway has been cleverly designed to serve as both a working winery and a welcome center for passing tourists. Despite its out-of-the-way location and low-key promotion, Lakeridge attracts a steady stream of visitors. I wonder if it's the free wine?

Tours run constantly, as long as there are people arriving, and take about 45 minutes. After a short video about the history of wine making in Florida and Lakeridge's operations, you are taken on a short tour. It leads you, via an elevated walkway, over the compact wine making area at the back of the building, onto a terrace that overlooks the vineyards and the rolling, lake-dotted countryside of the Central Florida Ridge, and then back over the U-shaped wine-making room.

After the tour, there is a 15-minute **wine tasting** that lets you sample some of Lakeridge's wines, including Crescendo, their *methode Champenoise* sparkling wine. You will also get to taste their mulled wine and, if you like, purchase a bag of spices to make your own. And speaking of purchases, all of Lakeridge's wines are available for purchase. In addition to a varying menu of specials, full cases are sold at a 20% discount. Buy three cases and get 25% off. Lakeridge also sells its own line of salad dressings, sauces, mustards, jams, and jellies.

The winery throws special events on a regular basis throughout the year, ranging from "Jazz at the Winery" to vintage auto shows. There is an admission of $2 for most of these events, although some are **free**.

Nearby: Citrus Tower, Presidents Hall of Fame.

Magical Midway

7001 International Drive, Orlando 32819 ～ (407) 370-5353
www.magicalmidway.com

Cost:	Rides $3 to $7, $7 for go karts, $25 for 3 hours of unlimited rides and go karts
Hours:	Monday and Tuesday 2:00 p.m. to 10:00 p.m.; Wednesday to Friday to midnight; Saturday and Sunday 10:00 a.m. to midnight
Location:	On I-Drive, two blocks south of Wet 'n Wild

Magical Midway is a smaller version of *Fun Spot Orlando,* described above, but due to the absence of kiddie rides it draws an older teen clientele. The main attractions are the two elevated wooden go-kart tracks, but there are also midway-style rides including a scaled-down version of Universal's *Dr. Doom* shot tower ($5). Since it's easy to burn through a lot of money paying for individual rides, the $25 pay-one-price option quickly begins to make sense.

There is also a giant slingshot that will shoot two riders ($25 each) some 370 feet into the air where they tumble and bounce for a while before being reeled back in.

You can document your insanity on video for an extra charge. It's only competition for sheer terror is the **Starflyer**, which flings riders around like a "carousel on steroids" at 230 feet ($7).

Nearby: Fun Spot Orlando, iFly, Ripley's Believe It Or Not, Titanic, Universal Orlando, Wet 'n Wild, WonderWorks, World Bowling Center.

Old Town

5770 West Irlo Bronson Highway, Kissimmee 34746 ~ (407) 396-4888
www.myoldtownusa.com

Admission:	**Free**. Rides are extra.
Hours:	Daily noon to 11:00 p.m.; Rides operate Monday to Friday from 2:00 p.m.; Saturday and Sunday from noon
Location:	About 1 mile east of I-4, just past Mile Marker 9

Take away the window dressing and Old Town is just a mall filled with gift, novelty, and souvenir shops. But the window dressing is fun and obviously popular with the crowds that make Old Town a lively place to visit and shop during those sultry Florida evenings.

Behind a small, brightly lit amusement park facing Route 192, a vaguely Western Main Street stretches through a few blocks of 70-plus shops, cafes, and entertainments to a tiny carousel, a mini roller coaster, and other rides on the edge of the Kissimmee night. It's pedestrians only, with frequent benches for weary strollers and a constant swirl of visitors from around the world.

The dozen or so rides are of the carnival midway variety and are paid for with tickets purchased from a booth at the front ($1 per ticket). Rides cost anywhere from 2 to 5 tickets, so a $25 ride-all-day pass will pay for itself fairly quickly. The **AMPventure** Ropes Course, Rock Wall, and Zipline are priced separately (3 to 10 tickets) or included in a $35 all-day pass. A tiny go-kart track collects a separate fee of $6 for a 13-lap, 4-minute ride. Old Town also boasts a haunted house, the **Haunted Grimm House**. Admission is $12.50 ($6.75 for kids 10 and under) for a 5- to 10-minute stroll through 20 rooms of shocks and surprises courtesy of special effects and a handful of live actors. If you absolutely must visit a haunted house, the Grimm establishment is satisfactory.

Lazer Tag ($5) works an interesting variation on the theme—the floors are inflated and the walls padded, allowing the shoeless players to dive and roll like action movie heroes as they fire off their laser weapons at all and sundry. The collection of rides at the end of Old Town's main street includes two coasters. The **Wacky Worm** (2 tickets) is a scaled-down kiddie coaster while the **Windstorm Coaster** (5 tickets) provides more grown-up thrills although it can't match the coasters at the major theme parks.

Old Town lays on a number of **free** events to draw crowds and keep them entertained between bouts of shopping. An outdoor stage down one of the side streets offers musical entertainment like Latin Sundays sponsored by a local Latino radio station on an irregular schedule. More predictable is the 8:30 p.m. **Friday and Saturday Night Cruise** of vintage automobiles. Over 350 cars show up on the average Saturday, and Old Town claims it's the largest such event in the world. It's great fun for anyone who grew up in the age of those great finned monsters. Live rock 'n' roll adds the perfect musical accompaniment to the nostalgia.

There's food, too, most of it of the ice cream, popcorn, hot dog, and candy variety. But there are fast food eateries dishing up Tex-Mex and Chinese fare and the Blue Max Tavern offers decent burgers and sandwiches in a friendly pub atmosphere with karaoke every night.

Nearby: Arabian Nights, Fun Spot Kissimmee.

Orlando Ghost Tours

(407) 256-6225

www.americanghostadventures.com

Admission:	Adults $30; children (6 to 12) $15; seniors, teachers, students, and military $25
Hours:	Daily at 8:00 p.m.
Location:	Meets in front of the Dessert Lady, 120 West Church Street, downtown Orlando

It turns out you don't need a centuries-old castle to have a haunted house. Orlando has plenty of haunts and most of them date to the early twentieth century. This low key operation will help you find them.

You meet your group of intrepid ghost hunters on downtown Church Street, steps away from the struggling restaurant complex known as Church Street Station, which turns out to be a hotbed of paranormal activity. The various buildings here, some of Orlando's oldest, are haunted by the spirits of newborns murdered by their prostitute mothers, a piano player (who, until the building closed recently, liked to play for late night guests), and a can-can dancer who died while preparing to perform at Rosie O'Grady's.

Then it's off to scope out hauntings in one of several other downtown buildings. The evening often wraps up inside an old courthouse (now the Orange County History Center), where the tour goes high tech. Tour guests are issued electromagnetic detectors (or, if you prefer, bring a camera) to detect paranormal activity. On the tour I took, my detector started "spiking" wildly. I had apparently sparked the interest of Emily, a little girl who met a sad end in the city's foster care system years ago. The guide explained that Emily is drawn to father figures. As to why a little girl is haunting a courthouse, speculation has it that this is the last place she saw her family intact.

If you're a "sensitive," you will definitely want to take a tour like this. If you "ain't afraid of no ghosts" (as the song says), this is a good chance to test the courage of your convictions.

Presidents Hall Of Fame

123 U.S. 27 North, Clermont 34712 ~ (352) 394-2836

Admission:	Adults $14.95, children (5 to 12) $6.95, seniors/military/AAA $13.95, under 5 **free**
Hours:	Monday to Saturday 10:00 a.m. to 4:00 p.m., Sunday noon to 4:00 p.m.

• Chapter Fourteen: Another Roadside Attraction •

Location: About half a mile north of SR 50

Next to the *Citrus Tower* (see above) sits a small porticoed house that is home to an even smaller porticoed house. This is *Presidents Hall of Fame*, a meticulous scale model of the White House that has been the life's work of Orlando resident John Zweifel and his wife Jan. Anyone who's into modeling or anyone who's helped a child build a doll house will want to visit this astonishing work.

Inside you'll find life-sized wax-museum-style statues of all the U.S. presidents, from Washington on down, that are a fascinating chronicle of the evolution of upscale American male clothing over the years.

In the first of the two display rooms in this small museum is a 16-foot-square diorama depicting the building of the White House as it might have looked in 1797, three years before its completion. At a scale of three-quarters of an inch to one foot, we can watch the dozens of stonemasons, carpenters, and laborers ply their trade while George Washington himself surveys their progress. Washington, by the way, was the only president not to live in the White House, even though he supported the project.

The pièce de résistance, however, awaits in the much larger second room. Here you will find the 60- by 22-foot model of the White House executed in a scale of one inch to the foot. It took Zweifel, his wife, and hundreds of volunteers over 500,000 man-hours to bring the model to its present state and apparently they're not done yet, since the work is billed as an ongoing project. The result is impressive. They have re-created not just the main building but the East and West wings as well, all in astonishing detail.

As you enter the room, you see the front of the building. Peek through the windows and you can glimpse details of the rooms inside. But walk the length of the model and around to the back and the entire White House will be revealed to you. In doll house fashion, there is no rear wall and here the full extent of the Zweifels' accomplishment becomes apparent.

The scope of the re-creation and the attention to detail are astounding. You can spot pens on tables, cigar burns on tabletops, even the occasional gravy stain. The clocks tick, the phones ring, the television sets are on (picking up Orlando stations oddly enough). Along the wall behind you are dioramas of the Oval Office as decorated by a series of recent presidents.

The gift shop offers a surprising number of books about the White House and the presidents who have lived in it along with an assortment of more traditional souvenirs. A few items (not for sale) are worthy of *Ripley's Believe It Or Not!* You can see, through magnifying lenses, the flags of all nations painted on a grain of wheat or a portrait of the Kennedys, John and Jackie, executed on the head of a pin. What possesses people to do this sort of thing?

Some of the exhibits go on tour from time to time and so may not be there when you visit (*Tribute to the Presidents*, for example, traveled to the 2000 Republican Convention). On the other hand, the *Presidents Hall of Fame* sometimes hosts exhibits on loan from presidential libraries and other museums.

Nearby: Citrus Tower, Lakeridge Winery.

Ripley's Believe It Or Not

8201 International Drive, Orlando 32819 ~ (407) 363-4418

www.ripleysorlando.com

Admission:	Adults $19.99, children (4 to 12) $11.99, plus tax; parking is **free**
Hours:	Daily 9:30 a.m. to midnight
Location:	Next to the Wyndham Resort on I-Drive

Is that an ornate Italian villa sliding into a Florida sinkhole on International Drive or is it just *Ripley's Believe It Or Not?* It's Ripley's, of course, and the zanily tilted building is only one of the illusions on display here (and one of the best).

Robert Ripley was a newspaper cartoonist whose series on oddities and wonders, man-made and natural, made him a very wealthy man and an American institution. The Orlando Ripley's is one of several monuments to Ripley's weird and wonderful collections, gathered in the course of visits to some 198 countries at a time when such globe-trotting travel was still a challenge. On display here are objects collected by Ripley himself, along with others gathered after his death, and a series of show-and-tell displays illustrating a variety of optical and spatial illusions.

Where else are you going to see a real two-headed calf? Or the Mona Lisa re-created in small squares of toasted bread? Or a three-quarter scale Rolls Royce crafted from over a million matchsticks? Most displays here are fascinating, although a few are not for the squeamish and some may strike you as tasteless. Best of all are the show-and-tell displays, like an elaborately tilted and skewed room in which the balls on a pool table seem to roll uphill. There is also a giddily disorienting catwalk through a rock-walled tunnel. From the outside, it is obvious that the walls are moving, but step inside, onto the catwalk, and suddenly the walls seem to be rock solid and it is the catwalk that seems to be rotating.

Nearby: Fun Spot Orlando, iFly, Magical Midway, SeaWorld, Titanic, Universal Orlando, Wet 'n Wild, WonderWorks, World Bowling Center, YMCA Aquatic Center.

Spook Hill

www.spookhill.info

Admission:	**Free**
Hours:	24 hours
Location:	South on 27 to 17A (before Lake Wales), turn left (east) and follow signs

I don't get it. A sign at this "attraction" (which is just a line drawn on a road in the small town of Lake Wales) talks about a legendary Indian chief, an epic battle with an alligator, and the belief of early pioneers that the place was somehow haunted. Then you are instructed to stop your car on the white line painted in the street, place it in neutral, and then marvel as the car mysteriously rolls backwards uphill!

The only problem with this scenario is that it seems to me screamingly obvious that your car is rolling downhill. Maybe I'm perceptually challenged. Or maybe the locals are hiding in the bushes laughing at tourists making fools of themselves on Spook Hill. But what the heck, it's a local legend, it's free, and it's on the way to Bok Tower

Gardens if you're heading that way. Maybe you can explain it to me.

Nearby: Florida Skydiving Center, Legoland, Bok Tower Gardens, Lake Wales Arts Center.

Titanic, The Experience

7324 International Drive, Orlando 32819 ~ (407) 248-1166
www.titanictheexperience.com

Admission:	Adults $21.95, children (5 to 12) $12.95, plus tax
Hours:	Daily 9:00 a.m. to 9:00 p.m.
Location:	On I-Drive near Coco Kay Resort

Fans of the movie *Titanic* (and they are legion) will welcome the opportunity to visit this extremely well-done evocation of the most famous cruise ship in history. The exhibition takes the form of "guided tours" that depart every half hour or so and are led by actors representing historical characters, from the designers of the Titanic to crew members and passengers aboard the ship's ill-fated maiden voyage.

Among the highlights of the tour are re-creations of staterooms and other areas of the ship. And if the grand staircase looks smaller than the one in the film, that's because this one is accurate; the filmmakers took some liberties and made the staircase higher and broader. Then there are the artifacts, over 100 of which were salvaged from the actual wreck site, including playing cards, perfume bottles, and a 10-foot-long chunk of the hull. If you're in the right mood, these can be rather chilling. And some visitors may get a few goose bumps from seeing a costume worn by Leonardo himself in the movie.

But the real goose bumps come from the boarding passes you are handed at the start of your voyage into history. Each one bears the name of an actual Titanic passenger. At the end of the "voyage" you can consult a memorial wall and learn whether or not you survived. The historical character-guides handle their roles extremely well, giving equal time to historical trivia (like the fact that the ship's linoleum floors were the height of luxury at the time) and the somber human drama of the ship's tragic end.

The attraction's grand staircase has become a popular backdrop for weddings and events. A dinner show recreating the "Widener Party" features costumed actors interacting with you during a three-course meal, and costs $64.95 for adults, $39.95 for children. Call (407) 248-1166 for more information about either.

Nearby: Fun Spot Orlando, iFly, Magical Midway, Ripley's Believe It Or Not, SeaWorld, Universal Orlando, Wet 'n Wild, WonderWorks, World Bowling Center.

Warbird Air Museum

6600 Tico Road, Titusville 32780 ~ (321) 268-1941
www.vacwarbirds.org

Admission:	Adults $18, children (4 to 12) $5, military and seniors (55+) $15, plus tax; group and family rates are available
Hours:	Daily 9:00 a.m. to 5:00 p.m., except Thanksgiving, Christmas, New Year's Day
Location:	On SR 405, on the way from Orlando to Ken-

nedy Space Center, via routes 528 and 407; from
I-95, take Exit 215

The Valiant Air Command is a non-profit group dedicated to preserving historic aircraft and, not incidentally, putting on some smashing aerial demonstrations. This small museum, located on the grounds of the Space Coast Regional Airport, shows off their collection when it's not airborne. An anteroom to the hangar contains a grab bag of military and aviation memorabilia, most of it from World War II. There's a little bit of everything, from propaganda posters, to uniforms, to weapons and war trophies, to model airplanes. Overhead hangs a replica of a 1907 Epps Monoplane. Your interest in all this will no doubt depend on your personal connection to the subject matter.

In the hangar, however, just about everyone will find something worth oohing and aahing over. While there are a few WWII planes, the bulk of the collection dates from the fifties. The collection changes from time to time but there will be enough Dakotas, Messerschmitts, Wildcats, Crusaders, and Hueys to keep the military aircraft buff happy. There's even an F-5 once used by NASA in attempts to break the sound barrier. If seeing all these planes makes you itch to get airborne, that can be arranged thanks to Warbird Flights, a separate company operating out of the Warbird Museum. Their services are described in *Chapter 19: Moving Experiences*.

Nearby: Astronaut Hall of Fame, Enchanted Forest, Kennedy Space Center, Police Hall of Fame.

The Water Ski Experience

1251 Holy Cow Road, Polk City 33868 ~ (863) 324-2472
www.waterskihalloffame.com

Admission:	Adults $5, seniors (65+) $4, children (6 to 12) $3
Hours:	Monday to Friday 10:00 a.m. to 5:00 p.m.
Location:	From I-4 Exit 44, go north on SR 559, then right on CR 557A

If water skiing is your thing, then you might find a visit to this museum rewarding. Here you can gawk at the first ever pair of water skis, which dates back to 1922 and to the "father" of water skiing, Ralph Samuelson. There are also displays of antique outboard motors, water skis, and memorabilia of all sorts, with an accent on trophies. The Time Line Wall illustrates key developments in the history of the sport and the library boasts over a thousand videos that you can see on request. The earliest footage, silent and in black and white, dates from 1939.

Nearby: Fantasy of Flight, Frank Lloyd Wright Buildings, Polk Museum of Art.

WonderWorks

9067 International Drive, Orlando 32819 ~ (407) 351-8800
www.wonderworksonline.com/orlando

Admission:	Adults $24.99, children (4 to 12) and seniors (55+) $19.95, plus tax; with magic show, adults $43.99, children and seniors $34.99
Hours:	Daily 9:00 a.m. to midnight

Location: On International Drive, next to Pointe★Orlando

If you liked the subsiding building that houses *Ripley's Believe It Or Not*, wait until you see *WonderWorks*. The fantasy here is that a mysterious neoclassical building has crashed out of the sky, upside down, right in the middle of Orlando's glitziest tourist strip. Inside, the normal laws of physics are likewise turned upside down. The exterior of *WonderWorks* has become Orlando's most-photographed building.

In fact, *WonderWorks* is packed with the kind of games and gimmicks (over 100) used by science museums to teach basic principles of physics, and it turns them into a highly enjoyable interactive amusement arcade. Here, on three noisy levels, you can experience an earthquake or a hurricane and get some idea of what it would be like to fly a fighter jet or land a space shuttle. Then test your reflexes, your pitching arm, the strength of your grip, and your visual acuity. Or maybe you'd just prefer to play around with soap bubbles as big as you are. One of the most popular attractions, often spawning long lines, is a station where you can design your own roller coaster then climb into a simulator and find out what it would feel like to ride it.

There's plenty more to keep you amused and entertained for as long as you'd like to hang out. The "world's largest" laser tag arena occupies the third level. Single games are $7 and replays $3; unlimited play from 9:00 p.m. to midnight, Sunday through Thursday, is $13. Also in the "basement" is a 4-D simulator ride and 36-foot-tall ropes challenge course; one visit to each is included in general admission, or they can be experienced a la carte for $10 each. Next door is Pointe★Orlando, an elaborate shopping, dining, and movie venue that is an attraction in its own right.

WonderWorks is also home to a nightly magic show that comes with all-you-can-eat pizza and all-you-can-guzzle beer, wine, or soda. Special combination packages include both the show and the attraction. Show times are 6:00 p.m. nightly, plus 8:00 p.m. Friday and Saturday. A great way to experience *WonderWorks* is to catch the magic show first and then while away the rest of the evening exploring the attraction. The magic show is reviewed in *Chapter 13: Dinner Attractions*.

Nearby: Fun Spot Orlando, iFly, Magical Midway, Ripley's Believe It Or Not, Titanic, SeaWorld, Univeral Orlando, Wet 'n Wild.

WordSpring Discovery Center

11221 John Wycliffe Boulevard, Orlando 32832 ~ (800) 992-5433; (407) 852-3626
www.wycliffe.org/wordspring

Admission: Adults $8, seniors (55+) $7, students (grades 1 to 12) $6, children under 6 **free**

Hours: Monday to Friday 9:00 a.m. to 4:00 p.m.

Location: In southeastern Orlando; call for directions or get map on website

If you thought the Bible had long since been translated into every conceivable language, think again. Of the world's estimated 6,800 languages, only an estimated 392 have the entire Bible. Another 1,000 or so have a complete New Testament and 883 have at least one book of the Bible. Some 3,000 languages still do not have their own version of the Bible.

Wycliffe Bible Translators seeks to fill in most of the gaps and this compact and colorful multimedia museum chronicles the process and the challenges involved. Many of the interactive stations are designed with kids in mind, but adults will find them a lot of fun, too. At one, you can type in your name and get a printed certificate showing how it would look in six different languages from ancient Egyptian hieroglyphics to Klingon. At another, you can send an electronic postcard with your photo via email. Or you can listen in on Mazateco, a tonal Mexican language that can be spoken or whistled.

There are a number of special activities. Monday to Friday, from 9:00 a.m. to 3:00 p.m. at the top of each hour, there is a **guided tour** of the Discovery Center facility. At 1:00 p.m. on the same days, **Face To Face** features talks by various people involved in the Bible translation process. **A to Z Adventures** ($8 per child, $6 per adult), which is presented most weekdays, gives kids a window on the cultures of different countries around the globe.

There is a modestly priced cafeteria (open from 11:30 a.m. to 1:00 p.m.) and a small gift shop selling handicrafts from around the world at very reasonable prices.

Nearby: Jesus Film Studio Tour.

Chapter Fifteen:

Do It!

A VACATION IN ORLANDO DOESN'T MEAN ALWAYS BEING A SPECTATOR. THERE are plenty of activities that will put you right in the middle of the action. In this chapter, I will discuss some of them. Of course, there are many sports-oriented activities as well. They are discussed in *Chapter 20: Sports Scores*.

Bird Watching

Central Florida offers some excellent opportunities for birders, experienced or not. For the novice, there's the spectacle of the spring nesting season at Gatorland, described in *Chapter 7*. More experienced birders will want to head for the Merritt Island Wildlife Refuge (*Chapter 17*); during the winter months it is one of the country's premier birding destinations.

Bird watching is pretty much a do-it-yourself activity, but there are some organized activities. Several area Audubon Societies offer periodic field trips, which are listed on their websites:

Orange Audubon Society
  www.orangeaudubonfl.org
Kissimmee Valley Audubon Society
  www.kissimmeeaudubon.org
Ridge Audubon Society (Lake Wales area)
  fl.audubon.org/who_centers_Babson.html
Indian River Audubon Society (Kennedy Space Center area)
  www.spacecoastaudubon.org

A wealth of other information about birding in Florida can be found at the following websites

  www.americanbirdcenter.com/abc-florida.html
  www.camacdonald.com/birding/usflorida.htm

Boat Rides

There are many places in the Orlando area where you can take a pleasant water-borne ride—as a passenger. You will find them listed in *Chapter 19: Moving Experiences*. However, there is one place that lets you take control.

Lake Eola Swan Boats

Lake Eola Park, Orlando ~ (407) 246-4485
www.cityoforlando.net/fpr/Html/Parks/lakeeola.htm

Cost:	$15 per half hour, including tax
Hours:	Weekdays noon to sunset, weekends 10:00 a.m. to sunset.
Location:	Downtown, near the intersection of Rosalind Avenue and Robinson Street

Right in the heart of Orlando's super-serious business district is this charming bit of whimsy. Lake Eola is Orlando's signature park, with its spectacular floating fountain, recently restored with new lights. Along its shore, at a tiny dock next to the Relax Grill, you can rent paddle boats decked out as graceful white swans and take them for a spin on this picture postcard lake. Electric powered gondolas are available for the same price, and electric swans are on the drawing board. A sunset cruise on a swan makes a lovely way to get your evening off to a flying ... er, floating start.

Nearby: Orange County Regional History Center.

Bowling

This all-American pastime is alive and well in Central Florida and if you've never tried your hand at it, a Florida vacation might be a good excuse. It's not that hard to master the basics and bowlers are a friendly lot willing to offer helpful hints to beginners. I have singled out two locations that are ultra-convenient for most tourists; however, there are many others in the Orlando area. If you'd like to sample them, you can get good information at www.floridabowling.com, which sometimes features money-saving coupons.

Kissimmee Lanes

4140 West Vine Street, Kissimmee 34742 ~ (407) 846-8844
www.amf.com/kissimmeelanes

Cost:	All ages $5.20 per game ($3.95 before 5:00 p.m. Monday to Friday; $5 after 10:00 p.m.)
Hours:	Monday to Wednesday noon to midnight; Thursday 9:00 a.m. to midnight; Friday noon to 2:00 a.m.; Saturday 9:00 a.m. to 2:00 a.m.; Sunday 10:00 a.m. to 1:30 a.m.
Location:	East of *Medieval Times* on US 192

This is a friendly neighborhood place that draws a lot of tourists to its 32 lanes. There is a full snack bar and a bar to slake that deeper thirst. The website has an e-club you can sign up with for discounts. Shoe rental is $4.

Nearby: Medieval Times, Pirate's Island Adventure Golf, Skate Reflections.

World Bowling Center

7540 Canada Avenue, Orlando 32819 ~ (407) 352-2695

www.worldbowlingcenter.com

Cost:	Adults $4, children $3, seniors (60+) $3 per game
Hours:	Daily noon to 11:00 p.m.
Location:	Near *Pirates Dinner Adventure*

Here is a moderately priced, basic 32-lane bowling alley right in the heart of the I-Drive district. What makes World Bowling Center a bit out of the ordinary is the wacky decor, which features murals of astronauts bowling, among other whimsical touches, and the computerized Brunswick Vector scoring system. There are late-night specials on Tuesday, Friday, and Saturday, and on Sundays the adult price drops to $3 per game. Shoe rental is $3.

Nearby: Pirate's Dinner Adventure, Magical Midway, Ripley's Believe It Or Not, Titanic, Wet 'n Wild.

Canoeing & Kayaking

What easier way to appreciate the pristine wilderness of the "real Florida" than to glide gently past it in a canoe? Surprisingly close to downtown Orlando are a number of canoeing trails that offer a glimpse of a Florida few tourists see. The shoreline will vary from well-manicured backyards to impenetrable jungles depending on where you canoe, and much of the scenery is drop-dead gorgeous. In many places, the landscape is little changed from the days Florida was first settled by humans. There are plenty of turtles and birds to be seen and you might even glimpse an alligator.

The two closest spots to Orlando for paddlers are the Wekiva River basin to the north of the city and the Little-Big Econ Wilderness Area to the east. Most of the outfitters listed below will offer drop-off and/or pickup service. Plan on starting fairly early in the morning and ending in mid-afternoon. Some places offer overnight trips and will even rent you camping gear. A typical four- or five-hour outing will cost about $30 to $40.

I have restricted listings to the immediate Orlando area, but if you're willing to drive a bit, there are many more streams to explore. A good source of information is the **Florida Professional Paddlesports Association** at www.paddleflausa.com.

Adventures in Florida

2912 East Marks Street, Orlando 32803 ~ (407) 924-3375

www.adventuresinflorida.com

This eco-tour company offers day-long canoe or kayak expeditions, lunch included, to the Little-Big Econ area and the Wekiva basin ($40 to $80 per person). On nights of the full moon they organize nighttime paddles. They also offer a number of week-long expeditions (about $1,200 per person), including one in Central Florida that includes a lot of kayaking and snorkeling with a manatee. If you know a place you'd like to explore, they can also arrange for rental, drop off, and pick up.

King's Landing Canoe Rental

5722 Baptist Camp Road, Apopka 32712 ~ (407) 886-0859
www.kingslandingfl.com

If you want to explore Rock Springs Run in Kelly Park, this is a good choice. For $30, you can enjoy a leisurely four-hour paddle downstream to the takeout point at Wekiva Island (see below), or dawdle for a picnic lunch along the way. For more on Kelly Park, see *Chapter 17: Gardens & Edens*.

Kissimmee Outdoor Adventures

101 Lakeshore Boulevard, Kissimmee 34741 ~ (800) 247-1309
www.kissoutdooradventures.com

This outfit on the shore of Lake Tohopekaliga in Kissimmee rents one- and two-person "sit-on-top" kayaks for $15 or $30 an hour, or a full day for $55 or $65. For information on their other services see *Chapter 19: Moving Experiences*.

Wekiva Falls Resort

30700 Wekiva River Road, Sorrento 32776 ~ (352) 383-8055
wekivafallsresort.com

Canoe rentals at this funky RV resort are an extremely modest $7.50 for two hours, and available even if you aren't an overnight guest. From here you can explore the Wekiva River, but there is no pick-up service; you paddle out and paddle back.

Wekiva Island

1014 Miami Springs Drive, Longwood 32779 ~ (407) 862-1500
www.geocities.com/wekivamarina

Located about half-a-mile downstream from where the Wekiva River and Rock Springs Run join, this outfitter rents canoes ($30 to $35 a day, with discounts after noon) or lets you launch your own canoe, kayak, or motorboat (up to 25hp) for a $6 to $20 launch fee. Wekiva Springs State Park is a mile upstream; there is no pick-up service. Formerly known as Wekiva Marina, it was reconceived as a "carbon neutral oasis" with a laid-back Jimmy Buffett vibe; hence the available essential supplies like $2 beers.

Wekiwa Springs State Park Nature Adventures

1800 Wekiwa Circle, Apopka 32712 ~ (407) 884-4311
www.canoewekiva.com

There is a $6 per vehicle charge for entry into this charming park (See *Chapter 17: Gardens & Edens*). The rental concession is at the headwaters of one source for the Wekiva River and offers single and double kayaks as well as canoes. Canoe and single kayak rentals start at $17 for two hours plus $3 for each additional hour; double kayaks are $22 for the first two hours. Several set trips ($30 to $40) offer pick-up service; otherwise, you must return canoes to the landing. They will also completely outfit a canoe for an overnight camping trip for $132. A linguistic note: The local Indians used Wekiwa with a "w" to refer to still water and Wekiva with a "v" to refer to running water. Hence the variant spellings.

Climbing

Central Florida is pretty flat, but if you get an itch to scale a sheer cliff face there's a place just north of Orlando that can accommodate you.

Aiguille Rock Climbing Center

999 Charles Street, Longwood 32750 ~ (407) 332-1430
www.aiguille.com

Cost:	Adults $15, students with ID $10.75, bouldering only $8.50. Equipment rentals extra, $6.50 for basic package.
Hours:	Monday to Thursday 10:00 a.m. to 10:00 p.m., Friday 10:00 a.m. to 11:00 p.m., Saturday 9:00 a.m. to 11:00 p.m., Sunday 10:00 a.m. to 9:00 p.m.
Location:	From I-4 Exit 94 drive east on SR 434 for 3 miles, then right on Ronald Reagan, right on Marvin, and right on Charles.

Located in a spacious former warehouse, Aiguille offer 25 rope stations on cliff faces of up to 36 feet in height, studded with colorful hand holds and with plenty of challenging overhangs. You can boulder (climb up to 11 feet off the ground) by yourself, but if you want to go higher you'll need a belayer to hold your support rope. If you don't have a buddy along, you can hire a staffer for this chore for $35 an hour, but only with an advance appointment. There's plenty of room for non-climbers to relax and watch the show, which can be pretty entertaining. If you get inspired to give it a try, lessons are offered.

Nearby: Sanford Orlando Kennel Club.

Fishing

The best time to go fishing, the conventional wisdom has it, is when you can. And you can go fishing in Central Florida. Boy, can you ever. If you just want to throw a line in the water and drift into a semi-trance, you can do that just about anywhere. If you'd like to do some real fishing, I strongly suggest you hire a guide. There are a number of reasons for this:

- A guide has the in-depth local knowledge you lack.
- A guide may be your only means of access to private lakes that have not been overfished.
- A guide will provide tackle and bait.
- Many of Orlando's fishing guides are attractions in themselves, practitioners of a lifestyle that has all but disappeared in our homogenized fast-food culture.

Throughout much of the American Southeast, bass fishing is virtually a state religion, and most of the Orlando area fishing guides seem to specialize in this feisty game fish. There are, however, other fish to be caught hereabouts. Here is a list of Central Florida species, with notes on their seasons:

American shad: Optimum, February and March, so-so January, April, and May.

Bluegill: Optimum, April to June, so-so the rest of the year.

Channel catfish: So-so all year.

Crappie: Optimum, December to March, so-so April and May.

Largemouth bass: Optimum, January to March, so-so the rest of the year.

Shellcracker: Optimum, May to July, so-so the rest of the year.

Sunshine bass: Optimum, December to February, so-so March, April, October, and November.

Striped bass: Optimum, December to February, so-so March, April, October, and November.

What you go after, then, will be a function of the time of your visit and your guide's predilections. Where you go will depend to a fair extent on the guide you hire and his location; each has his favorite (or even exclusive) areas. Among the more popular fishing spots are the Clermont chain of lakes (west of Orlando), the Wekiva River and the St. John's River (north of Orlando), and West Lake Tohopekaliga (in Kissimmee). Serious fishermen will want to pick up a copy of Kris Thoemke's *Fishing Central Florida* (Pineapple Press, $10.95), which provides lake by lake, stream by stream commentary.

Guides do not come cheap; $350 for a full day and $225 for a half day is fairly standard, although some services charge as much as $450 for a full day and $250 for a half. The price covers two people, plus tackle and, sometimes, bait. If all you have time (or money) for is a half-day, make it the morning. Of course, you will also need a Florida State fishing license. A three-day license for a nonresident is $17, an annual one is $47. You can get one at any fishing camp, or your guide will help you obtain one.

Rather than provide a lengthy list of fishing guide options that I can't personally vouch for, I suggest you visit the websites www.centralfloridafishingreport.com and www.floridasportsman.com for comprehensive area angling information and active community forums.

Go-Karts

Go-karts, for the uninitiated, are miniaturized racing cars and they've been around for 50 years. Originally marketed as do-it-yourself kits to hobbyists, go-karts have become a popular form of recreation that appeals to kids and grown-ups alike, with commercial tracks popping up to let casual enthusiasts have a go.

Powered by small gas engines, karts can reach speeds of up to 50 mph, although the karts you'll encounter in Orlando, seldom top 25 mph. Go-kart tracks range from simple concrete tracks marked off by old tires to elaborate, multilevel wooden courses. The go-karts at Old Town, Magical Midway, and the Fun Spots were covered in *Chapter 14*, but there are a couple of independent tracks around town.

Kissimmee Go Karts

4708 West Irlo Bronson Highway, Kissimmee 34746 ~ (407) 390-7223

www.kissimmeegokarts.com

Cost:	$4 per lap, 6 laps for $20, 11 for $21.50
Hours:	Daily noon to 10:00 p.m.
Location:	1 mile east of SR 565 at Mile Marker 13

Nothing fancy here, just go-karts conveniently located on Kissimmee's main tourist strip. Go-karts come in three sizes here—a small single-seater, a two-seater, and a faster "Indy Kart" that costs a few pennies more. The almost one-mile track snakes around three loops with a bridge and overpass arrangement allowing the karts to end up where they started.

Nearby: Medieval Times, Pirate's Island Adventure Golf.

Li'l 500

150 Atlantic Drive (at US 17-92), Maitland 32751 ~ (407) 831-2045
www.lil500.com

Cost:	$4 per ride
Hours:	Monday to Thursday 10:00 a.m. to 10:00 p.m., Friday and Saturday 10:00 a.m. to 11:30 p.m., Sunday 1:00 p.m. to 10:00 p.m.
Location:	From I-4 Exit 92 drive east on SR 436, then south on US 17-92 1.5 miles

Located north of Orlando, outside the tourist zone, this family-oriented attraction offers three separate tracks. The Family Track is strictly for little kids, while the Moto Track and Fastrac appeal to teens and adults.

Nearby: Birds of Prey Center, Holocaust Memorial, Enzian Theater, Maitland Historical Museums.

Golf

For golfers, Central Florida is a sort of demi-paradise, with over 170 courses within a 45-minute drive of downtown Orlando. With that many, choosing one can be a daunting task. You can simplify matters by using the services of Tee Times USA, (800) 374-8633 or www.teetimesusa.com. They will help you pick a course and make the reservations for you; they'll even email driving directions to you. It's a free service and you will pay the regular greens fees. You'll get the best choice of courses and times if you book several months in advance, but they can arrange next-day tee times as well.

Instead of listing here all the golf courses in Orange and Osceola counties, I invite you to check out Visit Florida's comprehensive course listing at www.visitorlando.com/things-to-do/golf. Or visit orlando.golfersguide.com and download a copy of the Central Florida *Golfer's Guide*. You will also find an extensive listing of golf courses of all types in the Yellow Pages in your hotel room.

Guns

Nothing is quite so American as the belief in the inalienable right to bear arms. If shooting off something that packs a kick is your idea of the pursuit of happiness, your visit to Orlando offers a good opportunity to indulge yourself. As long as you have some sort of government-issued ID, foreign or American, you can exercise your Second Amendment rights.

Shoot Straight

4700 South U.S. Highway 17/92, Casselberry 32707 ~ (407) 834-2242
www.shoot-straight.com

Cost:	$35
Hours:	Monday to Saturday 10:00 a.m. to 8:30 p.m., Sunday 11:00 a.m. to 6:00 p.m.
Location:	North of Orlando on US 17/92; several other locations in Central Florida

This chain of gun stores also has shooting ranges. In addition to the Casselberry location (the closest to Orlando), there are ranges in Apopka, Lakeland, and Tampa if you are headed that way.

You must be a member to shoot here and most members use their own weapons. But a one-month membership is just $35 and includes one free gun rental. Regular shooting sessions are $13 apiece, so if you shoot twice during your Orlando visit, the total cost is $36. They have 3 lanes for rifles and 11 for handguns. Shotguns can be accommodated (no bird shot, please), as can machine guns if you have a "Class 3" license. At Casselberry, Monday night is Ladies' Night and the ladies shoot **free**! Did someone say "Cheap date?"

Nearby: Flea World, Orlando Jai-Alai, Semoran Skateway.

The Shooting Gallery

2911 West 39th Street, Orlando 32839 ~ (407) 428-6225
www.shootinggalleryrange.com

Cost:	$22 to $42 per hour, plus ammo and targets
Hours:	Daily 10:00 a.m. to 8:00 p.m.
Location:	From I-4 Exit 79, go south on John Young Parkway a quarter mile to Cox Plaza on your left

At The Shooting Gallery you can rent any of a wide selection of handguns or automatic machine guns to experience the thrill of slamming hot lead into the paper thin body of an imaginary enemy. Instruction is available (briefly) if you need it, but the experience here is pretty much point and shoot simplicity itself.

There are six booths looking down the shooting range where paper targets in the form of human silhouettes hang from wires. There is a range rental of $12 per hour with handguns going for $10 and submachine guns for $30. Ammo and targets cost extra. To give you an idea, the typical machine gunner will go through four to five 50-round boxes of ammo at $12 a box in an hour. Targets (some shaped like notorious baddies) run a few bucks. If business is light, they will often let you overstay your hour at no extra charge.

The Shooting Gallery is located in a downscale strip mall across the street from an Orange County correctional facility and is surrounded by bail bondsmen. Are they trying to tell us something?

Nearby: Holy Land Experience, Millenia Mall.

Hang Gliding

Hang gliding was invented in Australia, which may be why you hear so much Aussie slang among Orlando-area hang gliding enthusiasts. There are two hang gliding venues to Orlando's south and west. Both have an appealing, low-key, good-vibes atmosphere and, thanks to tandem (two-person) gliders, both are well equipped to introduce the novice to this exciting experience. A word of warning: hang gliding can induce motion sickness, especially when the air is choppy.

An experienced pilot goes aloft with you and keeps you safe, but you can do much of the actual flying if you wish. Flights last about 20 minutes, 10 up and 10 down. Experienced hang gliders can sharpen their skills and rent gliders if they haven't brought their own.

QuestAir

6548 Groveland Airport Road, Groveland 34736 ~ (352) 429-0213
www.questairhanggliding.com

Cost:	$125 for 15–20 minutes, $225 for 30+ minutes
Hours:	Daily 8:00 a.m. to sunset
Location:	Take State Road 50 (East Colonial Drive) west to State Road 33 and turn left. Look for sign on your left.

Tucked away in a bucolic setting west of Orlando, this small operation offers rides in ultra-light aircraft as well as tandem hang gliding experiences. Primitive camping, RV hookups, and clubhouse bunks are available for hang gliders.

Nearby: Seminole-Lake Gliderport, Wallaby Ranch.

Wallaby Ranch

1805 Deen Still Road, Davenport 33897 ~ (800) 925-5229, (863) 424-0070
www.wallaby.com

Cost:	$175
Hours:	Daily 8:00 a.m. to sunset
Location:	From I-4 Exit 55, drive north on US 27 and turn left at Deen Still Road; drive 1.7 miles to the poorly signed driveway on your left.

This is a hang gliding club with regular, and very friendly, get togethers. It is larger than *QuestAir* and has fairly extensive facilities. There is a barbecue and a screened-in eating area as well as a treehouse for kids, and tent and RV camping.

The 500-acre facility has plenty of room for running and mountain bike trails. There is also a pool, a trampoline, and a climbing wall. If you come to the Orlando area regularly, you can store your hang glider here.

Nearby: Seminole-Lake Gliderport, QuestAir.

Horseback Riding

Though several Orlando equestrian centers have shuttered, there are still a few places to go horseback riding in the Orlando area. Most stables offer leisurely trail rides of about an hour or so. Lessons are available at these stables. Also see Forever Florida and the Crescent J Ranch in *Chapter 17: Gardens & Edens.*

Horse World

3705 South Poinciana Boulevard, Kissimmee 34758 ~ (407) 847-4343
www.horseworldstables.com

Cost:	$44 (beginners, 60 minutes) to $75 (advanced, 75 minutes), plus tax
Hours:	Daily 9:00 a.m. to dusk.
Location:	About 12 miles south of Highway 192

Western-style riding on 750 acres. Riding lessons are offered, and they rent facilities for group events such as picnics.

Rock Springs Riding Ranch

31700 CR 433, Sorrento 32776 ~ (352) 735-6266
www.rsrranch.com

Cost:	$37 to $80 for one- to three-hour guided trail rides; $150 for all day
Hours:	Daily 8:00 a.m. to 5:00 p.m.
Location:	North of Orlando in the Rock Springs Run State Reserve

Western-style trail riding in a beautiful state park. See *Chapter 17: Gardens & Edens* for more on Rock Springs Run State Reserve.

Jet Ski Rentals

Jet skis, those noisy motorcycles of the seas, are becoming increasingly popular (much to the dismay of those who prefer their lakes quiet and peaceful). If you'd like to take one out for a spin, there are a number of places that will accommodate you. No experience is necessary and driving a jet ski is the soul of simplicity. Rentals start at about $55 for 30 minutes and go as high as $100 an hour for really fast three-seater machines. Some places may offer other activities, such as wakeboarding, water skiing, or fishing.

Buena Vista Watersports

13245 Lake Bryan Drive, Lake Buena Vista 32830 ~ (407) 239-6939
www.bvwatersports.com

Extreme Jet Ski of Orlando

4914 West Irlo Bronson Highway, Kissimmee 34746 ~ (407) 390-1888
www.extremejetskioforlando.com

Miniature Golf

Just as the amusement park was revolutionized by Walt, miniature golf, once a homey mom-and-pop sort of attraction, has become a multilevel "themed" extravaganza with entrepreneurs competing with each other to create the most unusual, most atmospheric, most elaborate course yet. And the Orlando area boasts some of the finest examples of the genre. For most visitors, there's nothing quite like this back home, and I think a visit to at least one miniature golf attraction should be included in every Orlando vacation.

Most of the courses are concentrated in the International Drive area of Orlando and along US 192 in Kissimmee. During the warmer months, it's best to avoid the torrid heat of the day and play at night. Don't worry, they all stay open late. Discount coupons to most (if not all) of these courses can be found in brochure racks and throwaway magazines. In 2012 Universal Orlando will debut a 36-hole course with a B-movie theme at its CityWalk complex; pricing and hours are not yet available.

Bonanza

7761 West Irlo Bronson Highway, Kissimmee 34746 ~ (407) 396-7536

Behind that towering rock formation over the Magic Mining Company restaurant ("Steaks & Seafood") lies a cleverly laid out miniature golf course with a Gold Rush theme. There are two complete 18-hole courses, "The Prospector" (the easier of the two) and "The Gold Nugget." Putt your way over this three-story mountain past cascading waterfalls, old mining sluices, trestle bridges, mountain pools, and cool grottoes. The course is compact, well maintained, and a lot of fun.

Prices: $10 per course adults and children over 3. The second 18 holes are discounted.

Congo River Golf

5901 International Drive, Orlando 32819 ~ (407) 248-9181
6312 International Drive, Orlando 32819 ~ (407) 352-0042
4777 West Irlo Bronson Highway, Kissimmee 34746 ~ (407) 396-6900
531 West SR 436, Altamonte Springs 32714 ~ (407) 682-4077
12193 East Colonial Drive, Orlando 32826 ~ (407) 823-9700
www.congoriver.com

Here you can putt your way up, through, around, and over Livingston Falls in a setting that evokes a storybook Africa and the memory of Stanley and Livingston. There are two complete 18-hole courses, with the "Stanley" course being the easier of the two. If you find yourself having difficulties making par, it's "Livingston," I presume. The holes on both courses are lined with small rocks and large boulders, making for erratic and unpredictable bounces. There are also live gators you can feed for a small fee, and an arcade. The 6312 International Drive location offers views onto Wet 'n Wild's lake (see *Chapter 12*), where you will see screaming riders in inner tubes being towed by jet skis.

Prices: $11 per adult for 18 holes, $9 for kids. A second round costs $5. The Altamonte Springs and East Orlando locations only have 18 holes.

Hawaiian Rumble Adventure Golf

8969 International Drive, Orlando 32819 ~ (407) 351-7733
13529 South Apopka-Vineland Road, Orlando 32830 ~ (407) 239-8300
www.hawaiianrumbleorlando.com

There are two courses here, Kahuna and Lani, with Lani being the more difficult of the two. The courses wind around and through a towering central volcano with thundering waterfalls substituting for lava. Each location has a small Internet cafe.

Prices: $10 for 18 holes, all ages; 36 holes are $12.

Mighty Jungle Golf

7792 West Irlo Bronson Highway, Kissimmee 34747 ~ (407) 390-6453
mightyjunglegolfgroups.com

Located west of I-4 on the fringes of Disney property, this course was voted Best Mini Golf by the readers of *Orlando Weekly* in 2011. There are two 18-hole courses dotted with life-size plaster elephants and giraffes.

Prices: Adults $9.95, children $8.95; all-day $14.95

Pirate's Cove Original Adventure Golf

8501 International Drive, Orlando 32819 ~ (407) 352-7378
Crossroads Center, 12455 SR 535, Lake Buena Vista 32836 ~ (407) 827-1242
www.piratescove.net

Adventure on the high seas is the theme here with two 18-hole courses named after Blackbeard and Capt. Kidd. "Blackbeard's Challenge" is the more challenging of the two. The design and execution of these courses is on a par with that seen at Congo River (see above). I give Pirate's Cove a slight edge, however, with the Lake Buena Vista location my personal favorite. It boasts extra height and higher waterfalls, not to mention its location next to a number of excellent restaurants and Downtown Disney. At all locations, the courses are punctuated with signs offering the real-life history of their namesake pirates. (Will this edutainment never stop!)

Prices: Adults $10, children (4-12) $9. Unlimited play $12.

Pirate's Island Adventure Golf & Pirate's Cove

4330 West Irlo Bronson Highway, Kissimmee 34746 ~ (407) 396-4660
2845 Florida Plaza Boulevard, Kissimmee 34746 ~ (407) 396-7484
www.piratesislandgolf.com

Once again the theme is piracy and once again the two 18-hole courses are named for Blackbeard and Capt. Kidd. These are some of the handsomest courses in the Orlando area, with spectacular waterfalls cascading down in stages to a series of lagoons complete with artificial mist. The courses are beautifully maintained, with smooth brick borders on each hole. There's edutainment here, too, with signs providing capsule biographies of well-known (and not so well-known) pirates.

Prices: Each course is $10.75 for adults, $8.75 for children 4 to 12; all-day unlimited play costs $5 more for all.

Putting Edge

Festival Bay Mall, I-Drive and Oak Ridge, Orlando 32819 ~ (407) 248-0700
www.putting-edge.com

Here's an interesting take on the mini-golf theme. The greens are black and you play in the dark. Well, not completely. Ultra-violet light turns this compact 18-hole indoor course into a psychedelic wonderland. Even the balls and putters glow in the dark and once you get used to it, it's surprisingly easy to play.

Prices: Adults $10.50, youths under 12 $8.50; second round is half price. Party packages are $10 to $19 per person.

Volcano Island Adventure Golf

7460 International Drive, Orlando 32819 ~ (407) 351-4653
www.facebook.com/VolcanoIsland

Here's another volcano-themed course, with a four-story caldera "erupting" on a regular schedule, as cooling waterfalls cascade around you. A river runs through it, too, complete with flamingo paddle boats. There are two 18-hole courses, Tiki Falls and Volcano Voyage.

Prices: Adults $12.95, children (4–12) $11.95 for each course; the "Big Kahuna" package ($15.95) gives you both courses and free ice cream!

Paintball

Hunkered down under a moonlit sky behind a sandbag bunker with a remorseless "enemy" bearing down on you or running like mad through the scrub forest from barricade to barricade, with bursts of gunfire going off all around, you begin to understand why paintball has been called "the ultimate adrenaline rush."

Paintball lets you play John Wayne (or Rambo, or Chuck Norris) in refereed "battles" that last about 15 minutes and pit two teams of five to eight players against each other. The challenge—and the fun—comes in the form of the tiny paintballs that give the game its name. Fired from small CO^2 powered guns, they zip along at 190 miles an hour, splatting against whatever they come in contact with, leaving a telltale mark. They hit with quite a sting and raise a lovely red welt so when you get hit, you'll know it. The games are highly structured with an emphasis on good sportsmanship and safety. Anyone breaking the rules will be removed from the game. According to paintball promoters, paintball causes fewer participant injuries than bowling and golf. And, lest you think paintball is a game just for young boys and grown men who act that way, a surprising number of women play—and play hard.

Most games are played outdoors, although there are some indoor courses. Some fields use inflatable barricades to provide cover, others use hard plastic; best of all, in my opinion, are the woods courses, in which most, if not all the cover, is natural. The fields I have played are very imaginatively designed, well executed, and meticulously maintained. The length of game session varies and sessions can last four or five hours. Night games are especially exhilarating and highly recommended.

There are a number of paintball fields in the Orlando area. Most are fairly modest operations and locations can change regularly and without notice. So can hours of operation. Schedules are somewhat loose and fields are sometimes booked by local groups. There's always a possibility that you'll be able to join a private group, so it's worth dropping by or calling in to check. Kids as young as 10 can play at some courses with signed parental approval.

Prices vary from place to place. Most charge about $10 to enter. The real money is in the paintballs, which can cost upwards of $65 a case of 2,000 rounds. Most places sell them in batches of 500. If you don't have your own paintball gun, not to worry. You can rent one for $15 or so; many rental packages include ammo. Budget a minimum of about $50 per person for your paintball adventure. Make sure to dress down for your game and make sure to wear the required footgear, either boots or athletic shoes. Some places rent jumpsuits, many of them camouflaged; they are highly recommended. They provide concealment and some protection from the sting of a direct hit.

Since the paintball scene changes so often, I strongly recommend you call to check location, hours, and pricing before driving long distances. Note that the addresses given may be the office location and not the field location.

Extreme Paintball Experience

3831 West Vine Street, Kissimmee 34741 ~ (407) 873-9793
www.xtremepaintballxperience.com

Extreme Paintball Experience's (XPX for short) outdoor courses offer a variety of playing areas, including six wooded playfields. Billing itself as a "theme park for paintball," they even hold themed "zombie adventures" around Halloween featuring costumed actors and pyrotechnics. The fields are located 4.5 miles south of US 192 (Irlo Bronson Highway), on Poinciana Boulevard, just before you get to Green Meadows Farm. The driveway is easy to miss, so be on the lookout on your right and drive carefully into the makeshift lot.

Nearby: Green Meadows Farm.

Orlando Paintball

7215 Rose Avenue, Orlando 32810 ~ (407) 294-0694
www.orlandopaintball.com

This 300,000-square-foot, air-conditioned, indoor playing area is housed in a former shipping warehouse well off the tourist track on the northeast side of Orlando. Indoor paintball is a different experience and is best in the cooler months or when it's raining. The floor here is well cushioned with sawdust, and the low-tech layout of plywood and rubber tire barricades is imaginative and challenging with many dangerous cul de sacs to trap the unwary. This is sort of the urban guerilla version of paintball and vaguely reminiscent of those post-apocalypse shoot-em-up movies. This is another location that's hard for out-of-towners to find. Call for directions.

Nearby: Ice Den.

Plane Rides

It may be hard to believe, but it is actually possible when in Orlando to take the controls of an airplane and really fly it—no experience necessary. You even have your choice of planes.

Stallion 51

3951 Merlin Drive, Kissimmee 34741 ~ (407) 846-4400
www.stallion51.com

Cost:	As low as $450 for the T-6 Texan. Call for details since the flights are customized.
Hours:	Monday to Friday, by appointment
Location:	At the Kissimmee Airport off North Hoagland Boulevard

Orlando's theme parks have their share of thrill rides, but none of them has anything that can match this. This is a three-hour orientation flight experience as opposed to a ride.

At the Kissimmee Airport, you can strap yourself into a beautifully maintained and painted P-51 Mustang and spend an hour soaring and swooping Central Florida. These World War II vintage warbirds are powered by V-12 Rolls Royce engines and are capable of speeds up to 500 mph, although you'll be held to a more sensible 280 or 300 mph. You're not alone, of course. These Mustangs have dual-control cockpits and you ride in back, but you will have actual control of the plane at least 90% of the time—if you want to, that is.

For the penny-pinchers, a less pricey alternative is a flight in a T-6 Texan Mustang trainer, billed by the company as the stepping stone from general aviation flying to vintage warbirds.

To make doubly sure you get your money's worth, your flight is meticulously documented on video using cameras mounted on the stabilizer and the glareshield. You also get a pre/postflight briefing, a cockpit briefing, a photo, and a certificate as part of the package. If you decide you're cut out to be an aerial ace, transition and formation training is available on the T-6 and the P-51.

Nearby: Green Meadows Farm, Warbird Adventures.

Warbird Adventures

233 North Hoagland Avenue, Kissimmee 34741 ~ (407) 870-7366
www.warbirdadventures.com

Cost:	$250 (15 minutes) to $740 (one hour)
Hours:	Daily, except Sunday, by appointment
Location:	At the Kissimmee Airport, south of US 192

If you blanched at the cost of flying one of those Mustangs at Stallion 51 (above), you'll be glad to know that just a short distance away, in more modest surroundings, you can fly their baby brothers at a fraction of the cost. The North American T-6/SNJ/Harvards flown here were the premier fighter-trainers of World War II, renowned for their excellence for teaching pilots and preparing them for bigger planes (like the Mustang).

The experience is similar to that offered at Stallion 51, except that here you get to pilot from the front seat. The planes are also not quite as zippy, although that will hardly matter to most folks. The Pratt and Whitney 1340 radial engines are capable of speeds up to 240 mph, although typical cruising speed during these flights is 160 mph. The three planes in the fleet are painted with the markings of the Navy, Marines, and the Army Air Corps; you have your pick.

Warbird Adventures uses an a la carte approach to pricing. It costs $250, $430, and $740 for 15-, 30-, and 60-minute flights, with additional charges for options like aerobatics ($35, included in the 60-minute flight), a DVD of your flight ($50), and so forth. Flights are timed from takeoff to landing.

Nearby: Green Meadows Farm, Stallion 51.

Skating & Skateboarding

Orlando and the surrounding suburban areas offer a good selection of roller skating and skateboarding venues. You can even go ice skating when you tire of the heat and humidity! They have patchwork schedules, so it's best to call ahead or check schedules on the websites given below.

Ice Den

8701 Maitland Summit Boulevard, Orlando 32810 ~ (407) 916-2550
www.rdvsportsplex.com

Cost:	$7 to $10 depending on venue and time
Hours:	Vary by day
Location:	From I-4 Exit 90 go west on Maitland Boulevard about a mile to Maitland Summit on your right

Located in a sprawling modern fitness complex on the north end of Orlando, the Ice Den is a compact ice skating rink with two-hour public skating sessions on an idiosyncratic schedule. Skate rentals are just over $3 and there is a snack bar.

Nearby: Orlando Paintball.

Ice Factory of Central Florida

2221 Partin Settlement Road, Kissimmee 34744 ~ (407) 933-4259
www.icefactory.com

Cost:	$6 to $7 per session; skate rentals $3
Hours:	Friday to Tuesday; call for precise hours
Location:	From Florida's Turnpike Exit 244, go straight from the toll plaza on Shady Lane, then left on Partin Settlement Road

There are two rinks here, a large main rink and a smaller "studio" rink. Saturday nights are family nights, with a group of five getting admission and pizza for $40.

Nearby: Boggy Creek Airboat Rides, Bob Mackinson Aquatic Center, Osceola County Stadium (Houston Astros).

Orlando Skate Park

400 Festival Way, Orlando 32803 ~ (407) 246-2800

www.ci.orlando.fl.us/admin/cfo/realestate/skatepark/index.htm

Cost:	$8 non-member day pass, $40 monthly membership; $7 BMX non-member day pass
Hours:	Monday and Thursday 11:00 a.m. to 10:00 p.m., Tuesday and Wednesday 2:00 p.m. to 10:00 p.m., Friday 2:00 p.m. to 11:00 p.m., Saturday 9:00 a.m. to 11:00 p.m., Sunday 9:00 a.m. to 9:00 p.m. Extended hours during spring, summer, and winter breaks.
Location:	From I-4 Exit 84, go east on Colonial about 3 miles, then right on Maguire to the corner of Livingston

This is a well-designed outdoor skateboarding park that looks like a large, empty swimming pool. Depths range from 5 to 11 feet, with interesting variations in terrain along the bottom. There's even a transfer ridge. The mandatory waivers can be downloaded from the website. Sessions for BMX bikes are held Wednesday and Sunday evenings. A variety of membership options may appeal to enthusiasts who will be in Orlando for a while.

Nearby: Orlando Museum of Art, Orlando Science Center.

Semoran Skateway

2670 Cassel Creek Boulevard, Casselberry 32707 ~ (407) 834-9106

www.semoranskateway.com

Cost:	$6.50 to $8; basic skate rental is $2.50
Hours:	Vary by day
Location:	Just west of SR 436 (Semoran Boulevard), near Lake Howell

Roller skating pure and simple is what's on tap at this venue, which lies somewhat north of the beaten tourist track. There's a large rink, a good snack bar, and upbeat music. It's a real neighborhood place and crowded at most sessions, so grown-ups might want to take advantage of the adult skates on Sunday evening and Tuesday morning. Monday, Wednesday, Thursday, and Tuesday afternoons are reserved for private parties; Saturday is Old School Jams Night.

Nearby: Orlando Jai-Alai, Shoot Straight.

Skate Reflections

1111 Dyer Boulevard, Kissimmee 34741 ~ (407) 846-8469; (407) 239-8674 (from Orlando)

www.skatereflections.com

Cost:	$6.50 to $7.50 plus $2 skate rental, varies by session
Hours:	Vary by day
Location:	Just south of Highway 192

This roller skating rink specializes in good clean fun with strict rules against smoking and gum chewing and a dress code that bans such things as "muscle shirts" and "obscene wording" on clothes. The large rink is impeccably maintained with subdued disco lighting and a snack bar area with plenty of seating. Monday, Tuesday, and Thursday nights are reserved for private parties. Sunday is family day with $25 admission for 5.

Nearby: Green Meadows Farm, Kissimmee Lanes, Medieval Times.

Skydiving

Florida Skydiving Center

Lake Wales Airport
440 South Airport Road, Lake Wales 33853 ~ (863) 678-1003
www.floridaskydiving.com

Ever feel like throwing yourself out of a plane? Then this is the place to come and test your resolve. Actually, it's remarkably easy, since someone else throws you out. Allow me to explain: Would-be skydivers can experience the joys of freefall on a "tandem jump." That means you are strapped securely to a certified instructor, who knows the ropes and controls the jump. After a flight to 13,500 feet, the fun begins, with a full minute of freefall and about five minutes under a parachute to landing. No experience is necessary, but jumpers must be at least 18 years of age and weigh no more than 230 pounds.

The cost, including tax, is $199. If you want your dive immortalized on video or DVD, add another $95. If you can talk two or more of your friends into jumping with you, you'll all receive a discount—$10 per person. For groups of seven or more people, the discount goes to $20 a head. Licensed skydivers with their own gear can jump for just $25.

The first jump is scheduled for about 8:00 a.m. and the last usually goes at sunset. But since the entire experience takes about four to six hours, including a very thorough pre-jump briefing, plan on arriving early. The best idea is to reserve your jump a few days in advance. Florida Skydiving Center is open daily year round but hours vary seasonally.

Nearby: Bok Tower Gardens, Lake Wales Arts Center, Legoland, Spook Hill.

Skydive Deland

1600 Flightline Boulevard, DeLand 32724 ~ (386) 738-3539
www.skydivedeland.com

Skydive Deland operates in much the same way as the Florida Skydiving Center. Here the price of a tandem jump is $179, with groups of four to six people paying $165 each and groups of seven or more paying $155. The cost of a video or DVD record of the experience is $90.

If you are trying to decide which of these two skydiving venues to use, it turns out that both are almost exactly the same distance from the Universal Orlando theme park complex. Deland is to the north, while Lake Wales is to the south. Lake Wales is closer to the Disney World area.

Swimming

Unless you are staying at one of the large resorts, the swimming pool at your hotel may seem a bit cramped. And even then, the pool may be so crowded that you won't be able to do much more than splash about. Fortunately, there are two municipal swimming centers that offer some room for dedicated lap swimmers.

Bob Mackinson Aquatic Center

2204 Denn John Lane, Kissimmee 34744 ~ (407) 870-7665
www.kissimmee.org/index.aspx?page=145

Cost:	$5 per day for non-residents of all ages over 2
Hours:	March to September; hours vary with the season; call
Location:	From Kissimmee follow US 192 (Vine Street) east, veer left onto Boggy Creek Road, then left onto Denn John Lane

This outdoor facility features an eight-lane competition pool with diving boards, a shallow depth play pool with a water playground, and a 150-foot water slide with plunge pool.

Nearby: Boggy Creek Airboat Rides, Osceola County Stadium (Houston Astros).

YMCA Aquatic and Family Center of Orlando

8422 International Drive, Orlando 32819 ~ (407) 363-1911
www.ymcacentralflorida.com/y-locations/aquatic-center/

Cost:	$10 per day for non-residents of all ages
Hours:	Monday to Friday 5:30 a.m. to 8:30 p.m., Saturday 8:00 a.m. to 4:00 p.m.
Location:	From I-4 Exit 74 drive east and turn right onto International Drive, then right onto Jamaican Court

This elaborate indoor complex, which hosts regular swim meets and competitions, has three heated pools, including a diving well. All pools have lanes set aside for long distance lap swimmers.

Nearby: Pirate's Dinner Adventure, Ripley's Believe It Or Not, Sleuths, Titanic.

Wakeboarding & Water Skiing

Central Florida is dotted with lakes, many of which make ideal venues for waterskiing and wakeboarding. Unfortunately, unless you happen to have friends with lakeside property and a properly equipped boat, getting in on the action is hard. Here are some helpful alternatives.

Buena Vista Watersports

13245 Lake Bryan Drive, Lake Buena Vista 32830 ~ (407) 239-6939
www.bvwatersports.com

Cost:	$85 for half an hour, $145 for an hour, including

Hours:	driver and gas Daily 10:00 a.m. to 6:00 p.m.
Location:	From I-4 Exit 68 take SR 535 south; Buena Vista is on your left

Water skiers and wakeboarders can rent a boat and driver at this location on a small lake very conveniently located in the tourist district. If you don't feel confident enough to take a spin on skis, you can opt for a tube ride. All you need to do is sit down and hang on tight!

Nearby: Hawaiian Rumble Adventure Golf, Lake Buena Vista Factory Stores, Medieval Times.

Orlando Watersports Complex

8615 Florida Rock Road, Orlando 32824 ~ (407) 251-3100
www.orlandowatersports.com

Cost:	Rates range from about $25 for an hour to $45 for an all-day pass. Weekly passes are $185 and annual passes go for $1,000.
Hours:	Daily 11:00 a.m. to 6:00 p.m.; closes at 8:00 or 9:00 p.m. from Spring through Fall
Location:	From I-4 Exit 74 take Sand Lake Road east, turn right on Orange Blossom Trail, left on Landstreet Road, and left on Florida Rock Road

Sort of a cross between (or among) water skiing, surfing, and skateboarding, wakeboarding is an increasingly popular sport, and this 50-acre facility has quickly become its Central Florida epicenter. Here you can take advantage of two "cableways," overhead tracks that take the place of the more traditional speedboats and tow you along an oval course past (or over) a series of ramps and obstacles at speeds of up to 36 mph. You can choose from the double skis popular with beginners or a variety of special discs and trick skis, but the platform of choice seems to be the wakeboard.

Although beginners are welcome (or at least tolerated), this place has become a hot spot for pros and semi-pros looking to brush up on their skills. The level of ability on display can be pretty intimidating for novices. If you'd just like to come and watch, that's okay, too. There is a snack bar and a terrace-like dining area with a good view of the action. A pro shop offers the latest in equipment and accessories.

Note: Professional events are held here from time to time, which will limit your access to the facilities.

Although the complex can be seen quite easily from the toll road to the airport, it's a little tricky to find. Perhaps the easiest route for tourists is to head south from Sand Lake Road on Orange Blossom Trail (US 17/441). Just before the junction with Florida's Turnpike, turn left on Landstreet Road and drive about two miles through a heavily industrial area before turning left onto Florida Rock Road.

Nearby: Florida Mall, SeaWorld.

Chapter Sixteen:

A Who's Who
of Zoos

ANIMALS HAVE ALWAYS HELD A FASCINATION FOR US HUMANS, ESPECIALLY THE younger members of our species. So it's hardly surprising that in a tourist-saturated area like Orlando, you'd find a number of attractions built around this ancient allure. The attractions I describe in this chapter run the gamut from a true zoological park, to road-side attractions, to Gatorland clones, to conservation and preservation efforts; what they have in common, of course, is animals even though the context may differ from place to place. Other animal-themed attractions such as SeaWorld, Discovery Cove, Busch Gardens, and Gatorland are described in earlier chapters.

Audubon Center for Birds of Prey
1101 Audubon Way, Maitland 32751 ~ (407) 644–0190
http://fl.audubon.org/audubon-center-birds-prey

Admission:	Adults $5; children (3 to 12) $4; under 3 **free**
Hours:	Tuesday to Sunday 10:00 a.m. to 4:00 p.m.
Location:	East of I-4, near Exit 88

One of the most enchanting animal encounters to be found in the Orlando area is also one of the cheapest. The Center for Birds of Prey is an endeavor of the Florida Audubon Society. Each year it takes in about 700 wounded and orphaned raptors from all over Florida, tends to their wounds, and nurses them back to health with the ultimate goal of releasing them back into the wild. About 40% make it.

You won't be able to see the rehabilitation process; these birds are shielded from public view lest they become habituated to humans, thus lessening their odds for sur-vival back in the wild. You will be able to view a behind-the-scenes video and see from a distance the "flight barn" and the "rehabilitation mews," odd-looking structures with slatted wooden walls, in which injured birds are nursed back to health.

You can also see, in a series of attractive aviaries, birds whose injuries are so severe that they cannot be released. Here they lead the good life (at least they eat well and regularly) and perform a useful role in educating Florida school children and others about the wonders of wildlife and the need to protect it. There are about 20 different species of raptors housed here. They range from tiny screech owls to vultures. There are also a fair number of ospreys, red-tailed hawks, kites, and others. A pair of bald eagles, Prairie and T.J., are particularly fascinating. A short video tells the story of their offbeat love affair and touching attempts to have young.

A visit here can be an educational as well as an uplifting experience. While here, I learned for the first time of the 1916 Migratory Bird Treaty Act that made it illegal to own or transport even a single feather from these birds. The Center collects every feather from molting birds, as well as feathers from specimens that don't survive. They are turned over to the government, which in turn distributes them to Native American tribes for whom the feathers of eagles and other species have ritual significance.

A boardwalk leads down to a charming gazebo set in the wetlands along the shore of Lake Sybelia. A small museum tells the history of the Florida Audubon Society. Guided tours are available by reservation for groups of 10 or more and it's a good idea to call ahead to find out when volunteers will be on hand to answer questions. If a group comes through while you are visiting, feel free to join it. Finding Birds of Prey is a little tricky but it's worth it. Call ahead for detailed directions.

Nearby: Li'l 500, Maitland Art Center, Maitland Historical Museum, Waterhouse Residence.

Back to Nature Wildlife Refuge

18515 East Colonial Drive, Orlando 32820 ~ (407) 568-5138
www.btn-wildlife.org

Admission:	**Free**. Donations requested
Hours:	Tuesday to Sunday 9:00 a.m. to 4:00 p.m.
Location:	East of central Orlando

Located incongruously next to an auto repair shop, with which it shares an office, this nonprofit organization is dedicated to the four R's—Rescue, Raise, Rehabilitate, and Release. In the average year, it plays host to some 2,500 critters, but unlike Birds of Prey (see above), Back To Nature Wildlife Refuge takes on all comers, except common household pets like dogs and cats. The ultimate goal is to release their charges back into the wild, a goal that often proves elusive. What you will see when you visit are the animals that, for a variety of reasons, will be living out their lives in captivity. Many of the cages are marked with the nicknames and histories of their occupants.

The tales told about these animals are a litany of abuse, abandonment, stupidity, and the random cruelty of nature and (more often) mankind. There are "throw away" pets sold by unscrupulous dealers and abandoned when their owners discovered that porcupines, raccoons, and wild African cats don't make the charming pets they'd imagined. Then there are the birds and beasts damaged by pesticides or wounded by bullets. There are also many animals orphaned in the wild or born with disabilities that would have quickly killed them had they not been rescued first. Among the more impressive residents here are cougars, bobcats, bald eagles, and ring-tailed lemurs. A small nursery looks after the littlest guests, including baby raccoons and fledgling birds.

Back To Nature was a labor of love for retired founders David and Carmen Shaw, and a dedicated group of volunteers keep it alive. Donations are requested subtly via donation boxes scattered throughout the property. Many of the animal enclosures bear the names of donors who made them possible. It is unlikely you will leave without becoming a donor.

Note: The refuge plans to relocate to a 20-acre parcel near Lake Nona in the summer of 2012. Visit their website for updates.

C.A.R.E. Foundation

4609 West Ponkan Road, Apopka 32712 ~ (407) 247-8948
www.thecarefoundation.org

Admission:	Varies; $25 for a 1-hour tour for 2 guests, up to $100 for a 2-hour tour for 6
Hours:	By appointment only
Location:	Just off SR 441 and SR 429

C.A.R.E. stands for Creating Animal Respect Education. Like Back To Nature, above, it is a scrappy little nonprofit organization dedicated to rescuing abandoned animals, with an accent on "exotics." It is also a working educational facility with a full schedule of programs on Florida wildlife that it provides for both the tourist trade and local schoolchildren, so advance reservations are a must. You will find it down a dirt road on ten acres of Florida pine woods, in a ramshackle collection of barns and volunteer-built animal pens. It's worth seeking out.

Among the more impressive animals here are an immense Siberian tiger, a pair of black bears, and several gorgeous Florida panthers. There are also homelier charges like Gisele, a dwarf goat, and Truffles, a Vietnamese potbellied pig.

Visitors are treated to a guided tour by a friendly and knowledgeable volunteer. You'll learn the stories behind the animals and may even get to pet one or two. One of the most enjoyable aspects of the tour is just getting to see the obvious affection and interaction between the volunteers and their charges; it's really something to see a panther light up and start purring when her best friend approaches the enclosure.

C.A.R.E. helps support itself by taking its animals to Orlando area resorts, festivals and such for educational displays. Check the website for a calendar of upcoming events.

Nearby: Central Florida Zoological Park, Kelly Park, King's Landing Canoe Rental, Rock Springs Run State Reserve, Wekiwa Springs State Park.

Central Florida Zoo & Botanical Gardens

3755 NW Highway 17-92, Sanford 32747 ~ (407) 323-4450
www.centralfloridazoo.org

Admission:	Adults $12.95, children (3 to 12) $8.95, seniors (60+) $10.95, annual memberships start at $50; **free** parking
Hours:	Daily 9:00 a.m. to 5:00 p.m. Closed Thanksgiving and Christmas
Location:	From I-4 Exit 104 drive south on US 17-92 and

follow signs, less than a mile.

The Central Florida Zoo can't hold a candle to its bigger cousins in the Bronx and San Diego, but it does wonders with what it has. The collection is small, with an understandable strength in local species, many of which will be found in the excellent herpetarium (snake house). Among the more "exotic" species are kangaroos, two elephants, a clouded leopard, and cheetahs in a lovely habitat viewed through one-way glass. Other impressive specimens include a rare and endangered Amur leopard and some delightfully colorful Hyacinth macaws.

What makes this zoo special is its design and layout. Lovely boardwalks carry you between exhibits arrayed under a sheltering canopy of oaks. Especially nice is the **Florida Nature Walk** that snakes through a wooded and swampy area of the zoo grounds. Signs along the way do an excellent job of explicating Central Florida fauna and explaining the way in which minor differences in altitude produce major differences in plant life. The **Butterfly Sensory Garden** has been planted with flowers and herbs that attract these colorful insects for your delight.

ZOOm Air Treetop Adventure is a trio of obstacle courses made of ropes woven among the treetops. Though on zoo grounds, the attraction is ticketed separately, and zoo admission is not included or required. Prices start at $17.50 for the kids course, to $45.95 for a combo of the two adult courses, including the 500-foot long "Big Zip."

On weekends and holidays there are animal demonstrations involving the elephants, along with primate and feline feeding programs. Volunteer docents also roam the park with one of some 40 species used for educational purposes. You may get a chance to touch a boa or pet a possum. The zoo has a bare-bones snack bar, serving inexpensive hot dog and burger fare, with a lovely outdoor seating area nearby. Across from the entrance, there are sheltered picnic tables and barbecue pits, as well as a small carousel ($2) and an eight-minute, three-quarter-mile miniature train ride (adults $3, children $2).

Nearby: C.A.R.E., Kelly Park, King's Landing Canoe Rental, Rock Springs Run State Reserve, Wekiwa Springs State Park.

Green Meadows Farm

1368 South Poinciana Boulevard, Kissimmee 34741 ~ (407) 846-0770
www.greenmeadowsfarm.com

Admission:	$23, including tax, for all those 3 years old and up; Florida residents $21; seniors (55+) $19; annual pass $40
Hours:	Daily 9:30 a.m. to 4:00 p.m.
Location:	Six miles south of Highway 192

This is where kids meet kids—and piglets, and ducklings, and chicks. If you have little ones between the ages of 3 and 7, this cleverly conceived and well-run petting farm is sure to be a favorite memory of their Orlando visit. Better yet, let their grandparents take them! Green Meadows is an ideal place for this sort of trans-generational bonding experience. Meanwhile, you and your spouse can take the in-room jacuzzi out for a spin.

The ethos of Green Meadows Farm is pretty well summed up by the quote from Luther Burbank that greets you on your arrival: "Every child should have mudpies, frogs, grasshoppers, waterbugs, tadpoles, mud turtles, elderberries, wild strawberries, acorns, chestnuts, trees to climb, animals to pet, hay fields, pine cones, rocks to roll, lizards, huckleberries, and hornets. Any child who has been deprived of these has been deprived of the best part of their education."

Green Meadows Farm is spread out over 50 acres under the dappled shade of moss-draped southern oaks. The farm is experienced via a guided tour that lasts about two hours. If the park is busy, you may be asked to wait until the next tour begins but on slower days you'll be escorted to the tour in progress. ("When you get back to the chickens, you'll know the tour's over.") If you like, you can simply stay with the tour and repeat it over and over.

The tour includes a short ride on the farm train and a bumpy tractor-powered hayride, but the real stars of the show are the animals. This is not a working farm but more of a "farm zoo" with widely spaced pens holding a fairly representative cross section of American farm animals. There are also a few more exotic species, like llama, buffalo, and ostriches, that are showing up on your trendier farms. Visitors can enter most of the pens for a close-up encounter. This is the city kid's chance to hold a chicken, pet a baby pig, feed a goat, milk a cow, chase a goose, and meet a turkey that has yet to be served at Thanksgiving. Squawking guinea hens and stately peacocks (including a stunning all-white specimen) roam freely about the grounds. And, of course, there is a pony ride. The little ones love every minute. For doting parents and grandparents, it's a photographic field day.

The tour guides are the antithesis of theme park attendants. There are no spiffy uniforms or carefully rehearsed spiels here. These folks look and talk like they're down on the farm, dirty jeans and all. It's truly refreshing. But don't expect to escape the edutainment. You'll be treated to spot quizzes ("Who can tell me what a baby goose is called?") and little known facts ("The pig is a very clean animal.") as the guide shepherds you from pen to pen. Thanks to this tour I now know that the gestation period of a pig is three months, three weeks, and three days.

Of course everyone's favorites are the farm babies; you can increase your odds of seeing them by visiting during spring or around harvest time. During October there is pumpkin picking, another winner with the wee set.

There's little in the way of food. At the General Store, sandwiches are about $3 and ice cream bars about half that. Soft drinks are available from vending machines. You can also bring a cooler and have a picnic. Judging from the number of tables provided, quite a few people do just that.

Remember to wear sensible shoes—this is a farm, after all, and after a rain, it can get muddy. The tour is long and covers a fair amount of ground. You can rent a "little red wagon" for $3 in which to lug the kids.

Nearby: Extreme Paintball Experience, Old Town, Osceola Environmental Study Center, Skate Reflections, Stallion 51, Warbird Adventures.

Jungle Adventures

26205 East Colonial Drive, Christmas 32709 ~ (407) 568-2885
www.jungleadventures.com

Admission:	Adults $21.95, children (3 to 11) $14.95, seniors (60+) $18.95, all plus tax; annual passes are $65.85, $56.85, and $44.85 respectively
Hours:	Daily 9:30 a.m. to 5:30 p.m.
Location:	On SR 50, about 17 miles east of Orlando

It's hard to miss Old Swampy. He's a 200-foot foam and cement alligator stretched smilingly alongside SR 50 on the way to the Space Coast. Step into (or more precisely, around) his jaws and you enter Jungle Adventures, a small attraction that has some things in common with Gatorland (see *Chapter 7*) but a few surprises of its own.

At its most basic, Jungle Adventures is a small zoo with a familiar cast of characters—black bears, some spider monkeys, some crocs, macaws and cockatoos, bobcats, wolves, and coatimundi. The zoo's most distinguished specimens are its hybrid panther-cougars. But mostly there are alligators. Jungle Adventures is part of a larger alligator farming operation. There are some 200 gators living in the 20-acre park but just a stone's throw away are 10,000 more being grown out for their skin and meat.

What sets Jungle Adventures apart, and makes a visit worth consideration, are its fascinating setting and its shows. The setting is in the midst of a swamp, with the main zoo across a bridge and completely surrounded by water fed from a sulfurous spring. At first it seems that there's something terribly wrong with the water; it's completely covered by what looks like a chartreuse slime. Actually, it's duckweed, a tiny four-leafed water plant that grows in the billions. It adds a marvelously primordial touch to the alligators that swim through it, coating their horny hides with gooey green. Two short **jungle nature trails** take you around the back of the animal cages and let you take a close look at the natural Florida setting from the safety of a boardwalk.

The shows at Jungle Adventures are refreshingly low key, one might almost say amateurish, although in the very best sense of the term. There are three shows and a boat ride that are timed so that you can move seamlessly from one to the next. A complete cycle takes about two and a half hours and there are four cycles each day.

The 15-minute **pontoon boat ride** circles the island zoo as gators swish through the duckweed, leaving a telltale trail on the water's surface. Along the way, your guide tells tales of Jungle Adventures' past and present, and its future plans. An eclectic **animal show** features a small alligator, which everyone gets a chance to hold while their picture is taken. Next comes a snake or two, draped languorously on the presenter's shoulders. And if you're really lucky, you'll get a chance to pet a cougar.

In the **Native American Village** tour, you will hear fascinating lore about the Calusa, Seminole, and Cherokee tribes and have the opportunity to buy Native American flutes, necklaces, and dream-catchers.

Finally, there is an **alligator feeding show** reminiscent of the *Jumparoo* at Gatorland. Sometimes, the gators are fed from a dock-like platform over the water, but from time to time the handler chooses to work the shore, drawing the enormous reptiles from the green waters to leap and snap just a few feet away from the audience.

A number of events like Dinner Adventures in the Jungle and various **"VIP" tours** are available at additional cost; check the website for details. On a more downbeat note, it must be said that Jungle Adventures is showing its age, with many signs of "deferred maintenance." I suspect this has more to do with budgetary restraints than willful neglect, but those who might be put off by this are hereby forewarned.

Nearby: Back To Nature Wildlife Refuge, Fort Christmas Historical Park, Orlando Wetlands Park.

Reptile World Serpentarium

5705 East Irlo Bronson Highway, St. Cloud 34771 ~ (407) 892-6905
www.reptileworldserpentarium.com

Admission:	Adults $6.75, students (6 to 17) $4.75, children (3 to 5) $3.75; prices include tax
Hours:	Tuesday to Sunday 9:00 a.m. to 5:30 p.m.
Location:	East of St. Cloud, about 9 miles east of Florida Turnpike Exit 244.

This unassuming cinder block and stucco building houses an impressive collection (over 50 species) of snakes from around the world, ranging from the familiar and innocuous to the exotic and deadly. Here you'll find the Australian taipan, considered by some to be the world's deadliest snake, as well as a splendid 18-foot king cobra. All told, there are six species of cobra and 11 kinds of rattlesnakes. There are also snakes you may never see elsewhere, like the brilliant pea green East African green mamba and its less startling but nonetheless beautiful West African cousin. The snakes are housed in modest glass-fronted pens along a darkened corridor. Snakes are the main course, but there are also a 14-foot gator sulking in a shallow, murky pool, a passel of iguanas, and a pond full of turtles.

If all Reptile World had to offer was its snake displays, it might be recommended only to the certified snake fancier. But this is a working venom farm (if that's the right term). Though there may be only 50 snakes on public display, behind the scenes are hundreds of venomous snakes just waiting to be milked for their valuable venom. Reptile World ships this precious commodity worldwide for use in medical and herpetological research. The regular milking of these dangerous snakes is done in public and makes Reptile World more than just another snake house.

Venom shows are scheduled at noon and 3:00 p.m. daily. Sometimes the shows start a bit late, but any wait will quickly be forgotten once the show starts. After bringing out a large snake for guests to hold, owner George Van Horn retreats behind a glass wall to take care of business. About half a dozen snakes are plucked from their boxes and coaxed into sinking their fangs through a clear membrane stretched over a collection glass. The glasses range in size from small test tubes used for coral snakes to hefty pilsner glasses used for large rattlers and cobras. The view can't be beat; you are just three feet away from these fanged wonders and will be thankful for the glass window between you and the snakes.

The entire show is fascinating but the large snakes are the most impressive. The Eastern diamondback rattlesnake, the largest of its kind, bares huge fangs and spits copious venom into the collection glass. The black and white spitting cobra requires special care. As its name suggests, it spits its venom into its victim's eyes and the recommended treatment is to wash the eyes with urine. The monocled cobra, so called because of the eye-like marking on the back of its head, emerges from its box with hood flaring and head darting rapidly about. This is serious, not to mention dangerous business. Van Horn once received a near-fatal bite from a king cobra while 30 school children looked on enthralled, convinced it was part of the show.

Reptile World is on the extreme outer fringe of the Orlando tourist circuit. For anyone who has ever been fascinated by snakes, it's well worth the detour. By all means time your visit to the venom shows.

Nearby: Antiquing in St. Cloud.

Chapter Seventeen:

Gardens & Edens

FOR THOSE WHO FEEL THE ORLANDO THEME PARK EXPERIENCE IS "SO PLASTIC!," help is at hand. Within the Orlando metropolitan area, or just a short ride away, are private gardens, public parks, and wilderness tracts where cool waters, fresh breezes, and quiet forests await to soothe the simulation- and stimulation-weary tourist.

Here I describe the Harry P. Leu Gardens, right in the heart of Orlando, and the spectacular Bok Tower Gardens in Lake Wales, a short drive from Orlando. Of course, these attractions involve the cunning hand of man and are, in a way, just as artificial as any theme park—although some would argue they are a good deal more beautiful.

Then there are the state, county, and city parks, many of which have been only slightly modified by humans. It comes as a surprise to many visitors that the "real Florida" (to use a phrase pushed by the state's public relations campaigns) lies all around them. Just a short drive from your motel, you can hike miles and miles of pristine trails and never see another human, or swim in a crystal clear spring bubbling up from deep in the earth, or canoe down a river that still looks much as it did when the first Europeans arrived in this part of Florida.

This is nature, let us not forget, so in addition to sunscreen, a good bug repellent will come in handy for hikers. Be aware too that deer ticks carrying Lyme disease are found here. Common-sense precautions should be used with wildlife—don't pick anything up and don't feed the alligators (it's against the law!). The words to live by when visiting these beautiful areas are: "Take nothing but pictures, kill nothing but time, leave nothing but footprints."

The parks listed here are just the beginning. If this type of unspoiled recreation is to your taste, you may want to venture farther afield—to Blue Springs State Park to the north, where manatees come to warm up in the winter, or to Homosassa Springs State Park to the west, or to Lake Kissimmee State Park to the south. An excellent guide to Florida's state parks is available at www.FloridaStateParks.org. For more on Orlando's city parks, go to www.cityoforlando.net/fpr/Html/Parks/index.htm.

Bok Tower Gardens

1151 Tower Boulevard, Lake Wales 33853 ~ (863) 676-1408
www.boktowergardens.org

Admission:	Adults $12, children (5 to 12) $3
Hours:	Daily 8:00 a.m. to 6:00 p.m. (last admission at 5:00 p.m.)
Location:	Off Burns Avenue in Lake Wales. Take US 27 South to Mountain Lake Cutoff and follow the signs

Once upon a time, before the age of Kim Kardashian and Donald Trump, the wealthy knew how to spend their money. One such individual was Edward W. Bok, a Dutch immigrant born in 1863 who came to the United States at the age of 6 and made his fortune as a writer and magazine publisher. In the twenties, after his retirement, he set out to create an Eden on an unprepossessing patch of land whose only claim to fame was that it was reputedly the highest point on the Florida peninsula. He enlisted Frederick Law Olmstead, Jr. (son of the creator of New York's Central Park and a major landscape architect in his own right) to do the landscaping and hired noted architect Milton B. Medary to build a setting for a very special musical instrument. In 1929, he presented the result as a gift to the American people. The "result" is the Bok Tower and its magnificent carillon that stands majestically in the midst of an artfully designed wooded park, specifically conceived as a refuge from the bustle of "the world."

Bok Tower Gardens, now a National Historic Landmark, is a very special and a very quiet experience. Unlike nearby Legoland's Cypress Gardens, where the landscaping is over-the-top and in-your-face, the effect here is far more subtle, almost ethereal. The bark-chip covered paths through the woods are meant for leisurely strolls and quiet moments alone with one's thoughts. The vistas, powerful as they are, are contemplative and softly romantic.

Olmstead's design is devilishly clever in the way he leads you to the tower. Your first glimpse is across a reflecting pool, framed by palm fronds and Spanish moss. Then it vanishes as you approach more closely. Suddenly, the tower rises above you, standing on an island barely larger than its base, surrounded by a moat crossed by marble bridges and guarded by massive wrought iron gates. It's as if you have come upon a magical remnant of an ancient city in a storybook land, part cathedral, part castle keep.

The storybook aspect is heightened by the pink and gray Georgia marble that forms the tower's base and accents its flanks, the odd and complex sundial mounted on the side of the south wall, the highly polished brass door on the north, the mysterious red door behind the ornately carved balustrade above the sundial, by the very fact that you cannot cross the moat for a closer look. It must be a wondrous experience on a foggy morning.

The tower was never intended to welcome guests; the only way to get a look inside is to see the orientation film screened at the **Visitors Center** on a regular schedule. The tower exists solely to house the 60 precisely tuned bronze bells operated by a massive keyboard played with the fists. The carillon occupies the upper third of the structure. The unique sound produced by this massive instrument rolls out across the surrounding woods through 35-foot-high grilles in the form of Art Deco mosaics of drooping trees and animals in colorful shades of turquoise and purple.

Every afternoon at 1:00 and 3:00 there is a 45-minute **carillon recital**. Many of the pieces played were composed specifically for carillon, others have been adapted to the unique requirements of the massive instrument. A schedule of "Daily Carillon Music" lists the day's program, everything from old folk tunes to opera. It's a wonderful experience on a warm, sunny day and, unless you're a carillon connoisseur, probably unlike any other concert you've ever heard. When the performance is live (rather than recorded), a video monitor mounted in what appears to be a small green shelter lets you watch the carillonneur play.

Tip: Most people sit on the grass or on benches under the shady oak trees near the tower's base during the recitals. You will have a better musical experience if you move somewhat farther away. Stroll down the slope away from the tower until the tower's mosaic grilles reappear over the tops of the oak trees. Then find a spot with an unobstructed view of the top of the tower. This way, the music will roll over the treetops and cascade down the slope toward you.

Don't leave without exploring the rest of the grounds. Past the reflecting pool that marked your approach to the tower lies an "exedra," a semicircular marble bench that looks out from the top of Iron Mountain to the west. At the northern edge of the grounds is a more recent, and ingenious, addition, the **Window By The Pond Nature Observatory**. It's a small wooden building on the lip of a pond. You sit behind a large picture window, unseen by the wildlife outside. A sign notes that this is nature's show and that the performance schedule is erratic. On the back wall are drawings of the local animals you might glimpse from your hiding place.

From here you can take a one-mile hike through the **Pine Ridge Preserve**, one of the few remaining fragments of the sort of longleaf pine forest that once covered millions of acres of the southeastern United States. Preserving this patch of woods is not as easy as it may sound. A carefully orchestrated series of controlled burns is used to mimic ageless natural processes. Otherwise, evergreen oaks would invade the habitat and eventually kill the pines with their shady branches. An informative brochure that explicates the habitat can be found at the trailhead.

The **Visitors Center** houses a modest but finely executed exhibit that provides background on Bok, the tower, and the carillon it houses. The cafeteria-style **Blue Palmetto Cafe** serves simple sandwich platters, salads, and hot dogs. There is also a tasteful gift shop where you can get cassettes and CDs of Bok Tower carillon recitals. It carries a good selection of books about gardening, wildlife, conservation, and Florida's natural wonders. Framed photos and posters of the gardens make nice souvenirs.

In 1970, the Bok Tower Gardens Foundation acquired the nearby **Pinewood Estate**, formerly known as "El Retiro," a palatial summer home built for a steel mogul. Although it dates to only 1929, it has the look of a much older Mediterranean villa and has been meticulously restored inside. Both the house and the grounds were designed by architects associated with the Olmstead firm. Tours are by appointment.

The estate is open to self-guided tours Monday to Saturday noon to 4:00 p.m., and Sunday 1:00 p.m. to 4:00 p.m. General gardens admission is required, a combo ticket including Pinewood admission is $18 for adults, $8 for children 5 to 12. From Thanksgiving to Christmas, the house is decorated for the holidays. To check the tour schedule (always a good idea) and make reservations, call (863) 676-1408.

The Gardens are accessible to the physically challenged. They offer a limited number of free strollers and mobility vehicles for a fee, on a first-come, first-served basis.

Nearby: Legoland, Florida Skydiving Center, Lake Wales Arts Center, Spook Hill.

Enchanted Forest Sanctuary

444 Columbia Boulevard, Titusville 32780 ~ (321) 264-5185
nbbd.com/godo/ef

Admission:	**Free**
Hours:	Daily 9:00 a.m. to 5:00 p.m.
Location:	From I-95 Exit 215 east on SR 405 for 3.7 miles

The Environmentally Endangered Lands Program of Brevard County has created this picture perfect learning vehicle to teach people about the unique and subtle topography of coastal Florida. There are attempts to do this in other parks around the region, but none that I've seen do it as well as the Enchanted Forest.

Some 3.7 miles of self-guided trails through a portion of this 393-acre preserve take the visitor through six distinct environments, from scruffy, sandy scrub ridges to lush tropical forests that seem, well, enchanted. You can use the laminated trail guides to educate yourself to what you're seeing or just use the beautifully maintained trails for rest, relaxation, or exercise. A small interpretive center offers well-designed exhibits that further explain the surprising way in which a few feet of elevation in the Florida ecosystem can mean a startlingly different plant environment. There's also a gift shop.

Nearby: Astronaut Hall of Fame, Police Hall of Fame, Kennedy Space Center, Warbird Air Museum.

Forever Florida EcoSafaris and Crescent J Ranch

4755 North Kenansville Road, St. Cloud, FL 34773 ~ (866) 854-3837, (407) 957-9794
www.floridaecosafaris.com

Admission:	**Free** admission and parking; there is a charge for most activities
Hours:	Varies, Visitor Center opens daily at 9:00 a.m.
Location:	Take US 192 east from Kissimmee for about 24 miles to Holopaw; turn south on US 441 for about 7 miles to the entrance on your left. (The address given above is the corporate office.)

Did you know that wild hogs kill more people than any other wild animal? Did you know that red carpet lichen grows only where the air is especially pure? Did you know that the berries of poison ivy plants are the sole source of vitamin C for the animals of Florida's forests? These are just a few of the facts you'll learn as you explore a patch of the "real Florida" that is as much a family affair as it is a tourist attraction.

Forever Florida, which also calls itself Florida EcoSafaris, was founded by Dr. Bill Broussard as a living monument to his son Allen, a devoted ecologist who died well before his time. The attraction combines Dr. Broussard's ranch (he's a tenth generation rancher as well as an ophthalmologist) with a swampy wilderness tract next door that had been sold in parcels as part of a classic Florida land scam back in the sixties. It was in these woods, that young Allen fell in love with Nature and found his vocation.

You begin your visit to Forever Florida at the **Visitor Center**, which contains a gift shop and restaurant. Near the Visitor Center are a free **petting zoo and pony rides** ($8 by reservation). But the real attraction here is access to the nearby wilderness, much of which has remained untouched by the hand of man, despite the fact that this part of Florida was a thriving logging center in the nineteenth century.

You can reach the wilds in a number of ways: by foot, on horseback, or on a wacky-looking green "Swamp Buggy" designed by Dr. Broussard and unique to Forever Florida. Most people choose the last alternative.

Your tour vehicle is a 32-seat open-sided coach raised well above the ground on large tractor tires. The bucket seats are comfortable and the tour guides extremely knowledgeable experts, many with degrees in biology or ecology.

There are tours at 10:00 a.m. and 1:00 p.m. On the tour I took, we sighted white-tailed deer, armadillos, gators, wild turkey, and gopher tortoises. We even sighted some of those elusive wild hogs, albeit in hog traps. One lucky tour group sighted the Florida panther that roams this preserve. There are fewer than 150 left in the wild, so don't count on seeing one on your visit. Photographers should make sure to bring along their best telephoto lenses.

The highlight of the tour is the narration by your guide. These folks love this scruffy patch of Florida wilderness and it shows. They mix an in-depth knowledge of the local ecology with a passion for its preservation. You will leave this tour knowing why you should never buy cypress mulch for your garden and why wild hogs (descended from those abandoned by the Spaniards when they discovered there was no gold in Florida) should be removed from the Florida ecosystem. In fact, you will see ample evidence of the damage the preserve's estimated 800 hogs inflict on the local ecology. Those trapped hogs, by the way, are fattened up on yummy farm feed and then relocated elsewhere or given away to local groups for barbecues.

The **motorized tours** cost $32 ($24 for children 6 to 12; kids under 6 are **free**) and last about two hours. The **guided horseback tours** are offered daily, by reservation only, and cost $60 for 1½ hours. A half-day "Rawhide Roundup" tour is $99, and a 2-day overnight "horseback safari" is $199 (four-person minimum). There is no reduced price for children (age 10 and up only) on these tours.

In 2009, Forever Florida jumped on the Zip-line bandwagon by building **Zipline Safari**, one of the area's largest and best examples. Their network of cables is strung above the treetops, up to 68 feet above the ground, and overlooks rich foliage and fauna—including wild panthers and alligators! The seven zip-segments and two "sky bridges" require tremendous nerve (and about 2½ hours) to navigate. I found it an unforgettably invigorating experience, but acrophobics are urged to avoid it. The cost is $85 for everyone over age 10; all participants must be between 70 and 275 pounds. Discounts are available if you also purchase a tour. If you want a similar high-flying perspective without the speedy sliding, the **Cypress Canopy Cycle** ($45, ages 10 and older) lets you hang in a tubular recliner at 25 feet above ground and leisurely pedal along a one-hour arboreal circuit.

The **Cypress Restaurant** offers a straightforward menu of country-style cooking, with grilled chicken, ham, and turkey sandwiches, and a daily BBQ special. It's open 11:00 a.m. to 3:00 p.m. daily and until 4:00 p.m. on Saturday and Sunday. The gift shop sells clothing, some interesting crafts, and books on Florida ecology and cooking.

Forever Florida offers an evolving menu of special events and programs. Typically, when a special event is on, there will be a modest parking charge. Call ahead or check the website to see what's going to be on during your visit.

Kelly Park, Rock Springs

400 East Kelly Park Road, Apopka 32712 ~ (407) 889-4179
apps.ocfl.net/dept/CEsrvcs/Parks/ParkDetails.asp?ParkID=22

Admission: $3 per vehicle for 1 or 2 people; $5 per vehicle for 3 to 8 people; and $1 for additional person/walk-ins/motorcycles/bikes.

Hours: Daily 8:00 a.m. to 8:00 p.m. in summer; 8:00 a.m. to 6:00 p.m. in winter

Location: Take Rock Springs Road north from Apopka; right onto Kelly Park Road and follow signs.

This 248-acre Orange County park is built around one of the Apopka area's crystal clear springs. As its name suggests, Rock Springs bubbles up from a cleft in a rock outcropping and, instead of spreading out into a pool, becomes a swiftly running stream that quickly slows to a meander. The activity of choice here, and the major reason for the park's obvious popularity, is riding down the stream in an inner tube or on a float.

Kids, and not a few grown-ups, jump into the headwaters by the dozens and bob and splash their way downstream for about a mile. The trip takes about 25 minutes at a leisurely float. There are exits from the river along the way, and a nicely maintained network of boardwalks (with flooring designed to protect the barefooted) lets you carry your tube back to the beginning for another go. You can also go down without a tube but, for most adults at least, the stream is too shallow for swimming during most of its course. At the middle of the tubing course, the stream blossoms into a series of lagoons and pools that form the centerpiece of the park. This is the place to come for a cooling, if somewhat crowded, swim. Or join the sunbathers thronging the shores and islands. This is a great park for kids and, if you don't have any, you may feel a bit overwhelmed by other people's.

Tubes are not available in the park, so unless you bring your own, stop at one of the tube rental shops near the park entrance. The cost is modest, about $5 for a day's rental. Most of the rest of the park is given over to nicely shaded picnic tables, most with a barbecue nearby. The park also offers camping sites ($18 a night for Orange County residents, $23 for all others). Your admission receipt lets you leave the park and return the same day. No pets are allowed in the park, and there's no fishing here.

Nearby: C.A.R.E., Central Florida Zoological Park, King's Landing Canoe Rental, Rock Springs Run State Reserve, Wekiwa Springs State Park.

Leu Gardens

1920 North Forest Avenue, Orlando, 32803 ~ (407) 246-2620
www.leugardens.org

Admission:	Adults $7, children (grades K–12) $2
Hours:	Daily 9:00 a.m. to 5:00 p.m. Closed Christmas day.
Location:	Take I-4 Exit 85 (Princeton Street), go east to Mills (US 17-92) and turn right. Turn left on Virginia Drive and follow signs.

Strolling through Harry P. Leu's magnificent formal gardens on the shores of Lake Rowena, it's hard to believe that you're in the heart of the city, just a short drive from the "Centroplex" as Orlando rather inelegantly refers to its central business district. There's nothing inelegant about this luxurious estate, however. Deeded to the city by a local industrial supplies magnate and amateur botanist, the 50 acres of manicured grounds and artfully designed gardens offer a delicious respite from the cares of the world.

Camellias were Harry Leu's first love and the place is full of them—over 2,000, making this the largest documented collection of camellias in North America. But there are many other trees, flowers, and ornamental plants to catch the fancy of amateur gardeners, who will appreciate the meticulous signage that provides the full scientific name for the thousands of species represented. They can also flag down a passing staff member, who will be more than happy to answer their questions. The rest of us will simply enjoy strolling through this artfully constructed monument to the gardener's art, stopping now and then to smell the roses.

The estate is given over to a number of gardens that blend seamlessly one into another. Camellias bloom under tall Southern oaks dripping with Spanish moss in the North and South woods, while the palm garden allows botanists to test the hardiness of various species during the nippy Central Florida winters. In the center is a formal rose garden that is at its best from April through October. The Tropical Stream Garden features tropical vines and plants that are native to or can be grown in Florida. By the lake, the Native Wetland Garden is home to swamp hibiscus, lizard's tail, loblolly, and dwarf wax myrtle, all under the shade of stately cypress trees.

Another not-to-be-missed highlight is the 50-foot floral clock. The mechanism was purchased in Scotland and now sits on an intricately planted sloping hill at the foot of a formal garden. Later, a stroll down to the lake takes you past the Ravine Garden, lush with tropical plants. At the water's edge a spacious wooden terrace offers a peaceful spot to sit and admire the wading birds. Benches and a gazebo encourage you to sit and stay awhile. Your patience may be rewarded with a glimpse of Lake Rowena's resident 8-foot alligator.

Every half hour from 10:00 a.m. to 3:30 p.m., except in July when it is closed, volunteers conduct tours through the **Leu house**. Don't miss it. You'll be treated to a wonderfully gossipy recounting of the building's evolution, through several changes of ownership, from humble farm house to rich man's estate, spiced with tales of a sheriff gunned down in the line of duty and a home-wrecking New York actress. (That's her as Cleopatra in the photo in the living room.) Nearby is a cemetery in which the unfortunate lawman lies buried with many of his kin.

The antebellum-style **Garden House**, where you pay your modest admission to the gardens, houses a 900-volume horticultural library (open to visitors) and spacious meeting rooms. The terrace at the back of the building offers a stunning view of the lake. There are frequent arts and crafts exhibits in the Garden House, as well as a regular schedule of musical events. Limited wheelchairs are available free of charge. Pets are not allowed in either the gardens or the houses.

Nearby: Mennello Museum of Folk Art, Orlando Fire Museum, Orlando Museum of Art, Orlando Science Center.

Little Econ Greenway

2451 North Dean Road, Orlando 32817 ~ (407) 254-9030
apps.ocfl.net/images/Maps/LilEconMap.pdf

Admission:	**Free**
Hours:	Daily sunrise to sunset
Location:	Off East Colonial Drive, approximately 10 miles east of I-4 Exit 84

7.4 miles of paved path wind alongside the Little Econlockhatchee River offering a smooth ride for cyclists, skaters, and hikers alike. Ospreys and red-tailed hawks, as well as alligators can be sighted here and a special garden has been planted to attract butterflies. You can enter the trail at Forsyth Road just north of Colonial Drive on the west and hike to Jay Blanchard Park, where a YMCA branch offers a smoothies bar to slake your thirst. Tell them you'd like to be a guest and they will give you a day's free access to their well-equipped gym and outdoor pool. The eastern terminus of the trail is currently at Alafaya Trail, near University High School. Plans are on the boards to extend the trail eastward to the University of Central Florida, creating a ten-mile path that will link with other extensive trail networks.

Nearby: UCF Arboretum.

Mackinson Island County Park

In Lake Tohopekaliga, Kissimmee ~ (407) 742-7800
www.osceola.org/parks/160-3272-0/makinson_island.cfm

If you really want to get away from the madding crowd, you'd be hard pressed to find a better spot than Mackinson Island, just a stone's throw from downtown Kissimmee and yet a world away. First of all, it really is an island and it can only be reached by boat. Second, there's pretty much nothing there except for some wild hogs, feral goats, deer, armadillos, and lots of silence. At 132 acres, it's big enough to provide a marvelous sense of isolation, which is what its former inhabitants, the Seminole Indians, were looking for when European settlers started getting too close for comfort. Since those days, the island has played a number of roles, as a farming and cattle operation, an asylum for alcoholics, and most recently as an exotic animal attraction. Today, under the guidance of the Osceola County Parks Department it has reverted pretty much to its primeval state, although it may take some time for vegetation to completely reclaim it.

There are primitive camps sites here (groups only, permit required), a picnic pavilion with cookout pits, and (mercifully) restrooms. There is also a well-developed network of hiking trails. If you are not towing your own boat on vacation, you can take a tour offered by some of the Kissimmee boat-ride purveyors listed in *Chapter 19*. One of them, Kissimmee Outdoor Adventures, offers ferry service for $20 a person, which should appeal to campers.

Nearby: Not a thing.

Merritt Island National Wildlife Refuge

State Route 402, east of Titusville ~ (321) 861-0667
www.fws.gov/merrittisland/

Admission:	**Free**
Hours:	Monday to Friday 8:00 a.m. to 4:30 p.m.;
	Saturday and Sunday 9:00 a.m. to 5:00 p.m.
Location:	Just east of Titusville on SR 406; from I-95, take
	Exit 229

Hard by Kennedy Space Center, surrounding it in fact, are 140,000 acres of pristine Florida coastal wilderness, home to some 500 species of wildlife, including 21 on various endangered and threatened species lists. With the possible exception of the West Indian manatee, the stars of the show here are the 311 species of birds that either make the Refuge their home or pass through en route to other climes. As a result, the Refuge is one of the prime birding spots in the Southeast and a must-see attraction for anyone with even a modest interest in bird watching. From the majestic American bald eagle, to the colorful Florida scrub jay, to the many varieties of ducks and wading birds that frequent the salt marshes, a visit here will provide ample opportunities to add to your list of species spotted. In between birds, be on the lookout for alligators cruising through the shallows, and if you're really lucky you might catch a glimpse of an elusive bobcat bounding across the road.

The aforementioned manatees gather at the Haulover Canal linking the Indian River with Mosquito Lagoon. They appear with such regularity at a certain spot that the Park Service has erected a **Manatee Observation Deck** to give visitors a better look. A stop here makes a perfect counterpoint to the manatee exhibit over at Sea-World.

The **Black Point Wildlife Drive** ($5 per car, $15 annual pass), a self-guided driving tour of the Refuge's natural marshes and man-made impoundments, is a popular diversion. Maps and recorded guides are available at the Visitors Center. About half way through, you can park and set off on the five-mile **Cruickshank Trail** for a closer look at this magnet for migratory birds.

The adjacent **Canaveral National Seashore** ($5 per vehicle charge) offers miles of pristine beaches along the Atlantic. You can spend a very full day or two exploring the rich variety of a landscape that has changed little since the days of Ponce de Leon.

Tip: If you are angling to go fishing at the Refuge, get a free permit from a kiosk near the entrance; otherwise you may find yourself slapped with a $125 fine.

Nearby: Kennedy Space Center.

Orlando Wetlands Park

25155 Wheeler Road, Christmas 32709 ~ (407) 568-1706
www.cityoforlando.net/wetlands/

Admission:	**Free**
Hours:	Daily, February 1 to November 14 only, sunrise to sunset
Location:	East on SR 50, then left on CR 420 (Ft. Christmas Road); go 2.3 miles and turn right onto Wheeler Road

Tucked away on the far eastern fringes of Orlando is an ingenious combination of the practical and the aesthetic. To the untrained eye, the "Iron Bridge Easterly Wetlands" that comprise this park look like a preserved sliver of the "real" Florida. It is, in fact, part of the City of Orlando's wastewater treatment system. Every day, 16 million gallons of highly treated reclaimed wastewater from parts of Orange and Seminole counties are pumped into this 1,650-acre, man-made wetlands where aquatic plants continue the process of removing nutrients as the water slowly makes its way to the St. John's River. If visions of open sewers spring to mind, banish them. The result is enchanting, combining open fields, gently rolling woods, a small lake, and a thick forest.

In the parking area, go to the wooden announcement board. There you can sign in (don't forget to sign out!) and pick up a park map and a *Field Checklist of Birds.* The best way to get acquainted with the park is to walk (or jog) the four-mile "walk/jog loop." If you'd like, you can veer off onto a more primitive hiking trail through the woods; it eventually rejoins the main trail. The map thoughtfully points out the best bird-watching spots along the park's 20 miles of raised roads. More than 150 species frequent the park. The *Checklist* lists them and the seasons in which they visit and notes whether they are common, uncommon, or rare.

Biking is permitted on the berm roads and there is a sheltered picnic area in a broad grassy area near the parking lot. The Florida Trail skirts the property, allowing serious hikers to extend their explorations. The Orlando Wetlands Park is a bit out of the way (it is about a 40-minute drive east of the city), but a visit will reward ardent bird-watchers and those looking for a more exciting jogging trail than the motel parking lot.

Nearby: Fort Christmas Historical Park, Jungle Adventures, Tosohatchee Wildlife Management Area.

Osceola Schools Environmental Study Center

4300 Poinciana Boulevard, Kissimmee 34758 ~ (407) 870-0551

Admission:	**Free**
Hours:	Saturday 10:00 a.m. to 5:00 p.m., Sunday noon to 5:00 p.m.
Location:	13 miles south of Highway 192

During the week, this 19-acre patch of Reedy Creek Swamp serves as an educational resource for the school children of Osceola County. On weekends, it's open to the public and well worth a visit from the wildlife-loving tourist. In the winter and spring, you might even be able to spot a nesting bald eagle.

Begin at the Visitors Center, which houses one of the best introductions and reference guides to Central Florida wildlife you are likely to find. If you've spotted some critter that you can't identify, you'll probably find it here. Most impressive are the taxidermy of birds like the bald eagle and osprey. There are also stuffed panthers and black bears. Most of these specimens were killed accidentally, typically by an automobile. Now they help teach school kids. These three-dimensional examples are supplemented by quite lovely color photographs of the native species taken right here at the Study Center. On another wall are photos of the local flora. Add to this charts of bird silhouettes and animal tracks and you have a remarkably complete resource for enjoying the Florida wilderness. Pick up a free copy of *The Reedy Creek Swamp Nature Guide* and the trail guides to guide the rest of your visit.

There are three short trails to explore. An 1,800-foot raised walkway takes you into Reedy Creek Swamp and its 400-year-old cypress trees. At the end, an observation platform lets you eavesdrop on the osprey nests. The short Pine Woods Trail features a reconstruction of the portable logging railroads that once ferried felled trees out of the swamp. The rails were made by Krupp, the famous German industrial giant. Another trail leads to a modest Indian mound formed by snail shells discarded by the aboriginal inhabitants. A small picnic area is available.

Nearby: Green Meadows Farm, Old Town.

Rock Springs Run State Reserve

31799 County Road 433, Apopka 32712 ~ (407) 884–2008
www.floridastateparks.org/rockspringsrun/

Admission:	$3 per vehicle (up to 8 people); $2 for walk-ins and bicyclists
Hours:	Daily 8:00 a.m. to 6:00 p.m.
Location:	From I-4 Exit 101C, take SR 46 West about 7 miles; turn left onto route 433

This sprawling park is bounded by Rock Springs Run and the Wekiva River, which might suggest that water activities abound. Not so. There is no water access and a sign at the gate directs you to nearby resorts and parks if that's what you have in mind.

What the Reserve has to offer, in abundance, is solitude and well-maintained hiking trails that meander through 8,750 acres of the kind of terrain that's referred to as "Florida's Desert." Depending on how far you trek, you'll see sand pine scrub, pine flatwoods, bayheads, hammocks, and a few swamps. If you're lucky, you may glimpse a black bear. If you do, report the sighting by calling (407) 884–2008.

There is one "primitive" camping site in the Reserve for those hardy enough to backpack to the far side of the park. Or you can ride your horse there. The camping fee is $5 per person (adult or child) plus tax per night. If riding is your cup of tea, the Rock Springs Run Riding Stables has horses for hire. (See *Chapter 15: Do It!*)

Nearby: C.A.R.E. Foundation, Central Florida Zoo, Kelly Park, King's Landing Canoe Rental, Wekiva Falls Resort, Wekiwa Springs State Park.

Showcase of Citrus Eco Tours

5010 Highway 27, Clermont 34711 ~ (352) 267-2597

www.showcaseofcitrus.com/eco-tour/

Admission:	Adults $20, children (4 to 12) $10, $80 minimum per trip
Hours:	By appointment
Location:	Take US 192 or I-4 west to US 27, then drive north; Showcase of Citrus is on your right.

The main business of Showcase of Citrus is selling oranges and other citrus products, but as a sideline they operate one-hour "eco tours" through the groves and surrounding woods and marshes. The tour uses an open, but shaded, black and yellow striped "Monster Truck" with enormous wheels that lift it high and dry above the swampy terrain. The palmetto, oak, and pine scrub habitats here offer shelter to a variety of wildlife and the swamps feature the ever-present alligators.

Nearby: Citrus Tower, Lakeridge Winery, Presidents Hall of Fame.

Sylvan Lake Park

845 Lake Markham Road, Sanford 32771 ~ (407) 665-2180

www.seminolecountyfl.gov/parksrec/sylvan/SylvanLakePark.aspx

Admission:	**Free**
Hours:	Monday to Friday 8:00 a.m. to 10:00 p.m., Saturday to Sunday 8:00 a.m. to 8:00 p.m. Closed Thanksgiving and Christmas.
Location:	From I-4 Exit 101A, drive west on SR 46 3.2 miles, turn left onto Lake Markham Road. Park is less than a mile on left.

This Seminole County park offers cut-rate tennis and racquetball, along with four soccer fields. Tennis courts are $4 an hour before 5:00 p.m. and $6 per hour thereafter; racquetball courts are $6 an hour at all times; soccer fields go for $16 an hour before 5:00 p.m. and $23 per hour thereafter. Use of the facilities is open to all, even to tourists, but you must call for reservations.

Otherwise, the park offers picnicking, a jogging trail, and an intricate network of boardwalks that take you through the woods and across the swampy fringes of Sylvan Lake, where you can sit in a spacious gazebo and bird-watch or just while away the time. A small dock offers fishing or a place to launch your own canoe or other non-motorized boat.

Tibet-Butler Preserve

8777 State Road 535, Orlando 32836 ~ (407) 876-6696

www.sfwmd.gov/portal/page/portal/pg_grp_sfwmd_landresources/pg_sfwmd_lan-dresources_recopps_ul_tbpa

Admission:	**Free**
Hours:	Wednesday to Sunday 8:00 a.m. to 6:00 p.m.
Location:	About five miles north of I-4 Exit 68

Just a stone's throw from Walt Disney World and SeaWorld, amid the gated communities of Orlando's burgeoning southwest district, lies this 440-acre patch of Florida wilderness. The spiffy Vera Carter Environmental Center building, with its state-of-the-art interpretive displays, is the kickoff point for four miles of beautifully maintained trails and boardwalks that meander through bay swamps, marshes, cypress swamps, pine flatlands, and Florida scrub. The park borders the Tibet-Butler chain of lakes from which it takes its name, but you can't get down to the water. You can get close, though, on a lovely pavilion at the end of Osprey Overlook Trail. This is a great spot for bird-watching and an excellent place to escape the bustle of tourist Orlando. The Preserve is home to bobcats and foxes, although it is unlikely you'll spot any of these elusive creatures. Special programs and guided nature hikes are offered from time to time. Call for details.

Nearby: SeaWorld, Discovery Cove.

Tosohatchee Wildlife Management Area

3365 Taylor Creek Road, Christmas, 32709 ~ (407) 568-5893
myfwc.com/viewing/recreation/wmas/lead/tosohatchee

Admission:	$3 per person, $6 per vehicle (up to 8 people)
Hours:	Daily 8:00 a.m. to sunset
Location:	3 miles south of SR 50 in Christmas

If you really want to get away from it all, this mammoth (28,000-acre) wilderness area is an excellent choice. I visited one Wednesday afternoon and was the only person there. The park borders 19 miles of the St. John's River and includes wetlands, pine flatwoods, and hammocks. The name is a contraction of Tootoosahatchee, an Indian word for "chicken creek," and the eponymous stream flows through the northern portion of the reserve.

Hiking, biking, and horseback riding are the activities of choice here. If you want the purest experience of this enchanting and sometimes spooky ecosystem stick to the primitive Florida Trail, marked with white (or sometimes blue) blazes. The trails marked with rectangular or diamond-shaped orange blazes allow bikes and horses (bring your own horse; there are none for hire here). Walking softly and quietly will increase your chance of spotting wildlife. There are white-tailed deer, bobcat, gray fox, and several varieties of raptors to be seen here. The Florida panther is said to put in a rare appearance. More likely, you will flush large vultures or hawks as you proceed through the semi-gloom of the forest past tea-dark streams and pools, their still surfaces like obsidian mirrors.

If a casual visit is not enough, why not spend a few days? The camping here is "primitive," that is no recreational vehicles or pop-up tent trailers are allowed. Most of the campsites have nearby parking areas but for the truly adventuresome, there are two backpacking campsites, one of them seven miles from the nearest road. Campers must make reservations by phone at least two weeks (but no more than 60 days) in advance. There is a fee of $4.50 per person per night (all ages). The regular admission fee is waived for campers.

When you arrive, sign in and pay your vehicle fee (envelopes are provided). You must also sign out to let the park caretaker know that you are not lying wounded in some far flung corner of the wilderness. Also, be aware that hunting is allowed in this park. The deer season runs from early October to about Thanksgiving. The wild hog (yes, wild hog) season is in January and February, and wild turkey have their turn in March and April. All of these hunting seasons have gaps, that is, periods of three days to two weeks when hunting is not allowed. Hikers are advised to steer clear of the woods when hunting is allowed; call to check the schedule, which is also posted at the sign-in area. If you want to hunt, you have to get a special permit from the state even if you are a local resident.

Nearby: Fort Christmas Historical Park, Jungle Adventures, Orlando Wetlands Park.

Turkey Lake Park

3401 Hiawassee Road, Orlando 32835 ~ (407) 246-4486, (407) 246-1298
www.cityoforlando.net/fpr/Html/Parks/BillFrederick.htm

Admission:	$4 per car ($2 if it's just the driver)
Hours:	Daily 8:00 a.m. to 5:00 p.m. November to March; 8:00 a.m. to 7:00 p.m. April to October
Location:	From I-4 Exit 75 take Kirkman north, turn left onto Conroy then right onto Hiawassee to park entrance, about 4 miles total.

Just a stone's throw from the hurly-burly of Universal Orlando, the city of Orlando has created a 300-acre oasis along the shores of Turkey Lake. Officially called the Bill Frederick Park at Turkey Lake, this beautifully landscaped and maintained park offers picnicking, hiking along seven miles of nature trails, biking along a three-mile bike path, and a number of other diversions. The picnic areas are close to the lake with beautiful shaded tables and "picnic pavilions" (additional charge). There are nearby kiddie play areas and sandy "beaches" but no lake swimming. Instead there is a large pool overlooking the lovely lake. A fishing pier lets you test your angling skills against largemouth bass and other species. If you prefer to fish from a boat, you can rent one ($23.42 for 4 hours) Thursday through Sunday from 7:00 a.m. to 11:00 a.m. Call (407) 299-1248 to make a reservation.

Across the park, an "all children's" playground offers an enormous wood and car-tire wonderland that will offer little ones hours of exploration and fun. Shaded gazebos nearby keep Mom and Dad out of the sun. No eating here, however, as food draws rats and other not-so-welcome wildlife. Next door is a "Cracker" farm featuring an authentic 100-year-old barn, to give kids an idea of what pioneer Florida looked and felt like.

There's camping here, too. Cabins that sleep up to 10 are available for $47.95 per night. "Family" camp sites for trailers and RVs are $19 per night including electricity and water. If you need a sewer hookup as well, the price is $23. The area is beautifully shaded, with picnic tables and barbecue pits. A "primitive" camping area nearby is less shady, but at $10 per four-person tent, the price may be right. If you want to camp you will have to make reservations.

Nearby: Universal Orlando.

University of Central Florida Arboretum
4000 Central Florida Boulevard, Orlando 32816-2368 ~ (407) 823-2761
www.arboretum.ucf.edu

Admission:	**Free**
Hours:	Daily from sunrise to sunset
Location:	On the UCF campus in east Orlando; ask at the campus information booth for directions

The University of Central Florida has a quite extensive "collection" of trees and other flora, and it is displayed in this tranquil oasis in the midst of its ultramodern campus on the eastern fringes of Orlando. The emphasis is on Florida species but the collection ranges far and wide. A maze of nature trails takes the visitor through a number of plant "communities," including oak hammock, cabbage palm, and pond pine. Informative signage identifies individual species and, when appropriate, gives tips to gardeners. There is also a "community garden" where local volunteers grow food. Best of all, secluded tables and benches, some with thatched shelters offer quiet spots for contemplation or study.

Nearby: Little Econ Greenway.

Wekiwa Springs State Park
1800 Wekiwa Circle, Apopka 32712 ~ (407) 884-2008
www.floridastateparks.org/wekiwasprings/

Admission:	$6 per vehicle (maximum of 8 people); single occupant vehicles $4; pedestrians, bicyclists $2
Hours:	Daily 8:00 a.m. to sunset
Location:	From I-4 Exit 94 take route 434 West to Wekiva Springs Road, then about 3 miles to the park entrance.

This gem of a park boasts what must be the most beautiful spot to take a swim in all of Central Florida. The spring that gives the park its name bubbles up at the base of an amphitheater of greensward, forming a crystal clear circular pool of pure delight. The water is a steady 72 degrees year-round, making for a bracing dip in the heat of summer and a heated pool for snowbirds in the winter. The pool is fairly shallow, seldom more than 5 feet deep. Bring a snorkel and mask for a peek down into the spring itself.

The spring is one source of the Wekiva River, which flows from here northeast to the St. John's River. If you wish, you can rent a canoe to explore this lovely stretch of river. (See the canoeing section of *Chapter 15: Do It!*) The river is gorgeous from a canoe but some daring souls snorkel it. The park police tell me this is a foolhardy venture given the population of large alligators who have lost their fear of man, thanks to being fed by ignorant tourists. Shortly before one of my visits to the park, an 11-foot gator was pulled from the waters of nearby Wekiva Marina. Because of its aggressive behavior and total lack of fear of humans, the trapper was forced to kill it.

If you get hungry after your swim, there's a bare-bones snack bar at the top of the hill. But a better choice might be the picnic area at the other end of the park, where you'll find a couple of dozen picnic tables artfully sited around the shores of Sand Lake.

There are alligators here, too, so be careful.

In between there are some beautifully maintained trails. If you begin from the spring-fed swimming pool, a boardwalk takes you from the swampy jungle of the river's edge to the sandy pine forest of the drier uplands. This is one of the nicest spots I found in Central Florida for a visitor to get a quick appreciation of just how different Florida's ecosystems are. There's plenty of wildlife, too. I've spotted white-tailed deer fawns leaping through the woods and armadillos grubbing in the underbrush.

Family campsites are available by reservation if you'd like to stay longer. The fees for up to eight people are $24 per site per night. Primitive camping is $5 per person per night. The park requires written proof that pets have had a rabies vaccination. Call Reserve America, (800) 326-3521, for campsite reservations. Call the park at (407) 884-2008 for more information.

Nearby: C.A.R.E. Foundation, Central Florida Zoological Park, Rock Springs Run State Reserve, Wekiva Falls Resort.

Chapter Eighteen:

Artful Dodges

THOSE WHO ASSUME THAT ORLANDO, WITH ITS HIGH CONCENTRATION OF THEME parks and "mindless" entertainments, is a cultural wasteland have got it dead wrong. In fact, the Orlando area boasts some world-class museums, a lively and growing theater scene, and a number of modest local history museums.

HISTORICAL & SCIENCE MUSEUMS

Fort Christmas Historical Park & Museum

1300 Fort Christmas Road, Christmas 32709 ~ (407) 568-4149
http://apps.ocfl.net/dept/CEsrvcs/Parks/ParkDetails.asp?ParkID=15

Admission:	**Free**
Hours:	Museum is open Tuesday to Sunday 9:00 a.m. to 4:00 p.m.; Gift Shop open Tuesday to Saturday 11:00 a.m. to 4:00 p.m. Park is open daily 8:00 a.m. to 8:00 p.m. (to 6:00 p.m. during winter months)
Location:	Two miles north of SR 50, a major artery between Orlando and the Kennedy Space Center

This is not the actual Fort Christmas but a re-creation. The original was built a short distance away in 1837 during the Second Seminole Indian War (1835-1842) and has long since rotted away. The re-created fort, with its log cabin-like blockhouses and pointed palisades, is remarkably evocative of a frontier that most Americans associate with the West, not the South.

Display cases in the blockhouses provide a fragmentary history of the Seminole Wars, the culture they destroyed, and the early days of white settlement. In the nearby **Visitors Center**, which is built in the style of a "Cracker" (old-time Florida cowboy) farm house, you can get a pamphlet that explicates the museum's exhibits and provides a short history of the Seminole Wars. Scattered about the property is a small but grow-ing collection of **original Cracker architecture** that you can poke through at your leisure. Yesterday, disreputable shacks. Today, cherished history.

Fort Christmas is also a county park complete with picnic tables (many with bar-becues), a shaded playground, a baseball diamond, and tennis, volleyball, and basketball courts. The website lists events on a handful of weekends between November and May like "Cowboy Reunion" and "Old Timer's Day."

Nearby: Jungle Adventures, Orlando Wetlands Park, Tosohatchee Wildlife Man-agement Area.

The Holocaust Memorial

851 North Maitland Avenue, Maitland 32794 ~ (407) 628-0555
www.holocaustedu.org

Admission:	**Free, donations accepted**
Hours:	Monday to Thursday 9:00 a.m. to 4:00 p.m.; Fri-day 9:00 a.m. to 1:00 p.m.; Sunday 1:00 p.m. to 4:00 p.m.
Location:	At Maitland Boulevard and Maitland Avenue, about a mile east of I-4 Exit 90

The Holocaust Memorial Resource and Education Center houses a modest and moving museum commemorating one of the darkest moments in human experi-ence—the martyrdom of the six million Jews ruthlessly exterminated by the Nazis in the 1930s and 1940s. A small chapel-like room houses "The Holocaust in History," a permanent collection of multimedia displays documenting the horrors of institution-alized hate. A separate room houses rotating exhibits on aspects of the Holocaust. A 6,000-volume library is devoted exclusively to Holocaust history.

A visit here can be a profoundly disturbing experience, which is not to say it is something to shy away from. It will put the pleasures of your Orlando vacation in a richer perspective.

Nearby: Birds of Prey Center, Li'l 500, Maitland Art Center, Maitland Historical Museum, Waterhouse Residence.

Maitland Historical & Telephone Museum

221 West Packwood Avenue, Maitland 32751 ~ (407) 644-1364
www.maitlandhistory.org

Admission:	Adults $3, seniors 55+ and children (4 to 18) $2
Hours:	Thursday to Sunday noon to 4:00 p.m.; closed major holidays.
Location:	From I-4 Exit 90 go east on Maitland Boulevard, turn right on Maitland Avenue and right on Pack-wood.

This modest museum, housed in a former residence next to the Maitland Art Center (see below), houses memorabilia of the tiny town of Maitland, which began its life as Fort Maitland in 1838, serving as a way station between larger forts in Sanford and

Orlando. There is a timeline of Maitland history supplemented by changing exhibits focusing on a theme. Past exhibits have highlighted Maitland's Girl Scout history and toys, games, and leisure activities of the late 1800s and early 1900s.

The real attraction here, however, is the **Telephone Museum** housed in a building out back. Telephone service in this part of Florida began in 1909, when the Galloway family grocery store installed 10 phone lines so their good customers could order by phone. The service mushroomed into what came to be known as the Winter Park Telephone Company, which remained independent and family-owned until 1976 when it was sold to the company that became Sprint. There are several old magneto switchboards here, dating back to 1900, and a large collection of phones, from the old-fashioned, wall-mounted, hand-cranked varieties to a sleek one-piece 1970 Swedish Ericofon. There are very few explanatory labels, so ask for a guided tour. On my visit, I was escorted by a charming lady who once worked for the Galloways themselves.

Nearby: Birds of Prey Center, Holocaust Memorial, Li'l 500, Maitland Art Center, Waterhouse Residence.

Orange County Regional History Center

65 East Central Boulevard, Orlando 32801 ~ (800) 965-2030; (407) 836-8500
www.thehistorycenter.org

Admission:	Adults $9, seniors (60+), students, and military $7, children (5 to 12) $6
Hours:	Monday to Saturday 10:00 a.m. to 5:00 p.m.; Sunday noon to 5:00 p.m.
Location:	In downtown Orlando; from the north take I-4 Exit 84, from the south Exit 83A.

Unlike most county historical museums, which are dusty hodgepodges of miscellaneous objects displayed in a donated and threadbare house of "historical" interest, Orange County's museum is housed in a magnificent 1927 courthouse, its collection attractively and professionally displayed. This is one of the best-looking local history museums I have visited and well worth a look if you venture downtown.

The impressive ground floor entrance features a marble inlay map of the world with Orlando at the center; above is a wonderfully zany multimedia sculptural dome dotted with references to Central Florida's natural, cultural, and social history. Your best bet is to head for the fourth floor, enjoy the short orientation film, and then work your way down through a chronologically arranged series of exhibit rooms.

A fascinating display on tourism takes us back to the 1920s and the first RVs, converted Model Ts that brought penny-pinching "tin can tourists." The then governor of Florida said of these pioneers, "They came with one pair of underwear and one 20 dollar bill and changed neither." How times change! Other highlights are a perfectly preserved courtroom and a display on the pre-World War II training of military pilots, when Central Florida was so little-known that it was the perfect place for a top-secret government base. Just to remind you why you came to Orlando, there's also an excellent exhibit on the arrival of Disney and the area's subsequent explosive growth.

Nearby: Lake Eola Swan Boats, Leu Gardens, Orlando City Hall Galleries.

Orlando Fire Museum

814 East Rollins Street, Orlando 32803 ~ (407) 898-3138
www.cityoforlando.net/fire/Museum.htm

Admission:	**Free, donations requested**
Hours:	Friday 9:00 a.m. to 3:00 p.m., Saturday 9:00 a.m. to 3:00 p.m. Group tours by appointment
Location:	From I-4 Exit 85, go east and follow Loch Haven Park signs about one quarter mile

The charming brick 1926 Fire Station #3 has been lovingly moved to this secluded location behind the Orlando Shakespeare Festival in Loch Haven Park. Here fire buffs can enthuse over meticulously restored fire engines, including a 1911 horse-drawn steam pumper, a 1915 LaFrance Fire Engine, and a 1919 LaFrance Ladder Truck. Photos and documents arranged chronologically around the walls document the department's proud history. You have to pass through the lobby of the Orlando Shakespeare Festival to reach the museum, tucked away in a quiet courtyard, but it's worth seeking out.

Nearby: Leu Gardens, Mennello Museum of Art, Orlando Museum of Art, Orlando Science Center.

Orlando Science Center

777 East Princeton Street, Orlando 32803 ~ (888) 672-4386; (407) 514-2000
www.osc.org

Admission:	Adults $17, seniors (55+) $16, youths (3 to 11) $12
Hours:	Sunday to Tuesday 10:00 a.m. to 5:00 p.m.; Thursday to Saturday 10:00 a.m. to 9:00 p.m.; Sunday noon to 5:00 p.m.
Location:	From I-4 Exit 85, go east and follow Loch Haven Park signs about one quarter mile.

The Orlando area is gaining a reputation as another high-tech business corridor with specialties in laser and simulation technologies. The Orlando Science Center's smashing home is a fitting monument to the technological explosion going on around it and should serve as a launching pad for future generations of scientists. The accent is on kids and science education but, thanks to its ingenious hands-on approach, the Center offers plenty to keep even the dullest adult occupied.

The Center's 42,000 square feet are crammed with eye-catching exhibits that illustrate the many faces of science in an entertaining way. **DinoDigs** lets kids uncover faux fossils and inspect dino eggs; **Our Planet, Our Universe** lets you drive a mini Mars rover; **KidsTown** is a tyke-sized city where tomorrow's laborers can role-play at picking produce and designing dams. The centerpiece of the atrium is **NatureWorks**, a multi-story simulation of a cypress swamp, complete with live turtles and gators. Temporary exhibits often explore science inside a pop-culture wrapper.

The 310-seat **CineDome** features large-format movies and planetarium shows on a screen eight stories high, with a state-of-the-art sound system. Seeing a nature movie on the vast curved screen is an experience not easily duplicated elsewhere. The films are included in the price of admission.

A couple nights each month, the **Crosby Observatory** on the top floor stays open late for skywatching. Special events through the year include the popular **Otronicon** video game expo each January. See the website for details.

There's a Subway sandwich shop on the ground floor so you can plan a visit around lunchtime and then spend the rest of the day exploring the wonderful world of science, with side trips to the nearby museums.

Nearby: Leu Gardens, Mennello Museum, Orlando Fire Museum, Orlando Museum of Art.

Spence-Lanier Pioneer Center

750 North Bass Road, Kissimmee 34746 ~ (407) 396-8644
www.osceolahistory.org

Admission: Suggested donation, adults $5, children $2
Hours: Thursday to Sunday 10:00 a.m. to 4:00 p.m.
Location: Just south of Irlo Bronson Highway (US 192)

Sometimes referred to as the Pioneer Museum, this open-air venue is a labor of love of the Osceola County Historical Society. The highlights are several old wooden buildings, rescued from oblivion and moved to this site as reminders of Central Florida's not too distant but nonetheless vanished past.

The Lanier House, which has been dated to about 1887, is a Cracker-style residence made from broad cypress boards that have aged to a lovely cafe au lait shade of beige. The broad, shaded porches and airy central breezeway, or "possum trot," were designed to let air circulate through the four rooms. The spare interior rooms, including a kitchen with a wood stove, touchingly evoke the rhythms of life in a simpler time. Next door is the smaller, two-room 1890 **Tyson Home,** now used to re-create a turn of the century general store. Books of local history and locally produced crafts are sold here. Other historic structures preserved here include a primitive Cracker cow camp, a one-room schoolhouse, and a citrus packing house circa 1880. A nearby modern prefab building houses the **Osceola County Historical Society Museum**, a growing collection of antiques and memorabilia donated by the local community.

Across the street from the four-acre site of the museum is the **Mary Kendall Steffee Nature Preserve**. This 7.8-acre patch of wilderness lies in the very heart of tourist Kissimmee and yet remains remarkably isolated. A short walk on marked trails brings you to a raised boardwalk that juts out into Shingle Creek Swamp. A shaded seating area beckons the footsore. Aside from the intermittent drone of small planes landing at the nearby Kissimmee Airport, this is an oasis of tranquillity where you can glimpse the occasional eagle or other large raptor.

Nearby: Medieval Times.

Waterhouse Residence & Carpentry Museum

820 Lake Lilly Drive, Maitland 32751 ~ (407) 629-1532
www.maitlandhistory.org

Admission: Adults $3, seniors (55+), children (4 to 18) $2
Hours: Thursday to Sunday noon to 4:00 p.m.

Location:	From I-4 take Exit 90 East onto Maitland Boulevard, then turn right onto Maitland Avenue and right onto Lake Lilly Drive.

William H. Waterhouse, a home builder and cabinetmaker by trade, came to Central Florida in the early 1880s and put his obvious skills to use building a handsome family residence overlooking tiny Lake Lilly. Today, it serves as a monument to gracious living in a simpler, less stressful time. Lovingly restored and maintained by volunteers, the house contains many items of furniture fashioned by Mr. Waterhouse in the carpentry shop behind the home. The home itself is furnished throughout and looks as if the Waterhouse family had just stepped out for a moment. Do-it-yourselfers will marvel at the fine detail work and the lavish use of heart of pine, a favorite of builders of the period because it was impervious to termites. It is rare today because few loggers are patient enough to let pines go unharvested long enough for this prime lumber to develop.

Tours lasting 30 to 40 minutes are conducted by knowledgeable volunteers who will provide you with insights into this charming home and the people who lived here.

Nearby: Birds of Prey Center, Maitland Art Center, Maitland Historical Museum.

Wells' Built Museum of African American History
511 West South Street, Orlando 32805 ~ (407) 245-7535
www.pastinc.org

Admission:	Adults $5, students and seniors (60+) $3, children (4 to 13) $2
Hours:	Monday to Friday 9:00 a.m. to 5:00 p.m.
Location:	Just west of I-4 near Church Street

Dr. William M. Wells was a prominent African-American physician in Orlando during the first half of the 20th century. He created the South Street Casino to host touring black bands and, since Orlando was rigorously segregated, he opened the Wells' Built Hotel next door to house the musicians. Ella Fitzgerald, Count Basie, Ray Charles, Cab Calloway, Ivory Joe Hunter, and many other musical greats played the Casino and stayed at the hotel over the years. White Orlando didn't know what it was missing. The Casino is gone now, but the hotel's original facade remains. It has been converted into a modest 6000-square-foot museum housing memorabilia of Orlando's African-American community and displays on the Civil Rights movement in Orlando.

Nearby: Orange County History Center, Orlando City Hall Galleries.

Winter Garden Heritage Museum & History Center
1 North Main Street, Winter Garden 34787 ~ (407) 656-3244
www.wghf.org

Admission:	**Free**
Hours:	Daily 1:00 p.m. to 5:00 p.m., except holidays.
Location:	In the center of downtown Winter Garden, 12 miles west of Orlando via SR 50

This is actually four attractions in one, all located within easy walking distance of one another in "historic" downtown Winter Garden, which looks much the way it did back in the 1920s and 30s. The **History Center** serves primarily as a research resource for Winter Garden family and business history, but it also presents displays of local history that change every three months. The **Heritage Museum**, located in the picturesque old train station, is typical of other local history collections, although the museum does boast the "largest collection of antique citrus labels from West Orange County."

Railroad buffs will most definitely want to visit the **Railroad Museum**, around the corner on South Boyd Street in yet another old train station, the "Tug and Grunt," so called for its role as a freight line and low-cost passenger line for locals. The collection is catch as catch can, but claims to be one of the largest of its kind. Back on Main Street, the **Garden Theatre** has been restored to its 1930s glory, with an auditorium decorated to evoke an Italian courtyard, complete with twinkling stars overhead. It now hosts local dance and theatre troupes and occasional showings of classic films.

Winter Park Historical Association Museum

200 West New England Avenue, Winter Park 32790 ~ (407) 647-8180
www.wphistory.org

Admission:	**Free, donations requested**
Hours:	Wednesday to Friday 10:00 a.m. to 4:00 p.m.; Saturdays in July only 9:00 a.m. to 2:00 p.m.
Location:	In downtown Winter Park next to the park

This fledgling historical museum is housed in one room around the corner from the building in which Winter Park's Saturday Farmer's Market is held. The display is simple, relying heavily on photographs of now-vanished buildings and assorted household items and artifacts that speak less of Winter Park than of American consumerism. The best part of this museum is the central display area, a sort of room within a room. It houses changing exhibits artfully put together using donated and loaned furniture and artifacts. Past exhibits have included a Victorian parlor decked out for a Christmas celebration and a history of Florida's turpentine industry.

Nearby: Albin Polasek Galleries, Cornell Fine Arts Museum, Morse Museum, Winter Park Scenic Boat Tour.

ART MUSEUMS & GALLERIES

Visitors to Orlando will find plenty of opportunities to buy schlocky "art" aimed at the tourist trade, but if you'd prefer to admire fine art without having to buy it, there are a growing number of venues to choose from.

Albin Polasek Galleries

633 Osceola Avenue, Winter Park 32790 ~ (407) 647-6294
www.polasek.org

Admission:	Adults $5, seniors (60+) $4, students $3, under 12 **free**
Hours:	Tuesday to Saturday 10:00 a.m. to 4:00 p.m.; Sunday 1:00 p.m. to 4:00 p.m.
Location:	From I-4 Exit 87, follow SR 426 East 3 miles.

The studio-home and gardens of the late Czech-American sculptor, Albin Polasek, have been turned into a loving memorial by his widow. The quietly luxurious home was designed by Polasek himself and constructed in 1950 overlooking Lake Osceola. Today it is on the Register of Historic Places and houses some 200 of his works. The paintings are originals while most of the sculptures are reproductions.

Polasek was a devout Roman Catholic and a self-taught woodcarver who, as a young immigrant, found work carving religious statues in the Midwest. Later, he received formal art training and eventually became a highly respected academic artist. The work on display here ranges from the mawkish to the quite impressive. He was a better sculptor than painter and some of his bronzes, like *The Sower* and *Man Carving His Own Destiny*, possess real power. The former is a classically inspired bronze, the latter depicts a muscular figure in the process of carving itself out of stone.

One of his most affecting pieces is *The Victorious Christ*, a larger-than-life sculpture of the crucified Christ gazing heavenward. The original hangs in a cathedral in Omaha, Nebraska. There are two reproductions here. One dominates his two-story studio but the real stunner is the bronze version in the back garden, facing the lake.

Nearby: Cornell Fine Arts Museum, Morse Museum of American Art, Winter Park Scenic Boat Tour.

Cornell Fine Arts Museum

1000 Holt Avenue, Winter Park 32789 ~ (407) 646-2526
www.rollins.edu/cfam

Admission: Adults $5
Hours: Tuesday to Friday 10:00 a.m. to 4:00 p.m.; Saturday to Sunday noon to 5:00 p.m.
Location: On the campus of Rollins College, at the foot of Holt Avenue

The Cornell Fine Arts Museum has luxurious digs overlooking Lake Virginia on the Rollins College campus. The collection's emphasis is on European and American painting of the last three centuries. It is the oldest art collection in the state and boasts a permanent collection of over 5,000 objects, ranging from Old Masters to twentieth century abstractionists.

Typically, two of the museum's six galleries are given over to special exhibitions, such as recent ones showcasing contemporary portraiture and Stephen Shore's photographs of Andy Warhol's Factory in the 1960s, while two other galleries feature some choice examples from the permanent collection. The remaining space is given over to the print collection and educational activities. The Cornell joins forces with smaller museums across the country to mount distinguished traveling shows. Exhibits, which run from six to eight weeks, range from retrospectives of a single artist, to highlights of distinguished private collections, to surveys of important movements, to themed shows illuminating genres and techniques.

Nearby: Albin Polasek Galleries, Morse Museum, Winter Park Scenic Boat Tour.

Frank Lloyd Wright Buildings at FSC

111 Lake Hollingsworth Drive, Lakeland 33801 ~ (863) 680-4597
www.flsouthern.edu/fllwctr

Admission: **Free**

Hours: Visitor Center is open Monday to Saturday 10:00 a.m. to 4:00 p.m.; grounds are accessible 24 hours a day

Location: On the shores of Lake Hollingsworth

Devotees of Frank Lloyd Wright (and they are legion) will want to make a pilgrimage to Lakeland, about 54 miles west of Orlando, to marvel at the largest group of Wright buildings in the world. Wright designed 18 buildings for Florida Southern, a liberal arts college affiliated with the Methodist Church. Twelve were built.

To get there from Orlando, drive west on I-4 and take Exit 32. Follow US 98 South. From Tampa take Exit 22 and follow US 92 East. The two routes join in downtown Lakeland. When they part ways again, follow route 98 and, shortly, turn right onto Ingraham Avenue. Follow Ingraham until it deadends at Lake Hollingsworth Drive (you'll see the campus of Florida Southern College on your right).

Turn right onto Lake Hollingsworth, then right again onto Johnson Avenue. Look for the parking lot on your right opposite the William F. Chatlos Journalism Building. If the "Child of the Sun" visitor center isn't open when you drop by, look for a red and white sign; on it is a clear plastic box containing brochures that outline a self-guided walking tour that circles the grounds.

If you want a guided tour, an hour version is offered at 11:00 a.m. for $20 per person; a two-hour "in depth tour" at 1:00 p.m. costs $35. Both tours are offered in the summer by appointment only; call in advance to schedule.

The buildings were designed for a tight budget (in fact, much of the early construction was done by students in the forties) but the results are impressive. Many buildings are unlocked and open to the casual visitor. Inside, look for the tiny squares of colored glass embedded in the exterior walls—a delightfully whimsical touch. Take a moment to sit in the quiet splendor of the **Annie Pfeiffer Chapel**; the smaller but equally arresting **Danforth Chapel** is nearby. One of the most interesting buildings to be seen here is the only **planetarium** Wright ever designed.

The buildings are starting to show their age, but Wright's designs are so idiosyncratic, his decorative elements so unique, that this extensive example of his "organic architecture" seems to exist outside the time/style continuum we carry around in our heads. Instead, it is easy to imagine you are in a city built a long time ago in a galaxy far, far away.

The buildings are linked by one and a half miles of covered esplanades that Wright, in his charmingly perverse way, scaled to his own rather short height. "It makes it kind of difficult to recruit a basketball team," a college executive confided. But for those who fit underneath, the effect is rather cozy and Florida Southern students must say a silent prayer of thanks to Wright as they scurry between classes during an afternoon downpour.

Nearby: Fantasy of Flight, Polk Museum of Art, Water Ski Experience.

Lake Wales Arts Center

1099 State Road 60 East, Lake Wales 33853 ~ (863) 676-8426
www.lakewalesartscouncil.org

Admission:	**Free** to exhibits; admission to events varies
Hours:	Monday to Friday 9:00 a.m. to 5:00 p.m.; call for Saturday hours
Location:	Take U.S. 27 south to SR 60 and turn left.

If the Lake Wales Arts Center looks like an old Spanish mission, that's because it used to be a Catholic church. Today it is home to a smorgasbord of art exhibits, concerts, and cultural enrichment programs. A rotating series of month-long art exhibits feature group shows of abstract and figurative art, with an emphasis on Florida artists. There are frequent municipal art shows and juried exhibitions, while the entertainment series showcases jazz, classical, and contemporary musicians from around the state and world.

Nearby: Bok Tower Gardens, Florida Skydiving, Legoland, Spook Hill.

Maitland Art Center

231 West Packwood Avenue, Maitland 32751 ~ (407) 539-2181
www.maitlandartcenter.org

Admission:	For the gallery, adults $3; seniors (55+) and children (4 to 18) $2
Hours:	Tuesday to Sunday 11:00 a.m. to 4:00 p.m.
Location:	From I-4 take Exit 90. Go east on Maitland Boulevard, then turn right onto Maitland Avenue and right onto Packwood.

The Maitland Art Center is both a gallery and a working art school. It was founded in the late 1930s by the artist and architect André Smith as a "laboratory" for the study of modern art. Smith built a charmingly eccentric complex of tiny cottage/studios for visiting artists. He decorated the modest buildings with cast concrete ornaments and detailing heavily influenced by the art of the ancient Aztecs and Maya.

Today the gallery plays host to a regular succession of exhibits by local and national artists, exhibits of private collections, and arts and crafts workshops that are open to the public.

After visiting the gallery, take some time to stroll the grounds. The place must have been idyllic in its heyday, before Maitland became quite so built up. Across the street from the gallery and studios is a roofless outdoor concrete chapel with a latticework cross. Shaded by oaks dripping in Spanish moss and surrounded by lush vegetation, the chapel offers a peaceful corner for contemplation. It is also the setting for some spectacular weddings. Right next to it is an open courtyard whose exuberant decoration owes a debt to the boisterous paganism of pre-Columbian Mexico; it makes for quite a contrast.

Nearby: Birds of Prey Center, Holocaust Memorial, Maitland Historical Museum, Waterhouse Residence.

Mary, Queen of the Universe Shrine

8300 Vineland Avenue, Orlando 32821 ~ (407) 239-6600
www.maryqueenoftheuniverse.org

Admission: **Free**
Hours: Shrine open daily 7:30 a.m. to 5:00 p.m. Museum open weekdays 10:00 a.m. to 4:00 p.m. (closed Wednesday); Saturday and Sunday to 6:00 p.m.
Location: Near I-4 Exit 68

This Roman Catholic shrine had humble beginnings as a tourist ministry; today it is a large modern cathedral named by the Pope as a "house of pilgrimage." There is some striking architecture and religious art to be seen here, especially a lovely, abstract, blue stained-glass wall in a chapel dedicated to Our Lady of Guadalupe. A museum off the gift shop hosts rotating exhibits of religious relics and art from around the world.

Nearby: Discovery Cove, SeaWorld.

Mennello Museum of American Art

900 East Princeton Street, Orlando 32803 ~ (407) 246-4278
www.mennellomuseum.com

Admission: Adults $4, seniors (60+) $3, students $1, children under 12 **free**.
Hours: Tuesday to Saturday 10:30 a.m. to 4:30 p.m.; Sunday noon to 4:30 p.m.
Location: In Loch Haven Park, near I-4 Exit 85

Art collectors Marilyn and Michael Mennello fell in love with the work of "naïve" artist Earl Cunningham and purchased virtually his entire life's output. The City of Orlando, meanwhile, had been collecting Florida and southern folk art as part of its Public Art Collection. Now these two visionary endeavors have been brought together in a small gem of a museum located in a renovated private residence overlooking picturesque Lake Formosa in Loch Haven Park.

Cunningham was a Maine sea captain who gradually worked his way south, all the while painting imaginative and idealized coastal landscapes with a Caribbean sense of color. His works form the backbone of the Mennello Museum's collection. They are displayed using a clever halogen lighting system, designed by the museum's director, that heightens the colors in the paintings to almost neon intensity. Other rooms in the museum showcase items from the Orlando city collection and traveling exhibits of other American artists. Don't miss the sculpture garden and mural outside.

Nearby: Leu Gardens, Orlando Fire Museum, Orlando Museum of Art, Orlando Rep, Orlando Science Center, Orlando Shakespeare Theater.

Morse Museum of American Art

445 North Park Avenue, Winter Park 32789 ~ (407) 645-5311
www.morsemuseum.org

Admission: Adults $5, seniors $4, students $1, children under 12 **free**. **Free** to all Friday 4:00 p.m. to 8:00 p.m.

	November through April
Hours:	Tuesday to Saturday 9:30 a.m. to 4:00 p.m. (Friday to 8:00 p.m. November through April); Sunday 1:00 p.m. to 4:00 p.m.
Location:	On Park Avenue, just past the shopping district

Could the Charles Hosmer Morse Museum of American Art be the best museum in Central Florida? Well, for my money, it's hard to beat the world's largest collection of Tiffany glass. That's Louis Comfort Tiffany, the magician of stained glass who flourished at the turn of the twentieth century. The works on display here are absolutely ravishing and, if you have any interest in the decorative arts, your visit to Orlando will be poorer for not having found the time to visit this unparalleled collection.

When most people think of Tiffany glass they think of those wonderfully organic-looking table and hanging lamps with the floral designs. Those are here, of course, as are some stunning examples of his large-scale decorative glass windows and door panels. But there's much else, some of which may come as a surprise.

As brilliant a marketer as he was an artist, Tiffany saw the World's Fair of 1893 as an opportunity to spread his fame worldwide. So he put his best foot forward by creating an enormous chapel interior for the exhibition. Everything in it, from a massive electrified chandelier, to a baptismal font, to intricate mosaic pillars to stunningly beautiful stained-glass windows was of Tiffany design. The surviving elements of the chapel have been lovingly restored by the Morse and displayed in a room that is entered through the chapel's original, massive wooden doors.

A newly built wing holds the other crown jewel of the Morse, the recently restored Daffodil Terrace from Tiffany's Laurelton Hall estate on Long Island. Rescued by Hugh F. and Jeannette G. McKean after fire destroyed the mansion in 1957 and painstakingly reassembled from over 600 fragments, the 576-square-foot outdoor entertaining area (featuring 11-foot-tall marble columns) shares the 6,000 square feet of added exhibit space with over 200 other exquisitely designed domestic objects salvaged from Tiffany's dining and living rooms, including a 6½-foot-wide chandelier.

The faces on Tiffany's glass pieces were painted with powdered glass that was fused to clear glass, but much of the other detail and molding is created by the rich colors and tonal fluctuations in the glass itself. Tiffany is less well known as a painter, but several of his paintings, including some very deft watercolors from his worldwide travels, are to be seen here. There are also miniature glass pieces, vases in delicate, psychedelic-colored favrile glass, inkwells, jewelry, and other decorative objects.

The Morse's collection focuses on the decorative arts and is extensive, comprising over 4,000 pieces. In addition to the permanent displays, the museum dips into its collection to mount special exhibits illuminating various aspects of American decorative arts, including "vignettes," small rooms in which interior designers show off the museum's collection of furniture and decorative objects as they might have looked in the well-to-do homes for which these lovely objects were created.

Nearby: Albin Polasek Galleries, Cornell Fine Arts Museum, Winter Park Scenic Boat Tour.

Orlando City Hall Galleries

Orange Avenue and South Street, Orlando 32801 ~ (407) 246-2221
www.ci.orlando.fl.us/arts/galleries.htm

Admission:	**Free**
Hours:	Terrace gallery open Monday to Friday 8:00 a.m. to 9:00 p.m.; Saturday and Sunday noon to 5:00 p.m. 2nd & 3rd floor open Monday to Friday 8:00 a.m. to 5:00 p.m.
Location:	Just off I-4 Exit 82

The City of Orlando has a long-standing policy of supporting the arts and an extensive public collection of art, much of which is on display at City Hall. The ground floor "terrace" gallery, just off the impressive entry rotunda, is used for special exhibits that rotate every three months or so. The third-floor gallery just outside the mayor's office displays selected works from the permanent collection; continue down the stairs to the second floor and see more art on display. In fact, if you wander through the building, you will see that most of the hallways are alive with art. Much of the collection focuses on Florida artists, with an accent on folk art, but some major artists with national reputations are also to be found here.

Nearby: Lake Eola Swan Boats, Orange County Regional History Center.

Orlando Museum of Art

2416 North Mills Avenue, Orlando 32803 ~ (407) 896-4231
www.omart.org

Admission:	Adults $8, children (4 to 17) $5, college students and seniors (65+) $7; more for special exhibits.
Hours:	Tuesday to Friday 10:00 a.m. to 4:00 p.m.; Saturday and Sunday noon to 4:00 p.m.
Location:	In Loch Haven Park, near I-4 Exit 85

The Orlando Museum of Art (OMA) was founded in 1924 to present local, regional, and national artists and develop art education programs for the community. Today, its handsome modern building with its arresting circular hub houses a permanent collection of nineteenth and twentieth century American paintings. There is also a distinguished collection of pre-Columbian art housed in its own gallery.

On any given day, the galleries may host a special exhibit, a selection of works on loan, and a selection of works from the permanent collection. The museum also offers regular video, film, and lecture series, most of which require an additional admission charge. Wheelchairs and lockers are provided free of charge.

A small but very classy gift shop offers a tasteful range of small art objects, reproductions, calendars, glossy art books, and artisanal works you are unlikely to find elsewhere. On the first Thursday of each month, from 6:00 to 9:00 p.m., the museum throws a party with a cash bar, live music from local bands, and themed art by local artists. The $10 admission also allows entry to the galleries.

Nearby: Leu Gardens, Mennello Museum, Orlando Fire Museum, Orlando Science Center, Orlando Shakespeare Theater, Orlando Skate Park.

Osceola Center for the Arts

2411 East Irlo Bronson, Kissimmee 34744 ~ (407) 846-6257
www.ocfta.com

Admission:	**Free** to art gallery; performances $15 and up.
Hours:	Monday to Friday 9:00 a.m. to 5:00 p.m.; also open whenever there is a stage show or event
Location:	A mile east of Florida Turnpike Exit 244

This community-based arts organization mounts exhibits of Florida artists. Based on what I've seen, the standards for exhibition are quite high. Exhibits change monthly. The Center also hosts special events, such as a recent exhibition of work by established and emerging local artists. In addition to presenting art work, the Center hosts theatrical and musical presentations. Among these are tours by local professional performing arts groups and the productions of an in-house community theater group.

Nearby: Ice Factory, Mackinson Aquatic Center.

Polk Museum of Art

800 East Palmetto Street, Lakeland 33801 ~ (863) 688-7743
www.polkmuseumofart.org

Admission:	Adults $5, seniors (62+) $4, students (K-12) and college students with ID **free**. **Free** to all Saturday mornings 10:00 a.m. to noon.
Hours:	Tuesday to Saturday 10:00 a.m. to 4:00 p.m.
Location:	Near Lake Morton in downtown Lakeland

If you're making the pilgrimage to Lakeland to see the Frank Lloyd Wright Buildings at Florida Southern College, it's worth taking a bit more time to visit this small museum. Housed in a handsome modern building with marble floors and high ceilings, the museum is notable primarily for the Taxdal Pre-Columbian Gallery, an impressive collection of ceramics from ancient American cultures ranging from Mexico to Peru.

Nearby: Fantasy of Flight, Frank Lloyd Wright Buildings, Water Ski Experience.

Zora Neale Hurston National Museum of Fine Arts

227 East Kennedy Boulevard, Eatonville 32751 ~ (407) 647-3307
www.zoranealehurstonmuseum.com

Admission:	**Free, donations appreciated**
Hours:	Monday to Friday 9:00 a.m. to 4:00 p.m., Saturday 11:00 a.m. to 1:00 p.m.
Location:	From I-4 Exit 88 take Lee Road east and turn left almost immediately on Wymore; at the next light turn right on Kennedy for about a quarter mile.

The tiny enclave of Eatonville is the hometown of the writer Zora Neale Hurston, one of the shining lights of the Harlem Renaissance of the 1920s. Her namesake museum, nicknamed "The Hurston," is a small gallery hosting rotating exhibits of African-American artists from Florida and around the nation. The shows change about every six months. The community also hosts an annual festival each January in Hurston's honor celebrating various aspects of African-American culture; see www.zorafestival.com for information.

Nearby: Birds of Prey Center, Maitland Art Center.

THEATER

Orlando and the surrounding communities have an extremely active theater scene, which is not surprising considering all the talent attracted to central Florida by the nearby theme parks. In addition to the companies listed here, there is also a goodly number of community theaters. You will find complete listings of the week's theatrical offerings in the "Calendar" section of the Friday *Orlando Sentinel,* and in the free weekly paper, *Orlando Weekly,* as well as on their respective websites.

The Abbey

100 South Eola Drive, Orlando 32801 ~ (407) 704-6261
www.abbeyorlando.org

Orlando's newest live venue sits on the edge of downtown's fashionable Thornton Park district, in the ground floor of the Sanctuary high-rise. No expense was spared in the design of this neo-gothic styled club, from the hi-def screen in the fireplace to the subway tile in the restrooms. Of special note are the concert-quality LED lighting rig and bleeding-edge sound-system, which promise to make even the dullest show colorful and excruciatingly loud (sit near the rear).

Early local productions at this fledgling location have included pop musicals *Altar Boyz* and *Hedwig and the Angry Inch,* alternating with touring musical acts and off-Broadway comedies. Prices vary by show, and the space can hold between 150 and 400, depending on the seating configuration, so contact the box office for updates.

Annie Russell Theatre

1000 Holt Avenue, Winter Park 32789 ~ (407) 646-2145
www.rollins.edu/annierussell/

The drama department of Rollins College holds forth in this lovely, 377-seat Spanish Mediterranean style theater, offering an eclectic season of modern classics, a contemporary musical, and an old farce or Shakespearean play. The season runs from August to April and ticket prices are a bargain—$20 a seat. The repertory is ambitious and the productions I have seen belie the fact that all the performers are undergraduates. There is also a Second Stage series presenting more experimental work and the occasional new play. The Annie, as it's known locally, also presents touring dance companies of international renown.

Bob Carr Performing Arts Centre

401 West Livingston Street, Orlando 32801 ~ (407) 849-2001, (407) 849-2020
www.orlandovenues.net

Located downtown within sight of I-4, the Bob Carr is Orlando's venue for touring Broadway shows and other high-ticket, high-attendance performing arts events, at least until the ultra-modern Dr. Phillips Performing Arts Center on the opposite side of the interstate is completed in 2014 or so. The aging 2,500-seat theater hosts the **Broadway Across America Series**, presenting a season of six or seven shows for runs ranging from one week to a month. These are either touring companies of current or recent Broadway hits, or revivals showcasing a star you've probably heard of. Tickets for this series range from $36 to $99, plus fees; visit broadway.orlando.com for show information.

The Bob Carr is the venue of choice for local groups like the **Orlando Philharmonic** and **Orlando Ballet**, described below, as well as one-night stands by comedians like Mike Epps, magicians like David Copperfield, and the usual mix of pop and rock.

Florida Opera Theatre

(407) 718-4365

www.floperatheatre.org

Dedicated to bringing the piercing sounds of Italians in pain to Central Florida, the Florida Opera Theatre emerged from the ashes of the Orlando Opera, which folded for lack of funds in 2009. They offer a limited three-show season, in collaboration with other local groups like the Orlando Philharmonic and the St. Augustine and Vero Beach Opera.

Recent productions include Menotti's *The Medium* and Rossini's *The Barber of Seville*. Most performances are given in the Bob Carr Performing Arts Center or the Orlando Repertory Theatre mentioned above and below. Prices for tickets to individual performances range from $20 to $50.

Mad Cow Theatre Company

105 South Magnolia Street, Orlando 32801 ~ (407) 297-8788

www.madcowtheatre.com

This is Orlando's version of New York's Off Broadway or London's Fringe. Mad Cow has moved several times over the years, each time getting a little bigger and a lot better. Their current home boasts two intimate theaters in an attractive modern downtown building. Stage Left is the larger space at 100 seats; Stage Right is just half that size.

In mid-2012, Mad Cow plans to move into a new permanent home on historic Church Street in the 54 West complex. There they will enjoy a custom-built facility featuring a 160-seat Arena stage and a 70-seat black box, along with a lounge and expanded backstage facilities. The company has now achieved professional status, employing both Equity and non-Equity performers in a ten-play season of new works and modern classics. The selection of plays is eclectic, everything from Ibsen's *Ghosts* to *Sweeney Todd*. Other recent productions include *Freud's Last Session* and *Next to Normal*.

Although the theaters are comfortable, don't expect Broadway-style production values. The budget for these shows ranges from the minuscule to the modest. But for those with an adventuresome taste in theater-going, Mad Cow will be well worth checking out. Tickets range from $29 to $34, with discounts for seniors and students and some "pay what you wish" nights thrown in for good measure. Parking at the Library garage across the street is $3 with validation.

Orlando Ballet

1111 North Orange Avenue, Orlando 32804 ~ (407) 426-1739
www.orlandoballet.org

From October to May, this homegrown ballet company, under the direction of Robert Hill, mounts three-performance runs of about five ballets, ranging from "timeless classics to innovative contemporary works." They draw on a permanent company of professional dancers and a number of apprentices, occasionally presenting guest artists and visiting choreographers. Each year during the Christmas season, they present the ever-popular *Nutcracker,* and have reached out to a more contemporary audience with *Battle of the Sexes* and *Vampires' Ball* events. Performances are usually given at the Bob Carr (see above). Single tickets range from $15 to $75.

Orlando International Fringe Festival

398 West Amelia Street, Orlando 32801 ~ (407) 648-0077
www.orlandofringe.org

If you're in Orlando during late May and your taste runs toward experimental theater, you won't want to miss this theatrical feast. For 13 days, from noon to midnight, the venues around Loch Haven Park are given over to an international smorgasbord of traditional theater, cabaret, performance art, and street acts. A typical Festival will see over 600 performances by more than 80 groups from around the world. Most of the fare is decidedly adult, sometimes X-rated, but a parallel **Kids Fringe** features fare for younger folks. Most of the shows are indoors, but there are some outdoor performance venues.

To attend, you must first purchase a $8 button, which serves as a sort of cover charge for the Festival's shows. You then pay an additional $1 to $11 for each show you see, although some shows are free; an additional $1 service fee is levied on all tickets. The Festival is geographically compact, mostly utilizing the Orlando Shakespeare and Repertory stages, and a printed program lets you know what's coming up next and helps you plan your route from site to site. Try quizzing others making the round of shows for suggestions on what's worth seeing and what should be avoided like the plague. Check the website above for the exact dates and location of this year's bash.

Orlando Repertory Theater

1001 East Princeton Street, Orlando 32803 ~ (407) 896-7365
www.orlandorep.com

This professional, non-Equity company is the only local troupe specializing in family and children's theater. Productions at "The Rep" range from Off-Broadway hits to adaptations like *Junie B. Jones* and *A Christmas Story*. Productions are of remarkably high quality in a well-appointed and comfortable 328-seat space in a beautiful modern building that allows room for expansion. The theater is located in the Loch Haven Park arts complex that includes the Shakespeare Festival, the Orlando Museum of Art, and the Orlando Science Center.

The season runs from September through May and typically features six productions, each running for about five weeks. Performances are typically Saturdays at noon and 4:00 p.m., and Sundays at 2:00 p.m. and 5:30 p.m. Ticket prices are $11 for children under 17, $15 for seniors and college students (the theater is in partnership with University of Central Florida), and $17 for adults.

Orlando Shakespeare Theater

812 East Rollins Street, Orlando 32803 ~ (407) 447-1700
www.shakespearefest.org

The Bard of Avon is alive and well in Orlando, thanks to this professional theater company whose home (renovated at a cost of some $3.1 million) in Loch Haven Park boasts three performance spaces. The 330-seat Margeson Theater features a thrust stage and plenty of theatrical bells and whistles, while the 120-seat Goldman Theater is for more intimate productions. There is also a 100-seat "black box" house for experimental shows, workshops, and readings.

The Shakes (to use their ghastly nickname) is arguably the best theater group in Orlando, and the shows I have seen, including top-notch productions of *Taming of the Shrew* and *Cyrano*, have been excellent. The theater also has a very loyal cadre of performers, which means regular theatergoers have the pleasure of seeing good actors tackle a wide variety of roles over the years. Each season, the Festival presents six plays that may or may not have a Shakespearean connection. One play a year is often an adaptation of a classic novel written by a local playwright.

If you are in Orlando in December, don't miss their Christmas show. The Festival has made something of a cottage industry of producing offbeat alternatives to those gaudy revivals of *A Christmas Carol*. Some of them, like *The Trial of Ebenezer Scrooge* and *Every Christmas Story Ever Told*, are side-splittingly funny.

In November there is PlayFest, a four-day series of professional readings of contemporary plays in development. There are also occasional **free** readings of classic scripts on Sunday nights. Otherwise, ticket prices range from $16 to $38. Mainstage plays run about six weeks with evening performances on Wednesday through Saturday and a matinee on Sunday.

In addition to their self-produced shows, the Shakes rents its stages to a number of local "gypsy" theater and dance troupes without buildings of their own. Some, such as The Empty Spaces Theatre Co., and PB&J Theater Factory have consistently garnered strong reviews from the local press. RedChairProject.com offers information and discounts on advance tickets for these companies and many others.

Parliament House

410 North Orange Blossom Trail, Orlando, Florida 32805 ~ (407) 425-7571
www.parliamenthouse.com

The Parliament House Resort bills itself as the "gayest place on earth." Well maybe (the current owners are reportedly a straight couple), but the place has been a gay landmark in Orlando for over 35 years and has seen its ups and down. The new management has sunk a fair bit of money into renovations and the result is that the place is now glitzier than ever. There is a 130-room hotel, a heated pool, multiple bars (one with a western theme), and clubs all catering to a predominantly gay clientele. There is also plenty of entertainment.

On Fridays, Saturdays, and Sundays, they present a show featuring female impersonators of varying degrees of talent and verisimilitude in the Footlight Theater; once a year "Miss Parliament House" is elected, and for chubby chasers there is the Miss Large and Lovely National Pageant. The **Footlight Theater** is also the venue for occasional productions of more traditional works. They range from well-known plays by prominent gay playwrights such as Paul Rudnick and Charles Ludlam to locally written and produced comedies. Among the more successful examples of the latter are the works of Michael Wanzie who has enjoyed an artistic partnership with Parliament House for some three decades. Wanzie produces both his own work and that of others working in the same vein, which is to say very broad and very gay. You can find out what he's up to lately at his website www.wanziepresents.com.

Prices are moderate, seldom rising above $20 a ticket and your ticket stub gets you into the clubs afterwards. The shows at Parliament House are obviously not for everyone and are as far from "family fare" as it's possible to get. But if you have a taste for gay humor and over-the-top outrageousness, then you might want to give it a try. Just be aware that the quality of shows is not consistent.

Pinocchio's Marionette Theater
451 East Altamonte Drive, Altamonte Springs, FL 32701 ~ (407) 834-8757
www.pinocchios.net

Tucked away in a shopping mall on the far northern fringe of metro Orlando is a delightful vest-pocket marionette theater that brings timeless children's stories to life while teaching kids basic theater etiquette. Don't let the shopping center location fool you, either. The technical and artistic quality of the productions here are first rate and the miniature sets (if expanded to three times their actual size) would be the envy of most Orlando area theaters. A visit here is definitely worth the trip.

Pinocchio's is a non-profit organization and the labor of love of David Eaton, who wrote most of the shows, and the late Pady Blackwood, a master puppeteer who worked with Howdy Doody. The set designers have worked for Disney and Universal, and it shows. The 2-foot-high marionettes, which are pre-Muppet stringed puppets, are all hand-crafted for each show and costumed with the elegance and attention to detail you'd expect of much grander theaters.

Admission is a mere $5 for adults and children age 2 and over; season tickets are only $25. There are special rates for groups of 10 or more. Birthday parties, which include a puppet show, can be arranged for up to 50 kids. Call for details.

The Plaza 'Live' Theatre
425 North Bumby Avenue, Orlando 32803 ~ (407) 228-1220
www.theplazatheatre.com

Slightly to the east of downtown Orlando, in a renovated sixties-era movie house, the Plaza Theatre used to be devoted to presenting "family-friendly" live theater but lately it has been booked with an eclectic array of independent live music acts, from the Galactic Troubab Krewe to the Old 97's. From time to time, the theater may be rented to a touring show or comedian. Shows at the Plaza are presented on a rather erratic schedule, so check the box office or website. Tickets start at around $10 and soar to $86, depending the act, with many shows below $20.

SAK Theatre Comedy Lab

29 South Orange Avenue, Orlando 32801 ~ (407) 648-0001
www.sak.com

In the heart of downtown you'll find the Orlando home of improvisational comedy. "Improv," as its practitioners invariably call it, involves a group of agile and quick-witted actors creating a coherent and hilarious sketch based on frequently bizarre suggestions from the audience. More often than not, SAK succeeds. Speaking of success, Wayne Brady of the TV show *Who's Line Is It Anyway?* is a SAK alumnus.

Typically, what you will see is *Duel of Fools*, which is described as "two teams of improv comedy stars . . . in an all-out battle for laughs with Olympic judges, official referees, the pink shoe of salvation, help from the audience, and free candy!!!" Popcorn, soft drinks, beer, and wine are served. Unlike many comedy clubs, SAK adheres to a strict PG policy; there's no bad language, making it a possibility for your hipper kids.

SAK is open year round, Tuesday to Saturday. There are performances on Tuesdays and Wednesdays at 9:00 p.m., and Thursdays to Saturdays at 7:30 and 9:30 p.m. Additional $10 "Early Show" performances are at 11:30 p.m. on Friday and Saturday. Tickets are $15 for adults, but Florida residents with photo ID, and all students, seniors, and military personnel with ID, get in for $12. The Tuesday and Wednesday performances are by SAK's student company and are cheap at $2 to $3.

In 2010, SAK relocated into its comfortable current space on the second floor of the CityArts Factory at the corner of Orange and Pine Street. Downstairs you'll find an ever-changing selection of commercial galleries and artist studios. They are open to the public Tuesday to Saturday from 11:00 a.m. to 6:00 p.m., with an open house held in conjunction with other nearby galleries on the first Thursday night of every month. See www.cityartsfactory.com for details.

Theatre Downtown

2113 North Orange Avenue, Orlando 32803 ~ (407) 841-0083
www.theatredowntown.net

Here is another Off-Off Broadway-style theater offering mostly hip contemporary fare like *Psycho Beach Party* and *Avenue Q* and the occasional classic at moderate prices. The theater, a converted industrial building, has a 115-seat main stage with the audience on three sides of the stage. The performers are non-Equity, many of them just starting out on the stage, so the performance quality varies. The rock musical I saw there was vastly entertaining thanks to a spirited cast that made up in energy whatever they may have lacked in the talent department. Shows run for about a month with performances on Thursday, Friday, and Saturday at 8:00 p.m., with a Sunday matinee at 2:30 p.m. Tickets range from $16 to $22; bring cash for beer and wine, which you can take into the show.

Winter Park Playhouse

711-C Orange Avenue, Winter Park 32789 ~ (407) 645-0145
www.winterparkplayhouse.org

Hidden in an inconspicuous storefront location, this Equity company specializes in small-scale musicals presented in an intimate and unpretentious space. Typical shows offered here include *I Love You, You're Perfect, Now Change*, a tribute to Cole Porter, and *Musical of Musicals: The Musical*. They also do the occasional straight play like Neil Simon's *California Suite* or a one-man show about Mark Twain.

The Playhouse's season runs from July to May. Show times are Friday to Sunday evenings at 7:30 p.m., with Sunday matinees at 2:00 p.m. General admission tickets are $38 for adults, $35 for seniors (62+), and $20 for students. Matinee tickets are $28 for all. The Playhouse also presents a "Spotlight Cabaret" series in their beautifully appointed piano bar, hosting gifted local and national voices.

FILM

Orlando has the usual quota of mall-based multiplex movie theaters offering the latest Hollywood entertainment. The typical admission price is about $9.25 to $10.50 for adults, with a $3 or $4 premium for 3-D or IMAX. (Be warned: the area's only true giant-screen IMAX is at Pointe★Orlando.) Some theaters have lower prices ($4.75 to $7) for showings prior to 5:00 p.m. or for one morning screening each day.

The **Colonial 6** (407) 888-8224, in east Orlando on Colonial Drive, shows slightly older films for $1 to $2.50. The "Calendar" section in Friday's *Orlando Sentinel* lists the movie theaters in the greater Orlando area (which extends to the Atlantic coast) along with helpful capsule reviews.

One local film venue deserves special mention. The **Enzian Theater** (1300 South Orlando Avenue in nearby Maitland, (407) 629-0054, www.enzian.org), is the local art house. It shows subtitled European imports and the more adventuresome independent American films. From time to time, it runs special series built around a specific theme. Best of all, the films are screened in a 225-seat movie theater-restaurant. You can have a full meal, washed down with beer or wine, while soaking up culture. They serve up appetizers, sandwiches, and pizzas with a variety of toppings. Beer is sold by the pitcher as well as by the glass. A very filling meal can be had for less than $20 per person. Tickets are $8 for matinees (before 6:00 p.m.) and $10 for evening performances. They also have the wonderful Eden outdoor bar open daily at 11:00 a.m., for your pre- and post-cinema sipping pleasure.

In March or April of each year, the Enzian hosts the **Florida Film Festival**, screening as many as 150 films in four venues. Many filmmakers journey to Orlando for the event and give seminars. Single tickets and festival passes are sold; visit www.floridafilmfestival.com for dates and prices. Two shorter festivals are held in September (the Global Peace Film Festival, www.peacefilmfest.org) and in October (the Orlando Film Festival, www.orlandofilmfest.com).

MUSIC

The Orlando music scene is far too fleeting and fluid to cover in a guidebook, but if you like your music live rest assured that you will have plenty of opportunity to indulge yourself during your Orlando vacation.

For classical music fans, there is the **Orlando Philharmonic Orchestra**, (407) 896-6700, www.orlandophil.org, which presents a dozen or so concerts each year in a variety of venues including the Bob Carr Performing Arts Center mentioned earlier. That same downtown arena plays host to the usual array of aging rock stars and pop headliners, while the local bar and club scene serves up a wide variety of musical offerings from folk, to ethnic, to rhythm and blues, to country-western. Orlando has also garnered a reputation as an incubator of teen pop groups. If your taste lies in this direction you may be able to catch some rising stars. And, of course, opera fans have **Florida Opera Theatre** (see above).

The best way to plug into the music scene is the free *Orlando Weekly* newspaper, available in red kiosks around town each Wednesday. The "Calendar" section in Friday's *Orlando Sentinel* also lists all musical performances for the week, arranged helpfully by genre, along with a list of websites for local bands.

For those whose taste runs to classical music, the magazine *Orlando Arts*, available at museums and other cultural hangouts, lists upcoming events.

Chapter Nineteen:

Moving
Experiences

NOT ONLY ARE THERE A LOT OF THINGS TO SEE IN THE ORLANDO AREA, THERE ARE A lot of ways to see them. If walking or driving around begins to seem a bit boring, why not try some of these alternate modes of taking in the sights? There are some sights you will be able to see in no other way. Then again, some of these experiences are ends in themselves, with the passing scenery merely a backdrop.

Balloon Rides

Up, up, and away in a beautiful balloon. It's a great way to start the day and, if floating along on a big bubble of hot air appeals to you, that's when you'll have to go—at dawn. The weather's capricious in Orlando and at dawn the winds are at their calmest. A number of companies offer ballooning experiences in the Orlando area, and they all operate in much the same fashion, providing much the same experience.

Typically, you make your "weather-permitting" reservation by phone; your flight is confirmed (or called off) the night before. Then it's up with the birds to meet at a central location in the predawn twilight for a ride to the launch site, which will be determined by the prevailing weather conditions. Most operators let their passengers experience the fun (or is it the hard work?) of unloading and inflating the balloon. When the balloon is fully inflated, you soar aloft on a 45-minute to one-hour flight to points unknown. Of course, the pilot has a pretty good idea of where he'd like to put down, but the winds have a way of altering plans. After landing, once the balloon is packed away, a champagne toast is offered. With photographs and certificates, the passengers are inducted into the confraternity of ballooning. Some excursions include breakfast. The whole experience takes anywhere from three to four hours.

The baskets that hang beneath the balloons hold anywhere from 2 to 20 people, with six- to eight-passenger baskets being the most common. Usually, then, you will be riding with other people. If a couple wants a balloon to themselves (a frequent request), the price goes up. A few balloon operators try to float over Disney World whenever the winds cooperate, but it's hard to guarantee. The Disney folks are (understandably) less than happy about balloons landing on their property, so pilots must plan with care. Typically, your flight will be over the less-populated fringes of the metro area.

Hot-air ballooning is not cheap (most operators accept credit cards). Figure on about $175 to $200 per adult, about $100 per child (based on age or weight), plus tax, for the brief flight and the attendant hoopla. Some operators offer kids-fly-free promotions. Special packages, such as a wedding flight, can cost upwards of $1,000. Hot-air balloon operators, I have discovered, are a prickly lot, who are reluctant to provide pricing information, citing frequent fluctuations in fuel and other operating costs. So use the listing below as a starting point for your own comparison shopping.

Reservations must typically be guaranteed with a credit card and there are cancellation penalties. Many of the outfits listed below offer Internet discounts.

A Hot Air Balloon Ride

(407) 897-5432 ~ www.ahotairballoonride.com

Post-flight festivities include a "special balloonists prayer," a certificate of ascension, a commemorative pin, and a "sparkling beverage" toast. Helping the crew inflate the balloon is optional.

Aerostat Adventures

(877) 495-RIDE ~ www.balloonflorida.com

Specializing in couples-only flights, this operator offers flights near Mt. Dora and Eustis, north of Orlando, as well as flights in the Disney area. Post-flight there is a "champagne brunch."

Bob's Balloon Charters

732 Ensenada Drive, Orlando 32825 ~ (877) 824-4606; (407) 466-6380
www.bobsballoons.com

Bob Wilamoski's three balloons and 100-plus takeoff and landing sites let you soar pretty much anywhere in the Orlando area; they say they'll even take off from your home if conditions are favorable. Another draw is that you can crawl around inside the balloon while it's being prepared.

Fantasy of Flight

P.O. Box 1200, Polk City 33868 ~ (863) 984-3500
www.fantasyofflight.com/balloon.htm

This roadside attraction reviewed in *Chapter 14* also offers balloon rides. You must book at least 48 hours in advance. Fantasy of Flight is about 50 miles west of Orlando off Exit 44 from I-4.

Magic Sunrise Ballooning

(866) 606-RIDE (7433) ~ www.magicsunriseballooning.com

Offers the standard range of flights and amenities and the least expensive wedding package I've seen.

Orlando Balloon Rides

P.O. Box 560572, Orlando 32856 ~ (407) 894-5040
www.orlandoballoonrides.com

Orlando Balloon Rides, which also operates under the names "Blue Water Balloons" and "Orange Blossom Balloons," is the largest such company in the area. They use 25 launch sites scattered around the Orlando area, but sunrise flights near Disney are the big draw. All flights include a champagne toast and an all-you-can-eat breakfast buffet served after the flight. Their latest claim to fame is an 11-story, 24-passenger balloon billed as the biggest in North America.

Painted Horizons Hot Air Balloon Tours

7741 Hyacinth Drive, Orlando 32835 ~ (866) 578-3031; (407) 578-3031
www.paintedhorizons.com

Couples-only "private" flights are available seven days a week. Flights end with champagne, cheese, pastries, and crackers.

Boat Rides

As you can easily see when you fly into Orlando, Central Florida is dotted with lakes, from the tiny to the fairly large. It also boasts its fair share of spring-fed streams and rivers, as well as acre upon acre of swamps. It should come as no surprise, then, that the Orlando area offers the visitor plenty of opportunities to get on the water.

The signature Central Florida boat ride is aboard an airboat. These craft were created to meet the challenges of Florida's swamps and shallow estuaries. The pontoons allow the craft to float in just inches of water, the raised pilot's seat allows the driver to spot submerged obstacles (like alligators) before it's too late, and the powerful (if rather noisy) airplane propellers that power them let the boats skim across the water at a remarkable clip. The airboat is a raffish, backwoods sort of vehicle and it is used to give tourists a taste of what the old Florida of trappers and hunters was like. The "prey" is much the same—gators and such—but these days the only thing that gets shot is photographs.

There are other ways to cruise Central Florida's waters. One of the most popular is the pontoon boat, a flat rectangle set on two buoyant floats and designed for leisurely lake cruising. For many of Florida's lakeshore residents, they serve as floating patios; for the tourist trade, they make excellent sightseeing vessels. Central Florida even lays claim to a sort of cruise ship that takes passengers out on the broad St. John's River for an elegant dinner. All these options are listed below, along with the major airboat excursion companies.

A-Awesome Airboat Rides

P.O. Box 333, Christmas 32709 ~ (407) 568-7601
www.airboatride.com

Cost:	$50 per person for 90 minutes; may vary with the cost of gas
Hours:	Daily, 24 hours
Location:	Meets on SR 50 at the St. John's River bridge

"Captain Gator Bruce" runs this low-key operation offering private airboat tours of the extensive St. John's River ecosystem near Christmas, to the east of Orlando. The 90-minute tours are by reservation only. They offer a close-up look at alligators, bald eagles (September through May), and other denizens of this starkly beautiful landscape.

You can take a trip in the middle of the night if you wish, but you are better advised to consult with Captain Bruce on the best time to go to see what you want to see. There are two six-passenger airboats, but if you have a large group, Captain Bruce can round up enough boats to accommodate 30 people. There is a minimum per boatload, which means that if only two people go they will be charged a premium.

Aquatic Adventures Air Boat Tours

2571 Ridgeway Drive, Kissimmee 34746 ~ (321) 689-4281
www.aaairboattours.com

Cost:	One-hour tours: Adults $40, kids under 12 $35; 90-minute tours: Adults $60, kids under 12 $55
Hours:	Daily 9:00 a.m. to 5:00 p.m.
Location:	On the west shore of Lake Toho, south on CR 531 from US 17/92; ask for directions when making reservation.

Captain Dave slips his airboat, the Black Pearl (which is a vivid yellow) with its "stadium seating," into a quiet boat ramp on Lake Tohopekaliga for 60- and 90-minute tours of the lake's less populated areas. The standard tours round up the usual suspects of Central Florida wildlife with Captain Dave providing a running commentary through aircraft style earphones that allow him to talk over the propeller's roar. Night tours and private tours are also available. Dave also offers a tour of Mackinson Island, once an exotic animal attraction, now an Osceola County Park. The $85 tour includes a lake tour and a one-hour hike in search of wild hogs, feral goats, deer, armadillos, and other local denizens

If wildlife watching is too boring for you. Captain Dave will take you on a gator hunt, a real one, between August 15 and November 1. You'll need a trapper's license ($52 online from myfwc.com), but Dave will supply all the gear. Cost varies depending on exactly what you're looking for; call for details. Oh, and Captain Dave says no refunds if you get eaten.

Big Toho Airboat Rides

17 West Monument Avenue, Kissimmee 34741 ~ (888) 937-6843; (321) 624-2398
www.bigtohoairboatrides.com

Cost:	One-hour tours: Adults $50, kids (3 to 12) $35; online discounts available
Hours:	Daily 10:00 a.m. to 4:00 p.m.
Location:	In downtown Kissimmee; tours leave from the Big Toho Marina on the lake.

The gimmick here is that you pay $50 ($35 for kids) to have your picture taken with a live alligator at Big Toho's downtown office. Then they throw in a one-hour "free" airboat tour as a way of saying thanks. The tour explores Lake Tohopekaliga in search of alligators, eagles, ospreys, and, on the shore, wild hogs. They can also arrange a parasailing outing in Cocoa Beach on the Atlantic shore.

Boggy Creek Airboat Rides

East Location: 3702 Big Bass Road, Kissimmee 34744
West Location: 2001 East Southport Road, Kissimmee 34746 ~ (407) 344-9550
www.bcairboats.com

Cost:	30-minute scenic tours: Adults $25.95, children (3 to 12) $19.95, under 2 **free**
Hours:	By reservation
Location:	East: About 8 miles from East Irlo Bronson Highway on the north shore of East Lake Tohopekaliga. West: On the north shore of West Lake Tohopekaliga, about 20 miles from US 192 on Poinciana Boulevard (which becomes Southport Road).

Boggy Creek Airboats operates half-hour scenic nature tours on 17-passenger boats that explore the shores of their respective lakes. The eastern location also covers the nooks and crannies of Boggy Creek, one of the few habitats of the endangered snail kite. On the wildlife menu for both are alligators, turtles, and a multitude of water fowl. The east location offers a one-hour version for $41.95 adults, $36.95 kids. The west location offers "VIP" 45-minute swamp excursions on 6-passenger boats for $56.95 per person. On warm summer nights, both run hour-long alligator tours by reservation only. The tab is $51.95 for adults and $47.95 for kids.

You'll find the Big Bass Road location at East Lake Fish Camp, a lovely camping and fishing resort. Several fishing guides operate from this base. You might want to consider spending a day (and perhaps a night) here.

Cypress Lake Airboat Tours

3301 Lake Cypress Road, Kenansville 34739 ~ (407) 957-2277
www.cypresslakeairboattours.com

Cost:	One-hour tours: Adults $45, children (3 to 12) $35
Hours:	Daily 9:00 a.m. to 6:00 p.m.; last tour 4:30 p.m. Closed Easter, Thanksgiving, and Christmas.
Location:	From US 193 East, turn right on Vermont Avenue (also known as Canoe Creek Road); go 11.6 miles and turn right onto Lake Cypress Road.

Operating on the lesser-known Cypress Lake, south of Lake Toho, this operator offers a standard one-hour ride aboard 12-passenger airboats with "stadium seating" for unobstructed views. The owner Captain Doug, a Kissimmee native and lifelong swamp lover, guarantees your nature-tour itinerary will be free of housing or other human developments. Nighttime gator hunts are also available.

Kissimmee Outdoor Adventures

101 Lakeshore Boulevard, Kissimmee 34741 ~ (800) 247-1309
www.kissoutdooradventures.com

Cost:	90-minute tours: Adults $30, child $20, minimum of $90 per tour
Hours:	Daily 10:00 a.m. to 4:00 p.m.
Location:	Big Toho Marina on Kissimmee's lakeshore

This operators offers a 90-minute narrated "eco-tour" aboard the 17-passenger, 24-foot Miss Toho pontoon boat. Gators and eagles are among the wildlife usually sighted. Birdlife is abundant as well; the Lake Toho area is home to more exotic tropical bird species than anywhere else in Central Florida, they say, and they offer special pay-by-the-hour charters to birders hoping to catch a glimpse of the endangered snail kite. They also offer tours of Mackinson Island (see *Chapter 17*) and provide a ferry service ($20 per person) for those who wish to take advantage of the "primitive" camping on this isolated Osceola County Park.

Old Fashioned Airboat Rides

24004 Sisler Avenue, Christmas 32709 ~ (407) 568-4307
www.airboatrides.com

Cost:	Adults $50, children (3 to 12) $40, including tax; no children under 3
Hours:	By appointment
Location:	SR 50 at the public boat ramp about 45 minutes to an hour from Orlando

Captain John "Airboat John" Long runs this operation from his home, specializing in private airboat tours on three 6-passenger boats. Make your arrangements by phone (don't drop by the office!) and make sure you bring along lunch or a snack.

John's 90-minute nature trips are leisurely by the standards of most airboat tours. They explore a 40-mile roundtrip swath of river and swamp. There's plenty of gators and bald eagles to be seen along this remote stretch. On one side is the Tosohatchee Wildlife Management Area (see *Chapter 17*), on the other private ranch land. You can stop at a small island cabin or an ancient Indian mound for lunch and a great **photo op** of the boat on the water.

In the warmer months, John runs night trips in search of alligators. Gators have a reputation for being stupid but they avoid the blistering summer sun, making them smarter than the average tourist in some people's estimation.

Expect to ride with other folks, unless your party is four or more people. "Those boats burn a lot of gas," John explains. "Private tours" of one or two people are offered at $200. John doesn't allow children under three for safety reasons. Payment is strictly in cash or travelers checks; no credit cards.

Rivership Romance

433 North Palmetto Avenue, Sanford 32771 ~ (800) 423-7401; (407) 321-5091
www.rivershipromance.com

Cost:	$38 to $53.75, plus tax, drinks, and tip
Hours:	Cruises at 11:00 a.m. Wednesday to Sunday, and 7:30 p.m. Saturday; year-round
Location:	From I-4 Exit 103, 4 miles east on SR 46

The Rivership Romance is a refurbished, 100-foot, 1940s Great Lakes steamer that plies the waters of Lake Monroe and the St. John's River for leisurely luncheon and dinner cruises. It's not quite the "Love Boat," but for a change of pace from landlocked dining, it will do quite nicely.

There are three-hour luncheon cruises on Wednesday, Friday, and Saturday; four-hour luncheon cruises on Thursday; and three-and-a-half-hour dinner cruises on Saturday. The Sunday cruise is a brunch. Live entertainment is featured on all cruises and there is dancing to a sophisticated combo on the evening cruises.

The dinner menu is short but sumptuous and, in true cruise-line tradition, the portions are generous. After starting off with salad, you can choose from St. John chicken breast, panko-crusted tilapia, Caribbean pork, beef loin, or vegetable penne.

The scenery's nothing to sneeze at either. The St. John's is one of just two large rivers in the world that flow north and during the four-hour luncheon cruise, you'll get to see some 25 miles of its history-steeped shores. There's not much to see at night, of course, except for the stars, which can be spectacular on a clear night. Reservations are required and all major credit cards are accepted.

Scenic Lake Tours

101 Lakeshore Drive, Kissimmee 34741 ~ (800) 244-9105
www.fishingchartersinc.com

Cost:	Adults $30, children under 12 $20 ($70 min.)
Hours:	10:00 a.m. to 4:00 p.m. Monday to Friday; 9:00 a.m. to 3:00 p.m. weekends; sunset cruises by request
Location:	Departs from the Big Toho Marina on the Kissimmee waterfront

"Captain Rick" runs this friendly tour operation offering 90-minute "scenic/eco tours" of Kissimmee's Lake Toho (Tohopekaliga) aboard a 24-foot, 6-passenger pontoon boat. Bald eagles and ospreys can sometimes be spotted around the lake, but gators are more frequently sighted. Cruisers can also see the island from which Chief Osceola himself ruled over his territory. Reservations must be made 24 hours in advance. Captain Rick also provides fishing charters for crappie and bass on the lake.

Wild Willy's Airboat Tours

4715 Kissimmee Park Road, St. Cloud 34772 ~ (407) 891-7955
www.wildwillysairboattours.com

Cost:	Adults $39.25, children (3 to 10) $34.58 for a 1-hour trip, plus tax.
Hours:	Daily, 7 tours from 7:45 a.m. to 3:30 p.m.
Location:	On the east side of Lake Toho

Formerly known as the "upscale" Glades Adventures, this location is now home to the decidedly more down-home Wild Willy and his colorful crew of airboat captains. Willy operates only smaller 6-passenger airboats on one-hour tours of Kissimmee's Lake Tohopekaliga. On this tour, you might spot (depending on the season) bald eagles, osprey, otters, deer, wild boar, and, of course, alligators. Sunset alligator hunts are also available by appointment for $50 from November to March, Sunday to Thursday.

Back at the dock, there is a small alligator nursery, which is primarily an opportunity for tourists to touch a real live (and small) alligator. There is also a bait and tackle shop selling chips and beer alongside the minnows and worms. Yum.

Winter Park Scenic Boat Tour

312 East Morse Boulevard, Winter Park 32789 ~ (407) 644-4056
www.scenicboattours.com

Cost:	Adults $12, children (2 to 11) $6, tax included
Hours:	Daily 10:00 a.m. to 4:00 p.m. on the hour
Location:	At the foot of Morse Boulevard, a short stroll from Park Avenue's fancy shops

The little town of Winter Park has 17 lakes. Thanks to the operators of these modest, flat pontoon boats, you can visit three of them on a leisurely one-hour cruise. You slip between the lakes through narrow canals originally cut by logging crews in the 1800s. It's not quite Venice but it makes for an unusual and relaxing outing.

There's plenty of bird life to be seen on this tour and your guide will dutifully point out herons, muscovy ducks, and ospreys. Less frequently sighted are alligators, some of them quite large. There's also local history to take in, from the campus of Rollins College to the palatial 1898 Brewer estate, which is on the National Historic Register.

But, this tour is really about real estate envy. As you glide past one gorgeous multimillion-dollar home after another, their impeccably landscaped backyards cascading down to boathouses that coyly echo the architecture of the big house, you will find yourself asking, "Why them and not me? Why, why, why?"

Helicopter Tours

Small operations offering guided aerial sightseeing by helicopter pop up (and disappear) with some regularity, all offering much the same menu of tours, ranging from short two- to three-minute hops for about $20 to half-hour surveys for about $200, with children's prices somewhat less. Flights typically require a minimum of two adult passengers, although some require a full craft for takeoff and some offer special one-person rates. Flights usually start at 9:00 or 10:00 a.m. and continue until sunset.

Tip: The farther they have to fly the more expensive the trip. So if you especially want to see Universal Orlando, pick a helipad on International Drive; if Disney World is on your must-see list, try a tour that leaves from Kissimmee.

Air Florida Helicopters

8990 International Drive, Orlando 32819 ~ (407) 354-1400
www.airfloridahelicopter.com

Just north of the Pointe*Orlando Shopping Center

Orlando Helicenter
4623 Irlo Bronson Highway, Kissimmee 34746 ~ (407) 396-6006
www.orlandohelicenter.com
East of I-4 Exit 64, near Mile Marker 14

Orlando Helitours
5519 West Irlo Bronson Highway, Kissimmee 34746 ~ (407) 397-0226
www.orlandohelitours.com
East of I-4 Exit 64, near Mile Marker 9

Sunshine Helicopters
5069 West Irlo Bronson Highway, Kissimmee 34746 ~ (407) 390-0175
www.sunshineheli.com
East of I-4 Exit 64, between Mile Markers 10 and 11

Plane & Glider Rides
If helicopters make you skittish, you can do your sightseeing from a small Cessna prop plane operating out of Kissimmee. Farther afield from Orlando proper, you will find plane and glider rides that are more about the experience itself than the sightseeing. If you'd like to be a little more "hands on," check out the plane rides listed in *Chapter 15: Do It!*

Mauiva Air Tours
3956 Merlin Drive, Kissimmee 34741 ~ (407) 551-0577
www.mauivaairtours.com

Flying out of Kissimmee's Ranger Aviation Airport a short drive from the heart of the tourism districts, Mauiva takes groups of up to three people off on 30-minute sightseeing flights over the major theme parks every half hour from 7:30 a.m. to 5:30 p.m. The Celebration Tour ($60 for all ages) covers the Disney parks and SeaWorld; the Grand Tour ($109 adults, $99 children 2-10) adds Universal Orlando and other sights. The Sunset Tour ($129 for all ages) is timed to Orlando's often spectacular sunsets. Perhaps their niftiest tour is the Fireworks Tour that lets you view Disney's nightly extravaganza from a unique perspective. For an additional $29, you can briefly take the controls, under the pilot's supervision, of course, and fly the plane yourself; this option does not apply to the Fireworks Tour. Other add-ons and videos are available for an additional cost. Your group of three cannot exceed 450 pounds total. Flights cancelled due to weather will be rescheduled.

Nearby: Stallion 51, Warbird Adventures.

Seminole-Lake Gliderport
P. O. Box 135516, Clermont 34713 ~ (352) 394-5450
www.soarfl.com

Cost:	$120 to $200, including tax
Hours:	9:00 a.m. to 5:00 p.m.; June to September, closed Monday and Tuesday; October to May, closed Monday only.
Location:	Just south of Clermont, at the intersection of SR 33 and SR 561

If you look up in the sky and see puffy cumulus clouds against a warm blue sky, it's perfect gliding weather. You might just want to pop over to the Clermont area for an air-powered glider ride. The folks at Seminole-Lake Gliderport will put you in a high-performance glider with an FAA-certified instructor, tow you into the wild blue yonder—and let you go.

The price depends on the altitude at which the flight starts and, hence, its length. A $120 20-minute flight starts from 3,000 feet. At $160 and 4,000 feet they'll throw in some aerial maneuvers for the 30-minute flight. The $200 flight tows you to 5,000 feet, offering a spectacular view of Central Florida on the 45-minute glide to landing.

Flights begin about 10:00 a.m., with the last flight about 4:00 p.m. Visa and MasterCard are accepted. Instruction is also offered; rated pilots can pick up a gliding add-on to their license in about three or four days for about $2,500.

Nearby: QuestAir, Wallaby Ranch.

Waldo Wright's Flying Service

1400 Broadway Boulevard SE, Polk City 33868 ~ (863) 873-1339
www.waldowrights.com

Cost:	$60 to $200 per person
Hours:	Daily 10:00 a.m. to 5:00 p.m. weather permitting, October through August only
Location:	Exit 44 off I-4, about 50 miles west of Orlando

Waldo Wright runs his antique airplane ride concession out of the Fantasy of Flight attraction. Get a look at Central Florida from a vintage 1929 New Standard open-cockpit biplane. No reservations are necessary for the $75, 18-minute flights. For $234, you can get a half-hour in a 1942 Boeing Stearman PT-17 and even get a chance to take the controls. (See *Chapter 14* for Fantasy of Flight's other attractions.)

Nearby: Fantasy of Flight, Frank Lloyd Wright Buildings, Polk Museum of Art, Water Ski Experience.

Chapter Twenty:

Sports Scores

THE MILD CLIMATE OF CENTRAL FLORIDA IS AN OPEN AND ONGOING INVITATION TO THE active life. Sportsmen and women will find a wide array of choices to fit every taste and every budget. These activities are listed in *Chapter 15: Do It!*

The more sedentary among us will find enough spectator sports in and around Orlando to keep them busy for quite some time. And if you visit in the month of March, then you should by all means sample the pleasures of baseball Spring Training— even if you don't fancy yourself much of a baseball fan.

With the notable exception of the Magic, Orlando's professional basketball team, tickets to most events are easy to come by and reasonably priced.

Arena Football

Arena football is a scaled-down, indoor version of pro football. Two eight-man teams square off on a field about half the size of the outdoor version. Adding interest to the game, six players on each team play both offense and defense. Otherwise, the rules are much the same as those for pro football. There are 18 professional arena football teams in the United States.

Orlando Predators

302 S. Graham Avenue, Orlando 32803 ~ (407) 648-4444
www.orlandopredators.com

Season:	March to July
Where:	Amway Center, 400 West Church Street, in downtown Orlando, just off I-4 Exit 82B
Ticket Prices:	$8 to $250

Auto Racing - Dragsters, Motocross

Amateurs race for the love of it at two sets of racing venues that lie within driving distance of Orlando's main tourist areas. One is to the east of Orlando on busy State Route 50 and the other a short drive down Interstate 4 at Exit 38 in Lakeland. If you're staying near Disney, it may be easier to get to the Lakeland tracks.

The Lakeland location has two distinct styles. The dirt or clay tracks (which are subject to the vagaries of the Florida weather) are where you want to be for BMX bicycles, motocross, stock cars, and four-wheel-drive Mud Boggs (modified trucks). The drag strips use a straight paved track with bleachers, including a platform for wheelchairs.

In Orlando, Bithlo Motorsports specializes in motocross, an especially exciting form of motorcycle racing featuring rugged bikes competing on bumpy dirt tracks. The drag strip in Orlando is much like that at Lakeland. There's usually something going on at all these tracks on the weekends, with additional events on some weeknights, but it's a good idea to call the track or check online for current information.

Bithlo Motorsports

19400 East Colonial Drive, Orlando 32833 ~ (407) 568-2271
www.bithlomotorsports.com
Season: Year-round, see website for schedule
Ticket Prices: $10 and up, varies by race

Lakeland Motorsports Park

8100 Highway 33 North, Lakeland 33809 ~ (863) 984-1145
www.lakelandmotorsportspark.com
Season: Year-round, see website for schedule
Ticket Prices: $10 and up, varies by race

Speed World Dragway

19442 East Colonial Drive, Orlando 32833 ~ (407) 568-5522
www.speedworlddragway.com
Season: Year-round, see website for schedule
Ticket Prices: $10 and up

Auto Racing - Stock Cars

There is no major stock car track in Orlando, but fans probably won't mind traveling a short distance to get their speed fix, especially since one of the nearby tracks is the Daytona Speedway. Daytona hosts NASCAR's legendary "Daytona 500" in February.

Daytona International Speedway

1801 West Int'l Speedway, Daytona 32114 ~ (800) PITSHOP; (866) 761-7223
www.daytonainternationalspeedway.com
Season: NASCAR races in February (the Daytona 500) and July; other events in other months
Ticket Prices: $35 to $230, varies by race

Baseball - Major League

Thanks to the arrival in 1998 of the Tampa Bay Rays, an expansion team in the American League, Central Florida boasts its own professional baseball team. Despite the name, the team plays in St. Petersburg, not Tampa.

Tampa Bay Rays

1 Tropicana Drive, St. Petersburg 33705 ~ (727) 825-3137
tampabay.rays.mlb.com

Season:	April to September
Where:	1 Tropicana Drive, St. Petersburg
Ticket Prices:	$9 to $175 for general admission

Baseball - MLB Spring Training

Many major league baseball teams find Florida's spring weather ideal for their preseason warm-ups. The training regimen includes a number of exhibition games in March that allow the teams a chance to limber up and practice under realistic conditions. They also give fans a chance to look over their favorite team's form and check out new players before the official season begins.

I have listed here the teams that have spring training camps within striking distance of Orlando, bearing in mind that a true fan's definition of "striking distance" could mean 100 miles. The closest teams to Orlando are the Braves (at Disney) and the Astros (in Kissimmee). The prices listed below are for the 2012 season.

I can't claim to have visited all of these parks, but I've been to a bunch. My favorites are the Astros field, for its intimacy, and the Phillies park in Clearwater, which is a model for what a modern small-scale baseball stadium should be.

Atlanta Braves

Champion Stadium
ESPN Wide World of Sports Complex, Lake Buena Vista 32830 ~ (800)-745-3000

Location:	West of I-4 in the Walt Disney World complex
Ticket Prices:	$15 to $51

Baltimore Orioles

Ed Smith Stadium
2700 12th Street, Sarasota 34237 ~ (800) 745-300

Location:	I-75 Exit 210, west to Tuttle Avenue, right on Tuttle to ballpark
Ticket Prices:	$8 to $32

Detroit Tigers

Joker Marchant Stadium
2301 Lakeland Hills Boulevard, Lakeland 33805 ~ (866) 668-4437

Location:	South of I-4 Exit 33 about 3 miles
Ticket Prices:	$9 to $28

Florida Marlins / St. Louis Cardinals
Roger Dean Stadium
4751 Main Street, Jupiter 33458 ~ (561) 775-1818
> *Location:*   I-95 Exit 83, then 1 mile east to South Central Boulevard; follow traffic circle to Main Street.
> *Ticket Prices:* $6 to $23

Houston Astros
Osceola County Stadium
1000 Bill Beck Boulevard, Kissimmee 34744 ~ (321) 697-3200
> *Location:*   Off US 192, just east of Kissimmee
> *Ticket Prices:* $15 to $27

New York Yankees
Steinbrenner Field
1 Steinbrenner Drive, Tampa 33614 ~ (813) 879-2244
> *Location:*   I-4 to I-275 Exit 41, Dale Mabry North
> *Ticket Prices:* $21 to $37.50

Philadelphia Phillies
Bright House Networks Field
601 Old Coachman Road, Clearwater 33765 ~ (727) 467-4457
> *Location:*   US 19 to Drew Street (SR 590); west on Drew to stadium
> *Ticket Prices:* $14 to $28

Pittsburgh Pirates
McKechnie Field
1611 9th Street West, Bradenton 34205 ~ (941) 747-3031
> *Location:*   I-75 Exit 220, west on SR 64, left on 9th Street West
> *Ticket Prices:* $10 to $22

Tampa Bay Rays
Charlotte Sports Park
2300 El Jobean Road, Port Charlotte, FL 33948 ~ (941) 206-4487
> *Location:*   I-4 W to I-75 S (Exit 9), take Exit 191 off I-75 towards North Port. Turn left on US 41, right on Enterprise, right on El Jobean
> *Ticket Prices:* $10.75 to $31.50

Toronto Blue Jays
Dunedin Stadium at Grant Field
373 Douglas Avenue, Dunedin 34698 ~ (727) 733-0429

Location: From US 19, west on Sunset Point Road, right on
              Douglas Avenue
Ticket Prices: $15 to $28

Baseball - Minor League

The Orlando area's four farm teams give you a chance to see some rising (and a few fall-ing) stars in action. Many devotees of minor league baseball say it takes them back to a simpler time, before players started commanding multimillion dollar salaries. The prices are comfortably old fashioned, too, with great seats to be had for under $10.

Not so old fashioned are stadiums like the Yankee's Steinbrenner Field, which is better than some major league parks, and Bright House Networks Field, as already mentioned, is a stunner. The season is April to September.

Clearwater Thrashers (Class A, Philadelphia Phillies)

Bright House Networks Field
601 Old Coachman Road, Clearwater 33765 ~ (727) 467-4457

Location: US 19 to Drew Street (SR 590); west on Drew to
              stadium.
Ticket Prices: $1 to $10

Daytona Cubs (Class A, Chicago Cubs)

105 East Orange Avenue, Daytona Beach 32114 ~ (386) 257-3172
daytona.cubs.milb.com

Location: Jackie Robinson Ballpark; from I-95 take Inter-
              national Speedway Boulevard exit (SR 92) east to
              Beach, then south to East Orange
Ticket Prices: $6 to $12

Lakeland Flying Tigers (Class A, Detroit Tigers)

Joker Marchant Stadium
2301 Lakeland Hills Boulevard, Lakeland 33805 ~ (863) 413-4140
www.lakelandflyingtigers.com

Location: From I-4 Exit 33 follow signs to SR 22 South; go
              south about 2.5 miles to stadium.
Ticket Prices: $6 to $10

Tampa Yankees (Class A, New York Yankees)

Steinbrenner Field
1 Steinbrenner Drive, Tampa 33614 ~ (813) 879-2244

Location: I-4 to I-275 Exit 41, Dale Mabry North
Ticket Prices: $4 to $6

Basketball

The Magic are definitely the hottest sports ticket in town. Don't be surprised if you find them sold out well in advance, especially if they are playing the Lakers or the Bulls. Still, tickets are sometimes available. You can always try your luck outside the Arena on the day of a game; someone just might have an "extra" ticket. Florida law prohibits the sale of a sports ticket for more than $1 over its face value, but scalpers have commanded from $225 to $1,000 for tickets to Magic playoff games.

Orlando Magic

400 West Church Street, Orlando 32801 ~ (407) 896-2442
www.nba.com/magic

Season:	October to April
Location:	Amway Center, in downtown Orlando, just off I-4 Exit 82B
Ticket Prices:	$10 to $290

Dog Racing

Orlando itself does not boast a greyhound track, but there's one just across the Seminole County line, north of the city. It operates year round. Admission is cheap, free for general admission grandstand seats and just $2 for the clubhouse. The racing schedule is typically Monday, Wednesday, Friday, and Saturday afternoons at 12:45 p.m. with evening races on Friday and Saturday at 7:15 p.m.

When you tire of betting on the dogs here, you can bet on dog and horse races elsewhere that are beamed in by satellite.

Sanford-Orlando Kennel Club

301 Dog Track Road, Longwood 32750 ~ (407) 831-1600
www.sanfordorlandokc.com

Season:	Year-round
Location:	From I-4 Exit 94 go east on SR 434, right on Ronald Reagan Boulevard and left on Dog Track Road
Ticket Prices:	Clubhouse $2, grandstands **free**

Ice Hockey

After a long hiatus, professional ice hockey returns to Orlando in October 2012 with the arrival of a new Solar Bears team in the East Coast Hockey League.

Orlando Solar Bears

400 West Church Street, Orlando 32801 ~ (407) 951-8200
http://orlandosolarbearshockey.com

Season:	October to April

Location:	Amway Center, in downtown Orlando, just off I-4 Exit 82B
Ticket Prices:	To be determined

Jai-Alai

Jai-Alai is played on a sort of elongated racquetball court but, instead of a racquet, the players use a long curved wicker basket, called a cesta, strapped to their right hand, to catch and return the pelota (or "ball") at blinding speeds. To facilitate betting, the game is played in round-robin fashion by eight single players or two-man doubles teams. The first to reach seven points wins, with second and third place determined by point totals. Playoffs settle ties.

Reflecting the Basque origins of the game, most of the players have Basque or Spanish surnames. The action is fast and often surprisingly graceful. Points are determined much as they are in racquetball or squash. As one player (or team) loses a point, the next player takes his place. Although the program gives stats on the players, betting seems more like picking the numbers for a lottery game.

If you tire of the action unfolding in front of you, you can repair downstairs and bet on jai-alai matches in Miami or horse racing at New Jersey's Meadowlands, all of them shown on large video screens. When live games aren't being offered you can still stop by for the simulcasts of events elsewhere.

Orlando Jai-Alai

6405 South U.S. Highway 17-92, Casselberry 32730 ~ (407) 339-6221
www.orlandojaialai.com

Season:	Live games January to March; simulcasts year-round
Ticket Prices:	$1 at the door (55 and older **free**)
Hours:	Monday to Saturday opens at 11:30 a.m.; Sunday at noon; game times vary.

Chapter Twenty-One:

Shop 'Til You Drop

SEEN ALL THE ATTRACTIONS? GOT SOME MONEY LEFT? NO PROBLEM! ORLANDO makes it easy to go home flat broke and maybe with a few genuine bargains to help convince the folks back home that you're not simply an unregenerate spendthrift. Of course, for many people shopping is an attraction in itself, bargain or no. Whatever category fits you best, you'll find plenty of opportunities to shop 'til you drop.

In this chapter, I have concentrated mostly on discount shopping opportunities on the theory that, a) you can always pay full price back home and, b) your wallet can probably use the break during an Orlando vacation. Basic information about other shopping venues in the Orlando area can be found on the Internet at orlando.retail-guide.com. And don't forget all those gift shops in the various attractions described in earlier chapters.

Upscale Shopping

There's a lot more to buy in Orlando besides the gaudy T-shirts and cheap souvenirs you'll find in the theme parks. In fact, for many foreign visitors, high-end shopping excursions are a big part of Orlando's appeal.

The major upscale shopping destination is the **Mall at Millenia** (Exit 78 on I-4), a super-deluxe mall anchored by three major department stores, including Bloomingdale's and Neiman Marcus. Elsewhere among the more than 100 merchants you'll find familiar names like Tiffany, Gucci, Burberry, Michael Kors, Jimmy Choo, and Hugo Boss. There's art, too, including the fine collectables at Swarovski. When you're ready for a break, fine dining at P.F. Chang's or the Brio Tuscan Grill beckons and when your shopping day is done you can unwind at the Blue Martini, which features live entertainment. The mall's website is www.mallatmillenia.com.

Another major shopping destination is the **Florida Mall**, Central Florida's largest, at the intersection of Sand Lake Road and South Orange Blossom Trail. It is conveniently located between the airport and the major tourist districts, so don't be surprised to see tour buses lined up outside. There are six major department stores here, including Nordstrom's and Saks Fifth Avenue along with over 260 other stores that run the gamut from Abercrombie & Fitch and Banana Republic to Victoria's Secret and Zales Jewelers. There's even a large shop devoted entirely to M&Ms candies! There's no fine dining here, just a large food court, and a handful of casual tableservice restaurants like Buca di Beppo and Ruby Tuesday.

For a more traditional, less frenzied shopping experience head for **Park Avenue** in **Winter Park,** just north of Orlando. Here, under the shade of moss-draped live oaks, you can stroll past upscale boutiques like Lily Pulitzer, Eileen Fisher, John Craig, Scott Laurent, and Jacobson's. There's also an outpost of Williams Sonoma, as well as The Wine Room, which sells fine wines by the bottle and by the glass, using a state-of-the-art dispensing system, the first one of its kind in Florida. There are some terrific restaurants as well, including Park Plaza Gardens. At the end of the street is the gift shop of the Morse Museum.

Speaking of museums, don't overlook the gift shops of museums listed in *Chapter 18* as sources for one-of-a-kind gifts for you or for that special someone. Even theme parks like SeaWorld and Discovery Cove offer some upscale items, usually art pieces, to lure the discriminating shopper.

Outlet Shopping

Once upon a time, "factory outlets" were just that—small shops located in or near the factory where seconds, rejects, overruns, and discontinued lines could be sold, at a discount, directly to the public. Factory outlets existed outside the standard retail channels and were a classic win/win proposition: The public got a bargain and the factory recouped at least some of its costs.

Today, factory outlets have become very much a part of the retail scene, located far from the factory in glossy malls and often featuring merchandise specifically designed for and marketed to the bargain-hunting segment of the market. And the words "Factory Outlet" have become a marketing buzzword used to suggest deep, deep discounts, whether they are there or not. Some factory outlets are run directly by the companies whose merchandise they sell. Others are run by entrepreneurs who contract with big name companies and then set their own prices. Still others are run by merchants who buy cheap merchandise from a variety of off-cost producers or from brokers who specialize in overstocked and "distressed" goods. All of which is to say that, when it comes to outlet shopping, the warning "caveat emptor" (let the buyer beware) is in full force. On the other hand, I do not mean to suggest that the outlet malls in the Orlando area are filled with shady operators out to fleece the unwary tourist. Far from it. Most of these outlets offer excellent deals on first-rate goods and any factory seconds or irregulars are clearly marked. Still, a wise shopper will arrive with a clear idea of what he or she is looking for and what the "going rate" for those items is back home.

What follows is a survey of the major factory outlet shopping venues in the Orlando area. Conveniently enough, most of them are located along International Drive in Orlando. I have listed them in the order you would encounter them when traveling from north to south along this well-traveled tourist corridor and then south to

Kissimmee. The list is not meant to be all-inclusive. You may find other bona-fide outlets. On the other hand, there are many shops that use the words "factory outlet" rather loosely.

Lake Buena Vista Factory Stores
www.lbvfs.com

Location:	15657 SR 535, 2 miles south of I-4 Exit 68
Information:	(407) 238-9301
Hours:	Monday to Saturday 10:00 a.m. to 9:00 p.m.; Sunday 10:00 a.m. to 7:00 p.m.

This mall of more than 40 shops is located on the well-traveled state road that links I-4 to US 192. There's a small food court if you get hungry and a playground for the kids. They offer free shuttle service from nearly 60 participating local hotels.

Orlando Premium Outlets, International Drive
www.premiumoutlets.com/international/

Location:	4951 International Drive, at the north end of International Drive, in Orlando
Information:	(407) 352-9600
Hours:	Monday to Saturday 10:00 a.m. to 11:00 p.m.; Sunday 10:00 a.m. to 9:00 p.m.

Orlando Premium Outlets's I-Drive location is the 900-pound gorilla of the outlet scene with two malls and several "annexes," including an upscale shopping area just a short hop down International Drive. The sprawling complex (formerly known as the Belz or Prime outlets) plays host to some 180 merchants. Register online for the VIP Club for extra savings or to check out current specials offered by mall merchants. Like any self-respecting mall, this one features food courts and snack kiosks to refuel the flagging shopper. There are also games and rides for the kiddies.

Orlando Premium Outlets, Vineland Avenue
www.premiumoutlets.com/vineland/

Location:	8200 Vineland Avenue, off International Drive just south of SeaWorld
Information:	(407) 238-7787
Hours:	Monday to Saturday 10:00 a.m. to 11:00 p.m.; Sunday 10:00 a.m. to 9:00 p.m.

The newest entry in the outlet shopping sweepstakes boasts 150 stores representing such upscale vendors as Brooks Brothers, Armani, Lacoste, and Burberry, plus a central food court with its own Starbucks. The same VIP club mentioned above is also honored here.

Flea Markets

The flea market is an Old World concept. Originally the term was applied to impromptu markets, the yard sales of their day, where enterprising individuals at the frayed edge of the merchant class displayed a grab bag of merchandise, some of dubious provenance—hence the alternate term:"thieves' market." Like the term "factory outlet," the term "flea market" has evolved over the years. Today, as practiced in Central Florida, a flea market is a sort of alternate shopping mall. The market owner provides, at a modest rental, simple booths in covered arcades. The merchants are, for the most part, full-time professionals with long-term leases on their booths who differ from their counterparts in the glitzy malls only in the matter of scale.

Whereas the old flea markets of Europe held out the lure of uncovering some priceless antique at an unbelievably low price, the modern Florida flea market more often offers inexpensive merchandise, purchased from a wholesaler and offered at a price that might not be any better than you could get at Kmart. Still, savvy shoppers can find bargains here if they know what they're looking for (and at). The best bets, in my opinion, are the secondhand dealers, the craftspeople, the fresh produce vendors, and the purveyors of the sort of wacky and offbeat stuff you don't usually see elsewhere.

Whatever the drawbacks of flea market shopping, there's no denying that the atmosphere of these bazaars is a lot of fun. There's plenty of greasy and fattening food to keep your energy up and the very challenge of navigating the seemingly endless rows of wares tends to keep you going. For those who have never experienced this particular slice of Americana, I recommend it highly. For those of you who simply love the flea market experience (and you know who you are), the following flea markets should keep you busy. If you must have more, just look in the Yellow Pages in your hotel room under "Flea Markets."

Flea World

www.fleaworld.com

Location: US 17–92 in Sanford; I-4 Exit 98
Information: (407) 330-1792
Hours: Friday, Saturday, and Sunday 9:00 a.m. to 6:00 p.m.

Flea World bills itself as "America's largest flea market" with 1,700 dealer booths, most of which are occupied on any given weekend. There are **free** circus acts here and an amusement park next door to keep the kids occupied.

International Drive Flea Market

Location: 5445 International Drive in Orlando, just east of Kirkman Road
Information: (407) 370-4992
Hours: Monday to Saturday 10:00 a.m. to 8:00 p.m.; Sunday 10:00 a.m. to 6:00 p.m.

This bare-bones operation has space for 350 booths, but they are far from full. Look for a mix of costume jewelry, inexpensive clothing, and toys.

Main Gate Flea Market

Location:	5407 Irlo Bronson Highway (Highway 192) in Kissimmee
Information:	(407) 390-1015
Hours:	Daily 10:00 a.m. to 8:00 p.m.

This market is housed in a series of long metal buildings set well back from the heavily traveled tourist strip of route 192, just east of I-4. There are over 400 booths here and a smattering of food stands, some of which offer some intriguing ethnic specialties.

192 Flea Market

www.192fleamarketprices.com

Location:	4301 West Vine Street (Highway 192) in Kissimmee
Information:	(407) 396-4555
Hours:	Daily 9:00 a.m. to 6:00 p.m.

This is Kissimmee's original flea market. Over 400 booths offer a variety of wares, including plenty of Disney souvenirs and Florida T-shirts for the budget souvenir hound. I especially like the fact that this market seems to attract the casual vendor who uses it as a sort of substitute yard sale.

Osceola Flea & Farmers Market

www.osceolafleaandfarmersmarket.com

Location:	2801 East Irlo Bronson Highway (Highway 192) between Kissimmee and St. Cloud
Information:	(407) 846-2811
Hours:	Friday, Saturday, and Sunday 8:00 a.m. to 5:00 p.m.

A little farther off the tourist track, this flea market offers more fresh produce than the others. It also has a "garage sale" section that draws folks with some junk to unload (as opposed to regular merchants). There used to be up to 900 booths selling everything from Disney souvenirs to home improvement items to car stereos, but vendors have lately dwindled down into the dozens.

Visitors Market

www.visitorsfleamarket.com

Location:	5811 Irlo Bronson Highway (Highway 192) in Kissimmee
Information:	(407) 396-0114
Hours:	Daily 9:30 a.m. to "evening" (9:30 p.m., or 6:00 p.m. in slower periods)

A modest market housed in a former retail location on Kissimmee's gaudy tourist strip, this one has space for 250 booths, most of which are open for business selling a wide variety of cut-rate merchandise.

Antiquing

Depending on what you're looking for, the greater Orlando area may hold some hidden treasures for the antique hound. Don't expect much in the way of fancy European antiques, but if your interest runs to American vernacular furniture of the twentieth century, you may be in luck. There are even some pieces dating to the nineteenth century to be found.

What you will find in abundance is *stuff*—Depression-era glass, weaponry, old toys (including some nifty Disney memorabilia), Art Deco and Art Moderne bric-a-brac, old orange crate labels, Highwayman art, the list goes on and on. If rummaging through aisle after aisle of assorted stuff in search of hidden gems is your idea of a great time, you will find plenty to keep you occupied.

There are a number of antiquing hotspots in the area. The toniest is **Antique Row in Orlando,** a collection of 14 shops that runs for several blocks along Orange Avenue, just north of Lake Ivanhoe (Exit 84 or 85 on I-4). A standout here is **Washburn Imports** (407-228-4403); stop in to see their Indian furniture, and stay for a beer at their in-store bar, the Imperial. Farther afield, a number of historic downtown areas in nearby towns offer concentrations of antique stores. To the south lie **Kissimmee**, where **Lanier's** (407-933-5679) is the most prominent merchant, and **St. Cloud**, whose downtown is a sort of time capsule of mid-twentieth century working class Americana. To the north lies the picturesque and more upscale village of **Mt. Dora**. Here, you will find an antique mall in the downtown area and just outside town, on Highway 441, the sprawling **Renniger's Antique Fair** (352-383-8393), featuring over 300 dealers. To the west of Orlando is **Winter Garden**, whose historic Plant Street has several shops selling vintage Americana. Winter Garden is also home to **Theme Park Connection** (www.themeparkconnection.com, 407-284-1934), a warehouse of old props, costumes, signs, and other castoffs actually used inside the local theme parks, salvaged for sale or trade.

As you explore, be sure to pick up a free copy of *The Antique Shoppe*, a monthly newspaper that will point you to other antiquing destinations within easy driving distance of Orlando. It also contains valuable information on antique shows, auctions, flea markets, and collectors' clubs. The website is www.antiqueshoppefl.com.

Index to Rides & Attractions

Free Updates

For free updates to this book and its companion volume, *Universal Orlando: The Ultimate Guide To The Ultimate Theme Park Adventure*, visit:

http://www.TheOtherOrlando.com/tooblog

Other Books from
The Intrepid Traveler

The Intrepid Traveler publishes money-saving, horizon expanding travel how-to and guidebooks dedicated to helping its readers make world travel an integral part of their everyday life.

For more information visit our web site, where you will find a complete catalog, frequent updates to this and our other books, travel articles from around the world, Internet travel resources, and more:

http://www.IntrepidTraveler.com

If you are interested in becoming a home-based travel agent, visit the Home-Based Travel Agent Resource Center at:

http://www.HomeTravelAgency.com